# *Handbook of*
# FAMILIES
# &POVERTY

# *Handbook of* FAMILIES & POVERTY

D. *Russell Crane* ▪ *Tim B. Heaton*

*Brigham Young University*

*Editors*

**⑤ SAGE** Publications

Los Angeles ▪ London ▪ New Delhi ▪ Singapore

*For information:*

Sage Publications, Inc.
2455 Teller Road
Thousand Oaks, California 91320
E-mail: order@sagepub.com

Sage Publications India Pvt. Ltd.
B 1/I 1 Mohan Cooperative Industrial Area
Mathura Road, New Delhi 110 044
India

Sage Publications Ltd.
1 Oliver's Yard
55 City Road
London EC1Y 1SP
United Kingdom

Sage Publications Asia-Pacific Pte. Ltd.
33 Pekin Street #02–01
Far East Square
Singapore 048763

Printed in the United States of America.

*Library of Congress Cataloging-in-Publication Data*

Handbook of families and poverty / editors, D. Russell Crane and Tim B. Heaton.
    p. cm.
Includes bibliographical references and index.
ISBN 978-1-4129-5042-8 (cloth)
  1. Poverty—United States.  2. Poor families—United States.  3. Family—United States.
4. Economic assistance, Domestic—United States.  5. Public welfare—United States.  I. Crane, D. Russell.  II.  Heaton, Tim B.

HC110.P6.H36 2008
362.5′560973—dc22                    2007018220

This book is printed on acid-free paper.

07   08   09   10   11   10   9   8   7   6   5   4   3   2   1

| | |
|---|---|
| *Acquisitions Editor:* | Cheri Dellelo |
| *Editorial Assistant:* | Lara Grambling |
| *Production Editor:* | Tracy Buyan |
| *Copy Editor:* | Robin Gold |
| *Typesetter:* | C&M Digitals (P) Ltd. |
| *Proofreader:* | Kevin Gleason |
| *Indexer:* | Sheila Bodell |
| *Cover Designer:* | Michelle Kenny |
| *Marketing Manager:* | Jennifer Reed |

# Contents

# Preface

The *Handbook of Families and Poverty: Interdisciplinary Perspectives* is intended to discuss the most recent research and issues related to this important topic for families. It is interdisciplinary in nature, beginning with a marriage and family therapist and a sociologist as the co-editors. The contributors represent a broad number of disciplines ranging from marriage and family therapy, sociology, nursing, political science, psychology, family studies, and business.

The *Handbook* began as an outgrowth of the Brigham Young University (BYU) biennial research conference in 2004 organized by the Director of the Family Studies Center (Crane) in the School of Family Life. The School of Family Life hosts a research conference every 2 years on an important topic related to family life. Other conferences in the series include "Families and Work" (2006), "Families and Health" (2002), and "Revitalizing the Institution of Marriage for the 21st Century" (2000). Scholars from around the world are brought to the BYU campus to present their latest research on the topics of interest.

The proceedings of the Families and Poverty Research Conference provided the nucleus of the present volume, with a number of scholars being invited to broaden the number of subjects discussed beyond what could be contained in a single conference.

The *Handbook* is intended for readers from a multidisciplinary audience. Just as we sought a wide range of scholars to contribute to the volume, we hope that readers in a number of different disciplines might find articles of interest in the *Handbook*.

## ACKNOWLEDGMENTS

Our first debt of gratitude is to our contributors. Obviously, this project would not be possible without them. We sincerely appreciate their willingness to write for this book. They have already published extensively on the topics they cover here, and we appreciate their willingness to contribute to this volume. They have given freely of their expertise that has been gained over years of commitment to issues of families and poverty, as well as much personal effort and sacrifice.

We thank our many friends and colleagues at Brigham Young University. We appreciate the support of the former administrative team of the School of Family Life at BYU: James Harper, Director of the School, and Susanne Olsen Roper and David Dollahite, Associate Directors, for their support of this project. We give special thanks to Yevon Romney, administrative assistant at the Family Studies Center, and Adam Olson who helped in the managing of this project and in the preparation of the manuscript.

Our deepest thanks to our Sage editors, Jim Brace-Thompson and Cheri Dellelo, for their support for this work. Their encouragement and guidance have been consistent and consistently appreciated.

Finally, we give our thanks and love to our respective spouses, Eileen and Tamara, our families, who made this effort possible.

Sage Publications gratefully acknowledges the following reviewers:

Danielle A. Crosby
University of North Carolina at Greensboro

Jean W. Bauer
University of Minnesota

Virginia Curran Shipman
University of New Mexico

Dale Walker
Juniper Gardens Children's Project,
University of Kansas

Scott A. Ketring
Auburn University

Pamela A. Schulze
University of Akron

Cynthia Needles Fletcher
Iowa State University

# Introduction

This *Handbook of Families and Poverty* began as an outgrowth of the 2004 biennial research conference at Brigham Young University (BYU), organized by the Director of the Family Studies Center in the School of Family Life, D. Russell Crane. At these conferences, scholars from many parts of the world come to the BYU campus and discuss the latest issues in research and practice on topics that relate to families. The proceedings of the conference on *Families and Poverty* provided the nucleus of this volume. Following literature reviews on various issues in poverty and families, we then invited additional scholars to broaden the perspective.

The purpose of the book is to explore the roadmap for the next generation of scholars in areas related to families and poverty. The chapters represent the state-of-the-art thinking related to the reciprocal influences of couple, marital, and family issues on poverty. Some explore the specific areas of policy, others discuss research, and others offer examples in practice. Other chapters are important sources of information on a wide range of diverse populations and settings.

## CONCEPTUALIZING FAMILIES AND POVERTY

Although poverty is measured in simple terms—income below the poverty threshold adjusted for household size—the phenomenon is much more complex. Poverty is influenced by, and in turn influences, a broad complex of social structural, family, and personal characteristics. Figure 1 provides a conceptual model of the various interrelationships between poverty, determined by income in a given year and household size, and these other characteristics.

Poverty implies a lack of capital. During the last few decades, social scientists have done extensive work to identify various types of capital. Originally, capital was assumed to be monetary. In contemporary industrial societies, other forms of financial capital such as homeownership, retirement savings, and savings and investments are also important. Financial capital reduces the chances of having inadequate income in a given year. For example, the elderly who have retirement savings are less likely to be poor. Poverty, especially when extended over a long period, makes it very difficult to accumulate financial capital such as savings, a home, and a pension plan.

Other forms of capital are also important for understanding poverty. The poor often do not have social networks (social capital) that can give assistance in overcoming poverty. Such networks could include institutions such as banks or places that provide job training, as well as individuals who could help with finding jobs or meeting other needs. Indeed, the social networks of the poor may contribute

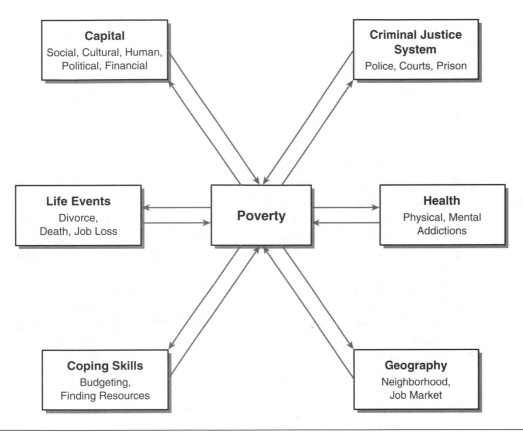

**Figure 1**    Links Between Poverty and Other Characteristics

to persistent poverty. Extended periods of poverty may also contribute to deterioration in social networks. Poverty is closely associated with the lack of skill (human capital) required to acquire jobs that pay a living wage, and poverty makes it more difficult to finish schooling or enhance one's skills. The poor have a weaker voice in political institutions (political capital), so governments are not always responsive to the needs of the poor. Finally, the poor may not have socially desirable attributes (cultural capital) such as language and dress that facilitate success in a capitalist economy, and the social isolation that comes with poverty makes it more difficult to acquire cultural capital.

Poverty increases the likelihood of experiencing negative life events such as divorce, unwed parenthood, becoming a victim of

crime, illnesses, death of a partner, or loss of a job. Certainly, all are at risk of bad luck, but the chances increase with poverty. The cycle becomes more vicious when these events increase vulnerability to long-term poverty. Health is of particular concern and so it is included as a separate category. As several authors in this volume note, the health-care systems of the United States and other societies give unequal treatment based on ability to pay. This is especially the case for health problems such as mental disorders and addictions that are less likely to be adequately covered by standard health insurance policies. Work conditions, stress, and environmental conditions increase the risk of health problems among the poor, and low-quality care available to the poor reinforces their vulnerability. Poor health, in turn, is a major barrier to finding good jobs. To the degree that those without access to good health care turn to self-medication with various substances, the risk of addiction increases. To date, most societies have not been successful in creating a health-care system that eliminates the vulnerability of the poor.

Critics of state-supported antipoverty programs often point to individual problems that contribute to poverty. For example, the term *culture of poverty* denotes behaviors and values of the poor that play a role in persistent poverty and the intergenerational transmission of poverty. If programs do not address such flaws, it is reasoned, the money will be wasted, at best. At worst, such programs facilitate the perpetuation of poverty. However, we find it more useful to consider a deficit of skills such as ability to budget, to deal with stress, and to locate resources that contribute to poverty. Conversely, poverty may interfere with acquisition and development of such skills. For example, a daily struggle to meet basic needs is not conducive to developing good long-term budgeting skills.

Chapter 16 explicitly addresses the relationship between poverty and the criminal justice system. To the extent that police are more likely to monitor the poor and the poor are less likely to receive good legal services, the poor are more likely to be convicted of criminal offenses. The risk is exacerbated when the poor turn to criminal behavior such as theft, prostitution, or dealing drugs because legitimate means are less accessible. Moreover, the criminal justice system is more likely to give prison sentences to the types of crime most common among the poor. The cycle continues because prisons do not adequately prepare inmates for reentry into paid employment upon release. In addition, the process of imprisonment separates inmates from their families and support networks. This process is especially difficult for poor families where the cost of transportation to and from a distant correctional facility may make visitation impossible.

Finally, geography plays a role. Whether in inner-city neighborhoods or depressed rural areas, the poor neighborhoods lack job opportunities and role models. Low income increases the likelihood that people will be compelled to live in disadvantaged neighborhoods and receive lower quality education and health-care services. Living in these neighborhoods increases the chance of continuing in poverty and reduces opportunities to get out of poverty.

In short, interrelationships between poverty and other phenomena are complex and interactive. Poverty increases the risk of being in circumstances that create major obstacles to getting out of poverty. The picture may not be so bleak for short-term episodes of poverty induced by acute illness or abrupt change in family circumstances. But extended periods of poverty create a vicious cycle. Policies and programs that conceptualize poverty solely in terms of inadequate income are doomed to failure because they do not address the host of interrelated conditions.

The central focus of this work is on the reciprocal relationships between family and poverty. Figure 2 summarizes some of the key aspects of these relationships. With the exception of people living alone, with unrelated individuals, or in institutions, the family is generally the unit that acquires and distributes resources. Of course, the family can also play this role for members who are not currently living in the same household such as children living away or in institutions. As the definition indicates, income is the resource that determines poverty status. But the family also plays a vital role in most of the other sources of capital presented in Figure 1. Families acquire all forms of capital, jointly experience many life events, create the context for health and access to the health-care system, determine geographic location, and are interdependent when coping

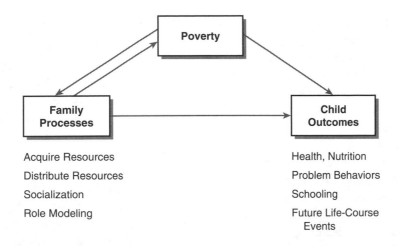

**Figure 2**     Family Processes and Poverty

with life's contingencies. In short, poverty and its connections are generally a family affair. Moreover, family processes influence and are, in turn, influenced by poverty.

One of the major concerns regarding poverty is that consequences for children are profound and detrimental. Poverty increases the likelihood of poor health and malnutrition for children. Children in poor families are more likely to exhibit problem behaviors and are less successful in the education system. Poverty also increases the chances that children will make early life-course transitions such as premarital pregnancy, marriage, and marital disruption. Such early transitions make it more difficult to escape poverty in adulthood.

Collectively, the chapters in this volume enhance our understanding of the linkages between poverty and other characteristics, the central role that the family plays in these linkages, and the consequences for children.

## OUTLINE OF THE BOOK

In the first section, we cover current issues related to welfare and social policy on the forefront of concerns among policymakers and professionals working to reduce or eliminate poverty. These include welfare policy and the outcome of "welfare reform" in the United States.

In the second section, we highlight issues of poverty among diverse populations and settings including families, children, Appalachian families, immigrant populations, Mexican Americans, Northern Cheyenne Nations, families dealing with issues of aging, families with a seriously mentally ill member, families with a substance-abusing member, families with incarcerated family members, and health outcomes for poor families.

The last section provides examples and explorations of specific interventions to potentially improve the lives of those living in poverty. For example, we address the role of Head Start, health care, microenterprise, the Triple P-Parenting Education Program, and the role of government in strengthening couple and family relationships.

## ORGANIZATION OF THE CONTRIBUTIONS

The domains discussed here are not organized in order of importance. Such an effort would be futile. We are concerned about all issues related to families and poverty, but we necessarily had to place one chapter in front of another. We hope our decisions in this regard are not taken as any signal of our regard for colleagues working in all of these important areas.

No handbook can adequately cover all important issues related to families and poverty. We expect this volume to be a beginning to provoke collegial discussion. In some cases, we were simply not able to secure authors in needed areas that met our time line. For example, an author on poverty issues of African Americans was not able to make the expected contribution. We offer only a sampling of important topics in helping families with poverty issues. We did not require contributors to adhere to a standard format for the chapters. Instead, we encouraged authors to write in the way that best addressed their areas of expertise. We think this approach should enrich the ongoing discussion among the disciplines.

## AUDIENCE FOR THE WORK

This is a beginning effort to include the perspective from a broad range of disciplines. It is a compilation rather than integration. To adequately address important needs of families, the next step for scholars is to do the hard work of integration and true collaboration. We look forward to works that bring scholars together in such integration.

The handbook is intended for readers from all areas devoted to the poverty of families. Just as we sought a wide range of scholars to create this volume, we hope that readers from all disciplines might be enriched by the work. We expect that researchers, practitioners, and students from many disciplines will find areas to entice their interests, provoke their thinking, and expand their practice. We hope that differences and commonalities of family issues will emerge in the study of the volume.

—D. Russell Crane and
Tim B. Heaton

# Part I

# WHAT WELFARE CAN AND CANNOT DO

# CHAPTER 1

# Innovation in Social Policy

## Evaluating State Efforts to Reform Welfare, Promote Work, and Help Low-Income Families

GARY BRYNER AND RYAN MARTIN

In 1996, Congress and the Clinton administration enacted a remarkable change in social policy in the United States, upending the conventional expectation that policy change only occurs incrementally. The new welfare law passed that year ended decades of a federal entitlement of cash assistance for poor families and gave states much more discretion to fashion the details of how they would help families move from welfare to work. Then presidential candidate Bill Clinton's promise in 1992 to end welfare as we know it put a Democratic imprimatur on welfare reform and created a political window for major policy changes, and the Republican takeover of Congress in the 1994 election ensured that conservative concerns would shape the policy changes. Welfare programs and agencies underwent a major transformation to help recipients prepare for and make the transition to the world of work.

A decade after the 1996 welfare reform law is a propitious time to explore lessons that can be drawn from this major policy experiment for the host of policies that are aimed at improving the life chances of low-income families. The goals of welfare policy address a wide range of issues, including how to strengthen two-parent families, discourage out-of-wedlock childbearing, provide effective job training and education, encourage improved parenting, and reduce poverty among children. The stakes are high for these families: policy reforms may help empower them to become productive and self-sufficient or may consign them to dead end lives of deprivation and discouragement with little hope for the future.

Welfare policy has been one of the most politically visible policies aimed at poverty in America, but it is only part of a suite of policies. Welfare policy has always been intertwined with health policy and Medicaid. Welfare policy intersects with educational policies such as Head Start, which is aimed at low-income children, and is increasingly tied to policies aimed at helping low-income fathers increase their income and strengthening marriage and encouraging two-parent families as a way to improve the well-being of children. Several chapters in this volume focus on these intersecting issues of health, family stability, fatherhood, and welfare. But understanding the policy debate surrounding these difficult issues also requires a clear understanding of the kinds of challenges facing low-income families, and a host of chapters here explore these challenges in detail, providing a rich portrait of the extent of poverty among children in America, elderly women, immigrant families, and other groups of society that are particularly vulnerable; how poverty interacts with mental health, hunger, limited access to health, childbearing, and incarceration; and the consequences of poverty on parenting, the way in which children use their time, and how families provide kinship care.

Given the visibility of welfare and the decades of policy frustration with the intractable problems it addressed, welfare policy is a good place to start. Welfare policy has been the source of more frustration, criticism, complaint, and reform proposals than perhaps any other social policy. The dramatic shift in policy in 1996, now a decade old, is ripe for analysis. What have been the goals of welfare policy reform and how well have those goals been achieved? What have been the consequences for poor children and their parents? What other policy changes could intersect with those made for welfare that could help improve the lives of those in our society who are most vulnerable? If there is indeed some policy success here and not just policy change, what lessons could be applied to engender more creative and effective policy reforms in other areas of social policy?

A primary goal of welfare is to move recipients from government dependency into jobs that will allow them to be self-supporting. The first part of the goal is relatively easy: through enforcement of time limits and other eligibility rules, the number of recipients can be significantly reduced. However, it is much more difficult to help recipients find and keep jobs that pay wages and benefits sufficient to sustain a family. For some recipients who

already have education, work experience, and other skills essential for workplace success, temporary assistance is all that is needed to help them prepare to reenter the workforce. For others who lack these things or have health or substance abuse challenges, significant caregiving responsibilities, or face other barriers to gaining employment, the task of moving them from welfare to work is much more complex.

Under the 1996 federal welfare reform law, states have the primary responsibility for designing and implementing welfare policy, and for finding ways to effectively move recipients from welfare to work. The federal government's role is to transfer funds to help states provide temporary cash assistance and related services, to place some limitations on state spending of federal dollars, and to ensure states meet federal participation requirements. Policy devolution to states is part of the New Federalism presidents have championed during the past three decades or so, but policy devolution became a particularly prominent part of welfare policy as frustration grew with expanding welfare rolls in the 1980s and early 1990s. Because it was unclear how welfare policy could produce self-supporting families, particularly if these families had a history of welfare dependency and numerous barriers to work, policymakers were willing to turn the problem over to states to experiment with alternative ways of solving these problems.

This chapter examines what states have done since 1996 to help recipients move into the workforce and become self-supporting. Because considerable variety exists in how states seek to promote work, their experience can suggest what policy innovations seem most promising as states continue to experiment with welfare policies. The devolution of welfare policy to states has important lessons for health care, education, food and hunger, immigration, and other policies where there is a similar belief that these difficult problems could be best addressed by states. And, as welfare policy becomes increasingly intertwined with efforts to strengthen two-parent families, it focuses even more attention on the importance of finding ways to encourage and support healthy families and help them work through the problems and difficulties they confront. The question of how successful welfare policy has been in promoting and supporting work among low-income families is critical because work is such an important element in the well-being of families, from securing income to promoting a sense of dignity and accomplishment to providing a model for children of how to productively contribute to society. This chapter (1) traces the evolution of welfare policy, (2) explores how states are encouraging work among welfare recipients, (3) examines how successful those efforts have been, and (4) suggests some implications for broader social policy.

## THE EVOLUTION
## OF WELFARE POLICY

For decades, states have been experimenting with ways to encourage work among low-income families, particularly those who have been receiving cash assistance. States were the first to create welfare programs aimed at ensuring mothers could be at home with their young children. In the early 20th century, states began enacting mothers' pensions laws that permitted widows to stay at home with their children rather than send them to orphanages. As the depth and breadth of the Great Depression overwhelmed the capacity of states to help poor families, the New Deal responded to the problems of poverty and unemployment, the fear of social unrest, and the growing belief that poverty was not the result of individual character flaws by calling for the federal government to take responsibility for helping to fund welfare (Bryner, 1998; Skocpol, 1992).

Title IV of the Social Security Act of 1935 created the Aid to Dependent Children (ADC)

program. The purpose of the program was to assist states, through matching federal funds, to "broaden and supervise existing mothers' aid programs." ADC was primarily aimed at helping widows care for their children, but evolved into a program to help divorced, deserted, and never-married mothers and their children as well. Six public assistance programs were created to give grants to states, each aimed at a different population: Old-Age Assistance, Aid to Dependent Children, Aid to the Blind, Maternal and Child Welfare (hospital, nursing, and public-health services for mothers and children), Vocational Rehabilitation, and Public Health. ADC was aimed at providing help to children who had been deprived of support because of the death or absence of a parent and to help keep families that had lost their primary breadwinner together. Each program had relatively specific standards for determining eligibility that were strictly enforced. Minimum benefit standards were set by the law that provided only meager assistance, but states could be more generous if they chose to.

The original act anticipated that welfare would primarily help states provide cash to needy children who had at least one disabled, unemployed, continually absent, or deceased parent. It evolved to also serve divorced, deserted, and never-married mothers and their children. By 1960, one of four children on welfare had been born out of wedlock, half lived in families split by divorce or abandonment, and half were black. As the task became more complicated, and more federal programs were added to promote employment, state experimentation through waivers became more important. Frustration grew along with the complexity of the program, and welfare reform became a regular refrain of presidential and congressional candidates.

Welfare was renamed Aid to Families with Dependent Children (AFDC) in a 1962 amendment to the Social Security Act. That law also provided increased benefits to help reduce poverty and funded more vocational training for welfare recipients. Most importantly, the program began permitting states to apply for waivers from federal rules for "experimental, pilot, or demonstration projects." The aggressive expansion of the welfare state under Lyndon Johnson's War on Poverty triggered a major effort at welfare reform under Richard Nixon. Reform was pursued through state experiments aimed at welfare recipients including mandatory job search, efforts to provide work experience, training programs, and an incentives approach that sought to increase the financial return welfare recipients received from working.

Ronald Reagan gave federalism and welfare reform new life in the early 1980s. The Reagan administration sought to delegate more discretion to states through block grants and gave states waivers from federal mandates that permitted them to place new requirements on recipients. As a result, states began to experiment with welfare-to-work proposals. Arkansas, for example, developed an innovative program under Governors Frank White and Bill Clinton that required welfare recipients to take job search classes, look for jobs under the supervision of a caseworker and, for a few recipients, do unpaid work for public and private employers for short periods. However, the Reagan administration ran into opposition when it tried to impose a major shift of responsibility for welfare to the states. States were unenthused, and Congress was hostile to the "New Federalism" idea of turning full responsibility for AFDC and food stamps to the states.

Governors played key roles in keeping welfare reform on the agenda and pushing Congress to pass the Family Support Act of 1988, which promised to "turn the welfare program upside down" and result in "lasting emancipation from welfare dependency" (Moynihan & Reagan, 1989, pp. 350–351). Governors forged common ground between conservatives, who came to accept that federal and state governments have a responsibility to provide education, training, and support services to help AFDC recipients obtain and keep jobs, and liberals, who came to see that mothers of even small children should work (Rovner, 1988). After 1988, welfare reform largely became a state venture. Although a 1962 amendment to the Social Security Act allowed state welfare programs to diverge from the federal requirements, states did not begin seeking waivers for their welfare programs in large numbers until the 1980s. Limited evaluation funds provided little incentive for states to follow through with quality evaluations, but the waiver process and the resulting evaluations served as important sources of information about the strengths and weaknesses of alternative approaches to changing welfare (Birnbaum, 1995). President George H. W. Bush's administration continued to encourage state experimentation. By 1996, 43 states had received welfare waivers; only Alaska, Idaho, Kansas, Kentucky, Nevada, New Mexico, Rhode Island, and the District of Columbia had not (Pear, 1996).

States took different approaches to welfare reform in the late 1980s and early 1990s. For some, welfare reform required building a new system from the bottom up through pilot or model projects. Other states built new systems from the top down by redefining agency missions, changing administrative structures, and redrawing agency boundaries. Still others pursued incremental changes in the way welfare systems operated (Waldfogel, 1994). A second dimension of reform centered on the basic direction states took. Some chose to operate a low-cost program that reached a substantial portion of the poor, others provided more intensive, higher-cost services to a smaller, more specific group, and a third group included both general low-cost services and specific, higher-cost programs for much smaller groups. A third set of choices focused on the goals of the welfare program. Some states sought to help recipients gain basic education, receive job training, and learn other skills, including long-term efforts where necessary. Others emphasized job placement and moving recipients as quickly as possible into the work force. The latter goal also coincided with the goal of reducing spending on welfare (Friedlander & Gueron, 1990). State experiments imposed time limits and work requirements, tightened child-support enforcement, allowed working families to keep more of their income, and eliminated benefit increases for mothers on welfare who had additional children (Cohen, 1994).

Bill Clinton's 1992 presidential campaign chose as one of its major planks the pledge to "end welfare as we know it." Part of his political claim to fame was that as governor of Arkansas he had led governors' efforts to reform welfare. He proposed a new approach that would provide health care and job training to welfare recipients and, after 2 years, require work of those who are capable. If private employment were not available, community jobs would be provided. Welfare reform was an important element of Clinton's electoral strategy. His focus on breaking the "culture of dependence" for the 20 to 25% of recipients who were enmeshed in a cycle of poverty and dependency was significant: finally, a Democrat was willing to take on the problem of the urban underclass, one of the most persistent and difficult public policy problems in America (Seib, 1993).

By the mid-1990s, there was more consensus about what to do about welfare than at any earlier time. However, the Clinton administration argued that health-care reform must come before welfare reform because lack of access to health care was a major cause of welfare participation. The administration's health-care initiative became bogged down, and the failure of Democrats to reform welfare (while leading the criticisms of welfare) left the door open for Republicans (DeParle, 1994). In September 1994, congressional Republicans released their "Contract with America," a campaign manifesto to which virtually all Republicans running for the

House swore allegiance. Among the proposals was a promise to reform welfare. Republicans effectively used the contract to focus attention on the failures of the Democratic Congress and swept to an astounding victory in November. The debate about what kind of welfare reform the Republicans had in mind started immediately. The new Speaker of the House Newt Gingrich said that Congress should consider cutting off welfare recipients after 60 days and turn over more care for the destitute to private charities and orphanages (Goodstain, 1994). The Republican Congress and Democratic White House fought throughout 1995 as welfare policy became intertwined with other contentious issues.

Governors also played major roles in the development of welfare proposals. Their power was a function of the alignment of governors who sought more flexibility and fewer mandates with Republicans in Congress who were in favor of a smaller national government. Republican governors also had some experience as welfare reformers and argued that they knew more than members of Congress about how to remedy welfare's defects. State successes with reducing welfare through work programs, time limits, and caps on benefits to children born to mothers on welfare were exactly the kinds of solutions members of Congress were looking for. As a result, Republican governors from Wisconsin, Massachusetts, and other states with extensive welfare reform programs in place worked closely with members of Congress.

After a deadlock over the federal budget and other disputes that led to two presidential vetoes of welfare bills, governors developed a bipartisan proposal for welfare reform that re-energized the federal debate (Derthick, 1979, p. 45). All 50 governors issued a joint welfare reform proposal in February 1996, and Republican congressional leaders worked with governors to come up with a proposal acceptable to them and to the Clinton administration. The impending 1996 presidential election created an incentive for everyone in Washington to show they could address a difficult issue, and the new welfare law was passed in August 1996, replacing AFDC with Temporary Assistance for Needy Families (TANF). The Personal Responsibility and Work Opportunity Reconciliation Act gave states considerable discretion as it replaced AFDC with a block grant, but it also imposed a host of requirements on states, such as requiring them to spend on welfare at least 75% of what they had spent in the past and place at least 50% of their caseload in statutorily specified work activities by 2002.

The 1996 act transformed welfare in a number of ways. It gave states much more flexibility and authority to design welfare policy, replaced the individual entitlement to cash assistance for low-income families with a $16.5 billion a year block grant to states, and gave them more discretion over spending, and set a lifetime limit of 60 months for receiving federally funded assistance. It transformed state welfare offices into employment agencies that emphasized moving recipients from welfare to work. Because of the impact of state welfare reform policies that were put in place before the 1996 law was enacted, the national policy changes in 1996, and a strong economy through the mid to late 1990s that produced low unemployment, welfare rolls fell dramatically from more than 14 million people in 1994 to 5 million in 2002, as welfare rolls drooped to their lowest level in 40 years (Pear, 2004). Other policies were also enacted during the time, such as a major expansion in the Earned Income Tax Credit (EITC), increased funding for child care, and broadened funding of Medicaid. These policy changes combined with welfare reform to help reduce the poverty level of children to 16.2% in 2000, the lowest rates since 1979 (Clinton, 2006). Between 1994 and 2001, the labor force participation rates of single mothers rose from 44 to 66% and the average incomes of single mothers grew from about $18,000 to $23,000 (Blank, 2006). The economic downturn in 2001 put a halt to the decline in welfare rolls, but the number of welfare families did not increase despite higher unemployment in the early years of the new century.

The 1996 law was scheduled to be reauthorized in 2002, but for 4 years, Congress and the states were unable to resolve controversies surrounding difficult issues of whether to increase the work requirements imposed on states, the amount of federal money available for child care, and how to reduce out-of-wedlock pregnancy, encourage two-parent families, and strengthen marriage (for a summary see Center for Budget and Policy Priorities, 2003). Each of these issues was contentious, but eventually the debate focused on how to increase expectations for states to engage recipients in work, despite the now decade-long consensus that welfare and work should be intertwined. During the first year of TANF, states were required to have 25% of recipients engaged in activities that were defined as work or preparing for work, and that figure was to rise to 50% by 2002. However, to reward states for moving families off the rolls, states were also given a caseload reduction credit that allowed them to reduce their required participation rate one percentage point for every percentage point reduction in TANF rolls. As a result, many states completely offset their work requirement by earning caseload reduction credits. On average, states only needed to achieve a 6% work participation rate in fiscal year 2004, although their actual performance was an average work participation rate of 33%. However, this figure varied dramatically across the nation, from 85% in Kansas to 8% in Georgia, and only one of the five states with the largest total welfare rolls achieved a rate greater than 50% (Pavetti, 2004). There was great variety in what states counted as work participation, and critics of state discretion seized on examples of state requirements that could be satisfied with educational and personal improvement activities that seemed far removed from work. In early 2006, Congress finally reauthorized TANF, increasing funding for initiatives to strengthen marriage and tightening the work requirements.

State experimentation is critical in policy areas such as welfare policy where it is not clear how best to solve difficult problems. But that also means that recipients of assistance residing in innovative and effective states get help in becoming more self-sufficient while those in other states may not get the support they need. The sections that follow describe state experiments aimed at encouraging work and examine what these experiments have achieved.

## HOW ARE STATES ENCOURAGING WORK?

State policies aimed at encouraging work among families receiving temporary assistance can be divided into three broad categories. First are eligibility rules that determine who can receive cash assistance and related services. Such rules can encourage work in the sense that the restrictions they place on participation in welfare can encourage work rather than the receipt of assistance (although they may not affect those who are not working and who are unable to find employment). More directly, these rules determine who can continue to receive assistance and who cannot, and thus shape decisions about who moves from welfare to work. Second, training and education programs, the development and enforcement of self-sufficiency plans, and other measures are aimed at helping recipients prepare to work. Third, child care, transportation assistance, and other services

are aimed at supporting recipients who have moved from welfare to work.

## *Eligibility Rules, Time Limits, and Other Requirements*

To encourage work, states have experimented with eligibility rules, self-sufficiency programs, and the structure of benefits, time limits, sanctions, provision of support services, and participation requirements. States have transformed their welfare systems from providers of cash assistance to employment offices. States have restructured state welfare and employment offices into employment-oriented departments and brought a number of social services under one roof. They have simplified the rules and streamlined the application forms for cash assistance, child care, Medicaid, and food stamps. The consolidation of these services in an employment department has helped cement the state's efforts to reorient its traditional welfare program toward work and provides a clear case of how government agencies can dramatically reorient the administration of social programs.

States typically require recipients to immediately begin applying for work, even before officials conduct assessments of employability and needs. This highlights the importance of work and uses the labor market to sort out which recipients are capable of working and which ones will need help before they can successfully compete for jobs. States have increased the amount of earnings and the value of assets (such as vehicles) that they disregard in determining eligibility to encourage work. Most states have eliminated rules that limited the number of hours two-parent family heads can work and still be eligible for assistance. States largely rely on unsubsidized jobs; only a few states have developed subsidized job programs or relied on public service employment. One important way in which states differ is that some emphasize sanctions, shorter time limits, and caseload reduction, whereas others take a different approach, emphasizing incentives and engagement in work. The first approach is usually associated with more restrictive eligibility thresholds for earnings, work requirements that take effect before assistance is approved, and lower benefits. The second approach typically includes more generous disregards of income and assets, and relatively high cash benefit levels (Gais, 2002).

According to the 2006 TANF annual report (Office of Family Assistance, 2006),

States have developed widely varying approaches to time limits. This is because states have broad flexibility in designing time-limit policies and because the federal 60-month time limit does not apply to state-funded benefits. As a result, states can continue to provide TANF or other cash benefits to families, or to the children in these families, using state-only funds. In

fiscal year 2003, 50 states and territories had time limits that can result in the termination of families' welfare benefits; 19 of those states had limits of less than 60 months. However, over half of the national welfare caseload is in a state that either has no time limit or a time limit that reduces or modifies benefits when the limit is reached.

## Education and Training Programs and Preparation for Work

States have emphasized the development of self-sufficiency plans. These plans are the primary means for structuring the interaction between caseworkers and recipients. Recipients must comply with the requirements of these plans to maintain their benefits. In many states, officials provide relatively generous support for recipients, but are also quite willing to impose sanctions if recipients fail to do their part. This approach raises interesting questions

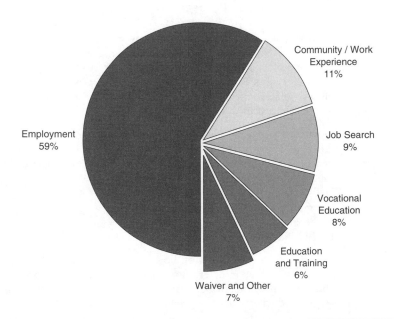

**Figure 1.1**    Total Hours of Reported TANF Participation, by Activity U.S. Monthly Average, Fiscal Year 2003

SOURCE: Office of Family Assistance, 2006.

about balancing the aggressive enforcement of requirements and creating a supportive environment that helps families become self-sufficient. Figure 1.1 shows the proportion of TANF recipients involved in different job-related activities in fiscal year 2003 (Office of Family Assistance, 2006).

### Support Services

There has been a dramatic shift in state spending toward support services. The amount states spend on cash assistance fell from 77% of total spending on welfare programs in 1997 to 44% in 2002, and the proportion of spending for services such as child care, training, and education rose from 23 to 56% (Pear, 2004). The devolution of welfare policy combined with giving states considerable discretion with federal mandates and incentives to encourage them to include certain provisions in their programs. The major provisions of TANF programs aimed at promoting work are summarized in Table 1.1.

**Table 1.1**    Overview of Work-Related Provisions of State Welfare Policies

| Policy | Description | Work-Related Goal |
| --- | --- | --- |
| Eligibility | | |
| Asset Test | This determines initial and continuing eligibility by specifying the value of assets a person can have to receive benefits. | To encourage families with resources to work rather than receive assistance |
| Income Test | This determines initial and continuing eligibility by specifying the amount of income a person can have to receive benefits. | To focus benefits on those with low incomes, and to control caseload size and cost |
| Diversion | This program is implemented to help families with short-term needs to not have to enter the TANF program. This may consist of a lump sum payment, job search services, or other benefits. Receiving diversion services often disqualifies the family from receiving TANF for a specified period. | To prevent those with short-term needs from applying for long-term assistance, and also to lower caseload size and program costs |
| Time Limits | Only U.S. citizens and legal immigrants (after five years of residency) are eligible. Federal TANF funds can only be received for a total of five years; state funding may be used for other groups and for funding beyond the 5-year limit. However, 20% of the state's caseload can be exempted for specific reasons. | To restrict or expand benefits to target groups, and to control caseload size and cost |
| Benefit Structure | This specifies benefit amount, how income is counted in determining benefits, and what disregards or other exemptions are applied when calculating benefits. | To provide supportive work incentives and to reward families for earnings |
| Sanctions | States may choose to sanction those not complying with various requirements of state TANF programs. These sanctions may decrease assistance (partial sanction) or eliminate benefits (full sanction) to the family, and they may be temporary or permanent in nature. | To provide punitive work incentives and to compel families to become self-sufficient |

| Policy | Description | Work-Related Goal |
|---|---|---|
| Other Compliance Requirements | States may also set various other compliance requirements. These may include income reporting, caseworker visit, or other meeting or reporting requirements. | To foster discipline or to restrict caseload to those in strict compliance |
| **Preparation for Work**<br>Training/Education | Programs include basic education, development of generic work-related skills, and specialized training to prepare recipients to work. | To provide skills and knowledge to aid the family in achieving self-sufficiency |
| Multiple Barrier Programs | Programs to give intensive services such as counseling, improved access to support services, and other help to families that have multiple barriers, such as health, permanent child care or aged care responsibilities, substance abuse, etc., to becoming self sufficient. | To overcome barriers that prohibit the family from becoming self-sufficient |
| Hourly Participation Requirements | States set minimum hours per week that recipients must be engaged in work-related activities. | To foster discipline and work ethic in recipients so they may become self-sufficient |
| **Supporting Work**<br>Childcare Exemption/Subsidy | These programs either exempt childcare costs from assistance calculations or offer subsidies for childcare expenses. | To provide supportive work incentives and to reward families for earnings |
| Transportation Exemption/Subsidy | States may choose to exempt transportation expenses when calculating benefits for transportation, or they may offer transportation subsidies. | To provide supportive work incentives and to reward families for earnings |
| Employment Subsidy | Subsidies offered to employers who hire current or former TANF recipients. This may be done either through direct payment to the employer or through tax incentives. | To create jobs for current and former TANF recipients, and to assist families in becoming self-sufficient |
| Individual Development Accounts | This program allows low-income individuals to save for asset investment. States can determine what spending is allowed, how much saving is permitted, and if funds will be matched by state money. | To encourage and reward savings by recipients, and also to assist them in becoming self-sufficient |
| EITC/Tax Incentives | These incentives are state or federal tax breaks for low-income citizens and those receiving assistance. These may include the federal EITC, state EITC, and other state tax deductions. | To provide supportive work incentives and to reward families for earnings |
| External Support Programs | These programs include Medicaid, Food Stamps, LIHEAP, housing subsidies, and other non-TANF federal and state programs. | Varies. Usually to provide low-income individuals with specific benefits (housing, food, health care, help with utility bills, etc.) |

## SUMMARY OF
## STATE TANF POLICIES

### Benefit Structure

One way that state reformers sought to increase work incentives was by increasing the benefits from working. To increase work incentives, many states increased the income disregards available to those receiving assistance. Many states also decreased the benefit reduction rate, or the rate at which assistance funding is lost as earned income increases. Doing this allows the worker to retain more of the earnings gained from an additional hour of labor. This increased state flexibility has led to a wide range of policy decisions as states were given complete discretion in how to calculate benefit amounts. The following tables have been created to help summarize and explain how state TANF programs now function (compiled from information in Office of Family Assistance, 2006; State Policy Documentation Project, 1999; Welfare Rules Database, 2005).

Table 1.2 shows that most states have an asset test of $2,000 for both applicants and recipients. Twelve states and territories have an applicant asset test of $1,000, but only eight use this same amount for recipients. Each of the eight that use it for recipients also use it for applicants, and the four that have different amounts for recipients all increase to at least $1,500. Table 1.2 also shows how most states treat applicants and recipients differently, and details regarding this difference will be discussed later in more detail. Table 1.2 also shows that most states disregard child-care expenses up to a maximum of $200 for children younger than 2 years old, and $175 for children older than 2 years old. Many states have diversion programs, and a three-month benefit equivalent is the most common limit states have when offering diversion. Table 1.3 shows the number of states with specified cash disregards.

States have also chosen to disregard a higher percentage of earned income than under AFDC. In addition, many states have chosen to change the percent of earned income disregarded depending on how long the recipient has had earned income. Figure 1.2 shows how the 17 states with changing percentage disregards change these disregards over time.

Most states treat applicants and recipients differently. In these states, applicants must meet either lower asset tests or lower income limits than would be required to receive benefits once on the program. Therefore, an individual in a given financial position may be eligible for benefits if already on the program, but that same individual can be ineligible based on application guidelines. This acts as a sort of financial trigger, where a strict threshold must be met initially, but then the person can continue to receive benefits once his or her financial position improves substantially. Only 15 states have the same asset test and disregards for applicants and recipients.

Some 30 states disregard a fixed percentage of earnings for recipients on the program at all times. These percentage disregards range from 20 to 100%. Seven states have a $90 and 0% disregard after 1 year of TANF assistance. In addition, 16 states disregard 0% of earnings after two years (15 after 1 year and one after 2 years). Although many of these states reduce their percentage earnings disregard after 1 year or more, four states disregard 0% of earnings immediately. Although all these states have a cash disregard of $90 or more (except for Wisconsin), these states still have a 100% benefit reduction rate for clients either immediately or after a period. This creates an interesting phenomenon for those states that increase the benefit reduction rate over time; as disregards change, the individual's total income will decrease if earned income remains constant. A total of 17 states have programs that will cause benefit amounts to decrease over time even if earnings are unchanged or even decrease.

**Table 1.2**     Summary of State TANF Policies in 2000 by Number of States in Each Category

| | *Number of States* | | | | |
| --- | --- | --- | --- | --- | --- |
| | *Policy 1* | *Policy 2* | *Policy 3* | *Policy 4* | *Policy 5* |
| **Asset Test**[1] | $1,000 | $2,000 | $2,500 | $3,000 | Other (all > $1,000) |
| Applicants | 12 | 27 | 4 | 6 | 5 |
| Recipients | 9 | 26 | 4 | 6 | 9 |
| **Income Test**[2] | | | | | |
| Cash Disregard | $0 | $90 | $120 | $200 | Other |
| Applicants | 16 | 21[3] | 4 | 3 | 10 |
| Recipients | 23 | 5 | 7 | 5 | 14 |
| Percent Disregard | 0% | 20% | 40% | 50% | Other |
| Applicants | 26 | 9 | 2 | 9 | 10 |
| Recipients | 4 | 3 | 4 | 14 | 29 |
| **Child Care Disregard** | | | | | |
| Children Under 2 | $0 | $200 | State Paid | Full Cost | Other |
| Applicants | 31 | 20 | 0 | 0 | 0 |
| Recipients | 16 | 35 | 0 | 1 | 1 |
| Children Over 2 | $0 | $175 | State Paid | Full Cost | Other |
| Applicants | 30 | 21 | 0 | 0 | 0 |
| Recipients | 16 | 35 | 0 | 1 | 1 |
| **Diversion** | Have Program | 2-Month Benefit Equivalent | 3-Month Benefit Equivalent | 4-Month Benefit Equivalent | Other |
| No. of States | 28 | 1 | 11 | 2 | 14 |

NOTES: 1. Count is for policy applying to cases with one adult in the assistance unit. 2. This count only includes those with a "pure" policy. For example, Nevada disregards $90 or 20 percent, whichever is greater. Also, some states disregard $0 only for a limited time. For purposes of this table, states with such policies are counted in the "Other" column. 3. North Dakota is not counted in this cell. Although they disregard $90, this disregard changes to 27 percent if income is greater than $334.

Tables 1.4 to 1.6 show how states compare on some other important provisions of state TANF programs. Table 1.4 outlines how states provide for intermittent and lifetime time limits for TANF participants. Table 1.5 classifies states by the maximum benefits they provide as a percentage of their median income and the federal poverty level. Table 1.6 classifies states according to the kinds of work activities they count as satisfying federal requirements. The 2006 reauthorization and subsequent regulations will likely result in major changes to those patterns of work requirements.

## HOW SUCCESSFUL ARE STATES IN ENCOURAGING WORK?

### Research on Specific State Policies: Eligibility

*Time Limits.* Although time limits undoubtedly decrease the welfare caseload and may

**Table 1.3** Number of States With Specified Cash Disregards by Time Receiving Earned Income, Counting Both States With Constant and Changing Policies Over Time

| Disregard | Time Receiving Earned Income | | | |
| --- | --- | --- | --- | --- |
| | Immediately | After 4 Months | After 6 Months | After 1 Year |
| $0 | 22 | 20 | 19 | 18 |
| $90 | 4[1] | 4 | 5 | 10 |
| $100 | 2 | 3 | 3 | 3 |
| $120 | 8 | 9 | 10 | 6 |
| $150-$200 | 8 | 8 | 8 | 8 |
| Other | 7 | 7 | 6 | 6 |
| Some $ Disregard | 29 | 31 | 32 | 33 |

NOTE: 1. North Dakota is not counted in this cell. Although they disregard $90, this disregard changes to 27 percent if income is greater than $334.

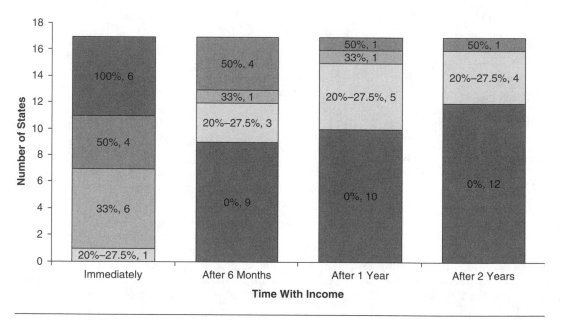

**Figure 1.2** Recipient Percent Earnings Disregards Counting Only States With Changing Disregards

**Table 1.4** Intermittent and Lifetime Time Limits for State TANF Programs

| Intermittent | No Intermittent Limit | 1 Year | 18 Months | 2 Years | 3 Years | Other |
| --- | --- | --- | --- | --- | --- | --- |
| No. of States | 38 | 1 | 1 | 10 | 1 | 0 |

| Lifetime | 2 Years | 3 Years | 4 Years | 5 Years | No limit | Other |
| --- | --- | --- | --- | --- | --- | --- |
| No. of States | 3 | 1 | 3 | 39 | 4 | 1 |

**Table 1.5**  States Classified by Maximum Benefits as a Percentage of State Median Income (SMI) and Federal Poverty Level (FPL)

| *Percent of FPL* | < 20% | 20%–30% | 30%–40% | 40%–50% | 50%–60% | 63% |
|---|---|---|---|---|---|---|
| No. of States | 7 | 14 | 18 | 7 | 4 | 1 (A.K) |
| *Percent of SMI* | < 7% | 7%–9% | 9%–11% | 11%–14% | 14%–18% | 23% |
| No. of States | 6 | 11 | 14 | 13 | 6 | 1 (A.K) |

**Table 1.6**  States Classified by Type of Work Activities Counted Toward Work Requirements Including Participation Time Limits, Combination Requirements, and Hours Required

| | *Count Toward Work Requirement* | *Participation Time Limit* | *Combination Requirement* |
|---|---|---|---|
| **Work Activity** | | | |
| Adult basic education/English as a second language | 50[1] | 12 | 17 |
| Vocational education | 49 | 39 | 15 |
| Education related to employment | 46 | 12 | 14 |

| | *Count Toward Work Requirement* | *Participation Time Limit* | *Hours/Contacts Required* |
|---|---|---|---|
| Job search | 51 | 21 | 23 |
| Job skills training | 46 | 14 | 11 |
| On-the-job training | 47 | 15 | 0 |
| Subsidized employment | 43 | 21 | 18 |

| | *Count Toward Work Requirement* | *Minimum Hours* |
|---|---|---|
| Community service | 35 | 20 |
| Work experience | 46 | 36 |
| Job readiness | 51 | N/A |

| | *2 Year Degree* | *4 Year Degree* | *Time Limit* |
|---|---|---|---|
| Postsecondary education | 43 | 36 | 29 |

NOTE: 1. Includes three states that allow local units to decide. In these tables and figures, the District of Columbia is counted as a state.

increase the employment of welfare recipients, research on the magnitude and value of these effects is limited. This is due to the limited number of families that have actually become subject to lifetime limits. There are three main reasons why many fewer families have been affected by the time limit than expected. First, many states continue to offer benefits to those who have reached the time limit through state funds. Second, states are allowed to exempt as much as 20% of their caseload from work requirements. Third, the Caseload Reduction Credit allows states to meet much lower participation requirements than required by law. For example, in fiscal year 2002 and thereafter, the work participation rate for single-parent families was 50%. However, states receive credits equal to the reduction in their current caseload from 1995 levels. Because of this, although the statutory rate requirement was 50%, the Caseload Reduction Credit afforded 28 states an adjusted requirement of 0% (Office of Family Assistance, 2003).

*Benefit Structure.* High benefit reduction rates decrease work incentives for those receiving TANF benefits (for a review of research on the effect of welfare programs on work incentives, see Moffitt, 2000, pp. 26–34). For example, reducing benefits dollar per dollar with income virtually eliminates the incentive to work as the person receives no monetary benefit from working. Research has shown that lowering the benefit reduction rate will increase the labor supply of those who receive benefits. However, if the person is required to meet hourly requirements to remain eligible, this may not be necessary to encourage work because it is mandated. In addition, decreasing the benefit reduction rate will decrease the work incentives of those newly eligible for the program because they can work less and keep the same income. Therefore, the expected effect of a decrease in the benefit reduction rate on overall work participation is ambiguous.

*Sanctions.* Studies on sanctioned families reveal that they are less likely to have jobs than are other welfare leavers. Sanctioned family members also appear to be less educated, be in worse health, and have fewer job skills than other recipients do (see Moffitt, 2000, p. 5, for a summary of these studies). In addition, a study of recipients in three major cities revealed that a large portion of sanctions are for non-work-related reasons such as missing a caseworker appointment or not filing paperwork on time (Cherlin et al., 2001). Therefore, although sanctions may act as a sort of stimulus to encourage work, it appears that those ultimately subjected to

benefit reduction or termination are often made worse off by these sanctions.

## Preparation for Work

*Training/Education.* The two major approaches to the employment of TANF recipients are the Human Capital Development (HCD) model, which focuses on education and training, and the Labor Force Attachment (LFA) model, which focuses on rapid job placement. A synthesis of research conducted by the Manpower Demonstration Research Corporation on 29 different reform initiatives reveals that a combination approach is the most effective. The study reports that even though job-search-first programs yielded higher income initially, the difference diminished over time. Also, although most programs resulted in increased work activities, the most effective programs relied on short-term education and training with a strong focus on job search. However, because of the structure of welfare benefits, even though these programs increased earnings there was little change to overall income. Because benefits decreased as work increased, many families were only marginally better off even though their earnings increased (Bloom & Michalopoulos, 2001).

*Multiple Barrier Programs.* Little research has been done on the effectiveness of counseling and treatment programs in relation to work participation rates. However, research has shown that almost half of TANF recipients have physical or mental health problems. In the 1997 Urban Institute National Survey of America's Families, 48% of TANF recipients reported having either poor mental health or poor general health, and 32% reported having very poor mental or general health (Zedlewski, 1999, p. 2). Therefore, the continuation and expansion of such programs is vital to increasing the earnings of TANF recipients.

## Supporting Work

*Child Care Exemption/Subsidy.* Child-care income exemptions or subsidies help encourage work among TANF recipients by lowering the cost of working. By disregarding income spent on child care or paying for it directly, states remove this financial barrier to employment. Undoubtedly, this has been seen as a strong work support, and is therefore offered by almost every state. In addition, most states offer to reimburse for child-care services through the Child Care Development Fund (CCDF), and TANF recipients are often given priority for such funding.

## Research on Overall TANF Effectiveness

The 2005 annual TANF report to Congress suggested some broad measures of the impact of state efforts to encourage work and promote self-supporting families:

*Earnings.* State-reported data for welfare recipients show that the average monthly earnings of those employed increased from $466 per month in fiscal year 1996 to $647 in fiscal year 2003, a 49% increase (Office of Family Assistance, 2006).

*Drop in Child Poverty Rate.* Between 1996 and 2003, the overall child poverty rate dropped 14%. In that same period, the African American child poverty rate dropped from 39.9 to 33.6%; the Hispanic child poverty rate dropped from 40.3 to 29.7%. In married two-parent families (in 2003), about 1 child in 12 (or 8%) is poor, but about 42% of the children living in a female-headed, single-parent family are poor (Office of Family Assistance, 2006).

*Employment and Earnings Gains Among Low-Income Families.* Most of the reforms that were introduced in the 1990s had positive effects on employment and earnings. Thus, welfare reform is likely responsible for a portion of the increase in work and earnings among single mothers during the last decade, as nearly all of the experimental and econometric evidence suggests (see Figure 1.3). Some welfare reform components raise incomes and reduce poverty, although this does not occur with all policy components, and some favorable effects probably will not persist over time. Generous financial work incentives—high earned income disregards inside the welfare system or earnings supplements outside the welfare system—generate the strongest income gains and antipoverty effects (Office of Family Assistance, 2003).

*Increased Financial Work Incentives.* The most favorable effects are associated with financial work incentives, most likely because of the increase in family income that results from combining work and welfare. Even for these programs, evidence shows unfavorable impacts for some subgroups of participants, particularly for adolescent children and for younger children of parents who do not experience large income gains. Work requirements do not appear to have strong impacts on children, although here, too, evidence indicates unfavorable impacts for adolescents, especially in school performance.

## WHAT ARE THE IMPLICATIONS FOR NATIONAL WELFARE POLICY?

A wide range of criteria can be used to assess efforts by states to encourage work among welfare recipients. If the goal is to reduce welfare rolls and move clients into the workforce, time limits, sanctions, job placement, and other services can effectively lead to its achievement. If the goal is to help families to become self-sustaining, how to do that is much less clear, particularly for families that face multiple barriers. More broadly, if the

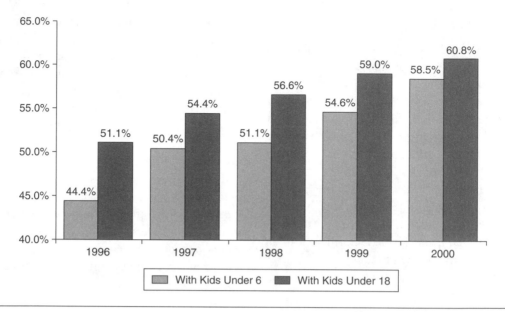

**Figure 1.3**   Employment Among Single Mothers Under 200% of Poverty

goal is to reduce poverty among families, welfare policies must interact with a host of other factors that determine how well that objective will be realized.

In promoting work, states have found that reducing the benefit reduction rate encourages work for those already receiving assistance because recipients are able to take home more of their earnings. Although this effect has been well documented, 14 states still at some point have a dollar-for-dollar reduction in benefits as earnings increase. Because work carries no financial incentive in these TANF programs, they rely on sanctions, time limits, and other compliance requirements to encourage work. However, the effectiveness of these punitive measures is questionable. As discussed earlier, sanctions appear to adversely affect those in the most difficult situations. In addition, the overall effect of time limits is yet to be well documented. Therefore, it appears that states should focus more on rewarding work than punishing noncompliance until more effective incentives can be constructed.

From the perspective of reducing welfare rolls and reorienting welfare agencies to employment offices, state welfare reform efforts have largely been a success. The number of recipients has fallen dramatically, and many have moved into the workforce. The most successful TANF programs are those that combine strong work incentives with training and education. Because of this, TANF policymakers must make a major investment in training and education programs. Although the costs of administering such a program will be higher than will a pure work-first approach, the benefits from using both strategies appear to be the most effective. Like most other policy areas, welfare policy is ultimately a question of trade-offs. Job preparation and education programs cost more in the short run, but are more likely to lead to independent families in the long run.

The goal of self-supporting families can mean earning enough to no longer qualify for cash assistance, or it can mean a job that pays enough to rise above poverty. The question of whether a state is doing enough to help families move from poverty to a sustainable level of income, rather than simply moving beyond the minimum income level provided by cash assistance is not just an empirical question but is also intertwined with an important normative debate. From one view, welfare reform is all about self-sufficiency—helping families who have been dependent on assistance getting off the rolls and becoming independent. Although some advocates of such a view want to reduce government spending, they more broadly represent the view that people are best served by being independent and self-sufficient—that it is in their own interest to be free from having to depend on others for their income. Others counter that interdependence, not independence, is the more appropriate social goal—that welfare should be built on the recognition that we are all dependent on each other, responsible for each other, able to call on each other for help, and committed to ensuring that those who have the most skills, resources, energy, and other productive attributes help those who have fewer resources.

Although some argue that there is now widespread agreement over the shortcomings of the old welfare system and the elements of the new one, others insist that the debate continue along these broad, ideological lines. Should the ultimate goal be minimal government, so that people are largely on their own, self-supporting and autonomous, or should the objective be a more connected community, with more interaction, responsibility, and sharing of resources? If the state opts for the latter, should that community be underwritten by government, or should it be voluntary, left to private groups and efforts? Should the state accept whatever poverty results from giving families 3 (or 5) years of assistance or should state officials and others continually seek ways to improve well-being, decrease inequalities, and increase opportunities? The former view largely dominates the national debate over reinventing welfare.

But strong voices defend the alternative view and are looking for a forum in which to explore the much broader agenda of reducing poverty and finding new ways to offer low-income families and their children in particular access to more opportunities for education, health, and progress.

Many people have declared welfare reform a success because rolls have declined and more single mothers are working. There is some room for celebrating the ability of the political system to come to some agreement about how to change a public policy, carry out the changes, and produce some positive results. Former President Bill Clinton wrote in August 2006 that although neither side got all of what it wanted, they were able to pass a bill that worked, that helped many families move into the world of work and toward the middle class (Clinton, 2006). Some conservatives have given Clinton the credit for reframing the debate regarding welfare reform by emphasizing how damaging the old system could be on women and children and on its failure to address the decline of two-parent families (Rector, 2006). Welfare reform has not reached the families that face the most difficult challenges of poor health, lack of education and work experience, domestic violence, substance abuse, inadequate housing, and other problems. Many of those families continue to survive only because they receive assistance through programs like food stamps, Supplemental Security Income, Medicaid, and housing aid. They cycle in and out of the cash assistance program and their dependency is largely hidden through these other programs (Besharov, 2006). Welfare reform did not occur in a vacuum and many other policies have been aimed at helping poor families, such as the EITC, an increase in the minimum wage, and broadening Medicaid coverage. But neither the combination of policies that are most responsible for the reduction in caseloads, nor how the caseload decline has affected the well-being of poor women and children is clear. More women are working and poor rather than not working and poor, and the intangible but real benefit that comes from being able to work is significant (Blank, 2006). But many families face such difficult barriers that they will not be able to simply move from welfare to work, and we have yet to figure out how to help those who most need our help.

Welfare policymakers and analysts have much to learn about the causes of poverty and how to design and implement policies that will help those most in need of assistance. Welfare is not yet a public problem that has been solved, but only a problem that is now beginning to be addressed differently than before. Policy innovation is a continuing public need in fashioning a new round of public policies, including state-private partnerships and other efforts that address the causes of poverty and the need for welfare, including spouse abuse, job discrimination, poor health, inadequate development of social skills, and poor education. The limited success of welfare reform is an encouraging sign that perhaps additional policy changes can address these root causes and prevent some of the problems that welfare systems are created to repair.

## REFERENCES

Besharov, D. J. (2006, August 15). End welfare lite as we know it. *The New York Times*. Retrieved from http://www.nytimes.com/2006/08/15/opinion/15besharov.html

Birnbaum, M. (1995). *Policy, planning and social experimentation: The sad case of the Wisconsin 100-hour rule experiment*. Madison: Department of Urban and Regional Planning, University of Wisconsin–Madison.

Blank, R. M. (2006, March). Was welfare reform successful? *Economists' Voice, 3*, Article 2. Retrieved from http://www.bepress.com/ev/vol3/iss4/art2

Bloom, D., & Michalopoulos, C. (2001). *How welfare and work policies affect employment and income: A synthesis of research*. New York: Manpower Demonstration Research Corporation.

Bryner, G. C. (1998). *Politics and public morality: The great American welfare reform debate*. New York: W. W. Norton.

Center for Budget and Policy Priorities. (2003). *Key provisions in TANF reauthorization bills passed by the Senate Finance Committee and the House*. Retrieved from http://www.cbpp.org/9-22-03tanf.htm

Cherlin, A., Burton, L., Francis, J., Henrici, J., Lein, L., Quane, J., & Bogen, K. (2001). *Sanctions and case closings for noncompliance: Who is affected and why?* Baltimore: Johns Hopkins University Press.

Clinton, B. (2006, August 22). How we ended welfare, together. *The New York Times*.

Cohen, D. L. (1994, February 9). Governors tout state welfare reforms. *Education Week*, p. 15.

DeParle, J. (1994, January 5). White House puzzle: How to let welfare reform wait while seeming to pursue it. *The New York Times*.

Derthick, M. (1979). *Policymaking for social security*. Washington, DC: Brookings Institution.

Friedlander, D., & Gueron, J. M. (1990). *Are high-cost services more effective than low-cost services? Evidence from experimental evaluations of welfare-to-work programs*. New York: Manpower Demonstration Research Corporation.

Gais, T. L. (2002). *Welfare reform findings in brief.* Albany, NY: Nelson A. Rockefeller Institute of Government.

Goodstain, L. (1994, November 15). Bishops critical of Gingrich on welfare cutback; Panel on sexual abuse recommends compassionate response to victims. *The Washington Post,* p. A3.

Moffitt, R. (2000). *Welfare programs and labor supply.* Baltimore: Department of Economics, Johns Hopkins University.

Moynihan, P., & Reagan, R. (1989). After years of debate, welfare reform clears. In *Congressional Quarterly Almanac 1988* (pp. 349–364). Washington, DC: Congressional Quarterly.

Office of Family Assistance, U.S. Department of Health and Human Services. (2003). *TANF Fifth Annual Report to Congress.* Retrieved from http://www.acf.hhs.gov/programs/ofa/annualreport5

Office of Family Assistance, U.S. Department of Health and Human Services. (2006). *TANF Seventh Annual Report to Congress.* Retrieved from http://www.acf.hhs.gov//programs/ofa/annualreport7/ar7index.htm

Pavetti, L. (2004). *The challenge of achieving high work participation rates in welfare programs* (Policy Brief No. 31). Washington, DC: Brookings Institution.

Pear, R. (1996, August 6). Changes in how welfare is operated, while sweeping, will be taking shape slowly. *The New York Times,* p. A11.

Pear, R. (2004, October 13). Welfare spending shows huge shift. *The New York Times,* p. A1.

Rector, R. (2006, August 24). Bill Clinton was right. *The Heritage Foundation.* Retrieved from http://www.heritage.org/Press/Commentary/ed082406a.cfm

Rovner, J. (1988). Welfare reform: The issue that bubbled up from the states to Capitol Hill. *Governing, December,* 17–21.

Seib, G. F. (1993, December 28). Clinton aides debate whether welfare reform will interfere with legislation on health care. *Wall Street Journal.*

Skocpol, T. (1992). *Protecting soldiers and mothers: The political origins of social policy in the United States.* Cambridge, MA: Harvard University Press.

State Policy Documentation Project. (1999). Washington, DC: Center for Law and Social Policy and Center on Budget and Policy Priorities.

Waldfogel, J. (1994). *Integrating child and family services: Lessons from Arkansas, Colorado, and Maryland.* Cambridge, MA: Malcolm Wiener Center for Social Policy, Kennedy School of Government, Harvard University.

Welfare Rules Database. (2005). *Welfare rules database: A longitudinal database tracking state AFDC/TANF policies.* Washington, DC: Urban Institute.

Zedlewski, S. R. (1999). *Work activity and obstacles to work among TANF recipients.* Washington, DC: Urban Institute Press.

# CHAPTER 2

# Social Policy and Marriage

## Lawrence M. Mead

What can government do to strengthen marriage? That is the most difficult question in national social policy today. I have not previously written much about this. Here are some preliminary thoughts.

To begin with, what is the marriage problem? I take it to mean two things. First, many fewer adults today marry and stay married than was once the case. One-fifth of adults have never been married at all, and about a half of marriages fail. Second, fewer children are born to or remain with married parents. A third of children are now born to unmarried mothers. These problems impose social costs that all poverty scholars acknowledge.

Like most social problems, the marriage problem has two dimensions. On one level, it affects the entire society, including the middle class, as is seen in the high divorce rates. Then, on a second level is a much more acute problem among the poor and racial minorities, seen above all in high rates of unwed pregnancy. In 2000, 27% of births were unwed among whites, but 43% among Hispanics and 69% among blacks (U.S. Department of Commerce, 2002, p. 59). That the middle class still marries at all, whereas the poor often do not, is widening inequality in America (Ellwood & Jencks, 2004). To strengthen marriage, we have to cause more adults to marry and stay married, so that more children have two parents, *and* we have to address the problem within both the middle class and the poor.

What has government done to strengthen marriage until now? My sense is—not much. Actually, government probably made the middle-class problem worse by making divorce easier than it was several decades ago. Some would say that government also undermined the poor family by permitting easier welfare for single mothers. The evidence for that is not so strong. But clearly government has not done much of anything to promote marriage. In social policy, marriage is virtually a new idea.

## WHY THE FOCUS ON WORK?

Instead, our recent innovations in social policy are centered mostly on getting poor adults to work. That has been the focus of welfare reform and many other policies going back 20 years. The welfare reform act of 1996 affirmed marriage rhetorically, but did much less to promote it than work. Why do we focus so much more on employment than the family? For three reasons.

First, lack of work is the more important cause of poverty, at least in the short run. That is, low family income is caused more clearly by low earnings than by whether the parents are married or not. Several research studies show this. In lifting families out of poverty, employment is paramount (Bane, 1986; Smith, 1988).

Second, government has done better at raising work level than at strengthening the family. Mandatory work programs tied to welfare showed a power to move poor adults into work, and therefore they became the centerpiece of our current welfare policy. These effects furthermore were certified by evaluations of high quality. Tougher work requirements appear to be the main reason why the welfare rolls have fallen by more than 60% since 1994—truly a revolution in social policy. And the effects of this, we know, were mostly good even for children and the family (Mead, 2001b). Recently, family programs have appeared that might be able to do something about marital problems, but they have yet to prove themselves, as I discuss later.

Third and most important, promoting work has been more popular than promoting marriage. The American public is willing to help the poor, but it insists that the adult poor work alongside the taxpayers. Americans do not object to helping people in need, but the adults must work if they can. So the public will to enforce work is clear-cut. Indeed, this will is so strong that the mystery is why welfare reform did not happen 20 years sooner. This was largely because a Democratic majority in Congress prevented fundamental change in welfare until the passage of the Personal Responsibility and Work Opportunity Reconciliation Act (PRWORA) in 1996 (Mead, 2001a).

Compared with work, Americans are unwilling presently to enforce marriage or pressure people to marry. According to polls, people are distressed by the decline of the family, but they are also tolerant of it. They wish it had not happened, but they are not willing to stigmatize single mothers (Thornton, 1995). Work, in contrast, is among what I call the common obligations— competences that we expect citizens to display. It is right up there with obeying the law and speaking English. Only because we believe this are we willing to enforce work on welfare adults, and bear the risks and costs of doing so (Mead, 1986, chap. 11). Marriage, however, people see as a private matter. They know marriage is important for society, but they are not yet willing to have government promote it. In enforcing work, we have both a mandate and means—a clear public will and effective programs. In promoting marriage, currently, we have neither.

## WHY MARRIAGE IS EMERGING

Nevertheless, the case for promoting marriage is getting stronger, also for three reasons. First, priorities have changed. We have addressed the work problem among the poor to a significant extent through welfare reform and other measures. We have not finished the job, but we are making progress. That makes the family problem relatively more important than previously. Most poor mothers gain by working and so do their children, but they would be a lot better off if they were married and the fathers of their children were pulling their weight. That would markedly improve the prospects of poor children. Second, the politics of the issue may be changing. Although most of the public is still ambivalent about promoting marriage, a pro-marriage movement has arisen. Third, promising programs may be appearing that could strengthen marriage.

As I see it, the marriage movement faces two challenges. One is to develop marriage programs and other policies to the point where they clearly and reliably succeed. The second task is political—to sell these policies to a broad public, to develop a constituency for promoting marriage, which we lack at present. These steps are interrelated. The programs are essential to get support for marriage policy, but equally, the programs cannot succeed unless there is broader support for enforcing marriage than we now see. Let me enlarge on each of these dimensions.

## PROGRAMS FOR THE MIDDLE CLASS

What new policies might we imagine to address the middle-class marriage problem, which primarily means divorce? The following are some preliminary ideas. Nonpoor people typically get married before having children, but then conflicts arise and they split. To counter this, first, we could roll back no-fault divorce. It seems apparent to me that many people get married, then divorce, without a serious effort to work out differences. That frees them from immediate distress, but it also costs them—and their children, and the society—much of the benefits of marriage. Covenant marriage has already arisen as an alternative to no-fault. But it may be necessary actually to undo the no-fault divorce reforms of the 1960s.

Second, in addition to tightening divorce rules, we may want to condition divorce on an effort to avoid it, to be sure parents have done all they can to stay together. Maybe divorce should not be allowed unless the parents undergo some form of counseling to see if reconciliation is possible. They would have to undertake it sincerely, not as a formality. In some cases now, judges already say to couples in court, "I don't believe you need to be divorced. Talk it over, and see whether this can be avoided." Maybe that effort should be mandated.

Third, it might be advisable to make it tougher to get married in the first place. Right now, to get a marriage license, you have to answer certain medical questions, but you do not have to show that you are emotionally ready to get married. What if couples who want a marriage license had to explain how they were going to handle issues that couples commonly break up over, such as where they are going to live, how they are going to support themselves, and whether and when they are going to have children? A couple would have to give credible answers to those questions before they could get a marriage license. If they could not do so, or if differences arose over the issues, this would postpone the marriage.

When churches marry people, they make them address these questions, by making them go through premarital counseling. Maybe churches could certify to government that the couples they marry had gone through this process. The government would provide counseling for people outside churches.

This implies that getting married would no longer be an automatic right. Rather, it would become a status requiring an element of preparation. It should not be exclusive, but qualifying should still make some demand. To graduate from high school, you have to pass a certain set of courses, and then we define you as employable. To get a driving license, you have to pass a driving test. The same here. You have to go through a marriage program, and then you are declared marriageable. Marriage is still a gamble, but there would be more chance that the newlyweds would stay together. And getting divorced would no longer be an automatic right either. You would have to show that you had made reasonable efforts to avoid it.

For a couple to form and have children without marriage would still be legal, much as people who drop out of school can still get jobs. But these would now be common-law marriages, without the direct sanction and approval of the society.

The reason for these requirements is simply that society has an important stake in marriages being strong and enduring. If we think this way, we are beginning to view marriage as among the common obligations. Marriage would never be mandatory, like death and taxes. To live a single life should always be permissible. But *if* you got married, you would have to approach it seriously. I realize that this suggestion is currently out of bounds. But that just gets to the key matter—the politics of marriage.

One less extreme measure would be to reduce the financial disincentives in welfare or the tax code that some think discourage marriage. But I see little evidence that disincentives affect actual marriage behavior. In terms of effects anywhere in social policy, incentives are not worth the analytic attention they receive.

## PROGRAMS FOR THE POOR

Now policies for the poor. Here the marriage problem is primarily the result of unwed pregnancy, the failure of parents to get married at all, rather than divorce. For starters, we should continue with the welfare work policies we have. They mainly target employment rather than marriage, yet evaluations show that they have some pro-marriage effects. In two studies, work requirements increased marriage (Gassman-Pines & Yoshikawa, 2006; Knox, Miller, & Gennetian, 2000). Welfare reform seems to be the main reason why, during the 1990s, unwed pregnancy declined but cohabitation rose. Although reform was aimed mainly at work, it sent a message about self-reliance that also altered sexual behavior in constructive ways (Sawhill, 2002, pp. 80–83).

When you require the mother to work, there is indirect pressure on the father to work

also, or to help out in other ways. Often, when the mother faces a work test, she takes a job and her spouse tends the children, an inversion of the traditional roles. Nevertheless, the father is back in the house, and on average that is good for the children. Here again, marriage promotion and preservation programs could well make a contribution, depending on the development going on now.

The other area that needs development is programs serving low-income men. The men, one could argue, are the immediate reason why we have a marriage crisis among the poor and minorities. Among these groups, most fathers of children fail to marry the mothers and take little responsibility for their children. The men, even more than the women, suffer from a lack of steady employment. Failure as a breadwinner is one reason the men desert their families—or are thrown out by the mothers (Edin & Kefalas, 2005, chaps. 2–3). For reasons nobody understands, the mothers are typically more employable than the fathers despite the impediments of caring for children. Government has learned how to promote employment among poor single mothers, but not yet among poor men.

Child support enforcement has improved, and that is good. Child support affirms an important social norm, and it brings families income that helps them leave welfare (Huang, Kunz, & Garfinkel, 2002). But cracking down on absent fathers is not sufficient. It may simply drive them underground, making them less likely to work in the legal economy. Toughening child support enforcement appears to be one reason why employment by low-skilled younger black men fell in the 1980s and 1990s, even as work levels for black single mothers rose because of welfare reform (Holzer, Offner, & Sorensen, 2005). The fathers also need help with their employment problems.

To me, the most promising development has been child support enforcement programs. In these, fathers who are jobless and behind on child support payments are required either to pay up or to participate in a work program, on pain of going to jail. Thus, there is a combination of help and hassle: You give the father some aid to work, and at the same time he has to pay up or perform in other ways. The leading examples are the Parents' Fair Share program, a national demonstration, and the Children First program in Wisconsin. In evaluations, both of these showed effects on child support payments by the fathers, chiefly by "smoking out" earnings they had not admitted to. But the programs did not show effects on the father's employment (Mincy & Pouncy, 1997). Further development is needed.

There may also be a need for amnesty programs. Some absent fathers roll up insupportable arrearages in child support that they owe. This happens when they have multiple children, do not work for long periods, or are incarcerated and judges do not adjust their judgments. We need fair procedures for reducing arrearages in cases where the fathers are overwhelmed. These would allow some reduction in their debts provided they worked steadily over some period.

In addition, many low-income fathers are imprisoned for criminal offenses. Like child support enforcement, incarceration is a reason why employment by young black men fell even during the prosperous 1990s (Holzer et al., 2005). And more than 600,000 ex-offenders are now exiting the prisons annually, many on parole (U.S. Department of Justice, 2006). Many of these men have families. To help them reconnect and avoid recidivism, they urgently need steady work. Several important experiments with prison reentry programs are now underway.

Government jobs are not in general needed to solve the employment problems of the poor. Lots of jobs are available in the private sector, as immigration shows. But for child support defaulters and ex-offenders— the most disadvantaged men—public employment may be necessary. For these groups,

government may need both to guarantee and mandate work in a hard-and-fast way that is possible only with public jobs. Men with serious child support debts and ex-offenders on parole might be assigned to government work crews, where their attendance and performance would be monitored for a period. After that, they would be placed in the private sector. Such positions are an aspect of some of the experimental programs just mentioned.

The goal is to make absolutely clear to these men that fathering children without commitment or committing crimes will not be tolerated. If you do that, the system will be all over you, and you are in for a life of trouble. But at the same time, if you go straight, society will help you fulfill your obligations. That is the same deal we struck with the welfare mothers.

## MARRIAGE PROGRAMS

All these policies, though constructive, support marriage indirectly. What about measures that attempt to promote marriage directly? They build upon counseling programs for promoting successful marriage, some of which have been favorably evaluated (Butler & Wampler, 1999; Markman, Renick, Floyd, Stanley, & Clements, 1993). The existing programs, however, were aimed largely at the middle class rather than at minorities and the poor—the groups with the most severe marriage problems. The evaluations are also less definitive than the studies we have on welfare work programs. Not all of them were experimental, and few had large numbers of clients.

The U.S. Administration for Children and Families (ACF) is now developing versions of these programs designed for the low-income populations. Among its initiatives are Supporting Health Marriage, which seeks to preserve marriage among couples who are already married, and Building Strong Families, which seeks to strengthen ties between parents who have had children before marriage. The agency plans to implement promising models, then evaluate them to see if they show impacts on the marriage problem. These initiatives are already funded and underway, and additional funding was approved as part of the 2006 reauthorization of Temporary Assistance for Needy Families (TANF).

Building Strong Families focuses on what are sometimes called fragile families programs. These try to build on the closeness that unwed parents typically feel at the time their child is born. The idea is to parlay that tie into a long-term relationship. Some view these programs as more promising than the child support enforcement programs mentioned previously. The latter take effect only after the parents have split, when it may be too late to repair their relationship. Fragile families programs aim at preventing the couple from breaking up in the first place. So far these programs have not shown convincing evaluation results that I know of.

## THE POLITICS OF MARRIAGE

Besides developing better policies, the other necessity is to develop more political support for strengthening marriage. The family has been neglected as a political issue until recently. Historically, it has never been the main subject of political controversy. Something else has always been more important. Governments worried about scarcity, war, religion, and class and racial conflict. The family and private life could never get on the agenda.

But now as Fukuyama says, we have reached the end of history. That is, the Cold War is over, and deep conflict over political fundaments is a thing of the past, at least within the West (Fukuyama, 1992). Even the war against terrorism is less threatening than were the struggles of prior centuries, because war against terrorism is largely external to our society. So with older issues quiescent, the family is at last getting on the front burner in politics, perhaps for the first time in history.

Civilization has long been in denial about the family problem. In ages past, marriages appeared stronger, and yet the society never faced up to the core question in marriage, which is how to maintain the relationship between the spouses. Robin Dion, one of the researchers developing marriage programs for ACF, remarked to me how the "family" programs we have are all about helping mothers and children. Nobody wants to talk about the relationship between the mother and the father, which is the real core of the problem. That has been true of the culture as a whole. We revere the family, but we evade the painful emotional dilemma at the heart of it.

Our sacred texts, such as the Bible, lay down a lot of rules about marriage, but they say remarkably little about how the spouses are to get along. And what the texts do say is too sacrificial in tone. The Bible often suggests that the way to make any relationship work is simply to bear all the burdens. Do what the other person wants. Be dutiful, obedient, and cooperative. Sacrifice yourself. That is the way to get into heaven. That does not sound like the good news. It is enough to scare anybody off marriage! Experience teaches that we cannot get along with people in this one-sided manner. You have to be considerate of others, but you also have to know and express your own needs. There has to be mutuality.

The marriage movement has dared to state that reality. Many of those who are trying to heal and promote marriage say the key is openness, as much as or more than sacrifice. Marriage manuals and courses talk about marriage in this new way. The movement is writing what amounts to a new scripture for this important question, and this *is* the good news. There still has to be commitment; marriage involves facing conflicts, not being deterred, not running away. But it is not simply bearing all the burdens, not simply bondage. I sense here a new maturity about this central human challenge. If this spreads, it will be of historical importance. Marriage could once again become a center for hope for our culture.

## APPEALING TO THE MIDDLE CLASS

How do we sell that idea to the middle class? For most Americans, marriage is far from dead. Most people do marry, and yet the high divorce rate indicates marriage has ceased to be a center of hope. Americans currently evince more doubts about marriage than they do about employment. Many today find their jobs more meaningful than their private lives. People once saw the family as a refuge from the competitive world of capitalism, but today the workplace often becomes a refuge from the family (Hochschild, 1997).

The marriage movement has not yet learned to turn this around. Some advocates for marriage talk about it in terms, again, that are too sacrificial. They say marriage is necessary for economic survival, or for the children. It is all about commitment. And again, that is what the sacred texts seem to say. But that is not a message that the middle class is able to hear.

The message is not even true. Going back to the book of Genesis, marriage is first for the spouses. Each of them is to have an adult companion to relate to. At its best, marriage allows adults to work through many of the emotional problems from their own pasts. When we fail to get along with other people, it is usually because our initial relationships with our parents or siblings were not constructive. In marriage, we may well repeat those errors, but we also have a chance to transcend them and build healthy relationships for the first time.

David Blankenhorn, who heads the Institute for American Values, once characterized marriage to me as "the whole enchilada." He meant that marriage is not without risk and difficulty, but that marriage is the best thing life has to offer for most people. For most adults, marriage should be the center of their lives. That's what middle-class Americans have to hear. They have to recover hope that this central institution can be a focus of meaning.

To accomplish that, we have to find a way to talk about commitment and at the same time allow second chances for people who have not made it the first time around. Many people are in that situation. We do this successfully in education and employment. We say you have to meet standards to get a degree or get ahead, but we will also give you more than one chance to make it. If you failed at school when you were young, you can go to community college later. If you failed in business, you can try again, and government will assist you. You have to take the initiative, and the standards remain high, but you can try again and again. In marriage, we have not yet found a way to combine serious standards with forgiveness and second chances. The suggestions I made earlier about making marriage and divorce more demanding aim to define a middle between serial relationships and no second chances at all.

## APPEALING TO THE POOR

Now how do we sell marriage to the poor? Their current attitudes are quite different from those of the middle class. Whereas the nonpoor often attempt marriage and fail, the poor tend to avoid it altogether. Most nonpoor people are more cautious about childbearing than they are about matrimony; they know parenthood involves a long-term commitment, one you cannot escape from as easily, under current policy, as you can from marriage. Low-income people, in contrast, are less guarded about parenthood than they are about marriage. They often procreate casually, but then treat marriage as a distant goal. They think marriage will be possible only after they become much more affluent and established. They see it as an achievement rather than a commitment. Certainly, mere pregnancy is no longer a reason to get married, as it once was (Edin & Kefalas, 2005, chap. 4).

The trouble, of course, is that this attitude involves serious costs for everyone involved and the society. Parents who procreate in advance of commitment to each other seldom stay together or get married later. At the time of the birth, they may intend to marry, but they seldom follow through. That leaves a future of single parenthood that is more barren for them and the children, on average, than if the family had truly formed.

As with the middle class, the case for marriage cannot stress only the gains to the children or the society. The parents have to see that marriage is central to *their* futures. For this population, that primarily means avoiding early pregnancy. Pregnancy is less often a prelude to marriage than a barrier to it. A single woman with children is much less marriageable than is one without children. Marriage advocates sometimes suggest that matrimony is a solution to teen pregnancy, but marriages before age 20 seldom last. For teenagers, the way forward is not to become pregnant *or* marry until they are out of their teens, and preferably through school and employed. Only if women remain childless this long are they likely to marry at all, let alone stay that way.

After age 20, the appeal of marriage has to be, less to the attractions of mutuality as with the better-off, than to practical advantages. For low-skilled people, the best hope for entering the middle class is teamwork. Poor parents who split up can expect a life of struggle with little mobility. Those who stay together and work side by side have a hope of affording a house in the suburbs. The main thing that distinguishes the black middle class from less fortunate blacks is a higher incidence of two-parent families. In the end, the attitude that low-income people have developed toward marriage, which can seem so liberated, is a dead end. They have to realize that, if they are to be parents at all, they can expect to prosper only if they get married and stay that way.

To reestablish that norm will require a struggle with the street culture of poor men. This chiefly means black men, but similar attitudes have developed among Hispanics, one reason marriage is in sharp decline among that group. Street culture allows men to abuse women, yet father children with them without thought of the consequences. The mothers are not innocent, yet in principle they would like to be married. For the men, that is less clear. Their exploitation of women appears to be a compensation for the failure most of them have known in the work world. So to reconcile poor men with marriage, the first necessity, again, is to confront their own employment problems, as suggested previously.

The stakes stretch beyond the family. A restoration of marriage is essential to improving racial integration in America. The main reason whites resist fuller integration with blacks and Hispanics is minority family patterns and their social effects. Most whites no longer believe that minorities as individuals are inferior, and integration in the university, the workplace, and other public settings is accepted. But many whites do resist living in the same neighborhoods as minorities and sending their children to the same schools. That is because in these settings they would have to confront the high rate of single parenthood among minorities and the high levels of crime and school problems associated with that.

The disorders are perpetuated by youths in gangs, but they occur because adult men are absent from these neighborhoods. Only husbands and fathers who stand by their families are able to control their own children, face down the gangs, and keep order. But to create more such men among minorities requires solving the marriage problem. Thus, restoring marriage to the point where two-parent families are again the norm among all racial groups, if not universal, is critical to advancing racial harmony.

The struggle is also with black and Hispanic opinionmakers. Minority leaders and professional people, including academics and clergy, recognize the problem posed by minority nonmarriage, but they hesitate to disapprove it. They fear stigmatizing the groups they want society to help. They have to be convinced that this is counterproductive. There are some favorable omens. In 1999, an important statement about the problem was developed by leading black and white experts acting together. This was a manifesto for change in which many leading blacks joined (Morehouse Research Institute & Institute for American Values, 1999). Another promising development was the Promise Keeper's movement of several years ago, where black men promised *en masse* to take their obligations more seriously. Talk is cheap, but this declaration was at least the end of denial.

## CONCLUSION

To conclude, in the struggle to restore marriage, politics and policy are intimately connected. We need better programs to promote and strengthen marriage, and there is some prospect that we will have them. But we also have to sell that mission to the American public. Only when such programs have a popular will clearly behind them will they be able to strengthen marriage.

Welfare reform offers a precedent. What changed the nature of welfare was not only the new work tests implemented in the 1990s but a political climate that legitimized those requirements. In Wisconsin, families began to go to work and leave welfare from the moment serious controversy about welfare broke out in the middle 1980s. They got a message that more self-reliance would be expected of them—before concrete requirements were even legislated, let alone implemented (Mead, 2004, chap. 9). Nationally as well, the welfare caseload fell sharply across the country from 1994, once a will to require work was clear—even before PRWORA was enacted in 1996 and even in states that did little to implement work tests "on the ground."

So too with the marriage problem. A will to address the problem is essential to developing better programs, and then those programs can strengthen a public commitment to proceed further, in a synergistic cycle. Attitudes and policies must shift together and in step. As Lincoln said, "We must think anew, and act anew. . . . and then we shall save our country" (Lincoln, 1989, p. 415).

## REFERENCES

Bane, M. J. (1986). Household composition and poverty. In S. H. Danziger & D. H. Weinberg (Eds.), *Fighting poverty: What works and what doesn't* (chap. 9, pp. 209–231). Cambridge, MA: Harvard University Press.

Butler, M. H., & Wampler, K. S. (1999). A meta-analytic update of research on the couple communication program. *American Journal of Family Therapy, 27*(3), 223–237.

Edin, K., & Kefalas, M. (2005). *Promises I can keep: Why poor women put motherhood before marriage.* Berkeley: University of California Press.

Ellwood, D. T., & Jencks, C. (2004). *The spread of single-parent families in the United States since 1960.* Cambridge, MA: Harvard University, Kennedy School of Government.

Fukuyama, F. (1992). *The end of history and the last man.* New York: Free Press.

Gassman-Pines, A., & Yoshikawa, H. (2006). Five-year effects of an anti-poverty program on marriage among never-married mothers. *Journal of Policy Analysis and Management, 25*(1), 11–30.

Hochschild, A. R. (1997). *The time bind: When work becomes home and home becomes work.* New York: Metropolitan Books.

Holzer, H. J., Offner, P., & Sorensen, E. (2005). Declining employment among young black less-educated men: The role of incarceration and child support. *Journal of Policy Analysis and Management, 24*(2), 329–350.

Huang, C. C., Kunz, J., & Garfinkel, I. (2002). The effect of child support on welfare exits and re-entries. *Journal of Policy Analysis and Management, 21*(4), 557–576.

Knox, V., Miller, C., & Gennetian, L. A. (2000). *Reforming welfare and rewarding work: A summary of the final report on the Minnesota family investment program.* New York: Manpower Demonstration Research Corporation.

Lincoln, A. (1989). *Speeches and writings, 1859–1865.* New York: Library of America.

Markman, H. J., Renick, M. J., Floyd, F. J., Stanley, S. M., & Clements, M. (1993). Preventing marital distress through communication and conflict management training: A 4- and 5-year follow-up. *Journal of Consulting and Clinical Psychology, 61*(1), 70–77.

Mead, L. M. (1986). *Beyond entitlement: The social obligations of citizenship.* New York: Free Press.

Mead, L. M. (2001a). The politics of conservative welfare reform. In R. M. Blank & R. Haskins (Eds.), *The new world of welfare* (chap. 7, pp. 201–220). Washington, DC: Brookings Institution.

Mead, L. M. (2001b). Welfare reform: Meaning and effects. *Policy Currents, 11*(2), 7–13.

Mead, L. M. (2004). *Government matters: Welfare reform in Wisconsin.* Princeton, NJ: Princeton University Press.

Mincy, R. B., & Pouncy, H. (1997). Paternalism, child support enforcement, and fragile families. In L. M. Mead (Ed.), *The new paternalism: Supervisory approaches to poverty* (chap. 4, pp. 130–160). Washington, DC: Brookings Institution.

Morehouse Research Institute & Institute for American Values. (1999). *Turning the corner on father absence in black America.* Atlanta: Morehouse Research Institute.

Sawhill, I. V. (2002). The perils of early motherhood. *The Public Interest, 146*(Winter), 74–84.

Smith, J. P. (1988). Poverty and the family. In G. D. Sandefur & M. Tienda (Eds.), *Divided opportunities: Minorities, poverty, and social policy* (chap. 6, pp. 141–172). New York: Plenum.

Thornton, A. (1995). Attitudes, values, and norms related to nonmarital fertility. In U.S. Department of Health and Human Services, Public Health Service, *Report to Congress on out-of-wedlock childbearing* (pp. 201–215). Washington, DC: U.S. Government Printing Office.

U.S. Department of Commerce, Bureau of the Census. (2002). *Statistical abstract of the United States 2002.* Washington, DC: U.S. Government Printing Office.

U.S. Department of Justice. (2006). *Bureau of Justice Statistics data on prison inmates returning to society.* Retrieved April 6, 2006, from the BJS Web site.

# CHAPTER 3

# Working Families Should Not Be Poor

## The New Hope Program

ANJALI E. GUPTA, JESSICA THORNTON WALKER, AND ALETHA C. HUSTON

In 1994, just 2 years before the passage of the Personal Responsibility and Work Opportunity Reconciliation Act (PRWORA), a group of concerned citizens in Milwaukee, Wisconsin, launched an employment-support program called New Hope.[1] The concept originated in response to structural factors in both the labor market and the welfare system that worked against low-income workers. Welfare rules that reduced benefits nearly one dollar for every dollar increase in earnings, low wages in the labor market, the necessity and expense of child care, and the unlikelihood of obtaining employer-provided medical insurance meant that leaving welfare for work often did not improve a family's economic status.

New Hope's founders thought Milwaukee—and perhaps America—could do better. In creating the program, they were guided by the notions that (a) people who are willing to work full time should be able to do so and (b) they should not be poor (Huston et al., 2003). New Hope's founders aimed to demonstrate a policy for working poor adults that would increase employment and earnings and decrease welfare use by addressing the problems of low wages, lack of health care, and lack of child care (Brock et al., 1997). Specifically, adults working full time (30 hours a week or more) were eligible to receive wage supplements to bring their incomes above the poverty threshold, subsidized health insurance, and child-care subsidies. Community service jobs were available to people who could not find regular employment.

In the United States, we live by simple math: Work leads to economic self-sufficiency and ultimately puts Americans ahead economically. Unfortunately, for many Americans the math doesn't always work out: Welfare leavers and other low-income Americans seldom experience substantial rewards from work, and many remain poor despite their work efforts. In the past decade, "working poor" has become an all-too-familiar catch phrase, representing individuals who, according to the U.S. Bureau of Labor Statistics (2006), spend 27 or more weeks per year in the workforce but do not earn enough to break the poverty threshold.[2] The working poor face practical constraints of adequate earnings, child care, and health insurance familiar to most working Americans, but these key work supports are generally out of reach. Lacking work supports can create chronic economic deficiencies and stress, which can ultimately harm parents' and children's well-being.

In this chapter, we consider New Hope—an experimental program that promoted full-time work and economic self-sufficiency among low-income adults by addressing key problems of the working poor (i.e., low wages, child-care costs, and the lack of health benefits). We examine the program's effectiveness in reducing poverty and improving the well-being of children and families. Its features are examined as model policies to aid working families.

## ISSUES FACING WORKING FAMILIES

The New Hope demonstration was carried out between 1994 and 1998, a time when welfare rolls were declining rapidly and many low-income parents were entering the workforce. Although many people believed that PRWORA would improve the lives of low-income children and families, the problems that New Hope targeted are very much still in evidence.

### Low Earnings

Since 1996, people have increasingly left the welfare system for employment, but many remain poor. This has led to a growing population of individuals who "play by the rules," relying on earnings rather than welfare, but have incomes below the poverty line. Surprisingly, more than half (58%) of the poor who worked in 2004 usually worked full time, and among all workers who usually had full-time wage and salary jobs, about 4.6 million lived in poverty in 2004 (U.S. Bureau of Labor Statistics, 2006). Overall, 4.3 million families are classified as working poor (U.S. Bureau of Labor Statistics, 2006). Although a decade has passed since PRWORA, the poverty rate of persons in the labor force is unchanged from 1997 levels (U.S. Bureau of Labor Statistics, 2006).

In recent years, large numbers of single mothers have joined the workforce and obtained jobs. In many cases, however, they exchanged welfare for earnings with little or no net gain (Bloom & Michalopoulos, 2001). Today, female heads of households are more than twice as likely as their male counterparts to be among the working poor (18.4% and 8.6%, respectively; U.S. Bureau of Labor Statistics, 2006).

One reason for poverty among the working population is wage stagnation. Economic growth used to improve earnings for all workers, but since the 1980s, large numbers of workers have remained poor in periods of prosperity. Real wages have fallen, especially at the low end of the continuum, and income inequality has increased (Blank, 1997; Blank & Schmidt, 2001).

### Child Care

Child care is an integral and expensive part of working-family life. In 2004, more than 62% of women with children under age 6 were in the labor force (U.S. Bureau of Labor Statistics, 2005). Concerns about safety, reliability, convenience, enrichment, and cost make obtaining child care a complicated venture for any worker, particularly one with low wages.

According to the National Association of Child Care Resource and Referral Agencies

[NACCRRA] (2006), child care consumes a large percentage of working families' resources. Families earning $18,000 or less and purchasing averaged-priced child care in one of 38 states would expend at least 30% of their annual income (NACCRRA, 2006). These figures are based on average prices and do not consider quality or accreditation. Overall, child care is a significant and necessary cash outlay for families with working parents—especially for single mothers without kith or kin child-care resources.

### Health Care

The United States continues to face a health insurance crisis. In 1996, nearly one-third (30.8%) of poor adults were without health insurance (Bennefield, 1997). The numbers have not improved. In 2004, 80% of the medically uninsured belonged to working families; this translates into more than 27 million workers without health coverage (Kaiser Family Foundation, 2006). Many low-wage jobs do not offer coverage, or if they do, the co-payments can be prohibitive.

### Work Supports

In summary, for many working Americans, earning wages does not equate to earning a living. Low wages for unskilled workers, high child-care costs, and lack of health insurance can relegate a working family to poverty. Bernheimer, Weisner, and Lowe (2003) aptly describe the situation as a "house of cards," highlighting the instability faced by America's working poor. With few resources, there may be little, if any, room for unforeseen or inescapable predicaments. A single, low-income, working mother without a back-up child-care plan may encounter a precipitous slope from a sick child to missed work, job loss, utility shut-offs, eviction, and perhaps even homelessness. Providing work supports can, as we will demonstrate, make crucial and positive differences in the lives of America's working families.

### NEW HOPE: A UNIQUE SOCIAL PROGRAM

In the 1990s, a number of antipoverty, employment, and welfare-to-work demonstration experiments were initiated to ascertain the effects of various welfare and employment policies.[3] New Hope stood apart. Where many were created to test welfare reform or elimination, New Hope offered a different solution, emphasizing gainful employment by providing a flexible menu of work supports. Where many were tied to the welfare system, New Hope originated from a movement to help all Americans have decent jobs. It was offered to adults with earnings below 150% of the federal poverty threshold regardless of their welfare or family status. Participation was also based on geographical residence within target zip codes, a minimum age of 18 years, and the desire to work full time.

Because the creators of New Hope wanted to demonstrate a policy that might be emulated elsewhere, they included a high-quality evaluation of its effects as part of the overall plan. They contracted with Manpower Demonstration Research Corporation (MDRC), a well-known independent evaluation firm, to conduct a study using a random assignment method. This evaluation demonstrated that New Hope achieved its intended direct effects: It increased participants' employment and earnings. Remarkably, the positive effects transcended the economic sphere. Children in the program families experienced a range of personal benefits, including higher academic achievement, more participation in structured activities, and more positive social behavior. These results are encouraging. They suggest that with adequate work supports low-income adults are better positioned to engage in work and that their children are better off academically and socio-emotionally.

## Program Components

The New Hope program supported participants' full-time work efforts by providing child-care subsidies and health insurance subsidies. It ensured that full-time work lifted participants out of poverty by providing a sliding-scale earnings supplement that buoyed incomes above the federal poverty line when combined with the Earned Income Tax Credit (EITC). In addition, all program group participants were assigned project representatives who explained program rules, answered questions, and supported them in identifying employment opportunities and accessing federal and state social services. Temporary community service jobs (CSJs) were available to those who could not find work. CSJs provided minimum-wage earnings and work experience and were subject to the employers' standard hiring and firing practices.

Because the child-care, health insurance, and income benefits were available only when work effort reached 30 or more hours per week, the program motivated participants to work full-time. At the same time, it did not discourage participants from working more than the required 30 weekly hours: Benefits were structured so as not to decrease as fast as earnings increased. Participation in New Hope did not preclude public assistance, so program and control group members remained eligible for state and federal social services. However, program group members who worked full time were unlikely to qualify for government benefits because of their work and New Hope-enhanced incomes.

The program package was offered cafeteria-style. Qualifying program group participants were free, but not obliged, to use any or all of the benefits. Ethnographic interviews suggest that participants tended to take up the particular combinations of New Hope benefits to which they did not previously have access or that best fit their daily routines, personal sociocultural beliefs and values, and financial and social-resource "configurations" (Gibson & Weisner, 2002; Lowe & Weisner, 2004). Although some used benefits selectively, others failed to qualify because their work level did not meet the 30-hour requirement.

During 3 years of eligibility, approximately 88% of program group members received some of the available program benefits for an average of 18 months. Earnings supplements were the most used benefit, taken by approximately 87% of participants for an average of 15 months. Approximately 56% of the participants used the health insurance benefit for an average of 12 months, and approximately 52% used the child-care benefit for an average of 16 months. Approximately 32% took CSJs (Huston et al., 2003).

## The Random-Assignment Evaluation

New Hope was evaluated with a rigorous experimental design using random assignment. Incorporating this experimental component gave New Hope broad policy relevance. A lottery-like process, random assignment created two groups equivalent on all baseline characteristics. The program group (N = 678) received the intervention but the control group (N = 679) did not. Random assignment permits evaluation of these groups during and after the experiment and the attribution of significant group differences to the New Hope program.

To document New Hope's effects on economic well-being, data on participants' work, earnings, and receipt of public assistance were examined. The state of Wisconsin and the New Hope program provided administrative records detailing welfare, payroll, and benefits receipt.

In addition to the economic factors targeted directly by the policy, New Hope's founders expected that the program would affect both parents' and children's well-being indirectly. Because New Hope provided work supports that might reduce poverty and improve child-care options, it had the potential for positive contributions to children's well-being. Therefore, the evaluation included an in-depth study of families and children to ascertain program and control group differences. Interviews and surveys were collected from parents, as many as two of their children, and the children's teachers at 2, 5, and 8 years after random assignment.

This study, called the Child and Family Study (CFS), consisted of 745 families with children ages 1 to 10 years at random assignment. It probed children's academic achievement, socio-emotional well-being, nonparental care, and extracurricular activities. Information was gathered on parents' economic and emotional well-being and parenting behavior. In addition, an ethnographic study was conducted with a randomly selected subset of 44 program and control group families to document New Hope's influence in a fluid and in-depth fashion.

Having multiple sources of data from child, teacher, and parent reports brings strength to the evaluation. Findings have higher validity when based on several sources. If only parent-based reports of child characteristics are gathered, such data can be confounded by the parent's well-being. A source outside of the family, namely a teacher, makes the findings more robust.

## Conceptual Framework

The New Hope program was not designed with the objective of direct effects on children and family life, but there were both theoretical and empirical reasons to expect that the economic changes in families would have indirect repercussions for families. The conceptual model guiding the evaluation is shown in Figure 3.1. It was based on two theoretical traditions designed to explain the relations of family income to children's development. We refer to these as (1) family resource and (2) socialization or family process theories.

*Family Resources.* Low family income, particularly during early and middle childhood, is associated with low school performance and behavior problems (McLoyd, 1998). According to the family resource model, the relation between income and child well-being is explained, in part, by the quantity and quality of goods that families consume, as well as by the environments that children experience in and out of the home—sometimes called material, human, and social capital (Becker, 1981; Coleman, 1988). Increased income may allow parents to spend more on their children's education, and health, thereby contributing to their children's achievement.

Family income also influences parents' decisions about child care and out-of-school activities. Children's experiences in these environments play an important role in their academic achievement and social development. In general, formal, center-based child care provides more educational opportunities, and, when quality is equivalent, it leads to more advanced cognitive and language development than informal child care does (National Institute of Child Health and Human Development Early Child Care Research Network [NICHD ECCRN], 2004). Some low-income mothers rely on relatives or friends, but many prefer center care, and use it when it is made available or when they receive subsidies to pay for it (Fuller, Kagan, Caspary, & Gauthier, 2002).

Environments outside the home are influential well beyond the preschool years. Participation in formal after-school programs that provide cognitive stimulation and positive adult interactions is associated with academic achievement among low-income children (Posner & Vandell, 1999). Increased

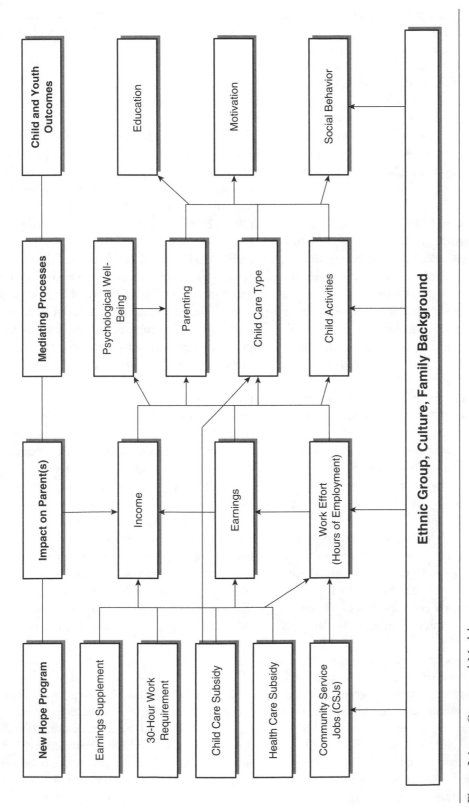

**Figure 3.1** Conceptual Model

income may also enable children to participate in organized extracurricular activities
(e.g., team sports or music lessons) that provide enriching experiences and supervision
while parents are working. To the extent that
they increase the use of high quality child
care and after-school programs, welfare and
antipoverty policies can be expected to have
positive effects on children's cognitive and
social development (Mahoney, Lord, &
Carryl, 2005).

*Socialization and Family Process.* According
to the socialization model, poverty reduces
parents' psychological well-being that, in
turn, affects parenting practices. For low-
income parents, such chronic stressors as single parenthood, financial worries, and the
constant struggle to make ends meet can take
a toll on well-being that, in turn, diminishes
their capacity to be sensitive and supportive
parents (McLoyd, 1998).

Paid employment often provides psychological benefits to low-income women,
despite the many challenges and stressors
that accompany it (D'Ercole, 1988). In addition to increasing financial security, employment often affords opportunities to lessen
social isolation and increase self-esteem
(Sears & Galambos, 1993). On the other
hand, dead-end, low-wage employment with
few benefits may increase a sense of time
pressure, work and family role strain, and
hopelessness about the future; such employment may also have deleterious effects on
parenting and child adjustment (Parcel &
Menaghan, 1997).

Both the resource and socialization models
suggest that the effects of a social policy will
depend on whether family income increases,
the circumstances and amount of parental
employment, the types of environments in
which the child spends time when the
parent(s) is away from home, and the parents'
psychological well-being and parenting practices. Hence, the intervening processes shown

in Figure 3.1 include parent psychological
well-being, parenting, child care, and child
activities.

## EFFECTS OF NEW HOPE

The results of the 2- and 5-year follow-up surveys and the ethnographic study are presently
available. Detailed presentations of the results
of the 2-year and 5-year follow-up periods
appear in Bos et al. (1999) and Huston et al.
(2001, 2003, 2005).[4] The New Hope program
had important and lasting advantages for
parents and children. It had statistically significant effects on families' economic well-being
and parents' psychological well-being, as well
as on children's academic achievement, socio-
emotional well-being, social behavior, participation in organized activities, and nonparental
care environments. In general, these effects
were positive. They existed during the experimental period (i.e., at the 2-year follow-up)
and were sustained even after the program
ended (i.e., at the 5-year follow-up), suggesting that New Hope fundamentally changed
the lives of some program group members.

Because of New Hope's work requirements and flexible program package, experimental effects represent the entire program
group whether the members took up any
benefits or not. Because the program lasted
3 years, findings do not represent what effects
New Hope or an analogous program might
have across a lifetime. Instead, they may provide a conservative estimate of lifetime effects.

### Effects on Parents

*New Hope Increased Earnings and Total
Income.* New Hope increased earnings-
related income and total income, although
the size of the effects diminished and were not
significant after year 3, when the program
supports ended. Across the first 5 years of
follow-up, the impact—program-versus-control

difference—for *earnings-related* income was 10% ($1,021).

Similarly, New Hope increased *average annual total* income during the 5-year follow-up period by about 7% ($883). Total income included earnings, EITC benefits, the New Hope supplement, welfare, and food stamps.

*New Hope Decreased Poverty.* Over the study period, the program group experienced less poverty than did the control group. New Hope substantially reduced poverty over the entire follow-up period, and the effects were equally strong in both the early and the later periods. Over the entire period, for example, 52.7% of the program group had incomes below the poverty line, compared with 66.3% of the control group. Neither welfare nor food stamp receipt differed significantly between the groups but welfare receipt declined dramatically across both groups.

*New Hope Increased Parents' Work Effort.* New Hope's effects on work effort were different depending on a person's employment status at random assignment. Among program group parents who were not employed at random assignment, work effort (average annual number of quarters employed) increased and was significantly higher than that of controls across 5 years after random assignment. These effects were strongest during the first 2 years after random assignment, and they were strongly related to New Hope's provision of CSJs.

By contrast, those who were employed at random assignment did not increase employment, and some who worked more than 40 hours a week reduced their work effort (Huston et al., 2003). Given that one of New Hope's aims was to increase employment, the slight decrease among those already employed at random assignment may appear to be a negative outcome. Instead, this result can be viewed in a positive light because it occurred for people working more than full

time. The program may have enabled parents to adjust their work levels, bringing them into balance with personal responsibilities and goals (e.g., family, community, and education), and maintain their earnings levels.

Although the positive effects on work did not last beyond the experiment's end, at the 5-year follow-up, most program group parents who worked in the program's first year remained employed longer than did their control group counterparts and in jobs that paid more (Huston et al., 2005).

*New Hope Had Few Effects on Parental Hardship and Psychological Well-Being.* At the 2-year mark, program parents reported reduced stress and increased feelings of social support, hope, and time pressure, but there were no effects on several other measures of psychological well-being. New Hope also decreased families' health-care-related material hardships: Program parents reported fewer experiences of going without medical or dental care because they could not pay for treatment. New Hope adults were more likely to have health insurance at the 2-year follow-up, but these effects had faded by the 5-year follow-up. There were no effects of New Hope on health insurance for children, possibly because Wisconsin established an extensive and comprehensive program of child health insurance in the mid-to-late 1990s; therefore, most children in program and control families were covered.

At the 5-year follow-up, only 1 of 10 indicators of psychosocial well-being differed for program and control group adults. Program group members reported a lower frequency of depressive symptoms than did controls, although absolute levels remained fairly high in both groups. Improved mental health could affect parenting, earnings, and household morale and, in turn, could influence children's academic and socio-emotional well-being. Thus, the positive effect on parents' levels of depressive symptoms may be important in the context of the positive child academic and socio-emotional effects described previously.

*New Hope Resulted in Few Parenting Effects.* According to the family process model, economic changes can affect parenting, but there were few effects of New Hope on the parenting practices that we measured. Among parents employed full time at random assignment, New Hope significantly increased parental warmth and parent-reported monitoring of focal—primary child under study—children's activities, but it had virtually no effects on parenting and parent-child relations. At the 5-year follow-up, parenting effects were few.

For older children (11–16 years old), program parents reported higher levels of effective child management: They reported fewer problems with control, less need to use punishment, and less parenting stress than did parents in the control group. Additional analyses suggested that parents' increased sense of effectiveness in controlling their sons at 5 years may have been an outcome of the children's improved behavior rather than a cause (Epps & Huston, 2006).

## Effects on Children

*New Hope Raised Children's Levels of Academic Achievement.* On the whole, New Hope led to improvements in academic achievement, especially for boys. These are apparent in teachers' reports of children's overall academic achievement and classroom study skills, parents' reports of children's reading skills, and children's scores on an individual test of reading achievement. Most of the 2-year program effects remained throughout the 5-year follow-up. That the effects endured 2 years beyond the program's end is important. As previously indicated, it suggests that the policy produced lasting, intrinsic changes in children's academic skills.

Some of the New Hope effects were greater for boys than for girls, partly because control group boys scored quite low. That is, the baseline level for boys was lower than for girls, so there was more room for boys to improve. Teachers rated New Hope boys higher than control boys on classroom study skills (e.g., paying attention, working independently), and New Hope boys were more likely to expect to attend and graduate from college than were control boys.

*For Boys, New Hope Improved Social Behavior.* Teachers rated children on positive social behavior—compliance to requests, sensitivity to others, and autonomy in the classroom—as well as on behavior problems—aggression, disobedience, anxiety, and social withdrawal. Parents also completed the same ratings. New Hope consistently improved the social behavior of boys and had mixed results for girls.

Compared with control families, program parents rated both their sons and their daughters higher on positive social behavior at both 2 and 5 years after random assignment. Interestingly, there were no significant effects on parent-rated problem behaviors.

Teachers' ratings differed by gender. Teachers rated program boys as having higher positive social behavior and fewer behavior problems relative to control group boys. They rated program girls as having lower positive social behavior and more problems than control girls.

*New Hope Increased Enrollment in Formal Child Care.* Relative to control group families, program group families used more formal child care (i.e., center-based care, preschool, Head Start, and school-based extended day programs). This was the case at both the 2- and 5-year follow-ups. At 2 years, children in the program group spent twice as much time as control children did in formal care. By 5 years, this difference had decreased slightly, but it remained robust as program group children spent 1.3 times as much time in formal care as controls even though parents no longer received New Hope subsidies. Although there were no significant effects on home-based care at 2 years, by 5 years program group children experienced significantly less home-based and unsupervised care (Huston et al., 2001, 2003, 2005).

These findings suggest that New Hope had lasting effects on parent's child-care choices, making them more inclined to select formal child care and less inclined to select home-based care. This may be because of the initial cost savings New Hope child-care subsidies provided, but it also may have been because program group parents' increased employment created the need for the safe, convenient, reliable, and stable care that is offered by formal care (Lowe & Weisner, 2004). Regardless, it seems that program group members' initial experiences with formal child care were positive enough for them to continue to prefer it to other alternatives.

*New Hope Increased Children's Participation in Structured Activities.* Children in the program group spent more time than control group children did in such structured, adult-supervised activities as lessons, coached sports, community/recreational center activities, clubs/youth groups, and religious activities. These patterns were most consistent for children in late elementary school and early adolescence.

New Hope promoted participation in a range of activities, including lessons, religious activities, before- and after-school programs, and club/youth groups. This may be an indirect effect of the program: Program group parents' increased employment may have heightened parents' desire to place their children, especially their boys, in safe, reliable, adult-supervised, out-of-school settings to reduce the likelihood of their involvement in risky behavior. That the rate of participation in any given activity varied across time may be explained by age-related changes in children's and parents' activity choices.

## Pathways of Influence on Children

The conceptual model shown in Figure 3.1 includes several possible pathways by which New Hope might have contributed to children's achievement and behavior. Each of these was measured in the evaluation. The family resource and family process models guided the conceptual framework.

The family resource model suggests that parents' economic circumstances and human capital strongly influence children's development, especially academic development, through the materials, opportunities, and experiences afforded them. This model is supported by consistent findings that poverty, particularly in early childhood, is related to low achievement (Duncan, Yeung, Brooks-Gunn, & Smith, 1998). Insofar as New Hope alleviated childhood poverty, it may have set children on a more positive academic path (Yeung, Linver, & Brooks-Gunn, 2002). New Hope's salutary economic effects may have enabled parents to provide their children more and higher-quality resources than they could have previously.

The family process model stipulates that the family economic context influences the relations and interactions within the family and that these in turn influence the children's development, especially socioemotional development. To the extent that New Hope reduced family economic pressure and bolstered parents' emotional wellbeing through increased employment and earnings, it may have enhanced the quality of parent-child relationships.

Overall, New Hope had some effects on income and financial resources, and it had large and lasting effects on children's childcare experiences and out-of-school activities, suggesting that these experiences constituted important pathways for effects. By contrast, there were small and scattered effects on parents' psychological well-being and parenting practices. Hence, it appears that changes in family resources may have accounted for the effects on children.

## SOCIAL SIGNIFICANCE OF EFFECTS

### Why Effects on Children's Well-Being Are Important

We have reported that New Hope had positive effects on program group children's academic achievement. These findings are important given poverty's strong association with deleterious academic consequences, including lower educational attainment and standardized-test scores and higher rates of course failure, grade retention, school dropout, and special-education placement (Duncan & Brooks-Gunn, 1997; McLoyd, 1998). That a program aimed at parents could have significant and lasting effects on children is remarkable. Moreover, the academic gains experienced by children in the program group may have lifelong implications. Early academic achievement can set children on positive academic trajectories that enable them to keep up in school and be at reduced risk for failure. Therefore, the fact that New Hope gave program group children an academic "shot in the arm" bodes well for their ongoing achievement.

The same is true for increased exposure to both structured activities and formal care. Participation in adult-supervised activities is associated with a range of benefits, including increased academic achievement and socioemotional well-being, and decreased risky behavior (Mahoney, Larson & Eccles, 2005). Formal care has a variety of developmental benefits, among them increased school readiness and academic achievement across time (NICHD ECCRN, 2004).

Also, New Hope provided some additional income and resources that allowed parents to purchase "extras" for their children. Some material goods may be important for reasons beyond the actual toy or clothing item. Peer pressure can be difficult for children with few resources, and a small extra can go a long way. As one mother said,

> I got both of my sons contact [lenses]. They had been wanting contacts for the longest. I couldn't even dream about it. But with that insurance, I paid just 20 dollars for each one. In that age group, you know, it's important how they look and all that. . . . I couldn't afford to buy them the kind of glasses they would have wanted.

Money spent on children may also have critical consequences as it counteracts negative neighborhood influences. One New Hope mother explained, "Not all places have gangs, but [my neighborhood] is infested with gangs and drugs and violence. My son, I worry about him. He may be veering in the wrong direction." Explaining why she buys her older sons extra items, such as 100-dollar gym shoes: "It's different for girls. For boys, it's dangerous. [Gangs are] full of older men who want these young ones to do their dirty work. And they'll buy them things and give them money."

### Why Effects on Parents Are Important

The low-income population suffers from mental health disorders at a higher rate than the nonpoverty population, and women consistently report more mental distress than men. Thus, it is not surprising that baseline measures of mental distress reveal that applicants to programs that aid the poor experience depression at much higher rates than in the general public (Quint, Bos, & Polit, 1997) and that both New Hope groups maintained rather high levels of depressive symptoms.

Even though New Hope's impact on depressive symptoms was small, it may have implications beyond psychological well-being. As seen in Figure 3.1, parental psychological well-being can affect the entire family via its effects on parenting. Earnings and work levels may also be affected by a person's mental health (Jayakody & Stauffer, 2000). Thus, mental health should be addressed by programs aiding low-income workers and parents.

Participants' life circumstances affected their ability to translate New Hope into improved economic circumstances. Ethnographic evidence suggests that such factors as a low education level, child-care responsibilities, an arrest record, and an inadequate work history affected participants' levels of employment and earnings. Over the entire sample, program effects on employment and earnings were consistently strong and significant for participants with one of these barriers. Among participants with no barriers or those with two or more barriers, New Hope had few effects on employment and earnings. These findings suggest that a program like New Hope is particularly advantageous to people who want to work but need a leg up. It has less to offer to those who want to work but have a more complex array of barriers or no apparent barriers (Huston et al., 2003).

### Understanding New Hope Within Its Economic and Sociopolitical Context

New Hope's positive effects on income and work effort must be interpreted in the context of the economic climate in which they occurred. First, in the booming economy of the 1990s, the program did not have much room to increase employment and earnings beyond the levels that control group members attained. Everyone had an easier time securing adequately paying work than they would have in leaner economic times. Second, New Hope overlapped with the national transition to PRWORA's welfare time-limits and sanctions, and Wisconsin was in the forefront of implementing an aggressive welfare-to-work initiative, known as Wisconsin Works or W2. Therefore, both program and control group members were experiencing considerable exogenous pressure to secure employment. Third, in the late 1990s, Wisconsin had more well-developed and advanced policies for the working poor than many states did, including a state EITC, a comprehensive health insurance system, and an expanded system of child-care subsidies. All these features made it possible for control group members to obtain some of the supports that New Hope offered and may have reduced the differences between the program and control groups.

In sum, New Hope's effects on employment and earnings probably represent a conservative estimate of what we would expect to see in a less advantageous economy, a state with less extensive work support policies, and a sociopolitical climate less intent on moving welfare recipients into employment (Bos et al., 1999). Further New Hope–like policies in other states and in varied economic and sociopolitical climates would be necessary to ascertain the full scope of possible effects.

## POLICY IMPLICATIONS

We have provided evidence to suggest that New Hope can stand as a model program and that certain aspects should be studied and incorporated into systematic government policies. New Hope and its contemporaneous PRWORA-era experiments should be viewed as pilot programs and used to inform social policies affecting low-income families. Together, they suggest an array of solutions to the problems of welfare and the working poor, and they provide evidence of their effectiveness. If applied effectively, lessons from New Hope and the other experiments can help create effective policies with meaningful, substantive solutions for low-income families.

Data on the working poor from the Department of Labor (aforementioned) highlight the need to redirect poverty policies away from an exclusive focus on welfare and former welfare recipients to include the working poor. New Hope was directed toward the working poor and designed so that receiving a supplement always added to a family's net income. New Hope's careful and intensive planning avoided the "earn a dollar, lose a dollar" feature of much welfare-to-work policy. Without this feature, the risk of work *disincentives* is present and, in turn, the national majority stance that "work pays" is jeopardized. New Hope illustrates how policies historically concerned with the "welfare poor" can transition to help today's "working poor."

Another innovative characteristic of the program was its cafeteria-style selection of benefits. Large-scale public policies rarely allow individuals to choose among benefits that best suit themselves and their families. Yet, people's lives are ever unique and the lives of the working poor are no more similar to one another than is the situation of any two random Americans. Policies to aid the working poor should attempt to empower individuals by bestowing on them some control in how they take advantage of available assistance.

Both the longitudinal and random experiment design provide considerable methodological strength. With these characteristics, robust *causal* effects can be calculated. The addition of deep ethnographic profiles brings qualitative human aspects to the research. The inclusion of face-to-face interviews provides the New Hope data set with a treasure trove of the personal experiences of America's working family life that provide a more informed notion as to why certain effects exist.

Although the New Hope demonstration limited individuals' eligibility to 3 years, it was not intended to be a time-limited program. The basic philosophy of New Hope was that individuals ought to be eligible for benefits as long as they met the criteria—low incomes and full-time work. Nevertheless, the evaluation did provide information about effects after the program ended. As one might expect, many of the effects, particularly the earnings and employment effects of New Hope, faded when the program ended after 3 years. Yet there were still effects on children's academic achievement and social behavior, and there were some lasting effects on family poverty.

Timing can be critical for certain effects as they affect children at particular ages or induce actions for workers at key times in their employment trajectory. If New Hope were funded in perpetuity, the effects found during its short 3 years would likely be sustained. But with limited public and private dollars, determining what limited years of funding can achieve in the long run is also important. Social interventions that set a child upon a better academic track can have positive repercussions throughout that child's life. Similarly, an incentive program that helps a parent secure a more stable and rewarding job can set that parent on a better career track for years to come.

Even though the direct intent of the program was economic, the myriad of positive outcomes realized by the New Hope children can serve as an impetus for future research. If a program not designed to achieve academic and behavioral improvements did so via supporting working families, how can future interventions and policies be created with more holistic and ambitious aims for America's working families?

The New Hope story is an optimistic one. If given moderate and flexible supports, even for a time as short as 3 years or less, individuals of few means can overcome structural and economic barriers to employment and become more financially self-sufficient. Moreover, a system that makes work pay and offers work supports that enable people to meet their responsibilities can have beneficial secondary consequences across children and families.

## NOTES

1. Technical information and further details about New Hope and the results reported in this chapter can be found in the 2- and 5-year New Hope reports (see Huston, A. C., Miller, C., Richburg-Hayes, L., Duncan, G. J., Eldred, C. A., Weisner, T. S., et al. [2003]. *New Hope for families and children: Five-year results of a program to reduce poverty and reform welfare*. New York: Manpower Demonstration Research Corporation; and Bos, J. M., Huston, A. C., Granger, R., Duncan, G., Brock, T., & McLoyd, V. C. [1999]. *New Hope for people with low incomes: Two-year results of a program to reduce poverty and reform welfare*. New York: Manpower Demonstration Research Corporation).

2. For additional information on the federal poverty thresholds and guidelines, visit the U.S. Census Bureau Web site, "How the Census Bureau Measures Poverty," at http://www.census.gov/hhes/www/poverty/povdef.html

3. For information on additional experiments, see Morris, P., Gennetian, L., & Duncan, G. J. (2005). Effects of welfare and employment policies on young children: New findings on policy experiments conducted in the 1990s. *Social Policy Report, 19*(2).

4. See also Duncan, G. J., Huston, A. C., & Weisner, T. (2007). *Higher ground: New Hope for working poor families and their children*. New York: Russell Sage.

## REFERENCES

Becker, G. S. (1981). *A treatise on the family*. Cambridge, MA: Harvard University Press.

Bennefield, R. L. (1997). *Health insurance coverage: 1996: Who goes without health insurance?* (Current Population Reports: Consumer Income, Report Number: P60-199). Washington, DC: U.S. Department of Commerce, Census Bureau. Retrieved June 15, 2006, from http://www.census.gov/hhes/www/hlthins/cover96/cov96asc.html

Bernheimer, L., Weisner, T. S., & Lowe, T. (2003). Impacts of children with troubles on working poor families: Mixed-methods and experimental evidence. *Mental Retardation, 41*(6), 403–419.

Blank, R. M. (1997). *It takes a nation: A new agenda for fighting poverty* (pp. 52–68). Princeton, NJ: Princeton University Press.

Blank, R. M., & Schmidt, L. (2001). Work, wages, and welfare. In R. M. Blank & R. Haskins (Eds.), *The new world of welfare* (pp. 70–102). Washington, DC: Brookings Institution Press.

Bloom, D., & Michalopoulos, C. (2001). *How welfare and work policies affect employment and income: A synthesis of research*. New York: Manpower Demonstration Research Corporation.

Bos, J. M., Huston, A. C., Granger, R., Duncan, G., Brock, T., & McLoyd, V. C. (1999). *New Hope for people with low incomes: Two-year results of a program to reduce poverty and reform welfare*. New York: Manpower Demonstration Research Corporation.

Brock, T., Doolittle, F., Fellerath, V., Wiseman, M., Greenberg, D., & Hollister, R. (1997). *Creating New Hope: Implementation of a program to reduce poverty and reform welfare*. New York: Manpower Demonstration Research Corporation.

Coleman, J. S. (1988). Social capital in the creation of human capital. *American Journal of Sociology, 94*(Supplement), S95–S120.

D'Ercole, A. (1988). Single mothers: Stress, coping, and social support. *Journal of Community Psychology, 16,* 41–54.

Duncan, G. J., & Brooks-Gunn, J. (Eds.). (1997). *Consequences of growing up poor.* New York: Russell Sage.

Duncan, G. J., Yeung, W. J., Brooks-Gunn, J., & Smith, J. R. (1998). How much does childhood poverty affect the life chances of children? *American Sociological Review, 63,* 406–423.

Epps, S. R., & Huston, A. C. (2007). Effects of a poverty intervention policy demonstration on parenting and child behavior: A test of the direction of effects. *Social Science Quarterly, 88*(2), 344–365.

Fuller, B., Kagan, S. L., Caspary, G., & Gauthier, C. (2002). Welfare reform and child care options for low-income families. *Future of Children, 12,* 97–120.

Gibson, C. M., & Weisner, T. S. (2002). "Rational" and ecocultural circumstances of program take-up among low-income working parents. *Human Organization, 61,* 154–166.

Huston, A. C., Duncan, G. J., McLoyd, V. C., Crosby, D. A., Ripke, M. R., Weisner, T. S., et al. (2005). Impacts on children of a policy to promote employment and reduce poverty for low-income parents: New Hope after 5 years. *Developmental Psychology, 41,* 902–918.

Huston, A. C., Granger, R., Bos, J., Duncan, G. J., McLoyd, V., Mistry, R., et al. (2001). Work-based anti-poverty programs for parents can enhance the school performance and social behavior of children. *Child Development, 72*(1), 318–336.

Huston, A. C., Miller, C., Richburg-Hayes, L., Duncan, G. J., Eldred, C. A., Weisner, T. S., et al. (2003). *New hope for families and children: Five-year results of a program to reduce poverty and reform welfare.* New York: Manpower Demonstration Research Corporation.

Jayakody, R., & Stauffer, D. (2000). Mental health problems among single mothers: Implications for welfare reform. *Journal of Social Issues, 56,* 617–634.

Kaiser Family Foundation. (2006). *The uninsured: A primer. Key facts about Americans without health insurance.* Washington, DC: Kaiser Family Foundation. Retrieved July 1, 2006, from http://www.kff.org/uninsured/upload/7451.pdf

Lowe, E. D., & Weisner, T. S. (2004). "You have to push it—Who's gonna raise your kids?": Situating child care and child-care subsidy use in the daily routines of lower income families. *Children and Youth Review Services, 26,* 143–171.

Mahoney, J. L., Larson, R. W., & Eccles, J. S. (2005). *Organized activities as contexts of development: Extracurricular activities, after-school and community programs.* Mahwah, NJ: Erlbaum.

Mahoney, J. L., Lord, H., & Carryl. E. (2005). An ecological analysis of after-school program participants and the development of academic performance and motivational attributes of disadvantaged children. *Child Development, 76,* 811–825.

McLoyd, V. C. (1998). Socioeconomic disadvantage and child development. *American Psychologist, 53,* 185–204.

National Association of Child Care Resource & Referral Agencies (NACCRRA). (2006). *Breaking the piggy bank: Parents and the high price of child care.* Retrieved May 22, 2006, from http://www.naccrra.org/docs/policy/breaking_the_piggy_bank.pdf

National Institute of Child Health and Human Development Early Child Care Research Network (NICHD ECCRN). (2004). Type of child care and children's development at 54 months. *Early Childhood Research Quarterly, 19,* 203–230.

Parcel, T. L., & Menaghan, E. G. (1997). Effects of low-wage employment on family well-being. *Future of Children, 7*(1), 116–121.

Posner, J. K., & Vandell, D. L. (1999). After-school activities and the development of low-income urban children: A longitudinal study. *Developmental Psychology, 35,* 868–879.

Quint, J., Bos, J., & Polit, D. (1997). *New chance: Final report on a comprehensive program for disadvantaged young mothers and their children.* New York: Manpower Demonstration Research Corporation.

Sears, H. A., & Galambos, N. L. (1993). The employed mother's well-being. In J. Frankel (Ed.), *The employed mother and the family context. Focus on women series,* (Vol. 14, pp. 49–67). New York: Springer.

U.S. Bureau of Labor Statistics. (2005). *Women in the labor force: A databook* (BLS Report 985). Washington DC: Author. Retrieved July 6, 2006, from http://www.bls.gov/cps/wlf-databook2005.htm

U.S. Bureau of Labor Statistics. (2006). *A profile of the working poor, 2004* (BLS Report 994). Washington, DC: Author. Retrieved July 6, 2006, from http://www.bls.gov/ cps/cpswp2004.pdf

Yeung, W. J., Linver, M. R., & Brooks-Gunn, J. (2002). How money matters for young children's development: Parental investment and family process. *Child Development, 73,* 1861–1879.

# CHAPTER 4

# Who Will Care When Parents Can't?

## An Overview of Trends in Kinship Care With a Focus on the Child-Only Provisions of the Temporary Assistance for Needy Families Program

KEVIN D. BLAIR AND DAVID B. TAYLOR

The care of children by relatives is not a new phenomenon. When a birth parent(s) can no longer provide for the child's basic needs, grandparents, aunts, uncles, and siblings often step forward and provide for the child (Jones, Chipungu, & Hutton, 2003). Historically, these arrangements have been informal and tended not to involve state child welfare agencies (Geen, 2003). Whether formal or informal, this practice is commonly known as *kinship care*. In recent years, the placement of children with relatives (and sometimes family friends) has become the foster care placement of choice for child welfare agencies (Murray, Ehrle, Macomber, & Geen, 2004). In addition to the formal use of kinship care by child welfare agencies, other types of kinship care have accelerated under provisions of the Temporary Assistance for Needy Families (TANF) Program. TANF provides income assistance to kinship caregivers who have taken over care of children whose parents are unable or unwilling to care for them (Geen, 2003). These situations are most commonly informal family arrangements that come to the attention of child welfare agencies only when the kinship caregiver applies for income assistance from the TANF program. These situations represent a special category of kinship care that is commonly referred to as Child-Only Cases. The Child-Only label is drawn from the Child-Only provisions of the TANF program that allow income assistance to be provided to a kinship caregiver of a child who is eligible for funds via TANF. Child-Only cases have many similarities to, but some significant differences from, typical kinship care cases, and pose unique challenges for child welfare programs in the United States (Blair & Taylor, 2004).

Regardless of whether a placement is a Child-Only placement or some other form of kinship care, the use of kinship care in general has become the object of increased scrutiny and debate by child welfare advocates and researchers (Jones et al., 2003). Specifically, child welfare advocates are concerned about the ability of kinship caregivers to properly meet the *best interests of the child* standard. According to the United Nations Convention on the Rights of the Child Fact Sheet (Child Welfare League of America [CWLA], n.d.),

> The best interests of the child must be a primary consideration in all decisions or actions that affect the child or children as a group. This holds true whether decisions are made by governmental, administrative, or judicial authorities or by families themselves.

The ability of many kinship caregivers to meet this standard is suspect and this is especially so in many of the Child-Only cases (Jones et al., 2003). In addition, the role of state and county child welfare offices in meeting the best interests standard in Child-Only kinship care cases is often vague and uncertain (Blair & Taylor, 2004; Geen, 2003; Murray et al., 2004). For example, in many states, kinship caregivers are not held to the same standards as are traditional foster caregivers (Murray et al., 2004). Furthermore, most kinship care cases are informal family arrangements. Murray et al. (2004) estimate that fully 77% of all kinship care cases do not involve child welfare agencies, thereby negating the ability of child welfare officials to provide any level of support services and quality assurance. The Child-Only cases often have an ill-defined status in child welfare offices that creates inequities in service and support. For example, Child-Only monies are typically far less than the monies provided to formal foster care arrangements (Blair & Taylor, 2004; Jones et al., 2003; Murray et al., 2004).

This chapter provides an overview of kinship care with a special focus on the TANF Program's Child-Only kinship care trend. The chapter begins with an overview of kinship care, the varying definitions and designations used across jurisdictions, and the historical role of the federal government that has led to the current Child-Only program. The chapter then examines current trends and issues in kinship care, including its dramatic growth in the United States during the past 10 years, and the increase in Child-Only kinship care cases. Finally, the chapter explores the benefits and problems associated with kinship care and speaks to the unique circumstances of these families, again with a special focus on the Child-Only cases. This section presents information gathered during a series of focus groups with Child-Only caregivers designed to highlight the challenges and struggles of Child-Only caregivers (Blair & Taylor, 2004). Next, the chapter discusses the current and critical policy issues surrounding kinship care, especially the role of child welfare officials. The chapter concludes with recommendations for improving Child-Only kinship care situations.

## KINSHIP CARE BACKGROUND AND DEFINITIONS

As noted by Geen (2003),

> Prior to the passage of the Adoption Assistance and Child Welfare Act of 1980, child welfare agencies rarely placed a child in need of foster care with relatives. However, Kinship care arrangements are not a new phenomenon. Anthropologists have documented the role that extended families play in raising children in cultures and communities around the world (Korbin, 1991; Young, 1970). Extended family members and other persons with a bond to the family have been particularly important in African-American families dating back to the time of slavery when parents and

children were often separated. In fact, the phrase *kinship care* was coined by Stack (1974) in work documenting the importance of kinship networks in the African American community. (p. 1)

Although the use of kin to care for children is not a historically new phenomenon, both the increased reliance on kin to provide foster care for children and the development of federal and state policies and programs that fueled these changes are significant. Given the increased use and reliance on kinship care, several scholars in the research community, as well as service providers, have begun to consider the impact of kinship care on both caregivers and children. Several issues have come to the forefront. What is the overall quality of care? Can kinship care be considered a permanent solution or is it only a stopgap strategy? What is the role of child welfare in kinship arrangements? Each of these issues remains open and requires further attention (Blair & Taylor, 2004; Geen, 2003), especially among the Child-Only cases.

## Definitions of Kinship Care

There is no one set definition of *kinship care*. In general, the term refers to any situation where a relative is taking care of a child (Murray et al., 2004). This situation may be formally arranged by a child welfare agency, or informally arranged by the family without state knowledge or intervention. Although roughly one half of the states limit their definition to family who are related to the child by blood, marriage, or adoption, 22 states use the term *kinship care* to include relatives, close family friends, godparents, congregation members, and essentially any adult who has an existing relationship with the child. Finally, five states have no definition of kin or of kinship care (Geen, 2003; Janz, Geen, Bess, & Scarcella, 2002). Regardless of the variations in the definition of kinship

care, the common thread is that the children are no longer living with their biological parents nor are they living in a traditional foster care arrangement with foster parents who have been through some type of screening, training, or licensing process.

Child-Only cases are typically viewed as kinship care cases, though most Child-Only cases arise from informal arrangements made by family members themselves and have little or no formal child welfare involvement or services (Blair & Taylor, 2004; Murray et al., 2004). In addition, a significant number of Child-Only cases are situations where the biological parent is disabled, is receiving Supplemental Security Income (SSI) assistance, and the children, who are living with him or her, are eligible for TANF Child-Only payments. In their study of one county in New York State, Blair and Taylor (2004) found that almost 50% of the Child-Only cases involved a disabled, rather than absent, parent. Thus, a large portion of Child-Only cases are not foster care cases in any traditional sense, yet they are lumped together with the kinship care Child-Only cases in most state child welfare offices. Clear differences exist between the needs of families that have taken over the care of a child whose parents cannot or will not care for the child and cases where a disabled parent is caring for his or her own child(ren) and receiving Child-Only monies (Blair & Taylor, 2004).

Differences in definitions of kinship care are not simply a matter of semantics, but have practical and real implications for the children and their caregivers, particularly in relation to the Child-Only aspects of both kinship care and the TANF Program. How caregivers are officially recognized and defined determines their legal status to the children in their care, as well as the types and amounts of assistance available. For example, whether a care provider is a *kinship caregiver* or a *kinship foster parent* determines the amount of financial assistance available to help care for the child (Hegar & Scannapieco, 1996). A kinship caregiver provides private, informal care with minimal resources or contact from child welfare agencies. Kinship foster parents are counted officially as part of the formal child welfare system, receive more financial assistance to support the childrearing effort, and experience greater support and involvement from child welfare agencies. In other words, foster parents, whether kin or nonkin, are held to more exacting standards and better reflect the *Best Interests* standards for the foster care of children. Thus, the difference between a foster parent designation and a Child-Only designation case is significant. The increasing use of kinship care, the rising number of Child-Only cases, and their use by both families and child welfare agencies, along with the somewhat hidden group of Child-Only children who are living with their biological parent(s), illustrates a shift in child welfare policy and practice that would have been unheard of before 1980. This shift in policy and practice has been shaped by changes in federal child welfare policy along with several other social forces.

## FEDERAL POLICIES, KINSHIP CARE, AND CHILD-ONLY CASES

Federal policy, and consequently state policies, toward the use of kinship care has been somewhat inconsistent over the years. Early policy generally favored the use of licensed foster parents over the use of kin, but it also created a split between the programs, services, and monies available to formal foster care providers versus the much more limited income assistance, often Child-Only monies, available to kinship caregivers (Geen, 2003). However, these early policies, especially the 1950 Amendment to the Social Security Act, allowed kinship caregivers to receive Child-Only payments if the children

in their care were eligible for assistance from the Aid to Families with Dependent Children (AFDC) program, the predecessor of TANF, even if the caregivers were not eligible for AFDC monies. This is a policy and distinction in providing assistance that has continued under the TANF program and its Child-Only provisions. This split between the services, especially monies, provided to formal foster care providers versus income assistance provided to kinship caregivers, has continued over the years and is reflected in the current TANF Program and the Child-Only grants that kinship caregivers may receive. To this day, most kinship caregivers are directed into income assistance programs rather than into foster care programs (Boots & Geen, 1999; Leos-Urbel, Bess, & Geen, 2002; Murray et al., 2004).

The first policy in the United States to officially recognize and require the use of family first or kinship care is the Indian Child Welfare Act of 1978, which mandates the use of kin for Native American children who are in need of foster care placement. Following closely on the Indian Child Welfare Act, the Adoption Assistance and Child Welfare Act of 1980 mandated that foster placement should be the "least restrictive, most family-like setting available located in close proximity to the parent's home, consistent with the best interests and special needs of the child" (Geen et al., 2001, Federal and State Kinship Care Policies section, 3). In general, states interpreted this Act as requiring kinship foster care as the first option, and, as a result, several states enacted legislation that expressed a preference for kinship foster care (Geen et al., 2001).

Geen et al. (2001) recently conducted a review of federal and state kinship care policies and observed that:

> More recently, the 1997 Adoption and Safe Families Act (ASFA) and the 1996 Personal Responsibility and Work Opportunity

Reconciliation Act (PRWORA) have articulated federal support of kinship foster care. ASFA indicates that, "a fit and willing relative" can provide a "planned permanent living arrangement" and that termination of parental rights does not have to occur within the allotted time frame if, "at the option of the state, the child is being cared for by a relative." (Federal and State Kinship Care Policies section, 3)

PRWORA has also had a major impact on foster care arrangements because it requires states to "consider giving preference to an adult relative over a nonrelated caregiver when determining a placement for a child, provided that the relative caregiver meets all relevant state child protection standards" (1996, § 505).

The Child-Only provisions of PRWORA, via the TANF Program, are a fast growing part of child welfare cases and an increasing focus of state and federal policymakers. The number of Child-Only cases grew to 978,000 in 1996, and then fell slightly to 918,000 in 1997, and in 1998 dropped to 743,000, before rising again in 1999 to 770,000 cases (Geen et al., 2001). Although these figures seem to show that the total number of cases has fallen somewhat, Child-Only cases continue to be a growing share of the total child welfare caseload, growing from 10% in 1988 to 29% in 1999 (Geen et al., 2001).

Finally, only in the last few years have researchers begun to monitor the Child-Only cases, with most of the data that are emerging consisting of demographics and general trends, with minimal information being available regarding the day-to-day lives and challenges of Child-Only kinship caregivers and their families (Blair & Taylor, 2004; Gordon, McKinley, Satterfield, & Curtis, 2003). According to Geen (2003), ASFA and PRWORA have increased the likelihood that kin will be the foster care placement of choice while ensuring that caregivers will have to make do with smaller assistance payments provided under the Child-Only provisions of TANF, along with significantly fewer services, training, and support than is provided to traditional foster care parents. All of this is happening despite evidence that kinship caregivers are typically very needy and the mounting evidence that Child-Only caregivers are as needy as and often needier than the typical kinship caregiver (Blair & Taylor, 2004; Geen, 2003; Gordon et al., 2003).

## CURRENT TRENDS AND ISSUES IN KINSHIP CARE

National statistics clearly show that kinship care has become the option of choice for a large number of children who are involved in the child welfare system. An unprecedented number of children are currently living outside of their immediate homes and with relatives (Murray et al., 2004). The following national statistics help create a picture of the growing use of kinship care:

- The Child Welfare League of America estimates about one-third of all children in foster care are currently placed with relatives and that this trend will continue for the foreseeable future (CWLA, 2005).
- According to the 2000 U.S. Census, more than two million grandparents are raising 4.5 million children, and other relatives are raising an additional 1.5 million children (U.S. Census Bureau, 2003).
- Nationally, 18% of out-of-home placements in 1986 were in kinship situations. This number jumped to 31% in 1990 and is now greater than 50% in many parts of the country (CWLA, 2005).

Although there is wide variation among states, states generally appear to be using kinship care more frequently to meet their foster care needs. The following three states illustrate this trend:

- In Illinois, in 1998, approximately 19,945 out of 34,650 children in out-of-home care were in kinship living arrangements. This equals 38% of all out-of-home placements in Illinois (CWLA, 2005).
- In Maryland, approximately 2,248 children were in kinship care as of December 2000 (Maryland Department of HRSSA, 2001).
- In New York, in 2001, 8,671 children were in kinship care out of 40,409 placed in out-of-home care, representing more than 21% of all out-of-home placements (New York Office of Children and Family Services, 2001).

The trend toward kinship placement is being fueled by several factors, chief of which is the declining availability of traditional foster home placements, family preservation—a belief that kin automatically provide better foster care than nonkin, the passage of the Adoption Assistance and Child Welfare Act of 1980 that shortens the time child welfare agencies have to find a permanent placement for a child, and financial pressures to seek out the lowest cost solutions.

## The Decline of Traditional Foster Homes

In 1985, approximately 147,000 foster homes were available nationally. By 1994, that number fell to 125,000, whereas the actual need for out of home placement of children rose (CWLA, n.d.). There is also a shortage of foster families with the necessary resources and willingness to parent children with certain characteristics or circumstances, for example, a shortage of foster families of color, foster families for sibling groups, emotionally disturbed teens, and medically fragile/complex infants. Although these numbers do fluctuate a bit with each new assessment, the consistent conclusion is that the overall number of traditional foster care placements remains far fewer than is needed (Jones et al., 2003).

The decline in traditional foster homes can be attributed to several factors, but it appears to be a phenomenon in need of further study. Changes in the American family, with the number of women now working outside of the home, is the most common reason cited as underlying the decline in traditional foster families (Jones et al., 2003; U.S. Department of Health and Human Services [U.S. DHHS], 2000). Other reasons include the aging out of experienced foster families, with fewer and fewer new families coming into the system to replace families that have aged out, and finally, unwillingness by families who are considering becoming foster families to take on children with difficult challenges and needs. Regardless of the underlying reasons, the decline in traditional foster families creates both incentive and pressure toward kinship care of children in need of foster care placement.

## Family Preservation

Partly by necessity and partly because of a changing level of awareness about the strengths of families, legislation, programs, and policies have entrenched notions that children should remain, if at all possible, with their families of origin (Gordon et al., 2003). Known as *family preservation*, this position holds that families should remain together except in the most extreme situations, situations that clearly endanger the child(ren) and that offer little or no hope of providing the child(ren) with a healthy and nurturing environment. From this perspective, assistance or treatment that is provided must occur within the family setting with the goal of preserving the family unit (Gordon et al., 2003). This strong federal preference to consider family as the best first option for children in need is clearly reflected in federal and state policy and is easily seen in any review of current child welfare policies and procedures.

Kinship care as the foster care arrangement of choice has, in actual practice, been controversial because at least some contemporary research suggests that the kin who are providing the care are often in crisis, at risk for a wide range of problems, and in need of much support and services (Blair & Taylor, 2004; Jones et al., 2003). These recent studies of kinship caregivers (Blair & Taylor, 2004; Gordon et al., 2003; Murray et al., 2004) have found kinship care providers in need of greatly expanded support services, and each study has concluded that child welfare agencies need to expand their support of these families.

### Financial Pressures

Two types of financial pressure can be seen when examining kinship care. The first is the financial pressure and hardship that is experienced by the vast majority of kinship caregivers (Murray et al., 2004), and the second is the financial pressure experienced by state child welfare agencies as they attempt to cope with the declining number of traditional foster families and the emphasis on family preservation (Blair & Taylor, 2004). Each affects the lives of kinship caregivers and Child-Only cases.

One of the most consistent findings of all recent studies of kinship caregivers and of the recipients of TANF Child-Only monies is that kinship caregivers receive less monies than they should and far less than they need (Blair & Taylor, 2004; Jones et al., 2003; Murray et al., 2004). In their recent study for the Casey Foundation, Jones et al. (2003) found that

> Temporary Assistance for Needy Families (TANF) and Child-Only grants provide benefits solely to children living with relatives other than birth parents. While these grants offer financial aid, the amounts are small (usually less than $200) and the paperwork requirements are substantial, so TANF is not fully utilized. (p. 14)

A series of focus groups and interviews with Child-Only caregivers conducted by Blair and Taylor (2004) reached similar conclusions and raised a number of questions regarding the role of caseworkers assigned to Child-Only cases in New York State. In every focus group, kinship caregivers described the tremendous financial pressures they were under and the minimal amounts of money and support they were receiving. Several of the caregivers questioned why county caseworkers did not help them find and apply for additional monies and services. In their focus groups with kinship caregivers in Baltimore, Gordon et al. (2003) found that kinship caregivers felt that the Department of Social Services used them as "babysitters" and pressured the caregivers to adopt the children in their care as a way of reducing caseloads and costs.

The financial problems facing kinship caregivers are well known and well documented (Murray et al., 2004). As Jones et al. (2003) state,

> One of the most pressing needs of kinship families is financial help. Government programs can provide some financial aid, but the amount is usually not enough to meet the family's needs and the processes required to receive funds can be complicated and disheartening. . . . While [the programs] are widely known, relative caregivers are often not making the most of them. (p. 14)

Murray et al. (2004) echo these concerns. Their findings show that despite being eligible for at least some types of income assistance, some 78% of kinship caregivers receive no financial assistance. In fact, some Child-Only caregivers may be eligible to receive monies as foster parents, typically a significantly greater amount of money and other supports. This possibility originated in 1979 when the Supreme Court decided

*Miller v. Youakim.* This decision held that relatives who meet foster care parent licensing requirements and who care for related children who are eligible for federally reimbursed foster care payments are entitled to receive the same federal benefits as nonrelative foster parents. In other words, this group of kinship caregivers, as long as they are licensed foster parents, is reimbursed at the same levels as traditional, nonkinship foster parents. However, then as now, most kinship caregivers with children in their care do not fall into this group, leaving them with the far more limited income assistance provided under TANF's Child-Only provisions (Boots & Geen, 1999; Geen, 2003).

## CHILD-ONLY CAREGIVERS AND THEIR NEEDS

Nationally, the typical kinship caregiver is a female (87.9%), African American (79%), unmarried (57.6%), poor (33% maintain income levels below $20,000), and undereducated (48.5% have high school education only or less). When compared with traditional foster care providers, kinship caregivers tend to be older, to have more health related problems, and to be less financially stable. They are more likely to be single and thus have to rely heavily on other family members to assist them in raising the child. Their levels of education, on average, are lower than are those of nonkin caregivers, as are their incomes. Both of these factors play heavily in their ability to fully provide for the many and varied needs of the children in their care (Jones et al., 2003).

In their needs assessment of Child-Only caregivers in one county in New York State, Blair and Taylor (2004) found that the Child-Only caregivers resembled the national picture of kinship caregivers in terms of financial need, levels of education, health related problems, and other pressures. Blair and Taylor also found that many of the Child-Only caregivers' financial needs exceeded the national averages and that the Child-Only caregivers also faced significant challenges in the areas of transportation—especially in rural areas—accessing health care, coping with school and the educational requirements of the children in their care, and obtaining needed legal advice—especially in the area of permanency planning.

Their study used a series of focus groups with Child-Only caregivers to both explore their needs and to develop a deeper understanding of the day-to-day lives and struggles of Child-Only caregivers. Blair and Taylor's findings confirmed the results of the focus group study conducted by Gordon et al. (2003), but also showed that each Child-Only caregiver situation was unique, requiring an individualized, case management approach to the provision of services. A sampling of the range of Child-Only cases found by Blair and Taylor is presented here:

1. *Case Example One:* D. is a 66-year-old recovering substance abuser. She shares her home with several adult children and many grandchildren, including three children who are part of the Child-Only population. The birth mother is drug-addicted and involved with the police and courts. D. is clearly overwhelmed by the situation in which she finds herself. On the one hand, she would very much like additional support from the county Department of Social Services (DSS). On the other hand, she is fearful that more DSS involvement will lead to the children's removal from her home and to more involvement with police, courts, and other aspects of "the system" that have typically proven less than helpful to her in the past.

2. *Case Example Two:* M. is a 24-year-old single female. M. has taken custody of her nephew from her drug-addicted brother and his wife. M. is employed in a position that she

describes as mid-level management. Her job is secure and pays well enough that the monies she receives as a Child-Only caregiver are used entirely as supplements, for example, to pay the costs of adding her nephew to her medical plan, day care services as needed, and so forth. M.'s primary concerns are legal; she is very concerned about making the custody permanent. In addition, she would like more information on parenting and support as a single parent. She is also unhappy with the treatment she receives from DSS. She feels that DSS does not treat her with the dignity and respect that she deserves.

3. *Case Example Three:* A. and B. are 50-plus-year-old grandparents who are raising their granddaughter. Their daughter comes and goes from their household, showing up for brief periods and then disappearing. A. and B. have many concerns surrounding permanency planning for their granddaughter, including their legal status as their granddaughter's guardians. They fear that their daughter will simply show up one day and announce that she is taking their granddaughter to live elsewhere. A. and B. also acknowledge any number of parenting mistakes with their own daughter and express concerns about not repeating them with their granddaughter. They too, express unhappiness with DSS. They view DSS as doing little other than sending them inadequate amounts of money and offering virtually no other support.

4. *Case Example Four:* G., a 30-plus-year-old female, is disabled and receiving SSI payments in addition to Child-Only monies. Unlike the previous examples, the children in G.'s home are her biological offspring. G.'s concerns deal far more with day-to-day functioning. She feels a great deal of financial stress as she tries to raise children with limited income and copes with a medical disability that prevents her from performing virtually any type of work that would raise her income. G. is very unhappy with her living situation, but feels she cannot afford a better apartment and still provide adequately for her children. Child support payments are also of concern to her. G. too is unhappy with DSS, feeling that they do little to help her other than sending her the Child-Only monies.

These four examples provide a sense of the range of challenges that the Child-Only caregivers face. As also uncovered by Gordon et al. (2003), though there are some overarching themes (permanency planning, long-term health of the children, legal status, and custody arrangements), each case is unique and in need of individualized planning and intervention.

## Are Kinship Caregivers Prepared for Their Roles?

In theory, kinship care provides an optimal alternative to both family preservation and traditional foster care. It removes the child from the home, arguably the source of the most imminent and most harmful elements. Yet, it keeps the child within the extended family, and the child does not have to go into foster care—the latter being a significant motivator in many Child-Only cases. Both D. and grandparents A. and B., described previously, cited the strong desire to keep their grandchildren out of "the system" as a major factor in their decisions to care for the children.

In addition, proponents of kinship care argue that placing the child with a relative causes the least amount of disruption to the child's life (Shlonsky & Berrick, 2001), and this is particularly true if the placement is the home of kin in which he or she may have already spent a considerable amount of time. Proponents of kinship placement also cite the opportunity for the birth parents to maintain some level of contact with their children (Dubowitz & Feigelman, 1993). In theory then, kinship placements offer stability, consistency, and security for the child. However, a closer look at both kinship care in general and at Child-Only Caregivers in particular raises a number of concerns regarding the quality of that care and the ability of kinship caregivers to fully provide for these children.

In particular, researchers have begun to question many aspects of the quality of care that kin can actually provide. Concerns include training and preparation for being kinship/foster parents, age and overall health of the caregivers, additional stressors and pressures that come from adding one or more additional children to any household, and finally, the lack of services and professional support given to kinship caregivers, especially in Child-Only cases (Blair & Taylor, 2004; Geen, 2003; Shlonsky & Berrick, 2001). It should also be noted that proponents of kinship care do not agree about the benefits and risks of maintaining contact with birth parents.

The 2000 Report to the Congress on Kinship Foster Care argues that although nonkin foster parents are well prepared to assume guardianship of children, relative caregivers are typically unprepared for the additional role and responsibilities (e.g., disciplining the child) and for the additional financial burden on often limited resources (U.S. DHHS, 2000):

> Kinship caregivers often become involved in a crisis situation with little or no notice. Not being prepared for the arrival of the children, they may not have adequate space, furniture (such as a crib), or other child-related necessities (e.g., toys or a car seat) . . . Unlike trained non-kin foster parents, kinship caregivers often receive little formal training, and may have a limited understanding of the child welfare system, what is expected of them, and the resources available to them. (p. 34)

In their focus groups with Child-Only kinship caregivers, Blair and Taylor (2004) found that more often than not the county department of social services only learned about the kinship care arrangement when the caregiver applied for Child-Only monies and that determining eligibility for the monies was the sole responsibility of the caseworker. In other words, the caseworker had no responsibility for quality assurance before or during the kinship care placement.

## Grandparents as Primary Caregivers

Though kinship care is not exclusive to grandparents, there is an overreliance on grandparents to provide kinship care. Research paints a troubling picture that suggests that the grandparents with the fewest resources and who are least able to provide for a child are the ones who are currently taking on this role. Scarcella, Ehrle, and Geen (2003) found that grandparents suffer from greater health and financial difficulties, and they tend to have less formal education than other relative caregivers. Grandparents also face additional difficulties such as transportation and mobility that impede or limit their ability to fully engage in their grandchildren's recreation and education/schooling.

When older nonrelative caretakers assume primary caretaking responsibilities, they are usually in better health and are more prepared to take on this role. Older relative caregivers typically take on this role willingly, but unexpectedly. They recognize what the alternatives would be if the children were either to remain in an at-risk situation with the birth parents or to be placed in the homes of strangers in foster care (Billing, Ehrle, & Kortenkamp, 2002; Harrison, Richman, & Vittimberga, 2000). As Shorr (2001), in his review of TANF and its impact on families, notes,

> It is a novel and an unexpected finding of recent studies that care by relatives is not, in

general, superior to the dubious care offered in most organized settings. This seems to mean that aunts or grandparents are now so stressed themselves that they take a child because the situation of the child and the child's mother is even more desperate than their own—the overwhelming fear, of course, is that the "county" will take the child. So, the relatives, reluctantly, take the child. (p. 43)

Examining physical and mental health data from the first two cycles of the National Survey of Families and Households (1987–1988 and 1992–1994), Fuller-Thomson and Minkler (2000) compared African American grandparent kinship providers with African American grandparent nonkinship providers. Fuller-Thomson and Minkler found that, compared with nonkinship providers, grandparent caregivers experienced a significantly greater number of physical and emotional limitations as reflected in the activities of daily living scale. It is unclear, however, whether these characteristics existed before becoming caregivers or whether these conditions could have been aggravated as a result of taking on the additional responsibilities of raising a child. Regardless, this is a disturbing observation because it again suggests that the grandparents least able to provide for a child are the ones who are currently taking on this role.

In addition, taking on the role and responsibilities of caretaker has affected the personal, work, home, and spiritual lives of many of the relative caregivers (Jones et al., 2003). This was seen also by Blair and Taylor, where 45% of the respondents in their study indicated that they agreed with the statement that taking on the role of caregiver has negatively affected family life. When asked to elaborate, caregivers spoke of financial pressures, parenting issues, and other issues that have been noted throughout this chapter.

## What Are the Most Important Needs?

Information from the Child Welfare League of America, a study conducted by Berrick, Needell, Barth, and Jonson-Reid (1998), along with the focus groups conducted by Blair and Taylor (2004) and by Gordon et al. (2003), found that kinship caregivers are in need of significant levels of support. In general, Berrick et al. found that kinship caregivers tend to have lower incomes, less education, and more health-care problems than do nonkinship caregivers. In addition, kinship caregivers tended to need more help with housing, clothing, transportation, and child care in general than did nonkinship caregivers. A 2000 report by the Department of Health and Human Services identified the following most frequently cited needs of relative caregivers: better preparation for caregiver role, financial assistance, mental health and emotional support, child care, transportation, tutoring, health insurance for the child, and legal assistance.

One important finding in the 2003 Casey Families Project report is that although there is some agreement about what the different needs are of the caregivers, the ranking of their importance is starkly different between agency personnel and the caregivers (Jones et al., 2003). For example, although agency personnel rank order the caregivers' needs as mental health services, financial assistance, respite care, and legal assistance, the caregivers ranked their top four needs as financial assistance, medical help for the children, respite care, and emotional and social support. Importantly, the caregivers also stated that the needs they had when they first gained custody of the child are much different than the needs they had when the child had been with them for some significant amount of time. In their respective focus group sessions with kinship caregivers, Blair and Taylor (2004) and Gordon et al. (2003)

consistently found similar concerns to those identified by the Casey Families Project.

All indications are that although kinship care offers some advantages over traditional foster care, it also creates a great many concerns, especially in the areas of support services for both the caregiver and children, permanency planning, and long-term stability of the child's life and environment. Concerns become more acute in Child-Only cases where supports are so minimal as to often be only a small amount of income assistance. Thus, although studies indicate that kinship care can offer a number of potential advantages over traditional foster care, many, if not most, of these potential advantages remain unrealized because the children and their kinship caregivers will not receive the services they need. In addition, kinship care tends to reduce the children's chances of obtaining other permanent legal status such as adoption or guardianship (Altstein & McRoy, 2000). In other words, although kinship care may be a better alternative in the short run, the long-term stability of the lives of the children who are placed into kinship care is a significant concern (Testa, 2001). These concerns need to be addressed with proper polices and programs that truly meet the best interests of the child standard.

## MEETING THE BEST INTERESTS STANDARD IN KINSHIP CARE AND CHILD-ONLY CASES

The history of child welfare could be characterized as a set of shifting dialectical arguments regarding what is in the best interest of the child and who is in the best position to serve, provide for, and protect those children who need to be removed from the care of their parents. This is also reflected in a pendulum swing that at times aims more toward formal forms of foster and institutional care but at other times aims more at kinship care and family preservation or reunification. The recent preference for kinship care has been fueled by the notion that placement with relatives serves as the optimal solution to serving the best interests of the child. Although the last 10 years have seen ebb and flow in overall kinship placements, the overarching trend is toward placement with relatives—a trend that has not seen an equal increase in child welfare policies, programs, and services that help ensure the best interests standards are being met via the increased use of kinship care and child-only cases. This is a troubling observation because the lives of a great many children and their caregivers are at stake.

The financial pressures on states to seek the lowest cost solutions also appear to be a factor that has speeded up the use of kin as primary caregivers. However, as noted by the kinship caregivers and Child-Only caregivers in the focus groups conducted by both Blair & Taylor (2004) and Gordon et al. (2003), asking families to care for children without providing the necessary resources and supports is, as one focus group participant noted, little more than "doing child welfare on the cheap" and might be stressing families out so much that it is undermining the benefits that kinship care can have relative to traditional foster care.

Many kinship caregivers are keenly aware that they receive significantly less monies and other forms of support than they need, and many are aware of the split between monies and support for traditional foster care parents and kinship caregivers. Addressing this disparity in financial assistance must be a key focus of federal and state child welfare policymakers. As Berrick and Needell (1999) noted more than 5 years ago, this issue is one that must be decided by policymakers and not researchers. They propose that the key question in coming years will be whether kinship caregivers most closely resemble informal family care or more closely resemble formal foster care (Berrick & Needell, 1999). Thus far, despite the obvious needs to do more, policymakers seem content to leave the inadequate monies and supports in place.

An equally important issue for policymakers surrounds the proper role of the state in providing quality assurance in kinship care and Child-Only cases. Blair & Taylor (2004) found that the caseworkers assigned to the Child-Only cases in their study had little or no case management responsibilities. In fact, the caseworkers' jobs would best be described as "Eligibility Technicians" rather than as caseworkers or case managers. This reality was frustrating and confusing to caregivers who wanted more help and support from their assigned caseworker. This does not appear to be a rarity, especially in the Child-Only case situations. There appear to be only some states that maintain a system of quality assurance that requires them to screen kinship caregivers before or during placements. To assess the quality of services provided to kinship caregivers and their children, and to guarantee a standard level of quality, states and counties should be required to implement quality assurance

safeguards to promote effective oversight and quality case management. Such provisions would permit child welfare agencies to identify any problems and to propose corrective actions to remedy any deficiencies.

In conclusion, although the need of kinship and Child-Only caregivers for financial assistance is an area that policymakers urgently need to address, the need for quality case management and support services, along with ensuring that kinship and Child-Only cases meet the Best Interests Standards, are areas equally deserving of critical attention from policymakers. Kinship and Child-Only caregivers deserve much better support and assistance than they are receiving. These are typically families with high levels of need, who are willing to open their doors to needy children. They have already demonstrated resourcefulness and a willingness to come forward without the expectation of a particular financial commitment by the county. They are more than carrying their share of the child welfare burden. It is time for child welfare policymakers to meet their responsibilities and provide the resources these families and children need.

## REFERENCES

Altstein, H., & McRoy, R. (2000). *Does family preservation serve a child's best interests? Controversies in public policy.* Washington, DC: Georgetown University Press.

Berrick, J. D., & Needell, B. (1999). Recent trends in kinship care: Public policy, payments, and outcomes for children. In P. A. Curtis & G. Dale (Eds.), *The foster care crisis: Translating research into policy and practice* (pp. 152–174). Lincoln: University of Nebraska Press.

Berrick, J. D., Needell, B., Barth, R. P., & Jonson-Reid, M. (1998). *The tender years: Toward developmentally sensitive child welfare services for very young children.* New York: Oxford University Press.

Billing, A., Ehrle, J., & Kortenkamp, K. (2002). *Children cared for by relatives: What do we know about their well-being?* (Assessing the New Federalism, Series B, No. B-46). Washington, DC: Urban Institute Press.

Blair, K., & Taylor, D. (2004). *Child only initiative grantees: A needs assessment of the COI grantees conducted for the Niagara County Department of Social Services.* Lewiston, NY: Niagara University.

Boots, S. W., & Geen, R. (1999, July). *Family care or foster care? How state policies affect kinship caregivers.* Washington, DC: Urban Institute Press. Available at http://newfederalism.urban.org/html/anf_34.html

Child Welfare League of America. (n.d.). *UN Convention on the rights of the child fact sheet.* Washington, DC: Author. Retrieved February 4, 2005, from http://www.cwla.org/programs/international/unfactsheet.pdf

Child Welfare League of America. (2005). *Kinship care fact sheet.* Washington, DC: Author. Retrieved May 24, 2007, from http://www.cwla.org/programs/kinship/factsheet.htm

Dubowitz, H., & Feigelman, S. (1993). A profile of kinship care. *Child Welfare, 72*(2), 153–169.

Fuller-Thomson, E., & Minkler, M. (2000). African American grandparents raising grandchildren: A national health profile of demographic and health characteristics. *Health and Social Work, 25*(2), 109–118.

Geen, R. (Ed.). (2003). *Kinship care: Making the most of a valuable resource.* Washington, DC: Urban Institute Press.

Geen, R., Holcomb, P., Jantz, A., Koralek, R., Leos-Urbel, J., & Malm, K. (2001). *On their own terms: Supporting kinship care outside of TANF and foster care.* Washington, DC: Urban Institute Press. Available at http://aspe.hhs.gov/hsp/kincare01

Gordon, A., McKinley, S., Satterfield, M., & Curtis, P. (2003). A first look at the need for enhanced support services for kinship caregivers. *Child Welfare, 82*(1), 77–95.

Harrison, K. A., Richman, G. S., & Vittimberga, G. (2000). Parental stress in grandparents versus parents raising children with behavior problems. *Journal of Family Issues, 21*(2), 262–270.

Hegar, R., & Scannapieco, M. (1996). From family duty to family policy: The evolution of kinship care. In E. P. Smith & L. A. Merkel-Holguin (Eds.), *A history of child welfare* (pp. 193–209). New Brunswick, NJ: Transaction.

Janz, A., Geen, R., Bess, R., Scarcella, C. A., & Russell, V. (2002). *The continuing evolution of state kinship care policies* (Assessing the New Federalism Discussion Paper No. 02-11). Washington, DC: Urban Institute Press.

Jones, E., Chipungu, S., & Hutton, S. (2003). *The kinship report: Assessing the needs of relative caregivers and the children in their care.* Seattle, WA: Casey Family Programs.

Korbin, J. (1991). Cross-cultural perspectives and research directions for the 21st century. *Child Abuse and Neglect, 151*(1), 67–78.

Leos-Urbel, J., Bess, R., & Geen, R. (2002). The evolution of federal and state policies for assessing and supporting kinship caregivers. *Children and Youth Services Review, 24*(1/2), 37–52.

Maryland Department of Human Resource Social Services Administration. (2001, August). Monthly Management Report.

Murray, J., Ehrle Macomber, J., & Geen, R. (2004, December). *Estimating financial support for kinship caregivers* (Assessing the New Federalism, Series B., No. B-63). Washington, DC: Urban Institute.

New York Office of Children and Family Services. (2001). New York Social Service Law § 384-b(1) {West, WESTLAW through L. 2003}

Personal Responsibility and Work Opportunity Reconciliation Act of 1996. H.R. 3734, 104th Congress, 2nd Session, § 505 (1996).

Scarcella, C. A., Ehrle, J., & Geen, R. (2003, August). *Identifying and addressing the needs of children in grandparent care* (Assessing the New Federalism, Series B, No. B-55). Washington, DC: Urban Institute Press.

Shlonsky, A., & Berrick, J. (2001). Assessing and promoting quality in kin and nonkin foster care. *Social Services Review, 75*(1), 60–83.

Shorr, A. (2001). *Welfare reform: Failure and remedies.* Westport, CT: Praeger.

Stack, C. (1974). *All our kin: Strategies for survival in a black community.* New York: Harper & Row.

Testa, M. (2001). Kinship care and permanency planning. *Journal of Social Service Review, 28*(1), 25–43.

U.S. Census Bureau. (2003). *Grandparents living with grandchildren: 2000.* Retrieved August 23, 2006, from http://www.census.gov/prod/2003pubs/c2kbr-31.pdf

U.S. Department of Health & Human Services. (2000). *Report to the Congress on kinship foster care* (Contract No. HHS-100-96-0011). Washington, DC: Author.

Young, V. (1970). Family and childhood in a southern Negro community. *American Anthropologist, 72*(2), 269–288.

# Part II

# POVERTY AMONG DIVERSE POPULATIONS AND SETTINGS

# CHAPTER 5

# Understanding the Processes Through Which Economic Hardship Influences Families and Children

RAND D. CONGER AND KATHERINE JEWSBURY CONGER

*The adverse effects of low SES on mental and physical health outcomes are as close to a universal truth as social science has offered.*

—Repetti, Taylor, & Seeman, 2002, p. 359

The economic changes of the last two decades in the United States (e.g., economic recessions and evidence of increasing income inequality) have enhanced ongoing interest in how social position and economic resources affect families and the development of children (Conger & Conger, 2002; Duncan & Brooks-Gunn, 1997). As suggested by the quote from Repetti and her colleagues that begins this chapter, research by developmental scholars joins with a broader initiative within the field of social epidemiology that focuses on *health disparities* or the general trend for more socially and economically disadvantaged people to suffer above-average rates of physical, emotional, and behavioral problems (Berkman & Kawachi, 2000; Oakes & Rossi, 2003). Consistent with this broader concern for social position and health in general, recent research and reviews of the literature provide significant evidence that economic hardship and disadvantage impair the functioning of parents (e.g., Conger, Rueter, & Elder, 1999) and threaten the physical, intellectual, social, and emotional health of children and adolescents (Bradley & Corwyn, 2002).

Indeed, a host of research now suggests a link between various dimensions of socioeconomic status (SES) and physical health, social-emotional well-being, and cognitive functioning for both children and adults (e.g., Berkman & Kawachi, 2000; Bradley & Corwyn, 2002; McLeod & Shanahan, 1996). With respect to the development of children and adolescents, recent findings demonstrate a clear connection between poverty and mental health (e.g., Ackerman, Brown, & Izard, 2004; Dearing, McCartney, & Taylor, 2001; McLeod & Shanahan, 1996), SES and cognitive development (e.g., Ackerman et al., 2004; Dearing et al., 2001;

Hoff, 2003; Hughes et al., 2005; Mezzacappa, 2004), and social class position and physical well-being (e.g., Evans & English, 2002; McLoyd, 1998). These findings lead to the important question of how SES might lead to these types of developmental consequences (Bradley & Corwyn, 2002; Hoffman, 2003).

This chapter evaluates two different theoretical approaches that have been proposed as possible explanations for the processes through which economic problems affect parents and children: the Family Stress Model and the Investment Model. These conceptual frameworks have intuitive appeal inasmuch as they are consistent with more general views about the ways in which family economic circumstances are experienced by family members. Thinking back to one of the most significant economic calamities in the history of the United States, the Great Depression of the 1930s, the newspapers of the time printed numerous stories about businessmen taking their lives in response to the collapse of the stock market in 1929. Similar reports occurred during the 1980s when farmers and bankers in the rural Midwest committed suicide at an increased rate during the economic crisis in agriculture (Conger & Elder, 1994). The Family Stress Model is consistent with these extreme consequences of economic problems in that it emphasizes the adverse emotional effects of economic hardship.

The Depression years also had a counterpoint to deprivation in the cartoon character of Little Orphan Annie. This orphan became the ward of a rich entrepreneur named Daddy Warbucks. As the story goes, he was able to provide Annie with the economic resources she needed to overcome the limitations imposed by a life of financial and social despair. During a time of economic chaos, this cartoon strip painted a picture of the possibility of overcoming the financial difficulties faced by far too many people in the United States. It also provides an extreme illustration of the Investment Model, which proposes that child development benefits from the wealth and investments of relatively well-to-do families. Although the suicides of stock brokers and the salvation of Little Orphan Annie represent extreme and even fictional representations of the influence of economic circumstances on children and families, they provide characterizations of these processes that are consistent with the two theories we next consider.

## THEORIES OF ECONOMIC STRESS AND INVESTMENT

The Family Stress and Investment Models are consistent with a *social causation perspective,* which argues that the social and economic circumstances in people's lives directly influence their emotions, beliefs, and behaviors (Conger & Donnellan, 2007). As we will discuss later in this chapter, this social causation approach to understanding the role of economic hardship in human development has been disputed and alternative theoretical frameworks have been proposed. For the moment, however, we focus on the stress and investment arguments and the empirical evidence related to them. The first theoretical paradigm, the Family Stress Model of economic hardship (FSM), proposes that financial difficulties have an adverse effect on parents' emotions, behaviors, and relationships, which, in turn, affects their parenting abilities or strategies (Conger & Conger, 2002). The second perspective, the Investment Model (IM), proposes that economic resources increase the investments parents make in their children's development, thus promoting a wide range of academic and social competencies that accrue to the benefit of the child (Bradley & Corwyn, 2002; Mayer, 1997). The FSM developed from a social psychological approach to understanding socioeconomic influences on families and children, whereas the investment perspective grew out of an economic view of these issues. These different intellectual heritages will become clear as we consider each of these theoretical frameworks in turn.

## The Family Stress Model of Economic Hardship (FSM)

The FSM builds on a tradition of research dating back to the Great Depression years of the 1930s. A series of studies at that time provided evidence that severe hardship could undermine family functioning and socialization practices in a fashion that negatively affected the lives of both parents and children (e.g., Angell, 1936; Cavan & Ranck, 1938; Komarovsky, 1940). Elder's research extended this earlier work in a series of reports demonstrating the response of depression-era parents to economic loss (Elder, 1974; Elder & Caspi, 1988). These themes have been carried forward in contemporary investigations that both support and modify many of the conclusions reached in these earlier studies (Leventhal & Brooks-Gunn, 2003; McLoyd, 1998). Mayer (1997) calls the conceptual ideas emanating from this line of research the "good parent theory," which proposes that poverty or low income has a negative impact on parents' psychological well-being. These psychological disruptions, in turn, are expected to reduce effective parenting practices.

Consistent with this line of research, Conger and his colleagues coined the term "family stress model," which was developed in their efforts to understand how financial problems influenced the lives of Iowa families going through a severe downturn in the agricultural economy during the 1980s (Conger, Rueter, & Conger, 2000; Conger et al., 2002; Conger & Conger, 2002; Conger & Elder, 1994). As shown in Figure 5.1, the FSM proposes that economic hardship leads to economic pressure in the family. Markers

of hardship include low income, high debts relative to assets, and negative financial events (i.e., job loss, increasing economic demands, or declining material resources). These hardship conditions are expected to affect family functioning and individual adjustment primarily through the economic pressures they generate. The FSM proposes that economic pressures include (1) unmet material needs involving necessities such as adequate food and clothing, (2) the inability to pay bills or make ends meet, and (3) having to cut back on even necessary expenses (e.g., health insurance and medical care). Conger and his colleagues argue that experiencing these kinds of pressures or strains gives psychological meaning to living with economic hardship (Conger et al., 1992, 1993, 1994, 2002; Conger & Conger, 2002; Conger & Elder, 1994).

In addition, the model predicts that when economic pressure is high, parents and other caregivers (e.g., members of the extended family) living with children are at increased risk for becoming emotionally distressed, as indicated by feelings of depression, anxiety, anger, and alienation. These markers of emotional problems are broadly conceived and may also be reflected in related problems such as substance use or antisocial behavior, as suggested by earlier research (Conger, 1995). According to the model, emotional distress predicts problems in family relationships, including increased conflict and reduced warmth and support in the relations between caregivers and also harsh and inconsistent parenting practices (Conger et al., 2000; Conger & Conger, 2002; Conger et al., 2002). Research indicates that the prediction of conflict and withdrawal holds not only for biological parents but also for stepparents, co-habiting unmarried romantic partners, and other caregiver relationships such as daughters and mothers raising a child together (Conger et al., 2002). The FSM also proposes that, in addition to parents'

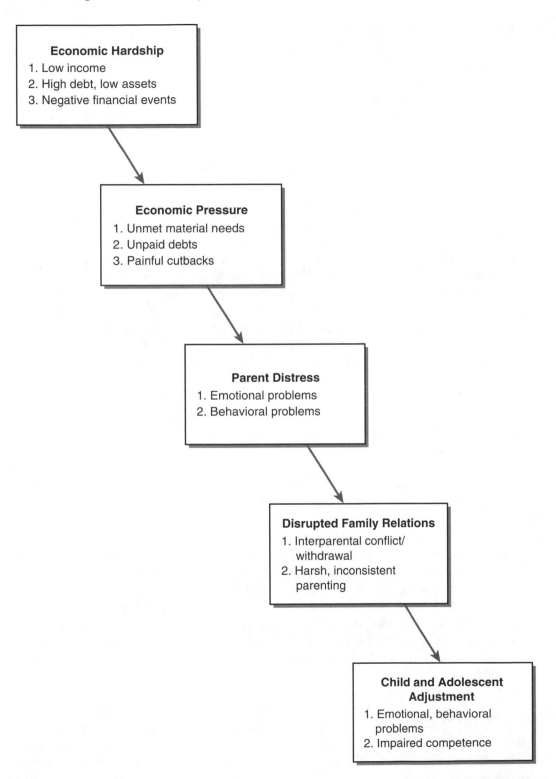

**Figure 5.1**    The Family Stress Model of Economic Hardship

emotional distress, interparental conflict and relationship problems will be directly related to disruptions in parenting.

In the cascade of influences depicted in Figure 5.1, the final step in the hypothesized stress process involves the connection between disrupted family relationships and child and adolescent adjustment. More specifically, the primary hypothesis is that disrupted parenting will mediate or explain the influence of parental distress and interparental conflicts on child development (e.g., Conger et al., 2000). According to the model, then, when families experience economic hardship, children are at risk for suffering both decrements in positive adjustment (e.g., cognitive ability, social competence, school success, and attachment to parents) and increases in internalizing (e.g., symptoms of depression and anxiety) and externalizing (e.g., aggressive and antisocial behavior) problems. The model also proposes, however, that these economic effects on children will only be indirect through their impact on the lives of parents and other family caregivers. For single-parent families, caregiver conflicts with one another may be omitted from the model or conflicts with an ex-spouse or current romantic partner might be substituted, as economic problems are expected to affect these relationships as well (Conger et al., 2002). Although elaborations of the FSM include factors that promote resilience or exacerbate vulnerability to these mediating pathways, the model in Figure 5.1 provides the basic tenets of this theoretical framework (Conger & Conger, 2002; Conger et al., 2002).

## The Investment Model (IM)

Whereas the FSM focuses on the hypothesized adverse emotional and behavioral consequences of low income and economic hardship, the IM is primarily concerned with the advantages that accrue to the developing child because of family wealth and financial prosperity (see Figure 5.2). The IM proposes that families with greater economic resources are able to make significant investments in the development of their children whereas more disadvantaged families must invest in more immediate family needs (Becker & Thomes, 1986; Bradley & Corwyn, 2002, 2003; Corcoran & Adams, 1997; Duncan & Magnuson, 2003; Haveman & Wolfe, 1994; Linver, Brooks-Gunn, & Kohen, 2002; Mayer, 1997). These investments involve several different dimensions of family support including (a) learning materials available in the home, (b) parent stimulation of learning both directly and through support of advanced or specialized tutoring or training, (c) the family's standard of living (i.e., adequate food, housing, clothing, medical care, etc.), and (d) residing in a location that fosters a child's competent development. For example, wealthier parents are expected to reside in areas that promote a child's association with conventional friends, access to good schools, and involvement in a neighborhood or community environment that provides resources for the developing child such as parks, playgrounds, and other child-related activities. In general, the IM predicts that economic well-being will be positively related to child-rearing activities expected to foster the academic and social success of a child.

Basically, the IM proposes that economically well-to-do families can provide a variety of resources that increase human capital for the developing child. The model reflects its economic heritage in this regard. That is, the theory proposes that families, just like businesses, invest in the products or services they provide. Presumably businesses with greater resources can make greater capital investments and, thus, maintain a competitive edge in the world of commerce. Similarly, families with greater resources can invest them in a fashion that will produce

**Figure 5.2** The Investment Model

a more competent and successful child. Children in more well-to-do families are more likely to have the nourishment, medical care, environmental safety and support, and educational and social opportunities they require to succeed in life.

## EMPIRICAL FINDINGS RELATED TO THE FAMILY STRESS AND INVESTMENT MODELS

In this section of the chapter, we review the research evidence related to the types of mediating pathways proposed by the FSM and the IM. Because several recent studies have been devoted to examination of the FSM, more evidence is available to consider for this theoretical perspective. However, an increasing number of studies have tested predictions from the IM and we consider this more limited evidence as well.

### The Family Stress Model of Economic Hardship

As shown in Figure 5.1, several elements in the FSM require empirical evaluation. To begin with, the theory proposes that there will be no direct connection between the exogenous variable in the model, economic hardship, and the endogenous variables involving emotional distress, close relationships of caregivers, socialization practices in the form of disrupted parenting, and child and adolescent adjustment. Rather, various forms of hardship such as low or unstable income, high debts relative to assets, acute economic setbacks, and increasing financial

demands, as might occur when an illness occurs in the family, are expected to lead to economic pressure. As noted earlier, economic pressure is central to the model in the sense that it captures the psychologically meaningful aspects of economic hardship, such as being unable to pay bills or purchase the necessities of life. High levels of economic pressure are expected to lead to the cascade of family disruptions illustrated in Figure 5.1. Because six independent studies involving highly diverse samples have now evaluated significant portions of the FSM using the same labels for constructs as described in Figure 5.1, we focus our review on the findings from these investigations. Following a short description of each study, we review the findings across the set of studies.

*The Iowa Youth and Families Project (IYFP).* The basic parameters of the model portrayed in Figure 5.1 were first proposed and evaluated in this study of 451 rural Iowa families. The focal children were in the seventh grade in 1989 when they were first interviewed with their parents. Initial findings were reported separately for the boys and the girls (Conger et al., 1992, 1993) who participated in the IYFP during seventh grade and who had complete data for the required analyses. These two-parent families were selected for study because they were experiencing the economic upheavals caused by the economic depression in agriculture during the 1980s. Given the ethnic structure of rural Iowa, all of these families were of European origin. The IYFP included assessments of all dimensions of the FSM as illustrated in Figure 5.1. Child and adolescent outcomes included negative adjustment (e.g., problem behaviors and emotional distress) and positive adjustment (e.g., school achievement).

*The Family and Community Health Study (FACHS).* The Family and Community Health Study replicated and extended the original Iowa research with rural families of European heritage in several important ways. First, it involved 422 two-caregiver African American families living in Iowa and Georgia who were raising the focal child, a fifth grader at study initiation. Second, these families primarily came from urban rather than rural areas, although these were not large urban centers of the type that have been the focus of most research with African American parents and children. They were recruited in a process that generated a true community sample with a wide range of SES characteristics from very poor to economically advantaged. Third, the caregiver relationship took several different forms including the married, biological parents of the focal child (39%), stepparents (33%), or children (28%) living with some other form of caregiver arrangement such as mothers and grandmothers. These important variations in caregiver relationships made it possible to determine if the processes described by the FSM would apply only to married biological parents, such as those in the IYFP, or to a broader array of possible care giving arrangements. As for the IYFP, the FACHS included measures for all the constructs in the FSM and also had indicators of both positive and negative child adjustment.

*The New Hope Project.* This study by Mistry, Vandewater, Huston, and McLoyd (2002) focused on a poor urban sample of primarily ethnic minority (57% African American, 28% Hispanic) families headed by a single parent (83%). Children ranged in age from 5 to 12 years for the 419 families in the study. The New Hope Project was an experimental study designed to determine whether financial assistance and job training efforts would improve the life conditions of poor families. Mistry and her colleagues examined how economic pressures influenced parenting behaviors and child outcomes using program evaluation data from the larger investigation. Because almost all of these families involved only a single parent, information was not collected on caregiver conflicts. Moreover, these investigators focused on two forms of parenting behavior, responsive parenting and effective discipline. For our purposes, we reverse the signs for their reported findings for parenting behaviors to be consistent with the idea of harsh, inconsistent, or disrupted parenting as proposed in the FSM. That is, we treat these variables as unresponsive parenting and poor discipline that are expected to be exacerbated by the economic stress process. Positive child adjustment was estimated by a measure of social competence and negative adjustment was indicated by externalizing problems.

*The Panel Study of Income Dynamics (PSID).* This study evaluates predictions from the FSM with younger children, ages 3 to 5 years. This report is based on the Panel Study of Income Dynamics, a nationally representative investigation of families and their economic experiences (Yeung, Linver, & Brooks-Gunn, 2002). The sample for the study is quite diverse in ethnicity, place of residence, SES, and family structure. Yeung and her colleagues examined predictions from the FSM for 753 preschool children, a relatively neglected age group in previous tests of the model. In their analyses, the researchers also examined predictions from the Investment Model, and we consider those results in the next section of this report. The results in the report considered here were based on information about the children and their mothers. Two forms of parenting were examined, warm (reversed for our review) and punitive. We focus on two child outcomes assessed in the study: externalizing behaviors (negative adjustment) and cognitive achievement (positive adjustment), measured by letter and word recognition. The relationship between caregivers was not examined in these analyses. Also important, all models were estimated controlling for mother's education and cognitive ability.

*The Finnish Replication Study.* In this research project, Solantaus and her colleagues attempted a major replication of the original IYFP findings based on an investigation of 527 two-parent families in Finland (Solantaus, Leinonen, & Punamäki, 2004). They included all of the major constructs in the model in their assessment package and predicted child externalizing and internalizing symptoms at time 2, controlling for the same problems at time 1, approximately 4 years earlier. Thus, they predicted rank order change in child adjustment. They did not include a measure of positive adjustment. In addition, all of the families included both a mother and a father along with a focal child between 12 and 13 years of age, characteristics consistent with the original IYFP. There were approximately the same number of boys and girls in the sample. The replication study took place during a period of economic crisis in Finland, similar to the agricultural depression experienced by the Iowa families. To our knowledge, this study represents the only attempted replication of the complete FSM outside of the United States.

*The Riverside Economic Stress Project.* Another important replication study of the FSM involved European American ($N = 111$) and Mexican American ($N = 167$) families of fifth graders who participated in the Riverside Economic Stress Project conducted in Southern California (Parke et al., 2005). This study included indicators for all of the major FSM constructs, including parental or caregiver conflict in these two-parent families. For the child outcome, the authors of the report used a combined measure of internalizing and externalizing problems, a marker of poor child adjustment, but they had no measure of positive child outcomes.

*A Review of the Findings.* Table 5.1 provides a summary of the results from each study in relation to predictions from the FSM (see Figure 5.1). The coefficients in the table are standardized estimates either from ordinary least squares regressions using manifest variables or from structural equation models with latent variables. These regression parameters are averaged within studies. For example, in the IYFP analyses there are four separate reports of the connection between economic hardship and economic pressure as estimated in four separate evaluations of the FSM: one for mothers and sons, one for mothers and daughters, one for fathers and sons, and one for fathers and daughters. The coefficient of .65 for the IYFP in the first row of the table represents the average of these four regression coefficients. In general, these averaged coefficients provide a good estimate of the findings for the separate studies. We discuss instances when the average estimate may be somewhat misleading. Cells with an NS in the table indicate the predicted association was not statistically significant. Cells with an NA indicate that a specific variable was not available for analysis. For example, the New Hope and PSID studies did not have a measure of conflict between parents or other caregivers in the family. Thus, any rows in the table that address the association between caregiver conflict and other variables in the model have an NA for these two studies.

The first row of the table addresses the FSM prediction that economic hardship will lead to perceptions of economic pressure by parents or other caregivers in the family. The degree of association ranged from .20 (New Hope Study) to .84 (Finnish Study), and all of the individual coefficients that were averaged

**Table 5.1**    Findings From Major Tests of the Family Stress Model With Standardized
Parameters Estimates

| | | | Research Studies | | | |
|---|---|---|---|---|---|---|
| Predicted Pathways | IYFP | FACHS | New Hope | PSID | Finnish Study | Riverside Project |
| 1. Economic hardship to economic pressure | .65 | .66 | .20 | .22 | .84 | .63 |
| 2. Economic pressure to parent/caregiver distress | .56 | .46 | .75 | .15 | .36 | .33 |
| 3. Parent/caregiver distress to caregiver conflict | .35 | .34 | NA | NA | .31 | .33 |
| 4. Parent/caregiver distress to disrupted parenting | .22 | NS | .47 | .08 | NS | .23 |
| 5. Caregiver conflict to disrupted parenting | .52 | .51 | NA | NA | .40 | NS |
| 6. Caregiver conflict to positive child adjustment | NS | NS | NA | NA | NA | NA |
| 7. Caregiver conflict to poor child adjustment | NS | NS | NA | NA | NS | .27 |
| 8. Disrupted parenting to positive child adjustment | −.35 | −.55 | −.20 | −.04 | NA | NA |
| 9. Disrupted parenting to poor child adjustment | .49 | .44 | .12 | .13 | .35 | .32 |

NOTE: NS = not statistically significant; NA = not applicable, measure not available.

to create these estimates were statistically significant. The findings with regard to this predicted association also underscore the importance of the FSM emphasis on a broad array of measures for economic hardship, including indicators of income, income loss, financial resources, and economic demands. That is, all of the studies that included multiple measures of economic hardship (IYFP, FACHS, Finnish Study, Riverside Project) produced much higher associations with economic pressure than those that only used a measure of family income (New Hope and PSID). We believe that these findings highlight the importance of the idea that an adequate evaluation of economic standing requires measures of other material resources and demands in addition to income, as proposed by the FSM. Also consistent with the model, the link between economic hardship and other endogenous variables was entirely indirect through economic pressure.

The next step in the FSM involves the path from economic pressure to parent or caregiver distress. Across the six studies, this predicted relationship ranged from .15 (PSID) to .75 (New Hope) and was always statistically significant. Given that many of the studies used different indicators for economic pressure and parental distress, this degree of replication is quite remarkable. The next prediction in the FSM (Figure 5.1) is that parental distress will lead to disruptions in family relationships. This hypothesis usually involves separate estimates from distress to caregiver conflict and then to parenting behaviors, as indicated in rows 3 and 4 of the table. For all of the tests of associations between these types of endogenous variables, earlier predictor variables in the model are controlled. Thus, the results in row 3 indicate that parent distress was directly related to caregiver conflict, for the studies that included the conflict variable, after controlling for economic pressure and economic hardship, the earlier predictors in the FSM. Parental distress also predicted disrupted parenting in four of the six studies, consistent with the FSM.

For two of the studies (FACHS and the Finnish Study), however, the results suggest that parental distress affects poor parenting only indirectly through conflicts between caregivers. For example, in the FACHS parental distress predicts caregiver conflict ($b = .34$) and caregiver conflict predicts disrupted parenting ($b = .51$; row 5, Table 5.1). A similar pattern of findings exists for the Finnish Study. These results suggest that parent emotional distress directly predicts caregiver conflict and either directly or indirectly influences disruptions in parenting through conflicts between caregivers. For two-parent or two-caregiver families of other types (e.g., mothers and grandmothers), conflicts between these caregivers appear to play a key role in the economic stress process in relation to disruptions of effective parenting practices. For single-parent families, emotional distress appears to directly affect the quality of parenting behavior.

Even though caregiver conflict seems to impair the parenting role, it does not relate directly to child and adolescent adjustment, as shown in rows 6 and 7 in Table 5.1. The only significant direct association ($b = .27$) between caregiver conflict and child outcomes occurs for poor child adjustment in the Riverside Project. Indeed, this averaged coefficient is misleading for the results of this study in an interesting way. For the Mexican American families in this study, caregiver conflict was a robust predictor of poor child adjustment ($b = .53$). For the European American families, the relationship was not statistically significant, consistent with the results from the five other studies considered here. It may be that this finding represents something unique about Mexican American families and children. For example, this interesting result may reflect the high value Mexican American parents and children place on the family unit. Because threats to the family itself engendered by interparental conflict may be especially distressing for Mexican American children, caregiver conflict may directly affect the emotional and behavioral problems of these children independently of styles of parenting (Parke et al., 2005). This possibility needs to be investigated in future research.

Finally, rows 8 and 9 in Table 5.1 provide findings related to disrupted parenting and child outcomes. Consistent with the FSM, problems in parenting impaired competent or positive child development in all studies that had a measure of positive adjustment. The low average coefficient in the PSID ($b = -.04$) reflects the fact that low parental warmth was not significantly associated with positive adjustment but parental punishment was. The findings in row 9 indicate that there was a significant association between problems in parenting and poor child adjustment for all the studies. Thus, as predicted by the model, disruptions in parenting behavior appear to play the key role in transmitting other elements in the economic stress process to the lives of children. Taken together, these studies suggest that the FSM provides a reasonably good heuristic model for helping to understand how economic hardship influences family members, socialization processes, and the positive or problematic adjustment of children and adolescents. Actually, given the wide variations in ethnicity, family structures, socioeconomic status and child ages in this set of studies, the degree of replication across them is quite remarkable.

## The Investment Model

Only a limited amount of recent research has been done on the IM (Figure 5.2). In part, this paucity of findings results from the fact that a demographic variable like family income is often treated only as a control variable in developmental research, rather than as a predictor of theoretical interest in its own right (Hoff, Laursen, & Tardiff, 2002; Hoffman, 2003). For that reason, a wide range of findings cannot be enumerated involving specific theoretical constructs from a number of theoretical tests of the model as we did for the FSM. Instead, we consider in some detail the small number of available tests that provide insights regarding predictions from the IM.

The emphasis in research on the IM has been on the means by which parents and other caregivers foster the academic, economic, and social success of children. For this reason, cognitive and academic performance has been an especially important focus in this line of research. The family stress perspective, on the other hand, has tended to focus on social and emotional adjustment problems of children and adolescents, consistent with the greater mental health orientation of the approach. As we saw with research on the FSM, however, some work in this area also addresses competent development, and the investment model has sometimes been used to predict behavioral and emotional problems. We consider some of these findings in this section of our review.

Several studies have confirmed the most basic propositions of the investment model; that is, that family income during childhood and adolescence is positively related to academic, financial, and occupational success during the adult years (Bradley & Corwyn, 2002; Corcoran & Adams, 1997; Mayer,

1997; Teachman, Paasch, Day, & Carver, 1997) and that family income affects the types of investments parents make in the lives of their children (Bradley & Corwyn, 2002; Mayer, 1997). The central aim of research on the model is to determine whether these investments explain the connections between income and developmental outcomes. With regard to the proposed association between income and investments, a seminal study by Bradley, Corwyn, McAdoo, and García Coll (2001) demonstrated the pervasiveness of this association.

Bradley and his colleagues used data from multiple waves of the National Longitudinal Survey of Youth to evaluate differences in parental investments and parental behavior, as measured by the Home Observation for Measurement of the Environment (HOME) scale (Bradley & Caldwell, 1980), for several thousand children ranging in age from infancy to early adolescence. For three major ethnic groups (European American, African American, and Hispanic American), the study indicated consistent differences on these dimensions between poor (families below the official poverty guidelines) and nonpoor families. For example, compared with poor families, parents in families with incomes above the official poverty guidelines were more likely to engage their children in conversation, learning activities, and discussions of events in their daily lives. Children in more financially secure families also had greater access to books, magazines, toys, games that stimulate learning, cultural events and activities outside the home, and special lessons that encourage particular talents in music, sports, and other specialized pursuits.

Parents in the nonpoor families also were more likely to demonstrate affection and respect for their children and less likely to use physical punishment or restraint. Moreover, the physical environments in which more advantaged children lived tended to be safer, cleaner, roomier, and less dark and cluttered.

This finding underscores the material disadvantage of poor children, which also extends to nutrition, medical care, clothing, and other basic necessities (e.g., Mayer, 1997). Finally, the poor children in the study were less likely to spend time with or even know their fathers, a reduction in the social capital available to them. Taken together, the results of this study of a large-scale, nationally representative, multiethnic sample of families demonstrate a clear link between family income and the investments that are made in the human capital of children (Bradley et al., 2001). Especially important, these investments extend beyond tutoring and material goods to include parental affection and respect as well.

Other research has shown that family income and the investments in children it predicts appear to have a beneficial influence on long-term developmental success. For example, children from more economically advantaged compared with poorer families accrue more years of education, are less likely to experience adverse events such as a teenage pregnancy, and are more likely to have an adequate income as an adult (Corcoran & Adams, 1997; Mayer, 1997). A significant limitation in most of this earlier research, however, is that the full mediating process proposed by the investment model has not been evaluated. That is, most researchers have not examined whether specific parental investments in children account for the connection between family income and child, adolescent, and early adult development. In a paper published in 2002, Linver et al. provided perhaps the best evidence for the set of empirical relationships proposed by the model.

In their report, Linver and her associates used information from several hundred families participating in the Infant Health and Development Program, a large-scale, multiethnic study of children from birth to 5 years of age at the time of their analysis. A particularly important feature of this study is that it examines economic influences at an early age, influences that likely set the stage for later child success or failure. Consistent with the IM, the association between family income and child cognitive development at ages 3 and 5 years (standardized intelligence test scores, $b = .70$ without control variables and .52 with control variables) was significantly reduced ($b = .36$) when the investment mediator was introduced into the analyses. A test of indirect effects also supported the conclusion that the influence of family income on cognitive development was partially the result of parental investments. The measure of parental investment was derived from the HOME, as in the Bradley et al. (2001) study just discussed, and included items related to parental behaviors expected to stimulate cognitive development such as language stimulation, teaching colors and numbers, providing books and other learning materials, and exposing the child to learning experiences outside the home. The investigators also found that the measure of parental investment completely mediated the association between income and child behavior problems at 3 and 5 years of age. Thus, the basic investment model in this study partially explained child maladjustment as well as child competence.

A particularly important feature of the Linver et al. (2002) study is that the investigators controlled for the influence of parent education and measured intelligence in the analyses, as well as other social-demographic characteristics. These controls assured that the results could not be attributed simply to the educational attainment and intelligence of the parent, which might indicate a direct genetic effect on the child's cognitive abilities. Thus, this report provides substantial support for the basic investment model. In a similar set of analyses using data from the PSID, Yeung et al. (2002) also controlled for parent personal and demographic characteristics in a test of the IM. Even with these controls, they found evidence that family income had an influence on child outcomes at least partly through parental investments in the competent development of children. These two studies provide suggestive evidence regarding the proposed importance of parental investments as the mechanism through which family income affects child and adolescent development.

To summarize available research on the IM, the connections between income and parental investment and between parental investment and child competence appear to be fairly well established (Bradley & Corwyn, 2002; Mayer, 1997). Required now are additional tests regarding the proposition that parental investments of various types actually account for the basic relationship between income and successful child development. Additional research on this hypothesized mediated pathway in the model is crucial for gaining additional understanding of how family income conveys developmental advantage across the life course.

## OVERVIEW AND DISCUSSION

We have considered two of the major theoretical frameworks that have attempted to explain how economic circumstances in family life affect the social, emotional, cognitive, and physical development of children. Six studies were identified that provide fairly explicit tests of the FSM and the full set of mediated pathways proposed in the model, beginning with economic hardship and ending with the developmental status of children and adolescents. These investigations varied substantially in ethnicity, family structure, and child age. Yet they all generated findings reasonably consistent with the overall model. We also found several reports that addressed various aspects of the IM; however, only two actually tested the proposed meditating role of parental investments in the connection between

family income and child development. Both of these studies provided some support for the hypothesized mediating process, and several studies were consistent with proposed connections between income and parental investments and parental investments and child development.

At this point, it would be relatively easy to conclude that the theories and results considered here provide substantial evidence that economic hardship and family income play a significant role in the lives of children and that the mediating mechanisms proposed in these models provide reasonably good explanations for how those economic influences might occur. We actually believe that these conclusions are reasonable and that they provide a good guide for future theoretical developments and empirical research. Theoretically, the findings suggest that the different approaches taken by the IM and FSM are complementary and may well be interrelated. Whereas the FSM focuses on the stresses and strains produced by economic disadvantage, the IM emphasizes the opportunities created by economic advantage. In reality, a more comprehensive theory could be developed if the two separate theories were combined into a single model of economic influences on family processes and child development. For example, the family stress processes proposed in the FSM result from low income; thus, they may also help explain the influence of income on parental investments. Future theoretical developments and theoretical tests should move in the direction of a more comprehensive and integrated model, as some researchers have proposed (see Conger & Dogan, 2006; Conger & Donnellan, 2007).

Despite this positive appraisal of the FSM and IM and the possibility of their combined use for a more general theory of economic influences on human development, others have proposed that these results may well be spurious (e.g., Mayer, 1997). As we noted earlier, the FSM and IM are based on the argument for social causation, which proposes that social and economic events and conditions play a causal role in the course of human lives. The counterargument is called social selection, which proposes that the attributes of individuals determine the kinds of social and economic events they will experience over time. According to this perspective, once these individual characteristics are taken into account, there is no expected relationship between SES and either parenting behaviors or the developmental outcomes of children. In other words, positive relationships between SES and childrearing practices or child adjustment are assumed to be spurious and would not exist if appropriate information were available about other parental characteristics. In addition, this perspective suggests that genetically transmitted abilities from parent to child, such as cognitive competence, may account for many of the connections between parental SES and child development.

Almost no research has been able to adequately address this counter proposal to the social causation argument; however, some interesting new findings are beginning to shed light on the issue. For example, two recent investigations found evidence that characteristics of family members may affect SES. In a study of preschool children, Hyde, Else-Quest, Goldsmith, and Biesanz (2004) discovered that a young child with a difficult temperament exacerbates feelings of parental incompetence and depressed affect for mothers. These maternal characteristics, in turn, reduce the quality and gratification of the mother's work life. Over time, one might expect that these types of family processes could actually reduce the mother's success in work and the family's overall SES. With regard to the FSM, Conger and Conger (2002) showed that parents who were high in mastery actually reduced their economic pressure over time, suggesting that this parental trait likely led to extra efforts to deal with economic problems. Presumably, this orientation to dealing with financial difficulties should help to maintain or improve family SES.

Perhaps even more relevant to the question of selection effects is a series of studies showing that the traits and dispositions of children and adolescents predict their SES as an adult. For instance, McLeod and Kaiser (2004) found that internalizing and externalizing problems occurring as early as 6 years of age predict lower adult educational attainment. In a separate study, Kokko and Pulkkinen (2000) showed that aggressive behavior at 8 years of age was related to long-term unemployment during the adult years. In their investigation, Feinstein and Bynner (2004) discovered that poor cognitive performance during early and middle childhood predicted lower educational attainment, lower income, and less work success during the adult years. Finally, Schoon et al. (2002) showed that low SES in a child's family of origin predicted lower academic achievement and continuing life stress across the years of childhood and adolescence. Lower academic competence and higher life stress, in turn, were associated with lower SES when the child became an adult. These results suggest a reciprocal process in which low SES in the family of origin is associated with low SES in the next generation of adults as a result of diminished academic performance and greater life stress.

Simply put, we expect that the FSM and IM are not incorrect, but they more than likely are incomplete. The research just cited suggests that personal characteristics affect the development of socioeconomic status, and these characteristics are likely to affect family functioning and family stress (Conger & Donnellan, 2007). Thus, combining the FSM and IM into a single comprehensive model of the relationship between SES and human development will still be insufficient to fully articulate the processes that may be involved. Emerging evidence suggests that the FSM and IM represent the social causation aspects of this relationship fairly well; however, mechanisms related to social selection also appear to account for at least some of the association between SES and human development. Conger and Donnellan (2007) provide a detailed examination of the possible interface between the social selection and social causation approaches to understanding the connection between SES and life course development, and propose a theoretical model that attempts to integrate these different perspectives. The important point for the moment is that SES and human development are likely intertwined in complex ways. Fully understanding these complexities will require additional research and theoretical development.

Although the research required to advance understanding of the linkages among economic circumstances, family life, and child and adolescent development will be both complex and demanding, we believe that such research is essential for the welfare of families and children, both today and tomorrow. For example, even though one might think that in the contemporary United States, social class differences are becoming less important and that the sorts of hypothesized SES influences discussed in this chapter are less relevant in the modern era, this point of view seems to be contrary to current realities. Even conservative commentators have recently noted the growing disparities in different aspects of SES and their important influence on the course of life (e.g., Brooks, 2005). More generally, the richest Americans have seen enormous increases in income and material wealth during the past two decades whereas most U.S. citizens have seen a decline in their financial well-being (Johnston, 2005; Magnuson & Duncan, 2002). Thus, the potentially negative influence of low SES on child development may well be more prevalent today than even a few years ago. Increased understanding of the mechanisms that lead from economic disadvantage to the life of the developing child will provide better information for the development of programs that can promote the well-being of families even in trying times and, perhaps, even help diminish the cycle of disadvantage from one generation to the next.

## REFERENCES

Ackerman, B. P., Brown, E. D., & Izard, C. E. (2004). The relations between persistent poverty and contextual risk and children's behavior in elementary school. *Developmental Psychology, 40,* 367–377.

Angell, R. C. (1936). *The family encounters the depression.* New York: Scribner.

Becker, G. S., & Thomes, N. (1986). Human capital and the rise and fall of families. *Journal of Labor Economics, 4,* S1–S139.

Berkman, L. F., & Kawachi, I. (Eds.). (2000). *Social epidemiology.* New York: Oxford University Press.

Bradley, R. H., & Caldwell, B. M. (1980). The relation of the home environment, cognitive competence, and IQ among males and females. *Child Development, 51,* 1140–1148.

Bradley, R. H., & Corwyn, R. F. (2002). Socioeconomic status and child development. *Annual Review of Psychology, 53,* 371–399.

Bradley, R. H., & Corwyn, R. F. (2003). Age and ethnic variations in family process mediators of SES. In M. H. Bornstein & R. H. Bradley (Eds.), *Socioeconomic status, parenting, and child development* (pp. 161–188). Mahwah, NJ: Erlbaum.

Bradley, R. H., Corwyn, R. F., McAdoo, H. P., & García Coll, C. (2001). The home environments of children in the United States: Part I. Variations by age, ethnicity, and poverty status. *Child Development, 72,* 1844–1867.

Brooks, D. (2005, June 1). Karl Marx updated for 21st century. *The Sacramento Bee,* p. B7.

Cavan, R. S., & Ranck, K. H. (1938). *The family and the depression: A study of one hundred Chicago families.* Chicago: University of Chicago Press.

Conger, K. J., Rueter, M. A., & Conger, R. D. (2000). The role of economic pressure in the lives of parents and their adolescents: The Family Stress Model. In L. J. Crockett & R. K. Silbereisen (Eds.), *Negotiating adolescence in times of social change* (pp. 201–223). Cambridge, UK: Cambridge University Press.

Conger, R. D. (1995). Unemployment. In D. Levinson (Ed.), *Encyclopedia of marriage and the family* (pp. 731–735). New York: Macmillan.

Conger, R. D., & Conger, K. J. (2002). Resilience in Midwestern families: Selected findings from the first decade of a prospective, longitudinal study. *Journal of Marriage and Family, 64,* 361–373.

Conger, R. D., Conger, K. J., Elder, G. H., Jr., Lorenz, F. O., Simons, R. L., & Whitbeck, L. B. (1992). A family process model of economic hardship and adjustment of early adolescent boys. *Child Development, 63,* 526–541.

Conger, R. D., Conger, K. J., Elder, G. H., Jr., Lorenz, F. O., Simons, R. L., & Whitbeck, L. B. (1993). Family economic stress and adjustment of early adolescent girls. *Developmental Psychology, 29,* 206–219.

Conger, R. D., & Dogan, S. J. (2006). Social class and socialization in families. In J. Grusec & P. Hastings (Eds.), *Handbook of socialization* (pp. 433–460). New York: Guilford Press.

Conger, R. D., & Donnellan, M. B. (2007). An interactionist perspective on the socioeconomic context of human development. *Annual Review of Psychology, 58,* 175–199.

Conger, R. D., & Elder, G. H., Jr. (Eds.). (1994). *Families in troubled times: Adapting to change in rural America.* Hawthorne, NY: Aldine de Gruyter.

Conger, R. D., Ge, X., Elder, G. H., Jr., Lorenz, F. O., & Simons, R. L. (1994). Economic stress, coercive family process and developmental problems of adolescents [Special issue on children and poverty]. *Child Development, 65,* 541–561.

Conger, R. D., Rueter, M. A., & Elder, G. H., Jr. (1999). Couple resilience to economic pressure. *Journal of Personality and Social Psychology, 76,* 54–71.

Conger, R. D., Wallace, L. E., Sun, Y., Simons, R. L., McLoyd, V. C., & Brody, G. (2002). Economic pressure in African American families: A replication and extension of the family stress model. *Developmental Psychology, 38,* 179–193.

Corcoran, M., & Adams, T. (1997). Race, sex, and the intergenerational transmission of poverty. In G. J. Duncan & J. Brooks-Gunn (Eds.), *Consequences of growing up poor* (pp. 461–517). New York: Russell Sage.

Dearing, E., McCartney, K., & Taylor, B. A. (2001). Change in family income-to-needs matters more for children with less. *Child Development, 72,* 1779–1793.

Duncan, G. J., & Brooks-Gunn, J. (1997). Income effects across the life span: Integration and interpretation. In G. J. Duncan & J. Brooks-Gunn (Eds.), *Consequences of growing up poor* (pp. 596–610). New York: Russell Sage.

Duncan, G. J., & Magnuson, K. A. (2003). Off with Hollingshead: Socioeconomic resources, parenting, and child development. In M. H. Bornstein & R. H. Bradley (Eds.), *Socioeconomic status, parenting, and child development* (pp. 83–106). Mahwah, NJ: Erlbaum.

Elder, G. H., Jr. (1974). *Children of the Great Depression: Social change in life experience.* Chicago: University of Chicago Press.

Elder, G. H., Jr., & Caspi, A. (1988). Economic stress in lives: Developmental perspectives. *Journal of Social Issues, 44,* 25–45.

Evans, G. W., & English, K. (2002). The environment of poverty: Multiple stressor exposure, psychophysiological stress, and socioemotional adjustment. *Child Development, 73,* 1238–1248.

Feinstein, L., & Bynner, J. (2004). The importance of cognitive development in middle childhood for adulthood socioeconomic status, mental health, and problem behavior. *Child Development, 75,* 1329–1339.

Haveman, R. H., & Wolfe, B. S. (1994). *Succeeding generations: On the effects of investments in children.* New York: Russell Sage.

Hoff, E. (2003). The specificity of environmental influence: Socioeconomic status affects early vocabulary development via maternal speech. *Child Development, 74,* 1368–1378.

Hoff, E., Laursen, B., & Tardif, T. (2002). Socioeconomic status and parenting. In M. H. Bornstein (Ed.), *Handbook of parenting: Vol. 2. Biology and ecology of parenting* (2nd ed., pp. 231–252). Mahwah, NJ: Erlbaum.

Hoffman, L. W. (2003). Methodological issues in the studies of SES, parenting, and child development. In M. H. Bornstein & R. H. Bradley (Eds.), *Socioeconomic status, parenting, and child development* (pp. 125–143). Mahwah, NJ: Erlbaum.

Hughes, C., Jaffee, S. R., Happé, F., Taylor, A., Caspi, A., & Moffitt, T. E. (2005). Origins of individual differences in theory of mind: From nature to nurture? *Child Development, 76,* 356–370.

Hyde, J. S., Else-Quest, N. M., Goldsmith, H. H., & Biesanz, J. C. (2004). Children's temperament and behavior problems predict their employed mothers' work functioning. *Child Development, 75,* 580–594.

Johnston, D. C. (2005, June 5). Richest are leaving even the rich far behind: Tax laws help to widen gap at very top. *The New York Times,* pp. 1, 17.

Kokko, K., & Pulkkinen, L. (2000). Aggression in childhood and long-term unemployment in adulthood: A cycle of maladaptation and some protective factors. *Developmental Psychology, 36,* 463–472.

Komarovsky, M. (1940). *The unemployed man and his family: The effect of unemployment upon the status of the man in fifty-nine families.* New York: Dryden Press.

Leventhal, T., & Brooks-Gunn, J. (2003). Moving on up: Neighborhood effects on children and families. In M. H. Bornstein & R. H. Bradley (Eds.), *Socioeconomic status, parenting, and child development* (pp. 209–230). Mahwah, NJ: Erlbaum.

Linver, M. R., Brooks-Gunn, J., & Kohen, D. (2002). Family processes as pathways from income to young children's development. *Developmental Psychology, 38,* 719–734.

Magnuson, K. A., & Duncan, G. J. (2002). Parents in poverty. In M. H. Bornstein (Ed.), *Handbook of parenting: Vol. 4. Social conditions and applied parenting* (2nd ed., pp. 95–121). Mahwah, NJ: Erlbaum.

Mayer, S. (1997). *What money can't buy: Family income and children's life chances.* Cambridge, MA: Harvard University Press.

McLeod, J. D., & Kaiser, K. (2004). Childhood emotional and behavioral problems and educational attainment. *American Sociological Review, 69,* 636–658.

McLeod, J. D., & Shanahan, M. J. (1996). Trajectories of poverty and children's mental health. *Journal of Health and Social Behavior, 37*, 207–220.

McLoyd, V. C. (1998). Socioeconomic disadvantage and child development. *American Psychologist, 53*, 185–204.

Mezzacappa, E. (2004). Alerting, orienting, and executive attention: Developmental properties and sociodemographic correlates in an epidemiological sample of young, urban children. *Child Development, 75*, 1373–1386.

Mistry, R. S., Vandewater, E. A., Huston, A. C., & McLoyd, V. C. (2002). Economic well-being and children's social adjustment: The role of family process in an ethnically diverse low-income sample. *Child Development, 73*, 935–951.

Oakes, J. M., & Rossi, P. H. (2003). The measurement of SES in health research: Current practice and steps toward a new approach. *Social Science and Medicine, 56*, 769–784.

Parke, R. D., Coltrane, S., Duffy, S., Buriel, R., Dennis, J., & Powers, J., et al. (2005). Economic stress, parenting, and child adjustment in Mexican American and European American families. *Child Development, 75*, 1632–1656.

Repetti, R. L., Taylor, S. E., & Seeman, T. E. (2002). Risky families: Family social environments and the mental and physical health of offspring. *Psychological Bulletin, 128*, 330–366.

Schoon, I., Bynner, J., Joshi, H., Parsons, S., Wiggins, R. D., & Sacker, A. (2002). The influence of context, timing, and duration of risk experiences for the passage from childhood to midadulthood. *Child Development, 73*, 1486–1504.

Solantaus, T., Leinonen, J., & Punamäki, R. L. (2004). Children's mental health in times of economic recession: Replication and extension of the family economic stress model in Finland. *Developmental Psychology, 40*, 412–429.

Teachman, J. D., Paasch, K. M., Day, R. D., & Carver, K. P. (1997). Poverty during adolescence and subsequent educational attainment. In G. J. Duncan & J. Brooks-Gunn (Eds.), *Consequences of growing up poor* (pp. 382–418). New York: Russell Sage.

Yeung, W. J., Linver, M. R., & Brooks-Gunn, J. (2002). How money matters for young children's development: Parental investment and family processes. *Child Development, 73*, 1861–1879.

# CHAPTER 6

# Early Childhood Education and Care

## An Opportunity to Enhance the Lives of Poor Children

ANNA D. JOHNSON, KATE TARRANT, AND JEANNE BROOKS-GUNN

The relatively recent surge in female labor force participation has led to a dramatic rise in the number of young children who experience nonparental care. For families with young children, the growth in dual wage-earning families and female-headed single parent households, combined with welfare-to-work requirements has changed the landscape of early childhood education and care, shifting away from maternal to nonmaternal care. In fact, child care beginning just a few months after birth is more common than not for many of America's young children (Bachu, 1995; Kamerman & Gatenio, 2003).

How children spend their early years is crucial. The first 5 years of life, often referred to as early childhood, are critical for cognitive, social, and behavioral development (Heckman & Krueger, 2004; Smith, Brooks-Gunn, & Klebanov, 1997). These years are also those in which children are most vulnerable to the well-documented negative effects of growing up poor; in particular, deep, persistent poverty that begins early in life is noted to be detrimental to healthy development (Duncan & Brooks-Gunn, 1997; Duncan, Yeung, Brooks-Gunn, & Smith, 1998).

Although research suggests that income is associated with young children's development during the preschool years, studies have likewise found that the poorest children may benefit the most from high-quality early childhood education and care (ECEC) (Brooks-Gunn, 2003). For children in poverty, high-quality ECEC may improve school readiness and subsequent chances for school success, financial independence, and social stability, thereby reducing achievement gaps between poor and more affluent youngsters (Heckman & Lochner, 2001). As a consequence, social scientists and policymakers alike have turned a great deal of their attention toward ECEC opportunities to promote school readiness skills in children who face considerable challenges with regard to school success.

This chapter reviews the research on the association between ECEC, childhood poverty, and child development. We review what is known about the link between poverty and early development, and then define ECEC as well as school readiness. We examine the prevalence and usage of ECEC, explore the effects of ECEC on young children's development and school readiness, and consider the aspects and measurements of quality of care in a variety of ECEC settings. We also discuss the influence of timing and intensity of children's participation in ECEC on child outcomes. Throughout the chapter, we consider the moderating influence of family income in relation to ECEC, and child development and school readiness. We conclude with a discussion of the policy implications of the research, calling for an expansion of high-quality ECEC to enhance the development of children growing up in poverty.

## POVERTY AND EARLY DEVELOPMENT

The noticeable shifts in who is caring for the nation's youngest citizens that have occurred in past decades have raised researchers' interest in the impact that ECEC has on children's development. Of particular interest is the potential of ECEC programs to address the school readiness gap experienced by disadvantaged children (Currie, 2001; Magnuson & Waldfogel, 2005; Vandell & Wolfe, 2000).

Few can disagree that growing up in poverty has adverse effects on child development. For instance, researchers have found that poverty is associated with approximately one-third of a standard deviation differential in achievement test scores between poor children and their nonpoor peers (Smith et al., 1997). Unfortunately, children in the United States are among the most likely age group to be living in poverty (U.S. Census Bureau, 2004), with nearly 20% of children younger than 5 years old living below the federal poverty line. Although developmental trajectories are believed to be malleable, children in families who live below the poverty line exhibit cognitive deficits when compared with their nonpoor peers (for a more thorough discussion of the cognitive and social outcomes associated with childhood poverty, please refer to Chapter 18, "Cognitive and Emotional Outcomes for Children in Poverty" by Barajas, Philipsen, & Brooks-Gunn). These differences become apparent around age 2, and persist to age 5 and beyond (Smith et al., 1997). Actually, recent studies suggest that the achievement gap between low-income children and their middle- and upper-class peers that is observed in the early grades continues, and may even widen, as children proceed through school (Baydar, Brooks-Gunn, & Furstenberg, 1993; Phillips, Crouse, & Ralph, 1998). Because childhood poverty is so pervasive and its impact so enduring, the influence of poverty on development, and what can be done to combat those negative effects, has become a central concern for researchers and policymakers.

## DEFINING ECEC

Research suggests that high-quality ECEC may be an effective way to support young children's development. Historically, ECEC programs for children before primary school entry have fallen into two categories: (1) child care and (2) early childhood education. Child care has, in the past, been thought to serve low-income children so that mothers can work, but early childhood education programs were originally conceived to offer educational experiences to middle- and upper-class youngsters before they entered primary school (Cahan, 1989; Kagan, 1991). Traditionally, child care and early childhood education programs have also had different goals and practices. An early childhood education program may be more focused on augmenting school readiness, so cognitive stimulation may be emphasized. A child-care program, on the other hand, may have the goal of supporting parents' work, so accessibility and availability of care might be emphasized. Although school readiness may be a secondary goal of child care, it is difficult to find current literature on child care that does not highlight child-care programs' effects on child developmental outcomes. Likewise, many early childhood education experiences are provided to children through centers at which children spend some or all of their days while their parents work.

In addition to being categorized according to their goals and purposes, ECEC programs may also be classified by setting, with ECEC taking place in a home-, center-, or school-based setting. Child care, as it is referred to in the developmental literature, generally takes place in either a home or in a center. Home-based care includes family child care, which is defined as care by a nonrelative in a child-care provider's home, and is typically regulated. Other types of home-based care include kith and kin care, which is care by a relative or friend that takes place either in the caregiver's home or in the child's home, and babysitter or nanny care, which is care by a nonrelative in the child's home (Capizzano & Adams, 2003). This form of care may also be referred to as family, friend, or neighbor care, or as license-exempt care.

Center-based settings include day care, nursery school, preschool, pre-kindergarten, and Head Start (Magnuson & Waldfogel, 2005). Furthermore, ECEC can also be classified according to the public policy that governs and subsidizes young children's early care and education, including child care, Head Start, pre-kindergarten, and special education. Funding for ECEC comes from the federal Child Care and Development Fund (CCDF), Temporary Assistance for Needy Families (TANF) funds, states' general revenues,

as well as through fees paid by parents; additional differences exist among center-based ECEC programs that operate for-profit or not-for-profit.

Despite divergent historical definitions, explicit goals, settings, and policy supporting child care and early childhood education programs, the distinctions between these types of ECEC have blurred. Some educators and policymakers have concluded that quality early childhood education and child care should be unified (Bowman, Donovan, & Burns, 2001; Brauner, Gordic, & Zigler, 2004). Therefore, in this chapter, we refer to ECEC to encompass the multitude of nonparental care arrangements that young children experience before school entry.

We also refer to school readiness as an outcome of interest throughout the chapter. As a result of findings reviewed in the present paper and elsewhere that suggest participation in ECEC before the start of formal schooling can improve later test scores, the role of quality ECEC in boosting children's readiness for learning upon school entry has received increased attention by researchers interested in development. *School readiness,* a child's preparedness both for learning and for the school atmosphere, is a term that has been used to encompass a range of concepts about early child development. In the literature, *school readiness* has been defined narrowly as the set of skills necessary for encouraging the growth of reading and reasoning skills. However, more comprehensive conceptions of school readiness, such as that put forward by the National Education Goals Panel, have emphasized child outcomes that are generally cognitive in nature but also may include social, physical, and health domains of child development (Kagan, Moore, & Bredekamp, 1995; National Education Goals Panel, 1997; Ryan, Fauth, & Brooks-Gunn, 2005; Scott-Little, Kagan, Frelow, 2005). Because ECEC focuses on children before primary school, school readiness is a reasonable outcome of interest for those concerned with the potential benefits of ECEC to consider.

## PREVALENCE AND USAGE OF ECEC

In the last few decades, the percentage of mothers with young children who work outside the home has increased substantially (Phillips & Adams, 2001). In fact, the overall labor force participation rate of women with children of any age increased from 38 to 68% between 1970 and 2000. For mothers of very young children, between birth and 3 years old, work force participation more than doubled during that time.

Interestingly, this current trend is consistent across families of different backgrounds and demographics. Where single mothers were far more likely to work, now single and married mothers, as well as poor and nonpoor mothers, are both more likely to be in the paid workforce today than they were several decades ago (Smolensky & Gootman, 2003). However, workforce participation rates do vary slightly for mothers with young children of different ages. Specifically, in 2004, almost 50% of married mothers with children in the first year of life were employed, compared with 53% of married mothers with children age 1 and 57% of mothers with 2-year-old children. For unmarried mothers, labor force participation rates also vary slightly by child age: 45% mothers of children in the first year of life work, compared with 56% of mothers of 1-year-olds and 61% of mothers of 2-year-old children (U.S. Bureau of Labor Statistics, 2006).

Although overall labor force participation rates for women with children have increased, the reasons driving workforce involvement by mothers of very young children may differ. Most obviously, changes that occurred as part of the broader welfare reform legislation of 1996 made benefit eligibility contingent upon employment. In many states, women are required to return to work as soon as 3 months after giving birth (Brady-Smith, Brooks-Gunn, Waldfogel, & Fauth, 2001; Chase-Lansdale et al., 2003). Thus, the influx of middle-class mothers into the paid labor force is partly the result of the closing of the gender gap differential, stagnant wages making two incomes necessary for many families, and the increase in divorce. The recent rise in the number of single mothers who work is partly because of the welfare reform requirements of mandated employment and time limits on welfare receipt. Both trends are associated with favorable economic conditions.

As a result of these increases in maternal labor force participation, the number of children who spend time in nonparental care has surged dramatically. By the turn of the century, 76% of children younger than 5 years old with working mothers were in some form of nonparental care arrangement for some amount of time (Capizzano & Main, 2005). Fewer children of working mothers were in full-time care; almost 48% of 3- and 4-year-olds, and approximately 38% of children younger than age 3 were in full-time care (Capizzano & Main, 2005).

Additional differences have been observed in the type of care used by children of different ages. The distribution of children in the various types of care settings is heavily concentrated in center-based or kith and kin care. Nationally, estimates of all children from birth to age 5 receiving any type of nonmaternal care reveal that 42% of children are in center-based care arrangements, 43% are in kith and kin care, and only 12% experience family child care (Capizzano, Adams, & Sonestein, 2000). Generally, infants and toddlers are more likely to experience relative care than are 3- and 4-year-olds. Among infants and toddlers, 17% are in family child care, 27% are in relative care, and 22% are in center care. Among 3- and 4-year-olds, 14% are in family child care, 17% are in relative care, and 45% are in center-based care (Capizzano et al., 2000).

Although there has been a dramatic rise in the overall percentage of children who are enrolled in nonparental care, the early care experiences of children growing up in poverty differ systematically from those of their relatively more advantaged peers. Research has shown an association between family income and children's participation in ECEC programs (Capizzano et al., 2000). Data from the Survey of Income and Program Participation child-care module suggest that in 2002, children in families above the poverty line used center-based care more than other care arrangements, but children from the poorest families were less likely to be in center-based care and more likely to receive relative care compared with middle- and upper-class children of the same age (Capizzano et al., 2000; Johnson, 2005). Researchers have highlighted cost of center care, hours of operation for child-care centers, and accessibility to center-based care in the community as explanations for the differences in type of care used by families of differing means (Capizzano, Adams, & Ost, 2006).

Similarly, children of less-educated mothers were less likely to be enrolled in an early childhood education program; although 70% of children whose mothers had graduated from college attended an early childhood education program, only 38% of children whose mothers had not graduated from high school were involved in such programs (Federal Interagency Forum on Child and Family Statistics, 2005). Reports suggesting that mothers with higher verbal scores on standardized measures tend to select higher quality care are also available (Fuller, Kagan, Loeb, & Chang, 2004), although this finding may be a function of maternal education.

Related to increases in child care, the proportion of children in the United States who attend early childhood education programs has swelled significantly. In fact, approximately 56% of 3-, 4-, and 5-year-olds were enrolled in a preschool program that was either center- or school-based in 2001, an increase of more than 40% from the 1970s, when just 23% of 4-year-olds were enrolled in such programs (U.S. Census Bureau, 1970; National Center for Education Statistics, 2002). Additionally, the number of early childhood education programs sponsored by school districts has also grown; two decades ago, only 10 states provided publicly funded pre-kindergarten programs, whereas approximately four times as many states offered such services by the beginning of the 21st century (Gilliam & Zigler, 2001).

Participation rates in all types of ECEC programs, both child care and early childhood education, vary by different racial and ethnic groups. Both non-Hispanic white children and non-Hispanic black children are more likely than are Hispanic youngsters to attend ECEC programs (Magnuson & Waldfogel, 2005). White and black 3-year-old children are similarly enrolled in center care, with Hispanic children lagging behind; in 2005, 49% of black 3-year-olds and 43% of white 3-year-olds were in center care, compared with only 23% of Hispanic 3-year-olds. The percentage of 4-year-old children in child care is higher, but racial and ethnic discrepancies persist: 71% of black, 68% of white, and 50% of Hispanic 4-year-olds attend center-based care (Federal Interagency Forum on Child and Family Statistics, 2005; Magnuson & Waldfogel, 2005).

## QUALITY IN ECEC

Quality in ECEC refers to aspects of developmental environments recognized by researchers to promote and enhance early learning. Two commonly used categories of quality include "structural" quality and "process" quality (National Institute of Child Health and Human Development Early Child Care Research Network [NICHD

Network], 2000; Peisner-Feinberg & Burchinal, 1997; Vandell & Wolfe, 2000; Whitebook, Howes, & Phillips, 1998).

*Structural quality* focuses on aspects of the child-care setting that may be objectively determined. Determinants of structural quality are those that pertain to the child-care environment itself, such as the ratio of children to staff members, the condition of the actual facility, teacher qualifications and training, and staff turnover rates. Aspects of structural quality differ depending on the type of care setting; distinctively, group size and adult-to-child ratios are smaller in noncenter care. The Fragile Families and Child Well-Being Study child-care component examined care patterns for 3-year-old children in 13 cities, and found that kith and kin care providers were responsible for an average of approximately 2–3 children, and family child-care providers cared for an average of approximately 6 children. In center-based care programs, those that were for-profit and not-for-profit, group size averaged approximately 12 children and 15 children, respectively (Rigby, Brooks-Gunn, & Ryan, 2006).

As structural dimensions of quality vary with the type of care provided, so does the relative importance of different elements of structural quality vary with the age of the children in care. For instance, research has demonstrated that group size and child-to-adult ratios are particularly important for infants in care, whereas caregiver education and qualification were more important for preschoolers in care (NICHD Network, 2000).

Government regulation of child-care providers on the state level has targeted structural aspects of care settings and included guidelines for appropriate group or class size, caregiver-child ratios, and caregiver qualification and experience that aim to ensure that young children are safely cared for in these settings (Gormley, 1991, 1995). However, states differ in the importance they ascribe to the different components of structural quality, with some of the 13 states included in the Fragile Families Study emphasizing teacher qualifications, and others highlighting the importance of child-to-adult ratio (Rigby et al., 2006).

In addition to being regulated, structural components can also be measured by accreditation standards such as those established by the National Association for the Education of Young Children (NAEYC) that are based on recommendations by child developmental scientists and educators and on practices that are believed to be developmentally appropriate. NAEYC accreditation is obtained by a self-assessment on 10 criteria: relationships, curriculum, teaching, assessment of child progress, health, teachers, families, community relationships, physical environment, and leadership and management. The center's assessment of itself is then verified by a NAEYC staff person. By meeting accreditation guidelines, programs demonstrate that they are able to offer children a high level of structural quality in a care setting, which has been shown to be associated with child cognitive and language outcomes (Shonkoff & Phillips, 2000). Studies that seek to evaluate the impact of child-care settings on child outcomes may compare the structural characteristics of a given center or set of centers to the previously mentioned regulations.

The other oft-referenced aspect of quality in a care setting is *process quality*, which refers to actual experiences of children and staff in care environments. Although structural quality easily lends itself to government regulation, process quality encompasses components of the care setting that lend themselves to observation. Process quality, which highlights the interactions between the child and caregiver, and between the child and other children, has been shown to be especially beneficial to young children's development (Blau, 2001). Process quality factors are evaluated based on observations made by trained teams of researchers who scrutinize the personal care practices, equipment, language experiences, motor and creative activities, social development, and staff needs of children and employees in care sites.

Process dimensions of quality are typically rated through the use of early environment rating scales. One such scale is the Observational Record of the Caregiving Environment (ORCE), used by the NICHD Study of Early Child Care. The ORCE requires qualified members of a research team to observe and record a target child's activities and interactions during a minimum of four 44-minute observation cycles, over two days. The ORCE can be used in all ECEC settings, on all young children, and measures caregiver responsiveness, warmth, and engagement with the child in cognitively stimulating interactions. One would expect that this system would yield more positive results for noncenter-based settings, where child-to-adult ratios and group sizes are smaller, and thus more interactions occur.

Two widely used observational scales that also measure process quality are the Family Day Care Rating Scale (FDCRS) for family care settings, and the Early Childhood Environment Rating Scale, Revised (ECERS-R) for center care arrangements (Harms & Clifford, 1989; Harms, Clifford, & Cryer, 1998). The ECERS-R contains 43 items organized into 7 subscales: space and furnishings, personal care routines, language-reasoning, activities, interaction, program structure, and parents and staff. The FDCRS has 40 items that make up 7 subscales: space and furnishings for care and learning, basic care, language and reasoning, learning activities, social development, adult needs, and provisions for exceptional children. The ECERS-R and FDCRS are limited in their abilities to capture the nature of caregiver-child interactions; moreover, the use of a composite score may mask individual contributions of the care environment that have particular importance for child development. Nonetheless, several

studies have used these measures of quality (e.g., Loeb, Fuller, Kagan, & Carrol, 2004; Love et al., 2003; Peisner-Feinberg et al., 2001) because of the scales' good psychometric properties, because they are easy to use in a reliable manner, and because they allow for cross-study comparisons because of their extensive use (Vandell & Wolfe, 2000).

Both the ECERS-R and FDCRS produce scores that range from 1 to 7; based on these scores, care settings are often grouped into four categories, where 1 indicates inadequate quality, 3 refers to minimal quality care, 5 suggests good quality care, and 7 is indicative of excellent quality in a care environment (Vandell & Wolfe, 2000). Using the ECERS-R, the Fragile Families Study found that, of the 13 cities sampled, 20% of centers were inadequate, 37% were minimal, 30% were good, and only 10% were excellent (Rigby et al., 2006). Similarly, the Cost, Quality, and Outcomes study revealed that most centers surveyed were mediocre, and a few were dangerously poor in quality (Helburn, 1995).

Research suggests that process quality and structural quality are correlated, with Pearson correlations ranging from 0.21 to 0.37 (Phillipsen, Burchinal, Howes, & Cryer, 1997; Shonkoff & Phillips, 2000), and that structural aspects of a care arrangement as well as process components can have both immediate and lasting effects on children's cognitive and social development (Fuligni, Brooks-Gunn, & Berlin, 2003). Prior work examining the impact of structural quality on child outcomes has demonstrated that optimal structural conditions facilitate better process conditions (Helburn & Howes, 1996).

However, questions remain regarding the relative importance of structural and process quality. From a policy standpoint, structural components are easier to measure and thus regulate; from a developmental perspective, process elements are especially important for early child development. Because the two dimensions are highly collinear, and because some research has found that the importance of structural or process quality varies with the age of the child in care (e.g., Burchinal, Roberts, Nabors, & Bryant, 1996), both structural and process quality must receive equal attention by researchers and policymakers.

## ASSOCIATIONS BETWEEN QUALITY ECEC AND CHILD DEVELOPMENT

High-quality ECEC is linked to better cognitive and social outcomes for young children (Burchinal & Cryer, 2003; Shonkoff & Phillips, 2000), and multiple studies have provided both theoretical and empirical support for associations between ECEC and enhanced child development (Bronfenbrenner & Morris, 1998; Lamb & Ahnert, 2006). In particular, several model early childhood education programs have concluded that early childhood intervention in the form of ECEC programming is one avenue through which children may be more successful in formal schooling (e.g., Barnett, 1995; Currie, 2001; Karoly et al., 1998; Yoshikawa, 1995). However, throughout this discussion of the impact of quality care on developmental outcomes, one must keep in mind that the relative importance of family background characteristics for child development is greater than that of ECEC, regardless of quality. Family factors and the relationship between a child and his or her mother are consistently more predictive of child outcomes than are child-care characteristics (Brooks-Gunn, Han, & Waldfogel, 2002; NICHD Network, 1997b).

The best evidence for the favorable impact that quality ECEC programming can have on development can be seen in the long-term follow-up studies of children who participated in early interventions such as the Perry Preschool Project, the Carolina Abecedarian Project, and the Infant Health and Development Program

(IHDP). These so-called "model" programs have contributed significantly to the extensive body of research suggesting that quality ECEC can enhance children's language and cognitive skills (Currie, 2001; Vandell & Wolfe, 2000). Additionally, these three studies were randomized trials, in which children were randomly assigned to a treatment group that received the intervention, or to a control group that did not. This type of study design largely rules out the effects of selection bias, a common methodological shortcoming of many studies of ECEC and child outcomes. When studies do not involve random assignment of participants to treatment conditions, the possibility exists that observed associations between early experiences and development are the result of preexisting, unobserved differences between the treatment and control groups.

The renowned Perry Preschool Project was an experimental study that randomly assigned a group of low-income preschool-aged children to an intense, high-quality ECEC intervention that included a weekday morning preschool routine combined with weekly home visits by program staff. The teacher-child ratio in the program classrooms was low, the teachers were professionally trained and qualified, and the program extended over 2 calendar years. In a 15-year follow-up study, children who had participated in the intervention demonstrated IQ increases in the years following the intervention. Children who participated in the program had higher achievement scores, spent fewer years in special education programs, and demonstrated fewer conduct and behavior problems than did those children who did not receive the intervention (Schweinhart, Barnes, & Weikart, 1993). Additionally, the positive effects of the intervention have persisted through age 40, as the "children" are now in their fourth decade of life (Schweinhart et al., 2005). Program participants displayed continued educational achievement, economic success, and lower overall rates of criminal arrests and delinquent behavior.

The Carolina Abecedarian Project is another example of an intense early education program administered to low-income children, with encouraging results. Also as an experimental design, program children were randomized at birth into a treatment or control group. The treatment group received enriched care in a center-based setting for 8 hours per day, 5 days per week, until the children were 5 years old. Teacher-child ratios were low and the educational curriculum was designed to enhance child development. When children in the treatment and control groups entered school, they were re-randomized so that half of each original group received school-age intervention during the primary school years, from 5 to 8 years old. Children who received school-age services also benefited from home visits and health services. Long-term follow-up studies of this high-quality ECEC program have found positive effects for program children at various points in their lives. At age 12, positive effects for the group of children that received treatment starting at infancy were found for cognitive and academic achievement (Campbell & Ramey, 1994). Children who received the intervention from infancy into elementary school demonstrated an IQ and achievement score advantage over those who did not participate in the early section of treatment, with effects persisting for 7 years after the program ended. Subsequent follow-up studies at ages 15 and 21 found that the children who participated in full-day programs from birth to kindergarten were more likely than were those who did not to achieve academic and school success, and less likely to experience negative outcomes typically associated with childhood poverty, such as teen pregnancy (Campbell, Ramey, Pungello, Miller-Johnson, & Sparling, 2002).

A third model program, the IHDP, was a randomized, multisite, clinical trial that offered full-time center-based care to low birth weight children from birth to age 3. Infants who were randomly assigned to the intervention group received educational programming via home visits and daily center-based ECEC beginning when they were 12 months of age. Intervention children's parents participated in support groups when their children began center care, and the center-based educational enrichment curriculum matched that of the earlier and successful Abecedarian Project. Findings from follow-up studies when children were 5 and 8 years old suggest that infants who were in the heavier low birth weight group experienced IQ gains of almost 4 points over their control group counterparts (McCarton et al., 1997), and recent findings imply that the cognitive benefits of the intervention were sustained for the heavier low birth weight treatment children through age 18 (McCormick et al., 2006).

Though not a randomized study, recent assessments of Oklahoma's universal prekindergarten (pre-K) program in Tulsa offer additional evidence for the positive impact that ECEC can have on early development (Gormley & Phillips, 2005). Pre-K programs in Tulsa are run by the public schools, and pre-K teachers have college degrees and are certified in early childhood education. Like other successful ECEC programs, the child-staff ratios in the pre-K classrooms are kept low. Although not a randomized study, researchers examining Tulsa's pre-K program and its effects on children employed a regression-discontinuity design, in which investigators matched children of similar ages and background characteristics who were enrolled in the pre-K program with children who were not yet enrolled. Thus, selection threats to the validity of the findings were minimized. Using test data for children who enrolled in pre-K in 2000 to 2001, researchers found that participation in Tulsa's pre-K program was associated with positive effects on language and cognitive skills (Gormley & Phillips, 2005). Although no long-term follow-up data are available for children who attended pre-K in Tulsa, one can assume that such a program that incorporates many of the elements that made earlier high-quality model programs successful in producing enduring positive effects for children will likely have a lasting impact on the children enrolled.

Oklahoma's program is not targeted specifically to poor children, but is a universal program available to all 4-year-old children in Tulsa. Data suggest, however, that the impact of ECEC programs like Tulsa's pre-K on child outcomes would differ for children from families of different financial backgrounds. Despite findings that children from families with low incomes tend to experience lower-quality child care (Fuller et al., 2004; Loeb et al., 2004; Phillips & Adams, 2001; Votruba-Drzal, Coley, & Chase-Lansdale, 2004), children from poor backgrounds have demonstrated substantial developmental gains when they are exposed to high-quality ECEC (Brooks-Gunn, 2003; Liaw & Brooks-Gunn, 1993). Indeed, researchers using data from the IHDP have provided evidence suggesting that children from poor families experienced more dramatic IQ effects at age 3 (Brooks-Gunn, Gross, Kraemer, Spiker, & Shapiro, 1992). Additionally, reports of improved socio-emotional growth in low-income children who received higher-quality care have also been published, along with findings implying that poor children who received extensive amounts of care, as long as it was not of low quality, demonstrated improved quantitative skills and a lower rate of behavior problems (Love et al., 2003; Votruba-Drzal et al., 2004).

Researchers have also found evidence that quality ECEC can act as a protective factor for children at risk. For instance, in a non-randomized study, higher-quality care was observed to moderate the impact of family poverty on young children's school readiness and language skills, suggesting that the positive impact of care on children in poverty depends on the quality of that care (McCartney, Dearing, & Taylor, 2003).

Another interesting effect of family income on the connection between ECEC and child development shines a light on the quality of care that many middle-income families are able to pay for. Although the quality of care that many poor families can afford is low, research implies that children from low-income families who qualify for child-care subsidies may experience better child care, and that high-quality child care made available to poor children at a very young age can produce lasting cognitive and social gains (Gomby, Larner, Stevenson, Lewit, & Behrman, 1995; Karoly et al., 1998; Yoshikawa, 1995). However, children from working-poor and middle-income families who can't afford center-based child care and don't qualify for child-care subsidies or quality early interventions may be enrolled in lower-quality child-care arrangements and thus do not reap the potential benefits that a child-care setting with high process and structural quality can offer. Children in poor families whose parents do not apply for or obtain subsidies for which they qualify likely also attend low-quality care.

## ASSOCIATIONS BETWEEN ECEC SETTING AND CHILD DEVELOPMENT

Recent studies using non-experimental data, such as the NICHD Study on Early Child Care (NICHD SECC) and the Early Childhood Longitudinal Study Kindergarten Cohort (ECLS-K), offer insight into the myriad ways ECEC can influence development (Magnuson, Meyers, Ruhm, & Waldfogel, 2004; NICHD Network & Duncan, 2003). It should be noted, however, that these non-experimental studies do not control for the effects of selection. As mentioned earlier, when random assignment is not used and instead families' child-care choices are observed and studied, there is always the possibility that family background characteristics are driving the observed associations between ECEC and child development outcomes. Despite these potential weaknesses in non-experimental studies, findings from such studies provide helpful insight into the features of ECEC programs that benefit development. Specifically, recent studies employing data from the ECLS-K and the NICHD SECC have explored how characteristics of ECEC programs, including the setting in which ECEC takes place, influence children's development and school readiness.

Findings from the nationally representative ECLS-K, which collected information on children's preschool experiences, found that children who attended center-based child-care, pre-kindergarten, or preschool programs generally exhibited higher reading and math scores than other children did. Specifically, children who attended some form of center-based care before formal school entry experienced a 0.15 standard-deviation gain in test scores over children who did not attend such programs (Magnuson, Meyers, et al., 2004). Another study using the same data concluded that children who attended pre-kindergarten scored 0.19 of a standard deviation higher on tests of math and reading ability than did their peers who were cared for exclusively by their parents in the year before kindergarten (Magnuson & Waldfogel, 2005).

Such findings are paralleled in reports using data from the NICHD SECC, which began in 1991 and has followed more than 1,200 families with children since the birth of their babies to observe and track their child-care choices. Recent research suggests that children who spent more time in high-quality center-based care experienced increases in cognitive scores; in particular, these children demonstrated higher math and reading scores that continued into the early elementary school years (NICHD Network, 2005b). Specifically, increases in center quality of 1 standard deviation were associated with 0.9 to 1.7 points of growth in child cognitive outcomes for children between the ages of 36 and 54 months, with effect sizes of care quality on cognitive scores ranging from 0.04 to 0.08 at age 4 ½ (NICHD Network & Duncan, 2003).

Other evidence for the relative benefit of center care over another care setting comes from a recent study using data from the IHDP (Hill, Waldfogel, & Brooks-Gunn, 2002), in which researchers found that high-quality center care can have a significant and lasting influence on children who would have otherwise been cared for either by their mothers or by another adult in a home-based setting. Indeed, research shows that center care can produce positive, sustained cognitive and social gains when at least one of the structural quality elements, such as a low ratio of children to staff members, is present (Burchinal & Cryer, 2003).

Although the model early childhood programs and data from the observational studies reviewed previously focus on center-based ECEC, many children (and especially very young children) experience home-based care. Studies on home-based care settings reveal that such arrangements typically offer lower ratios between adults and children, and many home-based providers demonstrate greater affect in their interactions with the children they care for (Phillips & Adams, 2001). Likewise, home-based care settings that contribute significantly to positive developmental outcomes are those that demonstrate certain characteristics of process quality, such as stimulating interactions between caregivers and children (NICHD Network, 2000; 2002a). Furthermore, for very young children and infants, home-based settings and the caregiver-child interactions they may foster can contribute to improved child outcomes; some research suggests that infants in home-based ECEC fare better than their peers in center-based arrangements (Phillips & Adams, 2001).

On the whole, the relative superiority of center-based or home-based care is unclear. Although research looking specifically at enrollment in center-based care, preschool, and pre-kindergarten programs has illuminated a connection between such programs and enhanced academic outcomes for children upon entering kindergarten (Bogard & Takanishi, 2005), other studies have found that center care is not always linked to positive outcomes. Attending center-based pre-kindergarten programs has been linked to negative effects for behavior (Magnuson, Ruhm, & Waldfogel, 2004), and a study of child care in four states concluded that 70% of child-care centers offered care that was mediocre, and more than 10% of centers provided care that was dangerously poor (Helburn, 1995). Recent findings from the Early Childhood Longitudinal Study Birth cohort (ECLS-B), a nationally representative study that is following children born in 2001, report that 9% of infants and toddlers in center-based care were in care that was of low quality, whereas 66% were in medium-quality centers, and 24% were in high-quality centers (Mulligan & Flanagan, 2006). Taken together, we must conclude that just because children are in center care does not guarantee positive outcomes across all domains of development, nor does it provide assurance that quality of care is exceptionally high.

Although the overall quality of center care has at times been found to be second rate, centers generally surpass home-based care on measures of quality (Kontos, Howes, Shinn, & Galinsky, 1995). Studies on home-based care settings have found that these arrangements may lack the stimulating materials that center-based programs tend to offer. Additionally, research suggests that home-based care providers may have less specialized training and be less well educated than the staff in center facilities (Kontos et al., 1995). Data from the ECLS-B imply that 36% of infants and toddlers in home-based care settings were in low-quality care, compared with 57% who were in medium-quality care, and only 7% who were in high-quality arrangements (Mulligan & Flanagan, 2006).

Family income can, to some extent, determine which care setting is most beneficial for the child; not surprisingly, the impact of diverse care arrangements and the quality of those ECEC settings differs for children from low-income families. Longitudinal research that explores associations between child outcomes and center-based ECEC among children from low-income backgrounds has demonstrated substantial positive program effects across a variety of developmental domains. For instance, center-based child care from birth to age 3 was linked with higher math skills in a low-income sample of children from the National Longitudinal Survey of Youth (NLSY) (Caughy, DiPietro, & Strobino, 1994).

Another study examined developmental outcomes for children in child care whose mothers participated in state welfare-to-work programs beginning when the children were between 1 year and 3 ½ years old (Loeb et al., 2004). Children in center-based care displayed stronger growth in cognitive development when the care administered was more sensitive and responsive; additionally, social growth was associated with caregivers who had higher levels of education. Meanwhile, children in home-based care exhibited increased behavioral problems at age 4.

## ASSOCIATIONS BETWEEN TIMING AND INTENSITY OF ECEC AND CHILD DEVELOPMENT

To further understand the link between ECEC and child development, a good deal of attention has been paid to the amount of ECEC children experience at different ages because evidence suggests that the amount of time spent in ECEC matters for child outcomes (Burchinal & Cryer, 2003).

In particular, researchers have focused their exploration on the influence of care on development for children age 1 and younger. Findings from the NICHD study indicate that about 1,000 children, out of the approximately 1,100 sampled, experienced some regular nonmaternal care in their first year of life; moreover, infants (once entering care) received an average of 29 hours of care per week (NICHD Network, 1997a; Vandell, 2004). The developmental literature suggests that children under the age of 1 who enter nonparental care can have vastly different experiences in child care, depending on a variety of factors. For those children who enter care in their first year, findings on the effects of such early enrollment have been mixed. Several studies have found that longer hours in nonparental care may negatively affect development for children less than 6 months old (e.g., Hill, Waldfogel, Brooks-Gunn, & Han, 2005; NICHD Network, 2004; Waldfogel, 2002).

Children who enter care when they are older have distinctly different experiences than their infant counterparts do. Data suggest that care initiated after a child's first year can elicit positive effects on cognitive development (NICHD Network, 1997c). For example, 3-year-old children who were enrolled at centers that met certain benchmarks of quality, namely those of caregiver education and qualification, exhibited higher school readiness and language comprehension scores (NICHD Network, 2005a). Recent findings imply that 2- and 3-year-old children who experienced more time in center care demonstrated stronger cognitive and language skills (NICHD Network, 2006).

Regarding behavioral development, the NICHD SECC found that 2-year-old children who attended centers that met standards for teacher-to-child ratios demonstrated more cooperative behaviors with their peers and a smaller number of behavior problems, and 3-year-olds who attended centers staffed by qualified caregivers had fewer behavior issues (NICHD Network, 2005a). However, there are more negative behavior findings for children after the first year of life who experience nonparental care than there are positive findings. For instance, 2-year-old children who had experienced multiple care arrangements demonstrated more frequent problem behavior (NICHD Network, 2000). By the time children in the NICHD SECC were in kindergarten, approximately one-fifth of those children who had been in care for more than 45 hours per week demonstrated above-average behavior problems (NICHD Network, 2003). In particular, children at 4 ½ years of age who had spent more hours in care were observed by their care providers, teachers, and mothers to be more fearful and shy, and children who spent more than 30 hours in care were considered to be more aggressive, than were their peers who had spent less time in care (NICHD Network, 2002b; 2003). Children at age 4 ½ who attended more hours of center care also had somewhat higher rates of externalizing behavior problems as reported by caregivers; however, these rates were not in the clinical or at-risk range (NICHD Network, 2004).

Like the impact of quality and setting on child outcomes, the influence of timing and intensity of child care on development may also be moderated by family income. For instance, findings from a recent study that examined the impact of center-based care on children of mothers who were welfare recipients suggest that attending more hours of center-based care was associated with better performance on measures of cognitive ability and school readiness, when compared with children who experienced home-based care (Loeb et al., 2004).

Although spending more hours in care has been shown to be related to stronger cognitive outcomes for children from low-income families, negative effects for behavior continue to be found. In particular, concerns about the detrimental impact of early and extended care on children's social and behavior outcomes that were raised 20 years ago persist (Belsky, 1986, 2001). However, these findings are far from conclusive. Although multiple studies have found negative relations between amount of time in child care and children's behavior problems (e.g., Belsky, 2001), evidence supporting the positive associations between behavior issues and extensive time in care specifically for low-income populations suggests that quality care in large doses may operate differently for poor children than it does for children from more advantaged backgrounds. As mentioned earlier in our chapter, spending more hours in quality care has been associated with some positive effects on behavior for low-income children (Votruba-Drzal et al., 2004), but other studies have found evidence for the negative impact of long hours in care for children in poverty (Magnuson, Ruhm, et al., 2004).

## CONCLUSION: AN AGENDA FOR ECEC RESEARCH AND POLICY

Based on the evidence we have reviewed, it seems that many in the scientific and policy communities can agree that quality ECEC has the potential to contribute to the healthy development of young children (Brooks-Gunn, 2003; Karoly et al., 1998; Lee & Burkam, 2002). Moreover, it seems that the timing, duration, and type of child care as well as characteristics of a child's home environment, such as family income level, can color the influence of ECEC on children's development. Indeed, when programs are administered early and in a comprehensive manner, and when recognized indicators of quality are met, early education programming can produce lasting gains in a variety of domains for children who otherwise may not start school on the same ground with their more privileged peers. The combination of increases in child-care use by American families and the widely accepted view among developmental researchers that early experiences can affect later development will, we hope, lead to continued concerted efforts by the scientific community to better understand the varying effects that ECEC can have on healthy child development.

An equal, if not greater, amount of scientific information exists explicating the well-documented effects of poverty on child development. As a result, there has been a need for studies that illuminate the nonparental care experiences of young children, and especially children from low-income backgrounds. In response to this need, researchers have devoted time to the exploration of experiences and outcomes of low-income children, specifically, who are in nonmaternal care.

Perhaps the best argument for making quality care available and affordable for all low-income families is that poor children have been shown to reap the greatest benefit from high-quality early childhood programs, and at the same time to be the most susceptible to low-quality ECEC and the negative effects of such poor care (Currie, 2001; Karoly et al., 1998). Although evidence from several studies points to the positive impact that quality center-based care can have on school readiness outcomes for all children, national data clearly demonstrate that very young low-income children are less likely to be in center care than are their more advantaged same-age peers (NICHD Network, 2004; Loeb et al., 2004).

Taken together, the recent flurry of research on ECEC suggests that important questions on the topic of how nonparental care can benefit child development should revolve less around whether it is helpful or harmful to young children's development and more around the nature of care arrangements that are most beneficial for children. Researchers have identified quality of care, type of care, and hours spent in care settings as factors that may mediate the influence of nonmaternal care on child development (Waldfogel, 2002). Consistently, studies have found that quality is the single greatest factor upon which the effect of child care may rest (e.g., NICHD Network, 2002b). Yet, whether the impact of ECEC on children's development is positive or negative depends on the characteristics of the care setting, the family environment, and the child; indeed, focusing on only one facet of child care, no matter how important that aspect of care is believed to be, fails to accurately depict the complete picture of the effects that child care can have on children.

If presenting the range of ECEC features that affect child development should be a priority in the research community, then so must increasing accessibility to quality ECEC for poor families become an urgent concern of policymakers. It has been 10 years since the enactment of welfare reform legislation resulting from the passage of the Personal Responsibility and Work Opportunity Reconciliation Act (PRWORA) in 1996. In some states, these reforms demanded that poor women return to work when their children were infants if they wanted to continue receiving welfare benefits. The same poor families who must place their children in care also lack the resources needed to enroll their very young children in a child-care setting that has high levels of process and structural quality.

Moreover, studies such as those reviewed in this chapter and elsewhere have found that children with more educated parents, parents with higher incomes, and mothers with higher verbal scores are more likely to receive center-based child care (Bainbridge,

Myers, Tanaka, & Waldfogel, 2005; Fuller et al., 2004). As reported in the present paper, however, disadvantaged children may stand to benefit the most from high-quality care. Researchers have posited that low-income children may suffer from a "double disadvantage," whereby children from disadvantaged families are both less likely to enjoy resources in the home that promote the development of skill sets needed for school success, and less likely to benefit from resources outside of the home that come from attending cognitively stimulating early care or education programs (Bainbridge et al., 2005; Meyers, Rosenbaum, Ruhm, & Waldfogel, 2004). Furthermore, increased funding for public early childhood education programming may have particularly positive returns in school readiness and healthy behavior for children in low-income families (Bainbridge et al., 2005; Brooks-Gunn, 2003). And recent findings make an extremely strong case: Universal enrollment in high-quality preschool could lessen the school readiness gap between black and white children by 20%, and between Hispanic and white children by 36% (Magnuson & Waldfogel, 2005).

These reported findings should serve as a call to action for policymakers; record numbers of children are in ECEC programs, income and quality care matter for children's healthy development, and poor children may have the most to gain from quality ECEC but are least likely to receive it.

Indeed, policies have to some extent been responsive to the cry for provision of quality ECEC services to low-income children. Programs such as Head Start, the comprehensive federally funded child development program available to poor children from birth to age 5, and pre-kindergarten programs in some states represent efforts to improve school outcomes for low-income children. In 2002, 65% of eligible 3- and 4-year-olds attended Head Start programs

(Magnuson & Waldfogel, 2005). However, even though low-income children age 3 and older have increasing access to center-based care programs such as Head Start and state-funded kindergarten, infants and toddlers in poor families are still at a disadvantage. For those children who do attend Head Start and state-funded pre-K programs, evidence from evaluations of both is encouraging, but there is room for improvement in each.

Findings from Head Start suggest that low-income and minority children can make significant gains in school readiness (Currie & Thomas, 1995). Similarly, as mentioned previously, recent reports on universal preschool programs in Oklahoma have indicated strong positive findings for minority children's cognitive skills in particular (Gormley & Phillips, 2005). Encouraging results from recent reports suggest that expanding pre-K to children in all 50 states, improving its quality, and making it available to all low-income 3- and 4-year-olds in poverty could significantly close the school readiness gap between white children and their black and Hispanic peers (Magnuson & Waldfogel, 2005).

However, not all the news is good. Research on children who attended ECEC programs such as Head Start indicates that positive program effects on children's school readiness dissipate as children enter primary school; positive effects of program participation get smaller but remain significant. This is likely because local public elementary schools that low-income children attend are of a substantially lower quality than is needed to maintain cognitive gains. Furthermore, lack of alignment between ECEC programs and policies may contribute to the observed reduction in positive effects over time (Kauerz, 2006). Thus, researchers and policymakers have called for the expansion of universal pre-kindergarten and for the alignment of elementary school services and curricula with those experienced by children in early

education programs like Head Start to address the short-lived positive effects of such programs (e.g., Bogard & Takanishi, 2005). Most importantly, the obvious weakness of existing pre-K programs is that they are not widely available to preschool-aged children in all states. And, as mentioned earlier, far fewer center-based services are available to infants and toddlers. In addition, for families living barely above the poverty threshold, those considered "near poor" with incomes between 100 and 200% of the poverty line (Duncan & Brooks-Gunn, 1997), services such as Head Start and subsidies for child care may not be available and thus the opportunities that their children will benefit from quality care are slim.

Much work remains to be done to realize the potential of ECEC to support poor children's well-being. Policymakers in general agree that 4-year-olds should have access to high-quality ECEC, but there is some disagreement about whether such programs should be offered universally or targeted to low-income families. Although most states now offer some form of public pre-K, programs vary between states with some (like Oklahoma) offering universal pre-K to 4-year-olds whereas other states offer ECEC programming that is targeted for limited populations. Likewise, there is some debate about whether 3-year-old children, especially those from low-income families, should also be assured access to high-quality center-based ECEC.

There is also some disagreement among states regarding program regulation and accreditation of ECEC. To ensure that more poor children have high-quality ECEC experiences, policymakers need to turn their attention to improving regulations and providing incentives to encourage all ECEC programs serving low-income children to reach program accreditation guidelines. To ensure that young children are more than safe and healthy, more stringent structural quality guidelines are needed; currently, most states incorporate program accreditation into public policy by offering accredited programs higher subsidy reimbursement rates than the rate that non-accredited programs receive (National Association for the Education of Young Children, 2006). All states must follow suit if all children are to receive quality early educations in optimal environments.

Without government intervention to increase access to and availability of quality care ECEC, the children who need stimulating ECEC most dearly are least likely to receive it. Therefore, it is imperative that researchers evaluate and policymakers promote the distinctive and influential role that all aspects of quality care can play in the development of young children from birth through later schooling.

## REFERENCES

Bachu, A. (1995). *Fertility of American women: June 1994* (U.S. Bureau of Census Current Population Report P20-482). Washington, DC: U.S. Government Printing Office.

Bainbridge, J., Meyers, M. K., Tanaka, S., & Waldfogel, J. (2005). Who gets early education? Family income and the enrollment of three- to five-year-olds from 1968 to 2000. *Social Science Quarterly, 86*(3), 724–745.

Barnett, W. S. (1995). Long-term effects of early childhood programs on cognitive and school outcomes. *Future of Children, 5*(3), 25–50.

Baydar, N., Brooks-Gunn, J., & Furstenberg, F. F. (1993). Early warning signs of functional illiteracy: Predictors in childhood and adolescence. *Child Development, 64*(3), 815–829.

Belsky, J. (1986). Infant day care: A cause for concern? *Zero to Three, 6,* 1–9.

Belsky, J. (2001). Developmental risks (still) associated with early child care. *Journal of Child Psychology and Psychiatry, 42*(7), 845–859.

Blau, D. M. (Ed.). (2001). *The child care problem: An economic analysis.* New York: Russell Sage.

Bogard, K., & Takanishi, R. (2005). PK–3: An aligned and coordinated approach to education for children 3 to 8 years old. *Social Policy Report, 19*(3), 3–24. Retrieved May 28, 2007, from http://www.srcd.org/documents/publications/SPR/spr19-3.pdf

Bowman, B., Donovan, M. S., & Burns, M. S. (2001). *Eager to learn: Educating our preschoolers.* Washington, DC: National Academy Press.

Brady-Smith, C., Brooks-Gunn, J., Waldfogel, J., & Fauth, R. (2001). Work or welfare? Assessing the impacts of recent employment and policy changes on very young children. *Evaluation and Program Planning, 24,* 409–425.

Brauner, J., Gordic, B., & Zigler, E. (2004). Putting the child back into child care: Combining care and education for children ages 3–5. *Social Policy Report, 18*(3), 3–15.

Bronfenbrenner, U., & Morris, P. A. (1998). The ecology of developmental processes. In W. Damon & R. M. Lerner (Eds.), *Handbook of child psychology: Vol. 1. Theoretical models of human development* (5th ed., pp. 993–1028). New York: Wiley.

Brooks-Gunn, J. (2003). Do you believe in magic? What we can expect from early childhood intervention programs. *Social Policy Report, 17*(1), 1–14. Retrieved May 28, 2007, from http://www.srcd.org/Documents/Publications/SPR/spr17-1.pdf

Brooks-Gunn, J., Gross, R. T., Kraemer, H. C., Spiker, D., & Shapiro, S. (1992). Enhancing the cognitive outcomes of low birthweight, premature infants: For whom is the intervention most effective? *Pediatrics, 89,* 1209–1215.

Brooks-Gunn, J., Han, W., & Waldfogel, J. (2002). Maternal employment and child cognitive outcomes in the first three years of life: The NICHD Study of Early Child Care. *Child Development, 73*(4), 1052–1072.

Burchinal, M. R., & Cryer, D. (2003). Diversity, child care quality, and developmental outcomes. *Early Childhood Research Quarterly, 18,* 401–426.

Burchinal, M. R., Roberts, J. E., Nabors, L. A., & Bryant, D. M. (1996). Quality of center child care and infant cognitive and language development. *Child Development, 67*(2), 606–620.

Cahan, E. (1989). *Past caring: A history of U.S. preschool care and education for the poor, 1820–1965.* New York: National Center for Children in Poverty, Columbia University. Retrieved from http://www.nccp.org/media/pch02-text.pdf

Campbell, F. A., & Ramey, C. T. (1994). Effects of early intervention on intellectual and academic achievement: A follow-up study of children from low-income families. *Child Development, 65,* 684–698.

Campbell, F. A., Ramey, C. T., Pungello, E., Miller-Johnson, S., & Sparling, J. J. (2002). Early childhood education: Young adult outcomes from the Abecedarian Project. *Applied Developmental Science, 6*(1), 42–57.

Capizzano, J., & Adams, G. (2003). *Research report: Children in low-income families are less likely to be in center-based child care* (Snapshots of America's Families III, No. 16). Washington, DC: Urban Institute Press.

Capizzano, J., Adams, G., & Ost, J. (2006). *Caring for children of color: The child care patterns of white, black, and Hispanic children* (Occasional papers No. 72). Washington, DC: Urban Institute Press.

Capizzano, J., Adams, G., & Sonestein, F. (2000). *Child care arrangements for children under five: Variations across states* (New Federalism: National Survey of America's Families. Series B, No. B-7). Washington, DC: Urban Institute Press.

Capizzano, J., & Main, R. (2005). *Research report: Many young children spend long hours in child care* (Snapshots of America's Families III, No. 22). Washington, DC: Urban Institute Press.

Caughy, M., DiPietro, J., & Strobino, D. (1994). Day-care participation as a protective factor in the cognitive development of low-income children. *Child Development, 65,* 457–471.

Chase-Lansdale, P. L., Moffitt, R. A., Lohman, B. J., Cherlin, A. J., Coley, R. L., Pittman, L. D., et al. (2003). Mothers' transitions from welfare to work and the well-being of preschoolers and adolescents. *Science, 299,* 1548–1552.

Currie, J. (2001). Early childhood education programs. *Journal of Economic Perspectives, 15*(2), 213–238.

Currie, J., & Thomas, D. (1995). Does Head Start make a difference? *American Economic Review, 85*(3), 341–364.

Duncan, G. J., & Brooks-Gunn, J. (Eds.). (1997). *Consequences of growing up poor.* New York: Russell Sage.

Duncan, G. J., Yeung, W. J., Brooks-Gunn, J., & Smith, J. R. (1998). How much does childhood poverty affect the life chances of children? *American Sociological Review, 63*(3), 406–423.

Federal Interagency Forum on Child and Family Statistics. (2005). *America's children: Key national indicators of children's wellbeing, 2005.* Washington, DC: Government Printing Office. Retrieved from http://childstats.gov/americ aschildren/pdf/ ac2005/ed.pdf

Fuligni, A. S., Brooks-Gunn, J., & Berlin, L. J. (2003). Themes in developmental research: Historical roots and promise for the future. In J. Brooks-Gunn, A. S. Fuligni, & L. J. Berlin (Eds.), *Early child development in the 21st century* (pp. 1–16). New York: Teachers College Press.

Fuller, B., Kagan, S. L., Loeb, S., & Chang, Y. (2004). Child care quality: Centers and home settings that serve poor families. *Early Childhood Research Quarterly, 19*, 505–527.

Gilliam, W., & Zigler, E. (2001). A critical meta-analysis of all evaluations of state-funded preschool from 1977 to 1998: Implications for policy, service delivery and program evaluation. *Early Childhood Research Quarterly, 15*, 441–473.

Gomby, D. S., Larner, B. S., Stevenson, C. S., Lewit, E. M., & Behrman, R. E. (1995). Long-term outcomes of early childhood programs: Analysis and recommendations. *Future of Children, 5*(3), 25–50.

Gormley, W. T. (1991). State regulations and the availability of child care services. *Journal of Policy Analysis and Management, 10*, 78–95.

Gormley, W. T. (1995). *Everybody's children: Child care as a public problem.* Washington, DC: Brookings Institution.

Gormley, W. T., & Phillips, D. (2005). The effects of universal pre-K in Oklahoma: Research highlights and policy implications. *Policy Studies Journal, 33*(1), 65–82.

Harms, T., & Clifford, R. M. (1989). *The Family Day Care Rating Scale.* New York: Teachers College Press.

Harms, T., Clifford, R. M., & Cryer, D. (1998). *Early Childhood Environment Rating Scale–Revised.* New York: Teachers College Press.

Heckman, J. J., & Krueger, A. B. (2004). *Inequality in America.* Boston: MIT Press.

Heckman, J. J., & Lochner, L. (2001). Rethinking education and training policy: Understanding the sources of skill formation in a modern economy. In S. Danziger & J. Waldfogel (Eds.). *Securing the future: Investing in children from birth to college.* New York: Russell Sage.

Helburn, S. W. (Ed.). (1995). *Cost, quality, and child outcomes in child care centers.* Denver: Department of Economics, University of Colorado at Denver.

Helburn, S. W., & Howes, C. (1996). Child care cost and quality. *Future of Children, 6*(2), 62–82.

Hill, J., Waldfogel, J., & Brooks-Gunn, J. (2002). Assessing the differential impacts of high-quality child care: A new approach for exploiting post-treatment variables. *Journal of Policy Analysis and Management, 21*, 601–627.

Hill, J., Waldfogel, J., Brooks-Gunn, J., & Han, W. (2005). Maternal employment and child development: A fresh look using newer methods. *Developmental Psychology, 41*(6), 833–850.

Johnson, J. O. (2005, October). *Who's minding the kids? Child care arrangements: Winter 2002* (Current Population Reports, pp. 70–101, U.S. Census Bureau). Retrieved from http://www.census.gov/prod/2005pubs/p70-101.pdf

Kagan, S. L. (1991). *United we stand: Collaboration for child care and early education services.* New York: Teachers College Press.

Kagan, S. L., Moore, E., & Bredekamp, S. (Eds.). (1995). *Reconsidering children's early learning and development: Toward shared beliefs and vocabulary.* Washington, DC: National Education Goals Panel.

Kamerman, S. B., & Gatenio, S. (2003). Overview of the current policy context. In D. Cryer & R. M. Clifford (Eds.), *Early childhood education and care in the USA* (pp. 1–30). Baltimore: Paul H. Brookes.

Karoly, L. A., Greenwood, P. W., Everingham, S. S., Hoube, J., Kilburn, M. R., Rydell C. P., et al. (1998). *Investing in our children: What we do and don't know about the costs and benefits of early childhood interventions.* Santa Monica, CA: Rand.

Kauerz, K. (2006). *Ladders of learning: Fighting fade-out by advancing PK–3 alignment* (Early Education Initiative: Issue Brief #2). Washington, DC: New America Foundation.

Kontos, S., Howes, C., Shinn, M., & Galinsky, E. (1995). *Quality in family child care and relative care.* New York: Teachers College Press.

Lamb, M. E., & Ahnert, L. (2006). Nonparental child care: Context, concepts, correlates, and consequences. In W. Damon, R. M. Lerner, K. A. Renninger, & I. E. Sigel (Eds.), *Handbook of child psychology: Vol. 4. Child psychology in practice* (6th ed., pp. 950–1016). New York: Wiley.

Lee, V. E., & Burkam, D. T. (2002). *Inequality at the starting gate: Social background differences in achievement as children begin school.* Washington, DC: Economic Policy Institute. Retrieved from http://www.epinet.org/books/starting_gate.html

Liaw, F. R., & Brooks-Gunn, J. (1993). Patterns of low birth weight children's cognitive development and their determinants. *Developmental Psychology, 29*(6), 1024–1035.

Loeb, S., Fuller, B., Kagan, S. L., & Carrol, B. (2004). Child care in poor communities: Early learning effects of type, quality, and stability. *Child Development, 75*(1), 47–65.

Love, J. M., Harrison, L., Sagi, A., van Ijzendoorn, M. H., Ross, C. M., Ungerer, J., et al. (2003). Child care quality matters: How conclusions may vary with context. *Child Development, 74*(4), 1021–1033.

Magnuson, K. A., Meyers, M. K., Ruhm, C. J., & Waldfogel, J. (2004). Inequality in preschool education and school readiness. *American Educational Research Journal, 41*(1), 115–157.

Magnuson, K. A., Ruhm, C. J., & Waldfogel, J. (2004). *Does pre-kindergarten improve school preparation and performance?* (Working Paper No. 10452). Cambridge, MA: National Bureau of Economic Research.

Magnuson, K. A., & Waldfogel, J. (2005). Early childhood care and education: Effects on racial and ethnic gaps in school readiness. *Future of Children, 15*(1), 169–196.

McCartney, K., Dearing, E., & Taylor, B. A. (2003, April). *Quality child care supports the achievement of low-income children: Direct and indirect effects via caregiving and the home environment.* Paper presented at the biennial meetings of the Society for Research in Child Development, Tampa, FL.

McCarton, C. M., Brooks-Gunn, J., Wallace, I. F., Bauer, C. R., Bennett, F. C., Bernbaurm, J. C., et al. (1997). Results at age 8 years of early intervention for low-birth-weight premature infants: The Infant Health and Development Program. *Journal of the American Medical Association, 277*(2), 126–132.

McCormick, M. C., Brooks-Gunn, J., Buka, S. L., Goldman, J., Yu, J., Salganik, M., et al. (2006). Early intervention in low birth weigh premature infants: Results at 18 years of age for the Infant Health and Development Program. *Pediatrics, 117,* 771–780.

Meyers, M., Rosenbaum, D., Ruhm, C., & Waldfogel, J. (2004). Inequality in early childhood care and education: What do we know? In K. Neckerman (Ed.), *Social inequality* (pp. 223–270). New York: Russell Sage.

Mulligan, G. M., & Flanagan, K. D. (2006). *Age 2: Findings from the 2-year-old follow-up of the Early Childhood Longitudinal Study, Birth Cohort* (ECLS-B). Washington, DC: National Center for Education Statistics. Retrieved from http://nces.ed.gov/pubsearch/pubsinfo.asp?pubid=2006043

National Association for the Education of Young Children. (2006). *State policies on accreditation and quality ratings systems and tiered reimbursement programs.* Retrieved from http://www.naeyc.org/ece/critical/chart1.asp

National Center for Education Statistics. (2002). *The condition of education 2002* (NCES 2002–025). Washington, DC: U.S. Department of Education. Retrieved from http://nces.ed.gov/fastfacts/display.asp?id=78

National Education Goals Panel. (1997). *Special early childhood report.* Washington, DC: Government Printing Office.

NICHD Early Child Care Research Network. (1997a). Child care in the first year of life. *Merrill Palmer Quarterly, 43*(3), 240–260.

NICHD Early Child Care Research Network (1997b). Familial factors associated with the characteristics of nonmaternal care for infants. *Journal of Marriage and the Family, 59,* 389–408.

NICHD Early Child Care Research Network. (1997c). Poverty and patterns of child care. In G. J. Duncan & J. Brooks-Gunn (Eds.), *Consequences of growing up poor.* New York: Russell Sage.

NICHD Early Child Care Research Network. (2000). Characteristics and quality of child care for toddlers and preschoolers. *Applied Developmental Science, 4*(3), 116–135.

NICHD Early Child Care Research Network. (2002a). Child-care structure→ process→outcome: Direct and indirect effects of child-care quality on young children's development. *Psychological Science, 13*(3), 199–206.

NICHD Early Child Care Research Network. (2002b). Early child care and children's development prior to school entry: Results from the NICHD study of early child care. *American Educational Research Journal, 39,* 133–164.

NICHD Early Child Care Research Network. (2003). Does amount of time spent in child care predict socio-emotional adjustment during the transition to kindergarten? *Child Development, 74*(4), 975–1005.

NICHD Early Child Care Research Network (2004). Type of child care and children's development at 54 months. *Early Childhood Research Quarterly, 19,* 203–230.

NICHD Early Child Care Research Network. (2005a). *Child care and child development: Results from the NICHD study of early child care and youth development.* New York: Guilford Press.

NICHD Early Child Care Research Network. (2005b). Early child care and children's development in the primary grades: Follow-up results from the NICHD study of early child care. *American Educational Research Journal, 42*(3), 537–570.

NICHD Early Child Care Research Network. (2006). Child-care effect sizes for the NICHD study of early child care and youth development. *American Psychologist, 61*(2), 99–116.

NICHD Early Child Care Research Network, & Duncan, G. J. (2003). Modeling the impacts of child care quality on children's preschool cognitive development. *Child Development, 74,* 1454–1475.

Peisner-Feinberg, E. S., & Burchinal, M. R. (1997). Relations between preschool children's child care experiences and concurrent development: The cost, quality, and outcomes study. *Merrill-Palmer Quarterly, 43,* 451–477.

Peisner-Feinberg, E. S., Burchinal, M. R., Clifford, R. M., Culkin, M. L., Howes, C., Kagan, S. L., et al. (2001). The relation of preschool child-care quality to children's cognitive and social developmental trajectories through second grade. *Child Development, 72*(5), 1534–1553.

Phillips, D., & Adams, G. (2001). Child care and our youngest children. *Future of Children, 11*(1), 35–52.

Phillips, M., Crouse, J., & Ralph, J. (1998). Does the black-white test score gap widen after children enter school? In C. Jencks & M. Phillips (Eds.), *The black-white test score gap.* Washington, DC: Brookings Institution.

Phillipsen, L. C., Burchinal, M. R., Howes, C., & Cryer, D. (1997). The prediction of process quality from structural features of child care. *Early Childhood Research Quarterly, 12,* 281–303.

Rigby, D. E., Brooks-Gunn, J., & Ryan, R. M. (2006, April). *Child care quality in different state policy contexts.* Paper presented at the annual meeting of the Administration for Children's Services Child Care Bureau Child Care Policy Research Consortium, Washington, DC.

Ryan, R. M., Fauth, R. C., & Brooks-Gunn, J. (2005). Childhood poverty: Implications for school readiness and early childhood education. In B. Spodek & O. N. Saracho (Eds.), *Handbook of research on the education of young children* (pp. 323–346). Mahwah, NJ: Erlbaum.

Schweinhart, L. J., Barnes, H. V., & Weikert, D. P. (1993). *Significant benefits: The High/Scope Perry Preschool study through age 27.* Ypsilanti, MI: High/Scope Press.

Schweinhart, L. J., Montie, J., Xiang, Z., Barnett, W. S., Belfield, C. R., & Nores, M. (2005). *Lifetime effects: The High/Scope Perry Preschool study through age 40.* Ypsilanti, MI: High/Scope Press.

Scott-Little, C., Kagan, S. L., & Frelow, V. S. (2005). *Inside the content: The breadth and depth of early learning standards.* Greensboro, NC: The Regional Educational Laboratory at SERVE.

Shonkoff, J. P., & Phillips, D. A. (2000). *From neurons to neighborhoods: The science of early childhood development.* Washington, DC: National Academy Press.

Smith, J., Brooks-Gunn, J., & Klebanov, P. (1997). The consequences of living in poverty on young children's cognitive development. In G. J. Duncan & J. Brooks-Gunn (Eds.), *Consequences of growing up poor* (pp. 132–189). New York: Russell Sage.

Smolensky, E., & Gootman, J. (Eds.). (2003). *Working families and growing kids: Caring for children and adolescents.* Washington, DC: National Academy Press.

U.S. Bureau of Labor Statistics. (2006). *Employment characteristics of families in 2005.* Retrieved from http://stats.bls.gov/news.release/famee.nr0.htm

U.S. Census Bureau. (1970). *School enrollment: Social and economic characteristics of students, October 1969* (Current Population Reports, P-20 Series). Washington, DC: U.S. Bureau of the Census.

U.S. Census Bureau. (2004). *The effects of government taxes and transfers on income and poverty: 2004.* Retrieved from http://www.census.gov/hhes/www/poverty/effect2004/effectofgovtandt2004.html#_iv._poverty

Vandell, D. L. (2004). Early child care: The known and the unknown. *Merrill-Palmer Quarterly, 50*(3), 387–414.

Vandell, D. L., & Wolfe, B. (2000). *Child care quality: Does it matter and does it need to be improved?* (Special Report No. 78). Madison: University of Wisconsin–Madison, Institute for Research on Poverty. Retrieved from http://www.ssc.wisc.edu/irp

Votruba-Drzal, E., Coley, R. L., & Chase-Lansdale, P. L. (2004). Child care and low income children's development: Direct and moderated effects. *Child Development, 75*(1), 296–312.

Waldfogel, J. (2002). Child care, women's employment, and child outcomes. *Journal of Population Economics, 15,* 527–548.

Whitebook, M., Howes, C., & Phillips, D. (1998). *Worthy work, unlivable wages: The National Child Care Staffing Study, 1988–1997.* Washington, DC: Center for the Child Care Workforce.

Yoshikawa, H. (1995). Long-term effects of early childhood programs on social outcomes and delinquency. *Future of Children, 5*(3), 51–75.

# CHAPTER 7

# Appalachian Families and Poverty

## Historical Issues and Contemporary Economic Trends

W. SEAN NEWSOME, KEVIN R. BUSH, CHARLES B. HENNON,
GARY W. PETERSON, AND STEPHAN M. WILSON

## DESCRIPTION OF THE REGION AND ITS PEOPLE

Appalachia is a vast area consisting of 200,000 square miles that stretches contiguously from southern New York to northern Mississippi and the upper two-thirds of Alabama. In total, the Appalachian region includes 410 counties in 13 states where approximately 23 million people live (Appalachian Regional Commission [ARC], 2006). Given the size and length of Appalachia, it is usually divided into northern, central, and southern regions. Northern regions are made up of New York, Pennsylvania, northern West Virginia, Maryland, and southeastern Ohio. Central regions are made up of eastern Kentucky, central Tennessee, southern West Virginia, and western Virginia. Southern regions are made up of Mississippi, Alabama, south and eastern Tennessee, Georgia, South Carolina, North Carolina, and eastern Virginia.

Although 93% of the population in Appalachia is of European descent, some assert that this population of mainly Scotch-Irish descendants has developed into its own ethnicity (Keefe, 1992; Keefe, Reck, & Reck, 1983). This process is thought to have occurred through generations of living in isolated mountainous areas in which a culture was developed based on shared beliefs (e.g., familism, love of place and land, neighborliness, and individualism) and ancestry. In addition, the social and geographic isolation helped facilitate a shared identity among individuals and families living in many of the northern, central, and southern regions of rural Appalachia (Keefe, 1992).

At the onset of the 1960s, however, the dire economic situation of rural Appalachia and its people was brought into public and national awareness. In order to address the economic issues facing rural Appalachia, and as a result of the 1960 presidential campaign of John F. Kennedy, who was profoundly affected by the geographic isolation and economic deprivation in Appalachia, the President's Appalachian Regional Commission (PARC) was created in 1963. Along with the creation of PARC in 1963, the Appalachian Regional Commission (ARC) was created on March 9, 1965, during President Lyndon B. Johnson's administration to address poverty and issues such as illiteracy, lack of health care, transportation, and human services. At the time of ARC's inception, one of every four Appalachians lived in poverty, and the per capita income was 23% lower than the national average (Owens, 2000).

Although the overall poverty rates in Appalachia have vastly improved since the 1960s, poverty continues to be a salient issue in many remote and geographically isolated areas of Appalachia. Although data from the 2000 census show that the overall poverty rate for the entire Appalachian area is only slightly above that of the United States, several Appalachian states and counties are much higher and display poverty rates well above the national average. Despite the prevalence of poverty in the Appalachian region, however, socioeconomic class distinctions among Appalachian people are made within communities and great contrasts currently exist between the wealthy and the poor (ARC, n.d.c).

The 1960s also witnessed many federal incentives that helped fuel the economy and infrastructure of the Appalachian region. Such federal incentives helped stimulate an economic infrastructure that also contributed to the increased diversity of Appalachian families. As a result, interstates, highways, and roads were constructed to provide more opportunities for movement into and out of the region. Such infrastructures during the 1960s resulted in a commonly held belief in central Appalachia and eastern Kentucky known as the Three R's (reading, [w]riting, and Route 23). For many Appalachians in this area,

such a belief was viewed as an opportunity for movement to the North and Midwest parts of the United States where manufacturing jobs in the automotive, steel, and rubber industries were flourishing.

The emerging infrastructure also resulted in the gradual expansion of various industries in Appalachia (e.g., timber and coal), which resulted in a migration to and from the region that influenced many rural Appalachian families (Rural and Appalachian Youth and Family Consortium, 1996). Despite such movements, families in rural Appalachia are generally described today as being more cohesive than many of their counterparts in the United States. As pointed out by many authors, most rural Appalachian families are nuclear in form and place greater emphasis on values of family over individualistic goals (Bush & Lash, 2006; Rural and Appalachian Youth and Family Consortium, 1996). Equally important, however, is that the extended family and kin network in rural Appalachia still plays an important role in daily life (Bush & Lash, 2006; Jones, 1991; Rural and Appalachian Youth and Family Consortium, 1996; Wilson & Peterson, 2000). In addition, extended families typically live in close proximity; therefore, more direct assistance from and involvement with kin is quite common. Even those who have migrated to urban areas in pursuit of employment or education retain close emotional ties to Appalachia and their kin network—so much so that many of them settle in urban areas where other Appalachians reside and routinely make frequent trips back "home" to Appalachia (Drake, 2003).

The family values that characterize the social orientation of many Appalachians differ also from the collectivistic orientation often associated with particular cultural and ethnic groups. For example, among Koreans and Chinese, collectivistic values have their origin in Confucianism and are viewed as a life philosophy, which is then incorporated into social institutions as well as the family. In contrast, family values among Appalachians tend to focus on the overall betterment of the family and family loyalty. Such emphasis on family loyalty is then oriented toward family survival—an approach to family that is not typically encouraged or endorsed by the broader "pick yourself up by your own bootstraps" U.S. society.

Young Appalachian adults are often expected to remain geographically close to their families and maintain strong interpersonal ties with their kin and community. However, such principles often conflict with the individualistic ideals of the larger U.S. society, which places expectations on geographic mobility. These contradictory value systems require many Appalachians to develop a bicultural identity for successful functioning within their families and in the broader U.S. society. As a result, many bicultural Appalachians find themselves changing the pronunciation of words and their use of language as well as their attitudes toward interpersonal relationships and social contexts.

In addition to strong family and kinship values and the historic patterns of geographic and social isolation experienced by many Appalachians, recent and current economic exploitation of the region's natural resources (e.g., coal and timber) have affected Appalachian families and their unique social-cultural environment (Wilson, 2002; Wilson & Peterson, 2000). As various outside interests have gained access to the region's natural resources, many Appalachians have changed from subsistence farming and other sources of family support to being employees in specific industries. Similarly, many of the young and highly educated have migrated out of rural Appalachia (ARC, 2006; Rural and Appalachian Youth and Families Consortium, 1996). The result has been a drain of human capital on many of the communities

in Appalachia. Such a drain of human capital leaves many Appalachian families with fewer role models to cultivate the importance of family and the Appalachian "way of life." Despite this, however, many of these migratory Appalachians retain close emotional and instrumental bonds with their families and communities, through frequent visits, phone calls, and subsequent return to the area.

## THE ECONOMICS OF THE REGION: ISSUES, TRENDS, AND FUTURE CONSIDERATIONS

Historically, the economic fortunes of Appalachia and its people reflected a trend of being narrow and self-supporting to that of being dependent on business and economic trends in the rest of the nation and the world (Hurst, 2006). During the early to mid-1900s, much of central Appalachia's economy was fueled by mining, agriculture (especially tobacco), and heavy industry. In fact, even though the number of jobs has declined in the extraction of coal, Appalachia still provides almost 40% of this natural resource to the United States.

During the past 15 years, however, the Appalachian economy has witnessed greater diversification and economic growth in the areas of government, retailing, furniture manufacturing, the lumber industry, tourism, and mini-industries (Hurst, 2006). Moreover, industries and companies such as Heinz, Deer Park, Kentucky Fried Chicken, Mountain Dew, Little Debbie, and the General Nutrition Center have been expanding. Employment in government services, tourism, retailing, mini-industries, and manufacturing continue to strengthen (Hurst, 2006). Tourism is becoming increasingly important in the more remote areas of Appalachia because many of these areas typically do not have other viable industries (Howell, 2006). Although tourism has long been a mainstay of the regional economy, today it is emphasized with developmental grants available for its promotion (Howell, 2006; Hurst, 2006).

In addition to tourism, manufacturing is still an economic mainstay but is no longer concentrated in a few major industries (Hurst, 2006). Although remaining more reliant on manufacturing and blue-collar employment than the rest of the United States, the region's economy and its families are now in many ways supported by greater diversification, and working to become more self-reliant and self-supportive. Although such changes might be associated with lower wages, some areas of the Appalachian region are experiencing lower levels of poverty than in previous years.

Besides the ever-changing and diverse areas of economic growth in Appalachia, the 1992 North American Free Trade Agreement (NAFTA, which took effect in 1994) appears to have led to a loss of jobs in large manufacturing companies and textiles. Automation and competition from imported goods also contributed to job loss. Several companies entered bankruptcy and moved jobs offshore to stay competitive with other manufactures. According to some, globalization has also resulted in many repercussions for Appalachian families' livelihoods and levels of poverty.

As the economy and job market have shifted in the Appalachian region, so have those counties and areas most affected by poverty. To better understand those counties and areas most affected by levels of poverty, researchers and authors have looked at the 410 counties composing Appalachia. They have classified the counties as being distressed (77), at-risk (81), transitional (222), competitive (22), and attainment (8) for fiscal year 2006. The classification is computed on a comparison of county and national rates on three economic indicators: 3-year average unemployment rate, per

capita market income rates, and poverty rates (ARC, n.d.a).

Families living in the 158 distressed and at-risk counties likely face the greatest risk for poverty. Distressed counties have 3-year unemployment rates of at least 1.5 times the national average, a per capita market income of no more than two-thirds the national average and rates of poverty at least 1.5 times the national average. For 2006, distressed counties reported an unemployment rate of 8.3%, a per capita income of $17,701 or less, and a poverty rate of 18.6% or higher (ARC, n.d.b). Most economically distressed counties are clustered in eastern Kentucky, central West Virginia, and the extreme southern edge of Appalachia in Mississippi and Alabama. No counties in Pennsylvania, Maryland, New York, Georgia, or South Carolina meet these criteria, with only a handful in Virginia, North Carolina, Tennessee, and Ohio. (See the map of counties categories by economic classification at www.gov/index.do? nodeld-58#econ; see ARC, n.d.b; see map at www.arc.gov/images/programs/distress/fy06 report/FY2006_Map1.pdf)

In addition to the most economically distressed counties being clustered in specific states, 81 at-risk counties are spread throughout the Appalachian region. Counties classified as being at-risk are those having a 3-year unemployment rate at least 1.25 times the national average, a per capita market income of no more than two-thirds the national average, and poverty rates at least 1.25 times the national average. Counties are also classified as at-risk if they meet two of the three indicators for distressed counties. Transitional counties are those with indicators that are worse than those for the national average in one or more of the three indicators used, but not meeting the criteria used for classification in the distressed and at-risk categories. There are 222 transitional counties, mostly in the most northern (New York and Pennsylvania), central (Ohio, West Virginia, Tennessee, and

North and South Carolina), and southern (Georgia and Alabama) areas of the Appalachian region (ARC, n.d.b).

The other classifications are competitive and attainment. Competitive counties have 3-year unemployment averages and poverty rates equal to the national averages, but per-capita market income between 80% and less than 100% of the national averages. There are 22 competitive counties, mostly on the edges of Appalachia. Counties are classified as attainment if they have economic indicators equal to or better than national averages. These 8 counties are also mostly found at the edge of Appalachia, but also include Allegheny in the state of Pennsylvania.

Although classification of counties might offer an ecological image of where families are susceptible to poverty, a portrayal of counties by rate of poverty can also be drawn as well as the overall poverty rate for the entire Appalachian region. As such, the poverty rate in 2000 for the Appalachian region was 13.6%; compared with 12.4% for the United States. In 1990, the rates were 15.4% and 13.1% respectively, and 14.1% and 12.4% in 1980. Although such data might suggest that the region is still suffering from higher poverty rates than the national average, and that the poverty rate is declining, a closer look by state and county levels indicates that many communities or local areas are still facing the challenges of poverty. Data in 2002 show that poverty rates ranged from 24.4% in Kentucky to 9.2% in Georgia. Within some states, the rates of poverty ranged widely across Appalachian counties: for example, from a low of 6.9% in Pike to a high of 18.8% in Centre (PA), 12.6% in Union to 32.8% in Noxubee (MS), 10.6% in Clark to 45.4% in Owsley (KY), and 9.3% in Putnam to 31.8% in Webster (WV). More than 25 Appalachian counties in 2000 had poverty rates between 27.6 and 45.4%, 60 counties had rates of 19.4 to 27.5%, and

more than 90 counties had rates between 13.5 and 19.3% (ARC, n.d.c; see poverty rates in the Appalachian region at www.arc .gov/index.do?nodeId=58#pov). With such disproportional rates of poverty, a disparity ultimately occurs that inevitably affects families and future generations in many of these areas and respective communities.

The disparate economic fortunes across the geographic regions of Appalachia are analogous to patterns of economic inequality among those living in these regions (Lichter & Campbell, 2005). In Appalachia, as in the rest of the United States, African Americans and other ethnic and racial minorities have higher rates of poverty compared with whites, regardless of family type. Among African American married couples with children, the poverty rate was generally greater than that for whites in the Appalachian region (46.4 compared with 37.4%), and Hispanic American married couples had higher rates of poverty than did other racial and ethnic groups. Overall, Hispanic Americans had lower rates of poverty than did African Americans. One explanation for this is that Hispanic Americans in the Appalachian region represent a much higher proportion of married-couple families than of single-parent families (Lichter & Campbell, 2005).

In Appalachia, as in the whole United States, the poverty rate for children exceeds that of the other age groups. This rate has fluctuated since 1959 when data were first available. The U.S. child poverty rate was the highest in 1959 (approximately 27%) and then declined and remained relatively stable through the 1970s (approximately 16%), increased between 1979 and 1982 (from 16 to 22%), fell during the 1980s, and then increased to 23% in 1993 (Lichter & Campbell, 2005). At the close of the 1990s, the poverty rate among children (16.6%) was its lowest since the late 1970s but, nevertheless, remained higher than rates for the elderly (8.5% among those age 65 to 74 and 11.5% among those age 75 and older) as well as for the nation's population as a whole (Lichter & Campbell, 2005).

Poverty age patterns in Appalachia mirror those represented by United States. Poverty rates among young adults and older adults (ages 18–64) in Appalachia were only slightly higher in 2000 than in the rest of the nation. However, there was a disparity in poverty rates among the elderly (12% in the Appalachian region compared with 9.6% nationwide). On the other hand, poverty rates among Appalachian elderly were lower than for most other age groups in Appalachia, a pattern similar to that found across the United States.

Similar to other parts of the United States, many feel that one approach to combat the issue of poverty is through educational attainment. Years of low educational attainment, chronic unemployment, and underemployment have been characteristics of poverty in Appalachia (Lichter & Campbell, 2005). In addition, a common perception among many families in Appalachia is that the benefits of education are offset by few employment opportunities. This perception generates disincentives for community investment in education, and for families encouraging their members to pursue more education. The belief held by many is that education does not pay off in better jobs and family life. However, an implication of one study shows an unexpected result. The "returns" to education in Appalachia, if considered relative to lower rates of poverty, show little difference in Appalachia relative to the rest of the nation. Across the United States, only 3.4% of people with college educations are classified as poor, compared with nearly 22% of those who drop out of high school. The association between education and living or not living in poverty is similar in Appalachia and non-Appalachia (Lichter & Campbell, 2005).

A review of geographic variations of educational inequality within Appalachia shows a complex portrait. Moreover, the complexities represent a continuum of differences between Appalachians with college educations living in counties with large metropolitan cities (with more than 1 million in population) and those with college educations living in completely rural counties. More importantly, data suggest that the greatest vulnerability to poverty is represented by the least educated groups in the less densely settled areas of Appalachia. Furthermore, in counties that are completely rural and nonadjacent to a metropolitan area, the poverty rate was nearly 100% larger than was the rate in the largest metropolitan counties (30.9 compared with 16.8%). A similar differential in poverty rates exists for high school graduates. More education is linked to lower rates of poverty and vice versa, with the linkage strongest in the most remote rural areas of the Appalachian region. However, this association does not reflect the benefits obtained from a college education in rural, relative to urban, Appalachia, but indicates that the consequences of low education result in higher rates of poverty (Lichter & Campbell, 2005).

Persistent challenges and economic distress continue to affect much of the Appalachian region. With limited employers paying adequate, middle-class wages and health benefits, many families or some of their members have left Appalachia in search of economic opportunities. In many cases, migration patterns can be characterized as the "best and brightest" leaving for better economic opportunities, whereas those remaining are the less educated, the unemployed, and the impoverished (Lichter & Campbell, 2005). Those families tend to have fewer job skills (i.e., human capital) and live in communities with fewer opportunities to break out of poverty (Mather, 2004).

## PERVASIVE FAMILY PATTERNS: EXTERNAL AND INTERNAL FORCES SHAPING FAMILIES AND POVERTY

In looking at the family patterns of the Appalachian region, many authors have historically cited the original Native Americans (e.g., Cherokee) and settlers from western and northern Europe that helped advance its family structure (Drake, 2003). As pointed out by many Appalachian scholars, such family and kinship structures contributed heavily to the rise of a specific folk-culture that centered on family relationships, kinship bonds, and the region's unique approach to territorial and physical conditions (Drake, 2003).

At the onset of the 20th century and before World War II, rural areas of southern and central Appalachia could be characterized more as collections of families and kinship communities rather than as a regional society (Beaver, 1986; Bryant, 1981; Hicks, 1992; Schwarzweller, 1970; Wilson & Peterson, 2000). For much of the 20th century, family life remained a central form of social organization in rural, southern, and central Appalachia. Because many residents of these isolated rural communities were members of overlapping kin groups, the lack of clearly defined boundaries between families and local communities often was evident. Across generations, these "kinship communities," or interlocking networks of extended families, were symbolically associated with a particular locale (e.g., a mountain, a "holler," a stream, or a county) and rooted deeply in the land (Batteau, 1982; Beaver, 1986; Bryant, 1981; Hicks, 1992; Wilson & Peterson, 2000). As a result, Appalachian folk culture and the concept of the "homeplace" became an important expression of such localistic ideas in rural

areas of southern and central Appalachia. More importantly, the concept of homeplace involved fond memories associated with a person's childhood home as well as feelings of attachment to place, fondness for the physical aspects of terrain and home, and one's loyalty to family (Cox, 2006). For many in this region, the Appalachian homeplace is laden with memories and emotional feelings that involve the integration between one's interpersonal and physical environments.

The current Appalachian region, however, is an amalgam of many cultures and is experiencing rapid socio-demographic change (Batteau, 1982; Burns, Scott, & Thompson, 2006; Klein, 1995; Wilson & Peterson, 2000). Besides the original indigenous people and the settlers of western and northern European origin, a considerable variety of Dutch, French, southern European (e.g., Greeks, Italians), African American, Hispanic, and Middle Eastern populations have become a part of the Appalachian tapestry.

Despite the current influx of race, culture, and ethnicity in many parts of Appalachia, one of the most common and long-held images of Appalachian families in the larger and broader U.S. context is that of an impoverished, backward, forgotten, and needy segment of America (Harrington, 1962). For some, the alleged root of Appalachian family "depravity" has often been described as a culture or subculture of poverty much in the manner conceptualized by anthropologist Oscar Lewis. According to Lewis, individuals and families who live in poverty share similar psychological and cultural qualities such as large families, poor education, deficient work ethic, and low expectations, which in turn buffer them from the worst consequences of marginalization and alienation but, nonetheless, trap them and their children in a culture of disadvantage (Lewis, 1963, 1968). Still others, however, point to the family as being a "culture of poverty" and cite the sources of traditionalism, fatalism, and a rejection of change sustained by the people and families of Appalachia (Weller, 1965). Many critics of this viewpoint, however, have pointed to the circular reasoning inherent in this perspective, particularly how it blames the victim and leaves the broader economic structure of Appalachia essentially unchallenged (Drake, 2003).

More recently, and partially in response to a culture of poverty perspectives, Appalachia has been defined as "America's Third World" (Lohmann, 1990), a colonized region in which its people are marginalized from mainstream American life, sharing common problems with other marginalized areas of North America (e.g., inner cities) and around the globe (e.g., the colonization of the Middle East for its oil resources) (Cécora, 1993; Couto, 1994; Day, 1987; Rosenberg, 1979; Wilson & Peterson, 2000; Wilson, Peterson, & Wilson, 1993). Such perspectives often portray economically deprived families of Appalachia as being representative of the "differentness" of this region, where the region's resources are often supported by outside interests. From this perspective, Appalachian families are viewed as living in a domestic colony whose economic and social capital are routinely exported to benefit external interests (Robertson & Shoffner, 1989; Wilson & Peterson, 2000).

Consequently, the denigration of Appalachian family life may be just another manifestation of exploitation, much like what has occurred for the region's land and natural resources. Thus, Appalachian families were poor, not because of their own culturally based psychological qualities, but because the region became increasingly connected with and exploited by the urban society at large as well as the industrialized and post-industrialized United States. With such considerations, many authors have suggested that like other aspects of American society, portions of Appalachia suffer from serious economic disadvantage that requires creative intervention efforts to address existing inequalities (Drake, 2003).

Closely related to such conceptions of endemic poverty have been the impressions of Appalachian families described by the "Local Color School" of writers that evolved after the Civil War and into the 20th century. Such authors helped foster the image of Appalachians in the modern mind as physically isolated, backward, quaint, parochial, and violent. Such imagery of Appalachian families frequently portray them as a deviant subculture whose very nature, despite substantial disadvantage, resists change in needed positive ways (Billings, 2006; Caudill, 1963). To the point, the stereotype of the "hillbilly" has been etched in popular culture as both an object of humor, derision, and social concern—the classic image being a lanky, gun-toting, hard-drinking, white male with little regard for the law, work, cleanliness, or education (Haskell, 2006). This image has been nurtured historically through comic strips like *Snuffy Smith* and *Li'l Abner* as well as through television and movies like *The Beverly Hillbillies, Hee Haw,* and *Deliverance*. The result has been that many Americans ascribe distinctive qualities to members of Appalachian families such as endemic poverty, clannishness, inbreeding, and illiteracy. However, the reality of the Appalachian region is much more complex than is conveyed by the dominant family caricatures portrayed by the popular media.

In addition to the various imageries portrayed by popular media, the complex and pervasive nature of Appalachian family life has spawned heated debates about its relative strengths and weaknesses. Deficit models have been proposed, with Appalachian familism being described as the source of many problematic psychosocial outcomes such as excessive emotional dependency or enmeshment, incest, diminished achievement motivation, inhibited socioeconomic mobility, extreme distrust of outsiders, and inability to cope with modernity (Weller, 1965; Wilson & Peterson, 2000). In contrast, the primary opposing view is more positive, with Appalachian families being portrayed as havens of security, as sources of stability, and as reservoirs of emotional support in times of crisis or stress (Brown & Schwarzweller, 1970; Dyk & Wilson, 1999; Hicks, 1992; Stephenson, 1968; Wilson, Henry, & Peterson, 1997). Positive aspects of Appalachian familism provide the necessary resources of having pride in one's heritage as well as providing a sense of having "roots" that then serves as a good background for identity development.

With such aforementioned considerations, Appalachian familism simply embodies the idea that one's individual welfare is best facilitated by fostering the interests of the group (or family) rather than focusing on the priorities of the larger society, such as self-interest, autonomy, and personal agency. Strong family values are neither inherently beneficial nor inevitably problematic for Appalachian family members. Instead, the essential issue is whether a particular family system has adapted itself to its surrounding social and physical ecology rather than having external standards imposed from the outside.

Certainly, the traditional folk culture of Appalachia, in its historic form, was highly adapted to a geographically isolated region in which the self-sufficiency of rural families was sustained by close-knit kin networks that provided a sense of security, stability, and strength. More importantly, family in Appalachia represents a set of attitudes about the importance of loyalty, bonds, reputation, and kinship ties that helps provide meaning and direction for many Appalachians. Family also represents a value system that may provide individuals who are a part of the Appalachian social experience with, at least in magnitude, some distinctiveness from the American mainstream.

## POLICY AND WELFARE REFORM: PAST AND RECENT POLICY MEASURES AFFECTING THE REGION

In addressing the sweeping policy and welfare reform measures that have affected many Appalachians, one must first identify and gain a better understanding of the socioeconomic and macroeconomic changes that have swept through the region. As pointed out by many, the Appalachian economy has routinely been more vulnerable to periods of recession and economic downturns than have other parts of the United States (Adams & Duncan, 1992; Drake, 2003; Sarnoff, 2003). Primarily, this has been the result of the Appalachian region being heavily involved in large and mini-manufacturing, and natural resource–dependent industries (e.g., coal and timber) that are often prone to macro and foreign policy initiatives (Drake, 2003). As a result, the Appalachian region has been susceptible to price fluctuations of natural resources, the impact of globalization, and the downsizing of large and mini-manufacturing industries resulting from the economic declines and policy initiatives during the 1980s and 1990s.

In addition to macroeconomic and policy changes that affected much of the Appalachian region during the 1980s and 1990s, many authors have also pointed to the growing inequality of income distribution throughout the Appalachian region and the United States. Central Appalachia continues to be one of the poorest regions in the country, but northern and southern Appalachia have become considerably less poor during the past 40 years (Sarnoff, 2003). Compared with the rest of the nation, central Appalachian wages are about 20% lower, whereas the northern and southern regions of Appalachia are about 10% lower. In addition, per capita income, perhaps the best overall indicator of economic well-being, declined only marginally from its peak of 83.2% in 1994 to 81.9% of the U.S. average in 1999 (Drake, 2003).

Although such data might suggest that the economic well being of individuals in the Appalachian region is making progress, a closer look indicates that many counties, communities and local areas in Appalachia are still facing the challenges of economic downturns that resulted from many policy and welfare measures initiated over the past 20 years. Coupled with the policy and welfare measures initiated over the past 20 years are various industry tax strategies as well as federal and state policies that resulted in high exit rates of manufacturing plants and job loss in northern, central, and southern parts of the Appalachian region. The movement of many of these manufacturers and industries is largely the direct result and influence of more liberal trade policies during the past two decades (Drake, 2003).

From the mid-1900s, however, income maintenance policies and welfare reform measures have played an important role in the Appalachian region. In the 1960s and 1970s, many of the social welfare reform measures looked to alleviate poverty, improve healthcare standards, and institute greater access to employment and education in Appalachia. During the 1960s, President Johnson initiated the "War on Poverty" in an effort to provide greater access to resources for needy families in Appalachia and the nation.

In President Johnson's attempt to create a "Great Society," many Appalachians benefited from numerous programs that were intended to create independency and support quality of life. Welfare reform programs that were initiated at the federal level such as the Economic Opportunity Act of 1964, the Food Stamp Act of 1964, the Social Security Act of 1964 and the Housing and Urban Development (HUD) Act of 1968, attempted to fight poverty in poor neighborhoods and communities, increase job opportunities, provide health care for needy children and families, and create greater accessibility to the "American Dream" (e.g., home ownership;

see Karger & Stoesz, 2005). Such large-scale federal efforts during the 1960s and 1970s contributed to many positive changes in the Appalachian region, despite Appalachian reluctance to want or desire federal government intervention through welfare reform programs. Moreover, data supports the likelihood that some of the most pressing concerns (e.g., poverty) facing the Appalachian region were improved through large-scale policy efforts at the federal level during the 1960s and 1970s (Sarnoff, 2003). Conversely, the end of federal and "big government" social welfare programs in the 1980s likely intensified some of the problems in the region (Drake, 2003). In addition, the shift from social welfare spending in the 1960s and 1970s to the slashing of social welfare spending during the 1980s brought about a sequence of events that left an indelible mark on the Appalachian region. Moreover, the inflation-fighting policies of the 1980s brought about a sequence of recessions that shocked many of the older manufacturing sectors of northern Appalachia and the coal industry of central Appalachia. The result was structural unemployment in many of the Appalachian regions (Drake, 2003).

In addition to the sequence of recessions that affected much of the Appalachian region during the 1980s, many parts of central Appalachia were also affected by the significant changes that occurred in the coal and steel industry. In particular, research has found that periods of boom and bust in the coal and steel industries results in significant decreases and increases in income maintenance programs instituted by the federal government (Black, Daniel, & Sanders, 2002; Black, McKinnish, & Sanders, 2003). Black and colleagues found that a 10% change in earnings in coal and steel counties was associated with a 9% to 10% change in Aid to Families with Dependent Children (AFDC) expenditures in that county (2002). As Black et al. pointed out, this relationship also worked in the opposite direction, so that during periods of earning, losses in the coal and steel industries resulted in rising AFDC expenditures and vice versa. Similar findings were also found in other income maintenance programs during the 1970s and 1980s. As such, Black et al. found that a 10% decline in county earnings resulting from a loss of steel or coal industry earnings led to a 7.9% increase in Social Security Insurance (SSI) benefit payments, an 18.7% increase in food stamp payments, a 26% increase in unemployment insurance payments, a 4.1% increase in Medicare and Medicaid payments, and a 1.5% increase in social security payments (2002). Even more important to these findings is that these increases in income maintenance expenditures came at a time when much of central Appalachia's population was declining and transitioning into a mini-manufacturing and service sector region.

During the 1990s, welfare and policy initiatives looked to provide a greater sense of individuality and independence. In fact, current welfare reforms have hoped to create less dependency on federal and state governments by creating greater job opportunities and work for many people in the United States as well as the Appalachian region. Most recently, welfare reforms such as the Personal Responsibility and Work Opportunity Reconciliation Act of 1996 (PRWORA) set out to consolidate three federal programs: Aid to Families with Dependent Children (AFDC), Emergency Assistance (EA), and the Job Opportunity and Basic Skills program (JOBS) into one block grant program called Temporary Assistance for Needy Families (TANF).

The overarching goals of TANF aimed at ending the dependency of needy families on government benefits, reducing the incidence of out of wedlock pregnancies, advancing the maintenance of two-parent families and establishing work participation rates (Greenburg &

Savner, 1996). As one of the most important pieces of welfare legislation to emerge since the Social Security Act of 1935, PRWORA delegates responsibility to states to implement and oversee—through the use of TANF block grant money—who will receive public assistance. However, such responsibility presents many challenges to state government officials for finding county and community ways to move people off public assistance and from welfare to work.

Although many proponents of TANF cite its success in dropping public assistance caseloads and returning adults to work, current data shows mixed results regarding its effectiveness in the Appalachian region (Karger & Stoesz, 2005). Specifically, TANF does not consider some of the most salient issues faced by many Appalachians. For example, TANF did not account for the "rural" obstacles presented by Appalachia and the issues these might result in concerning the required work agreement necessary to receive funds. Many central Appalachians live in counties and rural areas with constricted labor markets and other barriers (e.g., transportation) that may preclude their employment or ability to meet some of its requirements. Similarly, it has been pointed out that emphasis on "work-first" federal policies can result in a mismatch between local conditions, state expenditures, and federal wishes that neglects economically marginalized regions (Harvey, Summers, Pickering, & Richards, 2002).

In addition to the aforementioned concerns, TANF continues to perpetuate a climate of welfare behaviorism and stereotypes in an attempt to reprogram the behaviors of the poor. Although this type of welfare behaviorism is affecting the entire nation, nowhere is it more apparent than in Appalachia and the counties and states that make up central Appalachia. As such, welfare policy such as TANF sets out to "behaviorially change" the culturally and morally deviant, "bare-foot and pregnant" Appalachian female as well as the "lanky, gun-toting, hard-drinking, lazy," white Appalachian male who has little regard for work or education. Even more so, federal measures such as TANF do little to enhance human capital or tap into the strengths presented by many Appalachians. This is especially true of TANF and the potential impact it might have on the women of Appalachia. As a result, TANF does not recognize the strengths presented by many Appalachian women (especially in central Appalachia) and their long heritage of being the "backbone" of family. Besides the nurturing and attentive role many Appalachian women give to their immediate and extended families, many rely on such traditions as quilting, canning, farming, and digging "root" to help offset any economic downturns and family hardships. More common than not, women in this region represent a form of resiliency, stability and strength during the hardest of times, offering care, compassion, and understanding that punches no time clock and has helped maintain and perpetuate a culture of devotion to family and the Appalachian region.

However, federal policies that require work-first conditions potentially take many Appalachian women out of this role. When Appalachian women's work is forced into the labor market, there are fewer people to continue the long-standing tradition and importance placed on family. Such immediate concerns might also result in fewer individuals to care for children or the elderly. This is of special concern given the lack of children services in central Appalachia and the rising number of elderly that are dependent on family for support services (Miewald, 2003). This is also a concern given that young and old in many marginalized areas (including Appalachia) rely on women's labor for their health and well-being. Further complicating this issue is the lack of prolonged living-wage jobs in the Appalachian region. For example, in Appalachian Kentucky, single mothers are expected to go to work in an economy where unemployment approached 45% in 1996 (Collins, Eller, & Taui, 1996).

From the previous discussion, one can easily surmise that much of the welfare reform that has materialized at the federal level represents a long history of policies imposed by outsiders who have very little knowledge of Appalachian culture, economics, or politics. Therefore, future policy reform must look at creating relationships between Appalachian communities, institutions, and its people. Policy reform must be based on socioeconomic and macroeconomic assessments of the region rather than normative American culture values that exclude the experience of low-income Appalachians. Although some progress has been made in this direction, limited involvement in the creation of policy by those most affected by federal and state policy remains the norm.

In addition to the inclusion of Appalachians in the development of federal and state policy, future policy reform must also look to economic diversification efforts that cultivate job growth through an investment in human capital. Such investments in human capital should also recognize the changing role of manufacturing, industry, and the service sector in the Appalachian region. In most cases, this would mean greater emphasis placed on improving educational achievement in the areas of engineering, business, and service sectors (Hurst, 2006). Such an emphasis through education may result in an effective labor force that is sensitive to the current changes taking place in much of the Appalachian region and expands employment to the unemployed. However, given the limited resources for education in many northern, southern, and central Appalachian counties, such efforts must rely on policy initiatives at the federal, state, and local level.

Issues such as poverty, low wages, and limited employment in the Appalachian region must be reconciled through strategic national, state, and local efforts. Policy reform efforts must also tap the potential strengths of Appalachians and their understanding of what will potentially work and what will not work in rural areas. More importantly, strategic policy initiatives at the federal and state levels must assume that a "one size fits all" approach does not work when addressing many communities that occupy the Appalachian region.

## REFERENCES

Adams, T. K., & Duncan, G. J. (1992). Long-term poverty in rural areas. In C. R. Duncan (Ed.), *Rural poverty in America* (pp. 63–93). New York: Auburn House.

Appalachian Regional Commission. (2006). *Appalachian Regional Commission (ARC): Region.* Retrieved October 15, 2006, from http://www.arc.gov/index.do?nodeId=26

Appalachian Regional Commission. (n.d.a). *ARC-designated distressed counties, FY 2006.* Retrieved October 18, 2006, from www.arc.gov/index.do?nodeId=18

Appalachian Regional Commission. (n.d.b). *County economic status designations in the Appalachian region, FY 2006.* Retrieved October 18, 2006, from www.arc.gov.index.do?nodeId=2934

Appalachian Regional Commission. (n.d.c). *Poverty rates in Appalachia, 2000.* Retrieved October 21, 2006, from www.arc.gov/search/LoadQueryData.do?queryId=14

Batteau, A. (1982). Mosbys and Broomseldge: The semantics of class in an Appalachian kinship system. *American Ethnologist, 8,* 445–466.

Beaver, P. D. (1986). *Rural community in the Appalachian south.* Lexington: University Press of Kentucky.

Billings, D. B. (2006). Welfare and poverty. In R. Abramson & J. Haskell (Eds.), *Encyclopedia of Appalachia* (pp. 236–237). Knoxville: University of Tennessee Press.

Black, D., Daniel, K., & Sanders, S. (2002). The impact of economic conditions on disability program participation: Evidence from coal boom and bust. *American Economic Review, 92*(1), 27–50.

Black, D., McKinnish, T., & Sanders, S. (2003). Does the availability of high-wage jobs for low-skilled men affect welfare expenditures? Evidence from shocks to the coal and steel industries. *Journal of Public Economics, 87*(9–10), 1919–1940.

Brown, D. L., & Schwarzweller, H. K. (1970). The Appalachian family. In J. D. Photiadis & H. K. Schwarzweller (Eds.), *Change in rural Appalachia: Implications for action programs* (pp. 85–98). Philadelphia: University of Pennsylvania Press.

Bryant. F. C. (1981). *We're all kin: A cultural study of a mountain neighborhood.* Knoxville: University of Tennessee Press.

Burns, S. L. S., Scott, S. L., & Thompson, D. L. (2006). Family and community. In R. Abramson & J. Haskell (Eds.), *Encyclopedia of Appalachia* (pp. 149–154). Knoxville: University of Tennessee Press.

Bush, K. R., & Lash, S. B. (2006). Family relationships and gender roles. In R. Abramson & J. Haskell (Eds.), *Encyclopedia of Appalachia* (pp. 170–171). Knoxville: University of Tennessee Press.

Caudill, H. (1963). *Night comes to the Cumberlands.* Boston: Little, Brown.

Cécora, J. (1993). *Economic behavior of family households in an international context.* Bonn, Germany: Society for Agricultural Policy Research and Rural Sociology.

Collins, T., Eller, R., & Taui, G. (1996). *KRADD: Historic trends and geographic patterns.* Lexington: University of Kentucky Appalachian Center.

Couto, R. (1994). *An American challenge: A report on economic trends and social issues in Appalachia.* Dubuque, IA: Kendall/Hunt.

Cox, R. (2006). Homeplace. In R. Abramson & J. Haskell (Eds.), *Encyclopedia of Appalachia* (pp. 219–220). Knoxville: University of Tennessee Press.

Day, G. (1987). The reconstruction of Wales and Appalachia: Development and regional identity. *Contemporary Wales: An Annual Review of Economics and Social Research, 1,* 73–89.

Drake, R. B. (2003). *A history of Appalachia.* Lexington: University Press of Kentucky.

Dyk, P. H., & Wilson, S. M. (1999). Family-based social capital considerations as predictors of attainment among Appalachian youth. *Sociological Inquiry, 69*(3), 477–504.

Greenberg, M., & Savner, S. (1996). *A detailed summary of key provisions of the temporary assistance for needy families block grant H.R. 3734.* Washington, DC: Center for Law and Social Policy.

Harrington, M. (1962). *The other America.* New York: Macmillan.

Harvey, M., Summers, G. F., Pickering, K., & Richards, P. (2002). The short-term impacts of welfare reform in persistently poor rural areas. In B. A. Weber, G. J. Duncan, & L. A. Whitener (Eds.), *Rural dimensions of welfare reform.* Kalamazoo, MI: Upjohn Institute.

Haskell, J. H. (2006). In R. Abramson & J. Haskell (Eds.), *Encyclopedia of Appalachia* (pp. 216–218). Knoxville: University of Tennessee Press.

Hicks, G. L. (1992). *Appalachian valley.* Prospect Heights, IL: Waveland Press.

Howell, B. J. (2006). Tourism Section. In R. Abramson & J. Haskell (Eds.), *Encyclopedia of Appalachia.* (pp. 611-683). Knoxville: University of Tennessee Press.

Hurst, J. (2006). Business, industry, and technology. In R. Abramson & J. Haskell (Eds.), *Encyclopedia of Appalachia* (pp. 441–447). Knoxville: University of Tennessee Press.

Jones, L. (1991). Appalachian values. In B. Ergood & B. Kuhre (Eds.), *Appalachia: Social context past and present* (3rd ed., pp. 169–173). Dubuque, IA: Kendall/Hunt.

Karger, H. J., & Stoesz, D. (2005). *American Social welfare policy: A pluralist approach* (4th ed.). Boston: Pearson.

Keefe, S. E. (1992). Ethnic identity: The domain of perceptions of and attraction to ethnic groups and cultures. *Human Organization, 51,* 35–43.

Keefe, S. E., Reck, U. M. I., & Reck, G. G. (1983). Ethnicity and education in southern Appalachia: A review. *Ethnic Groups, 5,* 199–226.

Klein, H. (1995). Urban Appalachian children in Northern schools: A study in diversity. *Young Children, 50,* 10–16.

Lewis, O. (1963). *Life in a Mexican village: Tepoztlàn re-studied.* Champaign: University of Illinois Press.

Lewis, O. (1968). *La vida.* New York: Vintage Press.

Lichter, D. T., & Campbell, L. A. (2005, April). *Changing patterns of poverty and spatial inequality in Appalachia.* Retrieved October 21, 2006, from http://www.arc.gov/index.do?nodeId=2920#3

Lohmann, R. R. (1990). Four perspectives on Appalachian culture and poverty. *Journal of the Appalachian Studies Association, 2,* 76–88.

Mather, M. (2004). *Demographic and socioeconomic change in Appalachia: Households and families in Appalachia.* Report prepared by the Population Reference Bureau for the Appalachian Regional Commission (ARC). Washington, DC.

Miewald, C. (2003). Making experience count in policy creation: Lessons from Appalachian Kentucky. *Journal of Poverty, 7,* 163–181.

Owens, W. T. (2000). Country roads, hollers, coal towns, and much more. *Social Studies, 91*(4), 178–186.

Robertson, E. B., & Shoffner, S. M. (1989). Life satisfaction of young adults reared in low-income Appalachian families. *Lifestyles: Family and Economic Issues, 10,* 5–17.

Rosenberg, N. V. (1979). Regional stereotype and folklore: Appalachian and Atlantic Canada. *Appalachian Journal, 7,* 46–50.

Rural and Appalachian Youth and Family Consortium. (1996). Parenting practices and interventions among marginalized families in Appalachia. *Family Relations, 45,* 387–396.

Saranoff, S. (2003). Central Appalachia—Still the other America. *Journal of Poverty, 7,* 123–139.

Schwarzweller, H. (1970). Social change and the individual in rural Appalachia. In J. D. Photiadis & H. K. Schwarzweller (Eds.), *Change in rural Appalachia: Implications for action programs* (pp. 51–68). Philadelphia: University of Pennsylvania Press.

Stephenson, J. B. (1968). *Shiloh: A mountain community.* Lexington: University Press of Kentucky.

Weller, J. (1965). *Yesterday's people: Life in contemporary Appalachia.* Lexington: University Press of Kentucky.

Wilson S. M. (2002, July). *Child well-being in Appalachia. Report to the Appalachian Regional Commission on alternative definitions of child poverty.* Lexington, KY: Research Center for Families and Children.

Wilson, S. M., Henry, C. S., & Peterson, G. W. (1997). Life satisfaction among low-income, rural youth from Appalachia. *Journal of Adolescence, 20*(4), 443–459.

Wilson, S. M., & Peterson, G. W. (2000). The experience of growing up in Appalachia: Cultural and economic influences on adolescent development. In R. Montemayor, G. R. Adams, & T. P. Gullota (Eds.), *Advances in adolescent development: Vol. 9. Adolescent experiences: Cultural and economic diversity in adolescent development* (pp. 75–109). Thousand Oaks, CA: Sage.

Wilson, S. M., Peterson, G. W., & Wilson, P. (1993). The process of educational and occupational attainment of adolescent girls from low-income, rural families. *Journal of Marriage and the Family, 55*(11), 158–175.

# CHAPTER 8

# Poverty and Economic Polarization Among Children in Racial Minority and Immigrant Families

DANIEL T. LICHTER, ZHENCHAO QIAN,
AND MARTHA L. CROWLEY

Recent trends in child poverty and inequality can only be fully understood in light of America's growing racial and ethnic diversity, fueled largely by the massive new immigration from Latin America and Asia. Indeed, the racial and ethnic fabric of the United States changed substantially during the last half of the 20th century. In 1950, for example, the U.S. Census Bureau reported that 134 million, or nearly 90% of America's 151 million people, were white.[1] Blacks accounted for significantly more than 90% of the remaining nonwhite population (Gibson & Jung, 2002). Questions about race and inequality were considered almost exclusively in terms of black and white. The situation had changed considerably by the turn of the 21st century. Today, whites represent only 75% of America's population. Hispanics are now America's largest racial or ethnic minority—at 12.5%—whereas the black population has remained relatively constant at 10% to

12% since 1950.[2] A diverse Asian population accounts for about 4% of the U.S. population and comprises many different nationalities (Barnes & Bennett, 2002; Grieco & Cassady, 2001). Increasingly, minority population shares are especially apparent among children. Overall, in 2000, nearly two of five children were members of racial/ethnic minority groups or immigrant families (Hernandez, 2004).

Growing diversity raises the need to better monitor the changing economic incorporation of minority children, including immigrants, into American society. Recent trends among children also raise important new questions about racial stratification and persistent inequality in America's future. Unfortunately, one study after another has shown that poor children have a high probability of becoming poor adults because poverty is reproduced from one generation to the next (Gottschalk, 1997; Lichter, 1997). Racial and ethnic minorities also will represent a growing share of the population relative to America's aging white population. Thus, high rates of child poverty today, especially among the children of racial minorities and immigrants, may provide a portent of America's future—one characterized by growing racial and economic inequality.[3] It is more important than ever to evaluate the changing economic circumstances of America's increasingly diverse population of children. Such is our purpose.

In this chapter, we have two primary goals. First, we document changes in child poverty rates between 1990 and 2000 for different racial and ethnic groups. Like other studies (Lichter & Landale, 1995; Manning & Brown, 2006), we emphasize the role of family structure, including the rise in cohabitation, and increasing maternal employment in shaping children's economic circumstances. But we also highlight the new patterns of racial and ethnic variation in children's recent experiences. Second, unlike most previous studies, we evaluate children's changing location in the family income distribution (see Lichter & Eggebeen, 1993). Specifically, is there a growing gap between rich and poor children, and has this gap been reinforced by growing racial diversity and immigration over the past decade? These dual objectives are addressed using data from the 5% samples of 1990 and 2000 Public Use Microdata Samples from the U.S. Decennial Censuses.

## CHILD POVERTY AND RACIAL INEQUALITY

According to Bianchi (1999), poverty in America has become increasingly "juvenilized" during the past three decades. In the 1960s, child poverty rates were only about three-fifths as high as poverty rates among the elderly, but they were more than 80% higher in the early 1990s.[4] The economic roller coaster of the 1990s and early 2000s has also ushered in a new period of uncertainty in the family and economic lives of America's children (Lichter & Qian, 2004; Thomas & Sawhill, 2005). Poverty rates among children residing in the United States peaked during the 1993 recession, but subsequently declined by the end of the 1990s to their lowest levels (17.1%) in 20 years (U.S. Census Bureau, 2007a). Although this is welcome news, these national changes reflect the balance of poverty trends across a variety of population subgroups, including children in America's minority and immigrant families (Lichter & Crowley, 2004; Van Hook, Brown, & Kwenda, 2004). As such, they may conceal divergence among subgroups of children, some of which may not have benefited from the economic largesse of the 1990s.

Effective public policy aimed at reducing child poverty depends on improving our understanding of the forces underlying recent trends and racial differentials in child poverty. An Urban Institute report claimed that the 1996 welfare reform bill would doom an additional 1 million children to poverty (Zedlewski, Clark, Meier, & Watson, 1996). Clearly, these early forecasts have not materialized. Even the most prescient observers could not have anticipated the swift increase in employment rates among single mothers, from 60% in 1994 to 72% in 1999 (Moffitt, 2002). Recent estimates suggest that rising maternal employment, which some experts attribute to state "work first" welfare programs, may have accounted for as much as 50% of the post-1996 decline in poverty among children living in female-headed families (Lichter & Crowley, 2004). A burgeoning economy also played a large role. For example, Iceland (2003) and Gunderson and Ziliak (2004) showed that macroeconomic growth was strongly linked to declines in poverty during the 1990s. On the whole, it seems that economic growth, including rising maternal employment, has played a large role in shaping children's shifting economic circumstances.[5]

Changing family structure and child poverty have been inextricably linked during the past 40 years. In the 1960s, for example, most poor children lived with two parents who were married. By the end of the 1990s, 57% of poor children lived in female-headed families (U.S. Census Bureau, 2007b). Eggebeen and Lichter (1991) showed that about one-half of the rise in child poverty during the 1980s was caused by shifts in the child population from married-couple families to "high risk" female-headed families (cf. Cancian & Reed, 2002; Lerman, 1996; Thomas & Sawhill, 2002). The good news is that changes in family structure slowed significantly in the 1990s and were no longer associated with increases in poverty, even among children (Iceland, 2003; Lichter & Crowley, 2004). One policy implication is that any further reductions in child poverty may require more government, community, and faith-based efforts to promote marriage and strengthen fragile families. Indeed, the current Republican administration, through the Administration for Children and Families (ACF), has sponsored a "Healthy Marriage Initiative" that aims to stem unwed childbearing and help sustain healthy marital relationships, mostly through marriage education (e.g., relationship skills training) and counseling.

The negative economic implications of single parenthood and positive implications of maternal work in the 1990s for children's economic well-being have been unmistakable. Whether these patterns are also found among various racial and ethnic minorities or immigrant groups, however, is less clear. Despite declines in child poverty in the 1990s, large racial and ethnic differences persist while racial diversity in America has rapidly grown (Lichter, Qian, & Crowley, 2005; Manning & Brown, 2006). The children of minority and immigrant families have been affected in uncertain ways by long-term increases in maternal employment and family change. For example, the late 1990s brought especially large employment increases among African American single mothers, apparently in response to work-based welfare reform (Moffitt, 2002). On the other hand, inequality between blacks and whites, as measured by differences in child poverty, has been exacerbated over recent decades by growing racial differences in family structure (Eggebeen & Lichter, 1991). Unlike the situation for American-born blacks, differences in family structure accounted for only a small part of large Hispanic-white difference in child poverty during the 1980s. For Hispanic children, and especially Mexican-origin children, a large part of the poverty gap stems from differences in maternal employment (i.e., Hispanic mothers have lower employment rates).

Far less is known about the demographic and economic foundations of changing poverty rates among children in immigrant families, or immigrant-native differences (Crowley, Lichter, & Qian, 2006; Jensen & Chitose, 1994). A recent study by Hernandez (2004) showed that the poverty rate for immigrants was 50% higher in 1999 than was poverty among the native-born (21% vs. 14%). However, poverty rates among first- and second-generation immigrants declined slightly in the 1990s, after doubling (from 11.6% to 22.2%) during the preceding two decades (Van Hook et al., 2004). This study also reported that roughly one-half of the increase in immigrant poverty between 1969 and 1999 was attributable to changing economic conditions (as measured by parental work patterns). Child poverty rates in 1999 varied from a low of 9.5% among non-Hispanic whites to 32.9% among Mexicans. In 2000, the poverty rate for immigrants who entered the United States before 1970 was 8.3%. Rates for those arriving in the 1970s, 1980s, and 1990s were 11.5%, 15.2%, and 23.5%, respectively (Lichter & Crowley,

2002). These differences in poverty reflect the fact that recently arrived immigrants tend to be of childbearing age, are poorly educated, have fewer English language skills, and often lack the job skills necessary to avoid poverty. Measured poverty may veil even greater economic hardship if unsuccessful immigrants have returned to their countries of origin.

The typically positive interpretation given to widespread declines in child poverty during the 1990s, however, must be interpreted in light of America's rising overall standard of living (Eggebeen & Lichter, 1991; Rainwater & Smeeding, 2004). By definition, poverty income thresholds, if measured in constant dollars, have remained essentially unchanged since they were first introduced in the mid-1960s. Median family income, on the other hand, has increased substantially. Consequently, if compared with the national standard of living, the poor have fallen more deeply into poverty as the gap between average incomes of America's poor people and its middle-class and affluent people has grown (Iceland, 2003). In 1966, for example, the average income of the poorest one-fifth of U.S. families expressed as a ratio to mean family income was only .28. In other words, the income of poor families was 72% lower than the average U.S. family income. By 2001, the income of the poorest segment of the population was 79% lower. During that time, the mean income of the richest one-fifth of U.S. families rose dramatically in relation to the average family income—their income was 103% higher in 1966, and 139% higher in 2001 (see historical income figures in U.S. Census Bureau, 2007c, 2007d).

As the incomes of America's wealthiest families have burgeoned and average family incomes have grown, the U.S. government's poverty income thresholds have not kept pace. In 1980, for example, the median family income was 2.5 times greater than the poverty income threshold for a family of four. By 2001, this figure had climbed to 2.8,

indicating that the increases in absolute poverty thresholds have lagged behind the growth in family income during the past two decades.

One implication is that America's children may be on two different tracks into adulthood (e.g., Lichter & Eggebeen, 1993; McLanahan, 2004). One track is made up of poor and economically disadvantaged children living with single or divorced mothers or in two-parent working families struggling to make ends meet in a changing global economy. Many historically disadvantaged racial minorities and the "new" immigrant children fall into this population. A second track—so-called "cornucopia kids"—are living with two highly educated working parents. A disproportionately large majority of such children are white. Rising income inequality suggests that the economic trajectories of children on these two tracks may be diverging, despite widespread declines in child poverty during the late 1990s. Our primary goal is to document racial differentials in child poverty, while evaluating the potentially divergent economic paths among America's racial and ethnic minority children, many of whom are immigrants. The key question here is not whether racial minority children and immigrants are able to escape poverty but whether they are joining the American economic mainstream.

## DATA AND MEASURES

Our analyses are based on 1990 and 2000 data from the Integrated Public Use Microdata Samples (IPUMS) drawn from the decennial censuses (Ruggles et al., 2003). Data were weighted to correct for underrepresented segments of the population, ensuring a nationally representative sample that includes minorities and immigrants.

Our sample is limited to children aged 17 and younger who are related to the head of household, or whose parent is an unmarried partner of the household head (or householder).

Children who head households or who are married to household heads are excluded from our analysis. Each child is linked to family and parental information, including information on their parents' marital or cohabiting partners. A small number of cases lacking basic demographic information for the head of household are excluded from the sample. The total sample includes 3,208,706 children in 1990 and 3,577,175 in 2000.

We also draw secondary samples for the purpose of comparing the income distributions of families with and without children. Individuals aged 12 to 59 not residing in group quarters are weighted with the person weight and aggregated to the level of the household and then the family. This sample includes 3,935,446 families in 1990 and 4,727,901 families in 2000. Children were present in 51% of families in 1990 and 46% of families in 2000.

## Measures

*Poverty and Inequality.* Children are defined as poor when they live in families with incomes below the official poverty income thresholds for families with their specific size and configuration (i.e., adults and children), as determined by the Office of Management and Budget. Family income is measured in the year before the year of enumeration. This means that poverty status for 1990 and 2000 is based on money income and poverty thresholds for 1989 and 1999, respectively.

Officially, poverty is based on income of the family, but children may be living in households in which family members and nonfamily members pool incomes (Bauman, 1999; Carlson & Danziger, 1999). This is sometimes the case for children living with a cohabiting parent and partner. Nearly one in seven children living with a single mother actually resides with a cohabiting couple, and 43% of cohabiting couples live with children (Lichter & Qian, 2004). In our analysis, we redefine unmarried partners and their co-resident children as a social family (see Manning & Brown, 2006, for similar approach). We supplement official child poverty statistics with measures of child poverty adjusted for these living arrangements. For each cohabiting couple, we combine the household head's family income with that of the unmarried partner, and then compare this income to the appropriately adjusted poverty threshold (i.e., family size is adjusted upward to include the cohabiting partner and any additional children residing with them).

*Race, Nativity Status, and Family Structure.* Race and ethnicity data were used to identify five distinct subgroups of children: non-Hispanic white, non-Hispanic black, Native American, Asian and Pacific Islander, and Hispanic. With the exception of Native Americans, immigrant children were defined as those who are immigrants themselves (i.e., first-generation immigrants) or are the children of one or two immigrant parents (i.e., second-generation immigrants). Native children who were born in the United States to two native-born parents (i.e., third-generation) or who were born abroad to native-born Americans were identified as natives (for similar approach, see Hernandez, 2004; Van Hook et al., 2004).

For the first time, individuals in the 2000 census were able to claim more than one race. We used variables detailing Hispanic origins and race combinations to classify those claiming mixed race origins. Any person claiming Hispanic origin was classified as Hispanic; and any person claiming black, but not Hispanic, origin was designated as non-Hispanic black. Those claiming mixed white race, but not black or Hispanic background, were classified as non-Hispanic white. Asian-origin and Native American individuals with no specific black, Hispanic, or white claims were labeled Asian and Native American respectively. Depending on the analyses, we also classify children as living in (a) married-couple families, (b) various types of female-headed families, and (c) cohabiting-couple families (i.e., their unmarried parents are cohabiting). Children in female-headed families are further distinguished on the basis of their mothers' employment patterns during the previous year. Women who usually worked 35 or more hours per week were considered full-time workers; women who had jobs but worked fewer than 35 hours were labeled part-time. We also identified children whose mothers were unemployed or not in the labor force.

### Analytic Strategy

The first segment of our analysis focuses on racial differentials and changes in child poverty during the 1990s, and uncovers the extent to which they reflect new patterns of maternal employment and family structure. We use methods of direct standardization, as described in the Categorical Data Analysis System (CDAS), Version 3.5 (Eliason, 2002). Child poverty rates are calculated as the number of poor children divided by the total number of children, multiplied by 100. Overall poverty rates are the weighted sums of group-specific poverty rates. The overall poverty rate, for example, is equal to race-specific poverty rates, weighted by race groups' representation in the overall population and then summed. Thus, we can determine what the overall poverty rate would be given a differently distributed population. We can calculate, for example, what the 2000 poverty rate would have been if family structure remained unchanged since 1990 by applying 1990 population compositional "weights" to 2000 group-specific poverty rates.

By computing hypothetical poverty rates absent changes in composition, and comparing them to observed changes, we can demonstrate the degree to which compositional shifts (in family structure and maternal work) affect poverty trends. Subtracting the difference between the crude and composition-standardized rates from the difference in the crude rates, then dividing the result by the difference in the crude rates, yields the proportion of the crude rate change attributable to shifts in population composition. We can determine, for example, the degree to which declines in poverty between 1990 and 2000 may be attributed to shifts in family structure.

The second element of our analysis involves evaluating income growth and the changing distribution of poverty and affluence across racial groups and various subpopulations of America's children and families. Measures of income growth and inequality are based on income-to-needs ratios and their distribution across subgroups of children. Income-to-needs ratios are calculated by dividing children's family income by their family-specific poverty income threshold. An income-to-poverty ratio of 2.5 indicates that the child lives in a family with an income 2.5 times its poverty threshold.[6] Change in children's income inequality between 1990 and 2000 is measured with the ratio of the 80th to 20th percentiles in their income-to-needs distribution.[7] This provides a measure of the gap between rich and poor children. The ratio of the 50th to 20th percentiles shows the income gap between poor children and average children (i.e., children in families with incomes at the median). These analyses allow us to track changes in inequality within and between groups.

### RESULTS

### Changes in Child Poverty, 1990 to 2000

Data in Table 8.1 highlight recent changes in child poverty rates for whites, African Americans, Native Americans, Asian Americans, and Hispanics. In the 1990s, child poverty rates declined from 17.8 to 16.1%. These declines were not uniform across racial groups.[8] Declines were modest for non-Hispanic whites compared with those of racial minority children. African American children experienced declines in poverty from 39% in 1990 to 32% in 2000, and Native Americans had similarly large declines in poverty. Any optimism implied by substantial reductions in poverty over the past decade must be balanced by the fact that these minority children still had the highest poverty rates in 2000. Asian Americans, on the other hand, had the lowest poverty rate of all racial minorities in 2000.

Our results also indicate that children of immigrant families generally had higher poverty rates than their native counterparts did. Black children are the only group in which the poverty rate was substantially higher for natives than for immigrants. Nativity differences were less dramatic among Hispanics—undoubtedly reflecting the disadvantaged socioeconomic status of the native-born rather than upward mobility of Hispanic immigrants. Moreover, with the exception of Asians, trends in child poverty during the 1990s were more advantageous for natives than for immigrants. Among blacks and Hispanics, poverty rates declined faster for natives than for immigrants, and among whites, immigrant poverty rates rose whereas those of natives declined. For Asian and Pacific Islanders, the child poverty rate for immigrant children declined, while it increased among the native born from 9.7% in 1990 to 10.3% in 2000.

*Family Structure and Changes in Child Poverty.* Child poverty is strongly associated with family structure. Children in married-couple families are much less likely to live in poverty than are children in female-headed families. This raises an obvious question: Did declines in poverty reflect salutary changes in family structure over the 1990s?

Table 8.1 provides official and standardized child poverty rates for 2000. Standardized rates assume that children were distributed across family types in 2000 as they were in 1990. In other words, we imagine what poverty rates might look like had family structure not changed during the 1990s (i.e., the same shares of children lived with married couples, cohabiting couples, single male-headed families, single ever-married female-headed families, and never-married female-headed families). The results indicate that child poverty would have declined from 17.8% in 1990 (column 1) to about 15% in 2000 (column 3) in the absence of changes in children's living arrangements. The observed decline in child poverty during the 1990s was smaller. Similar patterns are observed for all racial groups except for Asian immigrants when we standardize by 1990 race-specific family patterns. Thus, for the decade of the 1990s, changes in family structure slowed the downward trend in child poverty rates (cf. Lichter & Crowley, 2004).

Column 4 presents standardized poverty rates for 2000 using family structure of the total population of children. In other words, how would child poverty rates differ if all children were uniformly distributed across married-couple and single-parent families? The results indicate that poverty rates would be higher among whites and Asian Americans, but lower among African Americans and Native Americans. This means that whites and Asian Americans are much more likely to live in low risk married-couple families, whereas African and Native Americans tend to live in single-parent families, which typically have high poverty rates. Child poverty rates for Hispanics change little with standardization because the family structure of Hispanic children is close to the national average for all children. Notably, Hispanic children of immigrant families are more likely than are third-generation Hispanic children (i.e., those with

**Table 8.1**     Child Poverty by Race, and Poverty Standardized by Family Structure, 1990 and 2000[1]

| | 1990 | 2000 | 1990 Standard[2] | 2000 All Races Standard[3] |
|---|---|---|---|---|
| **All Races** | | | | |
| | 17.82 | 16.07 | 15.02 | 16.07 |
| **White Non-Hispanic** | | | | |
| All | 10.82 | 9.10 | 8.42 | 11.30 |
| Native | 10.88 | 8.98 | 8.25 | 11.07 |
| Immigrant | 9.76 | 10.76 | 10.49 | 14.03 |
| **Black Non-Hispanic** | | | | |
| All | 39.24 | 31.86 | 30.72 | 21.30 |
| Native | 40.53 | 33.24 | 31.68 | 21.62 |
| Immigrant | 19.47 | 19.07 | 18.62 | 17.76 |
| **Native American** | | | | |
| All | 38.05 | 30.45 | 29.19 | 26.77 |
| **Asian and Pacific Islander** | | | | |
| All | 15.83 | 14.34 | 14.05 | 17.22 |
| Native | 9.72 | 10.28 | 9.15 | 10.88 |
| Immigrant | 17.15 | 14.92 | 14.63 | 18.30 |
| **Hispanic** | | | | |
| All | 31.35 | 27.11 | 27.01 | 26.72 |
| Native | 31.03 | 25.09 | 23.71 | 20.56 |
| Immigrant | 31.65 | 28.42 | 28.30 | 30.08 |

SOURCE: U.S. Census Bureau, IPUMS 5% sample.

[1]Family structure categories: married couple, cohabiting couple, single male head, single ever-married female head, single never-married female head.
[2]2000 poverty rates standardized by within-group 1990 family structure.
[3]2000 poverty rates standardized by all children's 2000 family structure.

native-born parents) to live with two parents, which places downward pressure on poverty rates. The important point, however, is that racial differences in family structure account for some, but not all of the differences in child poverty. For example, if black children lived in married-couple families in the same proportions as whites, their poverty rates would still be nearly double those of white children.

More than ever before, evaluating poverty among children living in single-parent families is made difficult by rising shares of children who also live with a parent's cohabiting partner (Lichter & Crowley, 2004; Manning & Lichter, 1996).

Indeed, as shown in Table 8.2, our estimates suggest that the share of children living in cohabiting-couple families increased from 3.46 to 5.43% of all children between 1990 and 2000. Increases were apparent for all racial minorities, and for both natives and immigrants, during the 1990s. However, children in immigrant families are less likely than are children with native-born parents (regardless of race) to live in cohabiting-couple families. In 2000, the shares of non-Hispanic black natives, Native Americans, and native-born Hispanics in these types of families were well above the national percentage.

**Table 8.2**   Official and Adjusted Poverty Rates for Children Residing With a Cohabiting Couple, 1990–2000

| | Percent of All Children | | Children Residing With a Cohabiting Couple | | | | All Children | |
| | | | Official Percent Poor | | Adjusted Percent Poor | | Adjusted Percent Poor | |
| | 1990 | 2000 | 1990 | 2000 | 1990 | 2000 | 1990 | 2000 |
|---|---|---|---|---|---|---|---|---|
| All Races | 3.46 | 5.43 | 43.29 | 35.07 | 25.12 | 20.15 | 17.19 | 15.26 |
| White Non-Hispanic | | | | | | | | |
| All | 2.78 | 4.41 | 37.93 | 29.12 | 18.04 | 13.58 | 10.26 | 8.42 |
| Native | 2.88 | 4.59 | 38.17 | 29.27 | 18.16 | 13.55 | 10.30 | 8.26 |
| Immigrant | 1.10 | 1.89 | 27.03 | 23.82 | 12.45 | 14.32 | 9.60 | 10.58 |
| Black Non-Hispanic | | | | | | | | |
| All | 5.35 | 7.50 | 50.00 | 41.95 | 33.21 | 25.99 | 38.34 | 30.66 |
| Native | 5.41 | 7.75 | 51.06 | 42.72 | 34.02 | 26.52 | 39.61 | 31.98 |
| Immigrant | 4.45 | 5.25 | 30.33 | 31.37 | 18.00 | 18.75 | 18.92 | 18.41 |
| Native American | 8.18 | 10.78 | 62.16 | 49.65 | 45.93 | 31.88 | 36.72 | 28.53 |
| Asian and Pacific Islander | | | | | | | | |
| All | 1.17 | 2.33 | 27.85 | 30.71 | 17.05 | 18.75 | 15.70 | 14.06 |
| Native | 3.22 | 4.88 | 27.40 | 29.87 | 15.63 | 15.94 | 9.34 | 9.60 |
| Immigrant | .73 | 1.97 | 28.27 | 31.00 | 18.40 | 19.75 | 17.08 | 14.70 |
| Hispanic | | | | | | | | |
| All | 5.32 | 7.66 | 49.91 | 40.94 | 34.65 | 28.30 | 30.54 | 26.15 |
| Native | 6.41 | 9.74 | 51.04 | 39.89 | 33.34 | 23.64 | 29.89 | 23.51 |
| Immigrant | 4.28 | 6.31 | 48.30 | 41.99 | 36.50 | 32.97 | 31.15 | 27.85 |

SOURCE: U.S. Census Bureau, IPUMS 5% sample.

Table 8.2 also includes the official poverty rate for children living with cohabiting parents, and an adjusted rate (columns 5–6), based on the combined incomes of each partner compared with an adjusted poverty threshold (because of adding an additional family member and any additional children residing with them). We assume, perhaps unrealistically, that partners pool their incomes to the benefit of co-residential children. By comparing the official and adjusted poverty rates, we can derive an upper-bound estimate of reductions in measured poverty if children's cohabiting partners married. Among all children residing in cohabiting-couple households, the 2000 child poverty rate would drop from 35% to 20%.[9] Reductions are evident among all groups. At a minimum, our results suggest that the official poverty rate is overestimated as a family-based measure, and has not kept pace with children's changing living arrangements, especially the rise in the percentage of children living with cohabiting couples.

The final two columns in Table 8.2 present overall 1990 and 2000 child poverty rates when adjusted poverty substitutes for official poverty among children living in cohabiting-couple families. By comparing these adjusted rates to the overall official rates presented in Table 8.1, we observe the effects of cohabitation on national estimates of child poverty. In 2000, the adjusted poverty rate was 15.26%, compared with an observed rate 16.07% (Table 8.1). The differences were also small for each race and nativity group. The measurement effects of cohabitation on overall child poverty rates are minimal. But they became larger during the 1990s with the rise in children living in such families.

*Maternal Employment and Poverty Among Children in Female-Headed Families.* Children living in female-headed families

have much higher poverty rates than do children living in married-couple families (Lichter & Crowley, 2004). Still, even among this disadvantaged population subgroup, racial differences in child poverty remain large. As shown in Table 8.3, poverty rates among children living in female-headed single families ranged from a high of more than one-half of immigrant Hispanic children (52%) to a low of less than 28% among white children with immigrant parents in 2000. The good news is that poverty rates for all such "at risk" children declined by nearly 10 percentage points (from 49 to 40%) during the 1990s, and economic gains are evident among all race and nativity groups. Yet, with the exception of Asians, poverty rates of children residing with native-born single mothers declined much more rapidly than among children with immigrant single mothers. For example, poverty among white children with native single mothers declined from 37% in 1990 to 29% in 2000, but declined far less—from 30% to 28%—among those with immigrant single mothers. Although these recent declines are encouraging, poverty rates among children living in female-headed families remain high by almost any standard.

Recent declines in poverty among children living in female-headed families imply that family changes alone cannot explain recent declines in child poverty. Previous studies indicate that changing maternal employment may have played a large role in the changing economic fortunes of such children (Lichter, Qian, & Crowley, 2005; Manning & Brown, 2006). Column 3 of Table 8.3 shows the standardized child poverty rate in 2000 using the 1990 race-specific employment rates of single mothers as the standard. Poverty among children living with single mothers would have declined to 43% rather than 40% if there were no change in maternal employment patterns during the 1990s. In other words, the rise in maternal

**Table 8.3**    Child Poverty by Race, and Poverty Standardized by Women's Employment Among Children Residing With Single Mothers, 1990 and 2000[1]

| | *1990* | *2000* | *1990 Standard*[2] | *2000 All Races Standard*[3] |
|---|---|---|---|---|
| All Races | 49.06 | 39.83 | 42.93 | 39.83 |
| White Non-Hispanic | | | | |
| All | 37.13 | 29.10 | 31.66 | 32.44 |
| Native | 37.35 | 29.15 | 31.82 | 32.63 |
| Immigrant | 29.73 | 27.92 | 27.97 | 28.10 |
| Black Non-Hispanic | | | | |
| All | 59.92 | 47.78 | 51.62 | 45.85 |
| Native | 60.63 | 48.46 | 52.34 | 46.35 |
| Immigrant | 37.32 | 34.90 | 34.95 | 36.61 |
| Native American | | | | |
| All | 61.24 | 49.38 | 53.02 | 46.42 |
| Asian and Pacific Islander | | | | |
| All | 40.76 | 33.12 | 35.39 | 32.13 |
| Native | 34.43 | 28.34 | 30.91 | 30.04 |
| Immigrant | 43.60 | 34.71 | 37.11 | 32.84 |
| Hispanic | | | | |
| All | 59.37 | 49.30 | 52.68 | 45.89 |
| Native | 60.22 | 47.55 | 53.52 | 44.83 |
| Immigrant | 57.62 | 52.00 | 51.89 | 48.02 |

SOURCE: U.S. Census Bureau, IPUMS 5% sample.

[1]Women's employment categories: full-time (35+ hours per week), part-time (fewer than 35 hours per week), unemployed, not in the labor force.

[2]2000 poverty rates standardized by 1990 women's employment patterns in this race group and family type.

[3]2000 poverty rates standardized by 2000 women's employment patterns among all races in this family type.

employment accounted for about one-third of the observed 9-percentage-point decline in poverty for children in single-mother families ([42.93–39.83] × 100 / [49.06–39.83]). Increases in maternal employment in the 1990s seem to have lifted many "at risk" children out of poverty.

Recent employment patterns among single mothers, however, had different effects on children of different racial and ethnic groups (Table 8.3). Among white children with native-born parents, the rise in maternal employment accounted for 33% of the 8-percentage-point decline in child poverty during the 1990s. For black and Native American children living in native-born single-mother families, the rise in employment accounted for about 31 to 32% of the roughly 12-percentage-point declines in child poverty. Rising maternal employment accounted for 47% of the decline among native-born Hispanics.

Among children residing with single immigrant mothers, however, maternal employment patterns can explain little of the recent changes in poverty. For example, changing maternal work patterns explain almost none of the 2- to 3-percentage-point poverty decline among children of white and black immigrant families. And, for children in immigrant Hispanic families, declines in child poverty during the 1990s would have been greater if 1990 maternal employment patterns had continued in 2000. Although welfare reform appears to have improved some children's economic circumstances by pressuring more single mothers to enter the labor force, this has not been the case for immigrant children.

Do differences in maternal employment account for racial and ethnic differences in female-headed families' rates of child poverty? To answer this question, we calculate employment-standardized child poverty for 2000. These figures assume that maternal employment patterns among single mothers in each racial group are identical to those of all single mothers. Our results indicate that racial differences in child poverty (column 2) are not simply the result of racial differences in the work habits of children's mothers. Blacks, Native Americans, and Hispanics—regardless of nativity status—would have much higher rates of child poverty than would non-Hispanic white or Asian children, even if maternal employment rates were the same for each racial group. Other explanations must be considered (e.g., differences in wage rates caused by low education, limited opportunities, or discrimination).

To sum up, recent declines in poverty rates among children living in single-parent families have been welcome news. Still, racial differences in child poverty remain large, with nearly half of all such African American, Hispanic, and Native American children living in poverty in 2000. Two countervailing factors have shaped recent trends in poverty—family instability and maternal employment. Differentials in child poverty rates were given impetus by the racial differences in female-headed families with children. On the other hand, maternal

employment among single mothers increased rapidly in the 1990s, which provided an important hedge against child poverty for most groups considered here. However, employment differences alone cannot explain differences in poverty rates across racial or immigrant groups of children.

## Changes in Income Inequality Among America's Children

The 1990s brought declines in child poverty rates for most racial, ethnic, and immigrant groups. But a narrow focus on declining poverty rates may cause us to overlook evidence that poor children may be poorer today than in the past, or that the incomes of poor children may have increased in absolute terms but declined *relative* to rising incomes of middle-class and affluent children. In other words, did income inequality among children increase (or decrease) during the 1990s as the income gap between poor and rich children widened (or narrowed)? Has growing racial diversity reinforced income inequality during the past decade? And has the racial distribution of affluent children become "whiter" whereas the poor increasingly comprise children of racial minority and immigrant families?

*Income-to-Poverty Ratios.* We begin with simple comparisons of trends in children's family incomes over the 1990s. Table 8.4 presents income-to-needs ratios for the overall population and for each racial and nativity group. Overall, the family incomes of poor children (i.e., children at the 20th percentile) increased from 10% over (1.10 times) the poverty threshold in 1990 to 19% over (1.19 times) the threshold in 2000. Income-to-needs ratios increased from 2.50 to 2.61 among children at the median of family income (i.e., the "middle class"), and from 4.31 to 4.74 among children at the top of the income distribution.

Evidence of whether income inequality increased in the 1990s is reflected in the ratio of the family income at the 80th percentile to the family income at the 20th percentile (last two columns, Table 8.4; see Danziger & Gottschalk, 2004, for similar approach). A higher ratio indicates greater income inequality. The ratio of income of affluent to poor children increased only slightly in the 1990s, from 3.92 to 3.98. In other words, affluent children have roughly 4 times as much family income as poor children. Based on this measure, there is little indication of large increases in income inequality among children in the 1990s.[10]

Our examination of racial and nativity differences in income and income inequality suggests at least three main conclusions. First, and perhaps most significant, the average family incomes of children at the bottom of the income distribution increased during the 1990s for each of the racial and immigrant groups considered here. Quite simply, the poor did not become absolutely poorer during the 1990s; indeed, their incomes grew. At the same time, income growth was also apparent at the 50th and 80th percentile for these groups of children, which raises questions concerning differentials in income growth across the income distribution (an issue to which we will return).

Second, racial and nativity differences in family income remain very large at each location in the income distribution. For example, for non-Hispanic white children at the 20th income percentile, their family income was 66% higher than the poverty income threshold. Among their non-Hispanic black counterparts, incomes were 39% *lower* than the poverty threshold. Clearly, America's poorest African American children are much poorer than America's poorest white children. Poor children of immigrant families (for each racial group except blacks) are poorer than poor children with native-born parents. At the other end of the income distribution, affluent white and Asian children, not surprisingly, had much higher incomes than the most affluent black, Native American, or Hispanic natives or immigrants (column 6, Table 8.4).

Third, for historically disadvantaged children, such as blacks, Native Americans, and Hispanics, income inequality decreased in the 1990s (except for black immigrants). This is indicated by the increasing ratio of the race-specific median incomes to the overall U.S. median income (columns 7–8). This also is indicated by the declining ratios of incomes at the 80th to the 20th percentiles. For example, among non-Hispanic blacks, the group with the highest income inequality, the incomes of affluent children were 6.6 times higher than the incomes of poor children (at the 20th percentile) in 1990. However, this figure declined to 5.4 by 2000. The decline reflects faster income growth (on a percentage basis) at the bottom than at the top of the income distribution for racial minority children. For these minority children, declines in child poverty during the 1990s were accompanied by the growth of income among poor children and declines in income inequality. This appears to be a significant departure from the results of past studies based on pre-1990 data (e.g., Lichter & Eggebeen, 1993).

*Distribution of Poverty and Affluence.* We have described income growth among poor, middle-class, and affluent children and changing inequality among racial and immigrant groups. But any interpretation of income growth must also consider the changing percentages of children in particular income classes. Indeed, it may be the case that more poor children are deeply impoverished today, or that poor children who escape poverty remain in families with modest incomes (i.e., the "near poor"). Any optimism implied by increases in income among poor children must be tempered if the percentage of poor and near poor increased during the past decade. A similarly less

**Table 8.4**  Ratios of Income-to-Needs Ratios: Group Median to Total Median and 80th Percentile to 20th Percentile, 1990 and 2000

| | Income-to-Needs Ratios | | | | | | Ratios of Income-to-Needs Ratios | | | |
| | 20th Percentile | | Median | | 80th Percentile | | Group Median to Total Median | | 80th Percentile to 20th Percentile | |
| | 1990 | 2000 | 1990 | 2000 | 1990 | 2000 | 1990 | 2000 | 1990 | 2000 |
|---|---|---|---|---|---|---|---|---|---|---|
| Total Population | 1.10 | 1.19 | 2.50 | 2.61 | 4.31 | 4.74 | 1.00 | 1.00 | 3.92 | 3.98 |
| White Non-Hispanic | 1.53 | 1.66 | 2.87 | 3.15 | 4.71 | 5.39 | 1.15 | 1.21 | 3.08 | 3.25 |
| Native | 1.52 | 1.67 | 2.86 | 3.14 | 4.67 | 5.35 | 1.14 | 1.20 | 3.07 | 3.20 |
| Immigrant | 1.69 | 1.59 | 3.20 | 3.32 | 5.46 | 6.16 | 1.28 | 1.27 | 3.23 | 3.87 |
| Black Non-Hispanic | .45 | .61 | 1.40 | 1.64 | 2.97 | 3.31 | .56 | .63 | 6.60 | 5.43 |
| Native | .43 | .59 | 1.34 | 1.57 | 2.91 | 3.22 | .54 | .60 | 6.77 | 5.46 |
| Immigrant | 1.01 | 1.05 | 2.16 | 2.25 | 3.82 | 4.03 | .86 | .86 | 3.78 | 3.84 |
| Native American | .53 | .67 | 1.37 | 1.60 | 2.77 | 3.11 | .55 | .61 | 5.23 | 4.64 |
| Asian and Pacific Islander | 1.21 | 1.30 | 2.81 | 2.95 | 5.08 | 5.62 | 1.12 | 1.13 | 4.20 | 4.32 |
| Native | 1.76 | 1.72 | 3.41 | 3.64 | 5.61 | 6.40 | 1.36 | 1.39 | 3.19 | 3.72 |
| Immigrant | 1.14 | 1.26 | 2.68 | 2.85 | 4.93 | 5.46 | 1.07 | 1.09 | 4.32 | 4.33 |
| Hispanic (Any Race) | .68 | .79 | 1.57 | 1.66 | 3.00 | 3.11 | .63 | .64 | 4.41 | 3.94 |
| Native | .64 | .81 | 1.73 | 1.94 | 3.34 | 3.69 | .69 | .74 | 5.22 | 4.56 |
| Immigrant | .72 | .78 | 1.45 | 1.54 | 2.66 | 2.73 | .58 | .59 | 3.69 | 3.50 |

SOURCE: U.S. Census Bureau, IPUMS 5% sample.

sanguine interpretation is required of income gains among the middle class or affluent if the percentage of middle-class or affluent children declined during the 1990s.

In this section, we calculate the percentage of children in *deep poverty*, which includes children in families with incomes less than one-half their poverty income threshold. *Marginal poverty* includes children with family incomes that are at least one-half, but less than 100% of their poverty threshold. Children in nonpoor families with incomes less than double their poverty threshold are included in the *near poverty* category. Children with family incomes at least four times their poverty threshold are considered *affluent* for our purposes. *Middle-class* children fall between the near poor and affluent, with family incomes that are at least double, but less than four times their family's poverty income threshold.

Overall, the percentage of children living in *deep poverty* declined from 8.3% in 1990 to 6.9% in 2000 (Figure 8.1). However, the percentage in *marginal poverty* or *near poverty* remained largely unchanged in the 1990s. The implication is significant: Overall declines in child poverty during the 1990s apparently reflected mostly the declining percentage of the most impoverished children. At the same time, the middle-class share declined slightly, chiefly because of increases in the share of affluent children.

Racial and nativity comparisons reveal some interesting facts. First, the percentage of children living in *deep poverty* generally declined in the 1990s, especially among African American children. Second, the percentage of children in near poverty increased for all groups except for native-born white, immigrant black, and immigrant Asian children. One implication is that increases may reflect declines in poverty as the poor have moved to the *near-poor* category. Third, among the most disadvantaged groups, including blacks, Native Americans, and Hispanics, the

poor and near poor outnumber the middle class and affluent. In 2000, 65% of Hispanic immigrants, and 60% of black natives and Native Americans, were poor or near poor, and 35 and 40 percent, respectively, were middle class or affluent. Fourth, the percentage of children living in *affluence* increased among every race/ethnic and nativity category. Not only did the income of the affluent increase, but also the share of affluent children increased. Fifth, among Hispanics and Asians, children in immigrant families had lower rates of affluence, but black and white immigrants had higher rates of affluence than their native counterparts. Among Hispanic immigrants, for example, only 8% were affluent in 2000—the smallest share of any race and nativity combination. Native-born Asians, on the other hand, had the highest rates of affluence—45% in 2000. These racial and immigrant differences in poverty and affluence clearly reveal inequality among American children.

Not surprisingly, these large racial and nativity differences in economic well-being reveal themselves in striking differences in the racial composition of the deeply poor, marginally poor, near-poor, middle-class, and affluent child populations. Figure 8.2 reveals that in 2000 the majority (more than two-thirds) of deeply poor children were racial minorities. Moreover, the small decline during the 1990s in the percentage of deeply poor children who were white or black was offset by increases in the percentage of Hispanic. By contrast, only 20% of affluent children in 2000 were racial minorities—with roughly equal shares of Asians, Hispanics, and blacks.

Figure 8.3 presents the changes in the percentage of children in female-headed families across the five income classes. The most striking finding is that most children in female-headed families—nearly 70%—are included in either deep poverty, marginal poverty, or near poverty. Although the share of these children in middle-class or affluent families increased in the 1990s, they nevertheless represent a very small proportion of such children. A similar conclusion applies to most of the groups considered here. Among native black, immigrant Hispanic, and Native American children, only a small fraction (about 20%) is middle class or affluent.

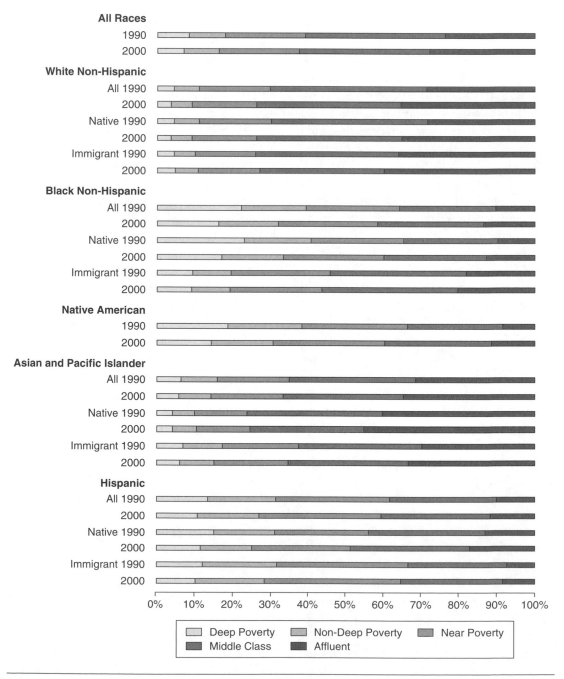

**Figure 8.1**   Child Poverty and Affluence by Race, All Families, 1990 and 2000

SOURCE: U.S. Census Bureau, IPUMs 5% sample.

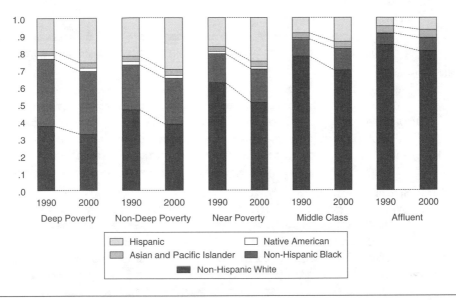

**Figure 8.2**     Race Distributions of Poverty and Affluence Groups, 1990 and 2000

Moreover, declines in deep and marginal poverty typically were offset by increases in the share of children who were near poor. Indeed, the near-poor category increased its population share by an amount equal to 41% of the decline in the share of poor children. The implication, of course, is that much of the decline in child poverty among female-headed families reflects shifts to near poverty rather than significant shifts to the middle class. Population shifts out of the near-poor category into the middle class likely deflate the true degree to which entry into the near-poor category offsets declines in poverty. In sum, many children in single-mother families moved out of poverty during the 1990s but few moved into the middle class. Indeed, most of these children remain economically disadvantaged but are not acknowledged as such in official government poverty statistics.

## Changes in Family Poverty and Affluence

We have focused our attention on racial and immigrant differences in poverty among children with different living arrangements. But how have families with children compared with those headed by similarly aged householders without children? Has the gap in economic well-being expanded during the 1990s as the proportion of families remaining childless has grown? We address these questions with 1990 and 2000 data on poverty for families with children (Figure 8.4) and without children (Figure 8.5).[11]

Overall, families without children were more likely than were families with children to be at the extremes of the income distribution. For example, a higher and growing percentage of families without children lived in deep poverty (8.1% in 1990 and 9.6% in 2000). For families with children, the comparable percentages of deep poverty were roughly one-half as large and declining—5.9% in 1990 and 5.2% in 2000. Roughly 40% of families without children were affluent both in 1990 and 2000. The percent of affluent families with children was lower but increased from 33% to 35% during the 1990s.

Similar patterns of inequality between families with and without children were apparent across racial groups.[12] That is, a larger

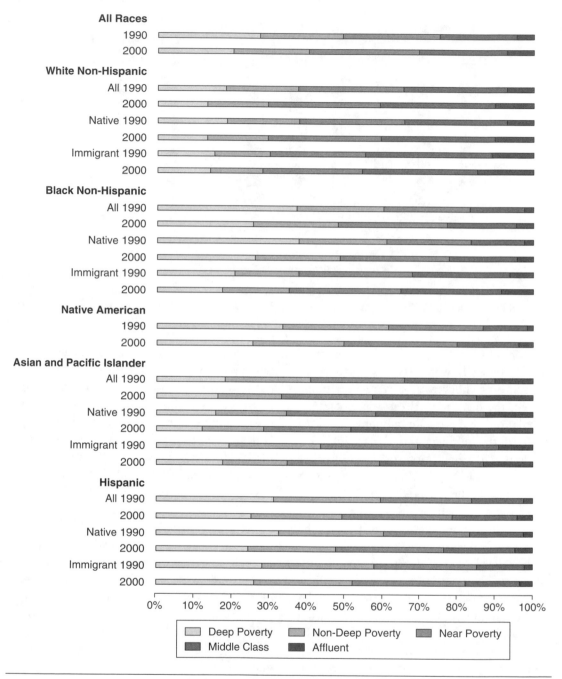

**Figure 8.3**    Child Poverty and Affluence by Race, All Female-Headed Families, 1990 and 2000

SOURCE: U.S. Census Bureau, IPUMs 5% sample.

share of families without children lived in deep poverty and in affluence. The one exception is Asian American families—the percent affluent is higher among Asian families with children than among their childless counterparts. In fact, more than one-half of native Asian American families with children were affluent, a percentage exceeding even that of whites. Racial differences in poverty also tend to be smaller when families rather than children are

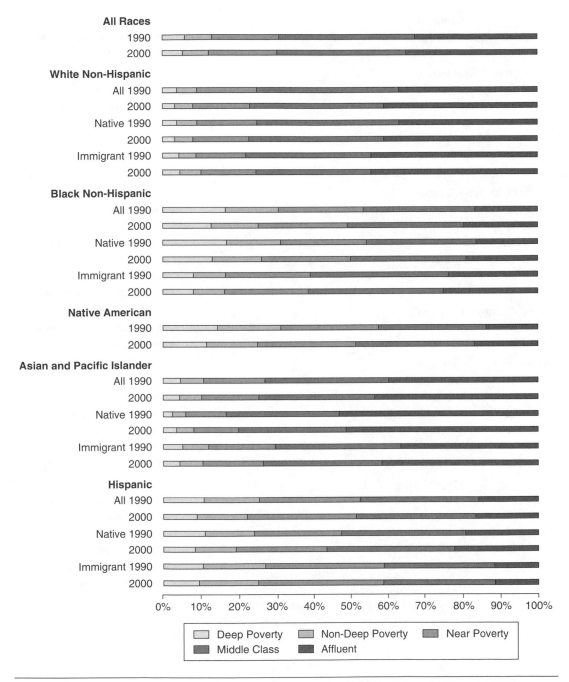

**Figure 8.4** Family Poverty and Affluence by Race, Families With Children, 1990 and 2000

SOURCE: U.S. Census Bureau, IPUMs 5% sample.

the unit of analysis (cf., Figures 8.1 and 8.4). This is attributable partly to family size and composition differences among families of different races and socioeconomic statuses. Analyses of families give equal weight to each family whereas analyses of children weigh families by family size, which is positively associated with poverty.[13]

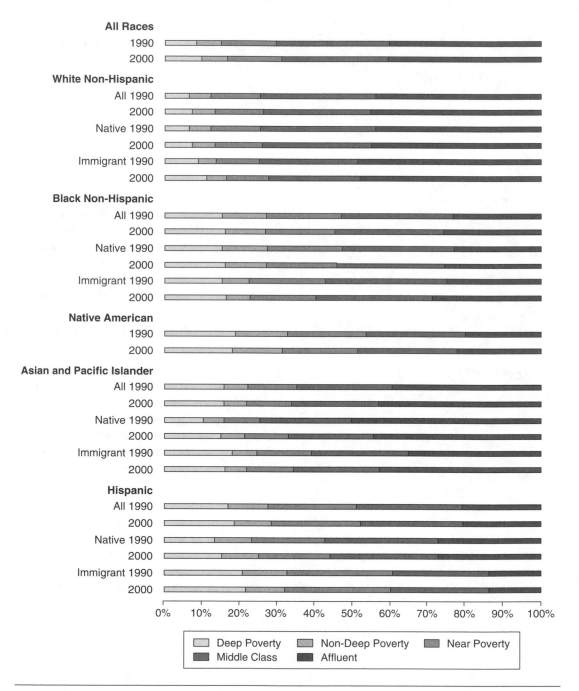

**Figure 8.5**    Family Poverty and Affluence by Race, Families Without Children, 1990 and 2000

SOURCE: U.S. Census Bureau, IPUMs 5% sample.

## DISCUSSION AND CONCLUSION

The 1990s ushered in a new period of growing racial and ethnic diversity in the United States. More than ever before, recent trends also have highlighted the need to better evaluate new patterns of economic incorporation of America's historically disadvantaged children of racial minority and immigrant families. As we have argued here, the current economic circumstances of America's minority children provide a window to the future of racial stratification and inequality. Our primary objective therefore has been to track trends in child poverty and income inequality among diverse minority groups over the 1990s. The 1990 and 2000 5% Public Use Microdata Samples provide samples of children of sufficient size and racial diversity to achieve this objective.

At the national level, our results indicate that the 1990s were a period of widespread declines in poverty among America's children. Each of the racial and ethnic groups considered here appears to have benefited from economic and employment growth during the 1990s. Indeed, our results suggest that increasing maternal employment rather than changing family structure accounted for the largest share of the recent declines in child poverty. Unlike the pre-1990 period, when children's living arrangements shifted them away from married-couple families to high-risk single-parent families, the 1990s brought little change in children's living arrangements (Lichter & Crowley, 2004; Iceland, 2003). Changing family structure is no longer giving demographic impetus to increasing poverty among children. Rather, the rise in maternal employment, especially among single mothers, has placed considerable downward pressure on child poverty rates nationally and across the population subgroups of minority children and children of immigrant families considered here (cf., Lichter & Crowley, 2004).[14]

We began with the assumption that national trends in child poverty could mask tremendous racial and ethnic diversity in children's economic circumstances. Our results, not surprisingly, do not lend themselves to simple conclusions. On the one hand, maternal employment played a large role in accounting for declines in child poverty among minority children. On the other hand, high rates of poverty among children of minority and immigrant families

cannot be explained away by existing differences in employment rates or work patterns among children's mothers. Conversely, although changes in family structure cannot fully explain trends in child poverty across population subgroups, racial differences in family structure continue to account for a significant portion of observed differences in child poverty across minority groups. Our results confirm the view that racial inequality among children cannot be discussed in isolation from the currently large group differences in out-of-wedlock childbearing, marriage, and divorce.[15]

At the same time, any analysis of trends and differentials in child poverty, if considered alone, may give a rather incomplete or even misleading picture of children's changing economic circumstances. Significantly, our results indicate that family incomes of America's poorest children, regardless of racial or ethnic background, increased during the 1990s at the same time poverty rates declined. Rates of deep poverty (i.e., below one-half of the poverty income threshold) also declined among children and families with children. Moreover, the growth in income inequality among children (e.g., Lichter & Eggebeen, 1993) apparently slowed significantly during the 1990s. These results provide a different picture than portrayed recently by McLanahan (2004), who suggested that the economic trajectories and resources of rich and poor children are now diverging. As we reported here, the family-size-adjusted incomes of the poorest children for most racial and ethnic groups increased at a similar or faster pace over the past decade than did the incomes of "average" or wealthy children (see Table 8.3). Yet, by definition, the absolute dollar gap in income between America's poor and affluent children increased during the 1990s.

Whether trends and racial differences in poverty and income during the 1990s should be viewed largely with optimism or pessimism is a matter of personal judgment or emphasis. There can be no disagreement, however, that racial and nativity differences in economic well-being remain large in the United States. And few observers will disagree that any progress toward racial inequality has been slow, or that continuing high rates of child poverty today will reinforce existing patterns of racial inequality in the future. Only by severing the link between childhood and adult poverty (e.g., through better education, a secure safety net, or economic opportunity) will America's future take a different or faster route toward racial economic equality.

## NOTES

1. Among the white population, only a small share was of Hispanic origin. Although data on Hispanic origin are not available from the 1950 census, the 1940 census indicated that 116 million of the 118 million white people were non-Hispanic in origin (Gibson & Jung, 2002). The heavy influx of Hispanics from Mexico and other Latin American countries did not begin until the 1960s.

2. The 2000 census indicates that nearly 35 million blacks lived in the United States, or roughly 12.3% of the total population (Grieco & Cassady, 2001).

3. Previous studies have demonstrated that childhood poverty compromises development trajectories, academic achievement, and social mobility. See Duncan and Brooks-Gunn's (1997) compendium of studies on the consequences of poverty for children's development.

4. Using data from the Current Population Survey and the Survey of Income and Program Participation, Iceland, Short, Garner, and Johnson (2001) found that child poverty rates continued to surpass those of other age groups, but that the gap between child and adult poverty rates is smaller when income calculations include noncash government benefits and the Earned Income Tax Credit.

5. From 1949 to 1969, Gottschalk and Danziger (1993) demonstrated that the large decline in poverty (–25.7 percentage points) were entirely attributable to changes in the economy. The subsequent period, from 1973 to 1991, showed little relationship between economic change and poverty.

6. We assume that the poverty income threshold for any given child represents need. Significantly, the income-to-poverty ratio also adjusts for family size and configuration—increasing with family size to reflect increased need and economies of scale.

7. The IPUMS family income-to-needs ratio is top coded at 5.01. Calculating 80th percentiles required us to replace top-coded values with our own income-to-needs computations, based on information about family income, size, and configuration.

8. Some additional analyses revealed that the child poverty rate would have declined to 14.9% (rather than 16.1%) during the 1990s if the racial/ethnic composition of the child population had remained unchanged after 1990. America's changing racial composition has put upward demographic pressure on child poverty rates. At the same time, the effects of changing immigrant composition on child poverty were modest. In the absence of changes between 1990 and 2000 in the share of first-, second-, and third-generation children, the child poverty rate in 1990 would have been 15.7% (rather than 16.1%).

9. Similar results are reported in a recent study by Manning and Brown (2006). They showed that the poverty rate was 7.6% for children living in married-couple families with both biological parents. For children living with cohabiting parents, the rates were 19.0 and 23.0%, respectively, for children living with both

biological parents or living with a biological parent and unrelated partner. Their analyses were based on the 1999 National Survey of American Families.

10. Conclusions about changing income inequality may be different if we compared other income percentiles, such as the 10th percentile to the 90th percentile. Blanket conclusions about changes in inequality based on these ratios are inappropriate. Income ratios and income differences among children at different locations in the income distribution may yield different interpretations. Our ratio measure in Table 8.3 indicates little change in income inequality during the 1990s. Absolute differences in income-to-poverty ratios of the poor and affluent, however, indicate large increases in inequality.

11. To be comparable, our sample of families without children includes only those in which the householder is 59 years old or younger.

12. Our secondary family samples were also classified by race. We categorized each family member's race as we did for children. But because children's race is often consistent with the mother's racial identification, we placed priority on adult females' race. For consistency, we did the same for families without children. In aggregating the sample, we selected the racial classification for the first-encountered adult female, adult male, female child, and male child, and our final family racial classification placed priority on racial identity in this order. If an adult female was present, our family race label reflects that person's race (or the race of the first adult female encountered in that family). If no adult female was present, our race variable reflects the first adult male encountered, and so on.

13. For example, a poor single mother with three children yields one poor family but three poor children.

14. Our analysis probably underestimates the effect of employment. It does not take into account the benefits of expansions in the Earned Income Tax Credit.

15. It is important to remember that eliminating racial and ethnic disparities in work and family will not completely end racial and ethnic economic inequality. These two factors are only part of the explanation and, as such, we must continue to look for additional explanations (e.g., low pay, discrimination).

---

# REFERENCES

Barnes, J. S., & Bennett, C. E. (2002). *The Asian population, 2000.* Census 2000 Brief 01–16. Washington, DC: U.S. Census Bureau.

Bauman, K. J. (1999). Shifting family definitions: The effect of cohabitation and other nonfamily household relationships on measures of poverty. *Demography, 36,* 315–325.

Bianchi, S. M. (1999). Feminization and juvenilization of poverty: Trends, relative risks, causes, and consequences. *Annual Review of Sociology, 25,* 307–333.

Cancian, M., & Reed, D. (2002). Changes in family structure: Implications for poverty and related policy. In S. Danziger & R. Haveman (Eds.), *Understanding poverty* (pp. 69–96). New York: Harvard University Press and Russell Sage.

Carlson, M., & Danziger, S. (1999). Cohabitation and the measurement of child poverty. *Review of Income and Wealth, 45,* 179–191.

Crowley, M., Lichter, D. T., & Qian, Z. C. (2006). Beyond gateway cities: Economic restructuring and poverty among Mexican immigrant families and children. *Family Relations, 55*(3), 345–360.

Danziger, S., & Gottschalk, P. (2004). *Diverging fortunes: Trends in poverty and inequality.* The America People Series. Washington, DC: Population Reference Bureau and Russell Sage.

Duncan, G. J., & Brooks-Gunn, J. (Eds.). (1997). *Consequences of growing up poor.* New York: Russell Sage.

Eggebeen, D. J., & Lichter, D. T. (1991). Race, family structure, and changing poverty among American children. *American Sociological Review, 56,* 801–817.

Eliason, S. (2002). *The categorical data analysis system.* Retrieved from http://www.soc.umn.edu/~eliason/CDAS.htm

Gibson, C., & Jung, K. (2002). *Historical census statistics on population totals by race, 1790 to 1990, and by Hispanic origin, 1970 to 1990, for the United States, regions, divisions, and states.* Working Paper No. 56. Washington, DC: U.S. Census Bureau.

Gottschalk, P. (1997). Is the correlation in welfare participation across generations spurious? *Journal of Public Economics, 63,* 1–25.

Gottschalk, P., & Danziger, S. (1993). Family structure, family size, and family income: Accounting for changes in the economic well-being of children, 1968–1986. In S. Danziger & P. Gottschalk (Eds.), *Uneven tides: Rising inequality in America* (pp. 167–193). New York: Russell Sage.

Grieco, E. M., & Cassady, R. C. (2001). *Overview of race and Hispanic origin.* Census 2000 Brief 01-1. Washington, DC: U.S. Census Bureau.

Gunderson, C., & Ziliak, J. P. (2004). Poverty and macroeconomic performance across space, race, and family structure. *Demography, 41,* 61–86.

Hernandez, D. J. (2004). Demographic change and the life circumstances of immigrant families. *Future of Children, 14,* 17–47.

Iceland, J. (2003). Why poverty remains high: The role of income growth, economic inequality, and changes in family structure, 1949–1999. *Demography, 40,* 499–519.

Iceland, J., Short, K., Garner, T. I., & Johnson, D. (2001). Are children worse off? Evaluating well-being using a new (and improved) measure of poverty. *Journal of Human Resources, 36,* 398–412.

Jensen, L., & Chitose, Y. (1994). Today's second generation: Evidence from the 1990 U.S. census. *International Migration Review, 28,* 714–735.

Lerman, R. I. (1996). The impact of the changing U.S. family structure on child poverty and income inequality. *Economica, 63,* S119–S139.

Lichter, D. T. (1997). Poverty and inequality among children. *Annual Review of Sociology, 23,* 121–145.

Lichter, D. T., & Crowley, M. L. (2002). Poverty in America: Beyond welfare reform. *Population Bulletin, 57*(June), 1–36.

Lichter, D. T., & Crowley, M. L. (2004). Welfare reform and child poverty: Effects of maternal employment, marriage, and cohabitation. *Social Science Research, 33,* 385–408.

Lichter, D. T., & Eggebeen, D. J. (1993). Rich kids, poor kids: Changing income inequality among American children. *Social Forces, 73,* 761–780.

Lichter, D. T., & Landale, N. S. (1995). Parental work, family structure, and poverty among Latino children. *Journal of Marriage and the Family, 57,* 346–354.

Lichter, D. T., & Qian, Z. C. (2004). *Marriage and family in a multiracial society.* The American People Series. Washington, DC, and New York: Population Reference Bureau and Russell Sage.

Lichter, D. T., Qian, Z. C, & Crowley, M. L. (2005). Child poverty among racial minorities and immigrants: Explaining trends and differentials. *Social Science Quarterly, 86,* 1037–1059.

Manning, W. D., & Brown, S. (2006). Children's economic well-being in married and cohabiting parent families. *Journal of Marriage and Family, 68,* 345–362.

Manning, W. D., & Lichter, D. T. (1996). Parental cohabitation and children's economic well-being. *Journal of Marriage and the Family, 58,* 998–1010.

McLanahan, S. (2004). Diverging destinies: How children are faring under the second demographic transition. *Demography, 41,* 607–627.

Moffitt, R. A. (2002). *From welfare to work: What the evidence shows.* Policy Brief No. 13, January. Welfare Reform and Beyond. Washington, DC: Brookings Institution.

Rainwater, L., & Smeeding, T. M. (2004). *Poor kids in a rich country.* Hoboken, NJ: Wiley.

Ruggles, S., Sobek, M., Alexander, T., Fitch, C. A., Goeken, R., Hall, P. K., et al. (2003). *Integrated public use microdata series: Version 3.0.* Minneapolis: Historical Census Projects, University of Minnesota.

Thomas, A., & Sawhill, I. (2002). For richer or for poorer: Marriage as an antipoverty strategy. *Journal of Policy Analysis and Management, 21,* 587–599.

Thomas A., & Sawhill, I. (2005). For love and money? The impact of family structure on family income. *Future of Children, 15,* 57–74.

U.S. Census Bureau. (2007a). History poverty tables. Table 3. Retrieved May 23, 2007, from http://www.census.gov/hhes/www/poverty/histpov/hstpov3.html

U.S. Census Bureau. (2007b). History poverty tables. Table 10. Retrieved May 23, 2007, from http://www.census.gov/hhes/www/poverty/histpov/hstpov10.html

U.S. Census Bureau. (2007c). Historical income tables—Families. Retrieved May 23, 2007, from http://www.census.gov/hhes/www/income/histinc/f03ar.html

U.S. Census Bureau. (2007d). Poverty thresholds. Retrieved May 23, 2007, from http://www.census.gov/hhes/www/poverty/histpov/hstpov1.html

Van Hook, J., Brown, S. L., & Kwenda, M. N. (2004). A decomposition of trends in poverty among children of immigrants. *Demography 41,* 649–670.

Zedlewski, S., Clark, S., Meier, E., & Watson, K. (1996). *Potential Effects of Congressional welfare reform legislation on family incomes.* Washington, DC: Urban Institute Press.

# CHAPTER 9

# Processes of Poverty and Social Exclusion in Poor Families

## ANGELA ABELA AND CARMEL TABONE

We are a clinical psychologist/ family therapist and a sociologist coming from the archipelago of Malta in the Mediterranean Sea. Given the general higher prevalence of poverty in families with children (Immerval, Sutherdal, & De vos, 2001; Micklewright & Stewart, 2000), we joined forces to research the dynamics of poverty and social exclusion amongst Maltese families, those with children in particular (Abela & Tabone, in press). Even though we inhabit a very small country with its distinctive, regional, cultural, and social differences (see Petmesidou & Papatheodorou, 2006), we believe that the concept of social exclusion that has certainly "achieved a wide currency in Western Europe" (Daly, 2002, p. 52)[1] may help us "grasp the multidimensionality and relational nature of being poor" (Saraceno, 2006, p. 95). We tend to endorse Saraceno's views and those of Fassin (1996) who suggest that this framework has now taken over that of the underclass common in the United States and that of the *marginalidad* in Latin America. In this chapter, we aim to highlight the interplay between poverty and social exclusion, keeping in mind the global perspective. We will use Malta as a case example.

Until recently, it has not been acknowledged that those coming from the lowest socioeconomic groups suffer more because of basic inequalities in society (Dallos & Draper, 2000). Their health problems, for example, were attributed to their fecklessness and poor eating habits. The perception of the Maltese about why some of them are poor is attributed mainly to laziness and lack of will power, with 50% choosing it as a main reason. We have often heard many say that the so-called poor are in fact cheaters beating the welfare system. Only 25% think that social injustice is the main reason for the prevalence of poverty. Other reasons include misfortune and inevitable progress (Abela, 2000). During the last decade, there has been a 10% decrease in those who believe that the poor themselves are to blame for their own situation. Abela (1998) points out, "A society which blames the poor for their condition can easily engender an increase in social exclusion" (p. 221).

Several authors point out that there are a number of complex pathways through which poverty influences the well-being of families and their members. These pathways highlight a strong link between the incidence and intensity of poverty and the relentless process of social exclusion. This connection exacerbates the chances for this sector of the population to come out of the poverty trap. Fernandez de la Hoz (2001) argues that whereas economic impoverishment is quantified more easily, social exclusion processes may operate at a more subtle level.

## DEFINITION OF POVERTY AND SOCIAL EXCLUSION

According to Brooks-Gunn, Rebello Britto, and Brady (1999), the poverty line is absolute in the United States. Income poverty is therefore defined by the poverty threshold. Household size is taken into account, and the threshold is based on what is called a thrifty food basket for families of particular sizes. In most Western countries, however, the concept of family poverty is measured in relative terms (Hernandez, 1997).

The European Commission (2001) in its Europe-wide research on Poverty and Social Exclusion measures poverty on the basis of income. The threshold is fixed at 60% of the national median *equivalized disposable income* of households. Equivalized disposable income is calculated on the collected total household income. Figures are given per "equivalent adult" to reflect differences in household size and composition. This scale gives a weight of 1.0 to the first adult, 0.5 to any other household member aged 14 and over, and 0.3 to each child (Dennis & Guio, 2003).

The Council of the European Union (EU) defines social exclusion as

A process whereby certain individuals are pushed to the edge of society and prevented from participating fully by virtue of their poverty, or lack of basic competencies and lifelong learning opportunities, or as a result of discrimination. This distances them from job, income and education opportunities as well as social and community networks and activities. They have little access to power and decision-making bodies and thus often feel powerless and unable to take control over the decisions that affect their day to day lives. (Joint Report on Social Inclusion, 2004, p. 10)

## PROCESSES OF POVERTY AND SOCIAL EXCLUSION

The Laeken European Council in December 2001 drew up a set of indicators to be used by both member states and the Commission in their Joint Report on Social Inclusion from 2003. They cover four important dimensions related to social cohesion: financial poverty, employment, health, and education.

Almost invariably, poor families tend to suffer from health problems, have a poor level of education, and hold vulnerable jobs or are unemployed. For children in particular, nutrition, parental mental health, parent-child interactions, the home environment, and neighborhood conditions also come into play (Brooks-Gunn et al., 1999). Conger, Rueter, and Conger's (2000) family stress model of economic hardship emphasizes how the emotional state and behavior of parents impinges on the lives of children. They argue that economic hardship and economic pressure is emotionally taxing for parents to the extent that their parenting behavior is disrupted.

Parental mental health has an adverse effect on the children. Depressed mothers tend to be disengaged from their children, less affectionate, and emotionally unavailable. Furthermore, parenting behavior tends to be harsher and less consistent and involved. The provisions for learning experiences in the home are somewhat limited. Brooks-Gunn et al. (1999) report that these account for as much as half of the effect of poverty status on the IQ scores of 5-year-olds.

Moreover, effects on the children's physical health and on their emotional and behavioral well-being have also been repeatedly referred to. Brooks-Gunn and Duncan (1997) report that poor children have a higher chance of experiencing low birth weight and growth stunting when compared with non-poor children and that this has been associated with reduced IQ and, in the case of reduced birth weight, increased rates of learning disability. The neighborhood environment also has a direct effect on the outcome of children and adolescents.

## THE FIVE MAIN INDICATORS OF SOCIAL EXCLUSION

In the sections that follow, we argue that social exclusion occurs primarily in the context of economic hardship. We also highlight the processes of social exclusion as they are manifested in one's low level of education, limited employability, poor health, and weak participation and integration in social life.

Data resulting from our study (Abela & Tabone, in press) will support our argument.

### Method

A full account of the Maltese empirical research on which this chapter is built may be found in Abela and Tabone (in press). A mixed methodological approach is adopted. In the quantitative analysis, 360 mothers living below the poverty line were interviewed. These had been classified as poor by the National Statistics Office in Malta through the Household Budgetary Survey, following the criteria adopted by the European Commission (National Statistics Office, 2003). A control group of 100 mothers

were selected at random from the remaining 85% of the Household Budgetary Survey. A questionnaire was used to compare the incidence of social exclusion indicators of families below the poverty line with families who are living above the poverty line. For the qualitative study, one-to-one interviews were held with 14 mothers. These were triangulated with focus groups held with the teachers of children from these families, and employment advisers. An interpretative phenomenological analysis (Smith, 1996; Smith, Jarman, & Osburn, 1999) was carried out.

### Economic Hardship

Economic hardship is still a reality among European countries. Despite the targets set up by the Lisbon agenda in 2000, poverty rates in the EU15 have gone up by 2 percentage points from 1999. Official Eurostat data show that, in 2004, after social transfers, 16% of persons in the EU25 have an equivalized disposable income below the at-risk-of-poverty threshold, when set at 60% of the national median equivalized disposable income. The figure rises to 17% if one considers only the EU15. It is important to keep in mind that percentages vary in the different European countries and range from 11 in Sweden, Finland, Luxembourg, and Denmark to 21 in Ireland, Portugal, and Slovakia.

An interesting indicator of poverty has to do with the distribution of income, with countries with higher rates of poverty having a wider distribution of income. This rate has showed slight changes across the years. In 2000 and 2001, the wealthiest 20% of the population in the EU countries had 4.5 times more income than did the poorest 20%. In 2003, this rate rose again to 4.6 and then to 4.8 in 2004. Data for 2004 are available for 14 countries, with ratios ranging from 3.3 in Sweden to 7.2 in Portugal.

Persistent poverty refers to those living on a low income for an extended period. More than half of those below the poverty line were persistently at risk of poverty in the EU between 1998 and 2000. The single elderly, single parents, couples with three or more children, the unemployed, and other inactive persons have high persistent income poverty rates. Those living in persistent poverty have a higher risk of being in social exclusion. They consistently find it difficult both to make ends meet and make back payments.

In countries where social transfers are limited, the preponderance of those suffering from economic hardship is higher, driving a bigger number of persons into social exclusion. The most recent available statistics show that in 2001, without social transfers, 22% of the EU population was below the relative median (60%) at-risk-of-poverty gap. Statistics are available for 26 EU and accession countries in 2003 and for 15 countries in 2004. Slovakia had the highest percentage (39%) of the population below the median 60% at-risk-of-poverty gap among the EU25, whereas the lowest percentage (15%) was held by the Czech Republic, Denmark, and Finland. Statistics for 2004 show the highest percentage (26%) to be in Portugal, followed by 25% in Germany, Greece, Spain, and Italy. Statistics for Slovakia are, however, not available for the year 2004. Finland had the lowest percentage of the population (14%) living below the relative at-risk-of-poverty gap in 2004. In 2004, it was estimated that without social transfers the at-risk-of-poverty rate in Malta would soar up from 15% to 30.2% (Dennis & Guio, 2004).

More females than males are below the at-risk-of-poverty-rate after social transfers in the EU25 with 17% females compared with 15% males. Children and youth in particular are a vulnerable group with 20% of children and youths of less than 16 years of age below the at-risk-of-poverty threshold after social transfers in 2004. The poverty curve goes down to 14% for the 25 to 49 age group, stays at 13% between 50 and 64 years but peaks at 18% for persons aged 65 years and over, the latter ranging from 6% in Luxembourg to 40% in Ireland.

The daily experience of those living below the poverty line is marked with stress and anxiety. In our in-depth interviews with 14 mothers (Abela & Tabone, in press), we asked them to explain to us what it means to them to live in poverty. The following are some of the answers obtained: "It is an everyday headache," "It is heart breaking to have to tell your children, 'We have to wait for payday,'" or "It means despair, quarrels in the family." Mothers have to struggle hard to cope with the cost of living. They cannot afford to buy a kilo of apples, which would cost approximately one Euro. At times, they even have to borrow money from their mothers to buy food items for their families.

This economic hardship exacerbates social exclusion. One mother pointed out to us that the dress she was wearing was 20 years old. She explained that she could not join other women in her town for a morning out and felt isolated and miserable. Another mother admitted that she cannot have a haircut when she needs it. Their families cannot afford simple luxuries like going out for a coffee once in a while or paying for the basic cable TV. Holidays are out of the question for them.

For single mothers, the situation seems to be worse. A widow admitted that she had back payments on water and electricity bills because she could not afford to pay for some time. During the interviews, we noticed that the houses of most single mothers were much more humble and located in poorer areas. The son of a single mother was sharing his mother's bedroom because of lack of space. Single mothers would like to go out and meet others, but cannot afford it.

## Unemployment

Unemployment, and long-term unemployment in particular, is one of the main factors of poverty and social exclusion (Dennis & Guio, 2003). Besides being a source of income, employment offers a valuable opportunity for social participation. Growing unemployment and job insecurity weaken welfare budgets and hit at vulnerable jobs.

In the EU countries, the frequency of unemployed persons in the low-income families is nearly three times higher than in the rest of the population (Mejer, 2000). In our research, the incidence of unemployment was significantly higher among the poor $(X (3) = 65.219, p > 0.00)$ (Abela & Tabone, in press).

When unemployment is long term (for at least 12 months), it is considered a stronger indicator of poverty and social exclusion. In 2005, in the 25 EU countries, 3.9% of the total active population or labor force was unemployed on a long-term basis. The long-term unemployment rate in Malta in 2005 stood at 3.4%, which is slightly below the EU25 average (Eurostat, n.d.).

Regarding the long-term unemployment rate, which is calculated as 24 months or more in search of a job, or since the last job was held, the EU25 rate in 2005 stood at 2.3%. This rate would be less (1.9%) if one were to consider only the EU15. The rate in Malta was 1.6% (Eurostat, n.d.).

Interestingly, the long-term unemployment EU25 average rate is higher among females than males, 2.6% compared with 2%. Additionally, in 2004, there was a 15% average difference in EU countries between men's and women's average gross hourly earnings, ranging from 4% in Malta and 5% in Portugal to 24% in Slovakia and Estonia and 25% in Cyprus (Eurostat, n.d.).

In 2005, 9.6% of children aged 0 to 17 years lived in jobless households. The rate in Malta is slightly below EU average, 8.9%. Caragata (2001) points out that unemployment among the poor is usually life long and multigenerational. The Maltese respondents revealed that there is a significant difference in intergenerational unemployment between poor and nonpoor $(X (1) = 5.541 p > 0.019)$.

Jobless households where no one is found to be working leave a "cumulative negative impact, at household level, of lacking contact with the world of work" (Dennis & Guio, 2003, p. 2). Moreover, as one of the employment advisors in our research pointed out, this situation also leaves a negative effect on children, creating a nonworking culture. These children are prepared to remain unemployed, and it is normal for them to have to register for work. In contrast, children of employed parents are almost shocked to hear that they could have to register to find employment.

The unemployed who otherwise fall in the low-income bracket rely more on unemployment benefits as their main source of income than do the unemployed in the rest of the population. This heavy dependence on unemployment benefits hinders such families from actively searching for jobs (Mejer, 2000). As Room (1999) argues, this may lead them to experience welfare services as disabling rather than empowering and may further exacerbate their social exclusion.

In the focus groups we held with employment advisors of the Employment and Training Corporation (ETC) in Malta (Abela & Tabone, in press), these advisors explained how a culture of unemployment is bred. One of the reasons for this is that unemployment benefits provide a stable income for vulnerable workers. In fact, 80% of the unemployed are low skilled and often feel a lack of respect and exploitation by employers. They could only earn the minimum wage. In the circumstances, they prefer to rely on benefits and increase their earnings by doing odd jobs unofficially, even more so when the difference between the benefits and the minimum wage in Malta amounts to 5 Maltese liras, which is approximately equivalent to 12 euros or 14 U.S. dollars.

Moreover, jobs are lost easily in low-level employment and going through the motions of applying for benefits all over again takes time. This means that such workers would have to endure the waiting time without any form of income. The employment advisors estimate that about 40% of the unemployed becomes caught in the benefit trap. According to the employment advisors, it takes between 6 months and a year of unemployment to fall in the benefit trap.

In an attempt to counteract the negative effects of unemployment benefits, Said and Said Camilleri (2003) studied the interaction of income tax and social benefit systems in Malta and its negative impact on the incentive to work. They suggest a series of options that the Maltese government could consider, including setting a threshold above which social security contributions are paid, and the tapering of unemployment benefits to persons moving from unemployment to employment. The researchers argue that the mentioned measures encourage the unemployed to actively seek employment. They also suggest that the average tax rates widen such that there is a perceived difference between unemployment benefits and income from work.

Addressing dependence on unemployment benefits as a way of redressing social exclusion is a complex issue. In America, following the 1996 welfare reform act, success in doing so was partial. Whereas the poverty rate dropped from 15.1% to 11.3%—that is, from 5 million families to 2 million families—10% to 15% are now neither working nor on welfare and depend on relatives for subsistence ("Helping the Poor," 2006). Many of these have mental or physical disabilities and cannot support their families by working. Courtney (2006) spent 4 years in Milwaukee County, finding out who these welfare applicants were. His team followed 1,075 parents, most of them mothers. More than three-quarters of these had at least one potential barrier to employment, including a disability, no high school diploma, poor health, a mental health problem, or an alcohol or drug problem.

More than half reported two or three barriers with 3 in 10 reporting three or more. Moreover, half of the parents had already been investigated for child abuse and about one-sixth had a child placed in foster care. Courtney concluded that most parents applying for welfare are not employable. Fighting unemployment and social exclusion is a long-term and complex process that includes both prevention and intervention policies targeting the various members of the family including babies and children, as we shall see in the education and health subsections.

Compounding the issue of poverty, social exclusion, and unemployment is the current flux of immigrants who are fleeing mostly from the sub-Saharan regions into rich countries. Because of its geographical position in the middle of the Mediterranean Sea, Malta has been a land of refuge for many on boats heading for the European mainland but who found themselves in dire straits. The statistics are indeed quite high when one considers our geographical size and population density.

While the World Trade Organization continues to bicker about how the richer countries can help these poor countries move their economies and sell their produce ("World Trade," 2006), inhabitants from these poor countries are escaping in droves in search for a better future. Unfortunately, they end up being exploited and mistreated wherever they go (see Martinez Veiga, 2006).

In Malta, the same dynamics come into play. The wife of a plasterer complained to us that irregular immigrants, which she grouped as "Arabs," were stealing her husband's job:

The problem is that there are a lot of Arabs. They take up work. I know that the Maltese are skilled, but if there is a block of flats they prefer to employ Arabs on it. That is a slap in the face . . . the big contractors tell you "if I have a piece of work I will give it to you, but for hotels and the like, I prefer having Arabs doing them."

In turn, employers exploit irregular immigrants by paying them a ridiculous amount or sometimes by cheating them in particularly mean ways. Employment advisors told us how employers themselves sometimes report immigrants for working without a permit to avoid paying them. As the immigrants are about to finish the work and get paid, they get reported instead and are caught by the police. (See Martinez Veiga, 2006, for similar mishaps in Spain.)

### Education

The ability to participate in society, including one's contribution in the world of work, depends on the educational attainment of the individual. The success or failure of the education system in a country is reflected in the proportion of people with low educational achievement. This is also an important indicator of a country's ability to fight poverty and improve social cohesion. According to the 2001 Labor Force survey in the EU, 19% of all 18- to 24-year-olds had lower education levels, ranging from 7.7% in Sweden to 45% in Portugal.

Eurostat research shows that, in 2002, 24.1% of all 25- to 34-year-olds in the EU15 had an International Standard Classification of Education (ISCED) of 2 or less, meaning that they possessed a pre-primary, primary, and lower secondary education. The percentage of early school-leavers in the EU25, has declined from 17.7% in 2000 to 15.2% in 2005. Malta has a high percentage of early school-leavers (41.2%).

Providing equal access to education is a complex endeavor. The problem of illiteracy of children at risk of poverty has long been perceived as an issue that has to be addressed before children start going to school. Initiatives carried out in the United States and United Kingdom, respectively, where child-care programs like Head Start

and Sure Start were launched, demonstrated that these children made significant progress in their developmental milestones. These preschool readiness skills were maintained during their school years, resulting in better outcomes in their educational attainment. Ramey et al. (1999) and Ramey and Ramey (1999) found that in the United States, these children benefited from more years of formal education because of higher IQs and better performance at school. Parenthood was left to a later stage in their life. Bradshaw and Bennett (2003) report that in the United Kingdom evaluations on Sure Start were positive.

In the meantime, parents living in conditions of poverty complain that the school does not relate empathically to them (ATD Fourth World, 2000). In our research (Abela & Tabone, in press) we specifically asked mothers what they think would help their children to get out of the poverty trap. They all agreed that a good education would definitely help their children. However, the mothers do not feel comfortable telling the school that the family is living in poverty. They think that their children will be stigmatized if the school knew about the situation. When we were conducting the quantitative part of our research, which took place in the first week of school term, one mother confided to our interviewer that at the moment she was not sending her children to school because the teacher was giving the children lists of stationery they needed to buy for that scholastic year and she could not afford to buy it. When the teachers learned about the views held by the parents of poor children, during a focus group we held with them, they were disappointed. Teachers called for more collaboration between the family and the school. They complained that many parents do not turn up for meetings. As the teachers were saying this, the first author could not help remembering that one single mother had told her that she had missed Parents' Day because she did not know how to read and had forgotten to ask her son to read the notice she had received from school. It is also worth remembering that as researchers, we had not relied on our original invitation letter when we contacted the teachers and asked them to participate in a focus group, but also made our respective mobile numbers available and had communicated by short message service through mobile phones with the teachers several times.

The teachers also told us that they would like parents to be more authoritative with their children and make them study when they are at home, but the parents complained that they are unable to continue helping children in their homework as they grow older. In their teenage years, these children end up roaming the streets after school. The following is a candid excerpt from the focus group interview between the first author and a teacher:

| | |
|---|---|
| *Teacher:* | These children have no one to guide them, or if they do, they have no idea how to guide them . . . a lot of parents already feel helpless in front of the children. The first thing I ask them is: Listen does the boy study at home? They tell you: "Eh . . . he comes home and goes out" . . . or they tell you: "No the boy is not interested in school, I don't know what I can do . . . " They don't tell them: "Sit down and study." I do not want to point a finger toward anyone, because we teachers point toward the parents and the parents point toward us. But I think that the parents have an important role to play. |

| | |
|---|---|
| *Author:* | How do you explain this behavior? |
| *Teacher:* | Everyone shirks (responsibility) a bit. |
| *Author:* | It's tough then, it must be very tough. |
| *Teacher:* | Often parents come to school and say: Sir I don't know what I am going to do with him. |

In an in-depth interview the first author of this paper had with a mother, the latter expressed her sense of helplessness with her eldest son who refuses to study:

> He tells me: "Did you study?" . . . and what can I tell him? I say I used to try my best when exams would be approaching. I used to open a book and study a bit not like you nothing at all. He tells me: "I study in vain, because I don't get it in, I forget."

Mothers feel that their own history of school failure impedes them from empowering their children any further at this point: "Because I cannot say that I am good at school and can help him make progress. I cannot do this, follow him in his studies, because I lack schooling myself."

Even though many parents coming from poor families feel disheartened and not able to help their children as the children grow older, this does not mean that they would not like their children to learn. In fact, we found no statistical difference between the poor and the nonpoor when it comes to the assistance in homework by parents. Parents coming from poor families also manage to find the money to send their children to private lessons after school. Even though private lessons are common in Malta (frequency in our research ranged from 15% for Maltese language to 20% for math), there was no statistical difference between the poor and the nonpoor regarding the children's attendance in private lessons. And yet, 9% of children living below the poverty line were found to have repeated the scholastic year at least once (X (1) = 3.931, $p > 0.047$).

This plight is to be found in many corners of the world. When the first author presented the qualitative component of our research at the European Family Therapy conference in Berlin in 2004, the chair, Toby Sigrun Herman, who is the current chair of International Family Therapy Association (IFTA) from Iceland commented: "It's the same story everywhere! The parents don't know what to do but the teachers expect more from the parents."

Similarly in her work at the Council of Europe, around parenting children at risk of social exclusion, the first author listened to parents of French, British, and Russian nationality who had come out of poverty giving their account on their personal experiences of parenting. The following is a summary of what the parents had to say about school:

> The parents were well aware that successful schooling was vital to improving their children's future prospects. And successful children would be able to teach their illiterate (or almost illiterate) parents a lot. Teachers, however, were generally speaking, unenthusiastic about giving extra help to these children, many of whom had learning difficulties. Nor did schools regard such parents as partners. (Abela & Berlioz, in press, p.12)

In the meantime, the perceptions of parents coming from poor backgrounds about their children's performance at school continue to fix a label of failure on them. These perceptions differ significantly between those who are below the poverty line and those who are above it. Only 13% of parents below the poverty line rate their children's performance as very good compared with 33.7% above the poverty line. Furthermore, 4% of parents below the poverty line rate

their children's performance as very bad. Parents above the poverty line did not even include their children in this rating. As one headmaster pointed out during the focus group, many poor parents end up criticizing their children with their friends and with the school. Most of these parents stop attending Parents' Day in the last 2 years of compulsory schooling between the ages of 14 and 16, implying that they have lost hope that the school could provide the skills that the children need.

Some of the Maltese mothers criticize the educational system. They think that streaming, which in Malta starts at the age of 9, exacerbates the children's sense of failure and should be disbanded. Mothers, who were interviewed separately from teachers, think that the school curriculum is not engaging their adolescent kids to learn. Mothers think that it would be more helpful if their kids were to learn a trade when in secondary school because this would give them the possibility of finding a related job when they finish school (Abela & Tabone, in press).

Mothers mentioned good teachers, a good head of school, more encouragement from school, instilling self-confidence in the child, and supervision during homework by them as helpful. Teachers need to learn more how to give feedback that would empower these children and their parents. They seem oblivious that parents are sensitive to criticism. One teacher in the focus group complained because a parent was very defensive when the teacher was trying to help the parent by giving her feedback about the girl.

The need for more collaboration between the school and home is also highlighted by Borg and Mayo (2001; see also Sefa Dei, Mazzucca, McIsaac, & Zine, 1997), who seek the views of parents, teachers and administrators of a school in a working-class community. Parents would like to be listened to by the school and feel empowered when their suggestions are implemented. The authors report that the teachers are often prejudiced toward the parents and are dismissive toward the children. In the international literature, it is argued that teachers find it difficult to empathize with these parents because of the different social class they come from. In Malta, however, many teachers hail from working-class backgrounds, but most still prefer to teach in schools where children are interested in getting good grades from their teachers.

An interesting initiative here in Malta that has been fairly successful in helping parents has been that of the Foundation of the Educational Services (FES). This foundation, which was set up in 2001, has taken a family approach to basic skills learning. Its programs complement schools' endeavors by helping parents through family literacy and parent empowerment programs to learn new skills to support their children's educational development.

One of the programs (Nwar), for example, offers literacy support to children at risk of significant failure and includes parents in the learning partnership on the premise that their participation will enhance pupil performance. An external evaluation in 2004 that included pre- and post-testing of the children in the program confirmed that gains in alphabet recognition, auditory blending, and oracy were statistically significant. We believe that schools have a lot to learn from this philosophy and that the concept of parent empowerment needs to be adopted more wholeheartedly in the schools.

However, the very poor, especially those who lead an unstructured life, fail to attend such programs with their children. This was confirmed by a telephone interview the first author had with the head of the service for children between 18 months and 3 years set up in an area in Malta that has a higher incidence of families living below the poverty line.

The challenges that parents and teachers alike passionately express about their struggle to overcome school failure highlight how the processes of poverty and social exclusion are difficult to overcome. Taking a more collaborative stance between the school and the family would certainly improve the life chances of these children and their parents. Nevertheless, for education to be successful in fighting poverty and social exclusion, it cannot be limited to schooling. Indeed these processes are often "inherited" from one generation to the other, leaving only limited opportunities for children to get out of the poverty trap. Prevention programs and early intervention are therefore necessary to step up the fight against poverty and social exclusion.

## Health

Ill health is closely linked to social exclusion. In our research, we found a higher incidence of long-term health problems among the poor. The difference between the poor and the nonpoor is statistically significant ($X$ (1) = 5.018, $p > 0.25$). Single-parent households with dependent children living below the poverty line have a higher rate of long-term health problems when compared with similar households above the poverty line ($X$ (1) = 8.315, $p > 0.004$) (Abela & Tabone, in press).

Health problems may be insidious and develop over time, but when they burst into full-blown conditions, the family often finds itself by the wayside. The disabling effects of ill health are far-reaching, triggering a series of problems that have a spiral effect, making it almost impossible for the family to get out of the poverty trap.

In our qualitative research, one of the mothers interviewed explained to us how her husband lost his job when he asked his employer to release him from working night shifts upon discovering that he was suffering from diabetes.

Why was he laid off?

Unjustly I think. He used to work as a security officer . . . and my husband suffers from diabetes, and the doctor told him: "in order to keep the diabetes in check don't work night duties. . . ." They used the certificate the other way round . . . I think it was an injustice.

This situation precipitated a big blow to the family, leading them to incur debts to make ends meet with the father's diabetes soaring even higher because of stress.

A similar situation occurred in another family where the father was suffering from thrombosis and could no longer work for long hours standing up as a glass blower. Given his low level of educational attainment, and the specialized skills that he developed over the years, he was unable to find a job that was suitable for him. His wife, in turn, sought work as a home help, but could not keep her part-time job because it aggravated her acute arthritis (Abela & Tabone, in press).

Mental illness prevails among the poor (Brooks-Gunn et al., 1999; Courtney, 2006). In our sample, we found a statistically significant higher incidence of mental illness among the adult population below the poverty line $(x (1) = 5.348, p > 0.21)$. Depression was almost three times more frequent (Abela & Tabone, in press). Abela (2002) also reports that women who live in poverty have higher rates of mental health problems and serious long illnesses when compared with other women coming from average or rich backgrounds.

Children who are brought up by depressed and distressed parents find themselves in a highly vulnerable situation. Marital conflict was also found to be significantly higher in poor families $(X (4) = 9.993 \ p > 0.041)$. In such circumstances (see also Conger et al., 2000), children find it extremely difficult to learn. They often feel unloved and abandoned and very angry and depressed about the world around them. In our sample, more children in poor families were found to have had emotional problems for at least 1 month. Nevertheless, treatment for emotional problems is much more common among nonpoor children (Abela & Tabone, in press).

One reason why poor families do not seek help regarding their physical and mental health is that they cannot afford to seek private health services. "We cannot cover all sickness costs. My husband is diabetic. The pink card[2] does not cover all the medicine. Some of the medicine obtained by pink card is not the best on the market." Even catching a cold is a burden on these families. One of the mothers exclaimed that they cannot afford an incidence of sickness in their family. "This winter all three children caught a cold, and I got it as well. We were running a fever and I spent LM25!" This cost amounts to the equivalent of almost half the weekly minimum wage.

Public health services, although free of charge, are not always convenient because no home visits are provided and waiting lists are long. Seeking psychological help is even more challenging for poor families. Moreover, services are not always accessible to the poor, as has been noted in the recommendations coming out of the Ministerial Family Conference in Lisbon.

In our in-depth interviews with the 14 mothers, we discovered that these mothers did not want to obtain help from social workers. Most of them wanted work and a good education for their children. Asking for help from social workers seemed to be perceived as another dent to their already fragile sense of dignity.

Abela and Berlioz (in press) summarize what the French, Russian, and British parents who had come out of poverty had to say about help for parents,

The greatest problem in their view was social isolation, accompanied by a feeling of rejection. . . . Their need for help was great. Paradoxically, however, they tried to avoid any contact with the appropriate social services, because they were afraid that their children would be taken away from them and placed elsewhere. Their fears were justified, because, at one stage or another, this was exactly what happened to them. The experience had been particularly painful for them, especially to those who had been similarly placed when they were young.

Even when parents did approach the social services, they found this process difficult and the services unfriendly. The British complained of being treated like little children and wondered how their own children could respect them if they were shown so little respect by others.

According to the guidelines provided for professionals working with children and parents at risk of social exclusion by the Council of Europe, which appear in the explanatory report of Recommendation 19 (Daly, 2006) on policy to support positive parenting, meeting such parents in their own environments and working in partnership with them are important examples of good practice.

The introduction of home visiting by a family nurse in the United States is one such example. Promising results have come from reliable longitudinal research on nurse home visiting. Nurses visited low-income mothers (most of whom were teenage mothers) in the prenatal period and during the first 2 years of the children's lives. Compared with those who only received developmental screening, these children and their mothers registered significant benefits 15 years later, including 46% fewer reports of child abuse and neglect and 56% fewer arrests. They also depended less on help by the state, and there were 28 or more months between first and second children (Olds et al., 1997, 1998).

### Integration in Social Life

Not surprisingly, those below the poverty line seem to be less integrated in social life ($X$ (1) = 13.647, $p > 0.000$). Few are members in cultural, sports, religious, or any other social organization when compared with those above the poverty line.

This is symptomatic of their exclusion from the rest of society. One teacher explained this phenomenon to us during the focus group. He teaches in a boys' secondary school in a deprived area. He is very aware that these boys are socially excluded:

> I understand that they need to have opportunities like other children . . . so that they would mix . . . so that they would know what is going on out there . . . I tried to make them join this sports club . . . they did not fit in.

He explained how out of place they felt when they had to play away from home during a basketball tournament with other schools. Once they were playing at a Catholic college that has a good reputation. Teams from various schools were in attendance. Most of the boys from the other teams were mixing and socializing whereas the boys from his team felt insecure and hovered around him. In the end, they wanted to quit the tournament. They preferred to relax in their own way. This was far too stressful, it seemed. In an in-depth interview, one mother told me that her son is always out running around in the streets on his bike after school. She tells him to study but he ignores her.

Several mothers told us during the interview about how embarrassing it is for them to confide in the school, the social services, or even their in-laws about their financial situations. Normally, the only person from whom the mothers interviewed would receive help is their own mothers who would often give them groceries to help them make both ends meet.

### FUTURE DIRECTIONS AND TRENDS

1. Research shows that it is a good idea to encourage the poor to work, leaving no loopholes for cheating or becoming dependent on welfare services (Dennis & Guio, 2003; "Helping the Poor," 2006; Said & Said Camilleri, 2003).

It appears, however, that despite such measures, a sizable number find themselves unable to cope on their own (Courtney, 2006).

2. One important focus should be on prevention and early intervention aiming to get children out of the poverty trap.

The UNICEF report (2005) highlights the fact that although welfare expenditure rose in most Organisation for Economic Co-operation and Development countries, this mostly went to retirement pensions and health. The report indicates that many of these countries have the potential to reduce child poverty below 10% without a significant increase in overall spending. A better distribution of resources, as advocated by UNICEF, is a long-awaited deliverable.

*The Economist* ("Helping the Poor," 2006) also thinks that helping the children of those parents who are facing a mental or physical disability is a priority ("Helping the Poor," 2006). Wisconsin officials who were involved in Courtney's research have admitted that they need to do more to help welfare applicants to address their personal challenges. Courtney thinks that voluntary parenting classes are very important (Courtney, 2006).

In 2004, the European Committee for Social Cohesion also chose to focus on parenting as a way of enhancing a revised strategy for social cohesion. Together with the Forum for Children and Families, it launched a project that was to be carried out by the European Committee of Experts on Children and Families with the aim of supporting parenting in the best interest of the child. Of particular interest is the work that was carried out around parenting children at risk of social exclusion and ways professionals can support good parenting. This work (see Daly, in press) was brought to the attention of all European Ministers responsible for family affairs at a conference held in Lisbon in 2006.

Examples of good practice such as the ones around early child-care programs like Head Start in the United States and Sure Start in the United Kingdom should be continued.

Home visiting by a family nurse with low-income mothers during pregnancy and after the birth of their children also obtained considerable benefits with low-income mothers as previously described.

Borg Xuereb (2005) argues that during prenatal classes, midwifery and obstetric services are helping partners to focus on the physical aspect of pregnancy, but miss the subtle, more complex psychological issues. In her study, Borg Xuereb is seeking the parents' views about what they would find helpful during these classes. Such help is particularly important for families who are socially excluded.

3. More parent friendly approaches that promote easier access to social services are also warranted. In its final communiqué, the 2006 Council of Europe Conference held in Lisbon on Parenting stressed the importance of major policies including employment, income support, housing and educational policies but also access to service provision in reducing poverty risk.

The ATD Fourth World, which is an international nongovernmental organization working with poor families has a lot to teach us about how to work with the poor, especially those living in great poverty (see ATD Fourth World, 2006; see also ATD Fourth World, 2005). The nonjudgmental approach and the ability to recognize that poor people have knowledge are important attitudes that help to build a healthy working relationship where the poor can process their past traumatic experiences and with help find the strength to become more in charge of their lives. In their work, the authors provide engaging narratives of how these voluntary workers accompany parents and their children, including the involvement of fathers whose support for their children is of utmost importance.

We believe that professionals working with the poor need more training in this regard.

4. A collaborative systemic approach when working with families in schools would

be particularly helpful to avoid symmetrical positions where parents blame teachers and vice versa. More family education is warranted in schools. More could be done to help young women stay in school and delay pregnancy, rather than ending up on welfare. Boys need to be more sensitive to issues around paternal responsibility from a young age. Adolescents' antisocial behavior warrants special attention. Multisystemic therapy (Henggeler, Schoenwald, Rowland, & Cunningham, 2002) is perhaps the most effective because it deals with the situation in the community and offers a variety of treatments depending on the special needs of a particular adolescent. Intervention at school, social skills, vocational guidance, and therapeutic work with families may be offered simultaneously. The active involvement of all parents, especially those who are socially excluded, is crucial in such endeavors.

## CONCLUSION

Until a few decades ago, when the world felt larger, it may have appeared rather strange to discuss processes of poverty and social exclusion from a global perspective by making use of the everyday experiences of a small state like Malta. With the advent of globalization however, we have come closer to each other and can readily identify similar processes taking place in the different countries of the industrial world including the Eastern European countries that are in the process of making the transition to a market economy. Moreover, the Lisbon Agenda in the year 2000, aiming to reduce poverty and social exclusion in the now 25 countries of the EU, has provided a context whereby knowledge from the respective countries has been shared. The Strategy for Social Cohesion of the Council of Europe developed between 1998 and 2004 has further enriched our understanding of the poor and the socially excluded, primarily by creating awareness that this section of the population has a right to an adequate standard of living and, above all, the right to the dignity of the human person. The increased knowledge, which is also reflected in the literature available, has certainly helped in bringing the subject on the family policy agenda alerting governments to step up their fight against poverty and social exclusion.

## NOTES

1. In October 1997, the Heads of State of the Council of Europe identified social cohesion as one of the foremost needs of the wider Europe. A new intergovernmental body, the European Committee for Social Cohesion, was set up within the Social Policy Department to devise a new vision for social cohesion in the 21st century.

2. The pink card entitles patients to obtain medicines free of charge from the Public Health Service.

## REFERENCES

Abela, A. M. (1998). A comparative analysis of poverty and social exclusion in Malta and Spain. In K. Korayem & M. Petmesidou (Eds.), *Poverty and social exclusion in the Mediterranean area*. Bergen, Norway: Comparative Research Programme on Poverty.

Abela, A. M. (2000). *Values of women and men in the Maltese Islands*. Malta: Commission for the Advancement of Women, Ministry of Social Policy.

Abela, A. M. (2002). *Women's welfare in society*. Malta: Commission for the Advancement of Women, Ministry of Social Policy.

Abela, A., & Berlioz, G. (in press). Support for parenting children at risk of Social Exclusion. In M. Daly (Ed.), *Parenting in contemporary Europe: A positive approach*. Strasbourg, France: Council of Europe.

Abela, A., & Tabone, C. (in press). *Family poverty and social exclusion with a special emphasis on children*. Malta: National Family Commission.

ATD Fourth World. (2000) *Education: Opportunities lost. The education system as experienced by families living in poverty*. Mery-sur-Oise, France: ATD Fourth World.

ATD Fourth World. (2005, May). *Valuing children, valuing parents*. Mery-sur-Oise, France: ATD Fourth World.

ATD Fourth World. (2006, January). *Comment favoriser la participation des familles en grande precarite aux reseaux découte, dáppui et dáccompagnement des parents* (REAPP). Mery-sur-Oise, France: ATD Fourth World.

Borg, C., & Mayo, P. (2001). From "adjuncts" to "subjects": Parental involvement in a working-class community. *British Journal of Sociology of Education, 22*(2), 245–266.

Borg Xuereb, R. (2005, July). *Supporting families through the transition to parenthood*. Paper presented at the 27th Triennial International Congress of the International Confederation of Midwives at the Brisbane convention and Exhibition Centre, Brisbane, Australia.

Bradshaw, J., & Bennett, F. (2003). *Report of United Kingdom national action plan on social inclusion 2001–2003*. Brussels, Belgium: European Commission.

Brooks-Gunn, J., & Duncan, G. J. (1997). The effects of poverty on children. *Futures of Children, 7*(2), 55–71.

Brooks-Gunn, J., Rebello Britto, P., & Brady, C. (1999). Struggling to make ends meet. In M. E. Lamb (Ed.), *Parent and child development in nontraditional families*. Mahwah, NJ: Erlbaum.

Caragata, L. (2001). A chip in the Canadian veneer: Family and child poverty as social exclusion. *Review of Social Work and Social Sciences, 9*(1), 36–53.

Conger, K. J., Rueter, M. A., & Conger, R. D. (2000). The role of economic pressure in the lives of parents and their adolescents: The family stress model. In L. Crockett & R. Silbereisen (Eds.), *Negotiating adolescence in times of social change* (pp. 201–233). Cambridge, UK: Cambridge University Press.

Courtney, M. E. (2006). *Welfare reform's shortcoming*. Retrieved August 2006 from http://www-news.uchicago.edu/citations/06/060724.courtney-wp.html

Daly, M. (2002) *Access to social rights in Europe*. Strasbourg, France: Council of Europe.

Daly, M. (Ed.). (2006). *Parenting in contemporary Europe: A positive approach*. Strasbourg, France: Council of Europe. Retrieved from http://www.coe.int/t/dg3/youthfamily/source/2006PositiveParentingMDrep_en.pdf

Daly, M. (Ed.). (in press). *Parenting in contemporary Europe: A positive approach*. Strasbourg, France: Council of Europe.

Dallos, R., & Draper, R. (2000). *An introduction to family therapy*. Buckingham, UK: Open University Press.

Dennis, I., & Guio, A. (2003). *Poverty and social exclusion in the EU after Laeken—Part 2* (Statistics in Focus, Theme 3, 9/2003). Luxembourg: Eurostat.

Dennis, I., & Guio, A. (2004). *Monetary Poverty in New Member States and Candidate Countries* (Statistics in Focus, 12/2004). Luxembourg: Eurostat.

European Commission. (2001). *Draft joint report on social inclusion* (Communication from the Commission to the Council 565). Brussels, Belgium: Rapporteur Anna Diamantopolou.

European Commission & Council on Social Inclusion. (2004). *Joint report on social inclusion.* Brussels, Belgium.

Eurostat, European Commission, EUROPA. (n.d.). Available from http://epp.eurostat.ec.europa.eu/

Fassin, D. (1996). Exclusion, underclass, marginalidad. Figures contemporaines de la pauvrete urbaine en France, aux états unis et en amerique latine. *Revue francaise de sociologie, 37*(1), 37–75.

Fernandez de la Hoz, P. (2001). *Families and social exclusion in the European Union.* A report submitted to the Coordination Office of the European Observatory on the Social Situation, Demography and Family, Brussels, Belgium.

Helping the poor. From welfare to workfare. (2006, July 29–August 4). *The Economist,* 44–46.

Henggeler, S. W., Schoenwald, S. W., Rowland, M. D., & Cunningham, P. B. (2002). *Serious emotional disturbance in children and adolescents: Multisystemic therapy.* New York: Guildford Press.

Hernandez, D. J. (1997). Poverty trends. In G. J. Duncan & J. Brooks-Gunn (Eds.), *Consequences of growing up poor.* New York: Russell Sage.

Immerval, H., Sutherdal, H., & De vos, K. (2001). Reducing child poverty in the European Union: The role of child benefits. In K. Vleminkx & T. Smeeding (Eds.), *Child well-being, child poverty and child policy in modern nations. What do we know?* Bristol, UK: Policy Press.

Martinez Veiga, U. (2006). Absolute poverty of illegal immigrants in Spain: A growing problem. In M. Petmesidou & C. Papatheodorou (Eds.), *Poverty & social deprivation in the Mediterranean.* Bergen, Norway: Comparative Research Programme on Poverty.

Mejer, L. (2000). *Social exclusion in the EU member states* (Statistics in Focus, Theme 3, 1/2003). Luxembourg: Eurostat.

Micklewright, J., & Stewart, K. (2000). *The welfare of Europe's children.* Florence, Italy: UNICEF Innocenti Research Centre.

National Statistics Office. (2003). *Household budgetary survey 2000.* Malta: Author.

Olds, D., Eckenrode, J., Henderson, C. R., Kitzman, H., Powers, J., Cole, R., et al. (1997). Long-term effects of home visitation on maternal life course and child abuse and neglect: 15-year follow-up of a randomized trial. *Journal of the American Medical Association, 278,* 637–643.

Olds, D., Henderson, C. R., Cole, R., Eckenrode, J., Kitzman, H., & Luckey, D., et al. (1998). Long-term effects of nurse home visitation of children's criminal and antisocial behavior: 15-year follow-up of a randomized controlled trial. *Journal of the American Medical Association, 280,* 1238–1244.

Petmesidou, M., & Papatheodorou, C. (Eds.). (2006). *Poverty & social deprivation in the Mediterranean.* Bergen, Norway: Comparative Research Programme on Poverty.

Ramey, C. T., Campbell, F. A., Burchinal, M., Skinner, M. L., Gardner, D. M., & Ramey, S. L. (1999). Persistent effects of early intervention on high risk children and their mothers. *Applied Developmental Science, 4,* 4–14.

Ramey, S. L., & Ramey, C. T. (1999). Early experience and early intervention for children at risk for developmental delay and mental retardation. In S. L. Ramey, C. T. Ramey, & M. J. Frielander (Eds.), *Mental retardation and developmental disabilities research reviews* (Vol. 5, pp. 1–10). New York: Wiley.

Room, G. J. (19990 Social exclusion, solidarity and the challenge of globalisation. *International Journal of Social Welfare, 8*(3), 166–174.

Said, E., & Said Camilleri, M. (2003). *The interaction of income tax and social benefit systems and its impact on the incentive to work*. Research presented to the Ministry for Social Policy, Malta.

Saraceno, C. (2006). Poverty and poverty discourses in Italy in comparative perspective. In M. Petmesidou & C. Papatheodorou (Eds.), Poverty *& social deprivation in the Mediterranean*. Norway: Comparative Research Programme on Poverty.

Sefa Dei, G. J., Mazzucca, J., McIsaac, E., & Zine, J. (1997). *Reconstructing "Drop-Out." A critical ethnography of the dynamics of black students' disengagement from school*. Toronto: University of Toronto Press.

Smith, J. A. (1996). Beyond the divide between cognition and discourse: Using interpretative phenomenological analysis in health psychology. *Psychology and Health, 11,* 261–271.

Smith, J, A., Jarman, M., & Osburn, M. (1999). Doing interpretative phenomenological analysis. In M. Murray & K. Chamberlain (Eds.), *Qualitative health psychology: Theories and methods*. London: Sage.

UNICEF. (2005). *Child poverty in rich countries*. Florence, Italy: Innocenti Research Centre.

World trade: In the twilight of Doha. (2006, July 29–August 4). *The Economist,* 65–66.

# CHAPTER 10

# Mexican American Families and Poverty

SCOTT COLTRANE, ROSS D. PARKE, THOMAS J. SCHOFIELD, SHIGUERU J. TSUHA, MICHAEL CHAVEZ, AND SHOON LIO

The year 2006 will be remembered in the United States for having seen the largest public demonstration by immigrants in the nation's history. Latino immigrants and their supporters took to the streets for the "Day Without an Immigrant March" to protest a congressional bill designed to keep Mexican nationals from crossing the U.S. border with a 700-mile fence and to criminalize illegal immigrants and those who assist or employ them (Gaouette, 2006). Political mobilization against immigrants and counter-movements for immigrant rights highlight the dramatic demographic shifts that have transformed the United States in the past two decades (Cauce & Domenech-Rodriguez, 2002). Latinos are already the largest ethnic "minority" in the nation, and by 2050, are projected to make up more than one-quarter of the U.S. population. It is important that urban poverty scholars, policymakers, and the general public understand the experiences of Latinos with poverty (Roosa, Morgan-Lopez, Cree, & Specter, 2002; Small & Newman, 2001). As we discuss in this chapter, Latinos

face substantial economic challenges, with rates of child poverty consistently much higher than are rates for non-Latino whites (Hernandez, 2004; Perez, 2004). In particular, this chapter will focus on Mexican Americans, who constitute two-thirds of the Latino population in the United States.

Past research has shown that a lack of financial resources jeopardizes the life chances of anyone who grows up poor (Duncan & Brooks-Gunn, 1997; McLoyd, 1998; Rank, 2004). Mothers with few resources experience higher infant mortality rates than do other mothers and are more likely to have premature or mentally retarded babies from prenatal malnutrition. People with lower incomes are more likely to get sick and stay sick longer because of deficiencies in diet, sanitary facilities, shelter, or medical care. Poor people have shorter life expectancies and are more likely to die from accidents, tuberculosis, influenza, and pneumonia. Youth raised in poverty are less likely to go to college and are more likely to be arrested, found guilty, and given longer criminal sentences for a particular violation. Finally, families with limited incomes are more likely than are families with more financial resources to experience child abuse, spouse abuse, divorce, and desertion (Coltrane & Collins, 2001). Because income disparities in the United States have been increasing in recent decades, concern has grown regarding how families and communities might ameliorate some of these negative outcomes (Edelman & Jones, 2004; Heyman, 2000). Research is now beginning to examine how culture, race/ethnicity, family structure, parenting practices, neighborhood context, or related factors might buffer families from the ill effects of poverty. Ultimately, this research might also help us design programs to meet the special needs of specific groups like Mexican Americans and, we hope, will lead to social policies that reduce overall levels of family and child poverty in the United States.

## DEFINING ETHNICITY

The labels "Latino" and "Hispanic" reflect a diverse ethnic identity based on tracing one's descent to Spanish-speaking countries. Very different groups are labeled Hispanic or Latino in American society, ranging from Mexican Americans (and Mexicanos, Chicanos, etc.) who make up about two-thirds of U.S. Latinos, to Puerto Ricans who make up more than 10% of U.S. Latinos, and Cubans who make up less than 5% of U.S. Latinos. The second largest group of Latinos in the United States is an aggregate category made up of persons from Central and South America (primarily El Salvador, Nicaragua, Colombia, Guatemala, Costa Rica, and Ecuador) who together constitute almost one-quarter of U.S. Latinos. These different Latino groups tend to live in different regions of the country, with Cubans concentrated in Florida, Puerto Ricans concentrated in New York, and Mexican American and Central and South American

peoples formerly concentrated in the southwest and in agricultural areas, but increasingly moving to urban centers and various communities throughout the United States.

Research has often idealized Latino and Mexican American families as monolithic (Cauce & Domenech-Rodriguez, 2002; Massey, Zambrana, & Alonzo Bell, 1995). In reality, family forms and practices vary substantially among any ethnic group, but perhaps especially among a group as large and diverse as those who trace their lineage to Mexico, or to Spanish land grants in the American southwest before the United States became a country (Baca Zinn & Wells, 2000). Although most Mexican Americans now live in urban or suburban neighborhoods, stereotypes about Mexican families have often been based on rural families from earlier historical periods and on assumptions about uniformly shared values (Halgunseth, 2004; McLoyd, Cauce, Takeuchi, & Wilson, 2000). The image of Mexican American families in popular culture and scholarly research has typically been homogenized and somewhat pejorative (see Mirandé, 1997), but contemporary Latino families are quite diverse in generational status, acculturation, economic conditions, and family practices (Buriel & De Ment, 1997; Cabrera & Garcia-Coll, 2004; Dohan, 2003; Leyendecker & Lamb, 1999; Lopez & Stanton-Salazar, 2001). To overcome such stereotypes, recent research has focused on variations among Mexican American families, often demystifying stereotypes and specifying the conditions under which different ideals and family practices occur (Baca Zinn & Wells, 2000; Coltrane, Melzer, Vega, & Parke, 2005; Coltrane, Parke, & Adams, 2004; Mirandé, 1997).

## MEXICAN AMERICANS AND POVERTY

The Mexican American population is characterized by disproportionate levels of poverty. Among both immigrants and the U.S.–born, Mexican Americans have remained at the lower end of the economic ladder. Morales and Ong (1993) and Ortiz (1996) suggest that the combination of high rates of participation in the labor market combined with consistently low wages contribute to the overrepresentation of Mexican Americans among the working poor. Mexican Americans tend to be employed in service sector or manual labor jobs with low pay, limited benefits, few opportunities for advancement, and periodic instability. Vélez-Ibáñez and Greenberg (1992) find that these families adapt by moving between sectors of the labor market, working multiple jobs, and pooling wages.

Economic marginalization profoundly affects Mexican American and other Latino children. A third of Latino children younger than 18 years of age live in poverty, which is three times the poverty rate among non-Latino white children (U.S. Census Bureau, 2004). Latinos are also disproportionately young, with almost 30% of Mexican Americans 14 years old or younger, compared with 19% for European Americans. Although most Mexican American white children live with both parents and in households with at least one employed adult, a disproportionate number are reared in situations with severely limited financial resources (Cauce & Domenech-Rodriguez, 2002).

Latino youth are at risk for a variety of negative outcomes, including violence, crime, and gang-related activity (Allen & Mitchell, 1998; Moore & Pinderhughes, 1993; Tapia, 2004; Wyche & Rotheram-Borus, 1990). Latino youth have the highest levels of drug and alcohol use, and the highest high school dropout levels of all ethnic groups (National Center for Education Statistics, 1998; Therrien & Ramirez, 2000). Latino youth rank second only to African American populations in prevalence of risky sexual activity, teen pregnancy, and gang-related behavior (U.S. Department of Education, 1995; National Centers for Disease Control, 2002).

Latino youth face other risks, such as increasing rates of suicide among adolescents (Chavez & Roney, 1990), poor physical health, and high levels of academic failure (Fuligni & Hardway, 2004). Despite a decline in some health-risk behaviors among American high school students, Latino adolescent problem behaviors appear to be on the rise (Guerra & Williams, 2006). According to the National Centers for Disease Control (2002), Latino children have a higher risk of maladaptive outcomes than do children from other minority groups at the same socioeconomic status (SES) level.

Mexican American families are of particular interest because of their high rates of poverty and high levels of child risk exposure, but also because of their traditional strengths, their high fertility rates, and their emphases on child rearing and extended family bonds. Mexican Americans typically have higher levels of extended "familism" when compared with other ethnic groups of various class levels (Vélez-Ibáñez, 1996). Familism is a central value reflecting strong family cohesion, with emphasis on the group over the individual and requirements for respect and obedience toward parents and other elders (Miranda, Estrada, & Firpo-Jimenez, 2000; Vega, Kolody, Valle, & Weir, 1991). Strong family cohesion and an extended family network can provide social, emotional, and instrumental support as family members share responsibilities, especially those related to child care. This system of social support creates a strong foundation for family life and increases available resources, even in the face of economic hardship. Familism has been described as essential for healthy adjustment in Mexican American families, especially for children (Gonzales, Knight, Morgan-Lopez, Saenz, & Sirolli, 2002; Vega et al., 1991).

Research has shown that family cohesion acts as a buffer against acculturative stress (Hovey & King, 1996; Salgado de Snyder, 1987), internalizing behavior (e.g., Lindahl,

Malik, Kaczynski, & Simons, 2004), external-izing behavior (Yahav, 2002), and academic failure (Prevatt, 2003). As these studies attest, most research has focused on family cohesion as a protective factor in relation to outcomes for youth (Cortes, 1995). In a recent extension of this research, we found that family cohesion mediates the relation between economic or life stress and parenting behaviors in both Mexican American and European American families, demonstrating that stress is more strongly associated with parenting behaviors in families that are less cohesive (Behnke et al., 2006). Although Mexican American families were more cohesive than their Anglo counter-parts, parenting practices in both ethnicities were similarly buffered from the effects of stress by family cohesion.

## ECONOMIC STRESS, PARENTING, AND CHILD DEVELOPMENT

In addition to problems directly associated with economic disadvantage, poverty has been shown to create ancillary problems in parenting and child development. Conger et al. (1992) developed an economic stress model that specified the following:

> Economic hardship would affect the lives of parents primarily through the noticeable financial pressures they create. In turn, these pressures were expected to have a direct impact on parents' demoralization and emo-tional distress. These mediating conditions, in turn, were predicted to have adverse con-sequences for the marriage and for skillful parenting. The end result of the hypothesized process was disrupted parenting and its neg-ative influence on the developmental trajec-tories of early adolescent males. (p. 537)

Such theoretical and empirical contribu-tions have expanded concerns about poverty beyond economics to the realm of family relations and child development. Thus, children can be seen as not only disadvan-taged in material and economic ways, but as subject to family practices shaped by reac-tions to economic stress that could poten-tially lead to psychological, emotional, or social maladjustment. This notion has been studied in relation to family life (e.g., Garbarino, 1976), with studies consistently confirming that poverty and economic stress are associated with reduced levels of family functioning (e.g., negative interactions; Gomel, Tinsley, Parke, & Clark, 1998) and problems for parents (e.g., Conger & Elder, 1994). Studies have shown that economic hardship is related to heightened family con-flict, negative parent-child interactions, and overall unhealthy family interactions (Behnke et al., 2006; Simons, Johnson, Beamon, Conger, & Whitbeck, 1996; Simons, Whitbeck, Conger, & Melby, 1990).

In a recent extension of this model to Mexican American families and children, we examined the impact of economic stress on children's adaptation (Parke et al., 2004). In this study, 278 Mexican American and European American families and their fifth-grade children were evaluated. Using measures derived from the Conger model, economic hardship was linked to indices of economic pressure that were related to depression symptoms for both mothers and fathers of both ethnicities. In structural equation models, depressive symptoms were linked to marital problems and hostile parenting. Hostile parenting, in turn, was strongly related to child adjustment prob-lems for European Americans, whereas mar-ital problems were more strongly linked to child adjustment problems for Mexican American families.

Why do marital problems appear to have a greater impact on children in Mexican American families? As noted previously, Mexican American families are characterized by high rates of marriage, high levels of family cohesion, and a high value placed on familism or family solidarity. From a family systems perspective, when the subsystems in the family are highly interdependent, problems in any subsystem are likely to have a more significant impact on other subsystems (e.g., the child) than in familial organizations in which family cohesion is lower. In addition, differences in the physical organization of space in Mexican American and European American households probably play a role in accounting for the links between marital problems and children's outcomes. Specifically, because Mexican American families usually are poorer than European American families, their houses are typically smaller and, in turn, children in Mexican American families are more likely to be exposed to ongoing parental conflict or be aware of parental marital difficulties. In contrast, European American families may be able to conceal their marital difficulties to a greater degree than Mexican American families can. This suggests that an ecological analysis of the links between privacy potentials in households, as well as children's exposure to displays of marital problems, would be worthwhile in future studies.

In both the European American and Mexican American families, hostile parenting—principally by fathers—was linked with higher levels of child adjustment problems. We interviewed fathers to determine what processes might be at work. Many Mexican American fathers talked about how work-related stress sometimes leads to harsh and explosive parenting. For example, one 36-year-old father who was a first-generation immigrant from Mexico said, "I get upset quickly, I get frustrated. Maybe it's because I'm so tired, I don't know, but I get upset, I get frustrated." Another father, a 30-year-old first-generation Mexican immigrant, when asked what he would like to change about his parenting, said, "Change my temper. I would change my character a little, my character

because of work, or financial worries, because of it, I'm a bit demanding."

A variety of mechanisms including modeling (Parke & Buriel, 2006) and coercive family process (Dishion, Patterson, Stoolmiller, & Skinner, 1991) have been suggested as explanations for this link between hostile parenting and child outcomes. Why is the father-child link stronger than the mother-child link, especially in European American families? The relative salience of father's discipline—in view of its relative intensity as well as its infrequency—may account for the stronger effect of paternal than maternal discipline. Alternatively, even though maternal hostility was not significantly directly related to child adjustment, mothers and fathers probably reinforce each other's level of hostility. By supporting paternal harsh parenting, mothers may have an indirect influence on child outcomes through the correlation between maternal and paternal hostile parenting. This hypothesis merits examination. More work is needed to understand better the differential influence of parenting and marital problems on children in these two groups.

For Mexican American families, the level of acculturation influenced the pattern of relationships. Maternal acculturation, which was highly correlated with paternal acculturation, was differentially linked with marital problems and hostile parenting. Maternal acculturation was associated with higher reported levels of marital problems but lower reported levels of maternal and paternal hostile parenting. Perhaps increased acculturation can be seen as being associated with a more individualistic orientation and a shift toward more egalitarian patterns of power relations in the family. Marital problems increased as women acculturated to the host country and began to expect more equality within the marriage (and between the parents and children) than did their husbands. Moreover, the empowerment that came as a result of children's linguistic and (host) cultural competence probably increased child-parent conflict because of the children's push for autonomy and greater decision making within the family. Similarly, conflict between parents and children tends to increase as children adopt norms of the host culture, with issues of dress codes, curfew, and activities with peers serving as flash points.

In our studies, we see these conflicts increase most dramatically for Mexican-born fathers as they attempt to control their adolescent daughters more tightly than their adolescent sons. One 52-year-old Mexican immigrant father discussed his worries about his daughter:

> I take her and bring her [to and from school]. And she tells me, "Don't go for me, I will walk," but I tell her, "I don't want you flirting." . . . She is old now and with any little thing that you do they are going to steal you. I tell her that "if you don't want any problems with any one, don't go with anyone if they ask you if you want a friendship, or a ride, or whatever." Tell them, "My dad is coming and he brings me and takes me so I don't need anything from no one."

In addition, as maternal acculturation increased, the level of both maternal and paternal hostile parenting decreased. This decrease is consistent with an increased awareness of alternative disciplinary strategies that are less harsh and punitive, such as reasoning, love withdrawal, and loss of privileges. At the same time, as acculturation increases, families become more acquainted with the relatively unfavorable attitudes that European Americans hold concerning the use of harsh and punitive disciplinary strategies (Straus, 1994). Finally, Mexican American parenting, particularly in immigrant families (Buriel, 1993), stresses greater accountability by children to help the family cope with its adjustment to life in the United States. Therefore, what is typically defined as "hostile

parenting" may be perceived differently in recent immigrant families if it helps promote the childrearing goal of accountability.

Although our findings revealed some differences across European American and Mexican American families, overall, the processes that characterized the operation of economic stress on family functioning were similar. This work underscores the robustness of the family stress model (Conger & Elder, 1994) and extends its applicability to Mexican American as well as European American and African American samples (Conger et al., 2002).

## A RISK AND RESILIENCE PERSPECTIVE ON POVERTY IN MEXICAN AMERICAN FAMILIES

To aid in understanding the effects of poverty in Mexican American families, a risk and resilience theoretical perspective is useful (Luthar, Cicchetti, & Becker, 2000). From this vantage point, children's successful adaptation given such stressful circumstances as family poverty varies as a function of two components: the form and frequency of risk and the protective or resilience factors that buffer the child from the adverse events. The value of this approach is that it focuses attention on the positive ways in which families can adapt and cope in the face of stressful circumstances such as poverty. This represents a shift away from a pathology or deficit view of poor families to a perspective that recognizes family strengths and the value of community social capital as assets that can be recruited to aid families in better managing the adverse events and circumstances associated with being poor.

Three sets of protective factors appear to buffer children from risk and stress and promote coping and good adjustment in the face of adversity. The first set of factors consists of positive individual attributes. Children who exhibit easy temperaments, high self-esteem, intelligence, and independence are more adaptable in the face of stressful life experiences (Rutter, 1987; Werner, 1993). Compared with boys and men, girls and women have a slight edge as well. The second set of protective factors is found in a supportive family environment. A close parent-child relationship or a satisfying marriage can buffer the adverse effects of poverty or other stressful conditions or events such as divorce or incarceration (Luthar et al., 2000). The final set of factors involves people outside the family, for example, individuals in the school system, peer groups, or religious institutions that support children's and parents' coping efforts. Later, we focus on individual family and community factors that help buffer children and adults from poverty's ill effects.

## INDIVIDUAL LEVEL FACTORS

As already noted, gender is an identified resilience factor, with Latino girls, especially at younger ages, being less reactive to stress than Latino boys. This has been attributed to *marianismo,* or the fact that Latinas are socialized to be self-sacrificing and obedient (Vega, 1990), and may develop an increased faculty to cope with adversity and avoid conflict (Flores, Cicchetti, & Rogosch, 2005). Although ethnic identity issues and expectations to help financially (Buriel, 1993) are risk factors for boys, Mexican American girls seem to show resilience, though the mechanisms are as yet unclear (Gonzalez & Padilla, 1997). Further research on gender is needed, however, because adolescent Latinas also experience high (and increasing) risks of suicide and other negative mental health outcomes. As noted previously, Mexican-born fathers tend to keep a tight rein on their daughters, which, in turn, may put the daughters at risk because of limited social opportunities and related conflicts with their needs or desires. Sons, on the other hand, are granted more autonomy than daughters are.

Individual personality traits such as self-regulatory skills may be important moderators of the effects of poverty as well. For example, moderate ego control is taught in Latino culture (de Rios, 2001; Simoni & Perez, 1995), as part of a value system teaching increased regulation of expressiveness and promulgation of emotional restraint. This has been found to buffer disadvantaged Latino children (Cicchetti, Rogosch, Lynch, & Holt, 1993). Masten et al. (1995) found that the causal influence tends to flow from school conduct to academic performance, rather than the opposite. This speaks to the value of the regulation and restraint championed in Latino culture for success in extra-familial settings such as the school. At the same time, the promulgation of expressive restraint may have unmeasured effects on the assertiveness and individual social and economic mobility of Latino youth.

Similarly, a sense of self-efficacy by children can be a protective factor (Bandura, 2006). Research by Small (2002) demonstrated how a taste of successful effort affords a sense of efficacy that can in turn be a catalyst for a proactive, involved community. In like manner, the development of a child's self-perception, self-evaluation, and self-respect forms a main element in the process of learning and experience that provides the ability to exert predictive and active control over the environment (Bandura, 1978, 2006; Harter, 2006). Such opportunities for Latino children in poverty can be curtailed by unstable employment of parents, lack of routines (Wilson, 1996), less predictable neighborhoods (Garbarino & Kostelny, 1992), disrupted social schedules because of family needs (Buriel, 1993), and increased arbitrary parental discipline (Elder, Nguyen, & Caspi, 1985).

In contrast to the adaptiveness of a child's sense of agency and efficacy, presence of an external locus of control (blaming poverty on social causes) leads children to lower educational goals (Murry et al., 2002). A central, often decisive role in the mediating mental processes that guide a person's purposeful dealing with the environment is played by the basic values, norms, goals, and motives relevant for the issue under consideration (Feather, 1980). Lowering one's educational goals would be a rational choice in a world where poverty was truly caused by social influences independent of a person's actions, and youth in poverty may make what they feel is a rational choice by lowering their educational goals. "Although poverty is objectively linked to social inequities and injustices such as racism, prejudice, and discrimination (Bobo & Smith, 1994; Wilson, 1996), messages that do not focus on victimization may enhance children's sense of control, optimism, and future orientation." (Murry et al., 2002, p. 118). Discrimination is a risk factor that many Latino children experience, (Flores et al., 2002), and even indirect exposure to discrimination through witnessed interactions or recounted episodes by others can influence a Latino child's social beliefs and expectations (Parke & Buriel, 2006). An additional way discrimination may exert influence is that experience channels our attention, and Latino children may become less aware of the world of social cues surrounding them as they are primed to detect hostile or discriminatory cues (Lemerise & Arsenio, 2000; Miller & Seier, 1994).

## FAMILY LEVEL FACTORS THAT MODERATE THE EFFECTS OF POVERTY

A considerable amount of research literature in the social and behavioral sciences suggests that poverty strongly influences parenting practices. Research investigating the mediating role of the family on the relationship between poverty and child outcomes has shown that mother-child interaction quality partially accounts for effects of social class

(Harnish, Dodge, & Valente, 1995). In addition to direct economic stress, parents living at or below the poverty level often have less understanding of children's behavior and development (Sameroff & Feil, 1985), and are less likely to ask children about wishes, reward positive behavior, or be responsive (Lareau, 2003; McLoyd, 1990). Parents in poverty also tend toward more hostile coparent relations (Brody et al., 1994; Conger et al., 1990). Low-income minority parents appear more likely to use parent-centered discipline strategies intended to result in short-term compliance (for a review, see Kelly, Power, & Wimbush, 1992). Although it has been suggested that personal resources might mediate the relationship between employment and parenting, this has not been consistently supported (Murry et al., 2002). Using a sample of low-income mothers to look at the mediators between maternal depression and parenting, Albright and Tamis-LeMonda (2002) found the same effects established for higher income families, suggesting that the relationship between maternal depression and child outcomes is not mediated by the presence or absence of books or toys, but of warmth and attention. This finding is relevant to the present discussion because Mexican American families, even when poor, tend to have high levels of maternal warmth and family cohesion. Researchers have yet to grasp the normative constellation of parenting elements among low-income parents (Brody & Flor, 1998; McGroder, 2000), especially Latinos (Hill, Bush, & Roosa, 2003). Although some work has suggested that the associations between poverty and parenting are not moderated by ethnicity (Gutman & Eccles, 1999), discussions of parenting among Latinos in poverty must consider the research showing that families in poverty frequently live in high crime neighborhoods (Rank, 2004), which often changes the type of parenting that is considered most adaptive (Furstenberg, Cook, Eccles, Elder, &

Sameroff, 1999; Parke & Buriel, 2006; see later discussion). However, we must not overstate the case for a new "adaptive" parenting for impoverished families in high-risk environments. Although some researchers suggest that decreased autonomy-granting by parents may be adaptive in low-income, high-risk environments, there are likely serious tradeoffs. For example, Crosnoe and Elder (2002) found that in low-income families, increased autonomy was associated with lower emotional distress among monozygotic twins. Although it has been suggested such authoritarian parenting is adaptive in high-risk contexts, the parenting goal of child compliance is simply one of many, including teaching, satisfying a child's emotional needs, and fostering familial relations (Magnuson & Duncan, 2002) This is implicitly acknowledged by Magnuson and Duncan, who praise interventions that result in parents being more sensitive, supportive, and positive, and less harsh and restrictive, as well as the resultant improved outcomes for the children of these parents (Brooks-Gunn, Berlin, & Fuligni, 2000; Olds et al., 1998)

Intergenerational residence, often associated with familism, may also increase resilience for families in poverty (Wakschlag, Chase-Lansdale, & Brooks-Gunn, 1996). Conversely, the potential negative consequences of familism are less recognized. Familism can lead to enmeshment in the family unit, which can become a liability if the family unit itself becomes dysfunctional. For example, in a study comparing Mexican Americans and African Americans from dysfunctional families, after controlling for SES, Mexican American youth evidenced higher levels of emotional disturbance, difficulty with peers, and lower adaptive functioning than did their SES-matched African American counterparts (Canino, Gould, Purpris, & Shaffer, 1986). Findings like these support the reasoning that when a child depends almost exclusively on the family unit

for support, guidance, and security, disruptions to the family system could be markedly more deleterious to the child.

For Mexican American immigrant children, the disruption of family ties that often accompanies life in the United States can be a risk factor because of the unavailability of extended family in the United States. In addition, family conflicts may arise during interactions with the host culture (i.e., cultural brokering) that can be disruptive to the harmony and structure of the family; this is especially salient in the context of familism where conflict is atypical. This disruption can be exacerbated by nonresident status, with the accompanying lack of access to social and community services and benefits. Nonresident status can even result in the nuclear family being split because of deportation for Mexicans who immigrated illegally. More than 5 million migrant workers, most of them Mexicans or Central Americans, experience stressors unique to their long hours, low income, and frequent relocations (Magaña & Hovey, 2003).

Acculturative stress affects the identity formation processes of Latino youth in ways that can increase risk of internalizing and externalizing. The stress of negotiating the expectations of the host culture and the heritage of the culture of origin can delay identity formation, or deflect the trajectories of Latino children toward maladjustment. Relative to ethnic identity, a bicultural trajectory (Clauss-Ehlers, 2004; Holleran & Jung, 2005) can allow children to enjoy the scaffolding of their culture of origin, while benefiting from the resources the host culture offers. Close family relationships or enmeshment with one's culture of origin can enhance a child's self-esteem, which has been shown to be a resilience factor for disadvantaged Latino children (Cicchetti & Rogosch, 1997).

Membership in an ethnic group does not necessarily mean a family shares the cultural beliefs or practices associated with that group, especially if they have lived in the United States for several generations. Traditional strengths such as close ties to extended family can themselves become risk factors, as illustrated by the work of Contreras, Manglesdorf, Rhodes, Diener, and Brunson (1999) showing that although greater support by a grandmother was related to less parenting stress among Puerto Rican mothers low in acculturation, the relationship reversed when the mothers were highly acculturated. Social networks, another resilience factor traditionally associated with Latino families, can become an additional source of stress (Belle, 1990), and level of acculturation may be the deciding moderator. The value of conformity over self-direction, a value emphasized in Latino culture, could start out as beneficial for recent immigrants, but become a risk factor for succeeding generations (Gecas, 1979).

## COMMUNITY LEVEL MODERATORS OF POVERTY

The school environment, although generally viewed as an asset to immigrant youth, can carry challenges for Latino children as well. Mexican American children attend more problematic elementary schools (larger, lower teacher experience, high percentage of minority students) than do their SES-matched counterparts from other ethnic minority groups (Crosnoe, 2005). Language barriers present their own set of challenges to Latino youth, creating obstacles to education and socialization (Parke & Buriel, 2006), as well as limiting peer associations, and creating a sense of alienation from the surrounding culture. The combination of poor schools and language barriers may contribute to the 30% dropout rate (Gonzalez et al., 2002) among Mexican Americans.

Our interviews with immigrant Mexican Americans suggest that it is harder for children whose parents went to school in Mexico compared with those whose parents went to school in the United States: "She sometimes wants us to help and sincerely we can't. We can't help in the language [English] and unfortunately, we can't even explain it to her in our language, no we can't . . . We feel bad. We want to help but we can't." Another Mexican immigrant father noted that he had difficulty dealing with his son's problems at school:

> If we go to school we try to find someone that can talk to me in Spanish. Yes, yes because . . . I normally understand a little, a little English but not a lot. I don't know how to speak it, darn. Like sometimes I tell him, when they are talking to me in English, I tell him to tell me what he is saying and he doesn't know how to tell me. He gets embarrassed and at the end he doesn't know how to say what it is that they are saying in English.

In addition, the modeling-based teaching pattern seen in rural Mexican culture, with much less praise directed toward the child and less emphasis on inquiry, may not prepare Mexican immigrant children adequately for American schools (Laosa, 1980). Poverty itself, and the language barrier between Mexican American children and many of their successful classmates may also be impediments to peer-mediated learning (Patterson, Vaden, & Kupersmidt, 1991; Teasley, 1995). In cases where these impediments compel Latino children to limit their peer associations, they are often required by their constricted range of peers to choose between two classic developmental tasks, academic success and peer acceptance (Holleran & Jung, 2005; Vigil & Long, 1981).

Like other immigrant families, Mexican parents use personal stories of hardship to encourage their children to work hard in school, and these stories have been shown to promote resilience (Tamis, 2005; Villenas

& Deyhle, 1999). One Mexican immigrant father who often told stories of hardship to his children started taking them to the fields to work when they were not in school:

> For example, all my kids know [how to work] the hoe, they know how to pick grapes—various jobs. So they see that the door is open for them to do more than those types of work. They always told me they were going to stay in school. And it made me happy to hear that, because I taught them how hard it was to work in the fields. (Lòpez, 2001, p. 430)

Beyond the proximal influence of poverty on the family, families in poverty are often compelled to live in disadvantaged neighborhoods. The disadvantages of such neighborhoods are clearly established in the literature (Leventhal & Brooks-Gunn, 2000). One key finding from our own research concerns the links between parents' perceptions of neighborhood and their parenting behaviors. Mexican American parents, especially fathers, in contrast to European American parents, perceived greater threats and danger in their neighborhoods; in turn, they were more restrictive and protective of their children as evidenced by higher levels of monitoring and supervision (Coltrane et al., 2005). Rather than viewing Mexican American fathers (or mothers) as simply restrictive, we can view them as protective and acting responsibly in response to the perceived level of neighborhood threat. Thus, parenting strategies may develop as an adaptive response to unsafe and unpredictable environments. The evidence for Mexican American parents' restrictiveness is consistent with earlier work with African American families (Brody et al., 2001; Furstenberg et al., 1999). African American parents residing in unsafe neighborhoods tended to use more authoritarian (i.e., restrictive and controlling) parenting strategies to protect their children. Moreover, children in these contexts benefited from these authoritarian parenting practices in their adjustment (Brody et al., 2001) whereas majority children are often harmed by the use of these authoritarian practices (Baumrind, 1978).

There are several reasons for the positive links between restrictive parenting in poverty neighborhoods and better child adjustment. First, greater control in harsh environments may actually protect children from potentially harmful threats (e.g., deviant peers, gangs, guns). Second, children in racial/ethnic minority groups may interpret parental behavior differently than majority white children do. The use of authoritarian tactics is generally more normative and viewed as an acceptable child-rearing style in ethnic neighborhoods (Corral-Verdugo, Frias-Armenta, Romero, & Munoz, 1995; Sonneck, 1999; for a similar argument about Asian Americans, see Chao, 1994). Third, the context in which parental restrictiveness occurs is critical to understanding its impact on children. For example, the link between harsh parenting and child outcomes may depend on whether parental disciplinary actions are carried out in the context of a warm, supportive family environment. To the extent that there is a supportive parent-child relationship and marital harmony, the effects of restrictive practices are likely to be more beneficial. Only when there is a hostile parent-child relationship will there be negative outcomes associated with the use of these practices.

Returning to our own findings, the relatively authoritarian practices we observed in response to neighborhood threat will likely have minimal detrimental effects on the children because these same Mexican American fathers reported more involvement with their children (e.g., walking and shopping together). In other analyses from our project, we discovered that less acculturated Mexican American fathers with traditional views about gender were highly involved with their children (Coltrane et al., 2004). We also discovered that overt conflict in Mexican American marriages was a better predictor of child emotional problems than was hostile parenting (Parke et al., 2004) and that father's use of physical punishment was associated with more behavior problems in children only when there was a hostile family climate. If there was a warm and supportive family atmosphere, the link between harsh fathering and child adjustment was not evident (Schofield, 2004). Hence, we must consider both the restrictiveness and the emotional warmth of the parent-child relationship to understand how parenting practices affect child development.

Community support is another resilience factor as Mexican American children living in poor neighborhoods fare better than do their counterparts living in lower-middle class neighborhoods, as long as the poor neighborhood has a significant Mexican American population, to serve as a social support network (Baca Zinn, & Wells, 2000). In both neighborhoods populated by recent immigrants and those populated by Latino families with a long history in the United States, residents are able to rely on extended family and social networks to negotiate economic stress by sharing housing, transportation, and childcare responsibilities (Dohan, 2003). That this is common to both immigrant and intergenerational families suggests a structural rather than cultural basis for the strong ties to extended family. Immigrants are likely to work longer hours to maintain sustainable wages whereas non-immigrants are more likely to resort to hustling and other nonsanctioned economic activities common in the barrio (Dohan, 2003).

Our research found high levels of co-ethnic support among low-income Mexican Americans living in impoverished neighborhoods, potentially explaining why Aneshensel and Sucoff (1996) found lower conduct disorder and depression for Latino youth living in low-income neighborhoods with a high concentration of Latinos, even when compared with Latino youth in higher SES neighborhoods (Coltrane et al., 2005). Research finding parental monitoring of early dating behavior to mediate the positive association between low-income neighborhoods and teenage childbearing (Hogan & Kitagawa, 1985) speaks to the benefit Latino children in poverty can gain from the high levels of monitoring reported by their parents (McLoyd et al., 2000).

Strong religious beliefs, which are on average higher among Latinos, have been identified as resiliency factors for other families in poverty (Brody, Stoneman, & Flor, 1996) if they lead to more child-centered and less controlling discipline. Cultural sanctions on particular risk factors such as divorce (Gonzalez & Padilla, 1997), as well as beliefs such as restrictions on use of alcohol and cigarettes among pregnant women (Bender & Castro, 2000) are aspects of Mexican American culture that promote resilience. Religious participation also creates an informal social support network, which can itself promote resilience. The effects of religiosity thus merit further study, particularly among high-risk groups like poor Mexican Americans.

## REMAINING ISSUES

Various issues merit further examination. First, the long-term effects of poverty on Mexican American families need to be traced. How many Mexican American families remain in poverty, and how many are able to move up the economic ladder in American society? Second, do improved economic circumstances always lead to better adaptation by parents and children? The challenge is to determine when upward economic mobility improves well-being and adaptation because of increased resources and improved neighborhoods and when such shifts—albeit positive in economic terms—are associated with weakening of community social ties or a reduction in the sense of cohesion among family members. Third, the impact of acculturation on cycles of poverty merits closer scrutiny, especially the role played by community capital in this process. How are employment opportunities related to acculturation and what impact does blocked mobility have on Mexican Americans who have lived in the United States for several generations? Fourth, treatment of acculturation as a family and community level variable rather than as an individual one might help researchers better understand the dynamics between the acculturation process and poverty fluctuations. Fifth, more focus on the effects of the "poverty gap" between generations within the same family would be worthwhile. If acculturated children fare better economically than their parents, for example, will this income discrepancy help or hurt family cohesion and a sense of familism? Sixth, more attention to the role of neighborhood contexts would be beneficial. We should focus not just on poverty per se but treat neighborhood as a resource for raising families out of poverty through the development of collective efficacy, a form of social capital in which the neighborhood is the identified unit of action (Bandura, 2006).

## CONCLUDING THOUGHTS

As our chapter suggests, the meaning and impact of poverty in Mexican American families is similar to, but also different from the experiences of European Americans. Some culturally unique aspects of Mexican American families' reactions to poverty caution us against generalizing findings across cultural groups. If we are to develop effective social policies to address the effects of poverty on Mexican American (or other Latino) children and families, we need to better understand both the similarities and differences across different cultural groups. Until we do, we will be poorly equipped to provide effective, culturally meaningful societal solutions to the adverse effects of poverty. Finally, to be successful, policies need to recognize and build upon the strengths of Mexican American families. Policies that incorporate positive aspects of Mexican American family life could serve as models for policy design for other ethnic groups as well. In the long run, members of the host culture, as well as all immigrant groups, will benefit.

## REFERENCES

Albright, M. B., & Tamis-LeMonda, C. S. (2002). Maternal depressive symptoms in relation to dimensions of parenting in low-income mothers. *Applied Developmental Science, 6,* 24–34.

Allen, J. P., & Mitchell, C. (1998). Racial and ethnic differences in patterns of problematic and adaptive development: An epidemiological review. In V. C. McLoyd & L. Steinberg (Eds.), *Studying minority adolescents: Conceptual, methodological, and theoretical issues* (pp. 29–54). Mahwah, NJ: Erlbaum.

Aneshensel, C. S., & Sucoff, C. A. (1996). The neighborhood context of adolescent mental health. *Journal of Health and Social Behavior, 37,* 293–310.

Baca Zinn, M., & Wells, B. (2000). Diversity within Latino families: New lessons for family social science. In D. H. Demo, K. R. Allen, & M. A. Fine (Eds.), *Handbook of family diversity* (pp. 252–273). New York: Oxford University Press.

Bandura, A. (1978). The self system in reciprocal determinism. *American Psychologist, 33,* 344–358.

Bandura, A. (2006). Toward a psychology of human agency. *Perspectives on psychological science, 1,* 164–180.

Baumrind, D. (1978). Parental disciplinary patterns and social competence in children. *Youth and Society, 9,* 239–276.

Behnke, A., MacDermid, S., Coltrane, S., Parke, R. D., Duffy, S., & Widaman, K. F. (2006). *Family cohesion in the lives of Mexican American and European American parents.* Unpublished manuscript (submitted).

Belle, D. E. (1990). Poverty and women's mental health. *American Psychologist, 45,* 385–389.

Bender, D. E., & Castro, D. (2000). Explaining the birth weight paradox: Latina immigrants' perceptions of resilience and risk. *Journal of Immigrant Health, 2,* 155–173.

Bobo, L., & Smith, R. A. (1994). Antipoverty policy, affirmative action, and racial attitudes. In S. Danziger, G. Sandefur, & D. Weinberg (Eds.), *Confronting poverty: Prescriptions for change* (pp. 365–395). Cambridge, MA: Harvard University Press.

Brody, G. H., & Flor, D. (1998). Maternal resources, parenting practices, and child competence in rural, single-parent African American families. *Child Development, 69,* 803–816.

Brody, G. H., Ge, X., Conger, R. D., Gibbons, F. X., Murry, V. M., Gerrand, M., et al. (2001). The influence of neighborhood disadvantage, collective socialization, and parenting on African American children's affiliation with deviant peers. *Child Development, 72,* 1231–1246.

Brody, G. H., Stoneman, Z., & Flor, D. (1996). Parental religiosity, family processes, and youth competence in rural, two-parent African American families. *Developmental Psychology, 32,* 696–706.

Brody, G. H., Stoneman, Z., Flor, D., McCrary, C., Hastings, L., & Conyers, O. (1994). Financial resources, parent psychological functioning, parent co-caregiving, and early adolescent competence in rural two-parent African American families. *Child Development, 65,* 590–605.

Brooks-Gunn, J., Berlin, L., & Fuligni, A. S. (2000). Early childhood intervention programs: What about the family? In J. P. Shonkoff & S. J. Meisel (Eds.), *Handbook of early childhood intervention* (2nd ed., pp. 549–589). New York: Cambridge University Press.

Buriel, R. (1993). Childrearing orientations In Mexican American families: The influence of generation and sociocultural factors. *Journal of Marriage and the Family, 55,* 987–1000.

Buriel, R., & De Ment, T. (1997). Immigration and sociocultural changes in Mexican, Chinese, and Vietnamese American families. In A. Booth, A. C. Crouter, & N. Landale (Eds.), *Immigration and the family: Research and policy on U.S. immigrants* (pp. 165–200). Mahwah, NJ: Erlbaum.

Cabrera, N., & Garcia-Coll, C. (2004). Latino fathers. In M. E. Lamb (Ed.), *The role of the father in child development* (4th ed., pp. 98–120). New York: Wiley.

Canino, I. A., Gould, M. S., Purpris, S., & Shaffer, D. (1986). A comparison of symptoms and diagnoses in Hispanic and black children in an outpatient mental health clinic. *Journal of the American Academy of Child Psychiatry, 25,* 254–259.

Cauce, A. M., & Domenech-Rodriguez, M. (2002). Latino families: Myths and realities. In J. M. Contreras, K. A. Kerns, & A. M. Neal-Barnett (Eds.), *Latino children and families in the United States.* Westport, CT: Praeger.

Chao, R. (1994). Beyond parental control and authoritarian parenting style. *Child Development, 65,* 1111–1119.

Chavez, J. M., & Roney, C. E. (1990). Psychocultural factors affecting the mental health status of Mexican American adolescents. In A. R. Stiffman & L. E. Davis (Eds.), *Ethnic issues in adolescent mental health*. Newbury Park, CA: Sage.

Cicchetti, D., & Rogosch, F. A. (1997). The role of self-organization in the promotion of resilience in maltreated children. *Development and Psychopathology, 9*, 797–815.

Cicchetti, D., Rogosch, F. A., Lynch, M., & Holt, K. D. (1993). Resilience in maltreated children: Processes leading to adaptive outcome. *Development and Psychopathology, 5*, 629–647.

Clauss-Ehlers, C. S. (2004). A framework for school-based mental health promotion with bicultural Latino children: Building on strengths to promote resilience. *International Journal of Mental Health Promotion, 6*, 26–33.

Coltrane, S., & Collins, R. (2001). *Sociology of marriage and the family*. Belmont, CA: Wadsworth.

Coltrane, S., Melzer, S., Vega, E., & Parke, R. D. (2005). Mexican American fathering in neighborhood context. In W. Marsiglio, K. Roy, & G. L. Fox (Eds.), *Situated fathering: A focus on physical and social spaces* (pp. 277–298). Lanham, MD: Rowman & Littlefield.

Coltrane, S., Parke, R. D., & Adams, M. (2004). Complexity of father involvement in low-income Mexican American families. *Family Relations, 53*(2), 179–189.

Conger, R. D., Conger, K. J., Glen, H., Elder, J., Lorenz, F. O., Simons, R. L., et al. (1992). A family process model of economic hardship and adjustment of early adolescent boys. *Child Development, 63*(3), 526–541.

Conger, R. D., & Elder, G. H., Jr. (1994). *Families in troubled times*. New York: de Gruyter.

Conger, R. D., Elder, G. H., Lorenz, F. O., Conger, K. J., Simons, R. L., Whitbeck, L. B., et al. (1990). Linking economic hardship to marital quality and instability. *Journal of Marriage and the Family, 52*, 643–656.

Conger, R. D., Wallace, L. E., Sun, Y., Simons, R. L., McLoyd, V. C., & Brody, G. H. (2002). Economic pressure in African American families: A replication and extension of the family stress model. *Developmental Psychology, 38*, 179–193.

Contreras, J. M., Manglesdorf, S. C., Rhodes, J. E., Diener, M. L., & Brunson, L. (1999). Parent-child interaction among Latina adolescent mothers: The role of family and social support. *Journal of Research on Adolescence, 9*, 417–439.

Corral-Verdugo, V., Frias-Armenta, M., Romero, M., & Munoz, A. (1995). Validity of a scale of beliefs regarding the "positive" effects of punishing children: A study of Mexican mothers. *Child Abuse & Neglect, 19*, 669–679.

Cortes, D. E. (1995). Variations in familism in two generations of Puerto Ricans. *Hispanic Journal of Behavioral Sciences, 17*, 249–255.

Crosnoe, R. (2005). Double disadvantage or signs of resilience? The elementary school contexts of children from Mexican immigrant families. *American Educational Research Journal, 42*, 269–303.

Crosnoe, R., & Elder, G. H. (2002). Adolescent twins and emotional distress: The interrelated influence of nonshared environment and social structure. *Child Development, 73*, 1761–1774.

de Rios, M. D. (2001). *Brief psychotherapy with the Latino immigrant client*. New York: Haworth Press.

Dishion, T., Patterson, G. R., Stoolmiller, M., & Skinner, M. L. (1991). Family, school, and behavioral antecedents to early adolescent involvement with antisocial peers. *Developmental Psychology, 27*, 172–180.

Dohan, D. (2003). *The price of poverty: Money, work, and culture in the Mexican-American barrio*. Berkeley: University of California Press.

Duncan, G. J., & Brooks-Gunn, J. (Eds.). (1997). *Consequences of growing up poor*. New York: Russell Sage.

Edelman, M. W., & Jones, J. M. (2004). Separate and unequal: America's children, race and poverty. *Future of Children, 14*, 134–137.

Elder, G. H., Nguyen, T. V., & Caspi, A. (1985). Linking family hardship to children's lives. *Child Development, 56*, 361–375.

Feather, N. T. (1980). Value systems and social interaction: A field study in a newly independent nation. *Journal of Applied Social Psychology, 10*, 1–19.

Flores, E., Cicchetti, D., & Rogosch, F. A. (2005). Predictors of resilience in maltreated and nonmaltreated Latino students. *Developmental Psychology, 41*, 338–351.

Flores, G., Fuentes-Afflick, E., Barbot, O., Carter-Pokras, O., Claudio, L., Lara, M., et al. (2002). The health of Latino children: Urgent priorities, unanswered questions, and a research agenda. *Journal of the American Medical Association, 288*, 82–90.

Fuligni, A. J., & Hardway, C. (2004). Preparing diverse adolescents for the transition to adulthood. *Future of Children, 14*, 99–119.

Furstenberg, F. F., Cook, T. D., Eccles, J. S., Elder, G. H., & Sameroff, A. (1999). *Managing to make it: Urban families and adolescent success*. Chicago: University of Chicago Press.

Gaouette, N. (2006, May 6). House GOP group targets bilingual ballots. *Los Angeles Times*.

Garbarino, J. (1976). A preliminary study of some ecological correlates of child abuse: The impact of socioeconomic stress on mothers. *Child Development, 47*, 178–185.

Garbarino, J., & Kostelny, K. (1992). Child maltreatment as a community problem. *Child Abuse & Neglect, 16*, 455–464.

Gecas, V. (1979). The influence of social class on socialization. In W. R. Burr, R. Hill, I. Nye & I. L. Reiss (Eds.), *Contemporary theories about the family*. New York: Free Press.

Gomel, J. N., Tinsley, B. J., Parke, R. D., & Clark, K. (1998). The effects of economic hardship on family functioning: A multi-ethnic perspective. *Journal of Family Issues, 19*, 436–467.

Gonzales, N. A., Knight, G. P., Morgan-Lopez, A. A., Saenz, D., & Sirolli, A. (2002). Acculturation and the mental health of Latino youths: An integration and critique of the literature. In J. M. Contreras, K. A. Kerns, & A. M. Neal-Barnett (Eds.), *Latino children and families in the United States: Current research and future directions* (pp. 45–74). Westport, CT: Praeger.

Gonzalez, R., & Padilla, A. M. (1997). The academic resilience of Mexican American high school students. *Hispanic Journal of Behavioral Sciences, 19*, 301–317.

Guerra, N. G., & Williams, K. R. (2006). Ethnicity, youth violence and the ecology of development. In N. G. Guerra & E. P. Smith (Eds.), *Preventing youth violence in a multicultural society* (pp. 17–46). Washington, DC: American Psychological Association.

Gutman, L. M., & Eccles, J. S. (1999). Financial strain, parenting behaviors, and adolescents' achievement: Testing model equivalence between African American and European American single- and two-parent families. *Child Development, 70*, 1464–1478.

Halgunseth, L. C. (2004). Continuing research on Latino families: El pasado y el futuro. In M. Coleman & L. H. Ganong (Eds.), *Handbook of contemporary families: Considering the past, contemplating the future* (pp. 333–351). Thousand Oaks, CA: Sage.

Harnish, J. D., Dodge, K. A., & Valente, E. (1995). Mother-child interaction quality as a partial mediator of the roles of maternal depressive symptomatology and socioeconomic status in the development of child behavior problems. *Child Development, 66,* 739–753.

Harrison, A. O., Wilson, M. N., Pine, C. J., Chan, S. Q., & Buriel, R. (1995). Family ecologies of ethnic minority children. In N. R. Goldberger & J. B. Veroff (Eds.), *The culture and psychology reader* (pp. 292–320). New York: New York University Press.

Harter, S. (2006). The self. In W. Damon, R. L. Lerner, & N. Eisenberg (Eds.), *Handbook of child psychology* (6th ed., Vol. 3, pp. 505–570). New York: Wiley.

Hernandez, D. J. (2004). Demographic change and the life circumstances of immigrant families. *Future of Children, 14,* 17–47.

Hernandez, M., & Nesman, T. M. (2004). Issues and strategies for studying Latino student dropout at the local level. *Journal of Child and Family Studies, 13,* 453–468.

Heyman, J. (2000). *The widening gap.* New York: Basic Books.

Hill, N. E., Bush, K. R., & Roosa, M. W. (2003). Parenting and family socialization strategies and children's mental health: Low-income Mexican American and European American mothers and children. *Child Development, 74,* 189–204.

Hogan, D. P., & Kitagawa, E. M. (1985). The impact of social status, family structure, and neighborhood on the fertility of black adolescents. *American Journal of Sociology, 90,* 825–855.

Holleran, L. K., & Jung, S. (2005). Acculturative stress, violence, and resilience in the lives of Mexican American youth. *Stress, Trauma and Crisis, 8,* 107–130.

Hovey, J. D., & King, C. A. (1996). Acculturative stress, depression, and suicidal ideation among immigrant and second generation Latino adolescents. *Journal of the American Academy of Child and Adolescent Psychiatry, 35,* 1183–1192.

Kelly, M. L., Power, T. G., & Wimbush, D. D. (1992). Determinants of disciplinary practices in low-income black mothers. *Child Development, 63,* 573–582.

Laosa, L. M. (1980). Maternal teaching strategies in Chicano and Anglo-American families: The influence of culture and education on maternal behavior. *Child Development, 51,* 759–765.

Lareau, A. (2003). *Unequal childhoods.* Berkeley: University of California Press.

Lemerise, E. A., & Arsenio, W. F. (2000). An integrated model of emotion processes and cognition in social information processing. *Child Development, 71,* 107–118.

Leventhal, T., & Brooks-Gunn, J. (2000). The neighborhoods they live in: The effects of neighborhood residence on child and adolescent outcomes. *Psychological Bulletin, 126,* 309–337.

Leyendecker, B., & Lamb, M. E. (1999). Latino families. In M. E. Lamb (Ed.), *Parenting and child development in "nontraditional" families* (pp. 247–262). Mahwah, NJ: Erlbaum.

Lindahl, K. M., Malik, N. M., Kaczynski, K., & Simons, J. S. (2004). Couple power dynamics, systemic family functioning, and child adjustment: A test of a mediational model in a multiethnic sample. *Development & Psychopathology, 16,* 609–630.

Lopez, D. E., & Stanton-Salazar, R. D. (2001). Mexican Americans: A second generation at risk. In R. G. Rumbaut & A. Portes (Eds.), *Ethnicities: Children of immigrants in America* (pp. 57–90). Berkeley: University of California Press.

Lopez, G. R. (2001). The value of hard work: Lessons on parent involvement from an (im)migrant household. *Harvard Educational Review, 71,* 416–437.

Luthar, S. S., Cicchetti, D., & Becker, B. (2000). The construct of resilience: A critical evaluation and guidelines for future work. *Child Development, 71,* 543–562.

Magaña, C. G., & Hovey, J. D. (2003). Psychosocial stressors associated with Mexican migrant farmworkers in the Midwest United States. *Journal of Immigrant Health, 5,* 75–86.

Magnusson, D., & Stattin, H. (1998). Person-context interaction theories. In W. Damon & R. M. Lerner (Eds.), *Handbook of child psychology: Theoretical models of human development* (Vol. 1, pp. 685–759). New York: Wiley.

Magunuson, K. A., & Duncan, G. J. (2002). Parents in poverty. In M. H. Bornstein (Ed.), *Handbook of parenting: Vol. 4. Social conditions and applied parenting* (pp. 96–121). Mahwah, NJ: Erlbaum.

Massey, D. S., Zambrana, R. E., Alonzo Bell, S. (1995). Contemporary issues in Latino families: Future directions for research, policy, and practice. In R. E. Zambrana (Ed.), *Understanding Latino families: Scholarship, policy, and practice. Understanding families* (Vol. 2, pp. 190–204). Thousand Oaks, CA: Sage.

Masten, A. S., Coatsworth, J. D., Neemann, J., Gest, S. D., Tellegen, A., & Garmezy, N. (1995). The structure and coherence of competence from childhood through adolescence. *Child Development, 66,* 1635–1659.

McGroder, S. M. (2000). Parenting among low-income African American single mothers with preschool-age children: Patterns, predictors, and developmental correlates. *Child Development, 71,* 752–771.

McLoyd, V. C. (1990). The impact of economic hardship on black families and children: Psychological distress, parenting, and socioemotional development [Special Issue: Minority children]. *Child Development, 61,* 311–346.

McLoyd, V. C. (1998). Socioeconomic disadvantage and child development. *American Psychologist, 53,* 185–204.

McLoyd, V. C., Cauce, A. M., Takeuchi, D., & Wilson, L. (2000). Marital processes and parental socialization in families of color: A decade review of research. *Journal of Marriage and the Family, 62,* 1070–1093.

Miller, P. H., & Seier, W. L. (1994). Strategy utilization deficiencies in children: When, where and why. In H. W. Reese (Ed.), *Advances in child development and behavior* (Vol. 25, pp. 107–156). San Diego, CA: Academic Press.

Miranda, A. O., Estrada, D., & Firpo-Jimenez, M. (2000). Differences in family cohesion, adaptability, and environment among Latino families in dissimilar stages of acculturation. *Family Journal, 8*(4), 341–350.

Mirandé, A. (1997). *Hombres y machos: Masculinity and Latino culture.* Boulder, CO: Westview Press.

Moore, J., & Pinderhughes, R. (1993). Introduction. In J. Moore & R. Pinderhughes (Eds.), *In the barrios: Latinos and the underclass debate* (pp. xi–xxxix). New York: Russell Sage.

Morales, R., & Ong, P. M. (1993). The illusion of progress: Latinos in Los Angeles. In R. Morales & F. Bonilla (Eds.), *Latinos in a changing U.S. economy: Comparative perspectives on growing inequality.* Newbury Park, CA: Sage.

Murry, V. M., Brody, G. H., Brown, A., Wisenbaker, J., Cutrona, C. E., & Simons, R. L. (2002). Linking employment status, maternal psychological well-being, parenting, and children's attributions about poverty in families receiving government assistance. *Family Relations, 51,* 112–120.

National Center for Education Statistics. (1998). Report on high school dropout rates of different ethnic groups. Washington, DC: National Center for Education Statistics.

National Center for Health Statistics. (2000). Retrieved January 2004 from http://www.cdc.gov/nchs/

National Centers for Disease Control. (2002, June 28). *Youth risk behavior surveillance.* Retrieved August 4, 2006, from http://www.cdc.gov/mmwr/preview/mmwrhtml/ss5104a1.htm

Olds, D., Henderson, C., Kitzman, H., Eckenrode, J., Cole, R., & Tatelbaum, R. (1998). The promise of home visitation: Results of two randomized trials. *Journal of Community Psychology, 26,* 5–21.

Ortiz, V. (1996). The Mexican-origin population: Permanent working class or emerging middle class? In R. Waldinger & M. Bozorgmehr (Eds.), *Ethnic Los Angeles* (pp. 247–277). New York: Russell Sage.

Parke, R. D., & Buriel, R. (2006). Socialization in the family: Ethnic and ecological perspectives. In W. Damon, R. L. Lerner, & N. Eisenberg (Eds.), *Handbook of child psychology* (Vol. 3, pp. 429–504). New York: Wiley.

Parke, R. D., Coltrane, S., Duffy, S., Buriel, R., Dennis, J., Powers, J., et al. (2004). Economic stress, parenting, and child adjustment in Mexican American and European American families. *Child Development, 75*(6), 1632–1656.

Patterson, C. J., Vaden, N. A., & Kupersmidt, J. B. (1991). Family background, recent life events and peer rejection during childhood. *Journal of Social and Personal Relationships, 8,* 347–361.

Perez, S. M. (2004). Shaping new possibilities for Latino children and the nation's future. *Future of Children, 14*(2), 122–126.

Prevatt, F. F. (2003). The contribution of parenting practices in a risk and resiliency model of children's adjustment. *British Journal of Developmental Psychology, 21*(4), 469–480.

Rank, M. R. (2004). The disturbing paradox of poverty in American families. In M. Coleman & L. Ganong (Eds.), *Handbook of contemporary families* (pp. 469–489). London: Sage.

Roosa, M. W., Morgan-Lopez, A. A., Cree, W. K., & Specter, M. M. (2002). Ethnic culture, poverty, and context: Sources of influence on Latino families and children. In J. M. Contreras, K. A. Kerns, & A. M. Neal-Barnett (Eds.), *Latino children and families in the United States* (pp. 27–44). Westport, CT: Praeger.

Rutter, M. (1987). Psychosocial resilience and protective mechanisms. *American Journal of Orthopsychiatry, 57,* 316–331.

Salgado de Snyder, N. (1987). Factors associated with acculturative stress and depressive symptomatology among married Mexican immigrant women. *Psychology of Women Quarterly, 11,* 475–488.

Sameroff, A., & Feil, L. (1985). Parental concepts of development. In I. Sigel (Ed.), *Parent belief systems.* Hillsdale, NJ: Erlbaum.

Schofield, T. J. (2004). *Parenting, marital quality, and child outcomes.* Unpublished M.A. thesis, University of California, Riverside, Department of Psychology.

Simoni, J. M., & Perez, L. (1995). Latinos and mutual support groups: A case for considering culture. *American Journal of Orthopsychiatry, 65,* 440–445.

Simons, R. L., Johnson, C., Beamon, J., Conger, R. D., & Whitbeck, L. E. (1996). Parents and peer groups as mediators of the effect of community structure on adolescent problem behavior. *American Journal of Community Psychology, 24,* 145–171.

Simons, R. L., Whitbeck, L. E., Conger, R. D., & Melby, J. (1990). Husband and wife differences in determinants of parenting: A social learning/exchange model of parental behavior. *Journal of Marriage and the Family, 52,* 375–392.

Small, M. L. (2002). Culture, cohorts, and social organization theory: Understanding local participation in a Latino housing project. *American Journal of Sociology, 108,* 1–54.

Small, M. L., & Newman, K. S. (2001). Urban poverty after *The Truly Disadvantaged:* The rediscovery of the family, the neighborhood, and culture. *Annual Review of Sociology* (27), 23–45.

Sonnek, S. M. (1999). *Perception and parenting style: The influence of culture (Hispanic American, Euro American).* (Doctoral dissertation, University of Wyoming, 1999). *Dissertation Abstracts International, 60*(6-B), 3021.

Straus, M. A. (1994). *Beating the devil out of them: Corporeal punishment in American families.* New York: Levington Books.

Tamis, A. M. (2005). Fostering academic resilience at home: Exploring contexts of parenting beliefs and behaviors within the families of low-income African American and Mexican American adolescents. *Abstracts International Section A: Humanities and Social Sciences, 66*(2-A). Abstract retrieved April 15, 2006, from PsychINFO database.

Tapia, J. (2004). Latino households and schooling: Economic and sociocultural factors affecting students' learning and academic performance. *International Journal of Qualitative Studies in Education, 17*(3), 415–436.

Teasley, S. D. (1995). The role of talk in children's peer collaborations. *Developmental Psychology, 31,* 207–220.

Therrien, M., & Ramirez, R. R. (2000). *The Hispanic population in the United States: March 2000. Current Population Reports.* Washington, DC: U.S. Government Printing Office.

U.S. Census Bureau. (2004). *Table 1.2 Population by sex, age, and Hispanic origin type: 2004.* Retrieved from http://www.census.gov/population/socdemo/hispanic/ASEC2004/2004CPS_tab1.2a.html

U.S. Department of Education, National Center for Education Statistics. (1995). *The condition of education.* Washington, DC: U.S. Government Printing Office.

Vega, W. A. (1990). Hispanic families in the 1980s: A decade of research. *Journal of Marriage and the Family, 52,* 1015–1024.

Vega, W. A., Kolody, B., Valle, R., & Weir, J. (1991). Social networks, social support and their relationship to depressions among immigrant women. *Human Organization, 50,* 154–162.

Vélez-Ibáñez, C. (1996). *Border visions.* Tucson: University of Arizona Press.

Vélez-Ibáñez, C., & Greenberg, J. B. (1992). Formation and transformation of funds of knowledge among U.S.–Mexican households. *Anthropology & Education Quarterly, 23*(4), 313–335.

Vigil, J. D., & Long, J. M. (1981). Unidirectional or nativist acculturation— Chicano paths to school achievement. *Human Organization, 40,* 273–277.

Villenas, S., & Deyhle, D. (1999). Critical race theory and ethnographies challenging the stereotypes: Latino families, schooling, resilience and resistance]. *Curriculum Inquiry, 29,* 413–445.

Wakschlag, L. S., Chase-Lansdale, P. L., & Brooks-Gunn, J. (1996). Not just "Ghosts in the Nursery": Contemporaneous intergenerational relationships and parenting in young African American families. *Child Development, 67,* 2131–2147.

Werner, E. E. (1993). Risk, resilience, and recovery: Perspectives from the Kauai Longitudinal Study [Special Issue: Milestones in the development of resilience]. *Development and Psychopathology, 5,* 503–515.

Wilson, W. J. (1996). *When work disappears: The world of the new urban poor.* New York: Random House.

Wyche, K. F., & Rotheram-Borus, M. J. (1990). Suicidal behavior among minority youth in the United States. In A. R. Stiffman & L. E. Davis (Eds.), *Ethnic issues in adolescent mental health* (pp. 323–338). Newbury Park, CA: Sage.

Yahav, R. (2002). External and internal symptoms in children and characteristics of the family system: A comparison of the linear and circumplex models. *American Journal of Family Therapy, 30*(1), 39–56.

# CHAPTER 11

# Mexican Immigrant Childbearing Women

## Social Support and Perinatal Outcomes

LYNN CLARK CALLISTER AND ANA BIRKHEAD

Hispanics are the largest and fastest-growing minority group living in the United States, currently constituting nearly 13% of the population of the United States (U.S. Census Bureau, 2004). Hispanics have been called the "silent or invisible minority" because of the lack of understanding regarding Hispanic health needs, status, behavior, and family roles (Agency for Healthcare Research and Quality [AHRQ], 2002). Because of high birth and immigration rates, by 2050 Hispanics are projected to represent 25% of the population of the United States (Mendelson, 2002).

Mexicans are the largest immigrant group in the United States, accounting for 28% (7 million) of the foreign-born population (Lagana & Gonzalez-Ramirez, 2003). More than 23 million people of Mexican descent live in the United States. Most Mexican immigrants are *mestizos,* a blend of Mexican Indian and Spanish cultures. Mexican Americans have the highest fertility rate of any ethnic or cultural group living in the

United States (dePaula, Lagana, & Gonzalez-Ramirez, 2001). The purpose of this chapter is to discuss social support and perinatal outcomes in Mexican immigrant childbearing women, using the research findings of the authors as an example.

## MEXICAN IMMIGRANT CHILDBEARING WOMEN

More than 17 million Hispanic women of childbearing age live in the United States (U.S. Census Bureau, 2004). Two-thirds of Hispanic births are to Mexican women, who have the highest fertility rate among Hispanic women (U.S. Department of Health and Human Services [USDHHS], Office of Research on Women's Health, 1998). Fifty-six percent of Mexican immigrant women fail to receive adequate prenatal care. Systems barriers include financial constraints, lack of insurance coverage, lack of culturally competent health care, linguistic barriers, long waiting times, lack of transportation, and lack of child care. Personal barriers include fears about immigrant status, lack of understanding of the importance of prenatal care, and low levels of maternal education. An additional barrier is a cultural orientation that views childbearing as a healthy experience requiring minimal medical interventions. These barriers result in Mexican women delaying entry into prenatal care, under-utilizing prenatal care, or not seeking prenatal care at all (AHRQ, 2002; Institute of Medicine, 2003; Robert Wood Johnson Foundation, 2001; Shaffer, 2002; Smedley, Stith, & Nelson, 2003; Zambrana & Carter-Pokras, 2001; Zambrana, Scrimshaw, Collins, & Dunkel-Schetter, 1997).

## Vulnerability, Socioeconomic Disadvantage, and Acculturation Stress

Vulnerable and socioeconomically disad-vantaged populations are social groups who have an increased risk of susceptibility to increased morbidity, premature mortality, and diminished quality of life. Many immi-grants have already experienced poverty and poor health care in Mexico (Tezoquipa, Monreal, & Trevino-Siller, 2005). Economic disadvantage is common among Mexican immigrants, with more than one-third of this population lacking health insurance. Many come to the United States "with little more than their motivation to succeed, their innate abilities, and the clothes on their backs" (Marin, 2003, p. 187). Poverty is high-est among Mexican immigrants, with a poverty rate of 24% compared with 12% in native-born Americans.

Educational levels are low among Mexican Americans, with only 8.6% being college graduates and less than 50% having graduated from secondary school. Only 22% of Mexican Americans earn $35,000 a year or more, with 27% living below the poverty line (Galanti, 2003). More than 50% of Mexican American women are employed, half in nonprofessional positions (Lagana & Gonzalez-Ramirez, 2003). The more edu-cated, urbanized, and acculturated Mexican American women are more likely to work outside the home.

In making the transition to living in the United States, Mexican immigrant women may experience a sense of uprootedness with the loss of cherished familial and social sup-port systems and identifiable resources, as well as dramatic shifts in cultural expecta-tions. There is a tendency toward feelings of alienation, fear, frustration, depression, sad-ness (*triste*), and isolation (Messias, DeJong, & McLoughlin, 2005; Siantz & Coronado, 2002). Poorer maternal mental health is asso-ciated with greater stress in Mexican immi-grant children (McNaughton, Cowell, Gross, Fogg, & Alley, 2004). Barriers to empower-ment include a reduction in support networks, chronic stress, helplessness and hopelessness, long-term poverty, and a perceived lack of control (Fraktman, 1998). Childbearing women with lower levels of support report poorer health; have higher levels of late, inad-equate, or no prenatal care; and experience more postpartum depression (Webster et al., 2000). These immigrant women "face new cultural customs, language barriers, and unfa-miliar health-care systems and medical man-agement plans" (Barron, Hunter, Mayo, & Willoughby, 2004, p. 331).

It has been suggested that socioeconomic disadvantage affects low birth weight when "women of color are no longer adequately protected by the affirming symbols of their native cultures and are simultaneously mar-ginalized both psychologically and economi-cally by mainstream United States culture" (James, 1993, p. 133). "There are diversities and complexities in women's health experi-ences" (Im & Meleis, 2001, p. 310). Stereo-typing by health-care providers marginalizes immigrants, and being marginalized defines women's perceptions, experiences, and responses to health-care encounters.

## PERINATAL OUTCOMES IN MEXICAN IMMIGRANT WOMEN AND NEWBORNS

A recent study established a database regarding the health of Mexican immigrant women and their newborns. Two hundred seventy-five Mexican immigrant childbearing women giving birth in Utah participated in the study. First-generation and less-acculturated women had more positive perinatal outcomes than did more-acculturated Mexican immigrant women (Callister, Birkhead, Vega, & Crookston, in review).

This study and others demonstrate that first-generation and less-acculturated Mexican immigrant women have the lowest rates of infant mortality and fewer low birth weight infants despite social risks such as low levels of education, income, and less use of prenatal care (Anachebe & Sutton, 2003; Balcazar & Krull, 1999; Crump, Lipsky, & Mueller, 1999). Less-acculturated Mexican immigrant women and their newborns who have a traditional cultural orientation appear to have a perinatal advantage despite greater poverty (Harley & Eskenazi, 2006; Morales, Lara, & Kington, 2002). Women who are highly acculturated are less likely to breastfeed (Gibson, Diaz, Mainous, & Geesey, 2005). According to Balcazar and Krull (1999, p. 420), "The process of acculturation is associated with negative birth weight outcomes after controlling for a wide array of biological, behavioral, medical, and psychosocial factors."

In most other populations, poverty has been associated with increased perinatal risk including higher rates of low birth weight infants and higher infant mortality (Seccombe, 2001). This is not the case with first-generation or less-acculturated Mexican childbearing women. More than two decades of studies have confirmed that this epidemiologic paradox exists (Callister & Birkhead, 2002; Rubio & Montgomery, 2003).

Social rather than genetic factors are postulated to be the chief contributors to these perinatal outcomes. Evidence indicates that Mexican immigrant women have existing cultural prescriptions for self-care to ensure healthy perinatal outcomes. These may be lost as they become increasingly acculturated (Acevedo, 2000; Callister et al., in review). Postulated protective cultural mechanisms in less-acculturated Mexican immigrant women supportive of positive perinatal outcomes include maintenance of their indigenous culture's dietary practices, promotion of a healthy lifestyle including low levels of substance use, caring and supportive family networks including "fictive kin," and value systems including a spiritual lifestyle and strong religious beliefs and practices (Harley & Eskenazi, 2006; Jones & Bond, 1999; Page, 2004; Warda, 2000). Childbearing and childrearing are highly valued roles and children are considered *angelitos*. Compared with other cultural groups who immigrate to the United States, Mexican Americans are highly protective of maintaining language, cultural beliefs, and cultural traditions. Assimilation is minimal. Often they congregate in ethnically segregated neighborhoods in urban areas, which buffer culture shock (Falicov, 1998; Peete, 1999).

### Social Support as an Ameliorating Factor

First-generation and less-acculturated Mexican women enjoy high levels of social support (Niska, 1999). Traditional Mexican concepts of *la familia* (family) include a large network of strong, enduring relationships (Friedman, Bowden & Jones, 2002). *Familism* produces a strong love for children emphasizing the importance of the mother's role in nurturing and protecting children before and after birth (Galanti, 2003; Jimenez, 1995). Major sources of social support include the baby's father, the maternal grandmother, other female extended family members, *compadrazo* or godparents, and female fictive kin. Family values espouse mutual obligations, support, and reciprocity (Friedman et al., 2002). Telleen and associates (1990, 1999) identified components of social support, including need for support, satisfaction with support received, number of people available to help, and those in the social network with whom the mother has a conflicted relationship. A social support network of diverse individuals provides diverse support (Falicov, 1998; Logsdon, Birkimer & Usui, 2000). Although social support among low-income families may not include financial support, emotional, instrumental, and informational support make an important difference (Henly, Danziger, & Offer, 2005). Social support activities for childbearing women include assisting these women in handling emotional distress, sharing tasks, giving advice, modeling parenting skills, and providing material resources (Barrera, 2000). Support has been described by Mexican-origin childbearing women as helping with daily hassles, showing love and understanding, and presence (Clark, 2001). In this study, 50% reported densely supportive networks; the others felt disconnected and expressed, "my family fails me." These findings are supported by Harley and Eskenazi (2006), who found that social support promotes health in Mexican immigrant childbearing women.

A touching account in the literature speaks of events surrounding the childbirth experiences of a first-generation Mexican immigrant couple and documents the strength of emotional and spiritual support offered by families. The paternal grandfather, a simple Mexican farmer, had been sitting in the waiting room for hours waiting for the birth of his first grandchild. There

was concern because of failure to progress and maternal exhaustion. Just before the laboring mother was to be taken to the surgical suite for a cesarean birth, she gave three pushes and her son was born. The new father told the grandfather, who knew of the young couples' fears, the happy news,

> Sitting alone in the waiting room, [the grandfather] had spoken with his grandchild in his mind, encouraging him to come and be born. He had shown the baby his memories of the beauty of the land [and] that he looked forward to walking together on the earth. He had spoken of the goodness of life, of friendship, laughter and good work. And lastly, he had spoken of his love for his family, of the joy they took in each other's lives. He had offered the baby his heart. [Parents in labor can] reach out to their unborn child in just the same way, sharing their love of life to strengthen and encourage the baby in this difficult passage. (Remen, 2000, pp. 260–262)

According to the 2000 census, nearly 20% of Hispanic households include six or more people living together. Among white households, only 10% have six or more sharing space. By pooling financial resources and sharing housing, food, and child care, Hispanics have better living conditions and are less socially isolated. This kind of cohesiveness among Mexican families demonstrates that social support is an important part of the Mexican lifestyle that has implications for health and well-being (Balcazar, Peterson, & Krull, 1997; Delgado, Metzger, & Falcon, 1995; Keefe, Padilla, & Carlos, 1979).

Benefits of social support to childbearing women include positive attitudes toward pregnancy, maternal/infant attachment, sense of control while laboring and giving birth, adherence with health-care recommendations, improved self-efficacy and self-esteem, improved functional status, improved coping, fewer low birth weight infants, increased incidence of breastfeeding, positive affect, the strengthening of family relationships, less substance use, reduced physical and physiological morbidity, and reduced sense of loneliness (Campero et al., 1998; Langford, Bowsher, Maloney, & Lillis, 1997; Logsdon, 2001; Logsdon & Davis, 2003; McNicholas, 2002; Zambrana, Scrimshaw, & Collins, 1997). Social support ameliorates the effects of poverty (Chavez, Hubbell, Mishra, & Valdez, 1997; Schaffer & Lia-Hoagberg, 1997; Sherraden & Barrera, 1996a, b) and is "an important family coping strategy" (Friedman et al., 2002, p. 528).

In a study of 20 less-acculturated women of Mexican descent living in a homogenous Mexican community, Domain (2001, p. 335) concluded, "Social support appeared to be a greater factor in positive birth outcomes than was socioeconomic status and formal prenatal care." In a grounded theory of Hispanic women's perceptions of pregnancy and prenatal care, Pearce (1998) found women sought healthy outcomes through receiving support from others. Types of support included instrumental support (housing, child care, transportation, money), emotional support (sharing problems, receiving reinforcement, confirmation, and encouragement), informational support (advice, counseling), and positive appraisal support.

Mexican cultural orientation or rootedness in cultural practices appears to have a protective effect on perinatal health. According to Stinson and associates (2000, p. 37), "Being born in Mexico is protective against low birth weight despite inadequate prenatal care and pregnancy complications if elements of a Mexican cultural lifestyle are maintained." It has been suggested, "The impact of Latina identity formation and cultural transformation on health behaviors, health risks, and protective coping strategies represents an emerging area of study" (Amaro & de la Torre, 2002, p. 528). The

following section reports a recent research study designed to shed light on cultural practices supportive of the health of Mexican immigrant women and newborns.

## PERCEPTIONS OF MEXICAN IMMIGRANT CHILDBEARING WOMEN

The purpose of this descriptive qualitative study was to explore the perceptions of Mexican immigrant women who had recently given birth in Utah regarding cultural beliefs, values, and practices associated with childbearing. "Despite the fact that Latinos are the fastest-growing ethnic group in the United States, clinicians and policy analysts have little data-based knowledge about the strengths of childbearing Latina women" (Heilemann, Frutos, Lee, & Kury, 2004, p. 89). The theoretical framework for this study was adapted from McCubbin and McCubbin's (1993) Resiliency Model. Resilience is the central focus of the model, which includes vulnerability (negative aspects or resiliency challenges such as culture shock, socioeconomic disadvantages, lack of maternal skills, literacy issues and low levels of maternal education, and lack of linguistic skills in English). Resiliency building or protective factors include social support, maternal role satisfaction, cultural valuing of childbearing and childrearing, positive adaptation, and spirituality/religiosity. Promotion of resiliency building factors can promote maternal/newborn health and the well-being of the family (Horowitz & Damato, 1999). In another study, personal strengths and resources in relationship to depressive symptoms in Mexican childbearing women were explored (Heilemann et al., 2004). Intrinsic strength factors such as a sense of mastery, resilience, life satisfaction, and spirituality; as well as extrinsic resources such as education, employment, access to transportation, income, and partner status were examined. Those who were more acculturated or who had lived longer in the United States were more at risk for depression, especially if they lacked social support. Sense of mastery and life satisfaction were postulated to have protective effects on emotional health. Social support also made a difference in the level of depression.

From the study of 275 Mexican immigrant childbearing women giving birth in Utah reported elsewhere (Callister et al., in review), a group of 20 first-generation, less-acculturated Mexican childbearing women were invited to participate in interviews. This subgroup was categorized as being "very Mexican" oriented in their beliefs and values, with scores ranging from five to eight. Maternal age ranged from 15 to 34 years, with a mean of 21 years of age. Maternal education level ranged from 1 to 14 years, with a mean educational level of 8 years. Sixty percent of the women were married and 40% were in committed relationships. Length of time living in the United States ranged from 1 month to 5 years. Thirty-eight percent were first-time mothers, and 62% had more than one child.

Acculturation scores were assessed by the General Acculturation Index (GAI) (Balcazar, Peterson, & Cobas, 1996). Following institutional review board approval, demographic and informed consent forms were completed, with those less literate receiving assistance in completing the forms. Interviews were conducted by bilingual perinatal nurses, with most held in the study participants' homes. The interviews began with "small talk" as culturally appropriate, to help the women feel comfortable with the research process and to have the sense that they were co-investigators (Sherraden & Barrera, 1995). The researcher shared how research results will help in designing better health care for Mexican immigrant women giving birth in Utah. Respect for cultural beliefs was demonstrated and attention given to recommendations for

vulnerable population research (Flaskerud & Winslow, 1998) and specifically research with Hispanic women (Naranjo & Dirksen, 1998). According to Marin and Marin (1991), Hispanics are less likely to self-disclose than are non-Hispanic whites, so the establishment of trust characterized the interviews. Each study participant was given a gift certificate as an expression of appreciation for participating in the study.

Questions included, "What kinds of things did you do during your pregnancy to keep healthy and to make sure you had a healthy baby?," "How did you handle the challenge of having a baby so far away from your family in Mexico?," and "What kind of support did you have?" Audiotapes were transcribed and translated concurrently into English, with attention paid to the linguistic nuances and sociocultural context. Several interviews were translated independently by a bilingual bicultural nurse to ensure inter-rater reliability and trustworthiness of the data attending to the specific vocabulary of those of Mexican descent (Marin & Marin, 1991). Narrative data were analyzed as appropriate for qualitative inquiry. Core concepts were identified and classified into conceptually relevant categories, reflecting the perspectives of the women. Trustworthiness of the data was established by having participants verify that the categories reflected their experiences and perceptions. Fittingness was established through saturation of categories. Saturation was reached when information became repetitive and data were fully explored.

Pervasive themes in the interviews were the importance of receiving support (recibir de consejo y ayuda) and accepting help from others (accceptar assitencia de otros). Roxanna expressed a longing for extended family members living in Mexico: "My husband gives me a lot of support but I feel alone. I wish in these moments that my mother was here. I think that if my mother were here, I would feel less alone."

Among Mexican immigrants, paternal involvement with the family is the culture norm in either a committed relationship *(union libre)* or marriage. When women leave behind extended families in Mexico, many Mexican immigrant fathers play a significant role in providing support (Domain, 2001; Guendelman, Malin, Herr-Harthorn, & Vargas, 2001). Paternal presence and involvement and valuing of the paternal role make an important difference. The couple relationship was characterized as supportive if there was an absence of controlling behavior, comfort with gender role flexibility, and a high degree of affection between the couple (Galanti, 2003; Guendelman et al., 2001; Lagana, 1996). Mexican immigrant women in committed relationships are more likely to access early and adequate prenatal care, demonstrate better perinatal outcomes, make a smooth transition to motherhood, and demonstrate positive maternal behaviors (Andresen & Telleen, 1992; Kalofonos & Planikas, 1999; Zambrana, Scrimshaw, Collins, & Dunkel-Schetter, 1997).

Concepcion described the strengthening of the couple relationship because they were far away from the benefits of extended family. She spoke of "the closeness me and my husband have gotten. We are closer now than we were before. He is a lot more understanding. It makes me happy." Eliana spoke of growing closer to her husband as they depended on each other,

> Without my family nearby it was very difficult. My husband and I prayed and grew together as a couple. We prayed a lot together. Pregnancy and birth is a time when a woman needs a lot of affection. My husband was working 12–18 hours a day and this made me sad. He was strong for me and told me to remember the baby. I was afraid I wouldn't be a good mother, and my husband would tell me stories about his mother, and this with the memories of my

own mother helped me to build the foundations of being a good parent. I tried to help my husband when he was homesick and missed his family. We had to depend on each other more and this helped us to grow close to each other.

Study participants also received support from female extended family members. Twenty-three-year-old Cristina, who had given birth to her second child, said,

> To have this baby it was hard to be away from family. My sister is the only one who lives here. The thing that helped me the most was to be able to go to my sister and [enjoy] her companionship.

Seventeen-year-old Teresa was fortunate to have her mother come from Mexico for the birth of her first child, a daughter. As she received emotional and spiritual support from her mother, she felt a sense of connectedness with her mother and other generations of women who have given birth,

> When the baby was born, I started to cry because I felt many things I can't describe. When you have a baby, you feel very beautiful and gentle. You feel scared, but it's still beautiful. It's difficult to express. When you are in labor you feel a lot of pain, but it's all taken away when the baby is born. You feel happy and well—so much so that the pain is alleviated.

Women supporting women offered informational support as *consejos*, the wise keepers of cultural values. As she gave birth to her third child, Maria expressed the sense she had from her mother, "It is a gift to be a mother. It is your purpose as a woman to be a mother. Therefore, when you feel the pains and all that accompanies having a baby, to be a mother compensates for all of this because you know why you feel that way."

The support of the maternal grandmother has a powerful stress-buffering effect that may contribute significantly to positive outcomes (Burk, Weiser, & Keegan, 1995; Sherraden & Barrera, 1996a). Many childbearing women cite their mother's advice, guidance, experiences, authority, and assistance as being invaluable at this time in their lives (Berry, 1999; Pearce, 1998).

Women also accessed circles of supportive women in the Mexican immigrant community for emotional, informational, and tangible support if it was not possible to have help from female extended family members. These *compadres* are referred to as "fictive kin" and are used when blood relatives were not available. According to Berry (2002, p. 366), "A strong mutual care bond develops and fictive kin are accorded a lifetime family status with reciprocal care practices. Fictive kin are often described in phrases such as, 'She's like my mother.'" The importance of such support has been documented in the literature (Lagana, 1996; Pearce, 1998). Fictive kin create new social networks with *compadres* who are also young childbearing women. Women participating in the study described fictive kin in phrases such as, "She's like a mother to me." The traditional cultural construct, *no preoccupada* or "do not worry" was used by experienced childbearing women to calm young inexperienced expectant mothers. Accepting help from others *(accceptar asitencia de otros)* was described by Maritza who spoke about the help provided by a dear friend,

> She helps me with the children, to prepare food, [and] tells me to take care of myself. She tells me, "No, rest." When I can't attend to my children, she will attend to them for me. I feel a lot of support. That helps me relax, makes me feel calmer.

Women expressed the sense that having a positive attitude and being happy, calm, patient, and relaxed during their pregnancy were very important. Emotional support was seen as essential in relieving stressors experienced during pregnancy. The Mexican culture does not espouse the fast-paced and highly technological health-care culture found in the United States. Pregnancy is seen as a time to be calm and serene and minimize stress (Guendelman et al., 2001). Maria said she thought Mexican women living in the United States longer had more problems with their pregnancy because they didn't have support to "slow down":

> The style of living here in the United States is very fast. Women have the stresses of working both in the house with the children and being pregnant as well as working outside the home. I think it is more difficult. There is a lot of stress with this rapid kind of life.

Emotional support was grounded in offering anticipatory guidance for those becoming mothers for the first time. This included sharing stories including birth narratives (Callister, 2004), assistance in problem solving, and praying to God. For example, Ramona was struggling with an insufficient supply of milk and had a strong desire to breastfeed. After listening to Ramona's concerns, a neighbor who was also breastfeeding her infant engaged in problem solving with Ramona. She made Ramona special teas from sesame and absinthe plants as is typical in northern Mexico to increase Ramona's milk supply. She breastfed Ramona's baby until Ramona's milk fully came in. This gift of self is typical of support offered by Mexican women. One participant described a circle of friends who often come together with their babies and young children just to talk, defined in Spanish as *"la tertulia"* or supporting each other.

Because faith in God is a major source of strength woven into the lives of Mexican immigrant women, praying both individually and together provided a significant means of support. Their spiritual lifestyle was definitely an ameliorating factor in perinatal outcomes. One woman felt the strength of prayers being offered for her by others and of her own personal prayers. She said that during her pregnancy,

> I would always ask God that He would take care of me and of my baby. The baby was born alive and healthy. I think it was because He was always helping me. My belief is that the baby was born healthy because I asked God and He listened.

Women trusted counsel given to them by other women more than counsel from health-care providers. Elena expressed frustration with her experience with health-care providers versus the advice given by other Mexican women who were experienced mothers,

> I don't like it as much here [in the United States] because they tell me that everything I am feeling is normal and they don't help me feel better and explain anything. If I tell them that I feel like this or hurt here, they tell me, "Oh, it is normal." Here they don't explain anything, they just say it is normal and I will feel better on my own. My mother tells me what I can do to minimize the discomfort of pregnancy and birth rather than just saying, "Oh, it is normal."

Childbearing and childrearing are highly valued roles among Mexican women and their families (Lagana & Gonzalez-Ramirez, 2003). This was expressed by one study participant who said, "It is part of God's plan to bring spirits into the world," and another who said, "I enjoyed my pregnancy just as my mom did." Because the maternal role is valued in the Mexican culture, social support is provided to childbearing women (Clark, 2001). The mother and the newborn are considered to be *muy delicados* or fragile and vulnerable. In traditional Mexican culture, *la cuarentena* is observed for 40 days postpartum, with dietary and behavioral restrictions.

During this time, enhanced social support is provided. According to Martinez-Schallmoser and associates (2003, p. 331), "During *la cuarentena*, the husband/partner, extended family members, and friends provide postpartum social support. Extraordinary care, thoughtfulness, assistance with housework and child care, and individual attention are traditionally provided to postpartum Mexican-American women."

Because generations of women value bearing and rearing children, Mexican women often possess a high degree of knowledge of health promotion strategies. Mexican immigrant women rely on self-care measures, family advice, and traditional methods of childbearing more than their Anglo counterparts do. This knowledge is passed down through generations of women. "Through face-to-face interactions with keepers of their most cherished cultural traditions, these women, with the help of kith and kin, can create supportive communities within which the most vulnerable members can be nurtured, affirmed, and strengthened" (James, 1993, p. 134).

## IMPLICATIONS FOR RESEARCH, CLINICAL PRACTICE, AND HEALTH AND SOCIAL POLICY

This study provided Mexican immigrant women with the opportunity to have a voice in developing interventions that more fully meet their health-care needs and eliminate health disparities (Amaro & de la Torre, 2002). Mexican immigrant women and their families have many intrinsic strengths despite educational and financial disadvantages and less access to health care (Heilemann, Lee, & Kury, 2005). The relationship between health policy and health outcomes in women merits further inquiry (Wisdom, Berlin, & Lapidus, 2005).

Researchers have concluded that less-acculturated and first-generation Mexican immigrant women and their newborns generally enjoy good health (Morales, Lara, & Kington, 2002). This is associated with sociocultural more than with physiological factors. Building on and respecting cultural practices passed down from generation to generation of women supportive of childbearing women is essential (Berg, 2003; Meleis, 2003; The Commonwealth Fund, 1998). Lothian (1998, p. x) expressed this thought:

> All women have a rich heritage of inner wisdom about birth that has been handed down through generations of women in their family. The beliefs, rituals, and traditions in every culture provide ways of caring and coping during pregnancy, birth, breastfeeding, and parenting.

Research with Mexican immigrant women as study participants will increase knowledge of the processes underlying the epidemiological paradox that may be relevant in other ethnic and racial groups (Amaro & de la Torre, 2002). More research is needed on the contextual and cultural coping strategies (both problem-solving and emotion-focused) that ameliorate negative outcomes (Franzini & Fernandez-Esquer, 2004; Juarbe, Turok, & Warda, 2003). Researchers should move beyond epidemiological studies to qualitative designs to gain insight into the lived experience of vulnerable and disadvantaged populations (Adams, 2004; Sandelowski, 2004).

Acculturation is a complex phenomenon (Arcia, Skinner, Bailey, & Correa, 2001; Balcazar & Krull, 1999; Beck, Roman, & Bernal, 2005; Cabassa, 2003; Franzini, Ribble, & Keddie, 2001; Friedman et al., 2002). Because there is no best measure of acculturation status, or a clear understanding of how acculturation measures compare, the refinement of acculturation measures to increase specificity and reliability is essential (Beck et al., 2005). Additional research is needed on access to services in social institutions, including health-care delivery systems, focusing specifically on subgroups rather than considering Hispanics as a homogenous group (Weinick, Jacobs, Stone, Ortega, & Burstin, 2004).

Measuring levels of social support during pregnancy may be helpful to assess perinatal risk in Mexican immigrant women (Clark, 2001). The Norbeck Social Support Questionnaire is a comprehensive, psychometrically sound tool (Norbeck & Tilden, 1983). Work has been done in Australia on a simple six-item, 5-point Likert scale screening tool, the Maternity Social Support Scale (MSSS) (Webster et al., 2000), which invites responses from "never" to "always" to the following statements: "I have good friends who support me," "My family is always there for me," "My husband/partner helps me a lot," "There is conflict with my husband/partner," and "I feel controlled by my husband/partner." However, this tool does not account for the fact that extended female family members may live some distance from the childbearing immigrant woman. Because of the critical role that social support plays in the health of Hispanic women, the development of culturally appropriate reliable and valid tools to measure social support is essential (Langford et al., 1997). According to Franzini and associates (2001), "It is not known if *familismo* actually increases the social support available to Hispanics . . . or simply provides a different, but qualitatively similar type of social support . . . The possible connection between this kind of social support and health has not been established." For at-risk women with inadequate social support, identifying community resources and enhancing professional support is essential. (See Table 11.1.)

Respecting and valuing cultural wisdom is an important part of overcoming barriers in health-care delivery. For example, one Mexican immigrant childbearing woman in the study said, "The doctors speak Spanish, but they still don't explain to me. The fact

**Table 11.1**    A Guide for Social Support Assessment in the Perinatal Period

- Can you describe the kinds of support you receive from your family and friends? Typically, women have some people who help with daily hassles, others who show love and understanding, and some who are just "there" to listen.

- Many women have people in their lives who are not supportive, but are antagonistic or abusive or distant. Do you have any relationships like that? Are you disappointed in how any of your family or friends are supporting you now?

- Can you share with me the nicest thing that someone has done for you during your pregnancy, and the meanest or worst thing that someone has done to you?

SOURCE: Clark, 2001, p. 1317.

that they don't explain, this is what I don't like. I don't know if they don't think I will understand." The American Public Health Association Maternal and Child Community Leadership Institute has developed a cross-cultural health information catalog summarizing cultural beliefs and practices that may be useful for health-care providers (http://www.apha.org/). Guidelines for developing multilingual resource manuals focusing on maternal-child and women's health topics have been described (Ridley, Naber, Florea, & Guminski, 2004). An excellent summary of issues related to caring for immigrants can be found at http://www.arhp.org/factsheets/crosscultural.cfm.

Respect for cultural values related to the importance of family support may also be lacking in the delivery of health care and social services. For example, one study participant explained that the lack of child care was problematic at the clinic where she received prenatal care:

Many times when we come in there is no one to watch our kids. My husband comes with me to the appointments and I want him in the room when the doctor is there but if the children become restless, it is necessary to take them out. Then I have to tell my husband afterward what happened and then he cannot ask any questions.

Stereotyping and marginalization unfortunately exist, and often this means daunting barriers to immigrant women accessing health care (Meleis, 2003). One Mexican immigrant woman reflected on her experience,

When they see you are brown they automatically think you are on Medicaid or they say, "So, are you going to be signing up for WIC and are you going to put the baby on Medicaid?" They assume that you don't have any money. Because of the way you look they assume that you are either here illegally or you are going to take government benefits. I could always say, "No, I have private insurance through my husband's job" and "Yes, we are here legally." It is always awkward.

Delivering culturally competent health care is grounded in an awareness of culturally diverse women's lives and includes provider attitudes, knowledge, and skills (Bunker, 2004; Callister, 2001; Meleis, 2003). Cultural competency reduces disparities in the delivery of health care when it includes respect for cultural practices that are protective of health (Brach & Fraser, 2000). Cultural competency is particularly significant because childbearing, as one of life's most significant events, is culturally shaped and socially constructed (Ottani, 2002). According to recommendations from the USDHHS Office of Minority Health, "Health care organizations should ensure that patients/consumers receive from all staff members effective, understandable, and respectful care that is provided in a manner compatible with their cultural health beliefs and practices and preferred language" (2001, p. 3).

With dramatic shifts in health-care delivery systems including a decline in public-funded maternal child health services and growing privately financed systems, vulnerable and socioeconomically disadvantaged women and children are at risk (Akukwe, 2000). Community partnerships are essential in the delivery of health care to Mexican immigrant women and their families (Barry & Britt, 2002; Poker, Hubbard, & Sharp, 2004). Wasserman and associates (2007) conducted a systematic review of published intervention studies of the use of preventive maternal and child health services by Latina women which documents the importance of such community partnerships. In Utah, health-care services are being developed to meet the special needs of Hispanic populations, including Mexican immigrants. For example, the University of Utah health-care system includes a clinic with bilingual health-care providers including Spanish speaking certified nurse midwives. Immigrant status is not an issue for receiving services. At McKay Dee Hospital in Ogden, Utah, peer support is provided for Hispanic childbearing women through the Hispanic Labor Friends initiative. These companions attend prenatal and postpartum appointments, support the women in labor, and participate in discharge teaching with the woman they are supporting. Through such programs, health and well-being is enhanced (Messias et al., 2005).

Building on the strengths of vulnerable populations, integrating the health beliefs and practices of those who are socially disadvantaged, helping women to access personal and professional support networks, and empowering vulnerable women, families, communities, and populations in shared partnership with health-care providers and social scientists are essential.

## REFERENCES

Acevedo, M. C. (2000). The role of acculturation in explaining ethnic differences in the prenatal health-risk behaviors, mental health, and parenting beliefs of Mexican American and European American at-risk women. *Child Abuse and Neglect, 24,* 111–127.

Adams, C. R. (2004). Linguistic differences and culturally relevant interventions for involving monolingual Latino individuals in research efforts. *Journal of Hispanic Higher Education, 3*(4), 382–392.

Agency for Healthcare Research and Quality (AHRQ). (2002). Health care for minority women. Retrieved August 4, 2006, from http://www.ahrq.gov/research/minority.htm

Akukwe, C. (2000). Maternal and child health services in the twenty-first century: Critical issues, challenges, and opportunities. *Health Care for Women International, 21*(7), 641–653.

Amaro, H., & de la Torre, A. (2002). Public health needs and scientific opportunities in research on Latinas. *American Journal of Public Health, 92,* 525–529.

Anachebe, N. F., & Sutton, M. Y. (2003). Racial disparities in reproductive health outcomes. *American Journal of Obstetrics and Gynecology, 188*(4), S37–42.

Andresen, P., & Telleen, S. (1992). The relationship between social support and maternal behaviors and attitudes: A meta-analytic review. *American Journal of Community Psychology, 20,* 753–774.

Arcia, E., Skinner, M., Bailey, D., & Correa, V. (2001). Models of acculturation and health behaviors among Latino immigrants to the United States. *Social Science and Medicine, 53,* 41–53.

Balcazar, H., & Krull, J. L. (1999). Determinants of birth-weight outcomes among Mexican American women: Examining conflicting results about acculturation. *Ethnicity and Disease, 9,* 410–422.

Balcazar, H., Peterson, G., & Cobas, J. (1996). Acculturation and health-related risk behaviors among Mexican American pregnant youth. *American Journal of Health Behavior, 20,* 425–433.

Balcazar, H., Peterson, G. W., & Krull, J. L. (1997). Acculturation and family cohesiveness in Mexican American pregnant women: Social and health implications. *Family and Community Health, 20*(3), 16–31.

Barrera, M. (2000). Social support research in community psychology. In J. Rappaport & E. Seidman (Eds.), *Handbook of community psychology* (pp. 215–245). New York: Kluwer Academic/Plenum.

Barron, F., Hunter, A., Mayo, R., & Willoughby, D. (2004). Acculturation and adherence: Issues for health care providers working with clients of Mexican origin. *Journal of Transcultural Nursing, 15*(40), 331–337.

Barry, K., & Britt, D. W. (2002). Outreaching: Targeting high risk women through community partnerships. *Women's Health Issues, 12*(2), 66–78.

Beck, C. T., Roman, R. D., & Bernal, H. (2005). Acculturation level and postpartum depression in Hispanic mothers. *MCN: The American Journal of Maternal Child Nursing,* 299–304.

Berg, J. A. (2003). Mexican American women's willingness to promote health. *Journal of Multicultural Nursing and Health, 9*(2), 34–43.

Berry, A. (2002). Culture care of the Mexican American family. In M. Leininger & M. R. McFarland, *Transcultural nursing* (3rd ed., pp. 363–373). New York: McGraw-Hill.

Berry, A. B. (1999). Mexican American women's expressions of the meaning of culturally congruent prenatal care. *Women's Health Issues, 10*(3), 203–212.

Brach, C., & Fraser, I. (2000). Can cultural competency reduce racial and ethnic health disparities? *Medical Care Research and Review, 57*(Supplement 1), 181–217.

Bunker, S. S. (2004). The lived experience of feeling cared for: A human becoming perspective. *Nursing Science Quarterly, 17*(1), 63–71.

Burk, M. E., Weiser, P. C., & Keegan, L. (1995). Cultural beliefs and health behaviors of pregnant Mexican-American women. *Advances in Nursing Science, 17*(4), 37–52.

Cabassa, L. J. (2003). Measuring acculturation. *Hispanic Journal of Behavioral Sciences, 25*(2), 127–146.

Callister, L. C. (2001). Culturally competent care of women and newborns: Attitudes, knowledge, and skills. *Journal of Obstetric, Gynecologic, and Neonatal Nursing, 30*(2), 209–215.

Callister, L. C. (2004). Making meaning: Women's birth narratives. *Journal of Obstetric, Gynecologic, and Neonatal Nursing, 33*(4), 508–518.

Callister, L. C., & Birkhead, A. (2002). Acculturation and perinatal outcomes in Mexican immigrant childbearing women. *Journal of Perinatal and Neonatal Nursing, 16*(3), 22–38.

Callister, L. C., Birkhead, A., Vega, R., & Crookston, L. M. (In review). *Perinatal outcomes in Mexican immigrant women giving birth in Utah.*

Chavez, L. R., Hubbell, F. A., Mishra, S. I., & Valdez, R. B. (1997). Undocumented Latina immigrants in Orange County, California. *International Migration Review, 31*(1), 88–107.

Clark, L. (2001). *La familia:* Methodological issues in the assessment of perinatal social support for Mexicans living in the United States. *Social Science and Medicine, 53,* 1303–1320.

Crump, C., Lipsky, S., & Mueller, B. A. (1999). Adverse birth outcomes among Mexican Americans: Are U.S.–born women at greater risk than Mexico-born women? *Ethnicity and Health, 4*(1/2), 29–34.

Delgado, J. L., Metzger, R., & Falcon, A. P. (1995). Meeting the health promotion needs of Hispanic communities. *American Journal of Health Promotion, 9*(4), 300–311.

de Paula, T., Lagana, K., & Gonzalez-Ramirez, L. (1996). Mexican Americans. In J. G. Lipson, S. L. Dibble, & P. A. Minarik (Eds.), *Culture and nursing care: A pocket guide.* San Francisco: UCSF Nursing Press.

Domain, E. W. (2001). Cultural practices and social support of pregnant women in northern New Mexican communities. *Journal of Nursing Scholarship, 33*(4), 331–336.

Falicov, C. J. (1998). *Latino families in therapy: A guide to multicultural practice.* New York: Guilford Press.

Flaskerud, J. H., & Winslow, B. J. (1998). Conceptualizing vulnerable populations health related research. *Nursing Research, 47*(2), 69–78.

Fraktman, M. G. (1998). Immigrant mothers: What makes them high risk? In C. G. Coll, J. L. Surrey, & K. Weingarten (Eds.), *Mothering against odds* (pp. 85–107). New York: Guilford Press.

Franzini, L., & Fernandez-Esquer, M. E. (2004). Socioeconomic, cultural, and personal influences on health outcomes in low-income Mexican-origin individuals in Texas. *Social Science and Medicine, 59*(8), 1629–1646.

Franzini, L., Ribble, J. C., & Keddie, A. M. (2001). Understanding the Hispanic paradox. *Ethnicity and Disease, 11,* 496–518.

Friedman, M. M., Bowden, V. R., & Jones, E. G. (2002). *Family nursing* (5th ed.). Upper Saddle River, NJ: Prentice Hall.

Galanti, G. A. (2003). The Hispanic family and male-female relationships. *Journal of Transcultural Nursing, 14*(3), 180–185.

Gibson, M. V., Diaz, V. A., Mainous, A. G., & Geesey, M. E. (2005). Prevalence of breastfeeding and acculturation in Hispanics. *Birth, 32*(2), 93–98.

Guendelman, S., Malin, C., Herr-Harthorn, B., & Vargas, P. N. (2001). Orientations to motherhood and male partner support among women in Mexico and Mexican-origin women in the United States. *Social Science and Medicine, 52,* 1805–1813.

Harley, K., & Eskenazi, B. (2006). Time in the United States, social support and health behaviors during pregnancy among women of Mexican descent. *Social Science and Medicine, 62*(12), 3048–3061.

Heilemann, M. V, Frutos, L., Lee, K. A., & Kury, F. S. (2004). Protective strength factors, resources, and risks in relation to depressive symptoms among childbearing women of Mexican descent. *Health Care for Women International, 25,* 88–106.

Heilemann, M. V., Lee, K. A., & Kury, F. S. (2005). Strength factors among women of Mexican descent. *Western Institute of Nursing Communicating Nursing Research Conference Proceedings, 38,* 161.

Henly, J. R., Danziger, S. K., & Offer, S. (2005). The contribution of social support to the maternal well-being of low-income families. *Journal of Marriage and the Family, 67*(1), 122–140.

Horowitz, J. A., & Damato, E. G. (1999). Mothers' perceptions of postpartum stress and satisfaction. *Journal of Obstetric, Gynecologic, Neonatal Nursing, 28,* 515–605.

Im, E. O., & Meleis, A. I. (2001). An international imperative for gender-sensitive theories in women's health. *Journal of Nursing Scholarship, 33*(4), 309–314.

Institute of Medicine. (2003). *Unequal treatment: Confronting racial and ethnic disparities in health care.* Washington, DC: National Academic Press.

James, S. A. (1993). Racial and ethnic differences in infant mortality and low birth weight: Psycho-social critique. *Annals of Epidemiology, 3,* 130–136.

Jimenez, S. L. M. (1995). The Hispanic culture, folklore, and perinatal health. *Journal of Perinatal Education, 4*(1), 9–16.

Jones, M. E., & Bond, M. L. (1999). Predictors of birth outcomes among Hispanic immigrant women. *Journal of Nursing Care Quality, 14*(1), 56–62.

Juarbe, T. C., Turok, X. P., & Warda, M. R. (2003). Coping strategies associated with physical activity and healthy dietary practice barriers among Mexican and Central American women. *Hispanic Health Care International, 2*(2), 51–59.

Kalofonos, I., & Planikas, L. A. (1999). Barriers to prenatal care for Mexican and Mexican American women. *Journal of Gender, Culture, and Health, 4*(2), 135–154.

Keefe, S. E., Padilla, A. M., & Carlos, M. L. (1979). The Mexican American extended family as an emotional support system. *Human Organization, 38,* 144–152.

Lagana, K. (1996). *Preventing low birthweight: Cultural influences on Mexican immigrant and Mexican American prenatal care.* San Francisco: UCSF Nursing Press.

Lagana, K., & Gonzalez-Ramirez, L. (2003). Mexican Americans. In P. F. St Hill, J. G. Lipson, & Meleis, A. I. (Eds.). *Caring for women cross-culturally* (pp. 218–235). Philadelphia: F. A. Davis.

Langford, C. P. H., Bowsher, J., Maloney, J. P., & Lillis, P. P. (1997). Social support. *Journal of Advanced Nursing, 25,* 95–100.

Logsdon, M. C. (2001). Helping hands: Exploring the cultural implications of social support during pregnancy. *Association of Women's Health, Obstetric, and Neonatal Nurses Lifelines, 4*(6), 29–32.

Logsdon, M. C., Birkimer, J. C., & Usui, W. (2000). Social support and postpartum depressive symptoms in African-American women with low incomes. *MCN: The American Journal of Maternal Child Nursing, 25,* 262–266.

Logsdon, M. C., & Davis, D. W. (2003). Social and professional support for pregnant and parenting women. *MCN: The American Journal of Maternal Child Nursing, 28*(6), 371–376.

Lothian, J. A. (1998). Culturally competent childbirth. *Journal of Perinatal Education, 7*(1), x–xxi.

Marin, B. V. (2003). HIV prevention in the Hispanic community: Sex, culture, and empowerment. *Journal of Transcultural Nursing, 14*(3), 186–192.

Marin, G., & Marin, B. V. (1991). *Research with Hispanic populations. Applied social research methods series* (Vol. 23). Newbury Park, CA: Sage.

Martinez-Schallmoser, L., Telleen, S., & MacMullen, N. J. (2003). The effect of social support and acculturation on postpartum depression in Mexican American women. *Journal of Transcultural Nursing, 14,* 329–338.

McCubbin, M. A., & McCubbin, H. I. (1993). Family coping with health crises: The Resiliency Model of family stress, adjustment, and adaptation. In C. Danielson, B. Hamel-Bissell, & P. Winsted-Fry (Eds.), *Families, health and illness.* New York: Mosby.

McNaughton, D. B., Cowell, J. M., Gross, D., Fogg, L., & Alley, S. H. (2004). The relationship between maternal and child mental health in Mexican immigrant families. *Research and Theory for Nursing Practice, 18*(2/3), 229–242.

McNicholas, S. L. (2002). Social support and positive health practices. *Western Journal of Nursing Research, 24*(5), 772–787.

Meleis, A. I. (2003). Theoretical considerations of health care for immigrant and minority women. In P. F. St. Hill, J. G. Lipson, & A. I. Meleis (Eds.), *Caring for women cross-culturally* (pp. 1–10). Philadelphia: F. A. Davis.

Mendelson, C. (2002). Health perceptions of Mexican American women. *Journal of Transcultural Nursing, 13*(3), 210–217.

Messias, D. K. H., DeJong, M. K., & McLoughlin, K. (2005). Being involved and making a difference: Empowerment and well being among women living in poverty. *Journal of Holistic Nursing, 23*(1), 70–88.

Morales, M. L., Lara, M., & Kington, R. S. (2002). Socioeconomic, cultural, and behavioral factors affecting Hispanic health outcomes. *Journal of the Poor and Underserved, 13*(4), 477–503.

Naranjo, L. E., & Dirksen, S. R. (1998). The recruitment and participation of Hispanic women in nursing research. *Public Health Nursing, 15*(1), 25–29.

Niska, K. J. (1999). Mexican American family processes: Nurturing, support, and socialization. *Nursing Science Quarterly, 12*(2), 138–142.

Norbeck, J. S., & Tilden, V. (1983). Life stress, social support, and emotional disequilibrium in complications of pregnancy: A prospective multivariate study. *Journal of Health and Social Behavior, 24,* 30–46.

Ottani, P. A. (2002). Embracing global similarities: A framework for cross-cultural obstetric care. *Journal of Obstetric, Gynecologic, and Neonatal Nursing, 31*(1), 33–38.

Page, R. L. (2004). Positive pregnancy outcomes in Mexican immigrants. *Journal of Obstetric, Gynecologic, and Neonatal Nursing, 33*(6), 783–790.

Pearce, C. W. (1998). Seeking a healthy baby: Hispanic women's views of pregnancy and prenatal care. *Clinical Excellence for Nurse Practitioners, 2*(6), 351–361.

Peete, C. T. (1999). The importance of place of residence in health outcomes research: How does living in an ethnic enclave affect low birth weight deliveries for Hispanic mothers? *Dissertation Abstracts, 60,* 1777-A.

Poker, A., Hubbard, H., & Sharp, B. A. C. (2004). The first national reports on United States healthcare quality and disparities. *Journal of Nursing Care Quality, 19*(4), 316–321.

Remen, R. N. (2000). *My grandfather's blessings: Stories of strength, refuge, and belonging.* New York: Riverhead Books.

Ridley, R. T., Naber, J. L., Florea, F. A., & Guminski, D. (2004). Development of a multilingual resource manual. *Journal of Transcultural Nursing, 15*(3), 231–241.

Robert Wood Johnson Foundation. (2001). New survey shows language barriers causing many Spanish-speaking Latinos to skip care. Fact sheet presented at press briefing, December 12, 2001. Washington, DC: Author.

Rubio, M., & Montgomery, K. S. (2003). Number of live births, body weight, and Latinas. *Hispanic Health Care International, 2*(3), 103–110.

Sandelowski, M. (2004). Using qualitative research. *Qualitative Health Research, 14*(10), 1366–1386.

Schaffer, M. A., & Lia-Hoagberg, B. (1997). Effects of social support on prenatal care and health behaviors of low-income women. *Journal of Obstetric, Gynecologic, and Neonatal Nursing, 26*(4), 422–440.

Seccombe, K. (2001). Families in poverty in the 1990s. In R. M. Milardo (Ed.), *Understanding families into the new millennium* (pp. 313–332). Lawrence, KS: National Council of Family Relations.

Shaffer, C. F. (2002). Factors influencing the access to prenatal care by Hispanic pregnant women. *Journal of the American Academy of Nurse Practitioners, 14*(2), 93–96.

Sherraden, M., & Barrera, R. E. (1995). Qualitative research with an understudied population. *Public Health Nursing, 7*(2), 105–110.

Sherraden, M., & Barrera, R. E. (1996a). Maternal support and cultural influences among Mexican immigrant mothers. *Families in Society: The Journal of Contemporary Human Services,* May, 298–313.

Sherraden, M., & Barrera, R. E. (1996b). Poverty, family support, and well-being of infants: Mexican immigrant women and childbearing. *Journal of Sociology and Social Welfare, 23,* 27–54.

Siantz, M. L. D. L., & Coronado, N. (2002). Factors associated with depression among Mexican immigrant farm worker mothers. *Hispanic Health Care International, 1*(2), 97–107.

Smedley, B. D., Stith, A. Y., & Nelson, A. R. (Eds.). (2003). *Unequal treatment: Confronting racial and ethnic disparities in health care.* Washington, DC: National Academy Press.

Stinson, J. C., Lee, K. A., Heilemann, M. S., Goss, G., & Koshar, J. (2000). Comparing factors related to low birth weight in rural Mexico-born and United States–born Hispanic women in southern California. *Family and Community Health, 23*(1), 29–39.

Telleen, S. (1990). Parental beliefs and help-seeking in mothers' use of a community-based family support program. *Journal of Community Psychology, 18,* 264–276.

Telleen, S., Herzog, A., & Kilbane, T. (1999). Impact of a family support program on mothers' social support and parenting stress. *American Journal of Orthopsychiatry, 59,* 410–419.

The Commonwealth Fund. (1998). *The Commonwealth Fund 1998 survey of women's health.* New York: Author.

Tezoquipa, I. H., Monreal, L. A., & Trevino-Siller, S. (2005). "Without money you're nothing": Poverty and health in Mexico from women's perspectives. *Review Latin American Enfermagem, 13*(5), 626–633.

U.S. Census Bureau. (2004). *2002 current population reports: The Hispanic population in the United States.* Retrieved July 10, 2006, from http://www.census.gov/population/www/socdemo/hispanic.html

U.S. Department of Health and Human Services, Office of Minority Health. (2001). *National standards for culturally and linguistically appropriate services in health care.* Rockville, MD: U.S. Government Printing Office.

U.S. Department of Health and Human Services, Office of Research on Women's Health. (1998). *Women of color health data book.* Rockville, MD: U.S. Government Printing Office.

Warda, M. R. (2000). Mexican American's perceptions of culturally competent care. *Western Journal of Nursing Research, 22*(2), 203–224.

Wasserman, M., Bender, D., Lee, S. Y. D. (2007). Use of preventive maternal and child health services by Latina women. *Medical Care Research and Review, 64*(1), 4–45.

Webster, J., Linnane, J. W. J., Dibley, L. M., Hinson, J. K., Starrenburg, S. E., & Roberts, J. A. (2000). Measuring social support in pregnancy. *Birth, 27*(2), 97–103.

Weineck, R. M., Jacobs, E. A., Stone, L. C., Ortega, A. N., & Burstin, H. (2004). Hispanic healthcare disparities: Challenging the myth of a monolithic Hispanic population. *Medical Care, 42*(4), 313–320.

Wisdom, J. P., Berlin, M., & Lapidus, J. A. (2005). Relating health policy to women's health outcomes. *Social Science and medicine, 61*(8), 1776–1784.

Zambrana, R. E., & Carter-Pokras, O. (2001). Health data issue for Hispanics. *Journal of Health Care for the Poor and Underserved, 12*(1), 20–34.

Zambrana, R. E., Scrimshaw, S. C. M., Collins, N., & Dunkel-Schetter, C. (1997). Prenatal health behaviors and psychosocial risk factors in pregnant women of Mexican origin: The role of acculturation. *American Journal of Public Health, 87*(6), 1022–1026.

# CHAPTER 12

# Food Insecurity and Provisioning

## Chronic Challenges Faced by Families Living in Poverty on the Northern Cheyenne Indian Reservation

ERIN FEINAUER WHITING AND CAROL J. WARD

Among families in poverty, one of the most important challenges is access to sufficient quantities and quality of food. In the early 1990s, about 10% of the U.S. population was estimated to suffer from poor nutrition associated with poverty (Barraclough, 1991). In 2002, the prevalence of all types of food insecurity in the United States was 11.1%, with the more severe form of food insecurity involving hunger affecting 3.5% (Nord, Andrews, & Carlson, 2003). According to research conducted by Bickel, Nord, Price, Hamilton, and Cook (2000), households headed by single women with children, those with incomes below the official poverty line, and minority households experience higher rates of food insecurity. Importantly, households with children experience food insecurity at twice the rate of households without children (Bickel et al., 1999). For these households and families, access to sources of food assistance is critical— an essential element of family survival. However, the impact of food insecurity on families involves more than meeting physical needs. Examining the social impacts of food insecurity among low-income households, Hamelin, Habicht, and Beaudry (1999) found that food insecurity includes psychological and socio-familial as well as physical experiences that disturb rituals of food consumption. Although households may be reluctant to participate in certain food provisioning activities at first, "eventually, the search for food takes precedence over previously held values" (Hamelin et al., 1999, p. 527S).

Recent research has addressed the effects of welfare policy reform on access to food assistance among poor populations, especially minorities. Among the populations studied, research on American Indians has examined how welfare reform has affected access to such food assistance programs as the Food Distribution program and food stamps (Brown & Cornell, 2001). These findings, along with research by Gundersen (2006), indicate that food insecurity remains high among American Indians, especially in communities where poverty rates are high, and access to food assistance varies with the degree of tribal control.

Both regional research (Bliss, 2004) and studies of specific reservation communities (e.g., Pickering, 2000; Ward & Whiting, 2006; Whiting, Ward, Hiwalker-Villa, & Davis, 2005) have demonstrated that increased levels of stress are associated with food insecurity. Although these studies show that high levels of stress are related to family food needs, little is known about the exact nature of the stressors and how they relate to food insecurity. Additionally, high stress levels have been associated with increasing mental health and health concerns. Therefore, greater understanding is needed about the relationship of stress to food insecurity and how stress is influenced by social and cultural factors, such as gender and race or ethnicity. For example, Siefert, Heflin, Corcoran, & Williams (2004) showed that women's physical and mental health were both adversely affected by food insecurity, and new research by Wu and Schimmele (2005) confirms the effects of food insufficiency on depression, especially among women. These findings suggest the need to examine more closely the nature and effects of stress related to food insecurity in populations that are especially vulnerable to these conditions. Important questions also remain about the use of food acquisition strategies and how particular social and cultural contexts affect experiences with food insecurity, hunger, and related stress factors.

This paper will present the findings of recent research designed to document the types and levels of food insecurity and related health concerns facing a reservation community, the Northern Cheyenne of southeastern Montana. This community is a particularly relevant setting for a case study because nearly 40% of Northern Cheyenne families have incomes below the poverty level (U.S. Bureau of the Census, 2000) and nearly 70% experience some form of food insecurity (Hiwalker

et al., 2002). The central purpose of this paper is to use household survey data to assess the relationships of background characteristics, food insecurity, and use of various food acquisition strategies to stress levels among reservation residents. Additionally, measures of stress will be examined in greater detail to learn more about the various types of stressors experienced. Qualitative data from in-depth interviews with reservation residents provide insights into the meaning of food in this community and the social and cultural influences on food security and stresses associated with accessing adequate food for families.

## LITERATURE REVIEW

Research on food insecurity during the last two decades indicates that food insecurity introduces stressors into the lives of adults responsible for feeding themselves and their children. Recent studies of the effects of welfare reform, which began in 1996 with the federal legislation that created Temporary Assistance for Needy Families (TANF), as well as efforts to document food insecurity levels among American subpopulations have contributed new insights into the relationships among poverty, food insecurity and health problems. These studies show that minority populations are particularly vulnerable. For example, Nelson, Brown, and Lurie (2000) reported that in a study of all patients admitted to an urban hospital in a two-week period, 50% were poor and minority, and a substantial proportion of the patients reported food insecurity. Of the 40% of the total sample ($N = 567$) that had received food stamps, half reported a loss of benefits and were more likely to report food insecurity and hunger. Among the conclusions of this study were that reductions in food stamps were associated with several measures of food insecurity and hunger, and that one-third of the hypoglycemic reactions reported by diabetics were related to an inability to afford food (p. 68).

Another study reported by Siefert et al. (2004) was designed to identify the independent effects of food insecurity and hunger on physical and mental health by analyzing their effects on poor women's health, while controlling for a broad array of potential common risk factors. Analyzing data at two time points, the authors found that women who were food insufficient in both years were more likely to report fair or poor health later (controlling for a range of factors). Food insufficiency at the second time point was significantly associated with diagnoses of major depression. The researchers' findings provide additional evidence that household food insufficiency can adversely affect physical and mental health. A recent study by Gray, Knudson, and Penland (2005) of Northern Plains Indians also supports this finding, but suggests that women and men may be affected differently by cultural identity, body mass index, and food insecurity.

Additional studies of the health and well-being of women have examined the effects of socioeconomic status. For example, Walker, Walker, and Walker (1994) found that despite the lack of differences between rural and urban mothers in most areas (such as perceived stress, parenting confidence, and body weight), socioeconomic status affected rural and urban women's levels of self-actualization, isolation, and nutritional status in different ways. The general importance of socioeconomic conditions is confirmed in other research which shows that families and households in poverty, including the working poor, experience financial insecurity, high levels of stress, and health problems (Newman, 1996; Vozoris & Tarasuk, 2003).

Several recent studies of poverty and the effects of welfare reform have focused on rural minorities. Research on several midwestern American Indian reservations (e.g.,

Harnack, DeRosier, Story, Himes, & Holy Rock, 2001; Pickering, 2000) suggests that food assistance and other social service needs remain high in the wake of welfare reform. In particular, food insecurity levels were high among research participants. Structural barriers specific to reservation life perpetuate such problems as food insecurity, and poor nutrition and health (Antell, Blevins, Jensen, & Massey, 1999; Pickering, 2000).

Research by Wu and Schimmele (2005) on food insufficiency and mental health effects provides particularly useful findings concerning the role of food shortages as a source of stress. This research asks the question, is food insufficiency a better indicator of depression than is socioeconomic status? The purpose is to examine two alternative explanations of depression in low-income populations: lack of socioeconomic resources that indirectly increases vulnerability to stress versus food insufficiency as a direct source of stress. Based on the work of Pearlin, Lieberman, Menaghan, and Mulla (1981), Wu and Schimmele define stress as a process involving exposure, resistance, and outcomes, and categorize sources of stress as life events and changes, chronic strains, and daily hassles. Food insufficiency, a more severe form of food insecurity, is identified as a "chronic strain," especially for individuals and families with low income. The authors cite several studies (e.g., Bandura, 1992; Fitchen, 1988; Hamelin, Beaudry, & Habicht, 2002; Lang, 1997; Rainville & Brink, 2001; Ross & Mirowsky, 1989; Siefert et al., 2004; Tarasuk & Maclean, 1990) that explore the effects of food insufficiency and identify such typical effects as the following: anxiety, guilt, shame, a sense of powerlessness, social friction, and exclusion. Another important finding is that food shortages result in individual preoccupation with obtaining food that diverts attention from other productive activities such as human capital development. Wu and Schimmele (2005) suggest that social support is an important resource for resistance to stress among vulnerable groups.

The findings of Wu and Schimmele's (2005) research involving a national Canadian sample with a range of income and ethnic groups (but excludes Canadian Indians on reserves) indicate that food insufficiency increases depressive symptoms among low-income groups. Their results show that although both socioeconomic measures and food insufficiency are important predictors of depression, food insufficiency is an independent, direct source of stress that affects depression. However, social support and social contact have significant mitigating effects in that they promote coping behaviors by helping individuals understand and manage negative life experiences and situational demands (p. 499). This study also confirmed that women tend to have more depressive symptoms than men do, and single-parent status is associated with an increase in the number of depressive symptoms individuals suffer (p. 494). Also important is that middle-aged persons suffer more depressive symptoms than do younger or older persons, whereas minority status is a protective factor.

Although Wu and Schimmele's research clarifies the relationship of food insufficiency to depressive symptoms, these findings are limited by the use of cross-sectional data which exclude persons living on Canadian Indian reserves. Additionally, this study does not include data on other types of stresses (negative life events, chronic strains, and daily hassles) that may be directly related to poverty and their relationship to food insufficiency. The latter is especially important because minority populations may experience multiple sources or types of stress.

Research supported by the John D. and Catherine T. MacArthur Network on Socioeconomic Status and Health (2005) at the University of California, San Francisco identifies stress as an important condition to examine in its own right because of its important effects on both physical and mental health. The specific effects of severe, prolonged stress include "suppression of the immune system," which

> ... makes the body more susceptible to everything from colds and flus to cancer. For example, the incidence of serious illness, including cancer, is significantly higher among people who have suffered the death of a spouse in the previous year.... Very often those under severe, prolonged stress may contract diseases related to immune deficiency and may even die of these diseases.... So it is very important that we recognize the cause for stresses and remove the causes to maintain a healthy lifestyle. (ICBS, 2006)

Focusing on how socioeconomic status influences the production and effects of stress, the mission statement of this network of researchers also asserts, "socioeconomic status and race/ethnicity interact in their associations with health" and calls for more research in this area. Both Pearlin (1989) and Aneshensel (1992) suggest the need to examine the role of social structural conditions in the stress process as well as how different stressors are related to each other. A recent review (Cohen, Underwood, & Gottlieb, 2000) of issues related to measurement of psychological stress cautions, however, that research on the multiple factors and dimensions of stress must use measures that address specific research questions and are sensitive to the population of interest.

Research that has attempted to address food insecurity and related stress among American Indian communities (Brown & Cornell, 2001) shows that a large proportion of both individuals and families experience food insecurity, and many experience hunger as well as the stresses related to accessing food. A recent study of the Northern Cheyenne reservation (Davis, Hiwalker, Ward, & Feinauer, 1999; Hiwalker, Davis, Ward, Youngstrom, & Feinauer, 2000; Hiwalker et al., 2002) revealed that more than two-thirds of reservation residents experience food insecurity and about 35% experience food insecurity with hunger. Findings of this study showed that food insecurity was a significant factor in the high levels of nutritional risk and poor nutritional health. Stress levels among study participants were also high for a substantial percentage of people. Qualitative data showed that sources of stress related to food shortages included barriers to obtaining food assistance (Davis et al., 1999; Hiwalker et al., 2000). Unlike the research by Wu and Schimmele, which assumed that using food assistance carries a social stigma, Northern Cheyenne research participants placed a higher value on obtaining food for their families than personal prestige. In this context, an important cultural norm involves sharing food with others in need as well as providing for your own family. Consequently, stress related to food shortages is not only a chronic strain, but can be a daily hassle involving role strain.

In research on other populations, studies examining household food provisioning show that households at risk for food insecurity typically participate in a myriad of food acquisition practices. Campbell and Desjardins (1989) found that household food provisioning for low-income households with children falls into three general categories: self-reliance, informal bartering, and formal institutions. Most interestingly, Campbell and Desjardins found that "most households used multiple approaches to take maximum advantage of their resource environments" (Campbell & Desjardins, 1989, p. 166).

Food acquisition research, which examines the coping and adaptive strategies of low-income families to achieve food security, documents types of household food provisioning activities. Adult participants are likely to skip meals or cut down on the amount of food they consume so that children will not go hungry (Ahluwalia, Dodds, & Baligh, 1998; Hoisington, Shultz, & Butkus 2002; Kempson, Keenan, Sadani, & Adler, 2003; Kempson, Keenan, Sadani & Rosato, 2002). Other frequently cited practices include borrowing and sharing food with social networks, accessing federal and community programs, as well as more extreme forms of food acquisition like salvaging food from dumpsters (Ahluwalia et al., 1998; Hoisington, Shultz, & Butkus, 2002; Kempson, Keenan, Sadani, & Adler, 2003; Kempson, Keenan, Sadani, & Rosato, 2002). Unsafe or risky food acquisition practices (Hoisington et al., 2002; Kempson et al., 2002, 2003) also include selling blood, collecting and eating road kill, and stealing or committing petty crimes to receive meals in jail (Ahluwalia et al., 1998; Hoisington et al., 2002; Kempson et al., 2002, 2003). Other practices include borrowing money, pawning items, restricting children's access to food supplies, begging, shoplifting, and living in abandoned buildings (Hoisington et al., 2002; Kempson et al., 2003).

Other sources of food include specific federal food programs such as food stamps, Head Start, Women, Infants and Children (WIC) and the school lunch/breakfast program, and more informal activities including attending events at churches, happy hours, and stores on days that offer food samples (Kempson et al., 2003). Hunting and gardening also supplement food resources (Hoisington et al., 2002; Kempson et al., 2002, 2003) along with local food pantries, soup kitchens, and other programs (Kempson et al., 2002, 2003; Tarasuk & Beaton, 1999).

Use of social support varies considerably among limited-resource families. Ahluwalia et al. (1998) found that among low-income families in North Carolina who relied on social networks for food assistance, information, and emotional support, family members were the primary social support resource, followed by friends, neighbors, and acquaintances. However, reliance on anyone was reported as distressing. These authors also found that reliance on social networks differed by ethnic group, with African Americans more often preferring formal assistance than whites because the people in their networks were "just as destitute as they were" (Ahluwalia et al., 1998, p. 605). When social networks failed, participants reported turning to community organizations that were seen as even less desirable, for example, food pantries and other agencies (Ahluwalia et al., 1998; Campbell & Desjardins, 1989). The severity of food insecurity is a factor in these food acquisition choices (Hoisington et al., 2002, p. 327). Using more desperate coping strategies as food becomes scarcer indicates that there may be a succession of strategies depending on both the severity of hunger and personal characteristics.

This review suggests several important questions that will be the focus of this chapter: (1) What are the effects of food insecurity on stress levels relative to other influences in this American Indian community, (2) how do food insecurity and specific food provisioning strategies relate to stress levels, and (3) what types of stresses are experienced by this particular population? Relatedly, we will explore how the local social and cultural context shapes the stresses related to food insecurity.

## RESEARCH CONTEXT, METHODS, AND DATA SOURCES

The context for this research is the Northern Cheyenne Indian reservation, established in southeastern Montana in 1884 by executive order. The reservation now includes 447,000 acres spanning 36 miles from east to west and 23 miles from north to south. It is the home of approximately 5,000 people, about 82% of whom are Northern Cheyenne, 13% are

members of other tribes, and 6% are non-Indian. Poverty on the reservation increased between 1979 and 1989 as the poverty rate for the surrounding areas dropped. The Northern Cheyenne reservation had the highest percentage (among the seven reservations in Montana) of persons and families below the poverty level in 1990, with 48% of adults and 44% of families living in poverty. It is important to consider the substantial proportion (40%) of Cheyenne families who continue to live under the poverty level today (U.S. Bureau of the Census, 2000) given today's $3-per-gallon gasoline and the remoteness of the Northern Cheyenne reservation (about a hundred miles from an urban center). Unemployment fluctuates between 60 and 85% because jobs are scarce on the Northern Cheyenne Reservation. Almost 42% of the reservation's people are under the age of 18, and another 50% are between the ages of 18 and 64.

## Food Security, Nutrition, and Health Survey

This research was conducted as part of several projects funded by the U.S. Department of Agriculture (USDA) small grants program from 1999 to 2001. One important part of the project involved a survey questionnaire developed in 2001 through a collaborative effort of researchers at Brigham Young University (BYU) and Chief Dull Knife College (CDKC). This survey uses the USDA Food Security Core Module (Bickel et al., 2000) to assess food use and acquisition decisions, and includes items on respondent use of food assistance programs and alternative food sources, standard assessments of nutrition and health risks (American Academy of Family Physicians, 2000; Martin, 1995), including risk factors associated with diabetes (American Diabetes Association, 2005), and life experiences and changes which can increase stress (Holmes-Rahe

Social Readjustment Rating Scale). Basic demographic data were also collected for respondents and for the household.

All parts of the instruments were field tested in the early spring of 2001 by CDKC project members and revised as needed. Respondents were informed about the purpose of the study and individuals who had problems with reading or understanding English were provided assistance from interviewers who would read or translate questions while allowing the respondents to privately record their answers. Everyone completing a questionnaire received a voucher that could be used in the local grocery store.[1]

*Sample.* The sampling frame for selection of survey participants was based on the enrollment lists of the Northern Cheyenne Nation. A stratified random sample was selected that represented both men and women across age groups in proportion to the population of the five primary communities on the reservation. Using age, sex, and community residence requirements of the sampling plan, research team members at CKDC identified and randomly selected eligible Northern Cheyenne tribal members for participation (see also Hiwalker et al., 2002).

Data on individual and household characteristics for this sample show that 52% of respondents reside in Lame Deer, which is the largest community and center of the reservation, 26% in Busby, 4% in Birney, 8% in Ashland, and 10% in Muddy Creek. This sample includes 209 (44%) men and 265 (56%) women. Just more than half (50.2%) of all respondents report being "married or with someone" at the time of the survey. Most households have less than three children (39% have 0–1, and 38% have 2–3). Fifteen percent of households report 4–5 children and 5% have more than 6 children under the age of 18. The age distribution of the sample reflects the sampling frame and resembles the distribution reported in the 2000 census (U.S. Bureau of the Census, 2000). Most respondents are from 25 to 44 years old, with 24% ages 25 to 34, and 22% ages 35 to 44. Slightly fewer are 45 to 54 years old (19%). Respondents reported full-time work (36%) and being unemployed (25%) most often, but about 17% reported part-time work and 15% seasonal work. Fifteen percent of respondents did not have a high school diploma, 39% had a high school diploma or GED, 39% had some college, and 8% had a college degree.

*Variables.* Data were collected about stressful life events experienced by respondents during the last 12 months using the Holmes-Rahe Social Readjustment Rating Scale. Although this instrument was developed in the 1970s for more general use, we believe it provides a useful starting point in identifying sources of stressful life events in this community. For descriptive purposes, these summed scores were grouped into levels of stress that include the following proportions of respondents: 44% demonstrated a low level of stress; 28% a medium level of stress; and 28% a high level of stress. Qualitative data collected through in-depth interviews with almost 100 persons are used to discuss types of stress associated with food insecurity and to supplement survey data.

Questions on food source use were developed from previous research with this population (Davis et al., 1999; Hiwalker et al., 2000, 2002). Through in-depth interviews on the Northern Cheyenne reservation for several years before the survey, 16 food sources were identified as being relevant to food provisioning. The survey asked respondents to use a five-point scale ("Don't use," "Use almost every month," "Some months but not every month," "Only 1 or 2 months," and "Don't Know") to indicate how often these sources were used to buy or obtain food. Besides wages, which is the most frequently used food source in our sample, food sources include formal food programs such as food stamps, the Food Distribution Program on Indian Reservations (FDPIR) program (usually called commodities), and Women, Infants, and Children (WIC). Other government programs include General Assistance and entitlement programs, including Social Security and Disability. Local programs and services consist of the Northern Cheyenne Food Bank, churches, and tribal food vouchers. Additional sources include relying on family or other subsistence activities, such as gardening, hunting, selling crafts, and working at odd jobs. Finally, pawning items was reported as an important source of food for many of the TANF (welfare) clients. Because some of the food sources were used relatively infrequently, dichotomous categories representing use and non-use were created for most of the analyses. Missing data were infrequent and were not significant in any analysis.

Levels of household food security are measured with the USDA Food Security Core Module (Bickel et al., 2000) regarding household experiences during the last 12 months. Of the 18 items, 10 are asked of all households but 8 pertain only to households with children under the age of 18. Therefore, this measure allows for a comparison between households with children and households without children. The USDA Food Security Core Module "is concerned only with food insecurity/hunger that occur because the household does not have enough food or money to buy food" (Bickel et al., 2000, p. 6). Specifically, questions are designed to assess the frequency of reducing food intake or adjusting normal food use, and the consequences of this choice, such as hunger or weight loss, for both adults and children in the household. Additional questions probe the perceptions of respondents about their experiences, including anxiety over food sufficiency and whether food was adequate in quality or quantity (Bickel et al., 2000). Because of the difficulty of measuring all aspects of food security, this scale is a partial measure; it does not measure nutritional status, safety, sources of food, social acceptability, or other social or physical barriers.

Additionally, respondents were asked about individual and household characteristics including age, gender, marital status, education level, and employment, and the number of children under the age of 18 in the household. Missing data represents fewer than 6% of any variable and is nowhere found to be significant.

*Analyses.* Stepwise ordinary least squares (OLS) regression is helpful for explaining the linear associations of independent variables with the dependent variable and is used in this analysis to understand the relative predictive importance of three sets of independent variables for overall stress levels. The relationship of food provisioning and food insecurity to stress outcomes is examined as demographic variables, food source use, and food security levels are regressed on stress levels using OLS regression.

## RESEARCH RESULTS

We begin with a description of frequencies for three central variables: stress levels, food security, and food provisioning. Multivariate analyses assess the relative effects of food security levels and food provisioning on stress levels. Descriptive statistics and qualitative data provide additional insights and illustrate some of the important themes identified in the analyses.

### Descriptive Statistics

*Stress Levels.* An analysis of stress levels for this sample indicates that most respondents experienced low and medium stress levels.[2] However, distributions of stress levels shown in Table 12.1 for several demographic variables indicate that females were more likely than males to have medium to high stress levels. Stress levels also declined with age, from 31–32% in the youngest age groups (18–24, 25–34, and 35–44 years) to 25–29% in the next age groups (45–54 and 55–64 years) and 16% among respondents 65+ years. Respondents with more schooling experienced higher stress levels than those with less schooling. Stress levels also increased with family and household size. Finally, stress levels varied by employment status. For example, about 60% of full-time or part-time workers reported medium to high stress levels whereas large proportions of the unemployed (64%) and retired workers (44%) had lower stress levels.

*Food Insecurity Levels.* Survey findings indicate substantial food needs in this population: 70% of all households were food insecure, and 34% experienced persistent hunger. Among households with children, 69% were food insecure, and 34% were food insecure with hunger.[3] Distributions of food insecurity levels, shown in Table 12.1, indicate that among households without children, 72% were food insecure, 35% of whom experienced hunger. Male and female respondents were similar in levels of food security although married respondents were more likely than single respondents to be food secure. Food security also differed by age: the most food secure age group is the youngest (18–24 years). However, food security declined with age: 36% for those 25 to 34 years, 25% for 35 to 44 years, 23% for 45–54 years, 21% for 55–64 years, and 22% for 65 years and older. Food security levels also differ by schooling and employment. Although 21% of survey respondents with less than a high school diploma were food secure, for subsequent levels of schooling food security increased: high school diploma or GED (27%), some college (36%), college degree (44%), and graduate degree (57%). Similarly, food security decreased with less stable employment:

full-time (41%), part-time (34%), seasonal/contract workers (22%), unemployed (20%), and retired (19%).

*Food Provisioning.* Food source variables, except wages, are grouped into four theoretically relevant categories based on source type: community, entitlement, informal economy, and welfare. Among welfare sources, the most frequently used sources were commodities (USDA food distribution) (31%) and food stamps (30%) followed by WIC and General Assistance. Family (29%) and tribal food vouchers (28.5%) were the most frequently used community sources, with smaller proportions of respondents using food banks and churches for food assistance. Odd jobs (26%), hunting (23%), and pawning items (22%) were the most frequently used informal economy sources. Finally, small proportions of respondents also reported that they gardened or sold crafts to get the money they needed for obtaining food, and small proportions also used entitlement programs, such as social security and disability benefits.

## Multivariate Analyses

Multivariate analyses presented in the following section show how the independent variables of interest—demographic characteristics, food insecurity, food provisioning types and strategies—are related to stress levels. We expect to find the following:

- Stress levels will increase with food insecurity levels and with less stable food sources or provisioning strategies.
- Stress levels will also be increased by less stable employment, gender (being female), age, higher levels of schooling, and number of children.

*Comparison of Stress Levels in Households With and Without Children.* Table 12.2 shows OLS regression analyses of the relative

**Table 12.1** Stress and Food Security Levels by Background Characteristics ($N = 474$)

| Demographic Variables | | Totals N (%) | Stress Levels Respondents | | | Food Insecurity Levels Households | | |
|---|---|---|---|---|---|---|---|---|
| | | | Low | Medium | High | Food Secure | Food Insecure Without Hunger | Food Insecure With Hunger |
| Gender | Male | 209 (44%) | 106 (51%) | 52 (35%) | 51 (24%) | 66 (32%) | 72 (35%) | 70 (34%) |
| | Female | 265 (56%) | 100 (38%) | 82 (31%) | 83 (31%) | 76 (29%) | 97 (37%) | 91 (34%) |
| Age Categories | 18–24 years | 72 (15%) | 22 (31%) | 28 (39%) | 22 (31%) | 33 (46%) | 26 (36%) | 13 (18%) |
| | 25–34 years | 114 (24%) | 48 (42%) | 30 (26%) | 36 (32%) | 41 (36%) | 37 (32%) | 36 (32%) |
| | 35–44 years | 103 (22%) | 42 (41%) | 29 (28%) | 32 (31%) | 26 (25%) | 41 (40%) | 36 (35%) |
| | 45–54 years | 92 (19%) | 42 (46%) | 27 (29%) | 23 (25%) | 21 (23%) | 35 (38%) | 35 (38%) |
| | 55–64 years | 48 (10%) | 21 (44%) | 13 (27%) | 14 (29%) | 10 (21%) | 18 (38%) | 19 (40%) |
| | 65+ years | 45 (10%) | 31 (69%) | 7 (16%) | 7 (16%) | 10 (22%) | 12 (27%) | 25 (51%) |

*(Continued)*

207

Table 12.1 (Continued)

| Demographic Variables | | Totals | Stress Levels Respondents | | | Food Insecurity Levels Households | | |
| --- | --- | --- | --- | --- | --- | --- | --- | --- |
| | | N (%) | Low | Medium | High | Food Secure | Food Insecure Without Hunger | Food Insecure With Hunger |
| Level of Schooling | Less than high school | 77 (15%) | 44 (57%) | 17 (22%) | 16 (21%) | 16 (21%) | 28 (36%) | 33 (43%) |
| | High school diploma/GED | 176 (39%) | 81 (46%) | 52 (30%) | 43 (24%) | 47 (27%) | 68 (39%) | 59 (34%) |
| | Some college/ associates degree | 160 (39%) | 50 (31%) | 51 (32%) | 59 (37%) | 57 (36%) | 57 (36%) | 46 (29%) |
| | College degree | 27 (6%) | 13 (48%) | 5 (19%) | 9 (33%) | 12 (44%) | 6 (22%) | 9 (33%) |
| | Graduate degree | 7 (2%) | 1 (14%) | 3 (43%) | 3 (43%) | 4 (57%) | 2 (29%) | 1 (14%) |
| Employment Status (over last 6 months) | Full-time | 165 (36%) | 27 (35%) | 22 (29%) | 28 (36%) | 68 (41%) | 62 (38%) | 35 (21%) |
| | Part-time | 77 (17%) | 27 (40%) | 23 (35%) | 17 (25%) | 26 (34%) | 29 (38%) | 21 (28%) |
| | Seasonal/contract | 67 (15%) | 54 (48%) | 29 (26%) | 29 (26%) | 15 (22%) | 28 (42%) | 24 (36%) |
| | Not employed | 112 (25%) | 23 (64%) | 6 (17%) | 7 (19%) | 22 (20%) | 33 (30%) | 56 (50%) |
| | Retired | 36 (8%) | 90 (44%) | 56 (27%) | 60 (29%) | 7 (19%) | 11 (31%) | 18 (50%) |
| Marital Status | Single/divorced/ widowed | 206 (46%) | 8 (42%) | 7 (37%) | 4 (21%) | 49 (24%) | 74 (36%) | 83 (40%) |
| | Married or with someone | 246 (54%) | 44 (57%) | 17 (22%) | 16 (21%) | 81 (36%) | 82 (36%) | 62 (28%) |

208

effects of background characteristics, food security levels, and food source types on stress levels for households with children compared with those without children. Modeling indicates some important differences in the effects of the independent variables on stress levels in the two types of households. For example, in neither model 1 nor 2 of households without children do background characteristics of respondents affect stress levels. However, in the analysis of households with children background characteristics of respondents have a much larger effect on stress levels. For example, models 1 and 2 for households with children indicate the importance of age, gender and schooling: model 1 shows that both being younger and having more years of schooling are associated with higher stress levels whereas model 2 indicates that being female and having more years of school increase stress levels. Finally in model 3, all three of these variables increase stress levels for households with children. In contrast, in model 3 for households without children, marital status has an important effect on stress levels.

Among the food source types, model 2 shows that use of the informal economy for food is the only food provisioning strategy that increases stress in households without children. In contrast, in households with children, four of the five food source types are significant for stress levels, as shown in both models 2 and 3. This finding suggests that the somewhat less stable food strategies increase stress in this population. In other words, use of food sources related to welfare, including specific formal food assistance programs, is less likely to produce higher stress levels.

Finally, model 3 shows the importance of food insecurity for both household types. As expected, being less food secure increases stress levels. Furthermore, food security is independently related to stress levels. A somewhat surprising finding is the absence of more differences between these two types of households, which suggests that the experience of food insecurity is stressful despite possible differences in food acquisition needs.

In sum, although food insecurity levels are important for both households with children and those without children, there are some important distinctions. For households with children, being younger, female, and having more years of schooling are associated with higher stress. Additionally, all of the other food strategies except welfare food sources lead to increased stress levels. In contrast, for respondents living in households without children, being single is associated with less stress whereas use of the informal economy food strategy and less food security increase stress.

## Additional Descriptive and Ethnographic Data

*Types of Stress Events Experienced.* The measurement of stress used in this research was based on the Holmes-Rahe Social Readjustment Rating Scale, an instrument that has been used in a variety of populations to measure experiences with life events and changes that produce stress. In this section, we use data collected with this instrument for exploratory purposes to describe the types of life events and changes most frequently experienced by research participants. Responses to life event items are organized into several categories, shown in Table 12.3, which have the most salience for this sample (i.e., at least 10% of the respondents indicated they experience the event, consequence, or concern).

In the area of health and health outcomes, the percentages reporting lack of sleep (46%) and change in sleeping habits (31%) indicate that sleep problems may be an important aspect of stress. Other frequently mentioned health concerns involve changes in eating habits, getting sick or being injured, and helping others with illness or crises. In the area of finances and work related events, 46% of respondents indicated they have experienced

**Table 12.2**   OLS Regression Coefficients for the Effects of Background Characteristics, Food Security, and Food Sources on Stress Levels for Households Without Children ($N = 127/445$) and Households With Children ($N = 318/445$)

| | Model 1 | | Model 2 | | Model 3 | |
|---|---|---|---|---|---|---|
| | *With Children* | *Without Children* | *With Children* | *Without Children* | *With Children* | *Without Children* |
| | Beta (S.E.) | Beta (S.E.) | Beta (S.E.) | Beta (S.E.) | Beta (S.E.) | Beta (S.E.) |
| **Background Characteristics** | | | | | | |
| Age | −.116* (8.467) | −.146 (11.780) | −.118 (8.888) | −.071 (12.477) | **−.181**** (8.960) | −.129 (12.360) |
| Gender[1] | −.092 (23.752) | −.070 (35.708) | **−.133*** (22.381) | −.120 (35.456) | **−.118*** (21.872) | −.108 (34.447) |
| Marital Status[2] | .070 (23.021) | −.174 (37.206) | .026 (21.490) | −.199 (36.577) | .000 (21.116) | **−.223*** (35.654) |
| Employment Over Last 6 Months | −.047 (9.040) | .073 (14.050) | −.091 (9.597) | −.023 (15.730) | −.155 (9.399) | −.041 (15.290) |
| Years of School | **.186**** (13.966) | .153 (20.434) | **.126*** (13.525) | .130 (20.013) | **.146**** (13.237) | .115 (19.454) |
| Number of Children < 18 in Household | .092 (13.729) | NA | .054 (12.558) | NA | .026 (12.358) | NA |
| **Food Source Type** | | | | | | |
| Wages | | | **.256***** (27.655) | −.106 (41.433) | **.263***** (26.969) | −.058 (40.731) |
| Community | | | **.187**** (11.558) | .058 (19.899) | **.122*** (11.671) | .018 (19.528) |
| Entitlement | | | **.145*** (25.599) | .003 (35.043) | **.163**** (25.024) | .035 (34.183) |
| Informal Economy | | | **.215***** (9.554) | **.355**** (21.066) | **.158**** (9.586) | **.343**** (20.465) |
| Welfare | | | .017 (13.445) | .008 (22.801) | .028 (13.119) | −.021 (22.259) |
| Food Security | | | | | | |
| *Food Security Level* | | | | | **.241***** (2.422) | **.255**** (3.998) |
| *Adjusted R²* | .053** | .016 | .221*** | .110* | .260*** | .162** |

NOTES: Food insecurity is scaled by the number of affirmative responses to food insecurity questions; levels are interpreted within the context of household composition.

1. Female is the omitted reference category.

2. Married (or with someone) is the omitted reference category.

*$p < .05$; **$p < .01$; ***$p < .001$ significant values are highlighted in bold.

**Table 12.3** Frequencies of Pertinent[§] Stress Variables by Category (*N* = 445)

| Dimension | Variable | N | % |
|---|---|---|---|
| Family | Death of a close family member | 186 | 41.8 |
| | Difficulties with family | 147 | 33.0 |
| | Change in health or behavior of family member | 126 | 28.3 |
| | Change in # of family "get-togethers" | 115 | 25.8 |
| | Gain a new family member | 107 | 24.0 |
| | Change in # of arguments with spouse | 85 | 19.3 |
| | Child leaving home | 73 | 16.4 |
| | Divorce or separation from spouse | 71 | 16.0 |
| | Trouble with in-laws | 65 | 14.6 |
| | Concern about pregnancy | 48 | 10.8 |
| Health | Lack of sleep | 207 | 46.5 |
| | Change in sleeping habits | 141 | 31.7 |
| | Change in eating habits | 122 | 27.4 |
| | Getting sick | 112 | 25.2 |
| | Serious illness in friend or family member | 106 | 24.1 |
| | Major personal injury or illness | 87 | 19.6 |
| | Depression or crisis in your best friend | 74 | 16.6 |
| | Drinking or use of drugs | 73 | 16.4 |
| | Negative consequences of drinking or drugs | 67 | 15.1 |
| Work/Financial | Financial difficulties | 205 | 46.1 |
| | Change in financial state | 164 | 36.9 |
| | Job changes (new job, hassles) | 106 | 23.8 |
| | Change in work hours/conditions | 104 | 23.4 |
| | Change to a different line of work | 76 | 17.1 |
| | Change in responsibilities at work | 75 | 16.9 |
| | Spouse begins or ends work | 64 | 14.4 |
| | Major business readjustment | 46 | 10.3 |
| Social | Death of a close friend | 107 | 24.0 |
| | Concern about your appearance | 103 | 23.1 |
| | Change in social activities | 102 | 22.9 |
| | Outstanding personal achievement | 88 | 19.8 |
| | Christmas | 81 | 18.2 |
| | Have boy/girl friend cheat on you | 68 | 15.3 |
| | Peer pressures | 63 | 14.2 |
| | Ending a steady dating relationship | 59 | 13.3 |
| | Change in recreation | 55 | 12.4 |
| | Getting in a physical fight | 51 | 11.5 |
| | Change in church activities | 51 | 11.5 |
| | Maintaining a steady dating relationship | 49 | 11.0 |

*(Continued)*

**Table 12.3** (Continued)

| Dimension | Variable | N | % |
|-----------|----------|---|---|
| | Jail term | 45 | 10.1 |
| | Vacation | 45 | 10.1 |
| Other | Change in housing situation | 135 | 30.3 |
| | Change in living conditions | 131 | 29.4 |
| | Begin or end school | 68 | 15.3 |
| | Attending school beyond high school | 64 | 14.4 |
| | Commuting to work or school (or both) | 63 | 14.2 |

SOURCE: Food Security, Nutrition and Health Survey, 2001.

§ Includes variables with greater than 10% of the sample indicating a positive response, or experiencing the event.

financial difficulties, and 37% reported changes in their financial state. Other important events include changes in working conditions, hours, or responsibilities. In the area of family relationships and circumstances, responses showed that nearly 42% of the sample had experienced the death of a close family member in the last year, and 33% of respondents reported family difficulties. Changes in family members—behavior or health, family get-togethers, gaining a new family member—were also reported by about 25% of respondents. Other important stressors include divorce or separation, a child leaving home, and arguments or trouble with a spouse or extended family members.

Finally, responses regarding social and other life events show that substantial percentages experienced changes in housing situation (30%) and living conditions (29%). Other important experiences included the death of a close friend (24%), concerns about appearance (23%), and changes in social activities (23%).

These data are important for suggesting the nature of the stressful life events measured by this instrument. They indicate that within the context of the Northern Cheyenne reservation, typical events and changes experienced by residents are related to health, finances, work and social relations or concerns. Although stress scores indicate that most respondents experienced low to medium levels of stress (as indicated by the numbers of events they identified), food insecurity is an important experience not represented in this instrument. Ethnographic data are an important supplemental source of insights regarding Northern Cheyenne reservation residents' experiences with the problems and stresses associated with food shortages and acquisition strategies.

*Stresses Associated With Food Acquisition.* Evidence from qualitative research involving in-depth interviews with more than 70 food program participants between 1999 and 2001 is useful for identifying the types of stresses that reservation residents experience related to food shortages, despite access to food assistance programs such as food stamps. Results of this research (Davis et al., 1999) indicate that most clients receiving food stamps were not able to meet the food needs of their children with the amount of food stamps they received. Interview data illustrate these problems and the strategies used to meet family food needs.

When interviewees were asked to discuss any problems they encountered in feeding their families with food stamps, they most frequently cited running out of food before the end of the month. The following quotes indicate the inadequacy of food stamps for feeding many clients' families:

> . . . running out of food. The food stamps we receive aren't enough to cover the number of people that is in my family.

> . . . running out of food, mainly in Birney, 'cause we are so isolated. We don't have any stores, like in emergency situations. We are always afraid of running out of food, especially like in the winter times when the roads are bad. That is when it is the hardest. . . . Usually the food don't last throughout the whole month. There is always the problem of buying more food with whatever cash you have when you run out of food stamps.

> We usually try to make them last the whole month, but like I said, we go shop at Billings so that we get more for what we receive. And I think it's really important that we, we have to really watch how we spend, so that we have enough each month.

> Sometimes it's just like the adults that go without. Like me and my husband, we'll go without just for our kids to eat.

Understanding the food shortages many food program participants face involves looking at both the problems they identify and how they access and use local resources for survival. One problem is the high price of food purchased locally, which is related to the costs of transporting food to a small store serving an isolated, rural reservation area; virtually everyone indicated that food prices are higher in reservation stores than off the reservation. A common coping strategy involved traveling to larger towns or cities to buy groceries at more reasonable prices. Although many clients lived near a local grocery store, they preferred to shop off the reservation where food stamps buy more.

Thus, a second problem is related to transportation. For example, if food stamps clients could go to Sheridan, Hardin, or Billings (50 to 110 miles away), or even Ashland or Colstrip (10 to 25 miles away), they could buy more food for the dollar than if they shopped in Lame Deer. However, this requires access to a vehicle to drive, or they must have the cash to pay someone to drive them. Thus, those able to make their food stamps last the month were people who had access to a reliable vehicle needed to shop off the reservation, or those who had additional cash or food to help make ends meet.

Another strategy was to cook meals more efficiently, often drawing on the recipes and knowledge of grandmothers and aunts to help to stretch the food. For example, cooking beef and vegetable stews, casseroles, and other such dishes helped to cut down on the use of expensive items such as meat. Survival strategies of those clients not able to solve their food shortages by shopping or cooking more efficiently meant the difference between children and adults going to bed hungry or not. Along with drawing on the help of immediate and extended family members, who shared food and helped prepare meals, these clients went to other local food assistance programs, such as tribal charities, the food bank, and local churches. Most clients interviewed cited at least one of these sources as very significant for meeting their food needs every month. Most cited more than one. The local safety net, comprising kinship groups, tribal programs, and local service organizations, was important for most of the interviewees.

Of the alternative sources of food used, more than half of the clients interviewed reported that family and friends were the sources on whom they could depend for getting the food items they needed or borrowing the money to buy groceries. About half of the interviewees reported using the Northern Cheyenne Nation's charities program (food vouchers) to feed families in need, followed by the local food bank.

Another important strategy for obtaining money for groceries was odd jobs, particularly, cleaning, babysitting, or manual work. Emergency food from churches and pawning household items to get money for groceries were important food sources for about a third of the clients. Other clients made money for groceries by selling homemade food, such as fry bread, or traditional beadwork. Despite the problem of having insufficient food supplies to meet their family needs, most clients also reported that, whenever they can, they help others who need food.

These qualitative data provide important insights into the experiences of Northern Cheyenne adults attempting to feed their families with scarce resources. Interview data show both the inadequacy of food stamps as an important food source in this community and the wide range of strategies used by families to make up for the resulting food shortages. Additional ethnographic data provide important details about the challenges faced by young parents, especially women, who experience high levels of stress. The higher stress levels experienced by those with more schooling and who use wages for food can be understood in relation to the high dependency ratio in this population, which means that those with more education (who are likely to have jobs) are responsible for supporting a comparatively larger number of persons (Ward, 1998). For many women, these challenges are related to starting families young and needing to help support their children while maintaining the traditional Cheyenne role of homemaker, which includes feeding the family (Hiwalker et al., 2000). When the problems these families experience are considered in light of the range of other stressful life events and changes described previously, food insecurity and use of certain food sources add to the challenges faced by members of this community. Additional data about the cultural meaning of food further clarifies this pattern.

*The Cultural and Social Significance of Food.*
Measuring stress related to food insecurity is especially important in the context of American Indian families and communities because of the cultural and social significance of food. Qualitative data collected through additional in-depth interviews identify some of the cultural norms and views of food that affect Northern Cheyenne community residents' responses to food insecurity. As part of the interviews about life on the reservation, interviewees articulated their thoughts and feelings about food.[4] Quotes from these interviews are presented here to illustrate major themes and concepts related to the social and cultural dimensions of food.

Food carries important cultural meanings for the Northern Cheyenne; it signifies a sense of community and cohesive group membership. Bringing food to community gatherings is a social tradition and one way that individuals can contribute to the group.

> When people used to get together, let's say for hand games, or some kind of a meeting, my grandmother always brought something. She would make soup, or maybe some bread, or choke-cherry pudding, and she would take it over, and all the families did that.

Food also represents support for neighbors and friends in the community when things are especially good, or when things are difficult.

> We usually have cookouts or something like that, sharing the will. And it's all in support of whosoever, has that happiness. On the other hand too, when you're going through difficult struggles, you can go to these people and just talk to them. And someone from families, you know, just might need help, but they're not sure how to go about getting what they need for themselves, you know. So you got these people there for you that will talk to these people, or will, you know, do something for these people. Either through prayer or some type of ceremony where people come together. People will bring food and things like that.

Food brings people together for a cause and creates a sense of unity.

> If we knew anybody was sick, we was all there, you know. We went over there, we was concerned about that person. We didn't care if he was Indian or white, you know. Everybody would take food over there to that family, you know.

Caring for the needs of others in the community is an important part of the Northern Cheyenne culture, which emphasizes sharing and aiding others. This cultural norm is particularly relevant to understanding the role of food and food distribution on the reservation. Because of the high value placed on sharing, people often offer to share even when they are struggling to make ends meet. Rejecting food that is offered is tantamount to rejecting the person offering it.

> I was taught, if they ask you to eat, eat what is put before you. Even if you don't like it, get rid of it. Don't say, "I don't like that. I don't want to eat it." Don't ever say that. That might be all that person has got to eat.

Besides the cultural implications of food for the Northern Cheyenne, there are also political ones. This is demonstrated by one man's description of what he sees as a lack of Cheyenne leadership currently on the reservation.

> Then the white people put them on the reservation, and when they did, they took away their horses, their rifles and everything, and they couldn't hunt for their own food anymore. They killed their buffalo off and said they would take care of them, and when they wanted something, then the Indians refused their leadership. And when the people would do that, they would take away their food. They wouldn't give them food, so the leadership [would] see their people die, and so the leaders had to bow to

the white people, get on their knees and say, "Yes, we'll do whatever you want."

These qualitative data are important for revealing the importance of food as both the means for meeting physical needs and as a source of community cohesion and participation. The multiple values that food represents have important implications for understanding food insecurity: Food shortages present community members with challenges both to their daily survival and to the ability to uphold important traditional community and family imperatives.

## DISCUSSION AND CONCLUSIONS

This analysis of Northern Cheyenne food insecurity, food provisioning, and stress was designed to respond to recent calls for research (Aneshensel, 1992; Pearlin, 1989; Wu & Schimmele, 2005) to consider how social structural conditions relate to stress and how different types or sources of stress relate to each other. Our analyses produced several conclusions. First, our results support Wu and Schimmele's findings that identified the salience of food insufficiency, a chronic strain, relative to individual and household characteristics for predicting stress levels. Despite its similarity in purpose to Wu and Schimmele's (2005) research, our study differed in its focus on an American Indian reservation population, use of a broader measure of stress related to the experience of life events and changes rather than depressive symptoms, and use of measures of food insecurity rather than food insufficiency. Nevertheless, our research shows that stress levels increased with the difficulties stemming from food insecurity, especially among households and families experiencing hunger. It also showed that food insecurity in both households with children and without children increases stress levels. Our statistical models also point to the importance of other independent variables: socioeconomic characteristics, such as age, gender, education, the number of children present, and use of specific types of food sources (daily hassles).

Second, use of different food strategies in this analysis adds a new dimension to understanding the relationships of food insecurity to stress by showing that experiences in food acquisitioning independently increase stress in this low-income, minority population. Similar to other studies (e.g., Ahluwalia et al., 1998; Campbell & Desjardins, 1989), Northern Cheyenne households used a variety of strategies to meet their food needs. However, the particular sociocultural context, which includes high unemployment and food insecurity rates along with local norms for accessing and sharing food, shapes food strategies in important ways. The analysis of different types of food strategies identified as meaningful in this community with both qualitative and quantitative data suggests that some food acquisition strategies may present additional sources of stress in meeting food needs. In particular, using food sources related to the informal economy (e.g., hunting, pawning, or working odd jobs) increases stress levels. In general, food acquisition practices are more stressful for households with children, possibly reflecting the challenges of providing food for larger households or families with scarce resources. Most importantly, these analyses of different food acquisition strategies indicate that the relationships of food sources to stress are neither simple nor straightforward. For example, our analyses show that stress levels of households may be influenced by the specific requirements for accessing each of the different types of sources.

Qualitative data provide some important insights for understanding how food insecurity and use of certain food sources contribute to the stress process. For example, ethnographic data indicate that low-income, food insecure, Northern Cheyenne households face significant challenges in accessing certain food programs and obtaining adequate food where local food prices are high, transportation is necessary to access reasonably priced sources of food, and lack of skills and knowledge among young adults prevents efficient use of food. Qualitative data also reveal how households draw on multiple sources of food when shortages occur. Additionally, women and those with more education are particularly stressed by the challenges of feeding their families, whether through work or other ways of acquiring the resources needed to feed their children. However, the cultural norm of sharing food remains strong despite food insecurity and the challenges and exertion often required for obtaining food for families.

As Gundersen (2006), Gray et al. (2005), and Bliss (2004) indicate, Northern Cheyenne families and households are not alone in experiencing the challenges associated with poverty. The results of this study suggest that both food insecurity levels and the strategies that households use to access food are likely to be relevant to understanding the stress levels associated with poverty in many American Indian communities. Moreover, findings of this study suggest that simply increasing food supplies is inadequate for addressing the needs of low-income American Indian families, especially in reservation areas. Decreasing the challenges associated with accessing the range of food sources may be equally important for lowering the stress levels faced by families in rural, reservation communities. However, because Indian communities also typically have strong cultural imperatives for sharing food and for women to maintain traditional roles in feeding families, lowering stress levels may also involve finding new ways to assist women and other caregivers within families who struggle to feed themselves and others.

## NOTES

1. Only two respondents refused participation and 21 surveys were not initiated or completed because of time constraints, leaving a response rate of 95% (477/500). Thirty-two cases were dropped from the final analysis because of missing data across variables indicating that they were not reliable, including cases of missing data on the dependent variable. Thus, the total number of usable cases dropped from 477 to 445, or a usable response rate of 89%.

2. Stress scores: Mean = 224.27, SD = 190.92 (max = 1005).

3. Food security in households with children: Mean = 6.0, SD = 4.99 (max = 18); food security in households without children: Mean = 5.5, SD = 4.37 (max = 18).

4. This research was conducted as part of a larger qualitative project in 1999 examining community attachment and the meaning of community membership on the reservation. Additional information can be found in Erin Feinauer (1999). *The Construction of Community among the Northern Cheyenne*. Master's Thesis, Brigham Young University.

## REFERENCES

Ahluwalia, I. B., Dodds, J. M., & Baligh, M. (1998). Social support and coping behaviors of low-income families experiencing food insufficiency in North Carolina. *Health Education and Behavior, 25*(5), 599–612.

American Academy of Family Physicians. (2000). *The nutrition checklist*. Nutrition Screening Initiative. Retrieved October 2005 from http://www.aafp.org/nsi/e-determ.html

American Diabetes Association. (2005). *National diabetes fact sheet, 2005*. Atlanta, GA: Centers for Disease Control and Prevention, U.S. Department of Health and Human Services. Retrieved April 4, 2006, from http://www.diabetes.org/diabetes-statistics.jsp

Aneshensel, C. (1992). Social stress: Theory and research. *Annual Review of Sociology, 18*, 15–38.

Antell, J., Blevins, A., Jensen, K., & Massey, G. (1999). *Residential and household poverty of American Indians on the Wind River Reservation*. Paper presented at the Joint Center for Poverty Research conference, Washington, DC.

Bandura, A. (1992). Self-efficacy mechanisms in physiological activation and health promoting behavior. In J. Madden, S. Matthysee, & J. Barchas (Eds.), *Adaptation, learning, and affect* (pp. 229–269). New York: Raven Press.

Barraclough, S. L. (1991). *An end to hunger? The social origin of food strategies*. London: Zed.

Bickel, G., Nord, M., Price, C., Hamilton, W., & Cook, J. (2000, March). *Guide to measuring household food security*. Alexandria, VA: U.S. Department of Agriculture Food and Nutrition Service.

Bliss, R. M. (2004, July). Breaking barriers to American Indian nutrition research. *Agricultural Research Magazine, 52*, 7.

Brown, E., & Cornell, S. (2001). *Welfare, work, and American Indians: The impact of welfare reform* (Policy Paper). Tucson: Udall Center for Public Policy, University of Arizona.

Campbell, C. C., & Desjardins, E. (1989). A model and research approach for studying the management of limited resources by low income families. *Journal of Nutritional Education, 21*, 162–171.

Cohen, S., Underwood, L., & Gottlieb, B. (Eds.). (2000). *Social support measurement and intervention* (pp. 29–52). New York: Oxford University Press.

Davis, J., Hiwalker, R., Ward, C., & Feinauer, E. (1999). *The impact of welfare reform on food assistance programs on American Indian Reservations: The Northern Cheyenne case study.* Washington, DC: U.S. Department of Agriculture, Report to Small Grants Program.

Fitchen, J. M. (1988). Hunger, malnutrition, and poverty in the contemporary United States: Some observations on their social and cultural context. *Food and Foodways, 2,* 309–333.

Gray, J., Knudson, A., & Penland, J. (2005). *Impact of food security on depression among Northern Plains Indians.* Paper presented at the 133rd Annual Meetings of the American Public Health Association, Philadelphia.

Gundersen, C. (2006, January). *Measuring the extent and depth of food insecurity: An application to American Indians in the United States* (NPC Working Paper #06-2). Ann Arbor: National Poverty Center, University of Michigan, Gerald Ford School of Public Policy.

Hamelin, A. M., Beaudry, M., & Habicht, J. P. (2002). Characterization of food insecurity in Quebec: Food and feelings. *Social Science and Medicine, 54,* 119–132.

Hamelin, A. M., Habicht, J. P., & Beaudry, M. (1999). Food insecurity: Consequences for the household and broader social implications. *Journal of Nutrition, 129,* 525S–528S.

Harnack, L., DeRosier, K., Story, M., Himes, J., & Holy Rock, B. (2001). *Prevalence of food insecurity and its relationship to obesity among American Indians in the Northern Plains.* Paper presented at the 129th Annual Meetings of the American Public Health Association, Atlanta, GA.

Hiwalker, R., Davis, J., Ward, C., Youngstrom, C., & Feinauer, E. (2000). *Is the food stamps program an adequate safety net for American Indian reservations? The Northern Cheyenne Case.* Washington, DC: U.S. Department of Agriculture, Report to Small Grants Program.

Hiwalker, R., Davis, J., Ward, C., Youngstrom, C., Li, W., & Whiting, E. F. (2002, February). *The relationship of food assistance program participation to nutritional and health status, diabetes risk and food security among the Northern Cheyenne.* Technical Report to U.S. Department of Agriculture.

Hoisington, A., Shultz, J. A., & Butkus, S. (2002). Coping strategies and nutrition education needs among food pantry users. *Journal of Nutrition Education and Behavior, 34,* 326–333.

ICBS. (2006). *Our body's reaction to stress (General Adaptation Syndrome [GAS]).* Retrieved July 10, 2006, from http://www.holisticonline.com/stress/stress_GAS.htm

John D. and Catherine T. MacArthur Network on Socioeconomic Status and Health. (2005). *Network mission.* Retrieved July 2006 from http://www.macses.ucsf.edu/Network/Mission.htm

Kempson, K., Keenan, D. P., Sadani, P. O., & Adler, A. (2003). Maintaining food sufficiency: coping strategies identified by limited-resource individuals versus nutrition educators. *Journal of Nutrition Education and Behavior, 35,* 179–188.

Kempson, K., Keenan, D. P., Sadani, P. S., & Rosato, N. S. (2002). Educators' reports of food acquisition practices used by limited-resource individuals to maintain food sufficiency. *Family Economics and Nutrition Review, 14*(2), 44–55.

Lang, T. (1997). Dividing up the cake: Food as social exclusion. In A. Walker & C. Walker (Eds.), *Britain divided: The growth of social exclusion in the 1980s and 1990s* (pp. 213–223). London: Child Poverty Action Group.

Martin, H. D. (1995). *How's your nutritional health?* Champagne: University of Illinois Cooperative-Extension Service.

Nelson, K., Brown, M., & Lurie, N. (2000). *Food insecurity and medical conditions observed in an adult population.* Paper presented at the Second Food Security Measurement and Research Conference, Economic Research Service, U.S. Department of Agriculture, Washington, DC.

Newman, K. (1996). The invisible poor. In M. L. Andersen & P. H. Collins (Eds.), *Race, class, and gender: An anthology* (4th ed., pp. 248–256). Belmont, CA: Wadsworth/Thomson Learning.

Nord, M., Andrews, M., & Carlson, S. (2003). *Household food security in the United States, 2002.* Washington, DC: Economic Research Service, U.S. Department of Agriculture.

Pearlin, L. (1989). The sociological study of stress. *Journal of Health and Social Behavior, 30,* 241–256.

Pearlin, L., Lieberman, M. A., Menaghan, E. G., & Mulla, J. T. (1981). The stress process. *Journal of Health and Social Behavior, 22,* 337–356.

Pickering, K. (2000). Alternative economic strategies in low-income rural communities: TANF, labor migration, and the case of the Pine Ridge Indian Reservation. *Rural Sociology, 65*(1), 148–167.

Rainville, B., & Brink, S. (2001). *Food insecurity in Canada, 1998–1999.* Hull, PQ: Human Resources Development Canada Publications Centre.

Ross, C. E., & Mirowsky, J. (1989). Explaining the patterns of depression: Control and problem solving—or support and talking? *Journal of Health and Social Behavior, 30,* 206–219.

Siefert, K., Heflin, C., Corcoran, M., & Williams, D. R. (2004). Food insufficiency and the physical and mental health of low-income women. *Women and Health, 32*(1/2), 159–177.

Tarasuk, V., & Beaton, G. H. (1999). Household food insecurity and hunger among families using food banks. *Canadian Journal of Public Health, 90*(2), 109–113.

Tarasuk, V. S., & Maclean, H. (1990). The food problems of low-income single mothers: An ethnographic study. *Canadian Home Economic Journal, 40,* 76–82.

U.S. Bureau of the Census. (2000). *Population and labor force reports.* Washington, DC: U.S. Department of Commerce, Government Printing Office.

Vozoris, N. T., & Tarasuk, V. S. (2003). Household food insufficiency is associated with poorer health. *Journal of Nutrition, 133*(1), 120–126.

Walker, L., Walker, M., & Walker, M. (1994). Health and well-being of childbearing women in rural and urban contexts. *Journal of Rural Health, 10*(3), 168–172.

Ward, C. (1998). The importance of context in explaining human capital formation and labor force participation of American Indians in Rosebud County, Montana. *Rural Sociology, 63*(3).

Ward, C., & Whiting, E. F. (2001). *Food Security, Nutrition and Health Survey.* Lame Deer, MT: Northern Cheyenne Reservation.

Ward, C. J., & Whiting, E. F. (2006). Food insecurity and diabetes risk among the Northern Cheyenne. *Journal of Hunger and Environmental Nutrition, 1*(2), 63–87.

Whiting, E. F., Ward, C., Hiwalker-Villa, R., & Davis, J. (2005). How does the new TANF work requirement "work" for rural minority communities? A case study of the Northern Cheyenne Nation. *American Indian Culture and Research Journal, 29*(4), 95–120.

Wu, Z., & Schimmele, C. M. (2005). Food insufficiency and depression. *Sociological Perspectives, 48*(4), 481–504.

# CHAPTER 13

# How Economically Disadvantaged Are American Elderly Women?

## Gender Differences in Economic Well-Being in Old Age

MARTHA N. OZAWA AND HONG-SIK YOON

The economic well-being of elderly people has greatly improved during the past several decades. This stems from concerted legislative initiatives at the federal level. Social Security benefits increased in 1968, 1969, 1970, and 1972. Automatic cost-of-living adjustments, enacted in 1972, ensure constant purchasing power to retired beneficiaries. American retirees also benefit from the Employee Retirement Income Security Act of 1974 (P.L. 93-406), which provides greater security for private pensions. Thanks to this act, minimum standards of administration and fiscal responsibility in pension plans have been strengthened, and the exclusion of differential treatment of most classes of employees has been prohibited. In addition, the 1984 Retirement Equity Act (REA) requires the spouse to agree in writing when a married worker chooses *against* the default option, which is the joint-and-survivor option (P.L. 98-397).

Moreover, the Supplemental Security Income (SSI) program, enacted in 1972, provides a basic minimum flow of income for the nation's elderly.

Because of all these legislative initiatives, the average income of older Americans increased from the 1960s to the 1980s at a faster rate than that of nonelderly people (Radner, 1987). This improvement in the income status of American elders is reflected in their steadily declining poverty rates. The poverty rate of the elderly (measured by the percentage of the elderly who are poor), which was extraordinarily high during the 1960s (approximately 35%), declined rapidly to 10.4% in 2002. Between 1973 and 1974, the poverty rate of elderly people declined to below that of children. And as of 2002, the poverty rate of elderly people was only 62% of the rate of children (16.7%) and was slightly below that of nonaged adults (10.6%) (U.S. Census Bureau, 1996, 2002).

Despite the apparent progress in the income status of elderly people, certain segments of the elderly population continue to be economically deprived. In particular, the plight of elderly women—especially women of advanced ages who are living alone—is of great concern. For example, in 1999, 18.7% of nonmarried women aged 85 and older were poor, compared with only 4.6% of married couples aged 65–74 (Social Security Administration [SSA], 2000b, p. 127). Race compounds economic standing in the United States, such that in the same year, 30% of nonmarried black women aged 75 and older were poor, compared with 15.9% of their white counterparts (SSA, 2000b, p. 133).

Thus, it is instructive to investigate the *net* gender differences in the economic well-being of American elders, controlling for other relevant variables. This article reports findings of our study on the following questions:

1. What were the differences in the economic well-being of elderly women and elderly men in 1969, 1979, 1989, and 1999?

2. What was the degree of economic inequality among elderly women and elderly men in 1969, 1979, 1989, and 1999?

3. What was the net effect of gender on the economic well-being of the elderly in 1969, 1979, 1989, and 1999, when age, race-ethnicity, marital status, number of children, and education were held constant?

4. How did age, race-ethnicity, marital status, number of children, and education correlate with the economic well-being of elderly women and elderly men?

## REVIEW OF THE LITERATURE

The economic condition of elderly people is determined by many factors. First, aging is associated with declining economic well-being. In 1998, the family income of nonmarried women aged 85 and older was only $13,814, which was 27% lower than that of nonmarried women aged 65–69 ($17,572). In contrast, the age differential in family income among nonmarried men was only 2% in the same year, and in 1996, the family income of nonmarried elderly men was $19,6161, compared with $14,966 for their female counterparts (SSA, 2000b, pp. 28–29).

Second, women's economic disadvantage is strongly related to their marital status in old age. A review of the literature indicated that women who eventually become widowed have a higher poverty rate before they are widowed and have an even higher poverty rate afterward than do women who stay married. Widowhood raises the already high poverty rate of eventual widows significantly (Holden, Burkhauser, & Myers, 1986) because the husbands of eventual widows tend to have lower earnings (Zick & Smith, 1991). Furthermore, widowhood abruptly increases the risk of becoming poor and increases it persistently thereafter because the tendency to fall into poverty over time is affected by aging, as well as by widowhood.

Widowhood appears to affect the income status of men and women differently. According to Burkhauser, Butler, and Holden (1991), on the death of a spouse, the chance of falling into poverty and facing a significant drop in income (measured by the income-to-needs ratio) dramatically increases for widows, but not for widowers. Also, whereas the income of women falls sharply when their husbands die, the income of men remains stable on the death of their wives (Holden, 1990).

Ozawa and Lum (1998) provided further insights into the effect of marital status on the economic well-being of women and men at the time of retirement in 1982 and 10 years later in 1992. Ozawa and Lum reported that at the time of retirement, the level of income status of women was more strongly affected by differential marital statuses than was that of men. For example, the income status of women who entered retirement as separated or divorced persons was 49.7% lower than that of married women, the income status of widows was 32.7% lower, and income status of never-married women was 38.4% lower. The economic disadvantage faced by men with the comparable marital statuses was milder: It was 25.7% lower for separated or divorced men, 6.8% lower for widowers, and 28.3% lower for never-married men. A similar pattern of economic disadvantage of nonmarried men and women was observed 10 years after these women and men retired.

Third, whereas being nonmarried generally works against women's economic well-being, education may provide a countervailing force. A study by Ozawa and Yoon (2003) on nonaged adults reported the stronger impact of education in shaping the economic well-being of women in the 1970s through the 2000s. For example, compared with the income status of women with a high school education, that of college-educated women was 53.1% higher in 1969 and 110.4% higher in 1999. The comparable figures for men were 45.9% and 82.6% in 1969 and 1999, respectively.

Fourth, children living at home may make a difference in the economic well-being of elderly women and men. However, the direction of its impact is ambiguous. Among nonaged women and men, children tend to make the income status of their parents lower because they incur extra expenditures within the family, as Ozawa and Yoon (2003) found. However, adult children of elderly persons may increase (or decrease) their parents' level of economic well-being, depending on the degree of financial contributions adult children make to elderly families' incomes.

Finally, because the American population is racially and ethnically diverse, the race-ethnicity variable should always be considered. For example, Ozawa and Yoon (2003) found that racial differences in the economic

well-being of the nonaged adults were larger than were gender differences.

## METHODOLOGY

### Source of Data

The data used in this study came from the 1970, 1980, 1990, and 2000 Current Population Surveys (CPSs) of the civilian noninstitutional population. The four surveys interviewed the following number of people aged 14 and over: 1970 survey, 104,400 people; 1980 survey, 135,000 people; 1990 survey, 114,500 people; and 2000 survey, 133,700 people. The CPS collects data on each respondent's level and sources of income, demographic background, education, living arrangements, employment, unemployment, wages and hours of work, occupation, industry in which employed, participation in publicly supported programs, and number of children in the family. The data are organized to enable researchers to investigate the economic lives of the U.S. population on the basis of individuals, families, or households. Because data for income are always for the year preceding the survey year, the variable economic well-being we developed is based on the income data for 1 year before the year of survey. All non-income-related variables are for the year of the survey (U.S. Census Bureau, 1984a, 1984b, 1991, 2000a). For our study, we selected women and men aged 65 and older.

### Conceptual Framework for Economic Well-Being

In our study, economic well-being was measured by the income-to-needs ratio, which was operationalized as the ratio of family income to poverty-line income. For example, an income-to-needs ratio of 2 means that the respondents were living at twice the poverty-line income. This procedure assumed that all the people in the same family had the same economic well-being. Thus, if the respondent was married, both spouses were assumed to have the same economic well-being. One advantage of using the income-to-needs ratio instead of other indicators, such as per capita family income, is that it incorporates the economy of scale as well as family size, making it possible to compare more precisely the economic well-being of one person with that of another person, regardless of the size of the families from which both came. Another advantage is that the income-to-needs ratio implicitly deals with price fluctuations, so we can compare economic well-being in various years.

## Definitions of Variables

*Dependent Variable.* The dependent variable for this study was the economic well-being of elderly adults aged 65 and older. As we stated earlier, this variable was measured by the income-to-needs ratio, which was obtained by dividing family income by the poverty-line income.

*Independent Variable.* The major independent variable was gender. A dummy variable was developed for this variable, assigning the value of 1 to women and zero to men.

*Independent Variables Used as Controls.* To net out the effect of gender on the economic well-being of elderly people, we included the following variables as controls: age, race-ethnicity, marital status, number of children, and education. Age and number of children living at home were continuous variables and are self-explanatory. To measure race-ethnicity, we developed two dummy variables—one for the black respondents and the other for the Hispanic respondents—assigning the white respondents to the reference group. Because of the lack of information on Hispanic versus non-Hispanic ethnic status in the 1970 CPS, we dichotomized race into white versus

nonwhite in that year. To measure marital status, we developed three dummy variables for divorced-separated, widowed, and never-married respondents, assigning married respondents to the reference group. To measure the level of education, we developed three dummy variables for those with less than a high school education, those with some college education, and those with a college education, assigning those with a high school education to the reference group.

## Analysis and Presentation of Data

First, we generated descriptive statistics on the backgrounds of the respondents from each survey. Second, we generated descriptive statistics on the income-to-needs ratios for 1969, 1979, 1989, and 1999 and calculated the percentage changes in the ratios from 1969 to 1979, from 1979 to 1989, from 1989 to 1999, and from 1969 to 1999. Third, we generated descriptive statistics on income inequality (measured by Gini coefficients) for 1969, 1979, 1989, and 1999 and observed the percentage changes between these years. We used the weight variable that was developed by the U.S. Census Bureau to generate descriptive statistics on all variables. This procedure was needed to adjust for the sampling, poststratification, and nonresponse biases in the CPS data sets.

Fourth, we conducted a series of ordinary least squares (OLS) regression analyses on the economic well-being of women and men. To net out the effect of gender, we included, as controls, age, race-ethnicity, marital status, number of children, and education. We further conducted OLS regression analyses for women and men, separately. This statistical procedure was used to investigate how age, race-ethnicity, marital status, number of children, and education were related to women's and men's economic well-being. For conducting OLS regression analyses, we transformed income-to-needs ratios into natural log because the distribution of income-to-needs ratios was skewed.

## FINDINGS

### Descriptive Statistics

*Backgrounds of the Respondents.* Two major trends may be seen in Table 13.1. First, the change in marital status among women was more drastic than that of men. The proportion of women who were married declined from 58.4% in 1970 to 42.9% in 2000, or a 27% decrease, whereas the proportion of men who were married declined 15%, from 88.5% to 74.1%. On the other hand, the proportion of men who were widowed increased faster than the proportion of women, although even in 2000, the proportion of women was three times as large as the proportion of men. Also, the proportion of men who were divorced-separated increased faster than the proportion of women: from 1970 to 2000, 825%, from 0.8% to 7.4%, compared with women's, which increased 376%, from 1.7% to 8.1%. In contrast, the proportion of women who are never married declined 28%, from 5% to 3.6%, during the same period, whereas that of men increased 56%, from 2.7% to 4.2%.

Second, the changes in the age composition of women and men differed greatly from 1970 through 2000. The proportion of women who were aged 75 and older increased 44%—from 33.3% to 48%, but the proportion of men in this age group increased by only 27%, from 33.2 to 42%. On the other side of the age continuum, the proportion of women who were aged 65 to 69 declined 33%—from 39.7% to 26.6%, compared with 29% for men—from 38.8% to 31.6%.

Third, the level of education increased immensely during the past 4 decades for both women and men. However, gender differences in educational attainment to the disadvantage of women still existed. In particular, the proportion of women with a college education increased 132% from 1970 to 2000, compared with 170% among men. In 2000, 11.3% of women had this level of education, compared with 21.3% of men.

Fourth, the pattern of change in the racial-ethnic composition of elderly women and men differed. Among elderly women, the proportion of black women increased 7% from 8.5% in 1980 to 9.1% in 2000, whereas among men it decreased 7%, from 8.8 to 8.2%. The proportion of Hispanic elderly people increased enormously among both women and men, but the rate of growth was greater among women: 153% among women versus 103% among men. The tremendous increase in the number of Hispanic elders stems from the growth in immigration in this group (see Ozawa, 1997).

Only in 1970, the likelihood of having at least one child living at home substantially differed between elderly women and elderly men, when 8.1% of elderly women and 5.2% of elderly men had at least one child living at home. In succeeding decades, the likelihood of having at least one child living at home declined considerably, with less than 3% of both elderly women and elderly men having at least one child at home.

*Level of Economic Well-Being (Income-to-Needs Ratios).* As Table 13.2 indicates, the level of women's economic well-being, which was measured by income-to-needs ratios, was exactly the same as men's in 1969. But women's income-to-needs ratio became significantly lower in the succeeding decades. From 1969 to 1979, women's income-to-needs ratio declined 8%, compared with an 8.4% *increase* among men. During the following two decades, the rate of growth in women's income-to-needs ratio was considerably lower than that of men. Thus, from 1969 to 1999, women's income-to-needs ratio increased only 20.4%, compared with a 51.6% increase for

Table 13.1  Backgrounds of Respondents (Percentage)

|  | 1970 | | 1980 | | 1990 | | 2000 | |
|---|---|---|---|---|---|---|---|---|
|  | *Female* (N = 4,837) | *Male* (N = 4,735) | *Female* (N = 11,183) | *Male* (N = 7,906) | *Female* (N = 10,994) | *Male* (N = 7,673) | *Female* (N = 9,031) | *Male* (N = 6,626) |
| **Age (Year)** | | | | | | | | |
| 65 to 69 | 39.7 | 38.8 | 33.7 | 38.5 | 32.1 | 37.3 | 26.6 | 31.6 |
| 70 to 74 | 27.0 | 28.0 | 27.0 | 28.4 | 25.8 | 27.9 | 25.4 | 26.4 |
| Over 75 | 33.3 | 33.2 | 39.3 | 33.1 | 42.1 | 34.8 | 48.0 | 42.0 |
| **Race** | | | | | | | | |
| White | 91.7 | 92.7 | 89.2 | 88.5 | 86.4 | 87.6 | 85.1 | 86.4 |
| Black (nonwhite)[a] | 8.3 | 7.3 | 8.5 | 8.8 | 10.3 | 10.4 | 9.1 | 8.2 |
| Hispanic | | | 2.3 | 2.7 | 3.3 | 3.8 | 5.8 | 5.5 |
| **Marital status** | | | | | | | | |
| Married | 58.4 | 88.5 | 38.7 | 76.8 | 40.6 | 75.1 | 42.9 | 74.1 |
| Widowed | 35.0 | 8.0 | 51.2 | 13.5 | 40.4 | 14.2 | 45.3 | 14.3 |
| Divorced-separated | 1.7 | 0.8 | 4.3 | 4.8 | 6.2 | 6.5 | 8.1 | 7.4 |
| Never-married | 5.0 | 2.7 | 5.9 | 4.9 | 4.9 | 4.3 | 3.6 | 4.2 |
| **Number of children** | | | | | | | | |
| None | 91.9 | 94.8 | 97.1 | 97.1 | 97.3 | 97.7 | 97.7 | 97.9 |
| One or two | 5.8 | 4.1 | 2.3 | 2.5 | 2.3 | 2.1 | 1.9 | 1.7 |
| Three or more | 2.3 | 1.1 | 0.6 | 0.4 | 0.4 | 0.2 | 0.4 | 0.4 |
| **Education** | | | | | | | | |
| Less than high school | 71.3 | 73.6 | 58.2 | 60.8 | 43.5 | 45.3 | 30.7 | 30.5 |
| High school | 17.3 | 12.0 | 24.6 | 20.2 | 34.6 | 27.3 | 39.8 | 30.4 |
| Some college | 7.1 | 6.5 | 9.8 | 8.7 | 12.1 | 12.4 | 18.2 | 17.8 |
| College education | 4.3 | 7.9 | 7.4 | 10.4 | 9.8 | 15.0 | 11.3 | 21.3 |

a. The "nonwhite" category is only for 1969.

**Table 13.2**     Income-to-Needs Ratio, 1969 to 1999

|  | 1969 | 1979 | 1989 | 1999 |
|---|---|---|---|---|
| | **Income-to-Needs Ratio** | | | |
| All | 2.75 | 2.71 | 3.29 | 3.68 |
| Women | 2.75 | 2.53 | 3.02 | 3.31 |
| Men | 2.75 | 2.98 | 3.68 | 4.17 |
| | **Percentage Change** | | | |
| | 1969 to 1979 | 1979 to 1989 | 1989 to 1999 | 1969 to 1999 |
| All | −1.5 | 21.4 | 11.9 | 33.8 |
| Women | −8.0 | 19.4 | 9.6 | 20.4 |
| Men | 8.4 | 23.5 | 13.3 | 51.6 |

men. As of 1999, women's income-to-needs ratio (3.31) was 21% lower than men's (4.17).

*Income Inequality.* Income inequality was measured by the Gini coefficient, which ranges from zero to 1. The higher the Gini coefficient, the greater the inequality. Table 13.3 indicates that the degree of income inequality among women was slightly higher than that among men in 1979 and 1989, but slightly lower in 1969 and 1999. From 1969 to 1999, the Gini coefficient for women increased 7.2%, compared with a 4.3% increase for men. Generally, women's level of, and pattern of change in, the Gini coefficient was similar to men's.

Although these descriptive statistics provide useful information on the income-to-needs ratios of women and men, OLS multiple regression analyses were performed to estimate the net gender differences in income-to-needs-ratios among elderly people.

## OLS Multiple Regression Analysis

Before we present the results of the OLS multiple regression analyses, it is important to recognize that regression coefficients in such analyses, in which the dependent variable is transformed into a natural log and independent variables take the form of dummy variables, need to be transformed. Halvorsen and Palmquiest (1980) argued that in such a situation, one could not use the regression coefficients to evaluate the relative effect of the independent variable on the

**Table 13.3**     Gini Coefficient of Income-to-Needs Ratio, 1969 to 1999

|  | 1969 | 1979 | 1989 | 1999 |
|---|---|---|---|---|
| | **Gini Coefficient** | | | |
| All | 0.410 | 0.396 | 0.425 | 0.437 |
| Women | 0.402 | 0.398 | 0.427 | 0.431 |
| Men | 0.418 | 0.388 | 0.417 | 0.436 |
| | **Percentage Change** | | | |
| | 1969 to 1979 | 1979 to 1989 | 1989 to 1999 | 1969 to 1999 |
| All | −3.4 | 7.3 | 2.8 | 6.6 |
| Women | −1.0 | 7.3 | 0.9 | 7.2 |
| Men | −7.2 | 7.5 | 4.6 | 4.3 |

dependent variable; rather, one would need to use transformed coefficients. In econometric terms, they argued,

$$C = ln(1 + g)$$

$$e^c = 1 + g$$

therefore,

$$g = e^c - 1$$

where $C$ = regression coefficient, and $g$ = relative effect.

Following this equation and applying the coefficient of 0.363, for example, one finds the relative effect $g$ to be 0.438, which can be interpreted as 43.8% greater. Thus, in the data analysis that follows, we used the procedure specified by Halvorsen and Palmquiest. We calculated the values of the relative effect $g$ (expressed in percentage by multiplying the transformed coefficient by 100) for all coefficients for dummy variables in the OLS multiple regression analyses that involved the natural log of income-to-needs ratios as the dependent variable and dummy variables as independent variables. (This transformation was not required for independent variables that were continuous variables.) We listed relative effects after $t$ values.

*OLS Multiple Regression Analysis of the Income-to-Needs Ratio (log): All.* Table 13.4 shows the net effect of gender on the economic well-being of nonaged adults in 1969, 1979, 1989, and 1999. It indicates that the gender differential in income-to-needs ratios was 8.3%, 6.2%, 8.6%, and 5.9% in 1969, 1979, 1989, and 1999, respectively, showing a decline in the gender differences as the decades progressed.

It is noteworthy that the race-ethnicity differential in income-to-needs ratios was higher than the gender differential in every year under investigation. As of 1999, black

persons were still 17.9% worse off than were white persons.

The effect of marital status on the income-to-needs ratios was found to be unique. Note that in 1969, the income-to-needs ratios of nonmarried persons (divorced-separated, widowed, or never married) were *higher* than that of married persons. One would expect that these persons are generally worse off than married persons. Why?

This unique finding had to do with two interrelated phenomena: The labor force participation of women and the economy of scale that is incorporated into the income-to-needs ratio. Because a relatively small proportion of women aged 65 and older in 1970 had worked during their working lives, the degree of financial contributions they could make toward their families' finances in old age was small. Government data show that the percentage of women who participated in the labor force in 1910 through 1960 was very small (23.4, 21.1, 22.0, 25.4, 30.9, and 34.9 in 1910, 1920, 1930, 1940, 1950, and 1960, respectively), and the women in this study were of working age precisely during these decades (U.S. Census Bureau, 1975, Series D-11–25, pp. 127–128). That is, the great majority of these women spent their adult lives as homemakers, not as paid workers. Thus, few women had incomes of their own when they became old and were economically dependent on their spouses.

When one of the spouses is completely dependent on the other, the economy of scale incorporated into the income-to-needs ratio works against them. Using the definition of poverty-line income developed by SSA (2000a), one sees that it takes only a 29% addition to the family income to enable a married couple to live at the same living standards as single persons with the same amount of income. If the other spouse brings in income that is larger than 29%, then the married couple's income-to-needs ratio increases accordingly. On the other hand, if

**Table 13.4**   OLS Multiple Regression Analysis of the Income-to-Needs Ratio (log): All

| | 1969 | | 1979 | | 1989 | | 1999 | |
|---|---|---|---|---|---|---|---|---|
| | Coefficient (t) | Relative Effect (%) | Coefficient (t) | Relative Effect (%) | Coefficient (t) | Relative Effect (%) | Coefficient (t) | Relative Effect (%) |
| Intercept | 2.236*** | | 1.690*** | | 2.033*** | | 1.821*** | |
| Age (Year) | -0.020*** (-10.44) | | -0.009*** (-7.83) | | -0.013*** (-10.58) | | -0.010*** (-6.46) | |
| Female | -0.087*** (-3.65) | -8.3 | -0.064*** (-3.94) | -6.2 | -0.090*** (-5.65) | -8.6 | -0.061** (-2.90) | -5.9 |
| Race | | | | | | | | |
| Black-nonwhite[a] | -0.526*** (-12.62) | -40.9 | -0.371*** (-13.31) | -31.0 | -0.371*** (-13.19) | -31.0 | -0.198*** (-5.50) | -17.9 |
| Hispanic | | | -0.277*** (-7.41) | -24.2 | -0.301*** (-9.09) | -26.0 | -0.378*** (-10.03) | -31.5 |
| (White) | | | | | | | | |
| Marital status | | | | | | | | |
| Divorced-separated | 0.303** (3.00) | 35.4 | -0.426*** (-11.60) | -34.7 | -0.338*** (-10.58) | -28.7 | -0.355*** (-9.51) | -29.9 |
| Widowed | 0.502*** (15.62) | 65.3 | -0.245*** (-13.42) | -21.7 | -0.238*** (-13.21) | -21.2 | -0.278*** (-11.39) | -24.3 |
| Never married | 0.174** (3.01) | 19.0 | -0.338*** (-9.99) | -28.7 | -0.297*** (-8.40) | -25.6 | -0.458*** (-8.92) | -36.7 |
| (Married) | | | | | | | | |
| Number of children | -0.060** (-3.16) | | 0.102*** (4.69) | | -0.093*** (-3.66) | | 0.072* (2.12) | |
| Education | | | | | | | | |
| Less than high school | -0.302*** (-9.44) | -26.1 | -0.302*** (-16.32) | -26.1 | -0.317*** (-18.21) | -27.2 | -0.314*** (-12.80) | -27.0 |
| (High school grad.) | | | | | | | | |
| Some college | 0.123* | 13.1 | 0.088** | 9.2 | 0.230*** | 25.9 | 0.163*** | 17.7 |

| | 1969 | | 1979 | | 1989 | | 1999 | |
|---|---|---|---|---|---|---|---|---|
| | Coefficient (t) | Relative Effect (%) | Coefficient (t) | Relative Effect (%) | Coefficient (t) | Relative Effect (%) | Coefficient (t) | Relative Effect (%) |
| College education | 0.371*** (2.40) | 44.9 | 0.403*** (3.12) | 49.5 | 0.494*** (9.43) | 64.0 | 0.506*** (5.78) | 65.9 |
| $R^2$ | 0.073 (6.91) | | 0.096 (13.48) | | 0.140 (20.00) | | 0.094 (16.78) | |
| F | 75.85*** | | 183.73*** | | 271.24*** | | 147.32*** | |
| N | 9,572 | | 19,089 | | 18,366 | | 15,656 | |

NOTES: $t$ values in parentheses.

*$p < .05$, **$p < .01$, ***$p < .001$.

a. The "nonwhite" category is only for 1969.

one of the spouses has no income, the couple's income-to-needs ratio decreases to 77% of the income-to-needs ratio of a single person. That is, the living standard of married couples, with only one spouse having an income, is 79% of the living standard of a single person with the same amount of income. One can surmise that the reason why married persons had lower income-to-needs ratio than did nonmarried persons in 1969 was that only one spouse in their families had income.

The effect of marital status on income-to-needs ratios in the subsequent decades was as expected. Generally, the income-to-needs ratio of nonmarried persons was lower than that of married persons. In particular, the economic disadvantage associated with divorce-separation was 34.7% in 1979, but narrowed to 29.9% in 1999. In contrast, the economic disadvantage associated with being never-married increased greatly, from 28.7% in 1979 to 36.7% in 1999. Likewise, the economic disadvantage associated with widowhood increased between 1979 and 1999, from 21.7% in 1979 to 24.3% in 1999.

The effect of educational achievement also increased enormously. For example, in 1969, the income-to-needs ratio of those with a college education was 44.9% higher than that of persons with a high school education. But in 1999, the income-to-needs ratio of those with a college education was 65.9% higher. The degree to which less-than-a-high-school education adversely affected income-to-needs ratios was stable throughout the decades under study, ranging from 26.1% to 27.2%.

Advancing age was associated with the decline in income-to-needs ratio in each year under investigation. In 1969, aging by 1 year meant a decline in the income-to-needs ratio of 2%, whereas in 1999, it meant a decline of 1%.

The number of children living at home exerted a negative pressure in the income-to-needs ratio in 1969 and 1989 and a positive pressure in 1979 and 1999. For example, in 1999, the addition of one child living at home meant an increase in the income-to-needs ratio of 7.2%.

*OLS Multiple Regression Analysis of the Income-to-Needs Ratio (Log): Comparison Between Women and Men.* Tables 13.5 and 13.6 show how the independent variables correlate differentially with the income-to-needs ratios of women and men.

Marital status affected the income-to-needs ratios of women and men differently. As Tables 13.5 and 13.6 indicate, for both women and men, 1969 was a unique year in that being nonmarried was not necessarily related to economic disadvantage. Specifically, among women, being divorced-separated, widowed, and never married were all positively related to the income-to-needs ratio. Among men, being widowed was positively related to the income-to-needs ratio, but being divorced-separated and being never married were statistically insignificant.

From 1976 on, the economic disadvantage associated with widowhood among women fluctuated from 25.6% in 1979, to 24.3% in 1989, to 28.3% in 1999, showing a gradual increase in the economic disadvantage associated with widowhood among women. The economic disadvantage associated with widowhood among women was always larger than among men; like women's situation, widowed men's disadvantage fluctuated, ranging from 12.5% in 1979 to 14.0% in 1999.

Coefficients of divorce-separation in 1979, 1989, and 1999 indicate that although the degree of economic disadvantage associated with this marital status was just about the same for women (35.3% lower) and for men (35.1% lower) in 1979, it steadily decreased for men, but not for women. As a result, in 1999, the income-to-needs ratio of divorced-separated women was still 31.8% lower than that of married women. The comparable figure for men was 28.3% lower.

**Table 13.5** OLS Multiple Regression Analysis of the Income-to-Needs Ratio (log): Women

| | 1969 | | 1979 | | 1989 | | 1999 | |
|---|---|---|---|---|---|---|---|---|
| | Coefficient (t) | Relative Effect (%) | Coefficient (t) | Relative Effect (%) | Coefficient (t) | Relative Effect (%) | Coefficient (t) | Relative Effect (%) |
| Intercept | 1.516*** | | 1.353*** | | 1.732*** | | 1.711*** | |
| Age (year) | −0.010*** (−4.19) | | −0.005*** (−3.35) | | −0.009*** (−5.96) | | −0.009*** (−4.63) | |
| Race | | | | | | | | |
| Black-nonwhite[a] | −0.547*** (−9.91) | −42.1 | −0.407*** (−11.26) | −33.4 | −0.319*** (−9.30) | −27.2 | −0.222*** (−4.92) | −19.9 |
| Hispanic | | | −0.207*** (−4.13) | −18.7 | −0.259*** (−5.72) | −22.8 | −0.339*** (−6.90) | −28.8 |
| (White) | | | | | | | | |
| Marital status | | | | | | | | |
| Divorced-separated | 0.294* (2.47) | 34.2 | −0.436*** (−9.00) | −35.3 | −0.391*** (−9.23) | −32.4 | −0.383*** (−7.92) | −31.8 |
| Widowed | 0.439*** (12.00) | 55.2 | −0.297*** (−13.65) | −25.6 | −0.278*** (−12.76) | −24.3 | −0.333*** (−11.40) | −28.3 |
| Never married | 0.179* (2.55) | 19.6 | −0.363*** (−8.37) | −30.4 | −0.285*** (−6.27) | −24.8 | −0.460*** (−6.74) | −36.9 |
| (Married) | | | | | | | | |
| Number of children | −0.027 (−1.19) | | 0.183*** (6.69) | | −0.024 (−0.81) | | 0.168*** (4.00) | |
| Education | | | | | | | | |
| Less than high school | −0.316*** (−7.78) | −27.1 | −0.311*** (−13.17) | −26.7 | −0.351*** (−15.56) | −29.5 | −0.284*** (−9.03) | −24.6 |
| (High school) | | | | | | | | |
| Some college | 0.155* (2.32) | 16.7 | 0.068 (1.93) | 7.0 | 0.213*** (6.68) | 23.7 | 0.205*** (5.73) | 22.8 |
| College education | 0.261** | 29.8 | 0.336*** | 40.1 | 0.480*** | 61.4 | 0.488*** | 62.9 |

(Continued)

**Table 13.5** (continued)

| | 1969 | | 1979 | | 1989 | | 1999 | |
|---|---|---|---|---|---|---|---|---|
| | Coefficient (t) | Relative Effect (%) | Coefficient (t) | Relative Effect (%) | Coefficient (t) | Relative Effect (%) | Coefficient (t) | Relative Effect (%) |
| | (3.22) | | (8.32) | | (13.79) | | (11.24) | |
| | 0.072 | | 0.089 | | 0.124 | | 0.085 | |
| $R^2$ | | | | | | | | |
| F | 41.9*** | | 109.2*** | | 154.7*** | | 83.9*** | |
| N | 4,837 | | 11,183 | | 10,994 | | 9,031 | |

NOTES: $t$ values in parentheses.

*$p < .05$, **$p < .01$, ***$p < .001$.

a. The "nonwhite" category is only for 1969.

**Table 13.6** OLS Multiple Regression Analysis of the Income-to-Needs Ratio (log): Men

| | 1969 | | 1979 | | 1989 | | 1999 | |
|---|---|---|---|---|---|---|---|---|
| | Coefficient (t) | Relative Effect (%) | Coefficient (t) | Relative Effect (%) | Coefficient (t) | Relative Effect (%) | Coefficient (t) | Relative Effect (%) |
| Intercept | 2.965*** | | 2.139*** | | 2.249*** | | 1.898*** | |
| Age (year) | −0.030*** | | −0.016*** | | −0.016*** | | −0.011*** | |
| | (−10.63) | | (−8.40) | | (−8.26) | | (−4.42) | |
| Race | | | | | | | | |
| Black-nonwhite[a] | −0.496*** | −39.1 | −0.315*** | −26.9 | −0.367*** | −30.7 | −0.154** | −14.3 |
| | (−7.89) | | (−7.21) | | (−8.83) | | (−2.61) | |
| Hispanic | −0.362*** | | −0.362*** | −30.3 | −0.349*** | −29.5 | −0.440*** | −35.5 |
| | (−6.46) | | (−6.46) | | (−6.94) | | (−7.50) | |
| (White) | | | | | | | | |
| Marital status | | | | | | | | |
| Divorced-separated | 0.311 | 36.5 | −0.434*** | −35.1 | −0.276*** | −24.1 | −0.333*** | −28.3 |
| | (1.70) | | (−7.72) | | (−5.43) | | (−5.64) | |
| Widowed | 0.605*** | 83.2 | −0.134*** | −12.5 | −0.119*** | −11.2 | −0.151*** | −14.0 |
| | (9.23) | | (−3.81) | | (−3.36) | | (−3.28) | |
| Never married | 0.146 | 15.7 | −0.311*** | −26.7 | −0.335*** | −28.5 | −0.467*** | −37.3 |
| | (1.48) | | (−5.70) | | (−5.71) | | (−5.99) | |
| (Married) | | | | | | | | |
| Number of children | −0.119*** | | −0.039 | | −0.162*** | | −0.099 | |
| | (−3.57) | | (−1.09) | | (−3.49) | | (−1.73) | |
| Education | | | | | | | | |
| Less than high school | −0.281*** | −24.5 | −0.286*** | −24.9 | −0.292*** | −25.3 | −0.358*** | −30.0 |
| | (−5.52) | | (−9.58) | | (−10.23) | | (−9.10) | |
| (High school) | | | | | | | | |
| Some college | 0.095 | 10.0 | 0.121** | 12.8 | 0.250*** | 28.4 | 0.102* | 10.6 |
| | (1.21) | | (2.60) | | (6.29) | | (2.23) | |

(Continued)

Table 13.6 (Continued)

| | 1969 | | 1979 | | 1989 | | 1999 | |
|---|---|---|---|---|---|---|---|---|
| | Coefficient (t) | Relative Effect (%) | Coefficient (t) | Relative Effect (%) | Coefficient (t) | Relative Effect (%) | Coefficient (t) | Relative Effect (%) |
| College education | 0.439*** (5.89) | 55.1 | 0.475*** (10.66) | 60.6 | 0.509*** (13.72) | 66.4 | 0.509*** (11.82) | 66.4 |
| $R^2$ | 0.080 | | 0.100 | | 0.129 | | 0.095 | |
| F | 46.0*** | | 87.8*** | | 113.7*** | | 69.7*** | |
| N | 4,735 | | 7,906 | | 7,673 | | 6,626 | |

NOTES: $t$ values in parentheses.
*$p < .05$, **$p < .01$, ***$p < .001$.
a. The "nonwhite" category is only for 1969.

Never-married women were economically disadvantaged, compared with married women, from 1979 through 1999, but their economic disadvantage was considerably worse in 1999, when their income-to-needs ratio was 36.9% lower than that of married women. Economic disadvantage associated with the never-married status steadily worsened even faster among men, with the result that in 1999, the income-to-needs ratio of never-married men was 37.3% lower than that of married men.

The negative effect of aging was *greater* among men than among women. The addition of 1 year of age meant a decline in the income-to-needs ratio by 3%, 1.6%, 1.6%, and 1.1% in 1969, 1979, 1989, and 1999 among men and by 1%, 0.5%, 0.9%, and 0.9% in 1969, 1979, 1989, and 1999 among women. One needs to remember, however, that women live longer, resulting in possibly a greater decline in their income-to-needs ratios by the time they die.

The impact of children living at home differed for women and men. For women, children positively affected the income-to-needs ratios in 1979 and 1999, but made no difference in 1969 and 1989. For men, the effect of children was negative in 1969 and 1989, but made no difference in 1979 and 1999. When the effect of children is positive and statistically significant, the addition of one child living at home meant a considerable improvement in women's income-to-needs ratio. For example, in 1999, the addition of one child at home was associated with an increase in women's income-to-needs ratio by 16.8%. Conversely, when the effect of children is negative and statistically significant, the addition of one child meant a considerable decline in men's income-to-needs. In 1989, the addition of one child at home was associated with a decrease in men's income-to-needs ratio by 16.2%.

The positive effect of a college education on women's income-to-needs ratios increased faster than on men's. From 1969 to 1999, the economic advantage associated with a college education increased 111%, from 29.8 to 62.9%, for women, but only by 20%, from 55.1 to 66.6%, for men. However, even in 1999, such an economic advantage was greater for men (66.4%) than for women (62.9%).

The impact of minority status on income-to-needs ratios differed between women and men. The economic disadvantage associated with being black was higher among women than among men in 1969, and the rate of decline in this economic disadvantage thereafter was slower among women than among men. As a result, in 1999, the income-to-needs ratio of black women was 19.9% lower than white women's, compared with a 14.3% differential between black men and white men.

## DISCUSSION AND CONCLUSIONS

To reiterate, this study found that the net gender effect on the level of income-to-needs ratio was not only relatively small, but declined as the decades passed. Marital status, race, and education were found to be stronger determinants than was gender. The regression, run separately for women and men, revealed the persistently greater negative effects of the divorced-separated and never married statuses on the income-to-needs ratio of women than on men's. The positive effect of a college education increased faster for women; however, even in 1999, its economic impact on women's income-to-needs ratio was still smaller than on men's. The economic disadvantage associated with being black became smaller among both women and men in the later decades, but a sizable racial difference still existed in 1999, although to a lesser degree among men. The economic disadvantage associated with being Hispanic grew larger because of the growth in immigration (Ozawa, 1997).

The most significant finding from this study was that the net gender difference in the income-to-needs ratios among elderly people was not only relatively small, but declined as the decade progressed. The level of, and the pattern of change in, the net gender effect among elders were in contrast to those among nonaged adults, whom we investigated in a separate study (Ozawa & Yoon, 2003), which used the same research method with regard to variables, measurement of income-to-needs ratio, and data source. Table 13.7 illustrates the difference.

Note, first, that the net gender effect on the income-to-needs ratio of elders was smaller than that of nonaged adults in each year under investigation, except in 1969, and, second, that the trend in the changes was opposite: Among the elderly, the ratio decreased, but among nonaged adults, it increased. All told, in 1999, the net gender effect among elders was only about one-third of the effect among nonaged adults. Why was there such a large difference in the net gender effect?

There are at least three reasons. First, as the rate of marriage disruption increases among nonaged adults, it inevitably leads to the care of children by women. Women's economic disadvantage under these circumstances is compounded by their relative low wages (U.S. Census Bureau, 2000b) and the poor enforcement of child support payments by noncustodial parents (Garfinkel, McLanahan, & Watson, 1989; U.S. Census Bureau, 2000b). Elderly people are not confronted with these problems. On the contrary, children living at home boosted the income-to-needs ratio of elderly women at least in 1979 and 1999 (see Table 13.5).

Second, earnings, which are a strong dividing factor between nonaged women's and men's economic standing, have become increasingly insignificant over the decades as the rate of labor force participation has declined among elderly persons—especially elderly men (U.S. Census Bureau, 2000b)—whereas social security benefits become an ever more important source of income. Furthermore, because the benefit formula for social security benefits is slanted in favor of low-wage earners—who are concentrated among women—the distribution of social security benefits is considerably more equal than are the distributions of earnings (Ozawa & Kim, 1989). The changing importance of social security benefits versus earnings works in favor of women.

Third, the development of public policy on income support for aged versus nonaged segments of the society differed diametrically. For the elderly, the United States has created a viable safety net based on the combination of the social security and SSI programs, both of which provide cost-of-living increases. A study by Ozawa and Yoon (2002) indicated that without these programs, the mean income of poor elders would have been only 11% of the poverty line. Social security and SSI together brought their mean income to 80% of the poverty line.

In contrast, payments under welfare programs (Aid to Families with Dependent Children [AFDC], now Temporary Assistance for Needy Families [TANF]), on which nonaged, mother-only families heavily depend, have not increased commensurate with

**Table 13.7**  The Net Effect of Gender on Income-to-Needs Ratios of Aged Versus Nonaged Persons (in Percentage)

|          | 1969  | 1979  | 1989   | 1999   |
|----------|-------|-------|--------|--------|
| Aged     | −8.3  | −6.2  | −8.6   | −5.9   |
| Nonaged  | −3.9  | −8.6  | −15.3  | −15.0  |

inflation. Governmental data show that AFDC provided no cost-of-living increases for many years, and, as a result, the median state AFDC payment level declined 47% in real terms from 1970 to 1994 (U.S. House of Representatives, 1994). In short, one can conclude that part of the explanation for the relatively small gender differences in the income-to-needs ratios of elders rests with the public policy on income support.

The favorable findings from this study notwithstanding, one needs to recognize that, in reality, women live longer, the positive impact of educational achievement on women's income-to-needs ratio is still smaller, and widowed or divorced-separated women pay a higher economic price than do their male counterparts. Moreover, if women are black, they pay an extra higher economic price than do men. If a woman has multiple risks working against her, her economic deprivation, indeed, will be horrendous. Thus, the findings from this study aside, public policy interventions on behalf of women at risk of being economically deprived are continuously called for.

## REFERENCES

Burkhauser, R. V., Butler, J. S., & Holden, K. C. (1991). How the death of a spouse affects economic well-being after retirement: A hazard model approach. *Social Science Quarterly, 72,* 505–519.

Garfinkel, I., McLanahan, S., & Watson, D. (1989). Divorce, female headship, and child support. In M. Ozawa (Ed.), *Women's life cycle and economic insecurity: Problems and proposals* (pp. 101–131). New York: Greenwood Press.

Halvorsen, R., & Palmquiest, R. (1980). The interpretation of dummy variables in semilogarithmic equations. *American Economic Review, 70,* 474–475.

Holden, K. C. (1990). The joint impact of retirement and widow(er)hood: Is there a double jeopardy? *Proceedings of American Council on Consumer Interest.* New Orleans, LA: American Council on Consumer Interest.

Holden, K. C., Burkhauser, R. V., & Myers, D. A. (1986). Income transition at older stages of life: The dynamics of poverty. *Gerontologist, 26,* 292–297.

Ozawa, M. N. (1997). Demographic changes and their implications. In M. Reisch & E. Gambrill (Eds.), *Social work in the 21st century* (pp. 8–27). Thousand Oaks, CA: Pine Forge Press.

Ozawa, M. N., & Kim, T. S. (1989). Distributive effects of social security and pension benefits. *Social Service Review, 63,* 335–358.

Ozawa, M. N., & Lum, Y. S. (1998). Marital status and change in income status 10 years after retirement. *Social Work Research, 22,* 116–128.

Ozawa, M. N., & Yoon, H. S. (2002). Social security and SSI as safety nets for the elderly poor. *Journal of Aging & Social Policy, 14,* 1–25.

Ozawa, M. N., & Yoon, H. S. (2003). Gender differences in the economic well-being of nonaged adults in the United States [Special issue on Rediscovering the Other America: The Continuing Crisis of Poverty and Inequality in the United States]. *Journal of Poverty: Innovations on Social & Economic Inequalities, 7*(1/2), 97–122.

Radner, D. B. (1987, August). Money incomes of aged and nonaged family units, 1967 to 1984, *Social Security Bulletin, 50*(8), 9–28.

Social Security Administration (SSA). (2000a). *Annual statistical supplement, 2000, to the Social Security Bulletin.* Washington, DC: Author.

Social Security Administration (SSA). (2000b). *Income of the population 55 or older, 1998*. Washington, DC: Author.

U.S. Census Bureau. (1975). *Historical statistics of the United States: Colonial times to 1970, Part 1*. Washington, DC: Author.

U.S. Census Bureau. (1984a). *Current population survey: Annual demographic file, 1970* (ICPSR 7561) (2nd ICPSR ed.). Ann Arbor, MI: Inter-University Consortium for Political and Social Research.

U.S. Census Bureau. (1984b). *Current population survey: Annual demographic file, 1980* (ICPSR 8040) (2nd ICPSR ed.). Ann Arbor, MI: Inter-University Consortium for Political and Social Research.

U.S. Census Bureau. (1991). *Current population survey: Annual demographic file, 1990* (ICPSR 9475) (2nd ICPSR ed.). Ann Arbor, MI: Inter-University Consortium for Political and Social Research.

U.S. Census Bureau. (1996). Income, poverty, and valuation of noncash benefits. *Current Population Reports* (Series P-60, No. 189). Washington, DC: U.S. Government Printing Office.

U.S. Census Bureau. (2000a). *Current population survey: Annual demographic file, 2000* (ICPSR 3048) (2nd ICPSR ed.). Ann Arbor, MI: Inter-University Consortium for Political and Social Research.

U.S. Census Bureau. (2000b). *Statistical abstract of the United States, 2000*. Washington, DC: U.S. Government Printing Office.

U.S. Census Bureau. (2002). Poverty in the United States. *Current Population Reports* (Series P-60, No. 222). Washington, DC: U.S. Government Printing Office.

U.S. House of Representatives, Committee on Ways and Means. (1994). *Overview of entitlement programs: 1994 green book*. Washington, DC: U.S. Government Printing Office.

Zick, C. D., & Smith, K. R. (1991). Patterns of economic change surrounding the death of a spouse. *Journal of Gerontology: Social Sciences, 46*, S310–S320.

# CHAPTER 14

# The Effect of Socioeconomic Status on the Community Functioning of People With Serious Mental Illness and Their Families

ERIC D. JOHNSON

A large body of social science research literature demonstrates a variety of negative effects of low socioeconomic (SES) status. This includes both main effects of SES itself, as well as indirect effects, including low and intermittent employment, dependence on public assistance, interrupted or inadequate housing, nutrition deficiencies, health-care maintenance and access to health-care services, social support, and personal resources limitations (Henly, Danziger, & Offer, 2005; Rank, 2001; Seccombe, 2000). These findings have been consistent across studies of adult functioning and distress outcomes (McLeod & Kessler, 1990; Turner & Lloyd, 1995), as well as child development outcomes (Conger et al., 2002; Evans, 2004).

In addition, a history of literature has documented consistent correlations between low SES and mental health problems, particularly attempting to assess whether the relationship is one of social causation or "drift-down" (Dohrenwend, Levav, Shrout, Schwartz, & Link, 1992; Dohrenwend et al., 1998; Miech, Caspi, Moffitt, Wright, & Silva, 1999; Weich & Lewis, 1998). Although many of these studies have focused more generally on emotional health, several have investigated the relationship between serious mental illness (particularly schizophrenia and major mood disorder) and SES (Cohen, 1993; Munk & Mortensen, 1992; Ritsher, Warner, Johnson, & Dohrenwend, 2001). Recent findings suggest that, whereas biological vulnerability accounts for up to 50% of the variance in serious mental illness problems, social environment factors may account for a significant proportion of the remaining variance (Draine, Salzer, Culhane, & Hadley, 2002; Hudson, 2005).

The compounding of vulnerable statuses has been a major complication in this research. Both ethnic minorities and single-parent households are overrepresented in the lower socioeconomic class, so there is often confusion about whether the problems are "best explained" by SES, race, family structure, or a combination (addition or interaction) of these variables (Fiscella, Franks, & Gold, 2000; Jaffee et al., 2005; McLeod & Owens, 2004). In addition, the frame of reference for analyzing "problems" among the lower class is almost invariably that which characterizes the middle class, without recognition that what represents a problem in a middle-class family may actually represent resiliency among the poor (McCubbin & McCubbin, 1988).

On the subject of families of the mentally ill, a significant body of literature focuses almost entirely on intra-family dynamics. This literature has examined three principal areas: (1) the effect of the family on the person with serious mental illness, principally focusing on the problem of "expressed emotion" (negative emotional over-involvement and criticism) predicting increased symptoms, or rehospitalization; (2) the effect of the ill member on the family, principally focusing on the problem of "family burden" (subjective sense of burden reported by caregivers) as an outcome of the ill member's illness or illness-related behaviors; and (3) the use of "psychoeducation" (a combination of education about the illness and problem-solving techniques) in helping family members understand and cope with the problems of having a seriously mentally ill member.

The "expressed emotion" (EE) literature over the past several decades has described a pattern of increased ill member relapse and rehospitalization, for both schizophrenic (thought disorder) and bipolar (mood disorder) patients, when the caregivers are arbitrarily discriminated between low and high EE (Hooley & Parker, 2006). However, recent cross-cultural studies suggest that this assessment may only be valid for Caucasians (Kealey, 2005; Kymalainen, Weisman, Resales, & Armesto, 2006; Rosenfarb,

Bellack, & Aziz, 2006a), and that the form and meaning of emotional expression are differently interpreted across cultural groups. In addition, it appears that EE is related to family members' attributions about the illness and sense of competence in managing the problems of the illness (Kuipers et al., 2006), and is bidirectional, being influenced by the IM, as it in turn affects the IM (Greenberg, Seltzer, Hong, & Orsmond, 2006; Lobban, Barrowclough, & Jones, 2006; Perlick et al., 2004).

The "family burden" (FB) literature has found significant correlations between IM problematic behaviors (especially noncompliance with prescribed medication, substance abuse, and increased symptomatology leading to rehospitalization), reported objective burden (loss of work time, increased expenses, disrupted family patterns), and reported subjective burden (the extent to which these objective burdens are perceived as distressing) (Perlick et al., 2006; Reinares et al., 2006; Rosenfarb et al., 2006b). However, cross-cultural investigations suggest that there is a poor correlation between objective burden and subjective burden, with Caucasian families frequently reporting less objective burden, but more subjective burden than do cultural groups with a more collectivist understanding of family (Biegel, Milligan, Putnam, & Song, 1994; Guarnaccia, 1998; Horwitz & Reinhard, 1995; Pruchno, Patrick, & Burant, 1997; Solomon & Draine, 1995).

The psychoeducation literature during the past few decades has documented significant improvements in family members' knowledge of mental illness symptoms, mental health resources, and problem-solving skills (Dixon, McFarlane, Lefley, Lucksted, & Cohen, 2001; Kuipers, 2006; Marsh, 2001). This approach has been adopted by the National Alliance for the Mentally Ill (NAMI) in their Family-to-Family self-help psychoeducation groups (Dixon, Stewart, et al., 2001). These programs have generally been in a multifamily group format, ranging in duration from a single day to ongoing groups that may exist for several years. Not surprisingly, the single-day approaches tend to provide families only with information, whereas the ongoing groups allow family members to explore different approaches to problem solving, and are more likely to demonstrate lasting change in the family structure (McFarlane et al., 1995; Pollio, North, Reid, Miletic, & Mcclendon, 2006; Solomon, Draine, Mannion, & Meisel, 1997).

Most of the literature that has examined the interface of family and social institutions with regard to families of the mentally ill has examined the relationship between patients, families, and mental health service providers (Harvey et al., 2002; Marshall & Solomon, 2004; Ware, Tugenberg, & Dickey, 2004), although a few studies have examined systemic barriers to receiving services and focused on health disparities (Biegel, Farkas, & Song, 1997; Dixon, Goldman, & Hirad, 1999; Shumway et al., 2003; Smith, 2003). These articles do not paint a rosy picture of a positive connection between front-line mental health providers and family members of the seriously mentally ill, nor does there appear to be much congruence between the values of policymakers (which are frequently economically based) and the concerns of the mentally ill and their families (which are focused on quality of life issues).

In sum, although substantial literature has examined family variables in relation to having a mentally ill member, and a separate body of literature has examined family variables in relation to the larger issue of SES, very few studies have examined the functioning of families of the mentally ill across socioeconomic categories, or have attempted to deconstruct differences based on a combination of demographic variables (Guarnaccia & Parra, 1996; Song, Biegel, & Milligan, 1997; Stueve, Vine, & Struening, 1997). Most of the articles that have examined a combination of demographic variables have primarily focused on ethnic issues or differences, rather than on SES differences.

The study reported in this chapter describes an interview study of 180 families with a seriously mentally ill member living in the community. The sample was stratified across SES, ethnic, gender, and urbanization categories, and examined both positive and negative influences on the community adaptation of people with serious mental illness and their families. The study was based on the theoretical propositions of McCubbin's Double ABCX Model of family stress and coping (McCubbin & Patterson, 1983). Expanding on Reuben Hill's ABCX Model of family crisis, in which A = the stressor, B = family coping resources, C = appraisal/interpretation, and X = extent of the crisis (Hill, 1949), McCubbin described the family's adaptation to an ongoing strain, in which AA = the "pile-up" of stressors, BB = original and revised coping resources, CC = original and revised appraisal/interpretation, and XX = the level of adaptation to ongoing (or chronic) strains. Because details of the study, including participant and measurement information, have been presented elsewhere (Johnson, 1998, 2004b), I will focus here on salient characteristics of the study, in order to focus on the findings regarding socioeconomic influence and related variables.

## METHODS

This study examined the negative effects of both environmental and illness-related strains, and the buffering effects of resources (family functioning, social support) and interpretation (family members' attributions about the illness, family members' sense of competence in managing the illness) on the adaptation level of mentally ill persons in the community, and on the perceived sense of burden experienced by family members.

The sample consisted of 180 families living in Mercer County, New Jersey. Each had a seriously mentally ill member (IM) currently living with them, or in regular (at least weekly) contact. (For purposes of this study, "seriously mentally ill" was defined as someone who has had at least one previous hospitalization for a psychotic episode involving mood or thought disorder, as defined by the *Diagnostic and Statistical Manual of Mental Disorders* [*DSM-IV*], American Psychiatric Association [APA], 1994.) Referrals came from a variety of sources, including inpatient programs, outpatient clinics, the community mental health center (CMHC) case management unit, the county jail system, and the local NAMI chapter. This diversity allowed for a stratified sampling approach that provided a mix of socioeconomic status: 39% of the sample were classified as upper-middle class (one or more family members with a professional job), 45% classified as lower-middle class (one or more family members with a blue-collar job), and 16% classified as lower class (welfare or the IM's social security providing the only income). In addition, the sample was stratified by ethnicity (58% European American, 32% African American, 10% Hispanic American), demographic distribution (56% urban families, 44% suburban families), and gender (56% male patients, 44% female patients). Diagnoses for the IM included six categories: thought disorder (schizophrenia, 22%), mood disorder (manic-depression, 10%), thought and mood disorder (schizoaffective, 29%), thought disorder and substance abuse (24%), mood disorder and substance abuse (4%), all three disorders (11%). Table 14.1 provides a summary of significant IM and family characteristics.

At a point as close as possible to the time when the IM had been released from psychiatric hospitalization for 6 months, at least one first-order relative (parent, sibling, spouse, adult child) who was living with or in frequent contact with the IM was interviewed, using a semi-structured interview schedule. Family members were interviewed at length (interviews lasted at least 2 hours in each case) by the author or one of four staff members of the Family Support Project (FSP). Attempts were made to include as many family members as possible in each case. In the case of multiple informants, a single-family summary score was derived for each of the variables.

Limitations in cognitive abilities and literacy were anticipated among a substantial portion of the sample, so self-report questionnaires were not used. Because all staff members of the FSP had previous experience in working with the mentally ill, and with family interviewing, ratings were based on staff assessments of family responses and interaction, after inter-rater reliability had been established for the instruments used.

Variables identified and investigated in this study included the following:

*Environmental Strain:* Environmental and demographic strains hypothesized to affect the family and IM, independent of the IM's mental illness (including neighborhood safety, family occupational stability, family health/disability, life-event changes in the past year, family size, gender, and race).

*Illness-Related Strain:* Conditions directly and specifically related to the course of the IM's mental illness—especially components of diagnosis, chronicity, severity, and substance use complications (including length of illness, number of hospitalizations, total number of mental health services received, substance use history, and psychiatric diagnosis).

*Family Functioning:* A combination of two measures of family functioning (Geismar, 1980; Olson et al., 1985), used to assess both internal family functioning (cohesion, adaptation, communication) and family-community interface (task performance, role satisfaction, deviance).

*Family Members' Sense of Competence:* A construct based on general measures of family

**Table 14.1** Demographics of Ill Member and Family Sample

| Category | Percent | Category | Percent |
|---|---|---|---|
| **IM Gender** | | **IM Race** | 58% |
| Female | 44% | European American | 32% |
| Male | 56% | African American | 10% |
| | | Hispanic American | |
| | | | |
| **IM Age** | 26% | **IM Education** | 23% |
| 20–29 | 38% | < High school | 35% |
| 30–39 | 22% | H.S. grad | 31% |
| 40–49 | 14% | H.S. + | 11% |
| 50–70 | | B.A.(+) | |
| **IM Marital Status** | 62% | **Psychotropic Meds** | 82% |
| Never married | 12% | Yes | 18% |
| Currently married | 26% | No | |
| Previously married | | | |
| **IM Diagnosis** | | **IM Diagnosis** | |
| Thought disorder | 22% | Thought and substance abuse | 24% |
| Mood disorder | 10% | Mood and substance abuse | 4% |
| Thought and mood | 29% | All 3 disorders | 11% |
| **IM Location** | | **Living Situation** | |
| Trenton | 56% | IM with family | 60% |
| Suburbs | 44% | IM elsewhere | 40% |
| **SES of Family** | | **Primary Caregiver** | |
| Upper middle | 39% | Parent | 70% |
| Lower middle | 45% | Sibling | 13% |
| Lower | 16% | Spouse | 6% |
| | | Adult child | 8% |
| **Problem Areas** | | **Problem Areas** | |
| Neighborhood safety | 30% | Occupational stability | 28% |
| Physical health/disability | 33% | Loss of family members | 15% |

resilience and hardiness (Antonovsky & Sourani, 1988; Kobasa, 1979), to assess family members' sense of managing the illness (and related problems) in the past, assessment of current coping strategies, and sense of challenge or threat of the future.

*Attributions:* The basis that family members attribute to the causation of the mental illness (including biological, social, religious), and the meaning that the illness has for them.

*Social Support:* The extent of available social support (kin networks, friendship and neighborhood networks, organizational networks), the use of the social support networks, and

family members' satisfaction with the social support received or used.

*Ill Member Level of Adaptation:* A measure of the IM's observable behavioral functioning, derived from National Institute of Mental Health (NIMH) assessment instruments (Carter & Newman, 1976), assessing functioning in five important areas of family and community living: activities of daily living (ADL) skills, problem behaviors, social functioning, emotional control, and active symptoms.

*Perceived Family Burden:* Family members' assessment of the amount of burden related to the IM's illness in several significant areas of family life (including finances, family routine, social and leisure activities, health, family interaction, and extra-family interaction).

## FINDINGS

Data were analyzed using multiple regression, direct and indirect effects, and structural equation modeling. Indices were evaluated by confirmatory factor analysis, scale reliability, and inter-rater reliability. Results confirmed the theoretical propositions of the Double ABCX Model, with both Environmental Strain and Illness-Related Strain having significant negative effects on Perceived Family Burden and Ill Member Level of Adaptation. Among mediating variables, Social Support failed to demonstrate significance. Family Functioning was unrelated to Perceived Family Burden, demonstrated a modest direct effect on the Ill Member Level of Adaptation, but had a strong positive effect on Family Members' Sense of Competence. Both family variables were found to buffer Environmental Strain, but had little effect on Illness-Related Strain. Most of the impact of Family Functioning on the Ill Member Level of Adaptation was mediated by Family Members' Sense of Competence, which proved to be the most important contributor to the Ill Member Level of Adaptation (Johnson, 2004b).

To determine whether there were significant differences in the influence of predictor variables for different socioeconomic and ethnic groups, split-file analyses were performed for these two covariates. There was a significant difference in the patterns displayed across SES groups versus ethnic groups. Although none of the mean scores on strain variables, family variables, or patient level of adaptation demonstrated a statistically significant difference among the ethnic groups, there was a distinct pattern of increase in stressors and decrease in functioning as SES

level declined. Table 14.2 presents information on a wide variety of variables in the study that demonstrated this pattern.

*Environmental Strain.* The following categorical variables, identified in the literature as likely to affect people with mental illness, were examined for their influence on the IM level of adaptation: environmental problems (neighborhood safety, family occupational stability, loss of family members, family physical health/disability); life-event changes (both positive and negative) in the past year; family (and household) size; location of residence; IM living with or away from family; age, race, and gender of the IM; age, gender, and family position of the primary caretaker; family history of substance abuse. Those variables that demonstrated sufficient differentiation among categories in a one-way analysis of variance (ANOVA), and were statistically significant at the $p < .05$ level when entered into a simultaneous multiple regression, were recoded to represent ordinal rankings from low to high strain. Five of the variables examined reached significance: (1) negative changes in the past year, (2) environmental problems, (3) larger family size, (4) (male) gender, and (5) (minority) race. A single score for Environmental Strain was created by adding the scores (ranks) from each of these five variables. A greater score represented a greater accumulated strain.

*Illness-Related Strain.* The following categorical variables, identified in the literature as likely to affect the IM's current level of adaptation, were examined: age at first hospitalization, number of hospitalizations, period of total hospitalization, length of time since the first hospitalization, psychiatric diagnosis, substance use history, previous mental health and substance use treatment services, family history of mental illness. A process identical to that of Environmental Strain was used. Four of the 10 variables examined reached significance:

**Table 14.2** Mean Scores by SES Levels

| Variable | Upper-Middle Class (N = 70) | Lower-Middle Class (N = 82) | Lower Class (N = 28) | | |
|---|---|---|---|---|---|
| Environmental strain | 7.5 | 10.2 | 13.1 | ** | ++ |
| Illness-related strain | 10.5 | 11.0 | 12.8 | ** | ++ |
| Family functioning | 6.6 | 5.7 | 4.9 | ** | ++ |
| Family sense of competence | 5.5 | 4.7 | 4.2 | ** | + |
| Family sense of meaning | 5.9 | 4.7 | 3.5 | ** | ++ |
| Ill member level of adaptation | 6.3 | 5.5 | 4.6 | ** | + |
| Problem behaviors | 5.9 | 8.5 | 11.1 | ** | + |
| Negative changes in past year | 0.7 | 1.1 | 2.2 | ** | ++ |
| Social support—use | 3.2 | 3.0 | 2.4 | | |
| Social support—satisfaction | 4.1 | 3.7 | 3.2 | * | |
| Perceived family burden | 4.6 | 4.8 | 5.2 | | |

\* Different from UMC at .01 level; \*\* Different from UMC at .001 level
⁺ Different from LMC at .01 level; ⁺⁺ Different from LMC at .001 level

(1) number of hospitalizations, (2) total number of mental health services received, (3) substance use history, and (4) psychiatric diagnosis. A single variable score for Illness Strain was created by adding the scores (ranks) from each of these four variables. Similar to Environmental Strain, a greater score represented a greater accumulated strain.

*Family Functioning.* Family functioning was assessed by FSP staff in interviews with family members, using two direct observation instruments that were derived from other instruments with a substantial history of use and verification. The Clinical Rating Scale (CRS) (Olson et al., 1985) is adapted from the Family Adaptability and Cohesion Evaluation Scale (FACES) of David Olson and associates. The Family Functioning Scale (FFS) (Geismar, 1980) is adapted from the St. Paul Scale of Ludwig Geismar and associates. Two scales were used because they examine different aspects of family functioning. The CRS assesses intra-family functioning in three dimensions: cohesion, adaptability, and communication. The FFS

assesses family functioning in the context of the community, along three different dimensions: task performance, role satisfaction, and deviance. Factor analysis supported the three categories of the CRS, but found the FFS to be essentially unidimensional. Both the CRS and FFS had similar correlations with the IM level of adaptation (CRS = .37; FFS = .44), and a moderately high correlation with each other (.68). It appeared that the two scales were measuring somewhat different, but complementary, aspects of family functioning. Scores from both scales were combined into a single Family Functioning score, with a greater score representing more successful functioning.

*Family Sense of Competence and Family Sense of Meaning.* The instrument developed for this study used the three-part frameworks developed by Kobasa (1979) and Antonovsky and Sourani (1988) to assess resilience and hardiness. These elements were modified to be appropriate to the experience of living with the mentally ill, and organized into a brief (12 item) index, composed of three dimensions: evaluation of the past, sense of competence in the present, and sense of meaning (future orientation). Scale reliability (Cronbach's alpha) = .85, and inter-rater reliabilities for the index ranged from .83 to .95. A single score for Family Sense of Competence and Family Sense of Meaning was determined by taking the mean of the individual items. Family Sense of Meaning was highly correlated with Attributions (that is, the cause attributed by family members for the mental illness). Higher scores on these two variables represented a greater sense of the family's ability to deal with the mental illness and attendant behaviors, and a stronger sense of meaning, purpose, and optimism about the future.

*Ill Member Level of Adaptation (IMLA).* The instrument developed for this study consisted of 46 items, which together provided a way of assessing the IM's observable behavioral functioning in six areas of family and community living. Through factor analysis, the IMLA index was reduced from 46 to 30 items (correlation = .99 with the original instrument). The revised index consisted of five factors, which roughly paralleled the categories of the original instrument and included (1) ADL skills (including hygiene, managing finances and transportation, work), (2) problem behaviors (including substance use, aggressive behaviors, legal involvement), (3) social functioning (including interaction with strangers, maintaining friendships, recreational activities), (4) emotional control (tolerating difference, handling conflict, emotional volatility), and (5) active symptoms (hallucinations, delusions, bizarre thoughts). Scale reliability (Cronbach's alpha) = .95, and inter-rater reliabilities for the index ranged from .94 to .99. A single variable score was determined by taking the mean of the individual items. A higher score represented more adequate functioning in the community context.

*Problem Behaviors.* This was a subset of the IMLA, described previously, that focused on substance abuse, aggressive behaviors, or legal involvement. Approximately 40% of the IM group in this sample had significant problems with one or more of these areas. A higher score represented more problematic behavior (lower functioning).

*Negative Changes in the Past Year.* Although positive changes in family life did not correlate significantly with overall functioning, negative changes did. Higher scores were correlated with more problematic functioning for both Family Functioning and IMLA.

*Social Support Use and Social Support Satisfaction.* Social support was examined in three dimensions: family members' assessment of the availability of support, the use that the family (especially the primary caregiver) made of available support, and family members' satisfaction with the social support. Each of these dimensions was ranked low, moderate, or high; they were further broken down by source of social support: kin networks, friendship and neighborhood networks, and organizational networks. They were not assessed according to the type of support (e.g., instrumental, emotional). Rankings were summed across all three sources of social support. Higher scores represented greater use of available (or perceived available) social supports, and greater satisfaction with the support received.

*Perceived Family Burden.* A family burden index, based on categories developed by Pai and Kapur (1981), examined the family members' assessment of the extent of burden that they attributed to the problems of the IM over the previous year, in the following categories: finances, disruption of family routine, disruption or postponing of family social and leisure activities, family health problems, conflictual family interactions, and problems (conflict or distance) in extra-family interactions. A single variable score was determined by taking the mean of the individual items. A higher score represented a higher level of burden perceived to be caused by the IM's illness.

As can be seen from Table 14.2, all of the variables in this study demonstrate a pattern of decline, such that the lowest SES class is significantly more disadvantaged than either the upper-middle or lower-middle classes. Given the number of variables analyzed in this study, very conservative significance levels have been used ($p < .01$ or less). Even among the variables that do not demonstrate statistical significance at this level (Social Support and Perceived Family Burden), a distinct pattern emerges.

Table 14.3 contrasts this pattern with mean scores across ethnic groups (African American and Hispanic American families have been collapsed into a single Minority category because of the relatively small size of the Hispanic American sample and similarities between scores of African American and Hispanic American families). Within each SES level, mean scores are quite similar for the European American and minority groups, and do not approach statistical significance. However, as SES declines, differences noted in Table 14.2 are apparent.

## DISCUSSION

The overall study described in this report investigated the theoretical propositions of the Double ABCX Model, with reference to the negative impact of strain variables, the potential mediating effect of family resource and interpretation variables, and the subsequent impact on both the community functioning of the ill member and the family's perceived sense of burden in managing the problem of serious mental illness. The negative impact of both environmental and illness-related strains on family and ill member variables were highly significant ($p < .001$) for all groups, regardless of SES, ethnicity, gender, or other demographics. These results strongly suggest that without a buffering influence, the negative effects of environmental and illness-related problems will take a devastating toll

**Table 14.3**  Mean Scores by Socioeconomic Status and Ethnic Group

| Variable | Environmental Strain | Illness-Related Strain | Family Functioning | Family Sense of Competence | IM Level of Adaptation |
|---|---|---|---|---|---|
| Upper-middle class—European American ($n = 47$) | −7.17 | −8.04 | 6.44 | 5.63 | 6.19 |
| Upper-middle class—minority ($n = 26$) | −7.04 | −8.04 | 6.41 | 5.84 | 6.49 |
| Lower-middle class—European American ($n = 43$) | −8.07 | −8.72 | 5.35 | 4.95 | 5.94 |
| Lower-middle class—minority ($n = 36$) | −9.13 | −9.54 | 5.48 | 4.68 | 4.96 |
| Lower class—European American ($n = 14$) | −10.57 | −10.50 | 4.47 | 3.81 | 5.19 |
| Lower class—minority ($n = 14$) | −11.07 | −10.43 | 5.00 | 4.37 | 4.04 |

on people with mental illness who are trying to function outside of the hospital environment. Of the mediating variables, only family members' sense of competence in managing the problem had significant correlations with the ill member level of adaptation ($p < .001$) and family sense of burden ($p < .01$) in multiple regression analyses.

The findings of this study support those of other recent studies that have examined the importance of "competence," "mastery," or "sense of control," demonstrating that a sense of meaning and competence can have significant effects on both psychological and physical outcomes, as well as a stress buffering effect (McCubbin, Thompson, Thompson, & Fromer, 1998; Mirowsky & Ross, 1990; Mueser, Corrigan, Hilton, Tanzman, & Schaub, 2002). This study has gone beyond the examination of personal competence and outcome to suggest that a family "atmosphere of competence" can contribute to the outcome of a vulnerable member. This has important implications for psychotherapeutic and psychoeducation work with families of the mentally ill, as well as with other families with vulnerable members (Dyck, Hendryx, Short, Voss, & McFarlane, 2002; Marsh, Lefley, Evans-Rhodes, Ansell, & Doerzbacher, 1996; McKay, Gonzales, Stone, Ryland, & Kohner, 1995; Walsh, 1996).

Several recent studies have documented the importance of family to the seriously mentally ill (Brekke & Mathiesen, 1995; Horwitz, Reinhard, & Howell-White, 1996; Pitschel-Walz, Leucht, & Bauml, 2001). Given the importance of the family sense of competence variable for IM functioning, and the necessity of family caregiving for many mentally ill persons in the community, mental health systems must incorporate services for families of the mentally ill into the continuum of mental health care. Recent reviews of empirically supported interventions with families of the mentally ill strongly encourage family support efforts as aiding families in

realizing and using their sense of competence (Dixon, McFarlane et al., 2001; Marsh, 2001). This is particularly significant for low-income families, as the strains are greater, the use of social support networks is less rewarding, and sense of competence in managing life generally, as well as managing the mental illness, is likely to be less.

However, it would be a great mistake to assume that education or therapy for low-income families of the seriously mentally ill will be sufficient to address the complex problems that these families face. Mental health practitioners must work in partnership with people with serious mental illness and their family members, to advocate for them, to empower them in making use of (and influencing) the structure of mental health services, and to support them in the face of economically driven policies and funding cuts that fail to recognize the harshness of their existence, with glib references to "entitlement" (Brown, 2002; Cohen, 2000). This support involves more than the self-righteous sense of "doing to" or "doing for" people with limited resources. It is a matter of listening to what they are saying about what they need (Corrigan, Thompson, Lambert, & Sangster, 2003; Johnson, 2004a; Rojano, 2004), and "doing with" them in a partnership that respects their voices (Johnson, 2001). In the world of mental illness, the stigma of the lower class is different from the stigma of the middle class. The stigma of the middle class is shame—the embarrassment of being different (Link, Struening, Neese-Todd, Asmussen, & Phelan, 2001; Wahl, 1999). The stigma of the lower class is impotence—not being heard, not being asked (Johnson, 2000; Ware et al., 2004). In both direct and indirect ways, low socioeconomic class burdens people with serious mental illness and their families. Partnership efforts require both direct interventions with families, and the indirect interventions of being "the flea in the ear" of mental health and social policymakers.

# REFERENCES

American Psychiatric Association (APA). (1994). *Diagnostic and statistical manual of mental disorders* (4th ed.). Washington, DC: Author.

Antonovsky, A., & Sourani, T. (1988). Family sense of coherence and family adaptation. *Journal of Marriage and the Family, 50,* 79–92.

Biegel, D. E., Farkas, K. J., & Song, L. Y. (1997). Barriers to the use of mental health services by African American and Hispanic elderly persons. *Journal of Gerontological Social Work, 29,* 23–44.

Biegel, D. E., Milligan, S. E., Putnam, P. L., & Song, L. Y. (1994). Predictors of burden among lower socioeconomic status caregivers of persons with chronic mental illness. *Community Mental Health Journal, 30,* 473–494.

Brekke, J. S., & Mathiesen, S. G. (1995). Effects of parental involvement on the functioning of noninstitutionalized adults with schizophrenia. *Psychiatric Services, 46,* 1149–1155.

Brown, S. L. (2002). We are, therefore I am: A multisystems approach with families in poverty. *Family Journal, 10,* 405–409.

Carter, D. E., & Newman, F. L. (1976). *A client-oriented system of mental health service delivery and program management: A workbook and guide.* Washington, DC: National Institute of Mental Health.

Cohen, C. I. (1993). Poverty and the course of schizophrenia: Implications for research and policy. *Hospital & Community Psychiatry, 44,* 951–958.

Cohen, C. I. (2000). Overcoming social amnesia: The role for a social perspective in psychiatric research and practice. *Psychiatric Services, 51,* 72–78.

Conger, R. D., Wallace, L. E., Sun, Y., Simons, R. L., McLoyd, V. C., & Brody, G. H. (2002). Economic pressure in African American families: A replication and extension of the family stress model. *Developmental Psychology, 38,* 179–193.

Corrigan, P., Thompson, V., Lambert, D., & Sangster, Y. (2003). Perceptions of discrimination among persons with serious mental illness. *Psychiatric Services, 54,* 1105–1110.

Dixon, L., Goldman, H., & Hirad, A. (1999). State policy and funding services to families of adults with serious and persistent mental illness. *Psychiatric Services, 50,* 551–553.

Dixon, L., McFarlane, W. R., Lefley, H., Lucksted, A., & Cohen, M. (2001). Evidence-based practices for services to families of people with psychiatric disabilities. *Psychiatric Services, 52,* 903–910.

Dixon, L., Stewart, B., Burland, J., Delahanty, J., Lucksted, A., & Hoffman, M. (2001). Pilot study of the effectiveness of the Family-to-Family education program. *Psychiatric Services, 52,* 965–967.

Dohrenwend, B. P., Levav, I., Shrout, P. E., Schwartz, S., & Link, B. G. (1992). Socioeconomic status and psychiatric disorders: The causation-selection issue. *Science, 255,* 946–952.

Dohrenwend, B. P., Levav, I., Shrout, P. E., Schwartz, S., Naveh, G., Link, B. G., et al. (1998). Ethnicity, socioeconomic status, and psychiatric disorders: A test of the social causation-social selection issue. In B. P. Dohrenwend (Ed.), *Adversity, stress, and psychopathology* (pp. 285–318). New York: Oxford University Press.

Draine, J., Salzer, M. S., Culhane, D. P., & Hadley, T. R. (2002). Role of social disadvantage in crime, joblessness, and homelessness among persons with serious mental illness. *Psychiatric Services, 53,* 565–573.

Dyck, D. G., Hendryx, M. S., Short, R. A., Voss, W. D., & McFarlane, W. R. (2002). Service use among patients with schizophrenia in psychoeducational multiple-family group treatment. *Psychiatric Services, 53,* 749–754.

Evans, G. W. (2004). The environment of childhood poverty. *American Psychologist, 59,* 77–92.

Fiscella, K., Franks, P., & Gold, M. R. (2000). Inequality in quality: Addressing socioeconomic, racial, and ethnic disparities in health care. *Journal of the American Medical Association, 283,* 2579–2584.

Geismar, L. L. (1980). *Family and community functioning* (2nd ed.). Metuchen, NJ: Scarecrow Press.

Greenberg, J. S., Seltzer, M. M., Hong, J., & Orsmond, G. I. (2006). Bidirectional effects of expressed emotion and behavior problems and symptoms in adolescents and adults with autism. *American Journal on Mental Retardation, 111,* 229–249.

Guarnaccia, P. (1998). Multicultural experiences of family caregiving: A study of African American, European American, and Hispanic American families. In H. P. Lefley (Ed.), *Families coping with mental illness: The cultural context* (pp. 45–61). San Francisco: Jossey-Bass.

Guarnaccia, P. J., & Parra, P. (1996). Ethnicity, social status, and families' experiences of caring for a mentally ill family member. *Community Mental Health Journal, 32,* 243–260.

Harvey, K., Burns, T., Fiander, M., Huxley, P., Manley, C., & Fahy, T. (2002). The effect of intensive case management on the relatives of patients with severe mental illness. *Psychiatric Services, 53,* 1580–1585.

Henly, J. R., Danziger, S. K., & Offer, S. (2005). The contribution of social support to the material well-being of low-income families. *Journal of Marriage & Family, 67,* 122–140.

Hill, R. (1949). *Families under stress.* New York: Harper & Row.

Hooley, J. M., & Parker, H. A. (2006). Measuring expressed emotion: An evaluation of the shortcuts. *Journal of Family Psychology, 20,* 386–396.

Horwitz, A. V., & Reinhard, S. C. (1995). Ethnic differences in caregiving duties and burdens among parents and siblings of persons with severe mental illnesses. *Journal of Health and Social Behavior, 36,* 138–150.

Horwitz, A. V., Reinhard, S. C., & Howell-White, S. (1996). Caregiving as reciprocal exchange in families with seriously mentally ill members. *Journal of Health and Social Behavior, 37,* 149–162.

Hudson, C. G. (2005). Socioeconomic status and mental illness: Tests of the social causation and selection hypotheses. *American Journal of Orthopsychiatry, 75,* 3–18.

Jaffee, K. D., Liu, G. C., Canty-Mitchell, J., Qi, R. A., Austin, J., & Swigonski, N. (2005). Race, urban community stressors, and behavioral and emotional problems of children with special health care needs. *Psychiatric Services, 56,* 63–69.

Johnson, E. D. (1998). The effect of family functioning and family sense of competence on people with mental illness. *Family Relations, 47,* 443–451.

Johnson, E. D. (2000). Differences among families coping with serious mental illness: A qualitative analysis. *American Journal of Orthopsychiatry, 70,* 126–134.

Johnson, E. D. (2001). The partnership model: Working with families of people with serious mental illness. In M. MacFarlane (Ed.), *Family therapy and mental health: Innovations in theory and practice* (pp. 27–53). Binghamton, NY: Haworth Press.

Johnson, E. D. (2004a). How family members of the mentally ill view mental health professionals: A focused ethnography. In A. R. Roberts & K. Yeager (Eds.), *Evidence-based practice manual: Research and outcome measures in health and human Services* (pp. 721–727). New York: Oxford University Press.

Johnson, E. D. (2004b). The role of families in buffering stress in persons with mental illness: A correlational study. In A. R. Roberts & K. Yeager (Eds.), *Evidence-based practice manual: Research and outcome measures in health and human services* (pp. 844–857). New York: Oxford University Press.

Kealey, E. M. (2005). Variations in the experience of schizophrenia: A cross-cultural review. *Journal of Social Work Research and Evaluation, 6,* 47–56.

Kobasa, S. C. (1979). Stressful life events, personality, and health: An inquiry into hardiness. *Journal of Personality and Social Psychology, 37,* 1–11.

Kuipers, E. (2006). Family interventions in schizophrenia: Evidence for efficacy and proposed mechanisms of change. *Journal of Family Therapy, 28,* 73–80.

Kuipers, E., Bebbington, P., Dunn, G., Fowler, D., Freeman, D., Watson, P., et al. (2006). Influence of career expressed emotion and affect on relapse in non-affective psychosis. *British Journal of Psychiatry, 188,* 173–179.

Kymalainen, J. A., Weisman, A. G., Resales, G. A., & Armesto, J. C. (2006). Ethnicity, expressed emotion, and communication deviance in family members of patients with schizophrenia. *Journal of Nervous and Mental Disease, 194,* 391–396.

Link, B. G., Struening, E. L., Neese-Todd, S., Asmussen, S., & Phelan, J. C. (2001). Stigma as a barrier to recovery: The consequences of stigma for the self-esteem of people with mental illnesses. *Psychiatric Services, 52,* 1621–1626.

Lobban, F., Barrowclough, C., & Jones, S. (2006). Does expressed emotion need to be understood within a more systemic framework? An examination of discrepancies in appraisals between patients diagnosed with schizophrenia and their relatives. *Social Psychiatry and Psychiatric Epidemiology, 41,* 50–55.

Marsh, D. T. (2001). *A family-focused approach to serious mental illness: Empirically supported interventions.* Sarasota, FL: Professional Resource Press.

Marsh, D. T., Lefley, H. P., Evans-Rhodes, D., Ansell, V. I., & Doerzbacher, B. M. (1996). The family experience of mental illness: Evidence of resilience. *Psychiatric Rehabilitation Journal, 20,* 3–12.

Marshall, T., & Solomon, P. (2004). Provider contact with families of adults with severe mental illness: Taking a closer look. *Family Process, 43,* 209–216.

McCubbin, H. I., & McCubbin, M. A. (1988). Typologies of resilient families: Emerging roles of social class and ethnicity. *Family Relations, 37,* 247–254.

McCubbin, H. I., & Patterson, J. M. (1983). The family stress process: The double ABCX model of adjustment and adaptation. In H. I. McCubbin, M. B. Sussman, & J. M. Patterson (Eds.), *Social stress and the family* (pp.7–38). New York: Haworth Press.

McCubbin, H. I., Thompson, E. A., Thompson, A. I., & Fromer, J. E. (Eds.). (1998). *Stress, coping, and health in families.* Thousand Oaks, CA: Sage.

McFarlane, W. R., Lukens, E. P., Link, B., Dushay, R., Deakins, S. A., Newmark, M., et al. (1995). Multiple-family groups and psychoeducation in the treatment of schizophrenia. *Archives of General Psychiatry, 52,* 679–687.

McKay, M. M., Gonzales, J. J., Stone, S., Ryland, D., & Kohner, K. (1995). Multiple family therapy groups: A responsive intervention model for inner city families. *Social Work with Groups, 18,* 41–56.

McLeod, J. D., & Kessler, R. C. (1990). Socioeconomic differences in vulnerability to undesirable life events. *Journal of Health and Social Behavior, 31,* 162–172.

McLeod, J. D., & Owens, T. J. (2004). Psychological well-being in the early life course: Variations by socioeconomic status, gender, and race/ethnicity. *Social Psychology Quarterly, 67,* 257–278.

Miech, R. A., Caspi, A., Moffitt, T. E., Wright, B., & Silva, P. A. (1999). Low socioeconomic status and mental disorders: A longitudinal study of selection and causation during young adulthood. *American Journal of Sociology, 104,* 1097–1129.

Mirowsky, J., & Ross, C. E. (1990). Control or defense? Depression and the sense of control over good and bad outcomes. *Journal of Health and Social Behavior, 31,* 71–86.

Mueser, K. T., Corrigan, P. W., Hilton, D. W., Tanzman, B., & Schaub, A. (2002). Illness management and recovery: A review of the research. *Psychiatric Services, 53,* 1272–1284.

Munk, J. P., & Mortensen, P. B. (1992). Social outcome in schizophrenia: A 13-year follow-up. *Social Psychiatry & Psychiatric Epidemiology, 27,* 129–134.

Olson, D. H., McCubbin, H. I., Barnes, H., Larsen, A., Muxen, M., & Wilson, M. (1985). *Family Inventories,* (Rev. ed.). St. Paul: Family Social Science, University of Minnesota.

Pai, S., & Kapur, R. L. (1981). The burden on the family of a psychiatric patient: Development of an interview schedule. *British Journal of Psychiatry, 138,* 332–335.

Perlick, D. A., Rosenheck, R. A., Clarkin, J. F., Maciejewski, P. K., Sirey, J., Struening, E., et al. (2004). Impact of family burden and affective response on clinical outcome among patients with bipolar disorder. *Psychiatric Services, 55,* 1029–1035.

Perlick, D. A., Rosenheck, R. A., Kaczynski, R., Swartz, M. S., Canive, J. M., & Lieberman, J. A. (2006). Components and correlates of family burden in schizophrenia. *Psychiatric Services, 57,* 1117–1125.

Pitschel-Walz, G., Leucht, S., & Bauml, J. (2001). The effect of family interventions on relapse and rehospitalization in schizophrenia: A meta-analysis. *Schizophrenia Bulletin, 27,* 73–92.

Pollio, D. E., North, C. S., Reid, D. L., Miletic, M. M., & Mcclendon, J. R. (2006). Living with severe mental illness—what families and friends must know: Evaluation of a one-day psychoeducation workshop. *Social Work, 51,* 31–38.

Pruchno, R., Patrick, J. H., & Burant, C. J. (1997). African American and white mothers of adults with chronic disabilities: Caregiving burden and satisfaction. *Family Relations, 46,* 335–346.

Rank, M. R. (2001). The effect of poverty on America's families: Assessing our research knowledge. *Journal of Family Issues, 22,* 882–903.

Reinares, M., Vieta, E., Colom, F., Martínez-Arán, A., Torrent, C., Comes, M., et al. (2006). What really matters to bipolar patients' caregivers: Sources of family burden. *Journal of Affective Disorders, 94,* 157–163.

Ritsher, J., Warner, E. B., Johnson, J. G., & Dohrenwend, B. P. (2001). Intergenerational longitudinal study of social class and depression: A test of social causation and social selection models. *British Journal of Psychiatry, 178,* s84–s90.

Rojano, R. (2004). The practice of community family therapy. *Family Process, 43,* 59–77.

Rosenfarb, I. S., Bellack, A. S., & Aziz, N. (2006a). A sociocultural stress, appraisal, and coping model of subjective burden and family attitudes toward patients with schizophrenia. *Journal of Abnormal Psychology, 115,* 157–165.

Rosenfarb, I. S., Bellack, A. S., & Aziz, N. (2006b). Family interactions and the course of schizophrenia in African American and White patients. *Journal of Abnormal Psychology, 115,* 112–120.

Seccombe, K. (2000). Families in poverty in the 1990s. Trends, causes, consequences, and lessons learned. *Journal of Marriage & the Family, 62,* 1094–1113.

Shumway, M., Saunders, T., Shern, D., Pines, E., Downs, A., Burbine, T., et al. (2003). Preferences for schizophrenia treatment outcomes among public policy makers, consumers, families, and providers. *Psychiatric Services, 54,* 1124–1128.

Smith, G. C. (2003). Patterns and predictors of service use and unmet needs among aging families of adults with severe mental illness. *Psychiatric Services, 54,* 871–877.

Solomon, P., & Draine, J. (1995). Subjective burden among family members of mentally ill adults: Relation to stress, coping, and adaptation. *American Journal of Orthopsychiatry, 65,* 419–427.

Solomon, P., Draine, J., Mannion, E., & Meisel, M. (1997). Effectiveness of two models of brief family education: Retention of gains by family members of adults with serious mental illness. *American Journal of Orthopsychiatry, 67,* 177–186.

Song, L. Y., Biegel, D. E., & Milligan, S. E. (1997). Predictors of depressive symptomatology among lower social class caregivers of persons with chronic mental illness. *Community Mental Health Journal, 33,* 269–286.

Stueve, A., Vine, P., & Struening, E. L. (1997). Perceived burden among caregivers of adults with serious mental illness: Comparison of black, Hispanic, and white families. *American Journal of Orthopsychiatry, 67,* 199–209.

Turner, R. J., & Lloyd, D. A. (1995). Lifetime traumas and mental health: The significance of cumulative adversity. *Journal of Health and Social Behavior, 36,* 360–376.

Wahl, O. F. (1999). Mental health consumers' experience of stigma. *Schizophrenia Bulletin, 25,* 467–478.

Walsh, F. (1996). The concept of family resilience: Crisis and challenge. *Family Process, 35,* 261–281.

Ware, N. C., Tugenberg, T., & Dickey, B. (2004). Practitioner relationships and quality of care for low-income persons with serious mental illness. *Psychiatric Services, 55,* 555–559.

Weich, S., & Lewis, G. (1998). Poverty, unemployment, and common mental disorders: Population based cohort study. *British Medical Journal, 317,* 115–119.

# CHAPTER 15

# Addiction and Medicaid

## A Prairie Sighting of Califano's "Elephant in the Living Room of American Society" and State Budgets

HARVEY H. HILLIN

In a survey of state budget directors conducted in 2001, former Secretary of Health and Human Services Joseph A. Califano, Jr., declared, "Substance abuse and addiction is the *elephant in the living room* of American society." No one was willing to seriously acknowledge the presence of the beast, much less to leave a trail of peanuts to coax it out of the living room. Califano goes on to say,

> Governors who want to curb child abuse, teen pregnancy, and domestic violence and further reduce welfare roles, must face up to this reality: unless they prevent and treat alcohol and drug abuse and addiction, their other well-intentioned efforts are doomed.
>
> Substance abuse is one of the largest state expenditures, but it is hidden in departments, categories, and services that do not bear the *substance abuse* or *addiction* label.

A 3-year study involving more than 40 researchers (funded by Robert Wood Johnson Foundation, Starr Foundation, Abercrombie Foundation, Primerica Financial Services, Carnegie Corporation of New York, National Institute on Drug Abuse, and National Institute on Alcohol Abuse and Alcoholism), surveying 45 states found addiction-related expenses consumed about 13% ($81.3 billion) of state budgets (total state resources spent) in 1998 ($453.5 billion). The study also found that on a per capita basis, each American spends $277 per year in state taxes to deal with the fallout from addiction and about $10 per year for treatment or prevention of addiction. This figure does not include the federal government costs in Medicare, Medicaid, private sector costs to employers, nor the incalculable toll of substance abuse and addiction on individuals and families. Of each substance abuse–related dollar spent by Americans, 96 cents is spent on the aftermath of addiction and 4 cents is used for prevention or treatment.

Substance abuse and addiction expenditures break down in the United States specifically as follows:

- 77% of justice spending ($30.7 billion for incarceration, probation, parole, juvenile justice and criminal court costs) at 6.3% of state budgets
- 25% of health spending
- 32% of child/family assistance
- 31% of mental health and developmental disabilities
- 25% of public safety
- 10% of education spending ($16.5 billion of $165 billion, which is 26% of state budgets)

In 1997, the Substance Abuse and Mental Health Services Administration (SAMHSA) of the U.S. Department of Health and Human Services estimated the cost of substance abuse treatment to be $276 billion (SAMHSA, 1997). And because estimates of addiction-related costs are often commingled with mental health costs, this estimate may be low. With the passage of the Mental Health Parity Act of 1996 (which does not apply to drug and alcohol abuse benefits), there is continual dislocation of patient care from private to public funding to deal with addiction (Cartwright, 1999).

## IN CONTEXT OF
## MEDICAID SPENDING

Medicaid provides health-care financing (including long-term care) for more than 58 million people in the United States (surpassing Medicare enrollment at 42 million) with greater than $300 billion in annual expenditures (Congressional Budget Office, 2005). As the largest health insurer, Medicaid is an integral element of the health-care system in all states. According to the National Association of State Budget Officers, health-care spending is about 17% (projected to be 24% by 2007) of state general fund spending, and comes

second only to education spending as a proportion of the total state budget (2002). As Medicaid goes, so goes the health-care infrastructure of the state. Medicaid is arguably one of the oldest examples of privatization in state government, and it is certainly the costliest. For states, Medicaid spending growth is driven by many factors beyond control (Smith & Moody, 2005). After 5 years of double-digit increases in overall health-care expenses, the rise has slowed to about 8% in 2006 (Perrin, 2005). Moreover, most private sector strategies to contain health-care costs (premiums, deductibles, co-pays, drops in coverage) are not available to Medicaid (Smith, 2005). Moreover, deep cuts in state Medicaid spending actually create economic problems for states because one dollar cut in state funds also loses one to three additional dollars in federal matching funds (Ku & Broadus, 2003).

The states still bear most addiction-related costs (Scanlon, 2002), and there is strong interaction with Medicaid costs. Evidence indicates that budgetary woes are shrinking funding despite growth in the need for services with increasing prevalence of addiction problems.

Prevalence of addiction issues in welfare cases are difficult to estimate (Frank, McGuire, Regeir, Manderscheid, & Woodward, 1994) and range from 6.6% to 37% of temporary assistance to needy family beneficiaries alone, which does not include child protection, juvenile justice, or disability-related costs (Jayakody, Danziger, & Pollack, 2000). In a 10-state study of Medicaid expenses, about one-third of high cost outliers (the top 10%) are users of mental health or substance abuse services (Buck, Teich, & Miller, 2003). There is little controversy that prevalence of addiction is higher among persons receiving public assistance than in the general population (Olson & Pavetti, 1996), and this fact was partially responsible for Congress passing the Personal Responsibility and Work Opportunity Reconciliation Act, which terminated addiction-related disability benefits.

Medicaid spending rose 25% from federal fiscal year 2000 to 2002 ($205.8 billion to $257.6 billion), which was actually lower than the increase in national per-person health-care spending or the increase in private health insurance premiums (Holahan & Bruen, 2003). And total health-care costs (private and especially employer-based health insurance rates) in the country rose at an even faster rate (Smith et al., 2004). Medicaid is a major payer for prescription drugs, which have risen about 15% annually for several years. Medicaid costs double each 5 to 6 years, and many of those cost increases are pharmacy driven. In Kansas Medicaid, hospitalization costs did not grow significantly in the decade of the 1990s because Kansas initiated prior authorization screening for psychiatric and substance abuse cases (which was a major driver of escalating Medicaid hospitalization costs in the 1980s), arresting the state's double-digit annual increases that took place in the previous decade (Hillin, 1989).

A small percentage of cases can drive a large percentage of costs in health-care reimbursement (Sharpe, 1999). In Medicaid, children and adults without disability (73%) account for only 32% of total expenditures (Liska, 1997). Addiction is almost always comorbid with mood symptoms (such as depression and anxiety) typically treated in psychiatric settings, and persistent substance abusers (particularly adolescents and young adults) have psychiatric hospitalization at twice the rate of others (Safer, 1987). Kansas parallels national mental health (which includes substance abuse) data, where 7% of consumers account for 53% of physician contacts and 64% of acute psychiatric bed days, in addition to a large proportion of emergency room visits.

## OTHER SOCIETAL CONSEQUENCES OF ADDICTION

A brief review of the extensive addiction and societal consequences literature proved overwhelming. About one-third of persons presenting for emergency psychiatric services are intoxicated with alcohol or other drugs (Breslow, Klinger, & Erickson, 1996; Rabinowitz et al., 1998). Marijuana use is widespread among persons with psychosis (Sembhi & Lee, 1999). High rates of substance abuse are comorbid with conduct disorders (Grilo, Becker, Fehon, Edell, & McGlashan, 1996; Young et al., 1995), suicide ideation (Alaja, Seppa, & Sillanaukee, 1999), public disruptions involving police referrals or involuntary referral (Schmidt, 1995), schizophrenia, bipolar disorders, personality disorders (Menezes et al., 1996; Piazza, 1996; RachBeisel, Dixon, & Gearon, 1999), and high rates of revolving door readmissions to inpatient care (Leon, Lyons, Christopher, & Miller, 1998). Testing at jails for all juvenile arrestees in the District of Columbia in 1997 (District of Columbia Pretrial Services Agency) showed 74% tested positive for marijuana (Shaffer, 1997), confirming similar upsurge data for the early 1990s by the National Institute of Justice Arrestee Drug Abuse Monitoring Program (ADAM), which averaged about 66% (Golub & Johnson, 2001).

There are five recent major national reports on challenges to the addictions and child welfare systems (Children's Defense Fund, 1998; General Accounting Office, 1998; Reid, Macchetto, & Foster, 1999; SAMHSA, 1999; Young, Gardner, & Dennis, 1998). A Columbia University survey of 915 child welfare professionals across the country finds that 80% said substance abuse is involved in three of four cases of child maltreatment (Reid et al., 1999). High-quality treatment alternatives are in short supply and face endangered or reduced funding.

There is little common knowledge, dialogue, or interdisciplinary training between child protection and addiction treatment systems. Substance abuse is also highly correlated with instances of abuse or neglect that drive children to out-of-home foster placement, but much controversy exists about how to successfully intervene in such situations in ways that promote recovery or family reunification (Department of Health and Human Services, 1999). In 2000, approximately 14 million Americans (6.3% of the population over age 12) used an illicit drug at least monthly (SAMHSA, 2000). The negative impact for both families and society as a whole is incalculable.

About 18% of persons with active addiction actually seek treatment (Green-Hennessy, 2002). However, more than four of five do not. This finding proved significant in the current review of Medicaid expenses.

## SOCIETAL CONSEQUENCES: TWO EXAMPLE DRUGS

### Alcohol

More than 130,000 deaths annually in the United States can be attributed to excessive alcohol consumption. The American Medical Association considers alcohol the third leading cause of preventable mortality in America after tobacco and diet-related patterns (McGinnis & Foege, 1993). About 25% of alcohol-related deaths are a result of drunk driving. Half of all boating fatalities involve alcohol intoxication (U.S. Coast Guard, 1994). Alcohol-related homicide accounts for 11% of the annual alcohol-related death total, and suicide accounts for 8%. The suicide rate for alcoholics is 55 times that of the general population. Comorbid alcoholism and depression are virtually always considerations in planning treatment and recovery and dominate the mental health literature (Thase, Salloum, & Cornelius, 2001).

More than 60 diseases have direct causal links to alcoholism (Gutjahr, Gmel, & Rehm, 2001). Several cancers of the gastrointestinal tract (including the esophagus, larynx, and oral cavity) are directly attributable to alcohol and comprise about 17% of annual alcohol-related deaths. About 9% of alcohol-related deaths are a result of stroke. Ninety-five percent of all cirrhosis deaths are alcohol related, which accounts for 18% of alcohol-related deaths (usually affecting people between 55 and 64 years old). Early heavy drinking can produce anemia, hypoglycemia, gastritis (often the first medical complaint in outpatient primary care), insomnia, lowered immune function, neuritis, pancreatitis, fatty liver, and hypertension. By the 1950s, alcoholism, which damages every major organ system, had replaced syphilis as the "great imitator" of other diseases.

The rate of traffic deaths (per 100,000 population) has gradually decreased since 1980, primarily because of improvements in traffic safety like seat belts, automotive engineering, air bags, and barriers between lanes on divided roadways, but perhaps also to more structured use of driving under the influence (DUI) programs (Doyle, 1996). Other mortality and morbidity data attributable to alcohol include 25% of all hospital visits (SAMHSA, 1993), 20% of suicide victims (National Institute on Alcoholism and Alcohol Abuse [NIAAA], 1993b), 40% of industrial fatalities and injuries (Bernstein & Mahoney, 1989), 65% of all cases of pancreatitis (NIAAA, 1993b), and increased risk for cancer (especially in the digestive tract, liver, breast, and colon). Alcohol is found in the victim, offender, or both in half of all homicides, serious assaults, sex crimes, robberies, and incidents of domestic violence (NIAAA, 1993a).

Approximately 12,000 babies with fetal alcohol syndrome (FAS) are born each year (SAMHSA, 1993), and alcohol is the leading known preventable cause of mental retardation in the Western world (Cook, Petersen, & Moore, 1990). Alcohol intoxication is a factor in the top four causes (motor vehicle crashes, unintentional injuries, homicide, and suicide) of youth deaths (Kann et al., 1998). Of nearly one million children found to be substantiated victims of abuse and neglect, at least 50% had chemically involved caregivers (Child Welfare League of America, 1997).

## Tobacco

The suspicion of a link between smoking and heart disease was first noticed in 1904 because intermittent claudication (pain in the calf of the leg caused by temporary narrowing of an artery) was a condition that appeared mostly in smokers. By 1934, epidemiological research showed increases in coronary heart disease (CHD) associated with increases in smoking after World War I (tobacco was a ration given free to American soldiers). In the 1950s, epidemiological evidence began to correlate lung cancer and smoking. When the *Reader's Digest* published "Cancer by the Carton" in 1952 (Norr, 1952), there was a drop in tobacco sales followed by introduction of the filter tip cigarette. By 1957, Surgeon General Leroy E. Burney reported excessive smoking among factors in lung cancer. On January 11, 1964, Surgeon General Luther E. Terry's advisory committee released "On Smoking and Health," which identified tobacco as addictive and carcinogenic. Also in 1964, tobacco industry funded research found nicotine to be addictive, but this information was withheld for another 30 years. In 1966, the Cigarette Labeling and Advertising Act took effect requiring warning labels on cigarette packaging. In 1967, Surgeon General William H. Stewart's report concluded smoking is the principal cause of lung cancer. In 1970, Congress strengthened the cigarette warning label act, and in 1971, TV and radio ads for cigarettes were banned. In 1973, the Civil Aeronautics Board required no-smoking sections on commercial flights, and in 1975, cigarettes were discontinued in military rations (tobacco companies knew that *donated smokes* in late adolescence and early adulthood guaranteed a paying customer base because of addiction).

In 1986, Surgeon General C. Everett Koop reported on exposure to second-hand smoke and, in 1988, declared cigarettes addictive again, as had his predecessors. In 1990, a federal ban on smoking on inner city buses and on flights lasting less than 6 hours was established. Then, in 1993, the Environmental Protection Agency identified second-hand smoke as a substantial health risk, and smoking was banned in the White House. In 1997, the attorneys general for Louisiana, Kansas, and several dozen other states in class-action lawsuit gained a settlement with the tobacco industry to reclaim billions of state Medicaid health-care costs attributed to smoking (not including 440,000 smoking-related deaths annually, and 30% of all cancer-related deaths), although most of these funds were plundered to other areas in most state budgets.

Tobacco is now responsible for one in five deaths in America, and more than 46 million Americans are smokers. Other significant findings about tobacco, illness, and other costs by the Centers for Disease Control (CDC), released by Dr. David Fleming (Acting CDC Director) on April 11, 2002 (McClam, 2002), follow:

- Each pack of cigarettes sold in America generates $7.18 in health-care costs and lost productivity.
- Americans buy about 22 billion packs of cigarettes annually, at an average cost of $2.92 in 1999.
- Nearly a half million Americans lose lives annually because of smoking-related illnesses.
- Smoking shortens the life of men by 13 years, and of women by 14.5 years.
- Smoking during pregnancy results in about 1,000 infant deaths per year.

Of drug dependencies comorbid with major mental illnesses (particularly depression, schizophrenia, and attention deficit hyperactivity disorder), nicotine (alone or in combination with alcohol, cannabis, and caffeine) is perhaps the most predominant (Breslau, 1995; Coger, Moe, & Serafetinides, 1996; Covey, Glassman, & Stetner, 1998; Dalack, Becks, Hill, Pomerleau, & Meador-Woodruff, 1999; Dursin & Kutcher, 1999; Fergussun, Lynskey, & Horwood, 1996; Hamera, Schneider, & Deviney, 1995; Kandel, Huang, & Davies, 2001; Rosen, Chase, & Dyson, 1999; Van Ammers, Sellman, & Mulder, 1997; Van Dongen, 1999). A consistent causal link exists from tobacco smoking to depressed mood in childhood and adolescence, but not vice versa (Wu & Anthony, 1999). Smoking is the horse before the depression cart. Moreover, it is rare to find a person with schizophrenia or bipolar disorder who is not also a tobacco smoker. Smoking costs account for about 6 to 8% of health-care expense in the United States (Warner, Hodgson, & Carroll, 1999).

About 46 million Americans smoke tobacco. Lifetime prevalence of nicotine dependence is found in 24% of the smoking population. The likelihood of a person becoming a lifetime smoker is highest for those who began smoking at or before age 16, after which the risk declines during the next 7 years (Breslau, Johnson, Hiripi, & Kessler, 2001). As David Kessler (former commissioner, Food and Drug Administration) suggested, nicotine addiction is a chronic disease with a pediatric onset (Gilpin & Ballin, 1996), and more than 3 million children in the United States now are smokers. Nearly a thousand of the 3,000 children who start smoking each day will die from a smoking-related disease. Smoking by American adolescents increased 78% from 1988 to 1996 (Kendell, 2000). In addition to correlations with mental health problems, delinquency, crossover to other addictive drugs in the stimulant class, and links to other physical health problems, smoking is highly correlated with poverty. In other words, the poorer one is, the higher the probability that one is also a smoker. Of drug-related Medicaid reimbursed

hospital care in the United States, cigarette smoking and illicit drug use count for 41% each of the total cost, followed by alcohol use at 18% (Fox, Merrill, Chang, & Califano, 1995). The CDC estimates 50 billion dollars was spent in 1993 for medical costs that were smoking related.

The average smoker in the United States will spend between $1,500 and $2,000 annually for cigarettes. These costs pale in significance when considering more than 430,000 annual smoking-related deaths (mostly from heart disease at roughly 36% of cases, and lung diseases like emphysema [Aubry, Wright, & Myers, 2000] and lung cancer, where smoking accounts for 86% of all cases), and 60 billion dollars in annual related health-care costs. Smoking and tobacco use will claim the lives of more than 500 million people worldwide (Henningfield, Fant, Gitchell, & Shiffman, 2000). The cost effectiveness of smoking cessation treatment is one of the highest in all of medicine (Harris, Schauffler, Milstein, Powers, & Hopkins, 2001).

## REVIEW OF KANSAS MEDICAID DATA

In a retrospective exploratory study of claims payments, several relevant questions occur with regard to the visible compared with the invisible costs of addiction as a portion of Kansas Medicaid expenses.

1. What are the directly identifiable Medicaid expenditures for a cohort of persons diagnosed with substance abuse disorders for a 4-year period (from 2000 through 2003), and is there a trend in expenses or volume, compared with the cohort of all other Medicaid recipients with medical claims?

2. What is the link between some known substance abuse–related conditions (like cirrhosis), Medicaid expenses, and the list of persons who got a substance abuse

diagnosis and actually got treatment for substance abuse in the same time frame? In simpler words, what is the *hit* rate for people with substance abuse problems actually getting treatment for substance abuse disorders?

Kansas Medicaid paid claims were examined for 4 years (calendar 2000–2003) to identify those clients who were treated directly for substance abuse–related diagnoses, using International Classification of Diseases (ICD–9th Revision) in the following ranges within the mental disorders nomenclature (which cross reference directly to the American Psychiatric Association's *Diagnostic and Statistical Manual,* 4th Revision, 1999):

> Alcoholic and drug-related psychoses: –291.0 through 292.9

> Acute alcohol intoxication through other mixed or unspecified drug abuse: –303.0 through 305.9

*Research Question #1: Diagnosed Substance Abuse Disorders and Impact on Medicaid.* Diagnosed substance abuse disorders would seem to be the most obvious place to look for the impact of substance abuse on Medicaid costs. In a 4-year period, a little more than 18 thousand (18,067) Kansas Medicaid clients met the criteria for a diagnosed substance abuse disorder. For this substance abuse diagnosis group, all medical claims were captured for those same years in three major categories: (1) pharmacy; (2) hospital and long-term care

(including nursing home); and (3) all other costs, such as physician and other professional charges, outpatient expenses, in Tables 15.1 and 15.2.

Total Medicaid costs trended upward each of the first 3 years, whereas there was a drop in 2003 for substance abuse group's medical costs (Table 15.3). There were similar upward trends in the percentage of substance abusers as a proportion of Medicaid clientele with costs, and in claims volume (Tables 15.4 and 15.5). Globally, there are three general cost drivers in such medical coverage programs. Those are (1) caseload increases (clients, covered lives), (2) utilization increases, and (3) price increases. Investigation revealed the most likely explanation for the downturn in medical costs for the substance abuse group was a mandate by the legislature to stop paying for transplants for adults in Medicaid (Kansas following the previous policy decisions of the state of Oregon in this case). These costly procedures usually included one or more liver transplants, so that even a few transplants had considerable effect on the arithmetic average (mean), as well as total costs for the cohort. The need for a liver transplant is quite often a result of damage to the liver from lifestyle decisions in relation to the active presence of addiction.

There was no comparable drop in the caseload of persons (total Medicaid beneficiaries and substance abuse group) served in Kansas in that same time frame. The portion of substance abusers served, however, did drop. In answer to research question one,

**Table 15.1**    Four-Year Claims by Cohort Group

| All Dollars | 2000 | 2001 | 2002 | 2003 |
|---|---|---|---|---|
| Pharmacy | $170,290,589 | $208,811,710 | $207,547,723 | $266,509,913 |
| Hospital/LTC | $742,743,514 | $716,899,373 | $713,393,715 | $662,750,603 |
| Physician/OutPt | $537,454,402 | $592,995,888 | $653,015,505 | $682,014,770 |
|  | $1,450,490,505 | $1,518,708,972 | $1,573,958,945 | $1,611,277,289 |

**Table 15.2**    Addiction

| Group | 2000 | 2001 | 2002 | 2003 |
|---|---|---|---|---|
| Pharmacy | $18,089,455 | $22,314,133 | $25,120,699 | $28,951,898 |
| Hospital/LTC | $42,376,268 | $41,631,340 | $45,398,061 | $37,197,026 |
| Physician/OutPt | $40,586,510 | $50,906,565 | $59,623,648 | $59,836,543 |
|  | $101,052,233 | $114,852,039 | $130,142,407 | $125,985,466 |
| Addiction % Costs | 6.97% | 7.56% | 8.27% | 7.82% |

**Table 15.3**    Average Annual Cost per Cohort

| Year | 2000 | 2001 | 2002 | 2003 |
|---|---|---|---|---|
| Controls | $7,259 | $7,448 | $12,262 | $6,733 |
| Addiction Group | $7,951 | $8,668 | $11,082 | $9,195 |

**Table 15.4**    Four-Year Caseload (Persons) by Cohort Group

| All Medicaid | 2000 | 2001 | 2002 | 2003 |
|---|---|---|---|---|
| Pharmacy | 146,522 | 160,051 | 122,620 | 176,508 |
| Hospital | 119,378 | 121,860 | 125,827 | 126,114 |
| Physician/Outpt | 199,829 | 203,915 | 128,360 | 239,315 |

**Table 15.5**    Substance Abuse by Cohort Group

| Substance Abuse Group | 2000 | 2001 | 2002 | 2003 |
|---|---|---|---|---|
| Pharmacy | 10,553 | 10,962 | 10,253 | 10,509 |
| Hospital/LTC | 8,542 | 8,988 | 8,962 | 8,471 |
| Physician/OutPt | 12,710 | 13,250 | 11,744 | 13,702 |
| Caseload % | 6.36% | 6.50% | 9.15% | 5.73% |

there was a modest increase of diagnosed and treated substance abuse over 4 years of Medicaid expenditures, comprising just under 7% of total costs in 2000 to about 8% of costs by 2003. However, national estimates of the costs to Medicaid for substance abuse and addiction are 30%. In other words, about 23% of those costs are not readily evident in claims data. Patients are treated for the physical sequels of addiction, rather than addiction itself. This also means this population is probably underdiagnosed and undertreated, which has health consequences for the addiction group, budget implications for government, and familial and societal consequences. Moreover, the average annual costs of the addiction group cohorts was trending upward until the year cost containment measures for transplants (2002) were implemented. Average costs for the addiction cohort climbed again in 2003, and their costs again exceeded all other recipients (controls).

*Research Question #2. Substance Abuse –Related Health Problems and Substance Abuse Treatment.* First, for persons with cirrhosis (known to be highly substance abuse–related) how many got addiction treatment? Of the 6,941 persons treated for cirrhosis in Kansas Medicaid, just less than one in five (1,359 or 19.5%) also got treatment for addiction. Conversely, just more than four out of five did *not* get referral or treatment. Does this mean a person can present for care, with a hardened liver the "size of an elephant's" and full-blown cirrhosis, and *not* get diagnosis and treatment referral for addiction? The data show that this is likely the case, and more specifically: more than four out of five times.

Second, for persons with esophageal diseases known to correlate highly with tobacco and alcohol use (esophagitis, reflux), how many got addiction treatment? Of 19,435 persons treated, 1,834 (10%) also got addiction treatment in that time frame. Conversely, 9 of 10 did not.

Much of the other budgetary research revealed primitive and fragmented systems for tracking expenses in relation to substance abuse, although there was general agreement among informants in state government that the problem pervades across systems.

## DISCUSSION

From this review of state budgets, Medicaid, and addiction-related spending, for every Medicaid dollar directly attributed to addiction-related disease, about four additional dollars are not identified. In the Kansas state budget, the visible part of the substance abuse and addiction elephant only represents 6.9% to 8% of the total costs, consistent with national data. The less-visible portion approaches one-third of total costs. There is support for the idea that substance abuse may likely be a significant cost driver in Medicaid, along with the overall increases in health-care costs.

Underdiagnosis of addiction is a second major finding. This finding led to further review of the literature on diagnosing habits of health-care professionals with regard to addiction. Indeed, inadequate preparation of physicians to diagnose or treat addiction means that a large percentage of persons with addiction go undiagnosed and untreated (Frost-Pineda, Van Susteren, & Gold, 2004; Miller, Sheppard, Colenda, & Magen, 2001; Moore & Malitz, 1986; Saitz, Mulvey, Plough, & Samet, 1997; Waller & Casey, 1990)—the possible exception to this underdiagnosis being when a patient is female and pregnant, when about 87% of primary care physicians are most vigilant about screening for substance abuse (Califano, 2000). Studies of the diagnosing habits of health professionals consistently find that the diagnosis of alcohol or drug abuse or dependence is routinely underused. Emergency room physicians miss more than half of the alcoholics they see in practice (Solomon, Vanga, Morgan, & Joseph, 1980). Primary care physicians will see more than one alcoholic a day who will not be properly diagnosed (Milhorn, 1988; Smith, 1983; Spickard, 1986; Ziring & Adler, 1991). Many physicians and nurses might consider attempts at further interventions in addictive diseases are a waste of time (McLellan, Lewis, O'Brien, & Kelber, 2000). Underdiagnosis, nonreferral, and lack of treatment can lead to dramatic health consequences for the individuals, families, and society.

In sum, confirmatory evidence indicates that the metaphoric "elephant" of substance abuse and addiction is alive and well in the living room of the Kansas Medicaid budget.

Former Secretary Califano's assertions are likely correct in citing that this is the case with other state budgets as well. Though part of the "elephant" stays covered up in departments, agencies, and services that do not bear the substance abuse or addiction label, the need to coax the costly and cumbersome animal out of the living room remains.

Rediscovery of fragmentation of government systems in relation to substance abuse is certainly not new or controversial. In that sense, state agencies mirror federal bureaus as "mini-me's." Substance abuse, mental health, public health, child welfare, education, and correctional systems are recognized as having different cultures, languages, funding streams, and methods. All view themselves as underfunded and fearful of cost shifting burdens. Advances in evidence-based practices during the past few decades present some unique opportunities.

Proportionately, why so few dollars are devoted to addiction treatment or prevention is beyond the scope of this chapter, but worthy of further consideration. Recognizing that some 40% of deaths are associated with behavior patterns that could be modified by preventive interventions (McGinnis & Foege, 1993; McGinnis, Williams-Russo, & Knickman, 2002), the case for more active public policy in dealing with such matters is apparent. The public health consequences, social consequences, toll on persons and families, and budgetary consequences are an overwhelming public burden.

## REGARDING FAMILIES AND POVERTY

The erosion and gradual disappearance of "intact" families in the United States has been a source of much academic and political debate for decades. Poverty has been with us for millennia, and has been rediscovered from time to time in the history of literature among several popular theoretical perspectives: (1) individual characteristics of the poor, (2) subcultures (more recently debates about the "underclass") as argued by Mead (1994) (3) structural or situational/circumstantial (political, economic, and geography to support livelihood), and (4) fatalism (Smith & Stone, 1989). In the politics of public policy debate, one's theory of poverty will predict policy preferences (liberals favoring the third theory, and conservatives divided along the lines of the first and second theories) (Schiller, 1989). The correlation of poverty and addiction is well established in the United States and many other "industrialized" societies. On a global scale, however, in many countries poverty (especially multigenerational poverty) does not correlate with use of intoxicants or addiction, with the exception of tobacco (Efroymson et al., 2001). Tobacco addiction brings a heavier burden on the poor (in Bangladesh, for instance) in both industrialized and non-industrialized countries alike. It might be unreasonable to suggest that addiction causes poverty. Addiction is spawned without respect for wealth or social class. Nevertheless, in the United States among working middle-class or upper-class families, addiction of a family member (especially one with parental responsibilities) can become an "off ramp" toward unemployment and poverty (as well as rejection by other family members, in the case of many homeless persons). Addiction in parents predicts poverty in children. Among already poor families, addiction rates are high. Moreover, the dislocation of families concurrent with addiction is well known. Based on strong correlation evidence in the literature, and in the data presented on health costs, it is more reasonable to assert that the two phenomena often are "seen together," with profoundly adverse effects on families, health care, and the economic well-being of the United States.

## REFERENCES

Alaja, R., Seppa, K., & Sillanaukee, P. (1999, May/June). Persistence of substance use related hospital utilization among psychiatric consultation patients. *Alcohol, 34*(3), 346–348.

American Psychiatric Association. (1999). *Diagnostic and statistical manual of mental disorders* (4th ed.). Washington, DC: Author.

Aubry, M. C., Wright, J. L., & Myers, J. L. (2000, March). The pathology of smoking related lung diseases. *Clinics in Chest Medicine, 21*(1), 11–35.

Bernstein M., & Mahoney, J. J. (1989). Management perspectives on alcoholism: The employer's stake in alcoholism treatment. *Occupational Medicine, 4*(2), 223–232.

Breslau, N. (1995, March). Psychiatric comorbidity of smoking and nicotine dependence. *Behavior Genetics, 25*(2), 95–101.

Breslau, N., Johnson, E. O., Hiripi, E., & Kessler, R. (2001, September). Nicotine dependence in the United States: Prevalence, trends and smoking persistence. *Archives of General Psychiatry, 58*(9), 810–816.

Breslow, R. E., Klinger, B. I., & Erickson, B. J. (1996, May). Acute intoxication and substance abuse among patients presenting to a psychiatric emergency service. *General Hospital Psychiatry, 18*(3), 183–191.

Buck, J. A., Teich, J. L., & Miller, K. (2003, September). Use of mental health and substance abuse services among high-cost Medicaid enrollees. *Administration and Policy in Mental Health, 31*(1), 3–14.

Califano, J. A., Jr. (2000, April 6). *Missed opportunity: National survey of primary care physicians and patients on substance abuse.* New York: National Center on Addiction and Substance Abuse at Columbia University.

Califano, J. A., Jr. (2001, January). *Shoveling up: The impact of substance abuse on state budgets.* New York: National Center on Addiction and Substance Abuse at Columbia University.

Cartwright, W. S. (1999). Cost of drug abuse to society. *Journal of Mental Health Policy and Economics, 2,* 133–134.

Children's Defense Fund. (1998). *Healing the whole family: A look at family care programs.* Washington, DC: Author.

Child Welfare League of America. (1997, February). Alcohol and other drug survey of state welfare agencies. Draft Report, Washington, DC, 1. Retrieved from www.cwla.org/programs/bhd/aod.htm

Congressional Budget Office. (2005, March). *An analysis of the President's Budgetary Proposals for Fiscal Year 2006* (Chapter 1, Table 1.4). Washington, DC: Author.

Coger, R. W., Moe, K. L., & Serafetinides, E. A. (1996, July–September). Attention deficit disorder in adults with nicotine dependence: Psychobiological factors in resistance to recovery? *Journal of Psychoactive Drugs, 28*(3), 229–240.

Cook, P. S., Petersen, R. C., & Moore, D. T. (1990). *Alcohol, tobacco and other drugs may harm the unborn* (Publication Number ADM 90-1711, p. 17). Rockville, MD: U.S. Department of Health and Human Services, Public Health Services, Alcohol, Drug Abuse and Mental Health Administration, Office for Substance Abuse Prevention.

Covey, L. S., Glassman, A. H., & Stetner, F. (1998). Cigarette smoking and major depression. *Journal of Addictive Diseases, 17*(1), 35–46.

Dalack, G. W., Becks, L., Hill, E., Pomerleau, O. F., & Meador-Woodruff, J. H. (1999, August). Nicotine withdrawal and psychiatric symptoms in cigarette smokers with schizophrenia. *Neuropsychopharmacology, 21*(2), 195–202.

Department of Health and Human Services. (1999). *Blending perspectives and building common ground: A report to the Congress on substance abuse and child protection.* Washington, DC: Author.

Doyle, R. (1996, December). Deaths caused by alcohol. *Scientific American, 275*(6), 30–31.

Dursin, S. M., & Kutcher, S. (1999, February). Smoking, nicotine and psychiatric disorders: Evidence for therapeutic role, controversies and implications for the future. *Medical Hypotheses, 52*(2), 101–109.

Efroymson, D., Ahmed, S., Townsend, J., Alam, S. M., Dey, A. R., Saha, R., et al. (2001) Hungry for tobacco: An analysis of the economic impact of tobacco consumption on the poor in Bangladesh. *Tobacco Control, 10,* 212–217.

Fergusson, D. M., Lynskey, M. T., & Horwood, L. J. (1996, November). Comorbidity between depressive disorders and nicotine dependence in a cohort of 16 year olds. *Archives of General Psychiatry, 53*(11), 1043–1047.

Fox, K., Merrill, J. C., Chang, H. H., & Califano, J. A., Jr. (1995, January). Estimating the costs of substance abuse to the Medicaid hospital care program. *American Journal of Public Health, 85*(1), 48–54.

Frank, R., McGuire, T., Regeir, D. A., Manderscheid, R., & Woodward, A. (1994). *Health care reform and financing of mental health services: Distributional consequences. Mental Health, U.S. Substance Abuse and Mental Health Services Administration* (DHHS, Publication SM 94–3000). Rockville, MD: Washington, DC: U.S. Government Printing Office.

Frost-Pineda, K., Van Susteren, T., & Gold, M. S. (2004). Are physicians and medical students prepared to educate patients about alcohol consumption? *Journal of Addictive Diseases, 23*(2), 1–13.

General Accounting Office. (1998, September). *Foster care: Agencies face challenges securing stable homes for children of substance abusers.* Washington, DC: Author.

Gilpin, B., & Ballin, S. (1996) Antidote for America's leading pediatric disease. *Circulation, 94,* 233.

Golub A., & Johnson, B. D. (2001, June 1). *Monitoring the marijuana upsurge with the DUF.ADAM arrestees, Final Report* (pp. 1–104). Washington, DC: National Institute of Justice.

Green-Hennessy, S. (2002, December). Factors associated with receipt of behavioral health services among persons with substance dependence. *Psychiatric Services, 53*(12), 1592–1598.

Grilo, C. M., Becker, D. F., Fehon, D. C., Edell, W. S., & McGlashan, T. H. (1996, July). Conduct disorder, substance use disorders, and coexisting conduct and substance use disorders in adolescent inpatients. *American Journal of Psychiatry, 153*(7), 914–920.

Gutjahr, E., Gmel, G., & Rehm, J. (2001, August). Relation between average alcohol consumption and disease: An overview. *European Addiction Research, 7*(3), 117–127.

Hamera, E., Schneider, J. K., & Deviney, S. (1995, September). Alcohol, cannabis, nicotine, and caffeine use & symptom distress in schizophrenia. *Journal of Nervous and Mental Disease, 183*(9), 559–565.

Harris, J. R., Schauffler, H. H., Milstein, A., Powers, P., & Hopkins, D. P. (2001, May–June). Expanding health insurance coverage for smoking cessation treatment: Experience of the Pacific Business Group on Health. *American Journal of Health Promotion, 15*(5), 350–356.

Henningfield, J. E., Fant, R. V., Gitchell, J., & Shiffman, S. (2000). Tobacco dependence. Global public health potential for new medications development and indications. *Annals of the New York Academy of Science, 909,* 247–256.

Hillin, M. R. (1989, July). *Personal communication, Prior authorization screening policies.* Kansas Department of Social and Rehabilitation Services, Medicaid Division, Topeka, KS.

Holahan, J., & Bruen, B. (2003, September). *Medicaid spending: What factors contributed to the growth between 2000 and 2002?* (pp. 1–17). Menlo Park, CA: Kaiser Commission on Medicaid and the Uninsured, Kaiser Family Foundation.

Jayakody, R., Danziger, S., & Pollack, H. (2000, August). Welfare reform, substance abuse, and mental health. *Journal of Health Politics, Policy, and Law, 25*(4), 623–651.

Kandel, D. B., Huang, F., & Davies, M. (2001, October 1). Comorbidity between patterns of substance use dependence and psychiatric syndromes. *Drug and Alcohol Dependence, 64*(2), 233–241.

Kann L., Kinchen, S. A., Williams, B. I., Ross, J. G., Lowry, R., Hill C. V., et al. (1998, August 14). Youth risk behavior surveillance—US 1997. *Mortality Weekly Report: Centers for Disease Control Surveillance Summary, 47*(3), 1–89.

Kendell, N. (2000, June 1). Medicaid and indigent care issue brief: Youth access to tobacco. *Issue Brief Health Policy Tracking Service,* 1–32.

Ku, L., & Broadus, M. (2003, January 13). *Why are states' Medicaid expenditures rising?* Center on Budget and Policy Priorities. Retrieved May 29, 2007, from http://www.cbpp.org/1-13-03health.htm

Leon, S. C., Lyons, J. S., Christopher, N. J., & Miller, S. I. (1998). Psychiatric hospital outcomes of dual diagnosis patients under managed care. *American Journal of Addiction, 7*(1), 81–86.

Liska, D. (1997, May). *Medicaid: An overview of a complex program (Policy Briefs/ANF: Issues and options for states* (A-8)). Washington, DC: Urban Institute. Retrieved from http://www.urban.org/url.cfm?ID=307044

McClam, E. (2002, April 11). *CDC: Economic loss from smoking at $7 a pack.* Associated Press, *Houston Chronicle,* from CDC news release.

McGinnis, J. M., & Foege, W. H. (1993). Actual causes of death in the United States. *Journal of the American Medical Association, 270*(18), 2207–2212.

McGinnis, J. M., Williams-Russo, P., & Knickman, J. R. (2002). The case for more active policy attention to health promotion. *Health Affairs, 21*(2), 78–93.

McLellan, T. A., Lewis, D. C., O'Brien, C. P., & Kelber, H. D. (2000, October). Drug dependence, a chronic mental illness: Implications for treatment, insurance, and outcomes evaluation. *Journal of the American Medical Association, 284*(13), 1693.

Mead, L. M. (1994). Poverty: How little we know. *Social Service Review, 68,* 322–350.

Menezes, P. R., Johnson, S., Thornicroft, G., Marshall, J., Prosser, D., Bebbington, P., et al. (1996). Drug and alcohol problems among individuals with severe mental illness in south London. *British Journal of Psychiatry, 168*(5), 612–619.

Milhorn, H. T., Jr. (1988, June). The diagnosis of alcoholism. *American Family Physician, 37*(6), 175–183.

Miller, N. S., Sheppard, L. M., Colenda, C. C., & Magen, J. (2001, May). Why physicians are unprepared to treat patients who have alcohol and drug related disorders. *Academic Medicine, 76*(5), 410–418.

Moore, R. D., & Malitz, F. E. (1986, January). Underdiagnosis of alcoholism by residents in an ambulatory medical practice. *Journal of Medical Education, 61*(1), 46–52.

National Association of State Budget Officers. (2002, Summer). *2001 state expenditure report* (Chapter 4, pp. 45–53). Washington, DC: Author.

National Institute on Alcoholism and Alcohol Abuse (NIAAA). (1993a). Alcohol, aggression, and injury. *Alcohol Health & Research World, 17*(2), 133.

National Institute on Alcoholism and Alcohol Abuse (NIAAA). (1993b). Medical consequences of alcoholism. *Alcohol Alert, 21*, 3.

Norr, R. (1952). Cancer by the carton. *Readers Digest, (December)*, 7–8.

Olson K., & Pavetti, L. (1996). *Personal and family challenges to successful transition from welfare to work.* (Final Report). Washington, DC: Urban Institute Press.

Piazza, N. J. (1996, January). Dual diagnosis and adolescent psychiatric inpatients. *Substance Use and Misuse, 31*(2), 215–223.

Rabinowitz, J., Bromet, E. J., Lavelle, J., Carlson, G., Kovasznay, B., & Schwartz, J. E. (1998, November). Prevalence and severity of substance use disorders and onset of psychosis in first admission psychotic patients. *Psychological Medicine, 28*(6), 1411–1419.

RachBeisel, J., Dixon, L., & Gearon, J. (1999, January–March). Awareness of substance abuse problems among dually diagnosed psychiatric inpatients. *Journal of Psychoactive Drugs, 31*(1), 53–57.

Reid, J., Macchetto, P., & Foster, S. (1999). *No safe haven: Children of substance abusing parents.* New York: National Center on Addiction and Substance Abuse at Columbia University.

Rosen-Chase, C., & Dyson, V. (1999, June). Treatment of nicotine dependence in the chronic mentally ill. *Journal of Substance Abuse Treatment, 16*(4), 315–320.

Safer, D. J. (1987, May). Substance abuse by young adult chronic patients. *Hospital and Community Psychiatry, 38*(5), 511–514.

Saitz, R., Mulvey, K. P., Plough, A., & Samet, J. H. (1997, August). Physician unawareness of serious substance abuse. *American Journal of Drug and Alcohol Abuse, 23*(3), 343–354.

Scanlon, A. (2002, December). *State spending on substance abuse treatment.* Retrieved from http://www.ncsl.org/programs/health/forum/pmsas.htm

Schiller, B. R. (1989). *The economics of poverty and discrimination.* Englewood Cliffs, NJ: Prentice Hall.

Schmidt, L. A. (1995, March). The role of problem drinking in psychiatric admissions. *Addiction, 90*(3), 375–389.

Sembhi, S., & Lee, J. W. (1999, August). Cannabis use in psychotic patients. *Australia and New Zealand Journal of Psychiatry, 33*(4), 529–532.

Shaffer, S. (1997, October 27). Record percentage of DC juvenile arrestees test positive for marijuana. *CESAR FAX: A weekly fax from the Center for Substance Abuse Research.* 6(42). University of Maryland: Center for Substance Abuse Research.

Sharpe, B. (1999, September 17). *Using evidence: Disease management and health benefit coverage options.* Tallahassee, FL: Florida Medicaid Agency for Health Care Administration.

Smith, J. W. (1983, November). Diagnosing alcoholism. *Hospital and Community Psychiatry, 34*(11), 1017–1021.

Smith, K. B., & Stone, L. H. (1989, March). Rags, riches and bootstraps: Beliefs about the causes of wealth and poverty. *Sociological Quarterly, 30*(1), 93.

Smith, V. K. (2005, October 18). *Medicaid in 2005: Issues, trends, and the outlook for the future.* Kaiser Employer Health Benefits, HRET survey, 2004 and 2005. Topeka, KS.

Smith, V., & Moody, G. (2005). *Medicaid in 2005: Principles and proposals for reform.* Lansing: MI: National Governors Association.

Smith, V., Ramesh, R., Gifford, K., Ellis, E., Wachino, V., & O'Malley, M. (2004, January). *States respond to fiscal pressure: A 50 state update of state Medicaid spending growth and cost containment actions* (p. i). Menlo Park, CA: Kaiser Commission on Medicaid and the Uninsured.

Solomon, J., Vanga, N., Morgan, J. P., & Joseph, P. (1980, May). Emergency room physicians: Recognition of alcohol misuse. *Journal of Studies on Alcohol, 41*(5), 583–586.

Spickard, A., Jr. (1986, December). Alcoholism: The missed diagnosis. *Southern Medical Journal, 79*(12), 1489–1492.

Substance Abuse and Mental Health Services Administration (1993, September). *National household survey on drug abuse: Main findings, National Institute of Alcohol Abuse & Alcoholism* (Eighth Special Report to the U.S. Congress on Alcohol & Health). Washington, DC: U.S. Department of Health and Human Services, SAMHSA.

Substance Abuse and Mental Health Services Administration (SAMHSA), Center for Substance Abuse Prevention, Toward Preventing Perinatal Abuse of Alcohol, Tobacco, and Other Drugs. (1993), *Technical Report* (9, 1). Washington, DC: U.S. Department of Health and Human Services, SAMHSA.

Substance Abuse and Mental Health Services Administration. (1997). *National estimates of expenditures for substance abuse treatment.* Rockville, MD: U.S. Department Health and Human Services, SAMHSA.

Substance Abuse and Mental Health Services Administration. (2000). Illicit Drug Use: Summary of findings from the 2000 Household Survey, Office of Applied Studies. Washington, DC: U.S. Department of Health and Human Services, SAMHSA.

Thase, M. E., Salloum, I. M., & Cornelius, J. D. (2001). Comorbid alcoholism and depression: Treatment issues. *Journal of Clinical Psychiatry, 62*(Supplemental, 20), 32–41.

Towers Perrin Associates. (2005, September). *Annual health care cost study* (p. 4). Stamford, CT: Authors.

U.S. Coast Guard. (1994, 9/95). *Boating statistics.* Washington, DC: U.S. Department of Transportation.

Van Ammers, E. C., Sellman, J. D., & Mulder, R. T. (1997, May). Temperament and substance abuse in schizophrenia: Is there a relationship? *Journal of Nervous and Mental Disease, 185*(5), 283–288.

Van Dongen, C. J. (1999, November). Smoking and persistent mental illness: An exploratory study. *Journal of Psychosocial Nursing and Mental Health Services, 37*(11), 26–34.

Waller, J. A., & Casey, R. (1990, November). Teaching about substance abuse in medical school. *British Journal of Addiction, 85*(11), 1451–1455.

Warner, K. E., Hodgson, T. A., & Carroll, C. E. (1999, Autumn). Medical costs of smoking in the United States: Estimates, their validity, and their implications. *Tobacco Control, 8,* 290–300.

Wu, L. T., & Anthony, J. C. (1999, December). Tobacco smoking and depressed mood in late childhood and early adolescence. *American Journal of Public Health, 89*(12), 1837–1840.

Young, N. K., Gardner, S. L., & Dennis, K. (1998). *Responding to alcohol and other drug problems in child welfare: Weaving together practice and policy.* Washington, DC: Child Welfare League of America.

Young, S. E., Mikulich, S. K., Goodwin, M. B., Hardy, J., Martin, C. L., Zoccolillo, M. S., et al. (1995, February). Treated delinquent boys' substance use: Onset, pattern, relationship to conduct and mood disorders. *Drug and Alcohol Dependence, 37*(2), 149–162.

Ziring, D. J., & Adler, A. G. (1991, April). Alcoholism: Are you missing the diagnosis? *Postgraduate Medicine, 89*(5), 139–141, 144–145.

# CHAPTER 16

# Incarceration, Poverty, and Families

## STEPHEN J. BAHR

A major social change in the United States is the increase in the prevalence of incarceration during the past 35 years. From 1970 to 2005, the incarceration rate per 100,000 U.S. residents increased more than seven times from 100 to 738 (Bonczar, 2003; Harrison & Beck, 2005; Stucky, Heimer, & Lang, 2005). Incarceration is most prevalent among young, minority males. In 2005, the incarceration rate was 1,366 per 100,000 for males compared with only 129 per 100,000 for females. Among men in their late twenties, 12% of African Americans were in prison compared with 3.7% of Latinos and 1.7% of whites (Harrison & Beck, 2006).

Those figures are based on snapshots of the number of people in prison at a given time. However, there is a constant flow of people in and out of prison, and some enter and exit prison a number of times. About 93% of all prison inmates eventually will be released to reintegrate into communities (Petersilia, 2005). More than 600,000 prisoners are released annually in the United States—an average of 1,600 per day (Petersilia, 2005). This is four times greater than the number of prisoners that were released 25 years ago (Visher & Travis, 2003).

In 2001, 4.3 million U.S. residents were former inmates (Bonczar, 2003). Among males ages 35 to 44, 22% of African Americans have spent time in jail or prison compared with 10% of Latinos and 3.5% of whites. If incarceration rates remain unchanged, 6.6% of U.S. residents will spend some time in prison. One-third of African American males and one-sixth of Hispanic males will spend time in prison compared with 1 in 17 among white males (Bonczar, 2003).

The extent of and reasons for the growth of incarceration in the United States have been well documented (Stucky et al., 2005). What has received less attention is how incarceration affects personal and family relationships. We do not understand well (1) how family relationships influence criminal behavior and the risk of incarceration, (2) how incarceration affects family members, particularly children, and (3) how families help prisoners after they are released (Uggen, Wakefield, & Western, 2005). The purpose of this chapter is to address these questions, paying particular attention to poverty and economic well-being. I take a life course perspective to explore the process of incarceration and reentry. To begin, I review the key concepts and assumptions underlying the life course perspective.

## LIFE COURSE PERSPECTIVE

The life course perspective explicitly assumes that motivations for and constraints against crime change as one passes through different developmental periods. Two key concepts in the life course perspective are trajectories and transitions (Elder, 2001; Sampson & Laub, 2001). Trajectories are long-term patterns and sequences. Family experiences influence choices and help establish patterns and sequences of behavior. Many individuals in prison have been on long-term trajectories that include unemployment, poverty, and crime. A key challenge as they reenter society is how to change their trajectories.

Transitions are special life events that are embedded within trajectories. Examples of transitions are obtaining a job, marrying, and becoming a parent. Entering and being released from prison also are key transitions. Many individuals who go to prison came from disadvantaged families where their parents had low levels of education, occupational status, and income (Hanlon, O'Grady, Bennett-Sears, & Callaman, 2005). In addition, many were delayed in the formation of their own families, partly because of their lack of occupational skills. Incarceration may exacerbate problems in fragile families by disrupting existing family bonds (Uggen et al., 2005). The life course perspective focuses on how certain transitions may help increase or disrupt social bonds, change social networks, and modify trajectories.

There has been much theorizing and research about why people commit crime but less study of why people who have committed criminal acts choose to desist from reoffending (Laub & Sampson, 2001; Maruna & Toch, 2005; Shover & Thompson, 1992). An advantage of the life course perspective is that it looks at individual stability and change over time. Most individuals do not suddenly commit a crime but have gone through a lengthy process of socialization to learn motivations and techniques for committing crime. Similarly, desistance from crime is a process in which an individual moves from a state of offending to a state of non-offending, which may take a considerable amount of time. The desistance process includes not only stopping criminal behavior but also disrupting existing roles and reorganization based on new roles. Occupation appears to be important in the reorganization of roles (Maruna & Toch, 2005).

The life course perspective integrates two major theoretical orientations. The first is social control theory, which uses social bonds to explain both the initiation into and the desistance from crime. As individuals become attached to conventional people and institutions, they develop a stake in conformity. On the other hand, individuals with weak or no ties are more likely to violate the law because they have fewer constraints and have less to lose if they are caught (Carlson, 2004).

When individuals are close to a parent, spouse, or child, they may feel constrained to obey rules and limit their deviant activities. However, those who do not have close family relationships may not feel as constrained to obey the law or conform to the desires of their family members. Similarly, one who is employed may have less time to "hang out" with friends and may limit criminal activities because of work involvement. In addition, employment may constrain illegal activities if individuals value their employment and perceive that criminal behavior may hurt their employment. On the other hand, if they are not employed or do not have a good job, they have nothing to lose by participating in illegal activities. Becoming married and employed appear to be important informal social controls that may help constrain individuals from criminal activities (Hirschi, 1969; Laub & Sampson, 2001).

Social learning theory is the second theoretical orientation often used by life course theorists. According to social learning theory, everyone is embedded in networks of relationships where they learn attitudes and behaviors, including motivations for and constraints against criminal behavior (Agnew, 2005). Individuals rarely begin committing illegal acts by themselves. They observe others and learn how to commit criminal acts from those with whom they associate (Elliott & Menard, 1996). Within small, informal groups people are taught, through imitation and reinforcement, to hold attitudes that are favorable or unfavorable to law violation (Akers & Sellers, 2004).

Although many social learning theorists focus on peers for criminal learning, families also are important for learning attitudes and behaviors about crime. In Sutherland's differential association theory, for example, learning takes place according to the frequency, duration, intensity, and priority of social interactions (Sutherland, 1947). Individuals are likely to acquire attitudes favorable to crime if they associate frequently with others who commit criminal acts and have favorable attitudes toward crime. If those interactions occur over a long period, internalization of pro-crime attitudes and behaviors is more likely than if the duration of the interactions is over a short period. Learning is more likely to occur when interactions are intense as opposed to casual and superficial.

Family relationships are likely to influence criminal learning because of their priority, intensity, frequency, and duration. One's family is the first social group many individuals belong to and individuals usually have frequent and intense interactions over a long period within a significant group. Family relationships also influence attitudes toward education and work and help structure economic opportunities.

From a social learning perspective, family ties may help individuals desist from crime because there is less time to associate with deviant friends. For example, when individuals marry, their networks may be altered so they spend less time with peers and have less exposure to others who are committing criminal acts (Laub & Sampson, 2001). With fewer friends to encourage and reward criminal behavior, motivation for committing crime may diminish (Maruna & Toch, 2005; Warr, 1998). Less time with peers translates into less modeling of and reinforcement of criminal behavior.

Both social learning and social control concepts are integrated in Agnew's general theory of crime (Agnew, 2005). He views crime as a function of motivations for crime and constraints against crime. Motivations for crime are assumed to be learned from exposure to criminal models and reinforcements for crime. Constraints against crime are assumed to result from informal social controls based on bonding.

In addition, Agnew postulates that motivations may arise from strains. For example, individuals may face strain if (1) they are prevented from achieving their goals (i.e., obtaining money), (2) valued possessions are removed or threatened to be removed, or (3) they are presented or threatened with noxious or negatively valued stimuli (Agnew, 2005). For example, if individuals are not able to get a good job, they may face economic strain because they have not achieved a goal. If they lose their job, they have lost something they need for economic support. Thus, economic strains appear to be important influences on criminal behavior.

In his theory, Agnew groups motivations and constraints into five major life domains: family, work, peers, school, and self (Agnew, 2005). He takes a life course perspective in that he views motivations and constraints changing according to one's social development. After reviewing existing research, he concludes that social support from a spouse is important in constraining criminal tendencies. One who is not married or is in an unhappy marriage will have fewer informal social controls to help constrain criminal tendencies. Similarly, those who are unemployed or employed in low-paying jobs will have a lower stake in conformity.

Another variation of life course theory is the Social Development Model (Catalano & Hawkins, 1996). This model takes a developmental perspective and identifies risk and protective factors that influence criminal behavior over time. Risk and protective factors are organized into several domains that are similar to the domains used by Agnew. According to the Social Development Model, helping individuals desist from crime requires strengthening attachment and commitment, providing modeling and positive reinforcement, and teaching pro-social attitudes. Family and work ties appear to be important in providing pro-social modeling and reinforcement.

In summary, according to the life course perspective, learning to commit crime and learning to desist from crime are long-term processes in which motivations and constraints change according to one's social development. All individuals are embedded in social networks that change as key life transitions are made, and those networks influence and are influenced by criminal trajectories. Economic transitions and strains are important elements that influence and are influenced by criminal trajectories

## METHODS

There has been extensive analysis of crime, incarceration, and reentry using large, national data sets (Bonczar, 2003; Langan & Levin, 2002; Travis & Visher, 2005b). The findings from these surveys have been valuable but are incomplete because of limited data from the perspective of the offender (Travis & Visher, 2005a). In this chapter, I report quantitative and qualitative data from interviews with 51 inmates as they were released from prison and with 140 jail

inmates soon before their release. The purpose of these two surveys was to obtain information on the actual life course of offenders from their perspective, including their family situations. Most of my analysis will focus on the 51 parolees, and the 140 jail inmates will be used as supplemental data. I turn now to a brief description of the procedures used to collect data from each of these two groups.

### Parolees

We sampled new parolees from Salt Lake City and Provo, the two major metropolitan areas in Utah. More than 85% of Utah's residents reside within these two urban areas. The parolees were interviewed right after release from prison, and at 1 month, 3 months, and 6 months after the first interview. By interviewing each parolee four times, we were able to capture the individual attitudinal and behavioral changes that occur as parolees go through the adjustment process.

The interview schedules were developed after an extensive review of the pertinent literature, observations of new parolees, discussions with parole officers, and consultation with colleagues. The first interview schedule included 129 quantitative and qualitative questions that asked about background, criminal history, family, housing, education, work, drug use, friends, recreation, and future plans. The second and third interview schedules included 79 follow-up questions, and the fourth interview schedule included 27 essential questions from the earlier interviews.

In Utah, all new parolees are required to attend an orientation meeting within the first month following their release. At the beginning of several of these meetings, we described the purpose of our study, invited the parolees to participate, and passed a sheet for volunteers to sign if they were willing to be interviewed. After the meeting, my research team and I interviewed parolees in a relatively private area within a large common room at the day reporting center. We were able to interview 51 of the total of 66 new parolees who attended the six meetings we attended (77%).

Parolees are a transient population that is difficult to track. We were able to obtain 1-month interviews from 31 parolees, 3-month interviews with 35 parolees, and 6-month interviews with 40 parolees. With cooperation from the Utah Department of Corrections, we were able to track all of our 51 respondents for a year to determine how many had returned to jail or prison.

The first interview averaged about 45 minutes, and the follow-up interviews took approximately 30 minutes each. The initial interviews were conducted from September to November of 2004 and the follow-up interviews were conducted from November 2004 to July of 2005. All initial interviews took place at the offices of Adult Probation & Parole. For the follow-up interviews, we called the parolees and arranged to meet them at the day reporting center at a time when they needed to meet with their parole officer or to attend a class. The fourth interviews were conducted by phone for those who were still in the community and in person for those who had returned to jail or prison by that time.

The 51 parolees had an age range from 22 to 56 with a mean of 35. Eight (16%) of the respondents were women. Thirty-eight (75%) said their ethnic status is white, eight identified themselves as Latino, one as Asian, and four as "other." Forty-three (84%) had at least graduated from high school or passed the General Educational Development (GED) test, but only one (2%) had graduated from college. Almost three-fourths (73%) were parents, and the number of children ranged from 1 to 6, with a median of 2. Thirty-six (71%) had been married but only eight (16%) were currently married. Almost all of the parolees (94%) said that they currently or previously had a drug problem. A summary

of the background characteristics of the 51 parolees is shown in Table 16.1.

## Jail Inmates

As part of an evaluation of a drug treatment program, we interviewed 140 individuals who were incarcerated in the Utah County Jail. Seventy were interviewed as they completed the On Unit Treatment (OUT) program, a drug treatment program for jail inmates. In addition, we interviewed 70 inmates not in the OUT program who were matched on age, gender, and type of offense. The interview schedule included 80 quantitative and qualitative questions that asked about background, criminal history, family, housing, education, drug use, friends, and future plans. Each interview took about 30 minutes and took place at the Utah County Jail.

The 140 jail inmates had an age range from 18 to 51 with a mean of 27. Sixteen (11%) were women. Almost two-thirds (64%) had never been married, 93% identified their ethnic status as white, and 56% were parents. Only one offender (0.7%) had graduated from college, 24% had received some college, and 46% had graduated from high school or received their GED. Almost all (98.6%) admitted to having a drug problem in the past (see Table 16.1).

Although the 51 parolees and 140 jail inmates appeared to be typical offenders, they were not a random sample of parolees or jail inmates in Utah or elsewhere. However, our purpose was not to describe the parolee population but to explore offending, incarceration, and reentry from the perspective of the offender. As noted by Travis and Visher (2005b), there is a dearth of information from the perspective of the individual parolee, and this type of data is needed to understand the process of prisoner reentry.

I now turn to the results of my analysis. I summarize recently published information

**Table 16.1** Prison and Jail Sample Characteristics and Comparison to Parolee Population in Utah and United States (by percentage)

| Variable | Categories | Prison Sample | Jail Sample | Utah Parolees | U.S. Parolees* |
|---|---|---|---|---|---|
| Sex | Male | 84.3 | 88.6 | | 93.3 |
| | Female | 15.7 | 11.4 | | 6.7 |
| Ethnicity | White or Anglo | 74.5 | 92.6 | 75.8 | 34.3 |
| | African American | 0.0 | 0.0 | 4.5 | 40.7 |
| | Native American | 0.0 | 0.7 | 2.9 | |
| | Hispanic or Latino | 15.7 | 4.4 | 11.9 | 19.2 |
| | Asian | 2.0 | 0.7 | 1.4 | |
| | Other | 7.8 | 1.5 | 3.5 | 5.8 |
| Marital Status | Married | 15.7 | 12.1 | | |
| | Divorced/separated | 52.9 | 24.2 | | |
| | Never married | 29.4 | 63.6 | | |
| | Widowed | 2.0 | 0.0 | | |
| Education | Less than high school | 14.0 | 30.0 | | 50.8 |
| | High school or GED | 62.0 | 45.7 | | 42.2 |
| | Some college or more | 24.0 | 24.3 | | 7.0 |
| | Mean age | 35 | 27 | | 34 |
| | Sample size | 51 | 140 | | |

*SOURCES: Harrison & Beck, 2005; Hughes et al., 2001.

that is relevant along with the results from the interviews.

## RESULTS

### Family Influences on Criminal Behavior and Incarceration

Recent research is consistent with the hypothesis that both the family of orientation and family of procreation influence crime and the risk of incarceration. Uggen, Wakefield, and Western examined family characteristics using data from a national survey of inmates in state and federal correctional facilities (Uggen et al., 2005). They observed that prisoners tend to come from disadvantaged families of orientation. Rates of single parenthood and poverty were considerably higher among families of inmates than in the general population and appeared to be related to criminal behavior. Uggen

et al. concluded that deficits in the family of origin were associated with increased criminal behavior of children from those families.

The researchers also found that the deficits in the family of orientation were associated with delays in family formation among the young adult children from those families. Their lower rates of marriage and education were associated with higher rates of crime. Similar results were reported in a recent study of 167 incarcerated women (Hanlon et al., 2005).

A profile of prisoners in the United States confirms that deficits in their families of orientation are associated with the risk of incarceration (Petersilia, 2005). One-third of the prisoners reported that their parents had abused drugs. Eighteen percent had a parent who had been incarcerated. Forty percent had a sibling, spouse, or child who had been incarcerated. Many came from single-parent families. One-fourth were separated or divorced.

In our interviews of Utah parolees, we asked detailed information about their families. Alcohol and drug problems among family members were common. Three-fourths said they had at least one family member with a drug or alcohol problem. More than 20% said their mother had a problem with alcohol, and 29% said their father had an alcohol problem. Ten percent said their mother used drugs, 18% said their father used drugs, and 42% said a sibling used drugs. Thus, alcohol and drug problems in families of orientation appear to contribute to their drug problems. Among the parolees, 82% said that drug use contributed to their incarceration.

Also, it was common for parolees to have family members who had been on probation or incarcerated. Two-thirds of the parolees said at least one family member had been on probation or in jail or prison. Twenty percent had at least one parent that had been on probation or in jail or prison. Forty-eight percent had a sibling who had been in prison or jail or on probation.

Similar problems seemed to be carried into their families of orientation. Twenty percent had a spouse or partner who had been on probation or in jail or prison, and 22% said they had a spouse or partner who had a problem with drugs. A summary of these characteristics is presented in Table 16.2.

A key issue in the study of crime is the extent to which economic problems contribute to crime. When individuals are under financial strain, one solution is to use illegal means to relieve the strain (Agnew, 2005). When criminals are asked why they engaged in crime, they commonly mention the need for money (Agnew, 2006).

We asked the 51 parolees what their financial situation was before they were first incarcerated. Twenty-nine percent said their financial situation was poor or very poor, and another 20% said it was only "fair." We also asked them if their financial situation

contributed to their being incarcerated. More than half (53%) responded "yes" to this question. Thus, according to their perceptions, economic strain was a factor that contributed to their incarceration.

A significant influence on financial strain is the lack of education. Many individuals who become involved in crime do not have the skills to obtain jobs that pay a living wage. Forty-one percent of released prisoners in the United States do not have a high school diploma and only a small percentage have completed college (Petersilia, 2005).

Only one of the 51 parolees we interviewed had completed college. Among the 140 jail inmates we interviewed, only one had a college degree. It appears that a lack of education is a factor associated with criminal behavior. I now turn to a discussion of how incarceration affects families.

## The Impact of Incarceration on Families

There has been relatively little study of how incarceration affects families, particularly its impact on children (Uggen et al., 2005). Incarceration has three possible effects on families. First, incarceration may have beneficial effects if it removes the negative influence of a child, spouse, or parent heavily involved in crime. Second, the incarceration might have little impact on families if the relationships were distant or fractured before the incarceration occurred. Third, the incarceration may weaken already fragile families if the family members depended on the member who was incarcerated for financial or emotional support.

In assessing the impact of incarceration on families, it is worth noting that prison policies tend to discourage family contact. Visiting hours are limited, phone calls are expensive, and inmates are often housed in prisons far away from their homes (Lynch & Sabol, 2001; Petersilia, 2003).

**Table 16.2**    Involvement of Family Members in Drugs and in Criminal Justice System: Utah Parolees

| Drug Use | Percent |
|---|---|
| At least 1 family member has alcohol or drug problem | 74.0 |
| Mother has problem with alcohol | 21.6 |
| Mother has problem with drugs | 10.0 |
| Father has a problem with alcohol | 29.4 |
| Father has a problem with drugs | 18.0 |
| Sibling has a problem with alcohol | 39.2 |
| Sibling has a problem with drugs | 42.0 |
| Spouse/partner has a problem with alcohol | 25.5 |
| Spouse/partner has problem with drugs | 22.0 |
| Drug use contributed to their incarceration | 82.4 |
| **Probation, Jail, or Prison** | |
| At least one family member has been on probation or in jail/prison | 66.0 |
| Mother has been on probation or in jail/prison | 6.0 |
| Father has been on probation or in jail/prison | 18.0 |
| At least one parent on probation or in jail/prison | 20.0 |
| Sibling has been on probation or in jail/prison | 48.0 |
| Spouse/partner has been on probation or in jail/prison | 20.0 |
| Sample Size | (51) |

The possible impact of incarceration on the parents of the inmate has been neglected by researchers. A recent study found mothers experienced grief and anxiety when their sons were incarcerated (Green, Ensminger, Robertson, & Hee-Soon, 2006). The incarceration increased their financial difficulties because many depended on their sons for financial support. It increased grandparent burden because the mothers had to help care for their sons' children. Yet some mothers had hope that the incarceration might help end the destructive lifestyles of their sons.

The next question is how incarceration influences relationships with spouses and partners. More than two-thirds of our parolee sample and one-third of our jail sample had been married, but only 16% and 12% were currently married, respectively. These inmates have a high rate of marital dissolution, but we do not know the extent to which their criminal behavior or their incarceration contributed to the dissolution of their marriages. Incarceration makes it more difficult to maintain marital bonds and, therefore, is likely to exacerbate existing marital problems.

As noted previously, there have been few empirical studies of how incarceration may affect the children of the offenders. Most prisoners lived with their child before incarceration and most attempt to maintain contact while they are in prison (Uggen et al., 2005).

Compared with children in the general population, children of incarcerated parents tend to have poorer school performance and health (Day, Acock, Bahr, & Arditti, 2005).

Among our interviewees, more than half (53%) of the jail inmates and more than two-thirds of the parolees (73%) were parents. Among the parents who had been in prison, three-fourths (76%) said they had some type of contact with their children while they were in prison, and 55% had contact at least once per month. Half of them were visited by their children, and the others had contact by phone or letter.

Forty-four percent of the jail inmates were not visited by their children while they were in jail, but 19% had weekly visits from their children and 25% were visited one to three times a month.

We asked the parolees what their biggest stress was while they were in prison. Half of all the parolees and 61% of the parents mentioned worries about their children or family.

We asked a series of questions about who cared for their children and what their concerns were regarding their children. The parent not in prison cared for the children in 65% of the cases, and 16% of the inmates relied on grandparents. When asked if their children were well cared for while they were in prison, 94% said they were.

Most of the inmates thought about their children regularly and were concerned about their welfare. Almost all (94%) of the inmates said they thought about their children daily. When asked about their concerns, they mentioned their children's feelings and emotional well-being, health, and schooling.

The impact of incarceration is felt long after prisoners are released. Following release, parolees face the task of reconnecting with family members. One of the first things inmates do upon release is contact family members. When we interviewed the newly released parolees, we asked them if they had any contact with family members. All but 1

of the 51 parolees already had made contact with a family member. Three-fourths had contacted their mothers, two-thirds a sibling, and half their fathers. Of those who were parents, 53% had made contact with their children.

The disruptive effects of incarceration are shown by comparing their living conditions before and after prison. Of the 18 parolees who lived with their children before incarceration, only 4 were living with their children after release from prison.

We asked several questions about frequency of contact with their children after release and the quality of their relationships. First, we asked them how difficult it has been to reconnect with their children. About half felt it has been easy or very easy, almost one-fourth were uncertain, and one-fourth said it has been difficult or very difficult.

When we asked about the quality of their relationships with their children, 63% of the parolees rated it as good or excellent, 26% said it was fair, and 11% said it was poor or very poor. When asked how frequently they see their child (or children), 34% responded not at all, 28% said 1 to 2 days per week, 13% said 2 to 6 days per week, and one-fourth said they see their children every day.

Overall, there was a bimodal distribution regarding the parolees' ability to reestablish relationships with their children. About half of them said it has been easy to reconnect with their children, saw their child at least once a week, and rated their relationship with their children as good or excellent. However, about one-third had not seen their children, had difficulty reconnecting with them, and felt their relationship was only fair or poor.

One of the major effects of incarceration is the stigma that affects the ability of individuals to obtain and maintain jobs. This effect was shown in a recent study of applicants to entry level jobs (Pager, 2003). An experimental audit procedure was used in which job applicants had identical credentials except the criminal record and race of the applicant varied. Among whites, only 17% of those with a criminal record received a call back compared with 35% among those without a criminal record. Among African Americans, the comparable percentages were 5 and 14, respectively. These data demonstrate how the stigma of incarceration limits opportunities for employment, and that this stigma is much more severe for African Americans than for whites. These findings suggest that the high rate of incarceration in the United States may be counterproductive because it interferes with employability even though employment is a consistent predictor of desistance from crime (Pager, 2003; Uggen, 2000). The inability to obtain employment affects the ability of parolees to reconnect with and support their families.

## Influences on Prisoner Reentry

After release from prison, individuals reenter society and attempt to reconnect with old networks or establish new relationships. Their adjustment to life outside of prison is influenced by their experiences before prison, during prison, and after release. Thus, reentry is a process that begins long before a prisoner is released (Visher & Travis, 2003). In this section, I discuss how family, work, education, and drug use are associated with successful adjustment following reentry.

*Family.* As individuals are released from prison, reconnecting with family members appears to be critical in successful adjustment, as illustrated by several recent studies. Sampson and Laub (1990) found that individuals who had strong ties to family were less likely to commit crime than were individuals with weak bonds. The social ties that developed during the transitions helped explain why they stopped committing criminal acts (Sampson & Laub, 1990).

In a related study (Laub, Nagin, & Sampson, 1998), standard predictors of crime

such as being a difficult child, having a low IQ, living in poverty, and poor parental supervision were unable to differentiate offending trajectories into mid-adulthood. However, marriages characterized by social cohesiveness had a preventative effect on crime. The effect of a good marriage grew slowly until it had a major impact on inhibiting crime (Laub et al., 1998).

Horney and colleagues (1995) introduced the concept of "local life circumstances" to explain changes in offending over relatively short periods. Their objective was to determine whether formal and informal mechanisms of social control affected the likelihood of committing nine major felonies. They analyzed month-to-month variations in the life circumstances and offending of convicted felons. Even though there was continuity over time, local life circumstances were associated with systematic changes in individual criminal behavior. The researchers observed that living with a wife was associated with lower levels of offending but living with a girlfriend was associated with higher levels of offending. Horney et al. concluded that individual trajectories of crime are influenced by local life circumstances such as quarreling with a family member, getting fired from a job, and drug use (Horney, Osgood, & Marshall, 1995).

Marriage, among other effects, may be important in reducing the amount of time ex-convicts spend with deviant friends (Warr, 1998). Marriage may help develop new networks that substitute for old deviant networks (Fagan, 1989). Stabilization of the new networks appears to be important. For example, when marriage is not stable, a return to drug use is more likely (Kandel & Yamaguchi, 1987). Similarly, new relationships and informal monitoring by a spouse appear to help individuals desist from using alcohol (Vaillant, 1995).

As noted earlier, we tracked the parolees for 1 year after release from prison to determine how they adjusted. At the end of 1 year,

19 of the 51 (37%) were back in jail or prison. We examined how characteristics measured just after release (first interview) or 1 month after release (second interview) were associated with their recidivism, which was measured by whether or not the parolee was back in jail or prison 1 year after release.

According to life course theories, bonds to family members may help individuals change their trajectories and remain crime free. First, we examined whether several family statuses were related to recidivism. Being a parent was not related to recidivism. However, being married had a modest, negative association with recidivism ($r = -.24$, $p = .048$). Those who were never married or were divorced were somewhat more likely to return to prison than were those who were married. For example, 44% (17 of 39) of the never married and divorced persons were back in prison within 1 year. Among those who were still married, only 2 of 12 (17%) were back in prison 1 year later (see Table 16.3).

More important than being a spouse or a parent is the quality of one's family relationships. We asked the respondents about their relationships with their own parents and children. Those who felt more close to their parents at the time they were released were somewhat less likely to be back behind bars 1 year after release. Twenty-nine percent of those who were close to their mother returned to prison compared with 58% of those who were not close to their mother ($r = -.26$, $p = .033$). For fathers, the comparable percentages were 25% and 50%, respectively ($r = -.26$, $p = .035$).

Children could play a critical role in desistance from crime. Love for and commitment to a child might help constrain an offender from associating with deviant peers and may motivate the offender to comply with his or her parole requirements. We measured the parent-child bond in two ways. First, we asked if their children ever visited them while they were in prison. Second, during the first interview, we asked them if they had any contact with family members since they were released, and if they said "yes," we asked who they have had contact with.

Those who were visited by a child in prison were less likely to recidivate than those who

Table 16.3    Percent Who Were Re-Incarcerated 1 Year After Release by Family Characteristics

|  | Re-Incarcerated | | |
|---|---|---|---|
|  | *No* | *Yes* | *R\** |
| **Married** | 44% | 17% | −0.24 |
| Sample size | (39) | (12) | |
| **Close to Mother** | 58% | 29% | −0.26 |
| Sample size | (12) | (38) | |
| **Close to Father** | 50% | 25% | −0.26 |
| Sample size | (22) | (28) | |
| **Child(ren) Visited Parent in Prison** | 46% | 13% | −0.36 |
| Sample size | (13) | (15) | |
| **Contacted Child(ren) Soon After Release** | 48% | 21% | −0.27 |
| Sample size | (31) | (19) | |
| **Family Members Provided Transportation** | 55% | 13% | −0.41 |
| Sample size | (31) | (16) | |

\* $p < .05$

were not. As shown in Table 16.3, only 13% (2 of 15) of those who were visited by a child were sent back to prison, compared with almost half of those who were not visited (6 of 13). Only 21% (4 of 19) of those who had contact with a child soon after release were back in prison 1 year later, compared with 48% (15 of 31) of those who did not have contact with a child soon after release.

When prisoners are released, they enter a very different world and one of their immediate needs is transportation. They are required to report to their parole officer, obtain employment, and attend various classes and counseling sessions. We asked each parolee how family members had been a help since they were released. Those who said their family members provided transportation were less likely to have recidivated than were those who did not list transportation as a resource provided by their families ($r = -.41$, $p = .002$; see Table 16.3).

Both of these sentiments are illustrated by the following comments of one respondent: "I have support from all my children right now and my sisters. They let me stay at their house and I helped them finish their basement while I was on home visits and my son gave me a truck and they're just really supportive. They told me they would go to all my classes with me if I wanted them to, so they really want to be involved."

*Employment.* When offenders are released from prison, they face the task of supporting themselves. A requirement of parole is to find employment even though many parolees have few marketable skills and have a history of underemployment and unemployment (Petersilia, 2005; Uggen et al., 2005). Finding employment is a critical step in the transition from prison to the community, so we expected that those who found work would be less likely to recidivate. This was not the case, however. At the first interview, 26 of our 51 parolees had already found work. Eight of the 26 (31%) who were employed at the first interview were back in prison 1 year later. Of the 25 who were not employed at the first interview, 11 (44%) were back in prison a year later (see Table 16.4). Although this difference is in the expected direction, it is not statistically significant for this small sample size. Further research is needed to explore this issue in more depth with a larger sample size.

We also examined their responses to a question about the difficulty in finding work. Again, those who said it was "very easy" to find work were somewhat less likely to recidivate (46% compared with 59%), but the difference was not statistically significant.

According to life course theory, what is important is not just getting a job but getting a high-quality job (Uggen et al., 2005). Steady work that provides sufficient hours is

**Table 16.4** Percent Who Were Re-Incarcerated One Year After Release by Work Characteristics

|  | Re-Incarcerated | | |
| --- | --- | --- | --- |
|  | No | Yes | R |
| Employed at Interview 1 | 44% | 31% | −0.14 |
| Sample size | (25) | (26) | |
| Has Specific Career Goals | 50% | 29% | −0.21* |
| Sample size | (20) | (31) | |
| Financial Situation Contributed to Incarceration | 25% | 48% | −0.24** |
| Sample size | (24) | (27) | |

* $p < .07$
** $p < .05$

critical if parolees are able to earn sufficient to support themselves. Not having a good-quality job puts added stress on the parolees, particularly if they have a family to support. This is illustrated by the following quote from a parolee who was arrested during Christmas for shoplifting:

> Because, I mean, if you want a job, you can get a job, if it's flippin' burgers. You know, so, you can get a job. But to get a, a good job, that pays, is harder. You know I can go get a cook job at Denny's or something, or Cracker Barrel or something like that and get nine, ten bucks an hour but it's nothin to support my family on, you know, so, minimum, bare minimum payments and rent and stuff but nothin to really support a family with.

The financial stress is illustrated by this parolee's explanation for his shoplifting:

> I started feeling like I had to make up everything for those last two years and stuff and for Christmas and stuff, and I—I wasn't, you know, I'd just barely got, you know, like a ten dollar an hour job and stuff, and trying to make up our bills and everything, and so I, I shoplifted, to try to get some extra money.

To support oneself, one must have a job with an adequate number of hours. Therefore, we looked at the number of hours the employed parolees were working each week. We found that those who were not re-incarcerated 1 year later were working significantly more hours soon after they were released from prison. They worked an average of 44 hours per week, compared with only 30 hours per week among those who were later re-incarcerated.

The finding that successful parolees worked an average of 14 more hours per week can be interpreted in several ways. Parolees may be constrained from committing further crimes by a lack of free time

to spend in criminal activities or with their friends. Those working fewer hours might not feel as committed to their jobs and may continue to feel victimized by society. Or, it could be that those who worked fewer hours simply lacked the motivation to work more. This lack of motivation to work is shown by a parolee who was applying for a job and who recidivated two times during the year.

*Parolee:*  They're probably not going to hire me, but I'm not worried about it.

*Interviewer:*  Might as well try.

*Parolee:*  I'm just doing it to make them (the parole officers) happy.

We also asked about their future career plans. Thirty-one had definite plans about their future career, and 20 did not have specific career plans. Among those with specific career plans, only 29% were back in prison 1 year later compared with 50% of those without specific career plans ($r = .21$, $p = .067$; see Table 16.4).

Those who said at their first interview that their financial situation before going to prison contributed to their latest incarceration were more likely to be re-incarcerated 1 year after release. They had financial strain initially and their ability to relieve that financial stress after incarceration apparently did not change.

*Education.* Education has been shown to be related to long-term financial well-being (U.S. Census Bureau, 2004). Parolees tend to have low levels of education and few marketable work skills (Petersilia, 2005; Uggen et al., 2005). In our sample of parolees, there was not a great deal of variation in their educational level. Therefore, for this part of the analysis, I divided them into two groups, those who had completed more than a high school education and those that had not. The modal education was a high school diploma or GED. Thirty-eight of the respondents were in the lower education category, high school education or less. We found a modest correlation between education and recidivism. Only 17% of those with *more* than a high school education were in prison 1 year later compared with almost half (45%) of those with a high school diploma or less ($r = -.25, p = .042$).

We also asked the parolees if they were currently going to school. Although only five were currently in school, none of them were in prison 1 year later. Among those not taking any classes, 43% (19 of 44) were in prison a year later ($r = -.27, p = .031$).

*Drugs.* One of the major risk factors for parolees is drug use. Most prisoners have had a problem with alcohol and other drugs (Petersilia, 2005). Forty-eight of our 51 parolees said they had a problem with alcohol or drugs in the past. Eighty-two percent said involvement with drugs contributed to their incarceration.

Among those who said drugs contributed to their incarceration, almost half were back in prison 1 year after release. However, among those nine who said drugs did not contribute to their incarceration, none were back in prison a year after release

(see Table 16.5). These findings illustrate how drug use contributes to incarceration and the difficulty many have in overcoming a drug problem.

During the first interview, we asked about drug use, and it was found to be predictive of later parole success. First, we asked them about the biggest challenges they faced since being released. Five of the parolees said "staying clean" was their biggest challenge and four of those five ended up back in prison, compared with only 33% of those who did not list "staying clean" as one of their biggest challenges.

In a related question, we asked, "Are you ever tempted to try alcohol or drugs?" Sixty-four percent of those who answered "yes" were in jail or prison by the end of the year compared with only 27% of those who answered "no."

We also asked the parolees about what classes they took while in prison, and now that they are out, which they felt were most helpful. Those who took a substance abuse class in prison were more likely to be successful parolees than were those that did not. Of the 36 who took a substance abuse class in prison, only 22% were back in prison a year later. Among the 12 who did not take a substance abuse class in prison, 9 (75%) were back in prison a year later (see Table 16.5).

Table 16.5    Percent Who Were Re-Incarcerated 1 Year After Release by Drug Use

| | Re-Incarcerated | | |
| --- | --- | --- | --- |
| | *No* | *Yes* | *R* |
| **Drugs Contributed to Incarceration** | 0% | 45% | .36** |
| Sample size | (9) | (42) | |
| **"Staying Clean" Listed as One of Biggest Challenges Since Release** | 33% | 80% | .29* |
| Sample size | (46) | (5) | |
| **Are You Ever Tempted to Try Alcohol or Drugs?** | 27% | 64% | .34** |
| Sample size | (37) | (14) | |
| **Took Substance Abuse Class in Prison** | 75% | 22% | –.48** |
| Sample size | (12) | (36) | |

\* $p < .05$
\*\* $p < .01$

Of course, we don't know if those with greater motivation to succeed were the ones who took the class or if the class actually helped individuals desist from drug use. Those who desist from crime may change their self-conceptions as suggested by Giordano et al. (2002). In their cognitive theory, they discussed how openness to change and mentally creating a replacement self are necessary steps in the desistance process (Giordano, Cernkovich, & Rudolph, 2002). The following quote is from a parolee who continued to define himself as an addict, did not change, and ended up back in prison:

> Yeah, you are always going to be tempted. There's not one day when you aren't tempted. Once you are an addict, you are always an addict. If it is around me, it is going to be really hard.

Conversely, the following quote is an example of a parolee who was attempting to create a positive replacement self:

> I don't believe in this "once an alcoholic always an alcoholic," "once a drug addict always a drug addict," "once a convict always a convict," you know, that's what they were pretty much saying, you know, and I don't believe that. I believe you're who you are and if you want to change you can, it's all a choice. The sooner you can stop saying that "I'm a convict or a drug addict," then you can go ahead with that logic.

*Multivariate Analysis.* Because of the small samples size, there is not sufficient statistical power to conduct a detailed multivariate analysis. However, to supplement the previous analyses and help control for other relevant variables, I used binary logistic regression to estimate how well the variables would predict recidivism during the year after release. The results are shown in Table 16.6. Those parolees that had specific career goals and who took a substance abuse class in prison were less likely to be back in jail or prison within the first year after release.

Of course, adjustment after release from prison is a process, and previous theory and research indicate that one key factor in this process is the ability to pay for necessities. Based on life course theory, I predicted that the quality of relationships with spouse/partner and children would be related to ability to pay.

In the first panel of Table 16.7, I limited the analysis to those with a partner or spouse ($N = 16$). The quality of the relationship with the partner was the independent variable. There was a positive relationship between the quality of the relationship with the partner and perceived ability to pay—those with a higher quality relationship had a greater ability to pay for their necessities.

In the second equation in Table 16.7, I limited the analysis to those with children

Table 16.6    Binary Logistic Regression of Recidivism by Selected Variables

| *Predictor Variables* | B | *Wald* | P | *Exp(B)* |
|---|---|---|---|---|
| Age | −0.08 | 2.29 | 0.13 | 0.93 |
| Gender | 1.65 | 1.94 | 0.16 | 5.18 |
| Education | −0.16 | −.07 | 0.79 | 0.85 |
| Drugs contributed to incarceration | 1.90 | 2.13 | 0.15 | 6.66 |
| Has specific career goals | −1.39 | 3.01 | 0.08 | 0.25 |
| Took substance abuse class in prison | −2.50 | 5.77 | 0.02 | 0.08 |

**Table 16.7**     Regression of Perceived Ability to Pay for Necessities by Quality of Relationships

| Predictor Variables in Equation 1 (N = 16) | B | Beta |
|---|---|---|
| Age | −0.01 | 0.04 |
| Gender | 1.37 | 0.41 |
| Quality of relationship with partner | 0.44 | .69* |

| Predictor Variables in Equation 2 (N = 34) | B | Beta |
|---|---|---|
| Age | 0.01 | 0.05 |
| Gender | 1.02 | 0.28 |
| Quality of relationship with children | 0.24 | .43* |

*$p < .01$

($N = 34$). I found a positive relationship between the quality of the relationship with their child (children) and their ability to pay for necessities.

Another important part of the reentry process is the ability to stay off drugs. At the first interview, we asked each of the respondents the following questions: "How difficult will it be for you to stay off alcohol or drugs?" Those who said they lived in neighborhoods with crime and drug selling said it would be more difficult (see Table 16.8). In addition, those parents who saw their children regularly were more likely to say it would be easy to stay off drugs.

## SUMMARY AND CONCLUSIONS

Because of the small sample size, the findings in this chapter are preliminary. However, the data are valuable because they provide qualitative and quantitative data from the perspective of the offenders. The parolee data is particularly valuable because the respondents were followed for 1 year.

The data suggest a reciprocal process between economic well-being and criminal activity. Before entering prison, a lack of education and few marketable skills made it difficult for many inmates to pay for basic necessities. Those who lacked the ability to

pay for necessities were more likely to become involved in criminal activities and become incarcerated. Involvement in drugs further compromised their economic abilities. Once they were incarcerated, their ability to become economically self-sufficient was further compromised because of the stigma of being an ex-con and the fact that they had not improved their economic skills while they were in prison.

Being able to stay off drugs is a key to successful reentry. Those parolees who took a substance abuse class while in prison were significantly less likely to return to prison within the first year after release.

Consistent with life course theory, family resources and adequate employment were related to successful reentry. Those who had specific career goals and who worked longer hours were more successful during the first year after release. In addition, having stronger family bonds (being close to a partner or children) was associated with a greater ability to pay for necessities. Apparently, having family ties provided resources that helped parolees pay for necessities. Those with family ties also had less difficulty staying off drugs.

As the incarceration rate has risen during the past quarter of a century, there has been relatively little study of how families are affected by it. In this chapter, I have shown that not only do family deficits lead to initial

**Table 16.8** Regression of Perceived Difficulty in Staying Off Drugs by Neighborhood Crime and Contact With Children

| Predictor Variables Equation 1 (N = 46) | B | Beta |
| --- | --- | --- |
| Age | 0.00 | −0.01 |
| Gender | 0.68 | 0.23 |
| Live in neighborhood with crime and drug selling | −0.88 | −0.30* |
| *Predictor Variables Equation 2 (N = 32)* | | |
| Age | 0.00 | −0.03 |
| Gender | 0.37 | 0.12 |
| Live in neighborhood with crime and drug selling | −1.15 | −0.42** |
| Number of days per week visit with children | 0.18 | 0.44** |

*p < .05
**p < .01

incarceration, but incarceration in turn affects families negatively. Thus, incarceration, which is supposed to protect society and help reduce crime, may actually help increase crime by interfering with family bonds and the ability of individuals and families to become self-sufficient economically. Society and families pay a heavy social, emotional, and economic price for the high rate of incarceration.

## REFERENCES

Agnew, R. (2005). *Why do criminals offend? A general theory of crime and delinquency*. Los Angeles: Roxbury.

Agnew, R. (2006). *Pressured into crime: An overview of General Strain Theory*. Los Angeles: Roxbury.

Akers, R. L., & Sellers, C. S. (2004). *Criminological theories: Introduction, evaluation, and application*. Los Angeles: Roxbury.

Bonczar, T. P. (2003). Prevalence of imprisonment in the U.S. population, 1974–2001. In Bureau of Justice Statistics Special Report, NCJ 197976 (pp. 1–12). Washington, DC: Bureau of Justice Statistics.

Carlson, P. M. (2004). Something to lose: A balanced and reality-based rationale for institutional programming. In J. L. Krienert & M. S. Fleisher (Eds.), *Crime and employment: Critical issues in crime reduction for corrections* (pp. 61–74). Walnut Creek, CA: AltaMira Press.

Catalano, R. F., & Hawkins, J. D. (1996). The social development model: A theory of antisocial behavior. In J. D. Hawkins (Ed.), *Delinquency and crime: Current theories* (pp. 149–197). Cambridge, UK: Cambridge University Press.

Day, R. D., Acock, A. C., Bahr, S. J., & Arditti, J. (2005). Incarcerated fathers returning home to children and families: A primer on doing research with men in prison. *Fathering, A Journal of Theory, Research, and Practice About Men as Parents, 3*(3), 183–200.

Elder, G. H., Jr. (2001). Time, human agency, and social change: Perspectives on the life course. In A. Piquero & P. Mazerolle (Eds.), *Life-course criminology: Contemporary and classic readings* (pp. 3–20). Belmont, CA: Wadsworth/Thomson Learning.

Elliott, D. S., & Menard, S. (1996). Delinquent friends and delinquent behavior: Temporal and developmental patterns. In J. D. Hawkins (Ed.), *Delinquency and crime: Current theories* (pp. 28–67). Cambridge, UK: Cambridge University Press.

Fagan, J. (1989). Cessation of family violence: Deterrence and dissuasion. In L. Ohlin & M. Tonry (Eds.), *Family violence.* Chicago: University of Chicago Press.

Giordano, P. C., Cernkovich, S. A., & Rudolph, J. L. (2002). Gender, crime, and desistance: Toward a theory of cognitive transformation. *American Journal of Sociology, 107*(4), 880–1064.

Green, K. M., Ensminger, M. E., Robertson, J. A., & Hee-Soon, J. (2006). Impact of sons' incarceration on African American mothers' psychological distress. *Journal of Marriage and Family, 68,* 430–441.

Hanlon, T. E., O'Grady, K. E., Bennett-Sears, T., & Callaman, J. M. (2005). Incarcerated drug-using mothers: Their characteristics and vulnerability. *American Journal of Drug and Alcohol Abuse, 31,* 59–77.

Harrison, P. M., & Beck, A. J. (2005). *Prison and jail inmates at midyear 2004* (NCJ 208801, pp. 1–14). Washington, DC: Bureau of Justice Statistics, U.S. Department of Justice, Office of Justice Programs.

Harrison, P. M., & Beck, A. J. (2006). *Prison and jail inmates at midyear 2005* (NCJ 213133, pp. 1–13). Washington, DC: Bureau of Justice Statistics, U.S. Department of Justice, Office of Justice Programs.

Hirschi, T. (1969). *Causes of delinquency.* Berkeley: University of California Press.

Horney, J., Osgood, D. W., & Marshall, I. H. (1995). Criminal careers in the short-term: Intra-individual variability in crime and its relation to local life circumstances. *American Sociological Review, 60*(5), 655–673.

Hughes, T. A., Wilson, D. J., & Beck, A. J. (2001). *Trends in state parole, 1990–2000* (NCJ 184735, pp. 1–16). Washington, DC: Bureau of Justice Statistics, U.S. Department of Justice, Office of Justice Programs.

Kandel, D. B., & Yamaguchi, K. (1987). Job mobility and drug use: An event history analysis. *American Journal of Sociology, 92,* 836–878.

Langan, P., & Levin, D. (2002). *Recidivism of prisoners released in 1994.* (NCJ 193427, pp. 1–16). Washington. DC: Bureau of Justice Statistics, U.S. Department of Justice, Office of Justice Programs.

Laub, J. H., Nagin, D. S., & Sampson, R. J. (1998). Trajectories of change in criminal offending: Good marriages and the desistance process. *American Sociological Review, 63,* 225–238.

Laub, J. H., & Sampson, R. J. (2001). Understanding desistance from crime. In M. Tonry (Ed.), *Crime and justice: An annual review of research* (pp. 1–69). Chicago: University of Chicago Press.

Lynch, J. P., & Sabol, W. J. (2001). *Prison reentry in perspective.* Washington, DC: Urban Institute.

Maruna, S., & Toch, H. (2005). The impact of imprisonment on the desistance process. In J. Travis & C. Visher (Eds.), *Prison reentry and crime in America* (pp. 139–178). New York: Cambridge University Press.

Pager, D. (2003). The mark of a criminal record. *American Journal of Sociology, 108*(5), 937–975.

Petersilia, J. (2003). *When prisoners come home: Parole and prison reentry.* Oxford, UK: Oxford University Press.

Petersilia, J. (2005). From cell to society: Who is returning home? In J. Travis & C. Visher (Eds.), *Prison reentry and crime in America* (pp. 15–49). New York: Cambridge University Press.

Sampson, R. J., & Laub, J. H. (1990). Crime and deviance over the life course: The salience of adult social bonds. *American Sociological Review, 55,* 609–627.

Sampson, R. J., & Laub, J. H. (2001). Understanding variability in lives through time: Contributions of life-course criminology. In A. Piquero & P. Mazerolle (Eds.), *Life-course criminology: Contemporary and classic readings* (pp. 242–258). Belmont, CA: Wadsworth/Thomson Learning.

Shover, N., & Thompson, C. Y. (1992). Age, differential expectations, and crime desistance. *Criminology, 30*(1), 89–104.

Stucky, T. D., Heimer, K., & Lang, J. B. (2005). Partisan politics, electoral competition and imprisonment: An analysis of states over time. *Criminology, 43*(1), 211–248.

Sutherland, E. H. (1947). *Principles of criminology* (4th ed.). Chicago: Lippincott.

Travis, J., & Visher, C. A. (2005a). Introduction: Viewing crime and public safety through the reentry lens. In J. Travis & C. A. Visher (Eds.), *Prisoner reentry and crime in America* (pp. 1–14). New York: Cambridge University Press.

Travis, J., & Visher, C. A. (2005b). *Prisoner reentry and crime in America.* New York: Cambridge University Press.

Uggen, C. (2000). Work as a turning point in the life of criminals: A duration model of age, employment, and recidivism. *American Sociological Review, 67,* 529–546.

Uggen, C., Wakefield, S., & Western, B. (2005). Work and family perspectives on reentry. In J. Travis & C. Visher (Eds.), *Prison reentry and crime in America* (pp. 209–243). New York: Cambridge University Press.

U.S. Census Bureau. (2004). *Statistical Abstract of the United States: 2004–2005* (124th ed.). Washington, DC: Bernan Press.

Vaillant, G. E. (1995). *The natural history of alcoholism revisited.* Cambridge, MA: Harvard University Press.

Visher, C. A., & Travis, J. (2003). Transitions from prison to community: Understanding individual pathways. *Annual Review of Sociology, 29,* 89–113.

Warr, M. (1998). Life-course transitions and desistance from crime. *Criminology, 36,* 183–216.

# CHAPTER 17

# Children's Time Use and Parental Involvement in Low-Income Families

W. Jean Yeung and Rebecca Glauber

Despite evidence of a small decline in child poverty during the second half of the 1990s, recent reports from the U.S. Census Bureau have shown that the number of children living in poverty increased by nearly one-half million in 1 year. In 2002, 16.7% of children lived in households where total household income was below the official federal poverty line. Children under age 6 and living in female-headed households are particularly vulnerable to poverty. In 2002, 48.6% of these children lived in households where total household income was below the official federal poverty line. This is five times the rate of poverty for children younger than age 6 living in households with two married parents (U.S. Census Bureau, 2003). Another recent trend that has significant policy implications is the steady increase in the percentage of poor children who live with working parents (Child Trends Databank, 2003). Twenty-seven million American children live in families in which their parents make less than twice the official federal poverty line, and more than 85% of these children have at least one working parent (National Center for Children in Poverty, 2004).

Recent welfare reform policies that have increased the work requirements of welfare recipients raise important and new questions regarding parents' work-family tradeoffs and the effects of these tradeoffs on children's well-being. Although some researchers and policymakers argue that children will benefit from the regularity and routine provided by working parents, others express concern over the likely negative consequences of employment policies that could potentially lead to a reduction in the amount of time that parents spend with their children (Huston, 2002).

Low-income families, including many single-parent families and working-poor two-parent families, face the challenge of supervising their children and spending time with their children on developmentally appropriate activities. Like other parents, low-income parents may make trade-offs between their work hours and their time spent with children. When employed, however, low-income parents often have less control over their work schedules and have fewer resources to purchase quality child-care services and provide for children's developmental needs. Thus, they are likely to experience intense work-family conflict. Scheduling conflicts, coupled with daily economic pressures may be detrimental to parents' psychological well-being, making them anxious or depressed, which in turn may lead to diminished energy in their provision of supportive interaction and a stimulating environment for children (McLoyd, 1990; Yeung, Linver, & Brooks-Gunn, 2002). However, employment can be beneficial to children if it results in additional income to provide better food, housing, medical care, a more stimulating and supportive environment for children, or improved parental psychological well-being, and a positive role model for children.

One potentially important aspect of children's well-being that has received little attention in poverty research is children's time use. Research has shown that children's productive use of time in activities such as reading, studying, extracurricular activities, and volunteer work tends to contribute to successful development (Eccles & Barbers, 1998; Leone & Richards, 1989; Timmer, Eccles, & O'Brien, 1985). Further, the time that children spend with parents, siblings, peers, and relatives is indicative of the quality of the social support network surrounding children, and it relates importantly to children's achievement. Time use studies, when used to complement traditional statistical information such as demographics, parents' earnings, and employment, can provide an otherwise unavailable glimpse of children's organization of life and social connections across multiple contexts (Folbre, 1997).

Our study uses both time diary data and nondiary data to address two research questions: (1) Do children in low-income families spend less time with parents or in activities that are conducive to learning or in activities that are associated with behavior problems?

(2) Do low-income working mothers have a lower level of involvement with children than nonworking low-income mothers do?

## LITERATURE REVIEW

Results from existing research on maternal employment and children's well-being have yielded mostly negligible or positive effects (Belsky, 1990; Parcel & Menaghan, 1994; Perry-Jenkins, Repetti, & Crouter, 2000), except for maternal employment during the very early stages of children's lives (Han, Waldfogel, & Brooks-Gunn, 2001; Rhum, 2004). Maternal employment is found to be associated with better maternal mental health (Hoffman & Youngblade, 1999). Much of this body of literature, however, has focused on middle-class two-parent families (Brooks-Gunn, Han, & Waldfogel, 2002; Harvey, 1999). Among low-income families, results from the literature range from no effect (Zaslow, McGroder, Cave, & Mariner, 1999) to a modest but overall positive effect of maternal employment on children's cognitive and social development (Moore & Driscoll, 1997; Vandell & Ramanan, 1992; Zaslow & Emig, 1997). Research examining parental work schedules shows that parents who work split shifts to reduce their paid child-care costs sacrifice important time with one another (Kiser, 2002; Presser, 1994). Research investigating the processes and mechanisms through which maternal employment affects children's well-being is more limited.

This chapter examines how maternal employment affects parents' psychological well-being and parent-child interaction. Maternal employment is seen to have a direct impact on family income, parents' psychological well-being, and their parenting behavior. Based on a large body of literature (Conger et al., 1992; Conger, Patterson, & Ge, 1995; McLoyd, 1990; McLoyd, Jayaratne, Ceballo, & Borquez, 1994), we hypothesize that a family's financial resources reduce economic pressure and parents' emotional stress, which in turn affect parenting behavior. Parents who have a healthy psychological well-being are more likely to be supportive of and involved with their children. We conceptualize parenting behavior broadly to include how parents structure their children's lives, parents' emotional support, as well as parents' involvement in their children's daily activities and in providing materials and experiences that are conducive to children's healthy development. These are important mechanisms identified in the literature through which income affects children's well-being (Demo & Cox, 2000; Guo & Harris, 2000; Mayer, 1997; Shonkoff & Phillips, 2000; Yeung et al., 2002).

A study on children in some local Head Start programs indicated that increased parental work hours and earnings are associated with improved maternal mental health and reduced punitive parenting behavior (Raver, 2003). Other studies, however, found that unless employment leads to a reduction in financial strain, mothers tend to become less supportive of and less involved in their children's lives (Jackson, Brooks-Gunn, Huang, & Glassman, 2000). These studies are limited in their generalizability because of the selective samples used.

Family income may also have a direct impact on parenting behavior as the time parents spend caring for children carries an opportunity cost of both wages forgone and human capital accumulation forgone (Mincer & Polacheck, 1974). Hence, parental involvement with children, particularly in the quantity of time with a child, may be reduced as parents' earning power increases. Studies by Hill and Stafford (1974) and Leibowitz (1974, 1977), however, indicate that mothers with high socioeconomic status spend significantly more time caring for their preschool children than do mothers with low socioeconomic status. A few recent studies also show that the substitution between

income and time with children is on a more limited scope as a desire for interaction with children leads parents in families with high income to spend more time with children during nonworking hours, particularly on weekends (Hallberg & Klevmarken 2003; Yeung & Stafford, 2003).

Spending time with children is an important way for parents to channel critical resources and values to children. Research in developmental psychology demonstrates that children of parents who provide a supportive environment and who spend direct time on important developmental activities have higher levels of cognitive skills and self-esteem (Eccles, Wigfield, & Schiefele, 1997; Maccoby & Martin, 1984). Recent research has also noted the potentially positive implications of family routines and rituals for children (Crouter & McHale, 2003; Fiese et al., 2002). These studies find that adolescents who are in families that share dinner together several nights a week or that share certain holiday rituals tend to do well in school, report lower levels of anxiety, and are less likely to engage in risky behavior.

Early sociological studies reveal that parents from different socioeconomic levels have different parenting practices (Kohn, 1969). Children's time use patterns reflect parents' values, resources, and constraints. More recent studies indicate that children of highly educated parents study and read more, watch TV less (Bianchi & Robinson, 1997; Yeung & Stafford, 2003), and participate in more organized activities (Hofferth & Sandberg, 2001; Lareau, 2002).

In summary, we propose that the key to understanding how parental employment affects children's well-being is through an analysis of how parents' employment affects their own psychological well-being, which in turn affects how parents structure their children's lives and the extent to which they are involved in their children's various activities. We use the data collected from children's time diaries to examine parental involvement in children's activities. Our effort in this paper focuses only on how employment and income affect parents' psychological well-being and parenting behavior. In future work, we will examine how parents' psychological well-being and parenting behavior affect various measures of children's well-being. Details on the data used are described in the next section.

## DATA AND MEASURES

We examined these issues through the study of children's time diaries and stylized survey data collected in the Panel Study of Income Dynamics (PSID). The PSID has collected annual data on the socioeconomic characteristics of a nationally representative sample of about 5,000 families since 1968. In 1997, the PSID conducted a Child Development Supplement (PSID-CDS), which contains child development information for approximately 3,600 children aged 0 to 12 years in 1997.

### Children's Time Diary Data

Unique to this data set is the detailed information about children's daily activities, which was collected in a time diary format in the spring and the fall of 1997. Each family was asked to complete a diary for as many as two children about what a child did, where the child was, who did the activity with the child, who was present but not involved, and what else the child was doing at that time. The diaries were collected for a random weekday and a random weekend day for each child.[1] From these diaries, researchers can construct children's activities over a week, and the role of caregiver, peers, kinship, and others in children's lives. The response rate for the time diary data was about 80%. Approximately 60% of these diaries were completed by the mother of the target child alone, 12% were completed by the mother and the target child together, 6% were completed by the target

child alone, 6% with the father present, and 12% were completed by someone else. We use all the diary data that are available for the analyses in this paper.

The validity of the time diary data has been assessed extensively in previous literature (Juster, 1985). This method is generally regarded as preferable to other methods of measuring time use in large samples. More traditional stylized questions that ask directly about the frequency and duration of time spent in various activities are affected by the predefined categorization of activities and possibly by systematic overestimate or underestimation by respondents of the actual time spent in those activities (Robinson, 1985; Stafford & Duncan, 1985). Time diaries have been found to be as accurate as, and possibly more accurate than, more expensive methods that assess time use sampled on a real-time basis. These include observationally based data and data from pager studies or Experience Sampling Methods (National Academy of Sciences, 2000). A schematic view and discussion of the coding system used for the PSID children's diaries and a detailed description of the codes is contained within the *PSID-CDS Coding Manual* available at the study Web site (http://psidonline.isr.umich.edu/CDS/TDqnaires.html).

We examined how much time children spent in schools, in day care, by themselves, and in various activities such as studying, reading, working on computers, watching TV, participating in arts or sports activities, sleeping, eating, doing housework, participating in religious activities, and in leisure activities. In addition, we examined time with parents, siblings, grandparents, other relatives, nonrelatives, and friends.

### Nondiary Data on Parenting Behavior

To supplement children's time diary data so that we could obtain a more complete picture of factors that affect parents' involvement in children's lives, we used other nondiary data such as parental involvement in various activities and parental monitoring behavior. Unfortunately, all of these involvement measures have been collected only for the primary caregiver of the target child, which is the mother in 95% of the cases. Therefore, our analysis is mostly limited to mother's behavior and well-being.

Parental monitoring behavior is assessed with an index based on the primary caregiver's knowledge of the child's close friends and with whom the child is when he or she is not at home. This index ranges from one to five, with five indicating the highest level of parental monitoring. Parental school involvement is measured by an index created from the average score of 11 items such as the frequency of volunteering in the child's school, observing the child's classroom, attending the child's school events, meeting with the child's teacher and principal, and attending parent teacher organization (PTO) or other such meetings. These items are measured on a three-point scale, with one indicating not having done the school activity in the current school year and three indicating having done the school activity more than once in the current school year.

Two other measures of parental involvement were used. They are based on the Home Observation for Measurement of the Environment scale (HOME)–Short Form from the Caldwell and Bradley HOME Inventory, Caldwell & Bradley, 1984). This scale assesses the cognitive stimulation and emotional support parents provide to children. The items are age-specific. The emotional support subscale includes interviewer's observation of the interaction between the child and the primary caregiver regarding the affection, warmth, and emotional support from the parent as well as reports from the primary caregiver about how often the parent spends time with the child, how close the child feels to the parents, and the parents' disciplinary approach. The

subscale for cognitive stimulation is based on a number of measures including the amount of time parents spend with children in outdoor activities, meal-eating, and outings to museums, theaters, or libraries; whether the child has access to toys, CD players or recorders, newspapers and magazines, or other materials to help learn; whether older children are engaged in extracurricular activities or read for enjoyment. Both subscales for emotional support and cognitive stimulation range from 2 to 14. For more detailed information about these measures, see the User's Guide for the PSID-CDS (Hofferth, Davis-Kean, Davis, & Finkelstein, 1997).

## Measures of Maternal Psychological Well-Being

Maternal emotional stress was assessed with the Composite International Diagnostic Interview (CIDI) (Kessler & Mroszek, 1994). Mothers responded to 10 questions, all prefaced by the question, "During the past 30 days, how often did you . . . ?" Example response-items include, "Feel tired out for no good reason," "Feel depressed," "Feel nervous," and "Feel worthless." Responses were on a Likert scale ranging from 0 (none of the time) to 4 (all of the time). An index was created by calculating the mean of all items (Cronbach's alpha was .90). This construct does not measure depression in a clinical sense but, rather, mother's depressive affect or emotional distress. A second measure of maternal psychological well-being examined in this chapter is an index of parental aggravation, measured by the extent to which the parent agreed to the following statement (one equals not at all true and five equals completely true): "[The child] seems to be harder to care for than most children," "There are some things that the child does that really bother me a lot," "I find myself giving up more of my life to meet [the child's] needs than I ever expected," "I often feel angry with [the child]," and " I would be doing better in my life without [the child]."

## RESULTS: DESCRIPTIVE ANALYSES

Using children's time diaries, we examined children's time spent with parents, family, and nonrelatives, and their time allocated to various activities. We constructed children's weekly time based on diary data collected for a randomly chosen weekday and a weekend day by calculating the sum of weekday time multiplied by five and weekend time multiplied by two.

Two levels of involvement are reported here, one accounts for only the time that a child is directly engaged with another person, the other includes the time that someone is available to the child but is not directly engaged with him or her in a certain activity. Following Lamb's convention (Lamb, Pleck, Charnov, & Levine, 1985), we refer to these two levels of involvement as "engaged time" and "accessible time." We compare the time use patterns for children across families at three poverty thresholds: (1) below the federal poverty level for the respective family size ($16,036 for a family of four in 1996), (2) at or above the federal poverty level, but at or below twice the federal poverty level for the respective family size, and (3) above twice the federal poverty level for the respective family size. The first two groups are both considered low-income families in this work. Whereas the first group falls under the official poverty definition, the second group also faces great challenges in caring for children but has received less attention in the literature and in policy considerations. We will call these three groups "poor," "near-poor," and "nonpoor" in subsequent sections.

Descriptive analyses reveal significant differences among income groups in both time allocated to various types of activities and in time children spend with kin and nonkin. We present data for preschoolers (aged 0 to 5 years) and school-age children (aged 6 to 12 years) separately as children's time use differs substantially by children's ages.

### With Whom Do Children Spend Their Time?

Tables 17.1 and 17.2 show children's mean weekly hours spent with parents, step-parents, siblings, grandparents, other relatives, nonrelatives, and friends for preschool age children and school-age children respectively. The top panel presents data for engaged time only, and the bottom panel presents data for engaged and accessible time. The most striking differences revealed in these tables are in the time that children from different income groups spend with their biological fathers. On average, preschool children in the poor group spend about 5 hours per week engaged with their fathers. This figure triples for nonpoor children, who spend an average of 16 hours per week engaged with their fathers. Children from near-poor families spend about 14 hours per week with their fathers. This pattern is also exhibited in the time that fathers are not only engaged with, but accessible to, their children. Children younger than age 6 from poor families spend an average of about 9 hours with their fathers either engaged with, or accessible to them. The corresponding level of time for nonpoor families is more than 28 hours.

Although children's time spent with fathers varies significantly across the three income groups, children's time spent with mothers does not. On average, mothers of children younger than age 6 spend about 30 hours engaged with their child and about 52 to 55 hours if we include the time when mothers are accessible to, but not directly engaged with, their child. This is more than twice the amount of time a child spends with his or her father, with the discrepancy particularly large

**Table 17.1** Time Children Aged 0–5 Spend With Others, by Income Group

| | Income Group | | |
|---|---|---|---|
| Total Weekly Engagement Hours (mean) | Poor | Near-Poor | Nonpoor |
| Mother | 29.64 | 33.56 | 30.92 |
| Father | 5.01[bc] | 14.03[a] | 16.27[a] |
| Stepmom | 0.13 | 0.12 | 0.03 |
| Stepdad | 0.28 | 0.40 | 0.14 |
| Siblings (biological or step) | 29.27 | 28.28 | 26.43 |
| Grandparents | 7.87 | 8.08[c] | 5.57[b] |
| Other relatives | 6.67[c] | 6.85[c] | 4.03[ab] |
| Other nonrelatives | 16.36 | 17.42 | 19.41 |
| Friends | 5.40 | 3.69 | 5.35 |
| Number of observations | 213 | 202 | 803 |

| | Income Group | | |
|---|---|---|---|
| Total Weekly Engagement + Accessible Hours (mean) | Poor | Near-Poor | Nonpoor |
| Mother | 52.91 | 55.35 | 51.97 |
| Father | 8.89[bc] | 20.43[ac] | 28.45[ab] |
| Stepmom | 0.22 | 0.15 | 0.06 |
| Stepdad | 0.56 | 0.57 | 0.26 |
| Siblings (biological or step) | 43.10 | 38.55 | 39.97 |
| Grandparents | 19.36[c] | 17.51[c] | 10.02[ab] |
| Other relatives | 12.40[c] | 12.96[c] | 7.08[ab] |
| Other nonrelatives | 36.72 | 34.88 | 40.52 |
| Friends | 6.68 | 4.44 | 6.41 |
| Alone | 0.34 | 0.29 | 0.47 |
| Number of observations | 213 | 202 | 803 |

a. Significantly different from mean of poor group at .05 level.
b. Significantly different from mean of near-poor group at .05 level.
c. Significantly different from mean of nonpoor group at .05 level.

for poor families because the majority of these families are single-mother families.

Tables 17.1 and 17.2 also reveal differences in the amount of time children spend with relatives, friends, and siblings. Children from poor or near-poor families spend significantly more time with relatives than do children from nonpoor families. On average, children in the two lower-income groups spend about 8 hours per week directly engaged with grandparents and about 7 hours per week directly engaged with other relatives, and children in nonpoor families spend about 2 to 3 hours less per week with grandparents and with other relatives. When we include the time that these relatives are accessible to them, the differences become magnified, with those in the nonpoor group spending more than 9 hours less with grandparents and more than 5 hours less with other relatives per week. These

**Table 17.2**   Time Children Aged 6-12 Spend With Others, by Income Group

|  | Income Group | | |
| --- | --- | --- | --- |
| *Total Weekly Engagement Hours (mean)* | *Poor* | *Near-Poor* | *Nonpoor* |
| Mother | 15.49 | 17.74 | 17.82 |
| Father | 5.19[bc] | 7.83[ac] | 11.70[ac] |
| Stepmom | 0.00 | 0.14 | 0.06 |
| Stepdad | 0.07 | 0.27 | 0.34 |
| Siblings (biological or step) | 29.02[c] | 28.01 | 24.47[a] |
| Grandparents | 2.21[b] | 4.14[ac] | 2.24[ac] |
| Other relatives | 6.59[bc] | 6.79[a] | 3.00[a] |
| Other nonrelatives | 37.93 | 35.52[c] | 38.99[b] |
| Friends | 7.47[bc] | 11.90[a] | 13.05[a] |
| Number of observations | 242 | 240 | 881 |

|  | Income Group | | |
| --- | --- | --- | --- |
| *Total Weekly Engagement + Accessible Hours (mean)* | *Poor* | *Near-Poor* | *Nonpoor* |
| Mother | 34.46 | 36.37 | 37.00 |
| Father | 8.88[bc] | 14.54[ab] | 23.52[ac] |
| Stepmom | 0.04 | 0.33 | 0.09 |
| Stepdad | 0.26 | 0.53 | 0.68 |
| Siblings (biological or step) | 40.75 | 42.02[c] | 37.05[b] |
| Grandparents | 4.65[b] | 9.29[ac] | 4.05[b] |
| Other relatives | 9.70[c] | 10.67[c] | 4.76[ab] |
| Other nonrelatives | 74.65 | 68.69[c] | 79.41[b] |
| Friends | 9.38[bc] | 13.90[a] | 14.69[a] |
| Alone | 3.60[c] | 2.83 | 2.29[a] |
| Number of observations | 242 | 240 | 881 |

a. Significantly different from mean of poor group at .05 level.
b. Significantly different from mean of near-poor group at .05 level.
c. Significantly different from mean of nonpoor group at .05 level.

results suggest that grandparents and other relatives often serve as child-care providers for parents who have scarce financial resources. A more detailed examination of the data reveals that this is particularly true for children younger than age 2 in poor or near-poor families who spend 8 to 10 hours per week directly engaged with a grandparent and 20 to 22 hours per week if we include the time a grandparent is accessible to them (data not presented). The implication of children's time with relatives and their well-being warrants future research. Although children may benefit from the kin support network, research shows that the quality of child care by relatives, in-home babysitters, and other informal providers is not always highly rated (Kontos, Howes, Shinn, & Galinsky, 1995).

No statistically significant differences are found across groups in children's time spent with others. On average, children aged 0 to 5 years spend 26 to 29 hours per week directly engaged with siblings, about 5 hours engaged with friends, and 16 to 19 hours engaged with other nonrelatives.

When we look at the patterns for children aged 6 to 12 in Table 17.2, we see that, consistent with previous literature, parents' time involvement decreases as children become older. This is mainly because of a decrease in children's need for personal care as they spend substantially more time in school. Data show that children who live in poverty continue to have a much lower level of contact with fathers in middle childhood than do those in nonpoor families.

Mothers of older children spend about 15 to 18 hours directly engaged with their school-age child, 35 to 37 hours if we include the time that a mother is accessible to the child. As with younger children, there are no statistically significant differences among income groups in the amount of time mothers spend with their older children, though mothers who live in poverty spend about 2 hours less with each child than do nonpoor or near-poor mothers. This pattern suggests that mothers who live in poverty, most of them single mothers, experience greater constraints in meeting their children's time needs or that their psychological well-being leads them to be less involved with their children. This also supports some recent findings that parents with high incomes substitute market child-care services for their own child-care time only in a limited scope, that is, they use high levels of child-care services on weekdays but also spend a substantial amount of time with children themselves, especially on weekends (Hallberg & Klevmarken, 2003; Yeung & Stafford, 2003).

As to time with relatives, school-age children spend a substantially lower amount of time with grandparents than children younger than 6—about 2.5 hours of engaged time per week for those in poverty and those who are above two times the official federal poverty level, twice as high when counting the accessible time. However, children from near-poor families spend twice the amount of time with grandparents, perhaps indicative of a great number of working-poor parents in this group who are in need of low-cost child care but who do not qualify for government subsidies. As with children younger than age 6, school-age children in the two low-income groups also spend more time with other relatives. They spend about 7 hours per week directly engaged with or in the vicinity of other relatives, as compared with the 3 hours for 6- to 12-year-olds from nonpoor families, reflecting a higher level of time children in nonpoor families spend in formal after-school care and extracurricular activities. These findings are consistent with recent ethnographic studies' findings that children in lower SES groups spend more time with their extended kin (Lareau, 2002). Older children in poverty spend significantly more time engaged with their siblings and less time with their friends than do children in nonpoor families. Interestingly, this pattern is not exhibited for younger children.

Table 17.2 also shows that children in poverty spend more time alone than do those in nonpoor families: 3.6 hours as opposed to 2.3 hours per week. The amount of time children are alone increases by children's age. Children aged 10 or older from poor and near-poor families average 5 hours alone per week, whereas children aged 10 or older from nonpoor families average 3.7 hours alone per week (data not presented).

## What Do Children Do?

Tables 17.3 and 17.4 reveal that across the income groups, children's lives are structured quite differently as well. For children younger than, those in nonpoor families spend more time reading and working on computers. On average, younger children from upper-income families spend about 1.7 hours per week reading, whereas younger children in poverty spend about .73 hours per week reading. These differences are also observed for school-age children. Children younger than the age of 6 who live in poverty spend about 13 hours per week watching television, compared with 10 hours for children in nonpoor families. The same pattern is exhibited for older children. Older children who live in poverty spend an average of 16 hours per week watching television, whereas children in upper-income families spend an average of 12 hours per week watching television. These results suggest that we may be able to trace gaps in children's cognitive and developmental outcomes to children's differential experiences at a very early age.

Three differences between younger and older children stand out: a large increase in the amount of time older children spend in school,

a modest increase in their studying time, and a decrease in their leisure time by about 50%. There are also significant differences across income groups in the amount of time children spend in school, in day care, and in visiting others. Poor children younger than age 6 spend more time in school than do near-poor children. This may be because of Head Start, a federally funded program that provides some preschool to young children from families that have an income level under the official poverty line. Older children from poor families similarly spend more time in school than do children from near-poor families. There are also significant differences among income groups in the amount of time children spend in day care. Across ages, children from poor families spend less time in formal day care than do children from the other two income groups,

**Table 17.3**   Time Allocated to Various Activities for Children Aged 0–5, by Income Group

| *Total Weekly Hours on Activities (mean)* | *Income Group* | | |
| --- | --- | --- | --- |
| | *Poor* | *Near-Poor* | *Nonpoor* |
| Studying | 0.31 | 0.43 | 0.28 |
| Reading | 0.73[c] | 0.80[c] | 1.66[ab] |
| Computer | 0.03[c] | 0.28 | 0.52[a] |
| TV | 13.03[c] | 13.66[c] | 9.69[ab] |
| Art | 1.56[bc] | 0.21[ac] | 0.89[ab] |
| Sports | 2.86 | 3.02 | 3.46 |
| School | 9.05[b] | 4.45[a] | 6.6 |
| Day care | 5.79[bc] | 10.82[a] | 9.91[a] |
| Sleep | 82.23 | 81.16 | 80.42 |
| Conversation | 0.96 | 0.68 | 1.06 |
| Eating | 11.11 | 10.17 | 10.33 |
| Household work and shopping | 3.88[c] | 4.61 | 5.81[a] |
| Market work | 0.01 | 0.01 | 0 |
| Religious activities | 0.29[bc] | 0.96[a] | 0.88[a] |
| Other leisure | 22.76 | 22.43 | 24.34 |
| Personal care | 9.33 | 9.1 | 8.75 |
| Visiting | 2.34[b] | 4.43[ac] | 2.66[b] |
| Number of observations | 213 | 202 | 803 |

a. Significantly different from mean of poor group at .05 level.
b. Significantly different from mean of near-poor group at .05 level.
c. Significantly different from mean of nonpoor group at .05 level.

**Table 17.4**   Time Allocated to Various Activities for Children Aged 6–12, by Income Group

| Total Weekly Hours on Activities (mean) | Income Group | | |
|---|---|---|---|
| | Poor | Near-Poor | Nonpoor |
| Studying | 2.82 | 2.01[c] | 2.96[b] |
| Reading | 1.03 | 0.60[c] | 1.33[b] |
| Computer | 0.18[c] | 0.73 | 1.10[a] |
| TV | 16.30[c] | 14.69[c] | 12.05[ab] |
| Art | 0.62 | 0.76 | 0.98 |
| Sports | 5.16 | 6.48 | 6.58 |
| School | 35.24[b] | 30.64[a] | 32.96 |
| Day care | 0.43[c] | 0.40[c] | 1.35[ab] |
| Sleep | 70.06[c] | 69.75 | 68.19[a] |
| Conversation | 0.32 | 0.37 | 0.52 |
| Eating | 7.58 | 7.45 | 7.6 |
| Household work and shopping | 3.80[c] | 5.08 | 5.81[a] |
| Market work | 0.15 | 0.32 | 0.24 |
| Religious activities | 1.13 | 1.34 | 1.47 |
| Other leisure | 11.78 | 13.82 | 13.36 |
| Personal care | 7.99 | 8 | 7.93 |
| Visiting | 2.42[c] | 3.82 | 3.72[a] |
| Number of observations | 242 | 280 | 881 |

a. Significantly different from mean of poor group at .05 level.
b. Significantly different from mean of near-poor poverty group at .05 level.
c. Significantly different from mean of nonpoor group at .05 level.

perhaps suggestive of parents from these families relying more on grandparents and other relatives for their day care needs.[2]

We also note that school-age children spend about 6 to 7 hours per week in arts and sports, with those in poverty spending about 5.8 hours and those in the nonpoor group spending about 7.6 hours in these activities, or about a third of the time they spend watching TV. Another interesting difference is that children in nonpoor families spend more time in household work and in shopping, averaging about 6 hours per week, compared with 3.8 hours for children in poor families. No significant difference is found across income groups in sports, eating, personal care, and other leisure activities.

## Low-Income Families

In the following sections, we provide a more detailed analysis of children from low-income families, defined in this paper as all children who reside in households with total family income under two times the official federal poverty line (both the poor and near-poor groups in previous tables). Children's time allocation may vary substantially by family structure and parents' work status, so we examine children's circumstances separately for those in single-parent families and those in two-parent families (including both biological parents and stepparents). For each type of family structure, we distinguish between working-poor and non–working-poor families.

We define working-poor families as those that have a family income below two times the official federal poverty line and two parents who work the equivalent of a full-time job (40 hours or more per week) or a single parent who works at least 20 hours per week. This group accounts for 62% of the single-mother low-income families and 73% of the two-parent low-income families.

Table 17.5 presents data for these low-income families. Comparing children from single-parent working-poor families with children from single-parent non–working-poor families, we see that children in working-poor families spend significantly less time with fathers, less time with both parents together, and less time with their friends, but more time with nonrelatives, perhaps day care providers or neighbors. They also spend 2 hours more per week watching TV and 2 hours less per week in sports and arts activities than do children from non–working-poor single-parent families. In addition, children in single-mother working-poor families spend 4 hours more per week in day care than do children from nonworking single-mother families. However, the total weekly time that children are engaged with their mothers is at a similar level for children from both working-poor and non–working-poor single-mother families. Although working-poor single mothers spend on average about one hour less with their children than do nonworking single mothers, this difference is not significant.

There is no significant difference in the monitoring behavior of working and non–working-poor single mothers. However, working-poor single mothers are less involved in their children's school—they volunteer and make presentations in class and attend PTO meetings less often than do non–working-poor single mothers. They are also more likely to cite work schedule conflicts and day care problems as barriers for becoming involved in schools. About 69% of working-poor single mothers, compared with 40% of nonworking single mothers, report that their work schedule

has impeded their involvement in their children's school more than once during the past school year. There are also significant differences between working-poor and non–working-poor single mothers' psychological well-being. Working-poor single mothers report less aggravation over caring for their child, and report less emotional stress than do non–working-poor single mothers.

When we compare the single mothers to two-parent low-income families, we see substantial discrepancies in the amount of time that children spend with their fathers, as well as the amount of time that children spend with both parents. Children from single-parent homes spend about 1.5 to 2 hours per week with both parents, whereas children from two-parent homes spend about 8 to 10 hours more per week with both parents. Children in two-parent low-income families spend less time in day care than do children in single-parent low-income families. Parents in two-parent low-income families also have higher school involvement, provide higher emotional support and more stimulating interaction with their children, and report less emotional stress.

In the following, we provide a comparison between children from two-parent working-poor families and children from two-parent non–working-poor families. Surprisingly, we find that children from working-poor two-parent families spend more time with both their mother and their father than do children from non–working-poor two-parent families. It is unclear why this is the case. Possibly, working-poor families value time with children more and make a special effort to spend more time with children during nonworking hours. However, the difference might also be a function of small sample sizes in these groups. With a response rate of 80%, we only have about 90 children in two-parent non–working-poor families in our sample. Children from working-poor two-parent families spend about twice as much time with grandparents as do children from non–working-poor two-parent families (6 hours as opposed to 3 hours

**Table 17.5**    Children's Time Use and Parental Involvement for Children Who Reside in Low-Income Households (Poor and Near-Poor)

| | Single-Mother Families | | Two-Parent Families | |
|---|---|---|---|---|
| | Working Poor | Non–Working Poor | Working Poor | Non–Working Poor |
| | (n=369) | (n=229) | (n=319) | (n=119) |
| **Children's Weekly Time With Others (in hours)** | | | | |
| Time engaged with mother | 22.5 | 23.4 | 27.01* | 22.51* |
| Time engaged with father | 2.03* | 3.7* | 15.25* | 10.41* |
| Time engaged with both parents | 1.28+ | 2.05+ | 10.67+ | 8.21+ |
| Time engaged with siblings | 29.36 | 25.7 | 29.03 | 29.6 |
| Time engaged with friends | 7.32 | 10.12 | 7.27 | 5.13 |
| Time engaged with grandparent(s) | 3.95 | 5.8 | 5.52* | 3.06* |
| Time engaged with other relatives | 6.65 | 6.16 | 5.97 | 7.58 |
| Time engaged with other nonrelatives | 33.29* | 27.91* | 23.93* | 30.53* |
| **Children's Weekly Time in Various Activities** | | | | |
| Achievement-related (studying & reading) | 2.22 | 2.3 | 2.39 | 3.18 |
| Watching TV | 15.66 | 13.68 | 13.03 | 13.91 |
| Arts, sport, and music | 5.06* | 7.10* | 4.89 | 4.68 |
| Other leisure activities | 16.57 | 14 | 18.66 | 18.71 |
| In day care | 6.14* | 2.51* | 3.18 | 1.28 |
| **Non-Time Diary Involvement Measures** | | | | |
| PCG monitoring/supervision behavior (1=low, 5=high) | 3.77 | 3.8 | 4.05 | 3.95 |
| % PCG volunteered in school more than once | 10.26* | 14.72* | 19.17* | 28.22* |
| % PCG attend PTA and like meetings more than once | 13.65* | 31.6* | 23.01 | 31.41 |
| Emotional support index (2-14) | 8.01* | 7.71* | 10 | 9.4 |
| Providing stimulating interaction (2-14) | 8.52 | 9.06 | 9.5 | 9.8 |
| **Barriers for School Involvement** | | | | |
| % work schedule a barrier more than once | 0.69* | 0.40* | 0.46* | 0.29* |
| % day care a barrier more than once | 0.15* | 0.03* | 0.05* | 0.13* |
| **PCG Psychological Well-Being** | | | | |
| Parental aggravation (4-25) | 8.60* | 9.90* | 8.16 | 8.93 |
| Primary caregiver emotional stress (0-4) | 0.78+ | 0.91+ | 0.56* | 0.81* |

* group means significantly different at .05 level; + group means significantly differently at .10 level.

per week). There is no significant difference in children's allocation of time to various activities between two-parent working and non–working-poor families. Parents in non–working-poor two-parent families are more involved in their children's school than are parents in working-poor two-parent families, with a larger proportion of mothers in two-parent working-poor families reporting that work schedule is a barrier for becoming involved in school in the past year. When we examine the psychological well-being of mothers, again we see that those in working-poor families report significantly less emotional stress than do those in non–working-poor two-parent families.

In summary, the descriptive statistics suggest substantial differences by family structure within low-income families, particularly in relation to the amount of time that children spend with their fathers and in day care. Within each family type, working-poor mothers are less involved in their children's school, though they are not less involved in monitoring their children's behavior or in spending time with their children. Mothers in working-poor families also seem to have better psychological well-being and provide more emotional support to their children.

## RESULTS: MULTIVARIATE ANALYSIS

In this section, we report results from multivariate analyses aimed at furthering our understanding of the relationship between parental employment and mother's involvement with children. Employment and family income data are measured for the year before the CDS: 1996. We measure weekly work hours as both a continuous variable and as a categorical variable. Results suggest that a nonlinear relationship exists, so we present findings from the models with categorical work hour variables. We also include a variable indicating whether the family is a working-poor

family or not. We experimented with different definitions of "working poor" with three cut-offs of the official poverty line: under 1, under 1.5, and under 2. Results are similar with these three different measures, so we present the version with a cut-off of twice the poverty line to be consistent with our descriptive analyses presented earlier. Our income measure is the total pre-tax income of all family members, inflated to 1997 price levels using the Consumer Price Index (CPI-UX1). We used a logarithmic transformation of family income in our multivariate analysis.

Our dependent variables include six measures: maternal psychological well-being, child's weekly engaged time with the mother, mother's provisioning of stimulating interactions, mother's provisioning of emotional support, mother's school involvement index, and mother's monitoring behavior index. We conduct Tobit analysis for the model of child's weekly engaged time with the mother, and ordinary least squares (OLS) regression for models with the other dependent variables. One limitation of the PSID data is that maternal psychological well-being is assessed at the same time as the collection of time diary data and other parenting behavior measures. These contemporaneous measures make it impossible to establish their causal relationship.

An important consideration is the extent to which selection effects (or omitted variables) obscure the relationship between maternal work and the processes through which employment affects children's well-being. In other words, there may be unobservable factors that lead parents to be employed in the labor market and to be more involved in childrearing. We address this issue in a limited way given that we only have one wave of CDS data. A set of child and family characteristics is included in the analyses as control variables. Children's characteristics included in the model are age, gender, and whether the child was born with a low birth weight. Mother's characteristics include education, her verbal test score that approximates her IQ (after controlling for her education), and whether or not she has received Aid to Families with Dependent Children (AFDC) at the time of the child's birth to capture her past economic well-being. These factors may potentially select mothers into different patterns of labor force participation and may also affect their parenting practices. Several other family characteristics are also controlled for—total family wealth collected in 1994,[3] the number of children under age 18 in the family, ethnicity of the family head, and family structure in 1997 categorized as two-parent families, single-mother families, mother with stepfather families, and other family structures.

We include families at all income levels in the analyses. Table 17.6 presents results for the entire sample with family structure variables as predictors in the models. Tables 17.7 and 17.8 present results for single-mother families and two-parent families separately. Table 17.6 shows that, controlling for child and a set of family characteristics, parents' work hours (combined work hours for two-parent families) have no effect on maternal emotional stress level and little effect on parental involvement, except that those who work 41 to 60 hours a week are significantly more likely to provide stimulating interaction to children and those who work 20 to 40 hours a week are significantly less likely to be involved in children's schools when compared with families with combined work hours of less than 20 hours a week. However, working-poor status is associated with less stimulating parent-child interaction. Family income is negatively associated with mother's emotional stress, but also negatively associated with both mother-child engagement time and the monitoring behavior index. High maternal emotional stress is significantly associated with four of the five parental involvement measures: less stimulating interaction, less emotional support, less school involvement, and less monitoring.

Factors other than employment, however, are important predictors of maternal emotional stress. Mothers with a higher educational level have a lower level of emotional stress, and black mothers have significantly higher emotional stress when compared with white mothers.

Family structure variables are also significantly associated with most of the parental involvement measures. Single mothers and mothers in stepfather families have higher levels of emotional stress than do those in two-parent families. Single mothers also provide less emotional support, are less involved in their children's school and in monitoring their children's daily activities. Other variables are significantly associated with mother's involvement with their child. Other than child's age and gender, human capital variables (education and verbal test scores) are positively associated with the provisioning of stimulating interaction, emotional support, the level of school involvement, and parental monitoring behavior. When compared with white mothers, black mothers provide less stimulating interaction, less emotional support, and are less involved in monitoring child's behavior.

Table 17.7 shows similar results for single-mother families. Mother's work hours have no effect on her psychological well-being and most involvement levels, except for a negative effect on school involvement for those who work 35 hours or more a week. Working-poor status has a marginally significant negative association with mother's provisioning of stimulating interaction to her child. Mothers with a higher income have lower emotional stress, but spend less time engaged with their child and are less involved in monitoring their child's whereabouts and friends.

In Table 17.8, we see that the amount of time mothers spend at work is negatively associated with the amount of time mothers engage with their children and with their children's schools. The working-poor status is

**Table 17.6** Estimates for Parental Involvement in All Families

| | Emotional Stress | Time With Mother (Marginal Effects) | Stimulating Interaction | Emotional Support | School Involvement | Monitoring Behavior |
|---|---|---|---|---|---|---|
| Combined weekly work hours of parents: | | | | | | |
| 20–40 | 0.00 | -0.97 | 0.28 | 0.19 | -0.27+ | 0.07 |
| 41–60 | 0.05 | 0.06 | 0.67* | 0.28 | -0.16 | 0.02 |
| 60 or more | 0.01 | -1.22 | 0.41 | 0.30 | -0.42* | 0.01 |
| Log family income | -0.05* | -.75* | -0.01 | 0.03 | -0.02 | -0.05** |
| Whether working poor | 0.04 | -0.57 | -0.64*** | -0.08 | 0.10 | -0.11 |
| PCG emotional stress | n.a. | -0.73 | -0.23** | -0.32*** | -0.11+ | -0.10*** |
| Child's age | 0.00 | -1.54*** | 0.15*** | 0.41*** | -0.02 | -0.02** |
| Whether girl | 0.06* | 2.61*** | 0.12 | 0.07 | -0.1+ | 0.05+ |
| Whether low birth weight | 0.08 | -1.20 | 0.16 | -0.11 | -0.08 | -0.05 |
| Black | -0.12* | -0.90 | -0.49*** | -0.53*** | -0.03 | -0.17*** |
| Hispanic | -0.07 | 1.74 | -0.82+ | 0.31 | 0.89 | -0.02 |
| Log family wealth | -0.01 | 0.10 | 0.02 | 0.00 | 0.01 | 0.00 |
| Parental education | -0.02* | 0.18 | 0.19*** | 0.08*** | 0.07*** | 0.01 |
| PCG verbal test scores | -0.01+ | -0.03 | 0.05*** | 0.02** | 0.00 | 0.02*** |
| Received AFDC when child born | 0.06 | -0.80 | 0.05 | 0.30* | 0.04 | 0.00 |
| Number of children | 0.01 | -1.59*** | -0.08+ | 0.04 | 0.00 | 0.01 |
| Single-mother family | 0.19** | -1.72 | 0.17 | -1.40*** | -0.32*** | -0.14* |
| Mother-stepfather family | 0.16* | -2.27* | -0.05 | 0.23 | -0.18 | -0.17* |
| Other family structure | -0.05 | -15.01*** | 0.08 | -0.57*** | -0.04*** | -0.18* |
| Whether in metropolitan | 0.04 | 0.23 | 0.01 | -0.08 | -0.03 | -0.05 |
| _constant | 1.65 | | 4.77 | 5.35 | 1.91 | 4.26 |
| R-squared/Wald chi-2 | 0.10 | 550*** | 0.24 | 0.64 | 0.08 | 0.11 |

*** significant at .001 level; ** significant at .01 level; * significant at .05 level; + significant at .10 level.

**Table 17.7**  Estimates for Parental Involvement in Single-Mother Families

| | Emotional Stress | Time With Mother (Marginal Effects) | Stimulating Interaction | Emotional Support | School Involvement | Monitoring Behavior |
|---|---|---|---|---|---|---|
| Parent's weekly work hours | | | | | | |
| 1–34 hours | −0.07 | −1.66 | −0.27 | 0.02 | −0.09 | 0.04 |
| 35 hours or more | 0.08 | 0.61 | −0.31 | 0.03 | −.36* | −0.03 |
| Whether working poor | 0.13 | 1.44 | −.51+ | −0.10 | −0.01 | −0.03 |
| Log family income | −0.09** | −.77* | −0.02 | −0.04 | −0.03 | −0.06** |
| PCG emotional stress | n.a. | 0.21 | −0.10 | −0.29** | −0.04 | −0.06 |
| Child's age | −0.02 | −1.55*** | 0.08** | 0.29*** | 0.00 | −0.05*** |
| Whether girl | 0.11 | 2.84** | 0.41* | 0.20 | −0.22* | 0.03 |
| Whether low birth weight | 0.05 | −4.25* | 0.35 | 0.09 | −0.08 | 0.02 |
| Black | −0.21+ | 0.15 | −0.83** | −0.77*** | 0.14 | −0.22* |
| Hispanic | −0.20 | −4.07 | −2.05* | −0.59 | −0.30** | 0.03 |
| Log family wealth | 0.00 | 0.12 | 0.01 | −0.02 | 0.01 | 0.00 |
| Parental education | −0.04 | −0.13 | 0.20*** | 0.05 | 0.06** | 0.02 |
| PCG verbal test scores | −0.02+ | −0.05 | 0.08* | 0.03* | −0.01* | 0.02* |
| Received AFDC when child born | −0.01 | 2.24 | 0.17 | 0.21 | 0.02 | −0.01 |
| Number of children | 0.02 | −1.61* | −0.19* | −0.08 | −0.03 | −0.03 |
| Whether in metropolitan area | −0.07 | 1.69 | −0.46* | 0.07 | 0.07 | −0.13 |
| _constant | 2.83 | | 5.12 | 5.92 | 1.85 | 4.45 |
| R-squared/Loglikelihood | 0.088 | | 0.218 | 0.488 | 0.097 | 0.113 |

*** significant at .001 level; ** significant at .01 level; * significant at .05 level; + significant at .10 level.

again negatively associated with stimulating parent-child interaction, and marginally associated with parental monitoring behavior. Family income has little effect on maternal involvement, except for a marginally positive effect on emotional support. We also see that maternal emotional stress is negatively associated with most of the involvement measures.

## DISCUSSION

In this initial exploration of children's time use and parental involvement in low-income families, we find two marked differences between children from low-income families and children from upper-income families, both of which most likely affect their overall well-being. First, we find that children from low-income families have substantially lower levels of involvement with their fathers and substantially higher levels of involvement with other kin, such as grandparents and other relatives. Although research on the positive effect of father's involvement is more readily available (Harris & Marmer, 1996; Lamb, 1997; Marsiglio, Armato, Day, & Lamb, 2000; Popenoe, 1996; Snarey, 1993; Yeung, 2004; Yeung, Duncan, & Hill, 2000), children's involvement with relatives

**Table 17.8**  Estimates for Parental Involvement in Two-Parent Families

| | Emotional Stress | Time With Mother (Marginal Effects) | Stimulating Interaction | Emotional Support | School Involvement | Monitoring Behavior |
|---|---|---|---|---|---|---|
| Parental weekly work hours | | | | | | |
| Head work hours | 0.00 | −0.01 | 0.00 | 0.00 | 0.00 | 0.00 |
| Wife work hours | 0.00 | −.08*** | 0.00 | 0.00 | −0.01* | −0.00+ |
| Whether working poor | −0.02 | 1.52 | −0.68** | 0.04 | 0.14 | −0.16+ |
| Log family income | −0.03 | −0.29 | −0.02 | 0.11+ | 0.01 | −0.01 |
| PCG emotional stress | n.a. | −2.56*** | −0.49*** | −0.36*** | −0.13 | −0.17*** |
| Child's age | 0.01 | −1.55*** | 0.17*** | 0.44*** | −0.04* | −0.01 |
| Whether girl | 0.03 | 2.05** | 0.14 | 0.07 | −0.07 | 0.07 |
| Whether low birth weight | 0.10 | 0.12 | 0.05 | −0.23 | −0.03 | −0.10 |
| Black | −0.07 | −1.17 | −0.56*** | −0.51*** | −0.02 | −0.17*** |
| Hispanic | −0.04 | 3.86 | −0.60 | 0.90* | 0.26 | −0.07 |
| Log family wealth | −0.01 | 0.085 | 0.03 | 0.02 | 0.00 | 0.00 |
| Parental education | −0.03* | 0.093 | 0.23*** | 0.10*** | 0.05* | 0.01* |
| PCG verbal test scores | 0.00 | 0.039 | 0.02 | 0.01 | 0.01 | 0.01** |
| Received AFDC when child born | 0.18+ | −3.23 | −0.52 | 0.18 | −0.13 | −0.23 |
| Number of children | 0.00 | −2.34*** | −0.01 | 0.10 | 0.03 | 0.04+ |
| Whether in metropolitan area | 0.05 | −0.54 | 0.18 | −0.08 | −0.06 | 0.00 |
| _constant | 1.36 | | 5.36 | 4.56 | 1.31 | 3.98 |
| R–squared/Wald chi–2 | 0.06 | 341.03*** | 0.22 | 0.62 | 0.06 | 0.12 |

*** significant at .001 level; ** significant at .01 level; * significant at .05 level; + significant at .10 level.

and the consequences to their well-being warrant more investigation in the future. Second, we find that school-age children from low-income families spend less time studying, reading, or in computer activities, and more time watching TV. These activities have been shown to have salient implication for children's school performance.

Our multivariate analyses provide little evidence that an increase in mothers' work hours compromises their involvement with their children, or leads to higher levels of emotional stress. Several previous studies also show that women's increased labor force participation has not affected the amount of time

that they spend with their children (Bianchi, 2000; Bianchi, Milkie, Sayer, & Robinson, 2000; Booth, Clarke-Stewart, Vandell, McCartney, & Tresch, 2002; Chase-Lansdale et al., 2003). Working mothers may find ways to remain involved in their children's lives by cutting back on sleep, housework, and leisure activities, or by engaging more intensively in selective activities that are conducive to child development during nonworking time such as on weekends. Our multivariate analyses do indicate lower levels of involvement in children's schools if children are from single-mother, full-time working families, or if children are from two-parent families where parents work more than 60 hours combined per week. A higher income is also associated with a lower level of maternal emotional stress, particularly for single-mothers, though it also has a negative association with two of the five parental involvement measures.

When we compare working-poor and non–working-poor families, there is little evidence that working-poor mothers are more emotionally stressed or less involved with their children. Working-poor status is significantly associated with only one of the parental involvement measures—the provisioning of stimulating interaction to their child, but not with the other four child-involvement measures. Working-poor single-mothers, in particular, tend to be less involved in their children's school and more often cite their work schedule as a barrier for becoming involved in their children's school. Children in working-poor families do spend significantly more time in day care than do those in non–working-poor families, especially those in working-poor single-mother families. Our results indicate a crucial need for policies attending to the quality of day care for children and allowing more flexibility for parents to participate in school activities in working-poor families. Making some current programs, such as Head Start, accessible to families with working parents that do not live under the official federal poverty line but near that line would benefit both parents and children.

Maternal emotional stress is a critical factor in mothers' involvement behavior. Our results, however, indicate that factors other than employment have a stronger effect on maternal psychological well-being and involvement with children. Family income, mother's education, family structure, and ethnicity are significant predictors of maternal psychological well-being. More educated mothers tend to be less emotionally stressed and more involved with their children. Single mothers in general are more stressed and less involved with their children. However, working-poor single mothers are less stressed and not less involved with their children, except for school involvement, than non-working single mothers. Hence, the critical policy considerations for low-income families should focus less on mothers' work hours, and more on increasing the human capital of low-income parents, providing adequate child care and flexible work hours to low-income parents, and providing adequate wages, particularly to single working-poor mothers. The lack of time for low-income working parents to be involved in schools is a serious cause of concern.

Our data do not allow us to examine the impact of parental work shifts, which are an important consideration for low-income families. In future work, we will construct better maternal work histories and incorporate maternal occupational status to examine in greater detail how maternal employment in low-income families affects their psychological well-being, family time use, and children's well-being.

---

## NOTES

1. There may be potential confusion in the time diary reports of school time and day care time so that these reports may not be the most reliable source of data on children's time in these institutions.

2. Acs, Ross-Phillips, and McKenzie (2000) used 200% of the federal poverty line and half-time employment as a cut off. In defining working-poor families, we also attempted different cutoff points of poverty levels including under 100% and under 150% as used by Wertheimer (1999). Because of sample size constraint, we decided to include in our analyses families that are under 200% of the federal poverty level.

3. We used the PSID data collected in 1994 about the value of owner-occupied real estate, real estate other than main home, vehicles or other assets on wheels, farm or business assets, shares of stock in publicly held corporations, mutual funds or investment trusts, including stocks in IRAs, checking and savings accounts, money market funds, certificates of deposit, savings bonds, treasury bills, and other investments in trusts or estates, bond funds, life insurance policies, special collections. Family wealth is measured as the sum of all previous items minus the value of debts other than mortgages, such as credit cards, student loans, medical or legal bills, or personal loans. We use a logarithmic transformation of family wealth in the multivariate analysis.

## REFERENCES

Acs, G., Ross-Phillips, K., & McKenzie, D. (2000). *Playing by the rules but losing the game*. Washington, DC: Urban Institute Press.

Belsky, J. (1990). Parental and non-parental child care and children's socio-emotional development: A decade in review. *Journal of Marriage and the Family, 52,* 885–903.

Bianchi, S. M. (2000). Maternal employment and time with children: Dramatic change or surprising continuity? *Demography, 37,* 139–154.

Bianchi, S. M., Milkie, M. A., Sayer, L. C., & Robinson, J. P. (2000). Is anyone doing the housework? Trends in the gender division of household labor. *Social Forces, 79,* 191–228.

Bianchi, S. M., & Robinson, J. P. (1997). What did you do today? Children's use of time, family composition, and the acquisition of social capital. *Journal of Marriage and the Family, 59,* 332–344.

Booth, C. L., Clarke-Stewart, A. K. Vandell, D. L., McCartney, K., & Tresch, O. M. (2002). Child-care usage and mother-infant "quality time." *Journal of Marriage and the Family, 64,* 16–26.

Brooks-Gunn, J., Han, W. J., & Waldfogel, J. (2002). Maternal employment and child cognitive outcomes in the first 3 years of life: The NICHD study of early child care. *Child Development, 4,* 1052–1072.

Caldwell, B. M., & Bradley, R. H. (1984). *Home observation for measurement of the environment*. Little Rock: University of Arkansas at Little Rock.

Chase-Lansdale, P. L., Moffitt, R. A., Lohman, B. J., Cherlin, A. J., Coley, R. L., Pittman, L. D., et al. (2003). Mothers' transitions from welfare to work and the well-being of preschoolers and adolescents. *Science, 299,* 1548–1552.

Child Trends Databank. (2003). *Child trends analysis of the March current population survey (CPS), 1996–2002*. Washington, DC: Author.

Conger, R. D., Conger, K. J., Elder, G. H., Lorenz, F. O., Simons, R. L., & Whitbeck, L. B. (1992). A family process model of economic hardship and adjustment of early adolescent boys. *Child Development, 63,* 526–541.

Conger, R. D., Patterson, G. R., & Ge, X. (1995). It takes two to replicate: A mediational model for the impact of parents' stress on adolescent adjustment. *Child Development, 66,* 80–97.

Crouter, A., & McHale, S. (2003, June). *Work time, family time, and children's time: Implications for child and adolescent relationships, development, and well-being*. Paper presented at Workforce/Workplace Mismatch?: Work, Family, Health, and Well-Being Conference, Washington, DC.

Demo, D. H., & Cox, M. J. (2000). Families with young children: A review of research in the 1990s. *Journal of Marriage and the Family, 62,* 876–895.

Eccles, J. S., & Barber, B. L. (1998). Student council, volunteering, basketball, or marching band: What kind of extracurricular involvement matters? *Journal of Adolescent Research, 14,* 10–43.

Eccles, J. S., Wigfield, A., & Schiefele, U. (1997). Motivation. In N. Eisenberg (Ed.) *Handbook of child psychology* (Vol. 3, pp. 1017–1095). New York: Wiley.

Fiese, B. H., Tomcho, T. J., Douglas, M., Josephs, K., Poltrock, S., & Baker, T. (2002). A review of 50 years of research on naturally occurring family routines and rituals: Cause for celebration? *Journal of Family Psychology, 16,* 381–390.

Folbre, N. (1997, November). *A time (use survey) for every purpose: Non-market work and the production of human capabilities.* Paper presented at the MacArthur Network on the Family and the Economy, Washington, DC.

Guo, G., & Harris, K. M. (2000). The mechanisms mediating the effects of poverty on children's intellectual development. *Demography, 37,* 431–448.

Hallberg, D., & Klevmarken, A. (2003). Time for children: A study of parents' time allocation. *Journal of Population Economics, 16,* 205–226.

Han, W. J., Waldfogel, J., & Brooks-Gunn, J. (2001). The effects of early maternal employment on children's later cognitive and behavioral outcomes. *Journal of Marriage and the Family, 63,* 336–54.

Harris, K. M., & Marmer, J. K. (1996). Poverty, paternal involvement, and adolescent well-being. *Journal of Family Issues, 17,* 614–640.

Harvey, E. A. (1999). Short-term and long-term effects of early parental employment on children of the National Longitudinal Survey of Youth. *Developmental Psychology, 35,* 445–459.

Hill, C. R., & Stafford, F. (1974). Allocation of time to pre-school children and educational opportunity. *Journal of Human Resources, 9,* 323–341.

Hofferth, S. L., Davis-Kean, P., Davis, J., & Finkelstein, J. (1997). *The child development supplement to the panel study of income dynamics: 1997 user guide.* Ann Arbor: University of Michigan Press.

Hofferth, S. L., & Sandberg, J. F. (2001). How American children spend their time. *Journal of Marriage and the Family, 63,* 295–308.

Hoffman, L. W., & Youngblade, L. M. (1999). *Mothers at work: Effects on children's well-being.* New York: Cambridge University Press.

Huston, A. C. (2002). Reforms and child development. *Future of Children, 12,* 59–77.

Jackson, A., Brooks-Gunn, J., Huang, C., & Glassman, M. (2000). Single mothers in low-wage jobs: Financial strain, parenting, and preschoolers' outcomes. *Child Development, 71,* 1409–1423.

Juster, T. F. (1985). The validity and quality of time use estimates obtained from recall diaries. In T. F. Juster & F. P. Stafford (Eds.), *Time, goods, and well-being.* Ann Arbor: Institute for Social Research, University of Michigan.

Kessler, R. C., & Mroszek, D. (1994). *Final versions of our non-specific psychological distress scale.* Ann Arbor: Institute for Social Research, University of Michigan.

Kiser, J. (2002, January). *Offset schedules and child care choices by dual earner parents.* Paper presented at the Industrial Relations Research Association Conference, Atlanta, GA.

Kohn, M. L. (1969). *Class and conformity.* Homewood, IL: Dorsey Press.

Kontos, S., Howes, C., Shinn, M., & Galinsky, E. (1995). *Quality in family child care and relative care.* New York: Teachers College Press.

Lamb, M. E. (1997). Paternal involvement: Levels, sources, and consequences. In M. E. Lamb (Ed.), *The role of the father in child development* (pp. 66–103). New York: Wiley.

Lamb, M. E., Pleck, J. H., Charnov, E. L., & Levine, J. A. (1985). Paternal behavior in humans. *American Zoologist, 25,* 883–894.

Lareau, A. (2002). Invisible inequality: Social class and childrearing in black families and white families. *American Sociological Review, 67,* 747–776.

Leibowitz, A. (1974). Education and home production. *American Economic Review, 64,* 243–250.

Leibowitz, A. (1977). Parental inputs and children's achievement. *Journal of Human Resources, 12,* 243–251.

Leone, C. M., & Richards, M. H. (1989). Classwork and homework in early adolescence: The ecology of achievement. *Journal of Youth and Adolescence, 18,* 531–548.

Maccoby, E. E., & Martin, J. A. (1984). Socialization in the context of the family: Parent-child interaction. In P. H. Mussen (Ed.), *Handbook of child psychology: Socialization, personality, and social development* (Vol. 5, pp. 1–101). New York: Wiley.

Marsiglio, W., Armato, P., Day, R. D., & Lamb, M. E. (2000). Scholarship on fatherhood in the 1990s and beyond. *Journal of Marriage and Family Review, 62,* 1173–1191.

Mayer, S. E. (1997). *What money can't buy: Family income and children's life chances.* Cambridge, MA: Harvard University Press.

McLoyd, V. C. (1990). The impact of economic hardship on black families and children: Psychological distress, parenting, and socioemotional development. *Child Development, 61,* 311–346.

McLoyd, V. C., Jayaratne, T. E., Ceballo, R., & Borquez, J. (1994). Unemployment and work interruption among African American single mothers: Effects on parenting and adolescent socioemotional functioning. *Child Development, 65,* 562–589.

Mincer, J., & Polacheck, S. (1974). Family investments in human capital, earnings of women. *Journal of Political Economy, 81,* 76–108.

Moore, K. A., & Driscoll, A. K. (1997). Low-wage maternal employment and outcomes for children: A study. *Future of Children, 7,* 122–127.

National Academy of Sciences. (2000). *Time use measurement and research.* Washington, DC: National Academy Press.

National Center for Children in Poverty. (2004). *State policy choices: Supports for low-income working families.* Retrieved from http://www.nccp.org/pub_swf04.html

Parcel, T. L., & Menaghan, E. G. (1994). *Parental jobs and children's lives.* New York: de Gruyter.

Perry-Jenkins, M., Repetti, R. L., & Crouter, A. C. (2000). Work and family in the 1900s. *Journal of Marriage and the Family, 62,* 981–998.

Presser, H. B. (1994). Employment schedules among dual-earner spouses and the division of household labor by gender. *American Sociological Review, 59,* 348–364.

Popenoe, D. (1996). *Life without father.* New York: Free Press.

Raver, C. C. (2003). Does work pay psychologically as well as economically? The role of maternal employment in predicting depressive symptoms and parenting among low-income families. *Child Development, 74,* 1720–1736.

Robinson, J. P. (1985). The validity and reliability of diaries versus alternative time use measures. In T. J. Juster & F. Stafford (Eds.), *Times, goods, and well-being* (pp. 33–59). Ann Arbor: Institute for Social Research, University of Michigan.

Ruhm, C. (2004). Parental employment and child cognitive development. *Journal of Human Resources, 39,* 155–192.

Shonkoff, J. P., & Phillips, D. A. (2000). *From neurons to neighborhoods: The science of early childhood development.* Washington, DC: National Academy Press.

Snarey, J. (1993). *How fathers care for the next generation.* Cambridge, MA: Harvard University Press.

Stafford, F. P., & Duncan, G. J. (1985). The use of time and technology by households in the United States. In T. F. Juster & F. Stafford (Eds.), *Time, goods, and well-being* (pp. 245–288). Ann Arbor: Institute for Social Research, University of Michigan.

Timmer, S. G., Eccles, J. S., & O'Brien, K. (1985). How children use time. In T. F. Juster & F. Stafford (Eds.), *Time, goods, and well-being* (pp. 353–382). Ann Arbor: Institute for Social Research, University of Michigan.

U.S. Census Bureau. (2003). Poverty in the United States: 2002. In *Current population reports: Consumer income.* Washington, DC: U.S. Government Printing Office.

Vandell, D. L., & Ramanan, J. (1992). Effects of early and recent maternal employment on children from low-income families. *Child Development, 63,* 938–949.

Wertheimer, D. (2001). *Working poor families with children: Leaving welfare doesn't necessarily mean leaving poverty.* Research Brief. Washington, DC: Child Trends.

Yeung, W. J. (2004). Fathers: An overlooked resource for children's educational success. In D. Conley & K. Albright (Eds.), *After the bell: Solutions outside the school* (pp. 145–169). London: Routledge.

Yeung, W. J., Duncan, G. J., & Hill, M. S. (2000). Putting fathers back in the picture: Parental activities and children's adult attainments. In H. E. Peters, G. W. Peterson, S. Steinmetz, & F. Day, (Eds.), *Fatherhood: Research, interventions and policies* (pp. 97–113). Binghamton, NY: Haworth Press.

Yeung, W. J., Linver, M., & Brooks-Gunn, J. (2002). How money matters for young children's development: Parental investment and family processes. *Child Development, 73,* 1861–1879.

Yeung, W. J., & Stafford, F. (2003, March). *Intra-family child care time allocation.* Paper presented at 2003 Annual Meeting of Population Association of America, Minneapolis, Minnesota.

Zaslow, M. J., & Emig, C. A. (1997). When low-income mothers go to work: Implications for children. *Future of Children, 7,* 110–115.

Zaslow, M. J., McGroder, S. M., Cave, G., & Mariner, C. L. (1999). Maternal employment and measures of children's health and development among families with some history of welfare receipt. In T. L. Parcel (Ed.), *Research in the Sociology of Work* (Vol. 7, pp. 233–259). Greenwich, CT: JAI Press.

# CHAPTER 18

# Cognitive and Emotional Outcomes for Children in Poverty

R. Gabriela Barajas, Nina Philipsen, and Jeanne Brooks-Gunn

For all its wealth, the United States has one of the highest rates of childhood poverty among industrialized nations. In fact, the average child in the United States is poorer than the average child in 12 of the 14 most developed nations (Rainwater & Smeeding, 2003). Today, roughly one in five of America's children are raised in poverty (DeNavas-Walt, Proctor, & Lee, 2005). Although the poverty rate fell between 1993 and 2000, current trends in the nation's poverty rate are not encouraging. Since 2000, the percentage of Americans living in poverty has increased from 11.3% to 12.7% (U.S. Census Bureau, 2004). Of the 37 million Americans living in poverty, children constitute a disproportionately vulnerable group; they compose 25.2% of the total population, yet they represent 35.2% of the people in poverty (DeNavas-Walt et al., 2005). Although white children constitute the majority of the poor in absolute numbers, Hispanic and African American children are overrepresented: 35% of African American

children and 28% of Hispanic children live below the poverty line compared with 10% of white children. The percentage of young children (age 5 and younger) living in poverty is higher than the percentage of older children (age 6 to 17) living in poverty: 20.5% versus 17%.

A child living in poverty lacks goods and services considered essential to human well-being (Betson & Michael, 1997). Not surprisingly, being raised in poverty has been linked with unfavorable early cognitive, verbal, and behavioral outcomes for young children (Aber, Bennett, Conley & Li, 1997; Brooks-Gunn & Duncan, 1997; Dearing, McCartney, & Taylor, 2001; Smith, Brooks-Gunn, & Klebanov, 1997). By age 2, differences on cognitive measures between children in and out of poverty tend to appear and such differences are of equal or greater size by age 5 (Duncan, Brooks-Gunn, & Klebanov, 1994; Klebanov, Brooks-Gunn, McCarton, & McCormick, 1998; Smith et al., 1997). Such delays in the preschool years increase the likelihood of lower achievement in school, grade retention, and school dropout (Brooks-Gunn, 2003; Brooks-Gunn, Guo, & Furstenberg, 1993; Campbell & Ramey, 1994; Patterson, Kupersmidt, & Vaden, 1990; Rouse, Brooks-Gunn, & McLanahan, 2005). Similarly, early behavior problems are associated with subsequent emotional problems, such as poor peer relations, conduct disorder, depression, and delinquency (Baydar, Brooks-Gunn, & Furstenberg, 1993; Dodge, Pettit, & Bates, 1994; Sampson & Laub, 1994). Moreover, studies have shown that the earlier poverty strikes in the developmental process, the more deleterious and long-lasting its effects (Duncan, Yeung, Brooks-Gunn, & Smith, 1998).

This chapter will explore the cognitive and emotional consequences of growing up poor, and examine how these effects are revealed during the preschool, elementary school, and, to a lesser extent, the high school years. First, we review the complexities of measuring poverty and isolating its effects on child well-being. Second, findings from key large-scale studies on direct associations between poverty and child's verbal, behavioral, and cognitive outcomes are reviewed. The extent to which the timing, depth, and persistence of poverty influence these associations will also be considered. Third, we consider the potential pathways, as illustrated by the family stress model and the investment model, through which poverty may influence child well-being. Finally, we consider the role of public policy in the lives of children growing up in poverty.

## Defining Poverty

The official poverty measure used in the United States is a monetary threshold known as the federal poverty level (FPL). Created in the 1960s, the federal poverty threshold represents the minimum standard of economic resources for families. Grounded in the assumption that food costs constitute one-third of a family's budget (or did in the late 1950s and early 1960s), the threshold is based on anticipated food expenditures (thrifty food basket), and multiplied by three (Citro & Michael, 1995). The threshold varies according to the size of a family and the age of its members and is adjusted annually for the cost of living based on the consumer price index. In 2004, the poverty threshold for a family of four (two adults and two children) was $19,157 (U.S. Census Bureau, 2004).

Although having a defined federal poverty level allows annual comparisons to be made, there are several criticisms of this measure. The first major criticism is that the measure is outdated: The changing face of the American economy and American family no longer falls in line with the measure that was created over four decades ago. As such, the measure does not accurately reflect differences in poverty across population groups and across time, nor does it account for the different needs of families in which parents do and do not work outside the home (parents who work outside the home have transportation, clothing, and child-care costs). Moreover, it does not consider the varied geographic differences in the cost of living, nor does it reflect the effects of policy initiatives (i.e., Earned Income Tax Credit [EITC] and health care) that significantly alter families' disposable income (Citro & Michael, 1995).

The second major criticism of the threshold is that it does not distinguish the degree of poverty a family is experiencing. Although the FPL allows for a dichotomous distinction between poor and nonpoor families, it underestimates the severity of poverty, as variations below the poverty line are extreme (Duncan & Brooks-Gunn, 1997). For example, nearly half of poor, young children live in households with incomes less than one half of the poverty line; in other countries, poor families are clustered more tightly around the line. This lack of sensitivity potentially underestimates material hardship (i.e., difficulty affording food and paying rent) for families (i.e., Mayer & Jencks, 1989). Moreover, many families are "near poor"—they have incomes between 100 and 200% of the poverty line. Because they may be ineligible for certain government programs (the cut-off for federal programs differs; Currie, 1997) the near-poor, despite having higher incomes, may have difficulty in making ends meet (Edin & Lein, 1997; Leventhal & Brooks-Gunn, 2002).

Finally, the U.S. poverty line is based on an absolute (an income cut-off defined in 1960 and carried forward with cost of living increases). Other countries use a line based on a percentage of median income. As overall income in a country increases, so does the poverty threshold. These changes over time reflect alterations in living standards. A measure that incorporates aspects of a relative threshold has been proposed by the National Academy of Sciences (Citro & Michael, 1995).

Policy scholars sometimes use the income-to needs ratio, which is calculated by dividing a household's income by the poverty threshold for that particular family. An income-to-needs ratio of 1.0 indicates that the family is living at the poverty threshold. Using this method, five different income-to-needs groups are identified: deep poverty ($< .5$), poverty ($.5$ to $1$), near poor ($1$ to $2.0$), lower-middle class ($2.0$ to $3.0$), middle class ($3.0$ to $4.0$), and affluent ($4.0$ and higher). Another measure involves calculating income quintiles; in general, the bottom quintile is poor, the second quintile is near poor. In either representation, about 40% of all children are poor or near-poor in the United States.

Relative poverty, the extent to which a household's financial resources fall below an average income (i.e., the median or mean income of all households in the United States), has been used as another marker of risk (Hernandez, 1997). Using this threshold, other families' incomes can change a family's poverty status, even if their income is relatively stable over time. Use of a relative poverty threshold gives a better picture of the uneven distribution of national wealth: Although living standards and real incomes have grown because of higher employment and sustained economic growth over recent years, gains in wealth have been unevenly distributed across populations. It is estimated that not until a family of four reaches twice the FPL ($40,000) can it adequately provide the basic necessities such as housing, food, and health care (National Center for Children in Poverty, 2005). Although 18% of children are technically poor (living at less than 100% of the FPL), another 22% (16 million) live in low-income households (household income between 100 and 200% of the FPL).

A family's economic situation changes over time: Job loss may push a family into poverty; an additional family member working may pull a family out of poverty. Such variation in families' economic histories has called for the need to also examine the timing, persistence, and depth of poverty in relation to child outcomes (McLeod & Shanahan, 1993). Persistence of poverty, measured via the number of years a family lives in poverty and whether a family cycles in and out of poverty, and depth of poverty (how far below the poverty threshold a family's income falls) have also been considered as moderators between poverty and child outcomes (Duncan & Brooks-Gunn, 1997).

Several mechanisms are driving today's poverty rates. Mainly, the rise in child poverty during the last 40 years is seen as resulting from changes in marriage and divorce rates, nonmarital fertility rates, and unemployment rates (Hernandez, 1997). The increase in number of single parents, both those who have children outside of marriage and those who experience divorce, is one of the most important causes of the rise in number of poor children: children in single-mother households are more likely to be poor than are those in two-parent households (McLanahan, 1997; McLanahan, 2004; McLanahan & Sandefur, 1994). For example among single-mother families, poverty rates for Hispanic, African American, and white families in 2004 were 39.3, 39.5, and 21.7%, respectively. The corresponding proportions for children in two-parent families were 21.2, 23.7, and 6.5%, respectively (DeNavas-Walt et al., 2005).

### Does Poverty Matter?

A consistent concern in studying the effects of poverty is that the estimated effect of income might be spurious. That is, unmeasured factors may in fact be responsible for the association between parental income and child outcomes (or at least a large part of the association). For example, perhaps parental mental health is the critical element in children's success. Researchers have attempted to disentangle this question and have found that poverty has a major effect on some child psychiatric disorders beyond family characteristics (Costello, Compton, Keeler, & Angold, 2003). In the Great Smokey Mountains study, a representative population sample of 1,420 rural children ages 9 to 13 years were given annual psychiatric assessments for 8 years. Halfway through that study, a casino opening on the Indian reservation gave every American Indian an income supplement that moved 14% of the study families out of poverty. Before the casino opened, persistently poor and ex-poor children had more psychiatric symptoms (4.38 and 4.28 respectively) than the never-poor children (2.75). After the opening of the casino, however, levels among the ex-poor fell to those of the never-poor children, whereas levels among those who were persistently poor remained high. Similar results were found in non-Indian children whose families moved out of poverty during the same period. If the reason for the association between poverty and child psychopathology was the poor mental health of families in poverty, relieving the poverty would have left the association intact. But this did not happen. Instead, this natural experiment found that removal from poverty brought children's psychopathology levels to the level of children who'd never been poor.

Using non-experimental data, researchers do find that income effects are smaller when a large number of other family characteristics are controlled (Blau, 1999; Klebanov, Brooks-Gunn, Chase-Landsdale, & Gordon, 1997; Mayer, 1997). Conventional methods probably overestimate the "true" effect of income by not controlling for the effect of all observed and unobserved parental characteristics (Mayer, 1997).

In an attempt to isolate the effects of poverty on children's development, more recent large-scale research initiatives have frequently over-sampled low-income families as well as included measures of these other known correlates to child development. The use of large, longitudinal studies such as the Infant Health and Development Program (IHDP), the Panel Study of Income Dynamics (PSID), the National Longitudinal Survey of Youth (NLSY), the National Institute of Child Health and Human Development's Study of Early Child Care (NICHD SECC) and the Early Childhood Longitudinal Study (ECLS-K) have remedied many methodological problems as they include adequate assessments of child development and families' economic status (Brooks-Gunn, Berlin, Leventhal, & Fuligni, 2000). These studies find significant income effects, although they are not as large as some of the earlier studies suggested (see also Duncan et al., 1998, for an example of a sibling-comparison model).

## LINKS BETWEEN POVERTY AND CHILDREN'S DEVELOPMENT

### Early Childhood

*Cognitive Outcomes.* The emotional, physical, and intellectual environment that a child is exposed to in the early years of life affects early learning, self-regulation, and perhaps brain organization (Carnegie Corporation,

1994; Shonkoff & Phillips, 2000). Consequently, young children may be more vulnerable to developmental problems should their environment prove especially impoverished. For example, children living below the poverty threshold are more than 1.3 times as likely as nonpoor children to experience learning disabilities and developmental delays (Brooks-Gunn & Duncan, 1997).

Measures of cognitive development include children's intelligence, verbal and reasoning skills, and scholastic achievement or, for young children, school readiness. Until recently, most poverty research comparing outcomes such as cognition, school achievement, and behavior problems in the poor and nonpoor has focused on older children and adolescents, rather than on young children, partly because most longitudinal data sets target adolescents and young adults (Brooks-Gunn et al., 2000; Brooks-Gunn, Duncan, et al., 1995; Brooks-Gunn, Klebanov, & Liaw, 1995).

Negative associations between family poverty and children's cognitive outcomes tend to emerge at age 2 years (Klebanov et al., 1998; Smith et al., 1997). Using the IHDP, a multisite, randomized intervention for almost 1,000 premature and low birth weight infants, Klebanov and colleagues (1998) tested the link between family poverty (defined as family income at or below 150% of the FPL) and child IQ scores measured at ages 1, 2, and 3 years. Family risk factors associated with poverty, such as single parenthood and low maternal education, were found to have a negative effect on age 1 IQ scores, whereas income itself did not. At age 2, however, both family risk and income predicted lower scores, with poor children's scores averaging 4.4 points lower than those of nonpoor children.

In addition to emerging at age 2, the negative effects of poverty on children's cognitive outcomes continue and may even increase throughout early childhood. Findings from the ECLS-K study found that during kindergarten, low socioeconomic status (SES) children caught up to their peers in basic

reading skills (i.e., letter recitation) but became even further behind their classmates on more complex skills (i.e., reading words; Denton, West, & Watson, 2003). Such results suggest that starting around age 2, children reared in poverty generally score between 15% and 40% of a standard deviation lower on standardized cognitive assessments compared with their nonpoor peers. These effects are sustained when children reach school age and are accompanied by lower levels of school achievement, higher levels of grade retention, and eventual dropout among poor children and adolescents (Aber et al., 1997; Brooks-Gunn & Duncan, 1997).

*Behavioral Outcomes.* The first years of life herald the development of capacity to form trusting relationships, which set the foundation for emotional regulation and subsequent relationships (Siegel, 1999). Although the link is not as strong as with cognitive outcomes, existing research indicates that young children living in poverty are more likely than nonpoor children to display emotional or behavioral problems (Lipman, Offord, & Boyle, 1994; Pagani, Boulerice, & Tremblay, 1997). Young children's social and emotional development is often measured through parental report of the child's behavior. These behaviors are often grouped along two dimensions: internalizing behaviors such as anxiety, withdrawal, and depression and externalizing behaviors such as aggression, fighting, and acting out (Brooks-Gunn & Duncan, 1997; McLeod & Shanahan, 1993). Three-year-olds in deep poverty displayed more internalizing behavior symptoms than did less poor children. Additionally, the gap between the groups widened by the time the children were 5 years old (Brooks-Gunn, Leventhal, & Duncan, 1999).

### Childhood and Adolescence

*Cognitive Outcomes.* Cognitive measures in childhood and adolescence are assessed via a child's school achievement, years of schooling, receipt of special education, grade failure, and general engagement in school. Although research on children's test scores at age 8 found that the effects of income on these scores were similar in size to those reported for 3-year-olds (Smith et al., 1997), few studies link long-term family income to cognitive ability and achievement measured during the school years (Brooks-Gunn & Duncan, 1997). The research that has related family income measured during adolescence on cognitive ability has found modest effects (Peters & Mullis, 1997), consistent with literature showing relatively small effects of income on school attainment. It should be noted, however, that such studies' measurement of parental income is restricted to the child's adolescent years, potentially biasing the findings.

To test the importance of timing on income effects, Duncan and colleagues (1998) estimated completed schooling models using three income measures: average parental income between birth and age 5, average income between ages 6 and 10, and average income between ages 11 and 15. The only stage for which parents' income significantly predicted high school graduation was early childhood. These findings suggest that the primary reason that parents' income during middle childhood or adolescence predicts completed schooling is that income during those periods is correlated with income in early childhood.

Other studies using the PSID and the NLSY have also found that poverty status has a small negative impact on years of schooling obtained (Haveman & Wolfe, 1994; Teachman, Paasch, Day, & Carver, 1997). Much of the observed association between income and schooling appears to be the result of confounding variables such as parent education, family structure, and neighborhood characteristics. In general, the links between poverty and school achievement in childhood and adolescence are likely to be statistically significant, yet small

(Brooks-Gunn & Duncan, 1997). For example, a recent study of the NICHD did find that children experiencing poverty later (ages 4–9 years) had less favorable developmental outcomes than those experiencing poverty in infancy (NICHD Early Child Care Research Network, 2005).

Research with other data sets examining measures of adolescent achievement and aspiration (such as high school rank and the number of courses taken) has also concluded that the effect of adolescent poverty on educational attainment appears to be limited. For example, the effect of poverty on continuation to postsecondary schooling in the Wisconsin Longitudinal Study (WLS) fell by 8% upon controlling for mental ability (Hauser & Sweeney, 1997).

*Behavioral Outcomes.* Social and emotional problems in late childhood are usually measured by teacher and parental reports, and focus on outcomes such as self-efficacy, self-esteem, depression, anxiety, and aggression. During the school years, economic circumstances seem to be important, but it is unclear whether behavior problems during this time merely reflect the continuation of problems that began in early childhood (Tremblay, Pihl, Vitaro, & Dobkin, 1994).

Studies looking at older children have found correlations between family income and number of behavior problems (Costello et al., 2003). In the Great Smokey Mountains study mentioned previously, an overall negative correlation was observed between family income and number of behavioral problems (i.e., depression, anxiety, conduct disorder, and oppositional defiance) in children ages 9 to 13. In the same sample, persistence of poverty was found to have varying effects on internalizing and externalizing behaviors. The children in this study who experienced an increase in income as a result of the introduction of a casino demonstrated a reduction in externalizing symptoms. Interestingly, their internalizing symptoms were unaffected by the change (Costello et al., 2003). Similar trends were observed in the internalizing symptoms of a subsample in the NLSY experiencing changes in family income. It is hypothesized that internalizing symptoms persist because income increases do not influence changes in the kinds of experiences that tie poverty to depressive symptoms (McLeod & Shanahan, 1996).

Gender differences have been reported in some but not most studies. Analyses from the Charlottesville Longitudinal Study on 8- to 10-year-olds revealed that the relationship between poverty and externalizing behavior was stronger for the boys than it was for the girls. Moreover, among children experiencing persistent poverty, the internalizing behaviors seemed to decrease over time for girls and increase over time for boys (Bolger, Patterson, Thompson, & Kupersmidt, 1995).

Few studies have focused on the behavioral outcomes for adolescents as they relate to income levels. However, some evidence indicates that adolescents' perception of family economic hardship predicts both increased levels of anxiety and decreased levels of self-esteem (McLoyd, Jayaratne, Ceballo, & Borquez, 1994).

In sum, the association between poverty and child development is observed more so in cognitive measures during the early years and in behavioral measures later in childhood and adolescence. We next consider the extent to which the depth, persistence, and timing of poverty influence these associations.

## DEPTH, PERSISTENCE, AND TIMING OF POVERTY

### Depth of Poverty

Links between income and child cognitive outcomes seem to be nonlinear because income has consistently been found to have a greater influence on child cognitive outcomes for those at the lowest end of the income distribution (Dearing et al., 2001; Duncan et al., 1998). For example, a comparison of the cognitive scores of 3- to 6-year-old children in six different income-to-needs groups: deep poverty (< .5), poverty (.5 to 1), near poor (1 to 1.5), lower-middle class (1.5 to 2), middle class (2 to 3), and affluent (> 3), found the largest cognitive deficits (8 to 12 points) for children living in deep poverty in comparison with those who were not poor (Smith et al., 1997). Similarly, another study comparing poor and middle-class children 3 years and older found that children living below the poverty line scored about 9 to 10 percentage points lower on math and verbal subtests than did children living at three times the poverty threshold. Children from families with incomes closer to, but still below, the poverty line also did worse than children in higher-income families, though the differences were smaller (Korenman, Miller, & Sjaastad, 1995). Such differences are significant because a 6- to 13-point difference might mean the difference between being placed in a special education class or not (Brooks-Gunn & Duncan, 1997).

The association between depth of poverty and behavioral outcomes is similar to effects on children's cognitive scores—the deeper the poverty, the stronger the negative impact on behavioral outcomes. Analyses from the IHDP revealed that 3-year-olds in deep poverty displayed more internalizing behavior symptoms than did less poor children, with an even greater difference between the groups at age 5 (Brooks-Gunn et al., 1999).

Such findings indicate that income may matter more at deeper levels of poverty and also suggest that the development of children in poverty may be more sensitive to changes in income than the development among nonpoor children (Duncan et al., 1998; Ryan, Fauth, & Brooks-Gunn, 2006). To test such a hypothesis, Dearing and colleagues (2001) used the NICHD Study of Early Child Care to model the associations between changes in income-to-needs and 36-month child outcomes, and found that when children from poor families experienced increases in income-to-needs that were at least 1 standard deviation (about 70%) higher than the mean change for poor families, they displayed outcomes similar to their nonpoor peers. Interestingly, similar changes in income-to-needs for children from nonpoor families proved to be of little importance, suggesting that poorer families benefit more from an increase in income than do nonpoor families. Analogous trends have been found between income and completed years of schooling (Duncan & Brooks-Gunn, 1997; Smith et al., 1997).

## Persistence of Poverty

Persistent poverty is consistently linked with more adverse effects on preschool children's cognitive development than is transitory poverty, with children experiencing either type of poverty scoring lower than never-poor children (Duncan et al., 1994; Korenman et al., 1995; Smith et al., 1997). Effect sizes are substantial. For instance, children in the IHDP who lived in poverty 4 of their first 5 years had IQ scores that were on average 9 points lower than those of nonpoor children (about three-quarters of a standard deviation). Children living in poverty for some but not all of the 4 years had IQ scores only about four points lower (less than a third of a standard deviation) than those of nonpoor children (Duncan et al., 1994). Smith and colleagues found similar results for children in the IHDP and NLSY datasets—children who experienced consistent poverty during the first 5 years had lower scores on all assessments compared with children who had been poor for transient periods (Smith et al., 1997). Such findings suggest that children who experience longer durations of poverty will lag behind nonpoor or temporarily poor classmates.

Persistence of poverty also has important associations with child behavioral development. In the IHDP, children who were persistently poor were more likely to display both internalizing and externalizing behavior problems when compared with never poor children (Duncan et al., 1994). Interestingly, children who experience persistent poverty did not display the same frequency or the same kind of behavioral problems as did children who experience short-term poverty. For example, 4- to 11-year-old children in the NLSY displayed more internalizing symptoms when persistent poverty was experienced and a higher presence of externalizing behaviors when current poverty was experienced. The different associations between behavior type and length of poverty suggests that persistent poverty evokes feelings of dependence, unhappiness, and anxiety, but current poverty has a larger influence on disruptive behaviors and peer conflict (McLeod & Shanahan, 1993; however, these findings are not consistently found). A second study using the NLSY data from children ages 3 to 11 also found that on average, children living in long-term poverty fared worse on behavioral outcomes, ranking 3 to 7 percentile points higher on behavior problems than did nonpoor children. However, children in long-term poverty experience fewer behavioral problems than did children who experienced only 1 year of poverty (Korenman et al., 1995).

## Timing of Poverty

Previous research has resulted in conflicting conclusions on the importance of timing of poverty on child cognitive and behavioral outcomes. Some findings suggest that poverty in infancy is more deleterious to long-term behavioral and achievement outcomes than is poverty in early childhood or adolescence (Duncan & Brooks-Gunn, 2000), but others suggest that children experiencing poverty later (ages 4–9 years) have less favorable developmental outcomes. Data from the NICHD Study of Early Child Care and Youth Development (SECCYD) were analyzed to determine the relationship between the duration and timing of poverty to children's cognitive and social development by comparing children who were never poor, poor during infancy (0–3 years of age), poor only after infancy (4–9 years of age), and chronically poor on measures of language and school readiness skills (NICHD Early Child Care Research Network, 2005). Where differences between early and late childhood occurred, children who experienced poverty after infancy had less favorable outcomes. Consistent with previous research, children in persistently poor families had the lowest levels of performance of the four groups on cognitive language skill measures, and their scores were significantly different from those in families that experienced shorter-term poverty. Moreover, the chronically poor families were more seriously and consistently disadvantaged than were those in transitory poverty on almost every indicator measured. Differences in the conclusions of these studies may be the result of differences in the study designs. Duncan and colleagues (1998) used sibling comparison, but the NICHD study (2005) did not, resulting in a stronger design that controlled for family variables caused by sibling design.

In sum, there exists an abundance of evidence indicating that family income can substantially influence child well-being. The association between income and child outcomes is particularly complex when one considers the effects of depth, persistence, and timing of poverty. Family income seems to be more strongly associated with children's ability and achievement-related outcomes than to emotional outcomes. In addition, the links are particularly pronounced for those who live in extreme poverty (< .5 FPL) and for children who live below the poverty line for multiple years. Although income effects on outcomes

such as depression and antisocial behavior are smaller than those on IQ, early poverty may put children at a disadvantage that does not abate even if families leave poverty. The frequency and type of behavioral problems experienced may depend on the persistence of the poverty. The next two sections describe processes through which poverty may cause these outcomes and the roles public policy can play in moderating these links.

## POVERTY PATHWAYS AND PROCESSES

The literature reviewed thus far highlights the cognitive and behavioral difficulties that poor children face but has not focused on the processes by which income might influence child development. In this section, a set of processes or "pathways" is discussed. By implication, each pathway is linked to both family income and one or more child outcomes (Brooks-Gunn & Duncan, 1997).

Economic deprivation may be negatively linked with parents' psychological health, parenting skills, the amount of time spent with the child, the social capital available to the family, the home environment, and parent-child interactions (Boisjoly, Duncan, & Hofferth, 1995; Dodge et al., 1994; McLoyd, 1990; Sampson & Laub, 1994). Consequently, most research examining potential pathways focuses on the family, home, and other aspects of a child's environment. Here, we will concentrate on two main theories relating poverty and family processes to child development: the "family stress theory," which focuses on the relationships and interactions within the family (Conger & Elder, 1994; Elder, 1999; Elder & Caspi, 1988), and the "investment model," which emphasizes the role of income in parents' ability to provide material goods, services, and experiences as well as human capital and home environment (Haveman &

Wolfe, 1994; Mayer, 1997). Disruptions in any of these areas have been linked to less than optimal child development both in the social and behavioral (Conger et al., 1992; Conger, Patterson, & Ge, 1995; Dodge et al., 1994; McLoyd, 1990; Sampson & Laub, 1994) as well as cognitive domains (Jackson, Brooks-Gunn, Huang, & Glassman, 2000; Linver, Brooks-Gunn, & Kohen, 2002; Yeung, Linver, & Brooks-Gunn, 2002).

## The Family Stress Model

Children show the healthiest outcomes when they experience parenting characterized by warm parent-child interactions, cognitive stimulation, clear limit setting, and adequate monitoring (Bornstein, 1995). In contrast, parenting that is erratic and harsh or emotionally detached has been linked to insecure infant-mother attachments, with potentially long-lasting effects on socio-emotional, behavioral, and cognitive outcomes (Shonkoff & Phillips, 2000). Research examining financial pressure and income deprivation has found that both seem to undermine parents' psychological and emotional resources, thereby disrupting parenting styles, parent-child interactions, and, consequently, child development (Conger & Conger, 2000; Conger & Elder, 1994; Dodge et al., 1994).

The family stress model was developed to examine how emotional distress and marital conflict, brought about by the demands of economic pressure, affect adolescent adjustment (Conger, Rueter, & Conger, 2000; McLoyd, 1989). Research on financial loss (resulting from unstable work, varying income levels, and unemployment) is distinct from poverty studies, in that the former examines how declines in income alter family dynamics, rather than how persistent deprivation shapes them (Ryan et al., 2006). This phenomenon was studied by Elder (1999), who found that parental emotional distress caused by income loss during the Great Depression led

to marital conflict and punitive parenting, especially by fathers. The children in this study, particularly the boys, who experienced the punitive and erratic parenting tended to have poorer adolescent adjustment and academic outcomes (Elder, 1999). Conger and colleagues found similar associations among families from rural farming communities in the Midwest (Conger et al., 1992), where economic pressure triggered maternal depression and marital conflict, decreasing nurturant parenting and resulting in a greater number of adjustment problems for children in their teenage years. Such findings indicate that a family's economic loss may influence child development indirectly through its emotional impact on parents.

The family stress model has been extended to address the effects of poverty on parents and children. Like families who experience income loss, parents in persistent poverty also struggle to supply food, shelter, safety, and clothing to their families. These struggles have been correlated with higher levels of depression and anxiety, which has been negatively associated with warm parenting (McLoyd, 1990). In fact, the association between parent stress and negative parenting is thought to be stronger for families with lower incomes because maternal depression and poor parenting practices appear to exert a stronger influence over the developmental outcomes of low-income children than of nonpoor children (Petterson & Albers, 2001). Additionally, the association between parenting and child outcomes is more pronounced for families with young children. This might be because infants and toddlers are more dependent on nurturance from parents than are older children (Elder & Caspi, 1988).

Parental stress caused by economic circumstance can influence a variety of parenting behaviors. For example, poverty has been linked to harsh parenting and physical disciplining practices (Dodge et al., 1994; Linver et al., 2002). This link might occur because parents resort to physical punishment to keep their children from engaging in dangerous or health-threatening activities, or as a direct result of increased parental stress. A second parent behavior influenced by poverty is parental supportiveness and warmth. Parent stress may lead parents to be less attentive and less responsive to the needs of their child (Dodge et al., 1994; Jackson et al., 2000; Smith, Brooks-Gunn, Kohen, & McCarton, 2001). Levels of parent supportiveness toward children may also be lower because poor parents often don't receive much social support themselves, which, when received, can mitigate parental stress (Jackson et al., 2000).

How parents adapt to the stress of poverty may influence how family poverty will influence children. If parents are able to maintain positive parenting behaviors, despite added stress, the negative effects of poverty might be buffered for the child. Families living in poverty with parents who develop positive and supportive relationships with children, create an environment that can reduce the developmental risks that are normally associated with economic deprivation for children (Cowen, Wyman, Work, & Parker, 1990; McLoyd, 1990). For example, fathers who experienced the economic effect of the Great Depression, but were able to maintain emotional stability despite financial losses, also experienced less marital conflict and were able to practice consistent parenting. These parental behaviors were most likely to influence the self-esteem and achievement among the children in the study (Elder & Caspi, 1988). Similarly, a more recent study found that for families in an economically depressed community, those that were able to remain nurturing and involved in parenting had children who were more likely to do well in school, have positive peer relationships, have more self-confidence, and exhibit less emotional distress (Conger & Conger, 2000).

Mothers who have stable emotional support are less likely than are mothers without social ties to report parenting in coercive and punitive ways (McLoyd, 1997). Although parents' resources somewhat determine the availability of social support, public policy initiatives such as social services and early intervention can help provide this kind of assistance. The roles of policies and programs in this regard are addressed in a later section.

## The Investment Model

Although the family stress model focuses on the association between economic deprivation and children's socio-emotional environment, the investment model focuses on the link between poverty and children's resources. Resources include money with which the family can purchase material goods, services, and experiences as well as other resources such as parental time, social capital, and the home environment. The most detrimental outcomes occur for families experiencing deficits in many of the resource categories considered under the investment model. The independent influences of these resources as mediating pathways are considered here. As with parenting behaviors, these pathways can serve as either protective or risk factors.

Limited income can influence the amount of cognitively stimulating materials found in a child's environment as well as the learning opportunities a child experiences. Data from the NLSY indicate that children of all ages from economically impoverished families have limited access to a variety of learning materials and experiences. These children are less likely to go to museums, experience the performing arts, or participate in lessons aimed at enhancing their skills (Bradley, Corwyn, Burchinal, McAdoo, & Coll, 2001). Researchers have found that if children are exposed to cognitively stimulating toys, books, and games, the negative effects of poverty on behavioral and cognitive child outcomes diminish (Yeung et al., 2002).

Moreover, the number of learning materials and stimulating experiences provided to a child explain a significant amount of variation in IQ scores during the preschool years (Duncan et al., 1994; Linver et al., 2002; Yeung et al., 2002). However, for young children, the value of learning materials and experiences is often mediated through capable adults or peers (Saegert & Winkel, 1990). Learning materials and activities can also provide opportunity for social exchanges, often engaging both the child and an adult and resulting in generally productive time spent together (Bradley & Corwyn, 2002).

The time a parent spends with his or her child is, in itself, a valuable commodity. Under the investment model, parental employment is both positive, because it increases income, and negative, because it decreases the amount of time spent on stimulating activities with the child. The challenge of balancing monetary and time-related resources is especially pronounced for low-income families, for although slight changes in income matter more for children in poverty than children at higher income levels (Dearing et al., 2001), low-income parents who work sacrifice time with their children without gaining much buying power in exchange (Ryan et al., 2006).

Social capital is another pathway through which poverty may be operating on children's outcomes. In short, social capital refers to help and support from family and friends in the form of both time and money (Boisjoly et al., 1995). Social support can help parents maintain emotional health and positive parenting in the face of economic adversity (Cowen et al., 1990). Mothers who receive social support may feel less isolated and less overwhelmed by their economic situation and therefore practice better parenting (McLoyd et al., 1994). When support comes in the form of financial assistance to the family, some of the economic strain and the negative outcomes associated with it may be relieved (Jackson et al., 2000).

The physical home environments of children in poverty play an important role in both cognitive and behavioral outcomes (Yeung et al., 2002). A study using data from the NLSY found that the physical environments of families in poverty are generally less safe, less clean, darker, and more cluttered than are those of nonpoor families. The same study found that these differences were the greatest during early childhood years, when poverty may have the greatest influence on child outcomes (Bradley et al., 2001).

Child health and nutrition is also influenced by parental income. Poor children suffer worse health than do middle-income children, who fare worse than the affluent (Case, Lubotsky, & Paxson, 2002). Poor children experience increased rates of low birth weight and elevated blood levels compared with nonpoor children (Brooks-Gunn & Duncan, 1997). These conditions have been associated with reduced performance on cognitive measures. In particular, low birth weight babies experience increased rates of learning disabilities and classroom behavior problems compared with those born of normal weight (Klebanov, Brooks-Gunn, & McCormick, 1994). Children in poverty also experience higher rates of growth stunting (low height for age), which is negatively linked with cognitive test scores and substantial short term memory impairment (Korenman et al., 1995).

The neighborhoods that families live in can also be considered an additional investment made by parents, as residence in impoverished neighborhoods has implications for child-care settings, schools, and peer groups (Mayer & Jencks, 1989; NICHD Early Child Care Research Network, 1997). A growing body of research suggests that the concentrations of poor and affluent neighbors have differential influences on child and adolescent development (Brooks-Gunn, Duncan, & Aber, 1997; Jencks & Mayer, 1990; Leventhal & Brooks-Gunn, 2000). For example, residence in neighborhoods with mean incomes greater than $30,000, compared with less affluent neighborhoods (mean incomes $10,000–$30,000) has been positively associated with 3-year-olds' IQ scores (Brooks-Gunn, Duncan, Klebanov, & Sealand, 1993). This positive association was sustained when children entered school 2 years later (Duncan et al., 1994). Conversely, studies have documented a negative association between neighborhood poverty and early school-aged children's math and verbal achievement (Chase-Lansdale, Gordon, Brooks-Gunn, & Klebanov, 1997). Neighborhood SES has also been positively associated with behavior problems, particularly internalizing symptoms (Chase-Lansdale et al., 1997).

Community analyses suggest that the structural and demographic features of neighborhoods and communities are likely to affect child and adolescent outcomes indirectly, through community level social and cultural processes such as community monitoring, the number and quality of social ties, organizational participation and value consensus. For example, neighbors may serve as role models and exercise social control, helping young people to internalize social norms and learn the boundaries of acceptable behavior (Gephart, 1997; Jencks & Mayer, 1990; Xue, Leventhal, Brooks-Gunn, & Earls, 2005).

## Child Care

In addition to the home environment and neighborhood, parents make investment in their children by placing them in nonmaternal child care. Research on child care suggests that children's experience in care can affect their cognitive and social development in early childhood. The size and direction of these effects, however, depend on age of entry into care, quality of care, and parents' poverty status (Brooks-Gunn, Han, & Waldfogel, 2002; NICHD Early Child Care Research Network, 2002). For an in-depth review of the effects of child care on developmental outcomes, please refer to Chapter 6 by Johnson, Tarrant, & Brooks-Gunn, also in this book.

In conclusion, the family stress and investment models have overlapping pathways through which poverty influences child outcomes. The impact of poverty on parents' mental health is one way in which children are negatively affected by economic impoverishment. A second way is via the limitations poverty places on a family's ability to obtain resources of varying kinds. These two models may work independently or may work concurrently while interacting with one another. Both models provide processes in which policy can intervene to improve the lives of poor children and their families. Such policies will be discussed in the next section.

## POLICY IMPLICATIONS

Based on evidence reviewed in the present chapter and elsewhere, little doubt should remain regarding the deleterious impact that growing up in poverty, especially deep, persistent poverty, can have on young children and their development. Because childhood is a period of both great opportunity and great vulnerability, several mechanisms for effective intervention have garnered increased attention in recent years. Of particular interest to those concerned with the well-being of children reared in poverty has been the initiation of income policies and in-kind support programs, which have both been shown to have an immediate impact on the number of children living in poverty and on the circumstances in which they live (Brooks-Gunn & Duncan, 1997). Given what is known about the pathways through which poverty affects early development, and specifically the mediating role that family stress and investment can play, social policies that increase family income and parental employment (cash or income transfer programs), and that provide in-kind services (such as nutrition, health care, and education) may mitigate the negative effects of poverty on development.

Here, we briefly consider several strands of cash transfer programs and in-kind services as modes for intervening in the lives of poor children by attempting to diminish family stress while increasing investments in children and improving overall family income. In particular, early intervention programs; welfare policies; the EITC; Women, Infants, and Children (WIC); food stamps; and free school lunch are mechanisms through which the negative effects of poverty on child outcomes may be limited.

### Early Intervention

Early intervention programs are a promising way to facilitate favorable outcomes among low-income children (Brooks-Gunn, 1993). Early intervention is a broad term that encompasses many ideas and programs, but usually refers to programs that target families with young children and provides some sort of center-based care, sometimes in conjunction with home visits, to improve both cognitive and behavioral outcomes for children. Early interventions target young children, sometimes starting during pregnancy, to increase the effect on outcomes before the child enters school. They operate under the theory that learning is cumulative, and that once a trajectory is set, it becomes increasingly difficult to change it over time.

Many early intervention programs have been evaluated for their short-term effects (before or at age 5) and long-term effects. The short-term findings from experimental studies on early intervention for at-risk children are consistent: "child focused" early care that provides an enriching learning environment can enhance disadvantaged children's cognitive, communication, and language skills (Barnett, 1995; Brooks-Gunn et al., 1994). Specifically, these programs

have been shown to arrest or reduce declines in poor children's IQ scores relative to non-poor children during the preschool years.

The Abecedarian Project began in the 1970s and has since served as an exemplar of early childhood programs. A randomized, controlled trial, the study included 111 children and involved an intensive, cognitive, language, and socio-emotional enhancing curriculum for the first 5 years of life (Burchinal, Campbell, Bryant, Wasik, & Ramey, 1997; Committee on Ways and Means, 2000). Short-term effects indicated elevated reading and math abilities for program children when compared with treatment children, and long-term assessments demonstrated sustained gains in IQ, math, and reading for program children through age 12; positive effects for reading continued to be found when program children were 15 (Campbell, Pungello, Miller-Johnson, Burchinal, & Ramey, 2001; Campbell & Ramey, 1994, 1995).

Studies such as Project CARE and IHDP have both shown substantial short-term gains in IQ and language skills. Both interventions used high-quality center care as part of their program models (Barnett, 1995; Brooks-Gunn, Klebanov, Liaw, & Spiker, 1993; Committee on Ways and Means, 2000). Long-term effects from IHDP have experienced "fade out" for the lighter low birth weight children from the sample; however, the heavier low birth weight children are still experiencing benefits from the intervention at age 18 (McCormick et al., 2006).

More recently, an experimental study of Early Head Start reported positive increases in children's cognitive outcomes at age three. The program also positively affected children's engagement with their parents, attentiveness during play, and decreased aggressive behavior (Love et al., 2002). In addition, long-term impact studies with Head Start participants have found higher scores on vocabulary tests, less grade repetition, and more years of completed schooling (Currie & Thomas, 1995; Garces, Duncan, & Currie, 2002).

Program evaluations that have examined long-term links between early intervention and children's behavior problems have mixed results. Participants in the Perry Preschool Program in Michigan, a model preschool program that emerged from the 1960s War on Poverty, experienced reductions in delinquent behavior in early adolescence and less involvement in the criminal justice system at 27 years of age compared with the children who did not participate in the intervention program (Schweinhart, Barnes, Weikart, Barnett, & Epstein, 1993). Similar findings, however, have not been found in other programs. For example, an examination of the long-term behavioral effects for Abecedarian children (after age 15) found no significant results (Campbell et al., 2001).

Although long-term effects have varied across studies, the short-term impact findings from experimental studies on early intervention for at-risk children suggest that early intervention programs can help close the achievement gap between poor and nonpoor children before they enter school. By providing a safe and enriching environment where children can play with learning materials, be read to, and go on field trips, center-based intervention programs influence processes within the family stress model as well as the investment model. Parents can improve their parenting skills by participating in parent involvement activities and by sharing information with center teachers and caregivers. In addition, for programs that also offer a home visiting component, home visitors often focus directly on teaching parents new skills. Home visiting may also result in parents feeling as though they have social support, thus potentially decreasing feelings of isolation and stress (Barnett, 1995; Brooks-Gunn, Duncan, et al., 1997; Shonkoff & Phillips, 2000).

## Welfare Reform

A second form of intervention is income supplementation or welfare. The Personal Responsibility and Work Opportunity Reconciliation Act of 1996 (PRWORA) marked the repeal of Aid to Families with Dependent Children (AFDC), and the creation of its present substitute, Temporary Assistance for Needy Families (TANF). Funded through block grants, TANF was designed to provide states with greater flexibility in determining eligibility and benefit levels. In addition, sanctions can be used by states to reduce or eliminate cash welfare benefits when recipients do not comply with work requirements or other program rules (Reichman, Teitler, & Curtis, 2005). Its purpose is fourfold: (1) to provide assistance to families in poverty so that children can remain in their homes, (2) to promote job training, work, and marriage, (3) to prevent childbirth outside of marriage, and (4) to encourage the formation of two-parent families (Greenberg et al., 2002).

The reform provisions that may have the largest impact on child outcomes include the work mandates, income supplements, time limits, and noncompliance sanctions (Duncan & Brooks-Gunn, 2000). Under TANF, recipients are required to work after 2 years of cash assistance or else face sanctions or other penalties. In addition, welfare is limited to a total of 60 months (consecutive or not) for any recipient. These changes as well as many others will affect the amount of income available to children living in poverty. Sanctions and restrictions are likely to lead to denial of benefits for the families with the youngest children if those children are born toward the end of the 5-year time limit of receipt for the family (Duncan & Brooks-Gunn, 2000). Researchers recommend that states consider exempting families with young children from time limits, sanctions, and restrictions. Evidence that this may give incentive for some mothers to continue bearing children to receive more welfare is weak (Duncan & Brooks-Gunn, 2000).

The literature regarding the impact of welfare receipt on children is mixed. One study found that welfare receipt at age 1 was negatively associated with age 3 IQ scores; scores were especially low for children who left AFDC by age 3 without leaving poverty (Smith et al., 2001). Other studies have found unemployment to be positively associated with children's behavior problems (Smith, Brooks-Gunn, Klebanov & Lee, 2000) regardless of welfare receipt, suggesting that low-income rather than welfare status could be driving negative effects on children. Inconclusive results with older children have also been documented. Some studies have found negative associations between family participation in a welfare program that mandated employment and provided earning supplements and 11-year-olds' achievement scores (Morris, Duncan, Clark-Kauffman, 2003), whereas other studies have found favorable school outcomes among preadolescent boys whose families participated in similar programs (Mistry, Crosby, Huston, Casey, & Ripke, 2001). These results suggest that the impact of altering parental investments in children in terms of time and money may vary given the context and population to whom the program is offered.

Welfare to work policies that impose recipient time limits have had differing effects on children based on the risk of welfare dependency of the family. In general, children may not benefit from parents' increased employment if it is not accompanied by sufficient increases in income to lift families out of poverty (Morris, Bloom, Kemple, & Hendra, 2003). Moreover, a small but growing literature on the effects of welfare sanctioning under PRWORA indicates that compared with non-sanctioned mothers, those who are sanctioned are at a high risk for food insecurity, utility shutoff, financial hardship, and homelessness or eviction (Reichman et al., 2005).

In addition to welfare benefits, other promising social policy programs aim to supplement the incomes of working families with children. Most notably, the EITC, a tax reduction and wage supplement for low- and moderate-income working families, lifts more than 4 million families and 2 million children out of poverty every year—making it the nation's most effective antipoverty program for working families (Nagle & Johnson, 2006). Additionally, in-kind programs like WIC, food stamps, and reduced price or free lunch and breakfast are services that seek to offer poor children additional supports that their families cannot afford.

## CONCLUSION

Although increasing family income and improving financial stability would likely lead to short- and long-term benefits in child cognitive and social development, and cash-benefit programs like recent welfare initiatives have the ability to contribute to family income in a meaningful way, policymakers must guarantee that such social policies enhance rather than limit children's healthy development. Recent findings on welfare benefit administration sound an alarming call to those concerned with child well-being; although welfare caseloads have fallen in the 10 years since the passage of the reform legislation in 1996, only 40 to 50% of mothers who have left the welfare rolls have secured full-time employment. Of those former welfare recipients who are now employed, their average yearly salary of $16,000 is not enough to keep a single mother of two children above the poverty level (Besharov, 2006). Without much-needed support and intervention, and the provision of services and benefits that truly pull families out of poverty, young children born into economically disadvantaged families will continue to fall behind their more advantaged peers in school and in later life experiences. However, with income supplementation, early intervention, and the implementation of well-researched and sound support systems, we can improve poor children's chances for life and school success.

# REFERENCES

Aber, J. L., Bennett, N. G., Conley, D. C., & Li, J. L. (1997). The effects of poverty on child health and development. *Annual Review of Public Health, 18,* 463–483.

Barnett, W. S. (1995). Long-term effects of early childhood programs on cognitive and school outcomes. *Future of Children, 5,* 25–50.

Baydar, N., Brooks-Gunn, J., & Furstenberg, F. (1993). Early warning signs of functional illiteracy: Predictors in childhood and adolescence. *Child Development, 64,* 815–829.

Besharov, D. (2006, August 15). End welfare lite as we know it. *The New York Times.*

Betson, D. M., & Michael, R. T. (1997). Why are so many children poor? *Future of Children, 7,* 25–39.

Blau, D. M. (1999). The effect of income on child development. *Review of Economics and Statistics, 81,* 261–276.

Boisjoly, J., Duncan, G. J., & Hofferth, S. (1995). Access to social capital. *Journal of Family Issues, 16,* 609–631.

Bolger, K. E., Patterson, C. J., Thompson, W. W., & Kupersmidt, J. B. (1995). Psychosocial adjustment among children experiencing persistent and intermittent family economic hardship. *Child Development, 66,* 1107–1129.

Bornstein, M. H. (1995). *Handbook of parenting.* Mahwah, NJ: Erlbaum.

Bradley, R. H., & Corwyn, R. F. (2002). Socioeconomic status and child development. *Annual Review of Psychology, 53,* 371–399.

Bradley, R. H., Corwyn, R. F., Burchinal, M., McAdoo, H. P., & Coll, C. G. (2001). The home environments of children in the United States, part II: Relations with behavioral development through age thirteen. *Child Development, 72,* 1868–1886.

Brooks-Gunn, J. (1993). Why do young adolescents have difficulty adhering to health regimes? In N. Krasnegor, L. Epstein, S. B. Johnson, & S. J. Yaffe (Eds.), *Developmental aspects of health compliance behavior* (pp. 125–152). Hillsdale, NJ: Erlbaum.

Brooks-Gunn, J. (2003). Do you believe in magic: What can we expect from early childhood intervention programs? *Social Policy Report of the Society for Research in Child Development, 17*(1), 1–14.

Brooks-Gunn, J., Berlin, L. J., Leventhal, T., & Fuligni, A. S. (2000). Depending on the kindness of strangers: Current national data initiatives and developmental research. *Child Development, 71*(1), 257–268.

Brooks-Gunn, J., & Duncan, G. J. (1997). The effects of poverty on children. *Future of Children, 7,* 55–71.

Brooks-Gunn, J., Duncan, G. J., & Aber, J. L. (Eds.). (1997). *Neighborhood poverty: Context and consequences for children* (Vol. 1). New York: Russell Sage.

Brooks-Gunn, J., Duncan, G. J., Evans, J., Moore, K., Peters, E., Runyan, D., et al. (1995). *New social indicators of child well-being.* Vienna, Austria: European Centre for Social Welfare Policy and Research, The Family and Child Well-Being Network.

Brooks-Gunn, J., Duncan, G. J., Klebanov, P. K., & Sealand, N. (1993). Do neighborhoods affect child and adolescent development? *American Journal of Sociology, 99,* 353–395.

Brooks-Gunn, J., Guo, G., & Furstenberg, F. F., (1993). Who drops out of and who continues beyond high school? A 20-year follow-up of black urban youth. *Journal of Research on Adolescence, 3,* 271–294.

Brooks-Gunn, J., Han, W. J., & Waldfogel, J. (2002). Maternal employment and child cognitive outcomes in the first three years of life: The NICHD study of early child care. *Child Development, 73,* 1052–1072.

Brooks-Gunn, J., Klebanov, P. K., & Liaw, F. (1995). The learning, physical, and emotional environment of the home in the context of poverty: The Infant Health and Development Program. *Children and Youth Services Review, 17,* 251–276.

Brooks-Gunn, J., Klebanov, P. K., Liaw, F., & Spiker, D. (1993). Enhancing the development of low birth weight, premature infants: Changes in cognition and behavior over the first three years. *Child Development, 64,* 736–753.

Brooks-Gunn, J., Leventhal, T., & Duncan, G. J. (1999). Why poverty matters for young children: Implications for policy. In J. D. Osofsky & H. E. Fitzgerald (Eds.), *WAIMH handbook of infant mental health: Vol. 3. Parenting and Child Care* (pp. 92–131). New York: Wiley.

Brooks-Gunn, J., McCarton, C., Casey, P., McCormick, M., Bauer, C., Berenbaum, J., et al. (1994). Early intervention in low birth weight, premature infants: Results through age 5 years from the Infant Health and Development Program. *Journal of the American Medical Association, 272,* 1257–1262.

Burchinal, M. R., Campbell, F. A., Bryant, D. M., Wasik, B. H., & Ramey, C. T. (1997). Early intervention and mediating processes in cognitive performance of children of low-income African American families. *Child Development, 71,* 339–357.

Campbell, F. A., Pungello, E. P., Miller-Johnson, S., Burchinal, M., & Ramey, C. T. (2001). The development of cognitive and academic abilities: Growth curves from an early childhood educational experiment. *Developmental Psychology, 37,* 231–242.

Campbell, F. A., & Ramey, C. T. (1994). Effects of early intervention on intellectual and academic achievement: A follow-up study of children from low-income families. *Child Development, 65,* 684–698.

Campbell, F. A., & Ramey, C. T. (1995). Cognitive and school outcomes for high risk African American students at middle adolescence: Positive effects of early intervention. *American Educational Research Journal, 32,* 743–772.

Carnegie Corporation. (1994). *Starting points: Meeting the needs of our youngest children.* New York: Author.

Case, A., Lubotsky, D., & Paxson, C. (2002). Economic status and health in childhood: The origins of the gradient. *American Economic Review 92,* 1308–1334.

Chase-Lansdale, P. L., Gordon, R. A., Brooks-Gunn, J., & Klebanov, P. K. (1997). Neighborhood and family influences on the intellectual and behavioral competence of preschool and early school-age children. In J. Brooks-Gunn, G. J. Duncan, & J. L. Aber (Eds.), *Neighborhood poverty: Context and consequences for children* (Vol. 1, pp. 119–145). New York: Russell Sage.

Citro, C. F., & Michael, R. T. (Eds.). (1995). *Measuring poverty: A new approach.* Washington, DC: National Academy Press.

Committee on Ways and Means. (2000). *The 2000 green book.* Washington, DC: U.S. Government Accounting Office.

Conger, R., & Conger, K. J. (2000). Resilience in midwestern families: Selected findings from the first decade of prospective longitudinal study. *Journal of Marriage & the Family, 64,* 361–373.

Conger, R. D., Conger, K. J., Elder, G. H., Lorenz, F. O., Simons, R. L., & Whitbeck, L. B. (1992). A family process model of economic hardship and adjustment of early adolescent boys. *Child Development, 63,* 526–541.

Conger, R. D., & Elder, G. H., Jr. (1994). *Families in troubled times: Adapting to change in rural America.* New York: Aldine de Gruyter.

Conger, R. D., Patterson, G. R., & Ge, X. (1995). It takes two to replicate: A mediational model for the impact of parents' stress on adolescent adjustment. *Child Development, 66,* 80–97.

Conger, K. J., Rueter, M. A., & Conger, R. D. (2000). The role of economic pressure in the lives of parents and their adolescents: The family stress model. In L. J. Crockett & R. K. Silbereisen (Eds.), *Negotiating adolescence in times of social change.* Cambridge, UK: Cambridge University Press.

Costello, E. J., Compton, S. N., Keeler, G., & Angold, A. (2003). Relationships between poverty and psychopathology: A natural experiment. *Journal of the American Medical Association, 290,* 2023–2029.

Cowen, E. L., Wyman, P. A., Work, W. C., & Parker, G. R. (1990). The Rochester Child Resilience Project: Overview and summary of first year findings. *Development and Psychopathology, 2,* 193–212.

Currie, J. (1997). Choosing among alternative programs for poor children. *Future of Children, 7,* 113–131.

Currie, J. M., & Thomas, D. (1995). Does Head Start make a difference? *American Economic Review, 85,* 341–364.

Dearing, E., McCartney, K., & Taylor, B. A. (2001). Change in family income-to-needs matters more for children with less. *Child Development, 72,* 1779–1793.

DeNavas-Walt, C., Proctor, B., & Lee, C. H. (2005). *Income, poverty, and health insurance coverage in the United States: 2004* (U.S. Census Bureau, Current Population Reports, pp. 60–229). Washington, DC: U.S. Government Printing Office.

Denton, K., West, J., & Watson, J. (2003). *Reading—Young children's achievement and classroom experiences* (NCES 2003–070). Washington, DC: U.S. Department of Education, National Center for Education Statistics.

Dodge, K. A., Pettit, G. S., & Bates, J. E. (1994). Socialization mediators of the relation between socioeconomic status and child conduct problems. *Child Development, 65,* 649–665.

Duncan, G. J., & Brooks-Gunn, J. (1997). *Consequences of growing up poor.* New York: Russell Sage.

Duncan, G. J., & Brooks-Gunn, J. (2000). Family poverty, welfare reform, and child development. *Child Development, 71,* 188–196.

Duncan, G. J., Brooks-Gunn, J., & Klebanov, P. K. (1994). Economic deprivation and early childhood development. *Child Development, 65,* 296–318.

Duncan, G. J., Yeung, W., Brooks-Gunn, J., & Smith, J. R. (1998). How much does childhood poverty affect the life chances of children? *American Sociological Review, 63,* 406–423.

Edin, K., & Lein, K. (1997). *Making ends meet: How single mothers survive welfare and low-wage work.* New York: Russell Sage.

Elder, G. H., Jr. (1999). *Children of the great depression: Social change in life experience.* Boulder, CO: Westview Press.

Elder, G. H., & Caspi, A. (1988). Economic stress in lives: Developmental perspectives. *Journal of Social Issues, 44,* 25–45.

Garces, E., Duncan, G. J., & Currie, J. M. (2002). Longer term effects of Head Start. *American Economic Review, 92,* 999–1012.

Gephart, M. A. (1997). Neighborhoods and communities as contexts for development. In J. Brooks-Gunn, G. J. Duncan, & J. L. Aber (Eds.), *Neighborhood poverty: Context and consequences for children* (Vol. 1, pp. 1–43). New York: Russell Sage.

Greenberg, M. H., Levin-Epstein, J., Hutson, R. Q., Ooms, T. J., Schumacher, R., Turetsky, V., et al. (2002). The 1996 welfare law: Key elements in reauthorization issues affecting children. *Future of Children, 12*(1), 27–57.

Hauser, R., & Sweeney, M. (1997). Does poverty in adolescence affect life chances of high school graduation? In G. J. Duncan & J. Brooks-Gunn (Eds.), *Consequences of growing up poor* (pp. 541–595). New York: Russell Sage.

Haveman, R., & Wolfe, B. (1994). *Succeeding generations: On the effects of investments on children.* New York: Russell Sage.

Hernandez, D. J. (1997). Poverty trends. In G. J. Duncan & J. Brooks-Gunn (Eds.), *Consequences of growing up poor* (pp. 8–34). New York: Russell Sage.

Jackson, A. P., Brooks-Gunn, J., Huang, C. C., & Glassman, M. (2000). Single mothers in low-wage jobs: Financial strain, parenting, and preschoolers' outcomes. *Child Development, 71,* 1409–1423.

Jencks, C., & Mayer, S. (1990). The social consequences of growing up in a poor neighborhood. In L. Lynn & M. McGreary (Eds.), *Inner-city poverty in the United States* (pp. 111–186). Washington, DC: National Academy Press.

Klebanov, P. K., Brooks-Gunn, J., Chase-Lansdale, P. L., & Gordon, R. A. (1997). Are neighborhood effects on young children mediated by features of the home environment? In J. Brooks-Gunn, G. Duncan, & J. L. Aber (Eds.), *Neighborhood poverty: Context and consequences for children* (Vol. 1, pp. 119–145). New York: Russell Sage.

Klebanov, P. K., Brooks-Gunn, J., McCarton, C., & McCormick, M. (1998). The contribution of neighborhood and family income to developmental test scores over the first three years of life. *Child Development, 69*(5), 1420–1436.

Klebanov, P. K., Brooks-Gunn, J., & McCormick, M. C. (1994). Classroom behavior of very low birth weight elementary children. *Pediatrics, 94,* 700–708.

Korenman, S., Miller, J. E., & Sjaastad, J. E. (1995). Long-term poverty and child development in the United States: Results from the NLSY. *Children and Youth Services Review, 17,* 127–155.

Leventhal, T., & Brooks-Gunn, J. (2000). The neighborhoods they live in: Effects of neighborhood residence upon child and adolescent outcomes. *Psychological Bulletin, 126,* 309–337.

Leventhal, T., & Brooks-Gunn, J. (2002). Poverty and child development. In *The international encyclopedia of the social and behavioral sciences* (Vol. 3, Article 78, pp. 11889–11893). Oxford, UK: Elsevier Science.

Linver, M. R., Brooks-Gunn, J., & Kohen, D. E. (2002). Family processes as pathways from income to young children's development. *Developmental Psychology, 38,* 719–734.

Lipman, E. L., Offord, D. R., & Boyle, M. H. (1994). Relation between economic disadvantage and psychosocial morbidity in children. *Canadian Medical Association Journal, 151,* 431–437.

Love, J. M., Kisker, E. E., Ross, C., Schochet, P. Z., Brooks-Gunn, J., Paulsell, D., et al. (2002). *Making a difference in the lives of infants and toddlers and their families: The impacts of Early Head Start.* Washington, DC: U.S. Department of Health and Human Services.

Mayer, S. E. (1997). *What money can't buy: Family income and children's life chances.* Cambridge, MA: Harvard University Press.

Mayer, S., & Jencks, C. (1989). Poverty and the distribution of material hardship. *Journal of Human Resources, 24,* 88–114.

McCormick, M. C., Brooks-Gunn, J., Buka, S. L., Goldman, J., Yu, J., Salganik, M., et al. (2006). Early intervention in low birth weight premature infants: Results at 18 years of age for the infant health and development program. *Pediatrics, 117,* 771–780.

McLanahan, S. (1997). Parent absence or poverty: Which matters more? In G. Duncan & J. Brooks-Gunn (Eds.), *Consequences of growing up poor* (pp. 35–48). New York: Russell Sage.

McLanahan, S. (2004). Diverging destinies: How children are faring under the second demographic transition. *Demography, 41,* 607–627.

McLanahan, S., & Sandefur, G. (1994). *Growing up with a single parent: What hurts, what helps.* Cambridge, MA: Harvard University Press.

McLeod, J. D., & Shanahan, M. J. (1993). Poverty, parenting, and children's mental health. *American Sociological Review, 58,* 351–366.

McLeod, J. D., & Shanahan, M. J. (1996). Trajectories of poverty and children's mental health. *Journal of Health and Social Behavior, 37,* 207–220.

McLoyd, V C. (1989). Socialization and development in a changing economy: The effects of paternal job and income loss on children. *American Psychologist, 44,* 293–302.

McLoyd, V. C. (1990). The impact of economic hardship on black families and children: Psychological distress, parenting, and socio-emotional development. *Child Development, 61,* 311–346.

McLoyd, V.C. (1997). The impact of poverty and low socioeconomic status on the socio-emotional functioning of African American children and adolescents: Mediating effects. In R. D. Taylor & M. C. Wang (Eds.), *Social and emotional adjustment and family relations in ethnic minority families* (pp. 7–34). Mahwah, NJ: Erlbaum.

McLoyd, V. C., Jayaratne, T. E., Ceballo, R., & Borquez, J. (1994). Unemployment and work interruption among African American single mothers: Effects on parenting and adolescent socio-emotional functioning. *Child Development, 65,* 562–589.

Mistry, R. S., Crosby, D. A., Huston, A. C., Casey, D. M., & Ripke, M. N. (2001). Lessons from New Hope: The impact on children's well-being of a work-based antipoverty program for parents. In G. J. Duncan & P. L. Chase-Landsdale (Eds.), *For better and for worse: Welfare reform and the well-being of children and families* (pp. 179–200). New York: Russell Sage.

Morris, P., Bloom, D., Kemple, J., & Hendra, R. (2003). The effects of a time-limited welfare program on children: The moderating role of parents' risk of welfare dependency. *Child Development, 74,* 851–874.

Morris, P., Duncan, G. J., & Clark-Kauffman, E. (2003). *Child well-being in an era of welfare reform: The sensitivity of transitions in development to policy change.* New York: MDRC.

Nagle, A., & Johnson, N. (2006). *A hand up: How state earned income credits help working families escape poverty in 2006.* Washington, DC: Center on Budget & Policy Priorities.

National Center for Children in Poverty. (2006, September). *Child poverty in 21st century America: Who are America's poor?* Retrieved May 31, 2007, from http://nccp.org/publications/pub_678.html

NICHD Early Child Care Research Network. (1997). Familial factors associated with the characteristics of nonmaternal care for infants. *Journal of Marriage and the Family, 59,* 389–408.

NICHD Early Child Care Research Network. (2002). Structure, process, outcome: Direct and indirect effects of caregiving quality on young children's development. *Psychological Science, 13,* 199–206.

NICHD Early Child Care Research Network. (2005). Duration and developmental timing of poverty and children's cognitive and social development from birth through third grade. *Child Development, 16,* 795–810.

Pagani, L., Boulerice, B., & Tremblay, R. (1997). The influence of poverty on children's classroom placement and behavior problems. In G. J. Duncan & J. Brooks-Gunn (Eds.), *Consequences of growing up poor* (pp. 311–339). New York: Russell Sage.

Patterson, C. J., Kupersmidt, J. B., & Vaden, N. A. (1990). Income level, gender, ethnicity, and household composition as predictors of children's school based competence. *Child Development, 61,*485–494.

Peters, E., & Mullis, N. (1997). The role of family and source of income in adolescent achievement. In G. J. Duncan & J. Brooks-Gunn (Eds.), *Consequences of growing up poor* (pp. 518–540). New York: Russell Sage.

Petterson, S. M., & Albers, A. B. (2001). Effects of poverty and maternal depression on early child development. *Child Development, 72,* 1794–1813.

Rainwater, L., & Smeeding, T. L. (2003). Doing poorly: U.S. child poverty in cross-national context. *Children, Youth and Environments, 13*(2).

Reichman, N., Teitler, J., & Curtis, M. (2005). TANF sanctioning and hardship. *Social Service Review, 79,* 215–236.

Rouse, C., Brooks-Gunn, J., & McLanahan, S. (2005). Introducing the issue. *Future of Children, 15,* 5–13.

Ryan, R. M., Fauth, R. C., & Brooks-Gunn, J. (2006). Childhood poverty: Implications for school readiness and early childhood education. In B. Spodek & O. N. Saracho (Eds.), *Handbook of research on the education of young children* (2nd ed., pp. 323–346). Mahwah, NJ: Erlbaum.

Saegert, S., & Winkel, G. H. (1990). Environmental psychology. *Annual Review of Psychology 41,* 441–477.

Sampson, R. J., & Laub, J. H. (1994). Urban poverty and the family context of delinquency: A new look at structure and process in a classic study. *Child Development, 65,* 523–540.

Schweinhart, L. J., Barnes, H. V., Weikart, D. P., Barnett, W. S., & Epstein, A. S. (1993). *Significant benefits: The High/Scope Perry Preschool Study through age 27.* Ypsilanti, MI: High/Scope Press.

Shonkoff, J. P., & Phillips, D. A. (Eds.). (2000). *From neurons to neighborhoods: The science of early child development.* Washington, DC: National Academy of Sciences.

Siegel, D. (1999). *The developing mind: How relationships and the brain interact to shape who we are.* New York: Guilford Press.

Smith, J. R., Brooks-Gunn, J., & Klebanov, P. K. (1997). The consequences of living in poverty for young children's cognitive and verbal ability and early school achievement. In G. J. Duncan & J. Brooks-Gunn (Eds.), *Consequences of growing up poor* (pp. 132–189). New York: Russell Sage.

Smith, J. R., Brooks-Gunn, J., & Klebanov, P. K., & Kee, K. (2000). Welfare and work: Complementary strategies for low-income women? *Journal of Marriage and the Family, 62,* 808–821.

Smith, J. R., Brooks-Gunn, J., Kohen, D., & McCarton, C. (2001). Transitions on and off AFDC: Implications for parenting and children's cognitive development. *Child Development, 72,* 1512–1533.

Teachman, J. D., Paasch, K. M., Day, R. D., & Carver, K. P. (1997). Poverty during adolescence and subsequent educational attainment. In G. J. Duncan & J. Brooks-Gunn (Eds.), *Consequences of growing up poor* (pp. 382–418). New York: Russell Sage.

Tremblay, R. E., Pihl, R. O., Vitaro, F., & Dobkin, P. L. (1994). Predicting early onset of male antisocial behavior from preschool behavior. *Archives of General Psychiatry, 51,* 732–739.

U.S. Census Bureau. (2004). *Poverty thresholds for 2004 by size of family and number of related children under 18 years.* Retrieved May 2, 2006, from http://www.census.gov/hhes/poverty/threshld/thresh04.html

Xue, Y., Leventhal, T., Brooks-Gunn, J., & Earls, F. J. (2005). Neighborhood residence and mental health problems of 5- to 11-year-olds. *Archives of General Psychiatry, 62,* 554–563.

Yeung, W., Linver, M. R., & Brooks-Gunn, J. (2002). How money matters for young children's development: Parental investment and family processes. *Child Development, 73,* 1861–1879.

# CHAPTER 19

# Challenging Social Inequalities in Health

## Michael Murray and David F. Marks

*Half the world—nearly three billion people—live on less than two dollars a day. . . . Nearly a billion people entered the 21st century unable to read a book or sign their names. . . . Less than one percent of what the world spent every year on weapons was needed to put every child into school by the year 2000 and yet it didn't happen.*

—Shah, 2006

Throughout the world millions of people continue to live in poverty. This is not just in the developing world, the Global South, but also in the developed world. Despite advances in overall wealth, substantial poverty still exists in many Western societies. In the United Kingdom, the proportion of individuals living in poverty increased from 15% in 1981 to 22% in 2002 to 2003, representing 12.4 million people (Paxton & Dixon, 2004). Other indicators of social inequality in the United Kingdom include the following:

- The richest people have increased their share of total income. The richest 1% increased their share of income from 6% in 1980 to 13% in 1999.
- The concentration of wealth continues to increase. The percentage of wealth held by the richest 10% of the population increased from 47% in 1990 to 56% in 2001.

In the United States, evidence shows a continuing increase in poverty. Using a more restrictive definition of poverty, the U.S. Census Bureau estimated that the proportion of Americans living in poverty increased from 11.3% in 2000 to 12.5% in 2003. In households of single mothers, poverty increased from 25.4% in 2000 to 28% in 2003 (DeNavas-Walt, Proctor, & Mills, 2004). According to figures from the Congressional Budget Office (2006), the inequality in income between the richest and poorest households in the U.S. continues to rise with the share of after-tax income going to the wealthiest one percent rising from 12.2 to 14% between 2003 and 2004, the largest one-year increase in 15 years.

## POVERTY AND HEALTH

### *Socioeconomic Status*

Health and wealth are clearly connected. Substantial research evidence from dozens of countries links socioeconomic status (SES) with health. These studies have consistently shown that the life expectancy of those in the lower social classes is lower than those in the higher social classes. Evidence also indicates that there is a social gradient in morbidity and mortality such that the social group one step down the social ladder is unhealthier than those at the top and so on. This persistent gradient is often referred to as the *health gradient.* When mortality is the measure, a more apposite term would be the "mortality gradient" or "death gradient." Death gradients have been observed in all human societies in both rich and developed countries (Kunst & Mackenbach, 1994) and in poor and developing countries (Marks, 2004).

The connection between SES and health occurs in the context of the family. SES is commonly evaluated in light of the occupation, education, or income level of the heads of each household. In the United Kingdom, for example, the head of a household consisting of a family is assumed to be the male parent (father). Yet the gradients we describe here are not restricted to fathers. They apply to all members of a family, and the effects of SES on health are replicated across gender and age. In the data shown in Figure 19.1, we can observe the impact of household economic status on the mortality rates among infants living in those households. Therefore, we can be quite certain that SES has a comprehensive impact on the health of all members of a household, both young and old.

Arguably, the impact may well be higher among mothers, daughters, and infants than on fathers and sons because of cultural assumptions favoring males to females in feeding habits, education, and employment.

The *death gradient* such as that shown in Figure 19.1 shows a steady increase in infant mortality as SES decreases.

Similar gradients exist in all societies including the United States, the United Kingdom, and all other industrialized and developing countries. If the gradient were stepped, or flat at one end of the range and steep at the other, it could be inferred that the causative mechanism(s) had a threshold value before any of the ill effects could appear. However, there is no evidence of any such thresholds. For most data, the gradient is a continuous one.

### *Black Report*

In 1977, the United Kingdom government established a working group to investigate the relationship between social position and health. The subsequent Black Report (Townsend & Davidson, 1982)—named after Sir Douglas Black, the working group chair—summarized the evidence on the relationship between occupation and health. It showed that those classified as unskilled manual workers (Social class V) consistently had poorer health status compared with those classified as professionals (Social class I).

The report clearly documented the link between social position and health and detailed four possible explanations:

- *Artifact explanations:* The relationships between health and social position are an artifact of the method of measurement.
- *Natural and social selection:* The social gradient in health is due to those who are already unhealthy falling whereas those who are healthy rise.
- *Materialist and structuralist explanations:* This explanation emphasizes the important role of economic and associated sociostructural factors.
- *Cultural and behavioral explanations:* These explanations "often focus on the individual

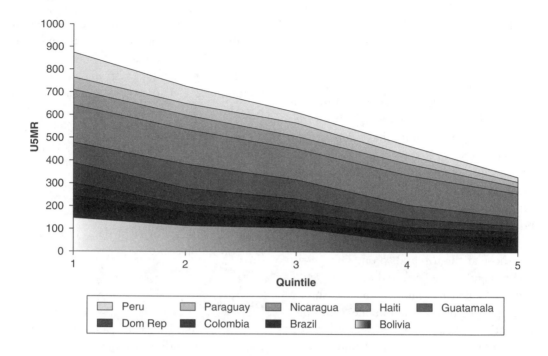

**Figure 19.1**  Under 5 Mortality in Latin America and the Caribbean According to Poverty Level Quintile From Poorest to Richest (from left to right)

as the unit of analysis emphasizing unthinking, reckless or irresponsible behaviors or incautious lifestyle as the moving determinant" (Townsend and Davidson, 1982, p. 23).

Although accepting that each explanation may contribute something, the report emphasized the importance of the materialist explanations and developed a range of policy options that could address the inequalities.

## Ecological Approach

The relationship between social position and health can also be considered from an *ecological perspective* or *systems theory approach*. Bronfenbrenner's (1979) ecological approach conceptualized developmental influences in terms of four nested systems:

- *Microsystems:* Families, schools, neighborhoods
- *Mesosystems:* Peer groups

- *Exosystems:* Parental support systems, parental workplaces
- *Macrosystems:* Political philosophy, social policy

These systems form a nested set, like a set of Russian dolls, microsystems within mesosystems, mesosystems within exosystems, and exosystems within macrosystems. In Table 19.1, we list some of the characteristics of low SES using Bronfenbrenner's systems approach. The table shows how many different disadvantages there can be across all four systems of the social, physical, and economic environment. In addition to these factors, we can add the low levels of actual and perceived injustice that many people with low SES experience and feel in their everyday lives.

Any explanation of the SES-health gradient needs to consider psychosocial systems that structure inequalities across a broad range of life opportunities and outcomes—health, social and educational. As illustrated in Table 19.1,

**Table 19.1**    Behaviors and Experiences Associated With Low SES

**Microsystems—families, schools, neighborhoods**

- Low weight births
- Family instability
- Poor diet/nutrition
- Parental smoking and drinking
- Overcrowding
- Poor schools and educational outcomes
- Poor neighborhoods

**Mesosystems—peer groups**

- Bullying, gangs, and violence
- Smoking and drinking
- Drugs
- Unprotected sex

**Exosystems—parental support systems, parental workplaces**

- Low personal control
- Less social support
- Unemployment or unstable employment
- High stress levels
- Low self-esteem
- Poorer physical and mental health

**Macrosystems—political philosophy, social policy**

- Poverty
- Poor housing
- Environmental pollution
- Unemployment or unstable employment
- Occupational hazards
- Poorer access to health services
- Inadequate social services

in comparison with someone at the high end of the SES scale, the profile of a low SES person is one of multiple disadvantages. The disadvantages of low SES accumulate across all four ecosystems and throughout the family.

This kind of *accumulation* and *clustering* of adverse physical, material, social and psychological effects helps explain the health gradient (Davey-Smith, Blane, & Bartley, 1994). Although each factor alone can be expected to produce a relatively modest impact on mortality, the combination and interaction of many kinds of ecosystem disadvantage are likely to be sufficiently large to generate the observed gradient.

## SOCIAL INEQUALITIES AND HEALTH

The distribution as well as the level of wealth and poverty in society are important. Much research has focused on the relationship between the extent of social inequality in a particular society and the extent of ill health. This research was particularly developed by Wilkinson (1996), who argued that overall health was poorer in the more unequal societies. Thus, health was affected not just by absolute deprivation but also by relative deprivation. This research has attracted substantial debate, and it would seem that the relationship is not as straightforward as was initially conjectured. Rather, there is much more to social inequality than inequality of income. We need also to consider inequality in access to resources and education and differentials in power between groups in society.

## Scientific Explanations

Contemporary research into explanations for social inequalities in health has been reviewed by Marinko, Shi, Starfield, and Wulu (2003). Their classification extends the four-fold explanation developed in the Black Report and is summarized in Table 19.2.

The psychosocial explanations are considered at both the more individual (micro) and the more social (macro) level. At the micro level, some argue that "cognitive processes of comparison," in particular perceived relative deprivation, contribute to heightened levels of stress and subsequent ill-health. At the macro-level, psychosocial explanations focus

on impairment of social bonds and limited civic participation, so-called social capital (see later), that flows from income inequality. These explanations are particularly favored by Wilkinson (1996) to explain the social gradient in health.

Material explanations focus on the importance of income and living conditions (see Macleod & Davey-Smith, 2003). At the micro-level, some argue that in a more unequal society, those worse off have fewer economic resources, which leads to increased vulnerability to various health threats. At the macro level, high-income inequality contributes to less investment in the social and physical environment. Those who favor the material explanations argue that the psychosocial explanations ignore the broad political context within which social and health inequalities are nested.

There are also the artifact and selection explanations of the social inequalities in health. Although these initially attracted

**Table 19.2**    Explanations for the Relationship Between Income Inequality and Health

| Explanation | Synopsis of the Argument |
| --- | --- |
| **Psychosocial (micro)** Social status | Income inequality results in "invidious processes of social comparison" that enforce social hierarchies causing chronic stress leading to poorer health outcomes for those at the bottom. |
| **Psychosocial (macro)** Social cohesion | Income inequality erodes social bonds that allow people to work together, decreases social resources, and results in low trust and civic participation, greater crime, and other unhealthy conditions. |
| **Material (micro)** Individual income | Income inequality means fewer economic resources among the poorest, resulting in lessened ability to avoid risks, treat injury or disease, or prevent illness. |
| **Material (macro)** Social disinvestment | Income inequality results in less investment in social and environmental conditions (safe housing, good schools, etc.) necessary for promoting health among the poorest. |
| **Statistical artifact** | The poorest in any society are usually the sickest. A society with high levels of income inequality has high numbers of poor and consequently will have more people who are sick. |
| **Health selection** | People are not sick because they are poor. Rather, poor health lowers one's income and limits one's earning potential. |

SOURCE: Based on Marinko et al. (2003).

attention, these arguments have less support today (Bartley Blane, & Davey-Smith, 1998).

## Lay Explanations

Recently, there has been increasing interest in what ordinary people have to say about social inequalities in health. This literature connects with the broader literature on popular health beliefs. In an early qualitative study of a sample of women in England, Calnan (1987) found that working-class women were reluctant to accept that they were less healthy than middle-class people. Those who did accept that wealthy people had better health attributed it to differential access to health care. Conversely, professional women were more likely to accept the existence of a health gradient and attributed the poorer health of working-class people to low job satisfaction, low wages, poor diet and the hazards of the working environment.

Chamberlain (1997) reviewed evidence from qualitative research concerning how people from upper and lower SES positions understand health and illness. These studies interviewed small groups of middle-class and working-class women and men classified on the basis of their occupations. Several differences are evident between these two groups. Working-class people tend to use more physicalistic terminology in their accounts of health and illness whereas middle-class people are more mentalistic and person-centered (Blair, 1993). Contact and communication with professionals can be affected by their class relationship with patients so, not surprisingly, surgeons and doctors are often perceived as "upper" class by working-class patients, whereas nurses are seen as more "down to earth."

Lay explanations about social inequalities in health are apparent from an early age. A study in Scotland (Backett-Milburn, Cunningham-Burley, & Davis, 2003) found that children identified social relationships and social life as important as material concerns in explaining health inequalities. This indicated that their direct experiences of relationships and unfairness were important to help them make sense of health inequalities. Further studies are needed to explore the relationship between social positioning and health experience.

## Power, Politics, and Health Inequities

Much of the research on social inequalities in health has focused on differences in income or wealth. As such, it has ignored issues of power and politics. A more inclusive approach has been developed by Hofrichter (2003), who considers inequalities in terms of class, gender, and race. These three social groupings are linked by issues of social and material exploitation. This approach enables the development of a more expansive approach to explaining health inequities not only in terms of income inequality and poverty but also in terms of institutional racism, gender discrimination, corporate globalization, degradation of the environment, destruction of the public sector, dangerous workplace conditions, and neighborhood characteristics.

An important factor in explaining these processes is the weakening of working-class power and the strengthening of capital during the past generation. Greater working-class power and political participation is associated with improved community health (Muntaner et al., 2002). Examples of the negative impact of increased corporate power itemized by Hofrichter (2003) include the following:

> Economic disinvestment in poor communities, extensive layoffs, mass firings and restructuring, gentrification, targeting of industrial and toxic waste facilities in communities of color, elimination of protective regulatory structures, profiteering by drug

companies seeking to maintain control of patents, financial speculation, use of dangerous technologies, restricting competition, shifting the tax burden to the less fortunate, tax subsidies to wealthy corporations, and failure to improve living conditions for farm workers. (p. 23)

These factors in turn threaten already weakened communities leading to further stress and ill health.

Coburn (2004) developed an integrative, class/welfare model, in which issues of income inequality and social cohesion are nested within a broader causal chain. This model argues that during the past 20 years, the power of business has increased but that of the working class has declined. This has been achieved through the introduction of neoliberal policies by the ruling class that have increased income inequality, led to poverty, and reduced access to services. In those countries with more social democratic rather than neoliberal governments, the power of capital has been resisted and the impact on health has been less. Coburn (2004) argues that this benefit to health has been achieved through both material and psychosocial advantages.

## HEALTH AND PLACE

Although the evidence linking ill health and poverty is clearly established, evidence also suggests regional or area variations. This has given rise to a growing program of research on health and place that has explored how major structural changes, such as those itemized earlier, lead to ill health. Features of unhealthy environments include threats to safety and to the creation of social ties (Repetti, Seeman, & Taylor, 1997). Conversely, healthy societies provide safety, opportunities for social integration, and the ability to predict and control our social world. Unhealthy environments are associated with chronic stress.

The social characteristics of a person's local neighborhood can act as an independent predictor of health. A study of four localities in the United States found that residents of disadvantaged neighborhoods had a higher risk of disease than did residents of advantaged neighborhoods, even after controlling for personal income, education, and occupation (Diez Roux et al., 2001). In an accompanying editorial, Marmot (2001) states,

Walk the slums of Dhaka, in Bangladesh, or Accra, in Ghana, and it is not difficult to see how the urban environment of poor countries could be responsible for bad health. Walk north from Manhattan's museum district to Harlem or east from London's financial district to its old East End, and you will be struck by the contrast between rich and poor, existing cheek by jowl. It is less immediately obvious why there should be health differences between rich and poor areas of the same city. It is even less obvious, from casual inspection of the physical environment, why life expectancy for young black men in Harlem should be less than in Bangladesh.

The findings of Diez Roux et al. (2001) suggest an important target for intervention: the neighborhood. This finding is exactly what would be expected from a community perspective.

Three theoretical approaches to the study of health and place have been identified (Curtis & Jones, 1998):

- *Hazard exposure:* Physical and biological risk factors are spatially distributed. This approach posits a direct pathway between hazard exposure and health risk.
- *Social relationships:* Space and place shape the character of social relationships and, in turn, psychosocial and behavioral risk factors.
- *Sense of place and subjective meanings:* This approach considers the shared social meanings people have of their communities.

The first explanation includes all aspects of the physical environment and includes environmental and occupational hazards, threats to personal safety, and the like. The second explanation connects with the growing literature on social capital, whereas the third is connected with the literature on community identity and community narratives.

## Social Capital

Social capital is increasingly used as an aid to explaining social variations in health. The concept has been especially promoted by Robert Putnam, who used it to characterize civic life in Italy (Putnam, Leonardi, & Nanette, 1993). He argued that certain communities had higher degrees of civic engagement, levels of interpersonal trust, and norms of reciprocity. Together, these characteristics contributed to a region's degree of social capital. Putnam (2000) subsequently explored the extent of social capital in the United States and argued that during the past generation, there has been a steady decline in participation in social organizations and thus a steady decline in social capital.

A series of studies have investigated social variations in social capital and its connection with health. Kawachi et al. (1994) found states with a low degree of income inequality also had low social capital as measured by group membership and social trust. Further, those states with high rates of social mistrust and low rates of membership of voluntary organizations had higher mortality rates.

A qualitative study by Campbell, Wood, and Kelly (1999) compared the sense of community engagement in two communities near London. They reported evidence that two aspects of social capital (trust and civic engagement/perceived citizen power) were higher in the "high health" community but two aspects (local identity and local community facilities) were higher in the "low health community." Campbell and Wood

suggested that certain aspects of social capital, in particular perceived trust and civic engagement, are more health enhancing than others are. Whereas Putnam et al. (1993) emphasized the importance of voluntary associations, Campbell and Wood found that these were rare in both communities. However, whereas the "low health" community made almost no reference to community-level networks in their community, these phenomena (e.g., residents' associations) were important in the "high health" community.

An important distinction that Putnam (2000) makes is that between bridging and bonding social capital. The latter refers to inward-looking social ties that bond the community together. Bridging social capital refers to links with diverse groups and provides an opportunity for community members to access power and resources outside their community. Both forms of social capital are essential in building healthy communities (Campbell & Murray, 2004).

Social capital has been widely criticized as an explanatory concept (e.g., Lynch, Due, Muntaner, & Davey-Smith, 2000). There is confusion about what exactly the term implies, there are debates about ways of measuring it, and there is ignorance of the broader political context. An interest in social relations does not preclude acceptance of the importance of political and material factors; however, Baum (1999, 2000) emphasizes caution in the use of the concept because "there are dangers that the promotion of social capital may be seen as a substitute for economic investment in poor communities particularly by those governments who wish to reduce government spending."

## Community Identity

An alternative to the rather behaviorist assumptions underlying much of the work on social capital is to consider the character of the community sense of meaning. The most comprehensive investigation of these processes is the work by Popay and colleagues (2003). They conducted a detailed ethnographic study of four neighborhoods in North West England. Popay et al. found that residents of the more disadvantaged neighborhoods identified *place* as the major explanation for health inequalities, whereas those in relatively advantaged areas preferred individualistic explanations. However, the residents often suggested a complex interaction of macro-structural, place, and lifestyle factors. For example, the residents of the more disadvantaged areas described how macro-structural factors interacted with place-based factors shaping particular lifestyle patterns. The mediating factor linking these factors was often seen as stress.

The way the residents described their communities was categorized into three normative guidelines:

1. *Relationships:* This guideline emphasized the importance of supportive social relationships with neighbors, trust and respect between people, and respect for property.

2. *Physical dimensions:* This guideline referred to aspects of safety, appropriateness, convenience, and cleanliness.

3. *Ontological identity:* This guideline is concerned with the relationship between one's sense of identity and place.

These guidelines helped distinguish between "good" and "bad" neighborhoods. It was not simply the material disadvantage of the neighborhood but, rather, the community dynamics and the extent to which the residents could identify with it. The residents of more disadvantaged areas reported more problems with their neighbors and less safety. These residents were also less likely to identify with their neighborhood. An important component of this research was the emphasis on the importance of community narratives (Popay, 2000; Williams, 2003). Attention to these narratives enabled the researcher to understand the lived experience of people's lives, of the connections between social and political change and everyday life.

## REDUCING INEQUALITIES

Reducing these social inequalities requires adopting a thoroughly multilayered approach. Whitehead (1995) identified four different levels for tackling health inequalities:

1. Strengthening individuals

2. Strengthening communities

3. Improving access to essential facilities and services

4. Encouraging macroeconomic and cultural change

These four levels correspond to the four layers of influence in Whitehead's "onion model" of the determinants of health. Extra microsystem and mesosystem levels, as in Bronfenbrenner's model, could be added to this list.

Interventions aimed at tackling inequalities at an individual level have shown mixed results. There are four possible reasons. First, people living and working in disadvantaged circumstances have fewer resources (time, space, money) with which to manage the process of change. Second, health-threatening behaviors such as smoking tend to increase in difficult or stressful circumstances because they provide a means of coping (Graham, 1993). Third, there may have been a lack of sensitivity to the difficult circumstances in which people work and live that constrain the competence to change. Fourth, there has been a tendency to blame the victim. For example, cancer sufferers may be blamed for the disease if they are smokers on the grounds that they are responsible for the habit that caused the disease.

Overall, efforts directed at the individual level have been inconclusive and small scale.

Because many health determinants are beyond the control of the individual, psychological interventions aimed at individuals are likely to have limited impact on public health problems when considered on a wider scale. This suggests a need for psychologists to work beyond the individual level, with families, communities, work sites, and community groups.

Efforts to tackle inequalities typically have two shortcomings (see Benzeval, Judge, & Whitehead, 1995):

1. Excessive attention is given to the health experiences of white males of working age compared with women, older people, people with disabilities, and minority ethnic groups. More attention needs to be given to the health concerns of these under-served groups.

2. The policy areas dealt with in detail— housing, income maintenance, smoking, and access to health care—are insufficiently comprehensive as an agenda for tackling inequalities.

Tackling health inequalities at the level of services to individuals is insufficient. The correction of inequalities in health demands "a wide-ranging and radical reshaping of economic and social policies" (Benzeval et al., 1995, p. 40). In other words, policy change at Levels 3 and 4 is required to bring about economic and cultural change.

## SOCIAL JUSTICE AND HEALTH

### Social Justice

Critics of the research into social inequalities in health often charge that social inequalities are both an inevitable part of life and also are necessary for social progress. An alternative perspective is to consider not simply inequalities *per se* but inequities in health. Health inequalities can be considered as inequities when they are avoidable, unnecessary, and unfair (Dahlgren & Whitehead, 1991). The issue of fairness leads us to consider the issue of social justice and health.

A useful starting point is the theory of "justice as fairness" developed by the moral philosopher John Rawls (1999). He identified certain underlying principles of a just society:

- Ensure people equal basic liberties including guaranteeing the right of political participation
- Provide a robust form of equal opportunity
- Limit inequalities to those that benefit the least advantaged

When these principles are met, citizens can be confident that they are respected by others and can acquire a sense of self-worth.

Adhering to these principles could begin to address the basic social inequalities in health. Daniels, Kennedy, & Kawachi (2000) detail a series of implications for social organization that flow from the acceptance of these principles. First, ensuring people have equal basic liberties implies that everyone has an equal right to fully participate in politics. This will in turn contribute to improvements in health because, according to social capital theory, political participation is an important social determinant of health.

Second, providing active measures to promote equal opportunities implies the introduction of measures to reduce socioeconomic inequalities and other social obstacles to equal opportunities. Such measures would include comprehensive child-care and childhood interventions to combat any disadvantages of family background. They would also include comprehensive health care for all including support services for those with disabilities.

Finally, a just society would allow only those inequalities in income and wealth that would benefit the least advantaged. This requires direct challenge to the contemporary neoliberal philosophy that promotes the maximization of profit and increasing the extent of social inequality.

## Health and Social Justice

To reduce the inequalities in health, a research and advocacy agenda on issues of social and economic justice needs to be developed (cf. Bullock & Lott, 2001). Such an agenda would be concerned not just with describing the impact of poverty and inequality on health and well-being but also with advocating for social and economic justice. It would include challenging the victim-blaming ideology that is often adopted in psychological approaches to the study of health and illness. It would also include defining health research as a resource for social change (Murray & Campbell, 2003; Murray & Poland, 2006). This would involve a variety of strategies and lead to a more politically engaged approach such as the one championed by Martin-Baro (1994), who challenged psychologists and social scientists to adopt a "preferential option for the poor."

Three approaches have been suggested by Fine and Barreras (2001):

1. *Public policy:* Documenting the impact of regressive social policies and agitating against such policies

2. *Popular education:* Challenging popular victim-blaming beliefs (common-sense) about the causes of ill-health

3. *Community organizing:* Working with marginalized communities and agitating for social change

The success of such a strategy requires building alliances with social groups most negatively affected by social inequalities. As Martin-Baro (1994) stressed, "The concern of the social scientist should not be so much to explain the world as to transform it" (p. 19).

## FUTURE DIRECTIONS

Research on social inequalities in health needs to be clearly connected to exploring various strategies to reduce such inequalities. These can range from macro-level strategies to micro-level strategies. Of primary significance is the SES of the family considered as a social unit. The effects of SES on health are transmitted through families, communities, and regions. SES is not simply an individual-level measure but a measure that applies to the entire family. More conceptual and theoretical effort should be allocated to the study of the mechanisms by which SES effects are transmitted across the whole family structure.

At the micro-level is a need to explore measures that can support healthy human development, especially in the early years. Studies of the health experiences of people from different socioeconomic backgrounds are particularly important to our understanding of the psychological mechanisms underlying health variations. Further research to explore the relationship between social positioning and health experience needs to connect with strategies for social and health professionals to engage with marginalized and disadvantaged sections of society.

At the meso-level is the need to intervene at the level of the group to explore ways of working in particular with disadvantaged young people who often feel isolated and rejected by mainstream society. In such a situation, they are more prone to engage in self-injurious practices.

At the exo-level is the need to evaluate various means of support especially for disadvantaged families and communities. Kim, Millen, Irwin, and Gershman (1999) called on researchers to adopt "a practice of 'pragmatic solidarity' . . . with and for the poor—acknowledging primary accountability to poor communities and their needs." In doing so, the aim is to develop effective action "to resist the multiple forces that threaten the health and survival of poor people today" (p. 391).

At the macro-level is a need to explore how widespread political changes affect the health of communities. This involves participating in ongoing critique and challenge to unjust social policies in developed and developing nations. In Africa and in many parts of Asia and Latin America, the levels of poverty are horrendous. In a world of plenty, it is intolerable that such levels of poverty continue to exist. Sachs (2005) estimates that poverty could be eliminated within 20 years through concerted international action. However, eliminating it requires widespread political action. In 2002, world leaders pledged to work toward a target of 0.7% of their national income in international aid. On average, the world's richest countries provide just 0.33% of their gross national product in official development assistance (ODA). The United States provides just 0.22%. If developed nations increased their ODA to 0.54% by 2015, they would contribute almost $200 billion, which would begin to end the extreme poverty throughout the world. However, money alone is not sufficient when developing nations are crippled by massive debt loads and world trading patterns continue to benefit the wealthier nations. More radical changes are needed in political arrangements.

In general, social research needs to move from observation and explanation of social inequalities in health to more action-oriented research that can challenge this social injustice and instead to develop strategies that in their practice lead to a more just and healthy society.

## REFERENCES

Backett-Milburn, K., Cunningham-Burley, S., & Davis, J. (2003). Contrasting lives, contrasting views? Understandings of health inequalities in differing social circumstances. *Social Science & Medicine, 57,* 613–623.

Bartley, M., Blane, D., & Davey-Smith, G. (1998). Introduction: Beyond the Black Report. *Sociology of Health and Illness, 20,* 563–577.

Baum, F. (1999). Social capital: Is it good for your health? Issues for a public health agenda. *Journal of Epidemiology and Community Health, 53,* 195–196.

Baum, F. (2000). Social capital, economic capital and power: Further issues for a public health agenda. *Journal of Epidemiology and Community Health, 54,* 409–410.

Benzeval, M., Judge, K., & Whitehead, M. (Eds.). (1995). *Tackling inequalities in health: An agenda for action.* London: King's Fund.

Blair, A. (1993) Social class and the contextualization of illness experience. In A. Radley (Ed.), *Worlds of illness: Biographical and cultural perspectives on health and disease* (pp. 27–48). London: Routledge.

Bronfenbrenner, U. (1979). *The ecology of human development: Experiments by nature and design.* London: Harvard University Press.

Bullock, H. E., & Lott, B. (2001). Building a research and advocacy agenda on issues of economic justice. *Analyses of Social Issues and Public Policy, 1,* 147–162.

Calnan, M. (1987). *Health and illness: The lay perspective.* London: Tavistock.

Campbell, C., & Murray, M. (2004). Community health psychology: Promoting analysis and action for social change. *Journal of Health Psychology, 9,* 187–195.

Campbell, C., Wood, R., & Kelly, M. (1999). *Social capital and health.* London: Health Education.

Chamberlain, K. (1997). Socioeconomic health differentials: From structure to experience. *Journal of Health Psychology, 2*(3), 399–411.

Coburn, D. (2004). Beyond the income inequality hypothesis: Class, neo-liberalism, and health inequalities. *Social Science & Medicine, 58,* 41–56.

Congressional Budget Office. (2006, December). *Historical effective federal tax rates: 1979 to 2004.* Washington, DC: Author. Retrieved from http://www.cbo.gov/ftpdocs/77xx/doc7718/EffectiveTaxRates.pdf

Curtis, S., & Jones, I. R. (1998). Is there a place for geography in the analysis of health inequalities? *Sociology of Health and Illness, 20,* 645–672.

Dahlgren, G., & Whitehead, M. (1991). *Policies and strategies to promote social equality in health.* Stockholm: Institute of Future Studies.

DeNavas-Walt, C., Proctor, B.D., & Mills, R.J. (2004). *Income, poverty, and health insurance coverage in the United States: 2003.* U.S. Census Bureau, Current Population Reports, P60-226. Washington, DC: U.S. Government Printing Office.

Daniels, N., Kennedy, B., & Kawachi, I. (2000). Justice is good for our health: How greater economic equality would promote public health. *Boston Review, 25*(1), 6–15.

Davey-Smith, G., Blane, D., & Bartley, M. (1994). Explanations for socioeconomic differentials in mortality. *European Journal of Public Health, 4,* 131–144.

Diez-Roux, A. V., Merkin, S. S., Arnett, D., Chambless, L., Massing, M., Nieto, F. J., et al. (2001). Neighborhood of residence and incidence of coronary heart disease. *New England Journal of Medicine, 345,* 99–106.

Fine, M., & Barreras, R. (2001). To be of use. *Analyses of Social Issues and Public Policy, 1,* 175–182.

Graham, H. (1993). *When life's a drag: Women, smoking and disadvantage.* London: Her Majesty's Stationery Office.

Hofrichter, R. (2003). The politics of health inequities: Contested terrain. In R. Hofrichter (Ed.), *Health and social justice: Politics, ideology, and inequity in the distribution of disease.* San Francisco: Jossey-Bass.

Kawachi, I., Colditz, G. A., Ascherio, A., Rimm, E. B., Giovannucci, E., Stampfer, M. J., et al. (1994). Prospective study of phobic anxiety and risk of coronary heart disease in men. *Circulation, 89,* 1992–1997.

Kim, J. Y., Millen, J. V., Irwin, A., & Gershman, J. (Eds.). (1999). *Dying for growth: Global inequality and the health of the poor.* Monroe, ME: Common Courage Press.

Kunst A. E., & Mackenbach J. P. (1994). The size of mortality differences associated with educational level in 9 industrialised countries. *American Journal of Public Health, 84,* 932–937.

Lynch, J., Due, P., Muntaner, C., & Davey-Smith, G. (2000). Social capital—Is it a good investment for public health? *Journal of Epidemiology and Community Health, 54,* 404–408.

Macleod, J., & Davey-Smith, G. (2003). Psychosocial factors and public health: A suitable case for treatment? *Journal of Epidemiology and Community Health, 57,* 565–570.

Marinko, J. A., Shi, L., Starfield, B., & Wulu, J. T. (2003). Income inequality and health: A critical review of the literature. *Medical Care Research and Reviews, 60,* 407–452.

Marks, D. F. (2004). Rights to health, freedom from illness: A life and death matter. In M. Murray (Ed.), *Critical health psychology.* London: Palgrave.

Marmot, M. (2001). Inequalities in health [Editorial]. *New England Journal of Medicine, 345,* 134–136.

Martin-Baro, I. (1994). *Writings for a liberation psychology* (A. Aron & S. Corne, Eds.). Cambridge, MA: Harvard University Press.

Muntaner, C., Lynch, J., Hillemeier, M., Lee, J., David, R., Benach, J., et al. (2002). Economic inequality, working class power, social capital, and cause specific mortality in wealthy countries. *International Journal of Health Services, 32,* 629–656.

Murray, M., & Campbell, C. (2003). Living in a material world: Reflecting on some assumptions of health psychology. *Journal of Health Psychology, 8,* 231–236.

Murray, M., & Poland, B. (2006). Health psychology and social action. *Journal of Health Psychology, 11,* 379–384.

Paxton, W., & Dixon, M. (2004). *The state of the nation: An audit of injustice in the UK.* London: Institute for Public Policy Research.

Popay, J. (2000). Social capital: The role of narrative and historical research. *Journal of Epidemiology and Community Health, 54,* 401.

Popay, J., Bennett, S., Thomas, C., Williams, G., Gatrell, A., & Bostock, L. (2003). Beyond "beer, fags, egg and chips"? Exploring lay understandings of social inequalities in health. *Sociology of Health and Illness, 25,* 1–23.

Putnam, R. (2000). *Bowling alone: The collapse and revival of American community.* New York: Simon & Schuster.

Putnam, R., Leonardi, R., & Nanette, R. Y. (1993). *Making democracy work: Civic traditions in modern Italy.* Princeton, NJ: Princeton University Press.

Rawls, J. (1999). *A theory of justice.* Cambridge, MA: Belknap.

Repetti, R. L., Seeman, T., & Taylor, S. E. (1997). Health psychology: What is an unhealthy environment and how does it get under the skin? *Annual Review of Psychology, 48,* 411–447.

Sachs, J. (2005). *The end of poverty: Economic possibilities for our time.* London: Penguin.

Shah, A. (2006). *Poverty facts and stats.* Retrieved July 22, 2006, from http://www.globalissues.org/TradeRelated/Facts.asp

Townsend, P., & Davidson, N. (1982). *Inequalities in health: The Black Report.* London: Penguin.

Whitehead. (1995). Tackling inequalities: A review of policy initiatives. In M. Benzeval, K. Judge, & M. Whitehead (Eds.), *Tackling inequalities in health: An agenda for action* (pp. 22–52). London: King's Fund.

Wilkinson, R. G. (1996). *Unhealthy societies: The afflictions of inequality.* London: Routledge.

Williams, G. H. (2003). The determinants of health: Structure, context and agency. *Sociology of Health & Illness, 25,* 131–154.

# Part III

# INTERVENTION AND EDUCATION FOR WORKING WITH POOR FAMILIES

# CHAPTER 20

# Giving Head Start a Fresh Start

## Douglas J. Besharov and Caeli A. Higney

From its earliest days, Head Start has been an extremely popular program because it is based on a simple idea that makes great intuitive sense: A child's early learning experiences are the basis of later development and, given the connections between poverty and low academic achievement, a compensatory preschool program should help disadvantaged children catch up with more fortunate children.

Who could be against a relatively low-cost, voluntary program that children and parents seem to love? Especially if evaluations show that it "works"? But the attractiveness of Head Start's underlying concept should not make it immune from constructive criticism. Given the results of recent evaluations, the program's continued defensiveness has become counterproductive. Head Start cannot be improved without an honest appreciation of its weaknesses (as well as strengths) followed by real reform.

The original Head Start model consisted of a few hours a day of center-based education

during the summer before kindergarten. After its first summer of operation, relatively informal evaluations suggested that Head Start raised the IQs of poor children. In the face of so many other programmatic disappointments, the Johnson administration latched onto these early findings. For example, in a September 1968 Rose Garden speech highlighting the "success" of Head Start, President Lyndon B. Johnson said, "Project Head Start, which only began in 1965, has actually already raised the IQ of hundreds of thousands of children in this country" (*Public Papers of the Presidents of the United States*, 1970, p. 973). And Sargent Shriver, who headed the War on Poverty, testified before Congress that Head Start "has had great impact on children—in terms of raising IQs, as much as 8 to 10 IQ points in a six-week period" (Zigler & Muenchow, 1992, p. 26).

No wonder that Head Start quickly expanded to every state and almost every congressional district. This early emphasis on

SOURCE: From Besharov, D., & Higney, C. (2006). Restarting Head Start: Why hasn't this program adapted with the times? *Public Policy: Current Thinking on Critical Issues*. Reprinted with permission of Maryland School of Public Policy, University of Maryland.

improved IQ scores, however, proved to be a doubled-edged sword. In 1969, the results of the first rigorous evaluation of the national Head Start program were released. Echoing the findings of many future evaluations, this Office of Equal Opportunity–commissioned study conducted by the Westinghouse Learning Corporation and Ohio University concluded that Head Start children made relatively small cognitive gains that quickly "faded out." (This was, to program advocates, the notorious "Westinghouse Study.") In the words of the report: "The research staff for this project failed to find any evidence in the published literature or in prior research that compensatory intervention efforts had produced meaningful differences on any significant scale or over an extended period of time" (Westinghouse Learning Corporation & Ohio University, 1969, pp. 26–31).

As a result, support for the program waned, and there followed a period of uncertainty about Head Start's future. Because the Westinghouse Study found that the academic-year version of the program had some measurable effects, the summer program was phased out, and Head Start took on its current shape: 4 to 7 hours a day from early September to mid-June.

By the early 1970s, Head Start advocates had regrouped. Ignoring the negative Westinghouse findings, they pointed to the apparent successes of other early childhood education programs, especially the Perry Preschool program and, later, the Abecedarian program. And, indeed, the public's impression that Head Start works stems largely from the widely trumpeted results of these two small and richly funded experimental programs from 30 and 40 years ago. Some advocates describe these programs as "Head Start-like," but that is an exaggeration: They cost as much as $15,000 a year in today's dollars (50% more than Head Start), often involved multiple years of services, had well-trained teachers, and instructed parents on effective

child rearing. These programs are more accurately seen as hothouse programs that, in total, served fewer than 200 children. Significantly, they tended to serve low-IQ children or children with low-IQ parents.

Most careful evaluations of *actual* Head Start programs are much less rosy. They have repeatedly shown either small effects or effects that, like those in the 1969 Westinghouse Study, fade out within a few years. No scientifically rigorous study has ever found that Head Start itself has a meaningful and lasting impact on disadvantaged young people. Upon reflection, this should not come as any surprise, given the large cognitive and social deficits that Head Start children evidence even after being in the program for 2 years (unless one thinks these children would be much worse off without Head Start).

After reviewing the full body of this research, a 1997 U.S. General Accounting Office (GAO) report concluded that there was "insufficient" research to determine Head Start's impact: "The body of research on current Head Start is insufficient to draw conclusions about the impact of the national program." The GAO added, "Until sound impact studies are conducted on the current Head Start program, fundamental questions about program quality will remain" (1997, p. 20).

## THE HEAD START IMPACT STUDY

Responding to the GAO report, in 1998, Congress required the U.S. Department of Health and Human Services to conduct another national evaluation of Head Start. To its credit, the Clinton administration took this mandate seriously and initiated a 383-site, randomized experiment (the gold-standard of evaluation) involving about 4,600 children. (In fact, throughout his presidency, President Bill Clinton and his appointees were strongly supportive of efforts to improve Head Start, even to the point of defunding especially mismanaged local programs.)

Sadly, the first-year findings from this Head Start Impact Study, released in June 2005, showed little meaningful impact on disadvantaged children (U.S. Department of Health and Human Services [HHS], 2005a).

For 4-year-olds (half the program), statistically significant gains were detected in only 6 of 30 measures of social and cognitive development and family functioning (itself a statistically suspect result). Of these 6 measures, only 3 measures—the Woodcock Johnson Letter-Word Identification test, the Spelling test, and the Letter Naming Task—directly test cognitive skills and show a slight improvement in one of three major predictors of later reading ability (letter identification). Head Start 4-year-olds were able to name about two more letters than their non–Head Start counterparts, but they did not show any significant gains on much more important measures such as early math learning, vocabulary, oral comprehension (more indicative of later reading comprehension), motivation to learn, or social competencies, including the ability to interact with peers and teachers.

Results were somewhat better for 3-year-olds, with statistically significant gains on 14 of 30 measures; however, the measures that showed the most improvement tended to be superficial as well. Head Start 3-year-olds were able to identify one and a half more letters and they showed a small, statistically significant gain in vocabulary. However, they came only 8% closer to the national norm in vocabulary tests—a very small relative gain—and showed no improvement in oral comprehension, phonological awareness, or early math skills.

For both age groups, the actual gains were in limited areas and disappointingly small. Some commentators have expressed the hope that these effects will lead to later increases in school achievement; however, based on past research, it does not seem likely that they will do so. As Jean Layzer of Abt

Associates points out, vocabulary and oral comprehension skills tend to be more indicative of later reading comprehension than the small increase in letter recognition (personal communication, July 29, 2005).[1]

These weak effects come as a tremendous disappointment. They simply don't do enough to close the achievement gap between poor children (particularly minority children) and the general population (HHS, 2005b).[2] And the absence of better short-term results is alarming, for it suggests that the quality of Head Start programs has deteriorated. In the past, the story of Head Start's impact was always one of fade out. But the Impact Study indicates that there are now few initial impacts to fade out. We should expect more of a program that spends about $9,382 a year on each child (University of Maryland, Welfare Reform Academy, 2006).[3]

Instead of acknowledging the troubling significance of these findings, the Head Start establishment and its allies immediately went on the offensive—perhaps because the reported effects imply that the program needs a major overhaul that would threaten vested interests. The National Head Start Association (2005), for example, claimed that the study is "good news for Head Start" and warned that "those who have resolved to trash Head Start at every turn will twist this data to their ends" as part of their "continued attempts to dismantle the program."

Whatever might be the motivations of the enemies of Head Start, many friends of low-income children find these results heartbreaking. Civilrights.org is a collaboration between the Leadership Conference on Civil Rights, the Leadership Conference on Civil Rights Education Fund, and 180 allied organizations. The best it could say about the study was that Head Start has a "modest impact" (Davis, 2005).

Sadly, the Head Start establishment's stonewalling seems to be working. Even responsible critics have been cowed into silence, or at least relegated to private muttering on the sidelines. As a result, instead of galvanizing action to improve the program, this most recent study will likely be ignored.

The same thing happened in 2001 when the equally heartbreaking results of the evaluation of Early Head Start were released. Started in 1995, Early Head Start is a two-generation program intended to enhance children's development and help parents to educate their young children. In 2004, it served about 62,000 children (HHS, 2005c) in about 1,300 centers, at a cost of about $10,500 per child (HHS, 2004). The program's total annual cost was about $677 million (HHS, 2005c).

The evaluation of Early Head Start, involving about 3,000 families, was also based on a rigorous random assignment design. Unfortunately, the effect sizes for virtually all important outcomes fell below levels that have traditionally been considered educationally meaningful. For instance, at age 3, Early Head Start children achieved a statistically significant, but small, two-point gain on the Bayley MDI, a standardized assessment of infant and toddler cognitive development (91.4 vs. 89.9 for control group children). In addition, a smaller percentage of Early Head Start children fell in the "at-risk" range of developmental functioning on the Bayley MDI (27.3% compared with 32.0% for the control group) (only statistically significant at the 10% level). But these effects are small, with the effect sizes just 0.12 and –0.10.

The HHS evaluation contractor's report was carefully worded to avoid claiming large gains while making the program seem a success: "The Early Head Start research programs stimulated better outcomes along a range of dimensions (with children, parents, and home environments) by the time children's eligibility ended at age 3" (Love et al., 2002, p. xxv). A press release about these findings issued by then Secretary of HHS, Donna Shalala, was not as careful. It was titled: "Early Head Start Shows Significant Results for Low Income Children and Parents" (HHS, 2001).

Both were misleading overstatements, but the tactic worked. There was no public dissent from this unjustifiably rosy interpretation of the findings—either from within the early childhood education community or even from more skeptical conservative observers. (After 5 years in office, the Bush administration has done little to provide a more realistic understanding of these disappointing findings.)

So, don't count on the politicians to do much on their own to improve Head Start. Republicans, worn down by years of battling, are reluctant to raise Head Start's problems, for fear that Democrats and liberal advocates will paint them, yet again, as being against poor children. And Democrats are afraid that honesty about Head Start's weaknesses will sharpen the knives of conservative budget cutters. In fact, even after the release of the Impact Study results, the relevant committees in both houses of Congress voted unanimously to expand eligibility for Head Start. The Senate bill would raise the income-eligibility cap from the poverty line to 130% of poverty (a roughly 35% increase in eligible children), and the House bill would allow programs to enroll more 1- and 2-year-olds, rather than their traditional target group of 3 and 4-year-olds (ultimately doubling the number of eligible children). At this writing, no final action has been taken, but it appears likely that the Senate will adopt the House provision.

## NOT WHAT PARENTS WANT

No single evaluation, of course, should decide the fate of an important program like Head Start, but this new study reinforces a developing professional consensus about Head Start's limitations. Many liberal foundations have already shifted their support away from Head Start and toward the expansion of preschool or pre-kindergarten ("pre-K") services—which siphon off hundreds of thousands of children from Head

Start programs. Many states have likewise begun funding expanded pre-K programs, again at Head Start's expense.

Perhaps the best indication of Head Start's slumping reputation comes from low-income parents themselves, who often chose not to place their children in Head Start. One can see this in the declining proportional enrollment of 4-year-olds, Head Start's prime age group. Between 1997 and 2004, even as Head Start's funded enrollment increased by 22%, the number of 4-year-olds in the program increased by only 2% (HHS, n.d.a; HHS, n.d.b).

To compensate for this drop-off in the proportional enrollment of 4-year-olds, Head Start grantees are signing up more 3-year-olds and encouraging them to stay in the program for a second year. Between 1997 and 2004, the number of 3-year-olds in the program increased by 38%, and their proportion of total enrollment increased from 30% to 34% (HHS, n.d.a; HHS, n.d.b). HHS strongly encourages grantees to serve 4-year-olds before serving other age groups. So, these age allocations, largely in the control of local grantees (except for Early Head Start), presumably reflect local needs and preferences.

This explains, by the way, why Head Start allies have pushed for an expansion of eligibility even in the absence of more funding. The program has essentially run out of eligible 4-year-olds to enroll (Besharov & Morrow, 2007). There has already been a notable loosening in the application of income-eligibility rules. By our calculation, about a quarter of the children in Head Start would not be income eligible if their income were measured at the time of enrollment or reenrollment (Besharov & Morrow, 2007).

A major reason for this shift away from Head Start is the increase in the employment, especially full-time employment, of low-income mothers (HHS, 1993).[4] When Head Start was first conceptualized in the 1960s, few low-income mothers (for that matter, few mothers in general) were in the paid labor force. So Head Start's part-time, part-year program was not an obstacle to participation. Since then, and especially after welfare reform, many more low-income mothers are working. Between 1996 and 2001, for example, the percentage of never-married mothers *working full time* rose from 36% to 52% (Bureau of Labor Statistics [BLS], n.d.a; BLS, n.d.b).[5] In almost all places, though, Head Start remains a part-time, part-year program, with half-day classes usually beginning in September and ending in mid-June.

The Head Start Bureau has actively encouraged grantees to provide more assistance for working parents, including targeted expansions for full-day programs and collaborations with child-care agencies. It has had real, but limited success. Some Head Start grantees have responded to the needs of working mothers by obtaining additional funding for "wrap-around" child-care services. But only about half of the Head Start children whose parents say that they "need" full-time/full-year care obtained it from Head Start in 2003 to 2004 (HHS, n.d.b).[6] Hence, the other half of mothers who work full-time and use Head Start must find some other child care for the rest of the day and the summer. About 230,000 mothers do just that (HHS, n.d.b).

The issue runs deeper, however. The evidence suggests that some parents simply do not want to use Head Start. Most income-eligible mothers who work full-time do not use Head Start, even though that means that they must spend more on child care (because of an often substantial co-payment) (HHS, 2002; Craig Turner, personal communication, June 22, 2005)[7]—more than 200,000 children in 2001. Or, instead, they rely on relatives to care for their children (another 200,000 plus children in 2001) (Besharov & Morrow, 2007).

Even many mothers who do not work, or who only work part-time and thus could use Head Start as a form of child care while they work, use relative care. In fact, we are told by a number of directors of local agencies that, when offered free Head Start in the summer, many parents who used Head Start during the school year prefer to leave their children home with older siblings.

Lastly, the new pre-K programs for low-income children established in many communities also seem to be siphoning off large numbers of children (GAO, 2003a).[8] Between 1990 and 2001, for example, the enrollment in public pre-K, which primarily serves low-income children, nearly tripled, increasing from about 300,000 to 800,000 children. This included, in 2001, about 111,000 Head Start-eligible 4-year-olds, already about a quarter of the number in Head Start—and, coincidentally, about the number of additional 3-year-olds added to Head Start. In 2005, for example, the Milwaukee *Journal-Sentinel* reported that competition from other early childhood programs had caused under-enrollment in some local Head Start programs (Carr, 2005). To increase Head Start enrollment among eligible 3- and 4-year-olds, school board members there have considered converting several pre-K classrooms to Head Start classrooms.

Why the apparent preference for pre-K programs? Perhaps parents find them more attractive than Head Start because of their seeming universality. Although most pre-K programs are directed to low-income children, they generally serve children from families with incomes as high as 185% of the poverty line (Barnett, Hustedt, Robin, & Schulman, 2003). Or perhaps it is because parents deem pre-K programs to be superior, especially because they are usually in school buildings and staffed by more highly educated teachers.

Some of the parents not using Head Start are undoubtedly making such choices involuntarily—because the Head Start program in their community has no vacancies or there are other barriers to enrollment. The weight of the evidence, however, indicates that this is not the predominant explanation. The lack of vacancies or other barriers would not explain the aggregate decline in the enrollment of 4-year-olds unless these problems were worsening over time. Even that, however, would not be consistent with the growing enrollment of 3-year-olds.

## PAST PROPOSALS

Despite congressional inaction, Head Start stands at a crossroads. The easiest course would be for the program to continue without modification and without responding to the major social and programmatic changes engulfing it. That would mean a continuing loss of 4-year-olds and an increase in the number of younger children in the program—with no substantial impact on their cognitive and emotional development.

The wisdom (and practical implications) of this shift in the program's primary target age on the organization of programs and their curricula should be carefully considered before grantee practices and expectations become too set to be changed. Other options that would meet the pressing needs of low-income children should also be considered before politically powerful vested interests are created.

Wishful thinking about Head Start's impact will not improve the life chances of disadvantaged children. A fundamental restructuring of the program is needed.

Some observers believe that Head Start should be expanded to meet the needs of working mothers, so that it would become a full-time, full-year program. Clinton proposed something along these lines when he was first elected president. But his plan stalled because of Head Start's high cost compared with other forms of child care, the substantial operational and administrative challenges in shifting facilities that are used for two Head Start sessions (morning and afternoon) or by other programs into full-time schedules, and, ironically, opposition from the Head Start community itself. (Much of the Head Start staff preferred to work only part-time and not in the summer.) Moreover, even this would be only a partial remedy for low-income, working mothers. Approximately 60% of low-income, working mothers have irregular hours and, thus, need child care at night and on weekends (Collins, Layzer, Kreader, Werner, & Glantz, 2000).[9]

Whatever were the merits of the original Clinton proposal, Head Start's cost structure is now an even greater obstacle to going full-time. After 15 years of cost increases mandated by Congress (at the behest of Head Start advocates) (Human Services Reauthorization Act, 1998; GAO, 2003b),[10] the average cost of a year of full-time Head Start (about $20,607 in 2004[11]) is about two and a half times the cost of center-based child care (about $8,100 in the 2001, the last year with data[12]) (University of Maryland, Welfare Reform Academy, 2006). Of course, Head Start supporters argue that the greater costs are because of greater quality. But the results of the Head Start Impact Study contradict their claims.

Furthermore, expanding Head Start in this way is no longer practical because the growth in government-subsidized child care (largely stemming from federal welfare reform legislation) means that Head Start is no longer the predominant form of child care for low-income families. In the 1980s and early 1990s, Head Start was by far the largest early childhood program, amounting to nearly half of total spending in some years (Besharov, Higney, & Myers, in press).[13] By 1999, however, Head Start accounted for only about a third of all federal and state child-care spending (Besharov, Higney, & Myers, in press). Moreover, because of federal legislation passed in 1990, the child-care world is now a vouchers-based system that accords parents at least some measure of choice about what provider to use. (At the same time, Head Start, not facing a similar market test, has become an even more defensive, entrenched interest, with federal re-funding all but guaranteed year after year.)

Responding to these changing realities, in 2003, President George W. Bush proposed a different approach to integrating Head Start into the wider world of child care. He wanted to give qualifying states control over Head Start funds. Opposition forced the House Republicans to limit the proposal to an eight-state demonstration program and to impose relatively stringent protections for turning the program over to a particular state. (According to the Congressional Research Service, to gain control over Head Start programming, a state was required to have "an existing state-supported system of public pre-kindergarten; standards for school readiness that are aligned with state kindergarten through twelfth grade; prior year state and local spending at a level of at least 50% of the federal Head Start funds to be allocated to the state; and an established 'means' for interagency coordination and collaboration. States would need to demonstrate that their standards 'generally meet or exceed the standards that ensure the quality and effectiveness of programs operated by Head Start agencies'" [Gish, 2003, p. 10]).

Despite these changes, Head Start advocates vigorously opposed the idea. The president of the National Head Start Association, Sarah Greene, called it a "radical proposal that dismantles the federal government's nearly four-decades-long commitment to getting at-risk children ready to learn" (National Head Start Association, 2003). In one particularly colorful phrase, Congressman George Miller (D-CA) said that handing control of Head Start over to states was "like handing your children over to Michael Jackson" (Miller, 2003). (Ironically, Congressman Miller seemed to think that Head Start was safer in the hands of a Republican President and Republican Congress than in the hands of the many states with Democratic governors or legislatures. But that particular rhetorical gap was not widely noticed.)

One must ask why the Head Start grantees and their allies were so opposed to this idea of a demonstration program, and would not accept an experiment in even a few states—unless they feared that the experiment would be successful. In any event, they were able to kill the Bush proposal, even after it had been substantially watered down.

## A FRESH START

In retrospect, a major element was missing from both the Clinton and Bush proposals: Although both proposals tried to align Head Start with state and local child-care networks, neither would have done anything to close the achievement gap for the most disadvantaged children.

One of Head Start's key weaknesses is its one-size-fits-all approach. Head Start does too much for some children—and too little for others. Despite the convenient rhetoric surrounding Head Start, not all poor children face the cognitive and developmental problems that animated Head Start's creation. Many poor children do not need the array of support services provided by Head Start and, based on the evidence, do just fine in regular child care when their mothers work. Children from the most troubled families (usually headed by young, single mothers), however, surely need much more than the program currently provides.

The current Head Start model is just not sufficient, in both its services and curriculum. It generally consists of only 4 hours a day of classroom instruction (some grantees provide more), for less than 9 months. And, despite Head Start's claims about "parent involvement," there seem to be no systematic efforts to include parents in the program or to give parents better child-rearing skills.

The best thing would be for Head Start to go back to its roots, to search for ways to make a meaningful improvement in the lives of the poorest, most disadvantaged children. It might, for example, provide services to

unwed teenagers that start during their first pregnancy. Head Start should not try to serve all families that happen to fall under the poverty line.

In the summer of 1968, I visited some of the first/earliest Head Start centers. They were in the Mississippi Delta, and I was a civil rights worker (from the despised North). What I saw was one of the most heart-warming and exciting scenes in my life. The children of sharecroppers and the dispossessed, victims of centuries of poverty and deprivation, were being given early education to help prepare them for school, as promised by President Johnson. In another room, their mothers were receiving training in homemaking and child-rearing skills. (This was, of course, long before we thought that mothers, especially low-income mothers, belonged at work.)

Focusing on the most in need, the new Head Start would be truly two-generational, that is, with real services for parents (not just the current lip service to parent involvement), and it would bring to bear all the programmatic services that have developed since Head Start was first conceived—Women, Infants, and Children (WIC), Medicaid, the Maternal and Child Health Block Grant Program, the Community and Migrant Health Center Program, and the Title X program, which seeks to reduce unintended pregnancy by providing contraceptive and related reproductive health-care services to low-income women.

In Head Start, as in the early childhood education field generally, there has been a shift away from direct, cognitive-oriented instruction and toward play-oriented and discovering-learning activities. Yet, according to Nicholas Zill, former director of Child and Family Studies at Westat, Inc., "The latest research evidence indicates that direct assessments of cognitive skills at kindergarten entrance are predictive of both early and later achievement, into the later grades of elementary school and beyond" (personal communication, May 3, 2006). Zill notes that new instructional methods and curricula aimed at bolstering children's language and literacy skills have been developed by education researchers and are currently being evaluated by the Institute of Education Sciences and the National Institute of Child Health and Human Development. If the results of the evaluations are encouraging, these new methods could inform a revamping of Head Start's curriculum and, possibly, result in a more effective early childhood education program.

In other words, if Head Start is to do a better job raising the intellectual and cognitive skills of disadvantaged children, it will need to alter its curriculum and teaching methods to emphasize such learning. This would, of course, require a major change in staffing and leadership and has been enough to raise the opposition of most Head Start administrators.

This would not be the first attempt to give Head Start a greater educational focus. In 1978, President Jimmy Carter also proposed that it be moved to the new Department of Education (as did George W. Bush more than 20 years later). The proposed transfer faced stiff opposition from Marian Wright Edelman, founder and president of the Children's Defense Fund, a notably liberal lobbying group. Civil rights groups, parents of children enrolled in Head Start programs, and child advocates also strongly opposed the proposal, arguing that the shift in focus to education would undermine the social services component of Head Start. Despite this, President Carter sent a bill to the Senate that would have made the proposed changes. After hearings, the Senate Operations Committee voted the bill down by a vote of 14 to 0 (Steinberg, 2001, p. A1; Zigler, 2001, p. A16).

The policy (and political) challenge would be to identify the children and parents needing this kind of intensive intervention. The other group needs an intense compensatory program for children and a seriously therapeutic program for parents. Research suggests that such a program would likely be much smaller than the current Head Start program (although total spending might not decrease) because it would serve only the identifiably at-risk children—perhaps identified at birth through WIC, Medicaid, Temporary Assistance for Needy Families (TANF), and other services for disadvantaged mothers and their newborns.

## A PLAUSIBLE SUBSTITUTE NEEDED

One hopes that the Head Start establishment, or at least major parts of it, as well as the larger child development community, will back such an endeavor. But after fighting many battles for survival over the past 40 years, they are understandably wary of those who question Head Start's effectiveness. Too often in the past, criticisms of the program have been used to justify dismantling the program, or at least curtailing its funding. They are unlikely to support real reform in the absence of a substitute programmatic model that is politically plausible—and that rigorous research indicates will do a better job than Head Start to narrow the achievement gap between poor and nonpoor children.

Hence, the strategy for real reform seems clear: Build a better early childhood intervention program somewhere—and prove that it *really* works. Based on past failures, this will be no mean feat. It will require a sustained, no-holds-barred inquiry into what is needed to improve the cognitive and social development of the neediest children.

Instead of expanding Head Start eligibility, therefore, Congress should mandate a systematic program of research and experimentation, one that tries and evaluates different approaches to see what works best. (Despite 40 years of operation, Head Start does not have a scientifically tested knowledge base about which approaches work—and for whom.) Needed is a scientifically rigorous inquiry into the comparative effectiveness of various curricula and program elements, such as full-day versus part-day and 1- versus 2-year programs, traditional 9-month versus full-year programs, classroom size (paralleling work on class size done at the elementary level), the training or formal education of teachers, and effective ways of helping parents do a better job meeting their children's needs. Most important, distinctions among children from different family backgrounds and with different degrees of need will be crucial.

Such a multifaceted research and development effort could be patterned after the new one for K–12 education established under the No Child Left Behind legislation. That effort enjoys a $400 million annual budget, compared with only $20 million for Head Start research. A tripling of Head Start's research budget would be a good start. If no new money is available, Congress could reallocate some of the $30 to $111 million now designated in the pending reauthorization bills for quality improvements (especially because about half of these funds go to raise the salaries of Head Start staff, already among the highest in the early childhood education world).

Conducting such an inquiry will require substantial intellectual and political effort—because of the turf battles it would trigger, the scientific challenges involved in designing so many multisite experiments, and the sustained monitoring and management needed. Nevertheless, without an effort on this scale and without such intellectual clarity, it is difficult to see how better approaches to child care and early childhood education can be developed.

Perhaps it is naive to think that Head Start can be operated on the basis of careful research rather than politics, but each year almost a million children pass through the program without getting the head start on learning they were promised. Shame on us.

---

## NOTES

1. The Impact Study itself also notes that vocabulary tests are "strongly predictive of children's general knowledge at the end of kindergarten and first grade." For more information, see HHS (2005a, pp. 5–8).

2. In this statement concerning the study's findings, the HHS (2005b) said that despite the gains shown in several areas, the Head Start programs "did not close the gap" between poor children and the general population. The statement continues: "The study found that Head Start produced small to moderate impacts in areas such as pre-reading, pre-writing, vocabulary and in health and parent practice domains. However, these impacts did not close the gap between low-income children in the Head Start program and the general population of three- and four-year olds. There were no significant impacts for three- and four-year olds in areas of early mathematics, oral comprehension and social competencies" (HHS, 2005b).

3. The Head Start Bureau reports an annual per child cost of $7,222. However, that figure (1) does not include all funds allocated to or spent by the program, (2) ignores the cost differences between part-day and full-day, center-based and home-based care, as well as between Early Head Start and regular Head Start.

*Total Head Start spending*: For the 2003/2004 program year, total Head Start expenditures (including support activities not counted by the bureau when calculating annual per child costs) were $6.774 billion ($6.074 billion excluding Early

Head Start costs). In addition, the Head Start Act requires that grantees provide an additional 20% to annual spending, which brings total spending to $8.129 billion ($7.289 excluding Early Head Start costs). The children in center-based Head Start also receive an additional subsidy through the Child and Adult Care Food Program (CACFP) of about $1,106. This brings the total spent on Head Start to $9.015 billion (8.175 billion excluding Early Head Start costs). In addition, various medical and other services are provided that are not quantified. We make no adjustments to our costs for these additional expenditures.

*Cost differences for part-day and full-day, center-based and home-based care, as well as between Early Head Start and regular Head Start:* Head Start data do not identify the different costs for these types of care, but they can be estimated by deriving hourly costs for each. First, we assume that hourly costs are the same for part-day and full-day care, and are 25% lower for home-based care compared with center-based care. We then derive an approximate hourly cost by taking estimated expenditures for part-day and full-day care (derived from the portion of spending on children in each, 29% and 71%, respectively) and dividing them by their respective durations (4 hours and 7 hours for 156 and 197 days, respectively, multiplied by the number of children for each category). After adjusting for the cost difference between center-based and home-based care, this results in annual per child costs of $6,081 for part-day and $13,438 for full-day center-based care. The respective figures for home-based care are $3,731 and $9,249. For Early Head Start, which is about 7 hours a day, we simply divide total expenditures ($677 million) by the number of children in the program (52,487) without including the pregnant mothers (5,896). The result is a 2004 estimated per child cost for Early Head Start of $12,899.

By applying these per child annual costs, we find a weighted average per Head Start child of $10,156 ($9,980 for part-day and full-day children), compared with the Head Start Bureau's estimate of $7,222.

For Head Start's calculation of annual per child costs, see HHS (2005c); for Head Start's total expenditures, authors' calculation based on HHS (2005c); for the 20% matching funds requirement under the Head Start Act, see Gish (2004); for the CACFP subsidy, authors' calculation based on U.S. Department of Agriculture (USDA) (2005).

4. The report by the Head Start Bureau (HHS, 1993) states: "Head Start must now fit into a diverse set of early childhood programs and resources at the federal, state, and local level. Some of the most dramatic changes in communities since the beginning of Head Start are reflected in the increased number and variety of programs sponsored by states and local education agencies, the increase in resources and mandates for serving children with disabilities, and the expansion and demand for full day services."

5. For 1996–2000, see unpublished tables from the BLS (n.d.a), "Table 15: Presence and Age of Own Children of Civilian Women 16 Years and Over, by Employment Status and Marital Status;" and for 2001, unpublished tables from the BLS (n.d.b), "Table 3: Employment Status of the Civilian Noninstitutional Population by Sex, Age, Presence and Age of Youngest Child, Marital Status, Race, and Hispanic Origin."

6. This is up from 41% in 1998 to 1999, although we have some questions about the accuracy of these data.

7. Even though child care for low-income families is subsidized, most states require co-payments that can be substantial, even for families under the poverty line. As of FY 2000, many states imposed co-payments for poor families as high as 10% of family

income. See HHS (2002), which states: "Co-payments are typically based on a percentage of family income, a percentage of the price of the child care, or a percentage of the State reimbursement rate." Thirty-eight states set co-payments on a percentage of the family income, often as much as 10%; five states set them as a percentage of the price of the child care; six states set them as a percentage of the state reimbursement rate; and one state allows but does not require counties to set co-payments at between 9 and 15% of the family's gross income, with the average, in FY 2001, being about 3.4% of family income. For a family of three (a mother and two children at the poverty line [$14,128]), that would be a co-payment of about $480 per year. Craig Turner states, "In FY 2001, the average co-payment as a percentage of income for families with incomes below the poverty line was 3.4%. In FFY 2002, it was 3.6% and in FFY 2003 3.8%" (personal communication, June 22, 2005). (These average payments include families with zero co-payment.)

8. The GAO (2003a) states, "Regional and grantee officials often indicated that competition from other early education or child care centers serving low-income preschool children contributed to Head Start underenrollment. . . . A large underenrolled grantee on the East Coast said that availability of pre-kindergarten programs at public and charter schools is the most important reason its delegate agencies are underenrolled."

9. For some discussion of working mothers' irregular hours and consequent need of child care, see Collins et al. (2000). In this study, "low-income" refers to children whose family income is at or below 200% of the federal poverty line.

10. The primary explanation for the increase in per child costs seems to be the growth in money spent on quality improvements. In 1991, 10% of the total Head Start appropriations were set aside for quality improvement activities. Beginning in 1992, the set-aside was modified to include 25% of all *new* funds. Half of these "quality monies" are to be used to raise the salaries of classroom teachers and other staff, for the putative purpose of helping programs recruit and retain quality staff. Quality improvement funds can also be spent on providing transportation, improving facilities, and expanding staff training and development. In 1999, the set-aside was increased to 60%, with the percent then declining to 50% in FY 2000, 47.5% in FY 2001, and back again to 25% in FY 2003. In FY 2001, quality improvement funding peaked at about $356 million. Because of slower growth in Head Start appropriations since then and a drop in the percent required to be spent on such activities, quality improvement funding dropped to about $32 million in FY 2003. See *Human Services Reauthorization Act* (1998), and the GAO (2003b).

11. To estimate an annual cost for full-time, full-year Head Start, we assume 8 hours of care for 5 days a week for 52 weeks a year. Applying the per hour cost of $9.74 derived previously, this comes to $20,259 per year per child. Authors' calculation based on data from HHS (2004).

12. For 2001, the most recent year for which we have data, combining Child Care Development Fund (CCDF) provider payments, administrative costs, CACFP subsidies, and parental co-payments results in an hourly cost of $2.36 ($2.52 in 2004 dollars). Assuming full-time, full-year care is 8 hours per day, 40 hours per week, 52 weeks per year results in a per year per child cost of $4,915 ($5,242 in 2004 dollars). We have no reason to think this cost substantially increased in 3 years. Authors' calculation based on the University of Maryland, Welfare Reform Academy (2006).

13. For an extended discussion of recent increases in child-care spending, see Besharov, Higney, and Myers (in press). The figure cited includes funds from the Child Care and Development Fund, Head Start, Temporary Assistance for Needy Families, the Child and Adult Care Food Program, and the Social Services Block Grant.

## REFERENCES

Barnett, W. S., Hustedt, J. T., Robin, K. B., & Schulman, K. L. (2003). *The state of preschool: 2003 state preschool yearbook.* New Brunswick, NJ: National Institute for Early Education Research.

Besharov, D. J., Higney, C. A., & Myers, J. A. (in press). *Federal and state child care and early education expenditures (1997–2005): Child care spending falls as pre-K spending rises.* College Park, MD: Welfare Reform Academy.

Besharov, D. J., & Morrow, J. S. (2007). *Is Head Start fully funded? Income-eligible enrollment, coverage rates, and program implications.* College Park, MD: Welfare Reform Academy.

Bureau of Labor Statistics, (n.d.a). Table 3: Employment status of the civilian non-institutional population by sex, age, presence and age of youngest child, marital status, race, and Hispanic origin. Unpublished tables from the Bureau of Labor Statistics.

Bureau of Labor Statistics, (n.d.b). Table 15: Presence and age of own children of civilian women 16 years and over, by employment status and marital status. Unpublished tables from the Bureau of Labor Statistics.

Carr, S. (2005, February 6). Head Start may need new direction. *Milwaukee Journal-Sentinel.*

Collins, A. M., Layzer, J. I., Kreader, J. L., Werner, A., & Glantz, F. B. (2000). State and community substudy interim report. In *National study of child care for low-income families.* Washington, DC: Abt Associates.

Davis, M. R. (2005, June 15). *Head Start has modest impact.* Retrieved May 15, 2006, from http://www.civilrights.org/issues/education/details.cfm?id=32351

Gish, M. (2003, December 17). *Head Start issues in the 108th Congress* (p. 10). Washington, DC: Congressional Research Service.

Gish, M. (2004, July 20). *Child Care issues in the 108th Congress* (CRS Report RL31817). Washington, DC: Congressional Research Service.

Human Services Reauthorization Act, 42 U.S.C. § 9801, section 6403. (1998). Retrieved May 19, 2005, from http://frwebgate.access.gpo.gov/cgi-bin/getdoc .cgi?dbname=105_cong_public_laws&docid=f:publ285.105.pdf

Love, J., Kisker, E. E., Ross, C. M., Schochet, P. Z., Brooks-Gunn, J., Paulsell, D., et al. (2002). *Making a difference in the lives of infants and toddlers and their families: The impacts of early Head Start: Vol. 1. Final technical report.* Washington, DC: U.S. Department of Health and Human Services. Retrieved December 30, 2002, from http://www.mathematica-mpr.com/PDFs/ehsfinalvol1.pdf

Miller, G. (2003, May 7). Panel one: Overview of administration plan and reaction from Capitol Hill. In *Head Start's future: Perspectives from the Bush administration, Congress, states, advocates and researchers.* Retrieved January 24, 2006, from http://www.brookings.edu/comm/events/20030507wrb.pdf

National Head Start Association. (2003, July 25). House Head Start bill vote, statement from Sarah Greene. Press Release. Retrieved January 18, 2006, from http://www.nhsa.org/press/pdf_docs/072503_NHSAstatement_%20onHouse_vote.pdf

National Head Start Association. (2005, June 9). New Head Start impact study shows "very promising" early results, points to success of program boosting school readiness of America's most at-risk children. Press Release. Retrieved January 18, 2006, from http://www.nhsa.org/press/News_Archived/2005/index_news_060905.htm

*Public papers of the presidents of the United States: Lyndon B. Johnson, 1968–69,* Book II. (1970). Washington, DC: Government Printing Office.

Steinberg, J. (2001, February 10). Bush's plan to push reading in "Head Start" stirs debate. *The New York Times,* p. A1.

University of Maryland, Welfare Reform Academy. (2006). Early Education and Child Care (ee/cc) Model.

U.S. Department of Agriculture, Food and Nutrition Service. (2005, July 15). Child & adult care food program: National average payment rates, day care home food service payment rates, and administrative reimbursement rates for sponsoring organizations of day care homes for the period July 1, 2004–June 30, 2005. *Federal Register, 69*(135), 42413–42415. Retrieved June 28, 2006, from http://www.fns.usda.gov/cnd/Care/Publications/pdf/2005notice.pdf

U.S. Department of Health and Human Services, Administration for Children and Families. (2005a). *Head Start impact study: First year findings.* Washington, DC: Author. Retrieved January 23, 2006, from http://www.acf.hhs.gov/programs/opre/hs/impact_study/

U.S. Department of Health and Human Services, Administration for Children and Families. (2005b, June 9). HHS releases Head Start impact study. *HHS News.* Retrieved May 22, 2006, from http://www.acf.hhs.gov/news/press/2005/head start_study.htm

U.S. Department of Health and Human Services, Administration for Children and Families, Child Care Bureau. (2005c). *Head Start program fact sheet, fiscal year 2004.* Washington, DC: Author. Retrieved June 28, 2006, from http://www .acf.hhs.gov/programs/hsb/research/2005.htm

U.S. Department of Health and Human Services, Administration for Children and Families, Head Start Bureau. (2004). *Early Head Start almanac.* Washington, DC: Head Start Information and Publication Center. Retrieved January 17, 2005, from http://www.acf.hhs.gov/programs/hsb/programs/ehs/ehsalmanac .htm

U.S. Department of Health and Human Services, Administration for Children and Families, National Child Care Information Center. (2002). *Child care and development fund report of state plans for the period of 10/01/99 to 9/30/01* (Part III, Section 3.5). Washington, DC: Author. Retrieved June 30, 2005, from http:// www.nccic.org/pubs/CCDFStat.pdf

U.S. Department of Health and Human Services, Administration for Children and Families Press Office. (2001, January 11). Early Head Start shows significant results for low income children and parents. *HHS News.* Retrieved January 18, 2006, from http://faq.acf.dhhs.gov/news/press/2001/ehs112.html

U.S. Department of Health and Human Services, Head Start Bureau. (1993). *Creating a 21st century Head Start: Executive summary of the final report of the advisory committee on Head Start quality and expansion.* Washington, DC: Author. Retrieved April 3, 2005, from http://www.acf.hhs.gov/programs/hsb/ research/21_century/part1.htm

U.S. Department of Health and Human Services, Head Start Bureau. (n.d.a). *Head Start program information report for the 1999–2000 program year.* Washington, DC: Author.

U.S. Department of Health and Human Services, Head Start Bureau. (n.d.b). *Head Start program information report for the 2003–2004 program year.* Washington, DC: Author.

U.S. General Accounting Office (GAO). (1997). *Head Start: Research provides little information on impact of current program* (GAO/HEHS-97-59). Washington, DC: U.S. Government Printing Office.

U.S. General Accounting Office (GAO). (2003a). *Head Start: Better data and processes needed to monitor underenrollment* (GAO-04–17). Washington, DC: Author. Retrieved April 3, 2005, from http://www.gao.gov/new.items/d0417.pdf

U.S. General Accounting Office (GAO). (2003b). Table 3. In *Head Start: Increased percentage of teachers nationwide have required degrees, but better information on classroom teachers' qualifications needed* (GAO-04–05). Washington, DC: Author.

Westinghouse Learning Corporation & Ohio University. (1969). *The impact of Head Start: An evaluation of the effects of Head Start on children's cognitive and affective development* (Vol. I, pp. 26–31). Athens: Ohio University.

Zigler, E. (2001, February 12). Head Start's history. *The New York Times,* p. A16.

Zigler, E., & Muenchow, S. (1992). *Head Start: The inside story of America's most successful educational experiment.* New York: Basic Books.

# CHAPTER 21

# Grandparents

## A Family Resource?

## Lynda Clarke

Recent changes in family life have meant that parents may be relatively poor in terms of time or human capital. Demographic and social changes have dramatically affected the living arrangements and family experiences of both parents and children in the last 30 years. Parents are often not married and may not even live together, families are diverse in their nature and operation, and family breakup is frequent. Family breakup may be extremely important for changing family relationships and has important implications for children in economic well-being and parental time. However, the nature of family life has changed also in other, less obvious ways. More families have two parents in paid employment than in previous generations and, though most mothers of small children work part time, the proportion of mothers who return to full-time work after maternity leave is increasing (Dex, 1999). There are also other important changes in domestic life and the nature of families. Family activities in the last 25 years have become much less home-centered and more individualistic and commercial. For example, the traditional activities of cooking, child rearing, and elder care have lost their central unifying role. These domestic activities have become less valued—labor-saving devices and pre-prepared foods are used to cut down on the time spent on these onerous tasks or help is "brought in" to assist with these roles.

The implications of these family changes for parents, children, and kin beyond the household, mainly grandparents, are potentially vast. For example, where both parents are working or where family breakdown has occurred, grandparents may be expected to care for grandchildren or to contribute to their support in financial or emotional terms. Other demographic changes have affected family roles. As a result of population ageing, new and extended family roles for older adults have been created, and a greater proportion of older people today are experiencing grandparenthood, and even great grandparenthood, than ever before. Older people, however, are living longer, and they are living healthier lives for longer. Attitudes toward older people's independence and autonomy are also changing. Supporting their children and grandchildren may, therefore, be at odds with their own desires to continue in paid employment or pursue other leisure interests.

Family interaction and support can be central to the well-being of both adults and children (Bowling, 1995). Support can take the form of economic contributions of cash or in kind, providing meals, clothes, or holidays for example, as well as emotional or practical help. The level and type of such family support is changing as a result of both demographic and social changes. It could be argued that population ageing and increasing family breakup, lone parenthood, and the increasing employment of mothers mean that support for children by kin from outside the household, especially by grandparents, may become increasingly important for modern families. Grandparents could be vital to providing stability when parental time or resources are stretched. Conversely, it could be postulated that older people have a desire for autonomy, which might mean that grandparents will not be available to provide child care, which is especially critical for poor families who cannot afford to pay for such care. However, for some families higher ages at first birth and the use of domestic aids and formal child care by mothers may mean that such support for grandchildren is not needed. It is not known whether any of these scenarios are true because little is known about family exchanges "beyond the household."

The British government's first consultation paper on "Supporting Families" recognized the role of the extended family and grandparents in supporting parents and children and providing stability (Home Office, 1998, pp. 18–19). However, the only evidence it quoted on the role of grandparents is from a small market research survey, and its recommendations to service providers

for encouraging grandparents to play a positive role in the lives of their families were somewhat vague and simplistic. The document briefly mentions the use of older people and grandparents by schools and as volunteers in the community, for example, as "grandparent mentors" in secondary schools. It identifies a threefold service provision to facilitate grandparent-grandchild interaction. First, local authority social services was urged to work with the extended family when relationships within the nuclear family are under stress and to consider grandparents as an "effective placement" when children have to be looked after by the local authority. Second, health visitors were encouraged to involve the wider family, and finally, housing departments were advised to "give due weight to the housing needs of grandparents . . . , for example by allocating homes so that wider families, particularly those with dependent children, are wherever possible living near to each other."

"Supporting Families" quotes a survey by Age Concern as showing that most grandparents are already involved with the care of their grandchildren. This survey showed that "92 percent of grandparents have regular contact with their grandchildren. They are the most important source of day-care of children: 47 percent help look after their grandchildren. Most children see their grandparents as important figures in their lives." There is no recognition in this document of the diversity of the role of grandparenting in Britain, what grandparents do for their families, and how happy they are with their role. Most importantly, there is no mention of grandparental rights or access to children after the divorce of their parents.

This chapter addresses whether grandparents can be viewed as a family resource especially in time of emotional or financial difficulty. First, it examines research evidence to date on the support that grandparents give to their families and their attitudes toward providing this assistance. Such support may take many different forms—from babysitting and looking after children while the parents are working to economic contributions of cash or in kind (providing meals, clothes, or holidays) as well as emotional or practical help. Second, evidence is presented from a national quantitative and qualitative research project in Britain on how much practical, financial, and emotional support grandparents gave to their families, how much variation there was both between grandparents and during the life cycle of the grandchildren, how it changed when family breakdown occurred, and grandparents' attitudes toward providing support.

## RESEARCH EVIDENCE ON GRANDPARENTAL SUPPORT

Despite the general acknowledgement of the importance of family relationships for personal well-being, we know little about the diversity of grandparental support in Britain, but in the United States, there is a well-established tradition of research on grandparents and their families. This has revealed that most practical support from grandparents takes place when grandchildren are young, a time when many grandparents babysit (Robertson, 1977) or provide child care while the parents are working or simply to give parents a break. Such support can be particularly important for lone parents who do not have a co-resident partner for such help. British research over many years has revealed that relatives and friends are the major providers of child care for most parents in work and that nearly half of preschool child care for lone mothers is being provided by grandmothers (e.g., Bradshaw & Millar, 1991). Similarly, research in America (Bloom & Steen, 1996) revealed that lone mothers compensate for the limited availability of the father by the greater use of

grandparents to provide child care (24.8% compared with 13.7% for married mothers with spouse present).

Other research on families has shown that many grandparents provide just part of the child care required for their grandchildren. A British study by Wilson (1987) asked 61 women about help provided by their parents. None of the women relied on grandmothers for the main responsibility of child care when they went out to work. Rather, grandmothers made themselves available for casual, rather than regular, babysitting and for help in emergencies, which was also found in another study (Cunningham-Burley, 1985).

More recently, authors of the 1998 British Social Attitudes Survey (BSAS), the first nationally representative view of British grandparenting, reported that they felt that levels of help with child care provided by grandparents were fairly low (Dench, Ogg, & Thomson, 1999). One quarter of grandparents with grandchildren younger than age 6 looked after them during the day and only 14% of grandparents with grandchildren younger than age 13 years took them to or from school at least once a week. Interestingly, the researchers found also that mothers working part-time had slightly higher rates of help than did mothers working full-time. The authors suggest that mothers working part-time are most likely to get family help with child care because their needs are more consistent with the type and level of help that grandparents are willing to provide.

The most extreme form of child-care provision by grandparents is undertaken by those who adopt a parental role. Unfortunately, we know very little about the extent and situation of custodial grandparenting in Britain. The only information we have comes from small-scale qualitative research (Laws & Broad, 2000; Pitcher, 1999). In stark contrast, this is an issue of increasing concern in the United States. The national census has been asking questions about grandparenthood in the

United States since 1970 and has shown a substantial increase in all types of households maintained by grandparents (Casper & Bryson, 1998). This has attracted much research in an attempt to understand the causes of this trend and also to document the effects on both grandparents and grandchildren as well as to profile grandparent-maintained households, documenting the relatively poor economic situation of these families (Casper & Bryson, 1998; Chalfie, 1994; Fuller-Thompson, Minkler, & Driver, 1997; Harden, Clark, & Maguire, 1997; Rutrough & Ofstedal, 1997). The main reasons found for grandparents adopting a parenting role were related to health, emotional, and economic problems experienced by these families; drug abuse among parents; separation and divorce; teenage pregnancy; single parenthood; mental and physical illness; AIDS; crime and imprisonment; child abuse; and neglect. Thus, grandparents were stepping in to care for and support their grandchildren suffering in such disadvantaged situations.

One repercussion of custodial grandparenthood, noted in other American research, is the physical and mental health of grandparents who look after their grandchildren. A number of studies have reported the health of these grandparents as poor compared with noncustodial grandparents (Burton, 1992; Emick & Hayslip, 1999; Fuller-Thomson et al., 1997; Marx & Solomon, 2000; Minkler, Roe, & Price, 1992). Contrastingly, benefits have also been found. Many studies report that, despite any problems arising, such care giving grandparents feel "useful," are happy to be able to "rescue" their grandchildren (Minkler & Roe, 1993; Saltzman, 1992) or report having more of a purpose for living (Jendrek, 1993). Thus, although raising a grandchild full-time has attendant problems, it can also be emotionally rewarding (Burton, 1992; Minkler & Roe, 1993).

As well as providing practical, childcare, or emotional assistance, grandparents sometimes offer quite substantial financial assistance to the parents of their grandchildren. In 1996, Fisher (1996) found that American grandparents spent an average of $400 per year on their grandchildren in the form of clothing, food, toys, educational materials, and financial and insurance products. Both grandmothers and grandfathers have been found to provide substantial financial assistance to their children by paying bills, buying clothes for the grandchildren, providing loans, or buying goods, for example, washing machines (Wilson, 1987).

American analysts have suggested also that in addition to the practical help and economic support that grandparents provide, they can perform a number of important symbolic or emotional functions for families. Global descriptions of grandparenthood have been proposed by a number of authors. Hagestad (1985), for example, described grandparents as the "family national guard" whose effects can be felt simply by their presence, not their actions. Similarly, Troll (1983) has described grandparents as "family watchdogs" who are there if they are needed. Grandparents are also portrayed as acting as "stress-buffers" when the family system or an individual member faces a crisis (Pearlin & Schooler, 1978) or being a "safety valve" or potential back up when something goes wrong (Rasmussen, 1983).

## BRITISH RESEARCH STUDY

One of the main findings of a recent British study was that government policy was ignoring the heterogeneity of grandparents' families and their roles (Clarke & Roberts, 2003). A national survey found that family relationships were complex but that grandparenthood remains an important family relationship, and in-depth interviews confirmed the importance of grandparents as a resource to families, especially when they were experiencing difficulties. This research project (Clarke & Roberts, 2003) explored various issues around grandparenting in Britain including the provision of child-care, financial, and emotional support by grandparents to their families. The study included two national surveys, a telephone interview of 870 grandparents in 2000, a further survey of 2,110 grandparents in the fall of 2001, and an in-depth study of 45 grandparents in 2001. The findings from both the national and qualitative studies will be used to explore the support provided by grandparents to their families and how this varies between families. Three main types of support were identified: practical, financial, and emotional.

## PRACTICAL SUPPORT

Standing in to help when there are problems or "being there" when needed was seen as one of the main obligations of grandparents by most of the grandparents we interviewed (Mason, May, & Clarke, in press). Acting as a custodial parent is perhaps the most demanding role taken on to support parents. However, as yet little evidence indicates that this form of support is growing in Britain. In this national sample, less than 0.5% ($N = 6/2001$) were looking after their grandchildren as a parent.

The other most important way in which grandparents might be involved in providing practical help for their children and grandchildren is by looking after their grandchildren when parents work, are under pressure, or pursue leisure activities. The quantitative results revealed that a high percentage of all grandparents (70%) lived within half an hour of at least one set of grandchildren, so the potential for grandparents to help out their children in this way was, therefore, quite high. Previous research has revealed that family type and mother's working status are the most important influences on whether

or not a child is looked after by grandparents in the day. Children in couple families and children with working mothers were more likely to be looked after by grandparents (Clarke & Cairns, 2001).

Taking care of grandchildren during the day is obviously related to the age of the child(ren) involved and the age of the grandparent because older children will not need day care, and older grandparents may not be able to cope with this demanding task. However, nearly two-thirds (61%) of grandparents with grandchildren younger than age 15 had provided day care for them during the last 12 months; for just under one-fifth (18%) this was for three or more times a week, and for a further quarter (25%) this was for one or two times a week on average. Multivariate statistical analysis of the quantitative data showed that providing day care was related to how close the grandchild(ren) was, the age of grandparent (most likely for grandparents younger than 70), and the age of youngest grandchild (most likely for preschool-aged children), as expected. Interestingly, the lineage of the grandchildren was also found to be important, with the children of sons being less likely to be provided with day care than were the children of daughters. If the grandchildren's parents had separated, then this difference was even more pronounced. There were no differences in the likelihood of grandparents providing day care between social classes or level of education nor whether the grandparent was working or not. Additionally, more than half of grandparents (55%) reported babysitting in the evenings; one quarter (25%) on a weekly basis and a further third (30%) at least monthly.

Grandparents were asked in the quantitative survey about the activities that they did with grandchildren, and more than half (52%) reported taking grandchildren to activities outside of the home, such as swimming, shopping, or special outings; more than one-quarter (28%) did this at least weekly, but this was linked to whether they provided daytime care for their grandchildren. More than half of the grandparents (53%) had grandchildren younger than 15 stay overnight—16% every week and 25% every month. This was also true for older grandchildren (23% with grandchildren ages 15 to 19, and 15% with grandchildren aged 20 or older), and some grandparents (13%) had taken grandchildren younger than age 15 on holidays.

Although grandparents were generally providing support of some kind for their families, this was not a universal fact. Some grandparents rarely saw their grandchildren, 10% only saw them during school holidays and 2% never saw grandchildren, but some of these grandparents did still act as sources of financial or emotional support. However, more than one-third of all grandparents (38%) reported that they had not done any of the activities asked about in the survey in the last 12 months for grandchildren, which included money contributions, day care, babysitting, and taking children out or having them to stay. This was also true for more than one-quarter (26%) of grandparents of grandchildren younger than 15, even though more than half of them saw these grandchildren weekly.

Whether or not the grandparents in the study supported their families in this way varied according to several different factors. The amount of babysitting and child care provided varied quite substantially from those who looked after their grandchildren just once or twice a year to those who helped out by looking after their grandchildren while the parents work. In the in-depth study of 45 grandparents, half (12) looked after grandchildren while the parents were working. Two grandparents regularly looked after their grandchildren during the day, but most either looked after grandchildren during the school holidays or took them to, or picked them up from, school or nursery.

The arrangements grandparents made with the parents varied according to the circumstances of both parties. The age of the grandchildren was important in determining the amount and type of child care provided, both changing as the grandparent and the child grew older. For example, one couple looked after their grandchild full time until she went to school:

> Well, from three months old we had her until she went to school because Sue was working so we more or less you know had her three or four days a week. But now that she's schooling, she used to come Tuesdays, now it's Wednesdays because he (grandfather) takes her up for horse riding on Wednesdays.

Some grandparents are doing a lot of practical support. One couple with three sets of young grandchildren were seeing them a lot. They had taken two granddaughters to school and collected them daily, had other grandchildren stay over every Saturday night and occasionally in the week, and offered a regular form of "break" to their lone-parent daughter with an autistic son by taking him "a couple of times a week." This amounted to a considerable involvement.

Interestingly, this couple did not find their current high involvement too much but contrasted it with earlier episodes when they "felt taken for granted."

> Sometimes haven't we as I say when they ring up and take you for granted which they do sometimes . . . But it's not too bad now. I mean when er Matlock went to school and Taylor we had him in the day and it got us down a little bit then when she first left [daughter had left her husband and they helped her to cope]. She lived over at R . . . then . . . but since she been in S, it's not been too bad for us now as she's only like, just over 5 minutes from us in the car.

Practical support, though, is very often particularly associated with younger children. One couple with two grandsons (aged 14 and 12) in the custody of their father saw their grandsons frequently but no longer offered this kind of support—"We have in the past, we've been over and fetched them from school, and we've done things like that. . . . But now they don't need it."

Grandparents who did provide such support tended to be quite flexible in what they were prepared to do and as circumstances changed, they were happy to step in and help the parents as and when required. As one grandparent put it, "No matter what you're going to do, if you've to do the housework or go somewhere, you'll drop it, or I do, drop anything for the grandchildren."

The family type of the grandchildren did not seem to affect the amount of babysitting or child care provided because this varied quite widely across both intact and separated families. A separation or divorce did have a greater impact, however, on the more extreme forms of support provided by grandparents. The BSAS asked grandparents about their satisfaction with their role (Dench et al., 1999) and found that the impact of family breakdown had quite a dramatic effect on grandparents' satisfaction and relationships with grandchildren, perhaps because grandparents felt obliged to provide greater help in such difficult circumstances. Indeed, family breakdown was associated with the highest level of grandparental help and with high rates of dissatisfaction. High input relative to child care appeared to be combined with low satisfaction with the grandparental role (Dench et al., 1999). Another study found that some grandmothers, especially paternal grandmothers, were reluctant to provide long-term child care for working mothers because they believed that they had brought up their own children and now it was their children's turn (Cotterill, 1992).

When the grandparents in the most recent British study were asked if they would be happy to provide more care for their grandchildren, most responded positively. Tension was apparent, however, where respondents felt their input was not sufficiently appreciated by the parents. As stated by one grandmother,

> She takes it for granted that we're going to have them and we will no problem, but she does take it for granted . . . we just wish that sometimes she would just ask us, she knows we wouldn't say no unless we were going somewhere, then that's different but she knows we wouldn't say no but she never asks.

Other grandparents who were also providing substantial amounts of care had limits on what they were prepared to do, principally because they wanted to do things for themselves. One grandmother had offered to help her daughter, but she would not give up the time she had put aside for herself for yoga classes. As she put it,

> It's just that I feel I've got to have a bit of time for myself now because I'm 70 now. I feel that I haven't got that much longer left and I've reared two children on my own and given all my time to them . . . I've helped them out in every way I possibly could so I just feel that I do really need a bit of time to myself. Is that selfish?

In this instance, even though the respondent had done an awful lot for her children, there was a sense of guilt that she wanted time, if only one day, for herself. We spoke to just two grandparents who categorically refused to babysit or look after the grandchildren unless it was an emergency. One felt that she had her own life to lead and said,

> I told them to count me out unless they're in real trouble, then I will. I'll be here but

I'm not just a built-in babysitter, I've got my own life and they all understand that so. It only arises if there's a real crisis then they know I would help but I'm not just a built-in babysitter.

Generally, practical help was seen as part of the territory of being a grandparent, but some grandparents appeared concerned that there was a *Hobson's choice* about the amount of child care they were called upon to do. They described their daughters or daughters-in-law as having to work to pay the mortgage and there being no other way to get child care the family either could afford or found acceptable. Some of them clearly resented this, but their inconvenience was the lesser of the two evils. Overall, it was clear from these grandparents' accounts that they were offering a range of support, most of it willingly but sometimes because there was no alternative source of help for their children and grandchildren, and in times of need, they felt they had to help.

## FINANCIAL SUPPORT

Giving money to grandchildren and their parents is often seen as an integral part of the grandparental role, being especially important when money is short or in times of need, for example, when children are born or when families separate. Two-thirds of the grandparents with grandchildren aged younger than 15 (65%) in the national survey had given them money in the last 12 months, and this was most common for grandchildren aged 5 to 14. One-third of grandparents (32%) had given money weekly, and a further 42% less than monthly. Multivariate statistical analysis shows that money gifts to grandchildren were related to the age of grandparent, the number of grandchildren, the age of youngest grandchild, the grandparent's income, and how close they lived to the grandchild. This was also true for grandchildren older than age 15,

where half (50%) of grandparents had given to grandchildren aged 15 to 19 and a quarter (25%) to those aged 20 or older.

Financial help and support varied enormously according to the income level and values of the grandparent and the circumstances of the child. In the in-depth study, it was obvious that some grandparents went out of their way to buy many extras and luxuries for their grandchildren: "We've bought bikes for them . . . they've had music centres . . . we bought their SKY-TV." Most of the grandparents in both the qualitative and quantitative (65–70%) studies provided some level of material support for their grandchildren and their families, and often there was a continuous flow of goods being passed from grandparents to their grandchildren. This ranged from toys and clothes to bigger items such as computers. Many of the grandparents with younger grandchildren bought them small things, such as sweets and toys, whenever they saw them whereas others routinely helped with things more likely to be necessities: "I'm the one who gets the shoes, grandma buys the shoes you know that sort of thing." Some grandparents gave pocket money each week; one grandmother, for example, gave her two teenage grandsons, both of whom had jobs, £5 each week. Some grandparents were upset that their own circumstances meant they could not do as much as they wanted either because of a lack of income or bad health.

The help that grandparents provided by buying things for grandchildren or providing financial assistance to their children very much depended on their own financial circumstances. This confirmed previous research findings where the most important factor affecting the help grandparents were able to give to their families was income level (Wilson, 1987). The lack of money to buy things for grandchildren in some cases caused considerable distress. One grandparent, for example, who was living on the basic state pension, was very restricted in what she could do for her granddaughter. She said,

Well, I can't buy her things, that hurts me because I can't buy her the things that I would like to buy her, it does it hurts. I mean I do buy her things and you know sweets and things like that but I can't do what I'd like to do.

The age of the grandparent and the grandchild did affect the provision of financial support. Older grandparents were more likely to have a lower income and poorer health and to have older grandchildren, whom the national survey showed tended to see grandparents less frequently. Previous research has suggested that as older grandparents tend to see less of their grandchildren than younger grandparents then, as a result, there may be less opportunity to buy things for them (Dench et al., 1999). There was awareness, particularly among the older grandparents, that as they got older, this would become more difficult when they had to rely on a pension and savings. As stated by one couple,

(Him) I mean we don't make it a policy to lend them or give them money on a regular basis, only in a crisis and I suppose the odd times we've had to say no because we haven't got it available without getting into debt ourselves.

(Her) And I mean we're not exactly in our eighties or anything so we've got quite a while to go before, hopefully, so we need to have a certain amount of money so it's not good saying all right we've got the money put away but we'll get it out. We can't because you know for old age, as long as what we do what we can do with our normal income then fair enough.

Being older affected grandparents' ability to offer financial support: several grandparents mentioned spontaneously, "Well we've helped in the past . . . but we're not really in a position to help them much," but even among younger grandparents in disadvantaged circumstances giving financial help to their children and grandchildren was difficult. One couple, where the grandfather was unable to work and the grandmother was retired, said they had not given financial help to the parents: "No never have done. Not only that we cannot really afford it anyway, my husband is on incapacity (benefit) and I'm not working so we only get a low income ourselves."

British research has revealed that certain norms shape or restrict grandparents' behavior with regard to their grandchildren (Cunningham-Burley, 1985; Mason et al., in press; Tunaley, 1998). The current qualitative study clearly revealed another such "guideline" that operated among the grandparents, that of treating all sets of grandchildren equally. Thus, when a grandparent bought something for one child the grandparent always made sure that the other children received the same. One grandparent, for example, said,

It's the same thing as with the others, if they need something she gets it and I try to keep them, if I've got something for Bethan I give to the rest at the same time. I keep it fair because I know that can cause friction in families, so therefore I keep it equal and there's not problems then, is there.

The one exception to this rule occurred where a separation or divorce had taken place and the grandparents felt that the grandchildren in those particular families were disadvantaged financially compared with other grandchildren. The statistical analysis of the national data showed that overall the grandchildren's family structure, that is whether both natural parents were living together or not, did not affect the amount of money being spent on grandchildren. However, some grandparents in the qualitative study were providing substantial financial support, for example, paying for nursery fees and holidays, and these tended to occur where family breakdown had taken place.

In helping out in this way, the grandparents provided considerable support to the mother with custody of the children, irrespective of whether she was their daughter or daughter-in-law. One couple, for example, said of their daughter-in-law at the time of the divorce,

> Yes she was very dependent in a way on us for a lot of things. Her own parents aren't particularly involved in any way so therefore it was us she turned to and also we felt it right for the children that they had strong back up. We needed to know for ourselves as much as for the children that they were OK.

Divorce and separation often meant grandparents stepped in to remedy financial difficulties. Among such grandparents, there was a sense of responsibility for the grandchildren to ensure that they did not miss the experiences of children in two-parent families. In this sense, they were prepared to pay for items that the mother could not afford. The reason that some grandparents interviewed gave more to the grandchildren in a separated family than to others in intact families was to offset any perceived imbalance. When asked if they buy the same amount of things for a grandchild whose parents were still together, one couple responded,

> We guarantee them a decent holiday, they can talk about it with their friends at school, it keeps them up with their cousins and things like that . . . Because of their financial situation I don't want them to lose out on the things that other children do. Therefore, we try to give them these experiences so that if they went anywhere that children have already done these things, they would have done them as well, they're not going to be held back in situations.

There were also instances of much more basic and everyday support being provided to lone mothers who were both daughters and daughters-in-law. One couple had moved back to Britain from Holland so that they could be on hand to take and collect children from nursery and school, provide meals, and have children in their house overnight several times a week while their daughter worked. The children had their own bedrooms in the grandparents' house and regarded it as their second home. The grandparents recognized that this would not have been the way they envisaged their retirement but saw it as their duty, which they enjoyed, to provide such support. They felt they did much more for these grandchildren than their other grandchildren but said that they would do the same for all of them if they needed help. For another couple, there was a sense of responsibility for the grandchildren where their son had left the marriage,

> (Grandfather) I mean I suppose we've had so much to do with the grandsons because of what Ben did. (Her) Yes, when he left his wife and she had two young, a baby and a little boy, so we were there all those years really for them.

As with child care, there was a great diversity in what grandparents provided financially for their grandchildren, as with other support that depended very much on the grandparents' own financial situation as well as the circumstances of their grandchildren's parents. Most of the grandparents, however, provided some level of financial assistance, and family breakdowns resulted in the greatest amount of assistance being offered if the grandparents could afford to do so. Most of the grandparents in the in-depth interviews felt that they would be happy to provide more for their grandchildren if they could afford it.

## EMOTIONAL SUPPORT

Emotional support in most families is a constant dimension of the give and take of family relationships and is particularly important during difficult times (Finch & Mason, 1993). In our study, such support was really only commented upon when it was recognized as being of abnormal levels, which was noticeably associated with family breakup. Many grandparents in this situation described how they both held back, tried not to take sides, but saw a key part of their role as providing "a stable platform for the kids." Some were even more involved in trying to help their very upset grandchildren: "We was always being sent for in the night if anything was wrong . . . and if Joseph was a bit upset which he used to be he'd crying for his dad, we'd bring him home with us." And grandfathers played a crucial role here with their little grandsons.

Eight of the 45 grandparents in the in-depth study allowed their children and grandchildren to temporarily move back into their homes. This was usually precipitated by a crisis; for example, one family had a house sale fall through and the family moved in with the grandparents until they made alternative arrangements. Separation or divorce also led to the same scenario. Seven of the grandparents interviewed had their daughter and her children or just the grandchildren live with them following family breakdown. As one grandparent recounted, she provided a home for their daughter when she separated from her husband: "When they split up she came to live here with us with the three children, they were here for about 12 weeks. It was very difficult."

Having grandchildren in separated families can affect grandparents' frequency of contact and level of contact. In one case where both their children had separated or were separating with children of similar ages (4 and 6), the difference between the frequencies of seeing or helping their daughter and her child was much greater than for their son and his daughter. However, the grandparents regretted this—it was not their choice but because access to their son's child was through their son; his decreasing frequency of contact with his daughter has reduced this. "We used to see more of her then because he used to pick her up on a Sunday and pop round," and not surprisingly, they would have preferred more contact, describing the amount of time with her as "it could be a lot better."

This was experienced and valued by many of the grandparents. One remarried couple with a set of grandchildren each spoke eloquently:

> I think the grandparents . . . are important for their grandchildren. From all the conversations I've had with them, it's always that they are happy with our existence and I think if anything happened to me they would be extremely sorry. No, I think they have derived emotional support and benefit from my existence and from my wife's [a step grandparent] as well because they look to her.

And the grandmother commented on her grandson's experience:

> Once he came here and spent his Christmas holidays with us and was quite astonished because then he was having problems with his father. I think then it was quite important that I could talk to him and he was really quite happy with this.

In two cases, the grandfathers also stepped into the shoes of the father who had left to provide a male figure in the lives of their grandchildren. Both grandfathers were able to calm their grandchildren in a way that the mothers were unable to: "We used to get a phone call, grandpa can you come up because Craig is upset. He just seemed to take notice of what I said you know, calm down, and put him to bed." Or to provide discipline,

> *(Him)* Well when Phillip moved away Shane wouldn't do what his mum said so she would phone up and say he's not doing

this, he's behaving badly or not doing that and I would go up and talk to him and he would listen to me.

*(Interviewer)* So he would respond to you rather than to his mother at that time?

*(Him)* Oh yes, all the time.

During the separation or divorce of the parents, some grandchildren found a safe haven in their grandparents, people who could provide the stability and support that they needed.

Although we only interviewed one custodial grandparent in our qualitative study, his experience is worth reporting here to illustrate the impact this undertaking can have on the life of the individual. This particular grandfather had taken on the care of his 2-year-old granddaughter following his daughter's increasing drug problem. Adopting this role had a major effect on his life, but not a fully positive impact. He strongly felt, however, that he wanted a relationship with his granddaughter whatever personal sacrifices he had to make. When asked how his life had changed, he said,

> I don't want to use the word burden but yeah it's changed my life and not for the better . . . If I hadn't stepped in and done this she would have been adopted and I wouldn't have seen her and that's why I stepped in and took custody. It wasn't ideal but then again I want to see my granddaughter so in a way I wouldn't say I've ruined my life but I've basically put, it's like putting your life on hold, you know, for what is going to be ten, fifteen years, I don't know.

Indeed, American research has found that becoming a custodial grandparent can have an enormous impact on the lifestyle of these individuals. Custodial grandmothers often report having to make dramatic changes, for which

they are unprepared, having assumed care of a grandchild (Fischer, 1983). One study found that the majority of 114 grandparents caring for their grandchildren needed to alter routines and plans, felt more physically tired, reported less time for oneself, and had less time to get things done (Jendrek, 1993). Many of the grandparents also reported less contact with friends and that they were less likely to do things for fun and recreation.

The custodial grandparent in this study also talked about the responsibility he had taken on. This affected his perception of himself as a grandparent and the role that he played. He had adopted a parental role and no longer perceived of himself as a "normal" grandparent:

> I'm a granddad now and I want to go down, I want to take her to the park, you know, for an hour or so, do you know what I consider normal grandparent things but obviously all that went different with Mandy and obviously it's not normal grandparent.

Again, this sentiment reflects American research that has found that the relationship with the cared for grandchildren may suffer. Grandparents in a position of authority tend to have a formal relationship with their grandchildren with less emphasis on indulging the grandchild in their care than traditional grandparents do (Emick & Hayslip, 1999). Custodial grandparents are, therefore, unable to have the traditional usually carefree relationship with their grandchildren that others often report.

The role of a grandparent was generally seen as a resource to be turned to if needed, "being there" was often seen as the defining nature of grandparenthood. The idea of "not interfering" but "being there" in times of crisis or upheaval was the ambivalence of this family role (Mason et al., in press). As one grandfather said, "A bad grandparent overindulges, interferes too much I think and is bossy perhaps. A good one, as I say, have them, love them and leave them alone is my motto 'Be supportive.'"

The changing nature of grandparenthood as children grow was exemplified by moving from direct, practical help to a more remote, latent, or emotional support. With adult grandchildren, it was often more a case of "they know we're here for them if they want us." Most grandparents in this study stated they would be happy to step in and help in an emergency, either financially or practically, and in this sense, they were providing emotional support. They were available and there emotionally for their families; the role described by Hagestad (1985) of "family national guard" could be ascribed to many of the grandparents in the study: Their effects were felt simply by their presence, rather than through their actions.

## CONCLUSIONS

This chapter has highlighted the great diversity in what grandparents do, and are willing to do, to support their families. In the British study, the grandparental role was shown to vary considerably, both between families as well as between different sets of grandchildren within families. It also varied between and within age groups and family types of the grandchild. It revealed that many grandparents provided child care for their young grandchildren and that financial support was often provided for grandchildren and their families, especially in times of need.

Three main types of support—practical, financial, and emotional—were identified. Multivariate analysis of the national data showed how contact, proximity, day care, and financial contributions varied between grandparents. These data are particularly revealing when considering low-income families in concert with how much grandparents can contribute to the well-being of their children's families. The most contact and

practical help was seen among younger grandparents with younger grandchildren, which was also true for financial support but income was also a factor here. Practical input from grandparents was not related to whether they were working or retired; however, lineage was an important influence on support, with the grandchildren of daughters generally having more contact and practical help from grandparents. The qualitative interviews, however, revealed that financial contributions from grandparents are guided by a sense of fairness with all sets being treated equally, except when a family is in need, for example, after family breakup.

Grandparents, particularly grandmothers, historically have played and still play a key role as additional source of child care and are routinely used for practical support in times of normal upheaval such as the arrival of new babies, moving, and the illness of parent, but they also took a key role in more protracted crises. Some reported having a separated child and family return "home" and found this difficult over a long period. Others stepped in to give practical help when the loss of a partner made practical life more difficult for their child and grandchildren. And at the extreme, one grandparent in our study had taken on the custody of his grandchild, still a rare occurrence in Britain, but likely to be a growing one.

Practical help was seen as "part of the territory" of being a grandparent. The study showed that many grandparents provided child care for their young grandchildren and that financial support was often provided for grandchildren and their families, especially in times of need. Emotional support was not explicitly recognized as such by grandparents but was evident when they described "being there" for their families if needed.

The family type of the grandchildren had a great impact across all three kinds of support examined. Family breakdown led to higher levels of all types of support being provided.

For example, some grandparents provided a home for their families or attempted to compensate financially or emotionally for the absence of a parent. In extreme circumstances, some grandparents were depended upon quite heavily by their families.

Although grandparents were generally providing support of some kind for their families, this was not a universal fact and should not be ignored by policymakers. Some grandparents never saw their grandchildren or saw them only rarely. Even though this does not mean they did not provide support to grandchildren, it does indicate that they were not available for direct physical assistance.

One of the main findings was the diversity of family lives and the great variation between grandparents in what they provided, how they helped, and what they were willing to do for their families. There was a considerable continuum of what people felt was appropriate. Most grandparents were generally prepared to step in to help their children with grandchildren when needed for child care, babysitting, or with help in times of family breakup or a crisis. But although some were clearly prepared to "drop everything for the grandchildren," others wanted time for themselves and set boundaries on what was legitimate or not. "I've told them to count me out unless there are in real trouble . . . I'm not a built in baby sitter . . . if there's a crisis then they know I would help."

Most of the grandparents in the study stated that they would be happy to provide more support to their families, although in some cases they expressed clear limits to this. This is perhaps a reflection that some of the grandparents felt that they had their own lives to lead and own circumstances to consider and that grandparenthood is not a direct relationship but is negotiated through the children's parents. The parents may act as gatekeepers in facilitating the interaction of grandparents and grandchildren or they may make demands felt inappropriate by the grandparents. It was important for them to achieve a balance between helping their families and doing what they themselves wanted to do. There was a life cycle nature of support, from being direct and practical in nature when children are young through to being more of a latent source of support, "being there," when the children are older. Also, it should be remembered that grandparents are likely to be providing care for elderly parents, so they are experiencing a double-burden of caring responsibilities.

Generally, most grandparents are a major source of practical, financial, or emotional help for their families, but this supporting resource cannot be presumed to always be available. Without accurate data, there has been a tendency in public policy to ignore the complexity of family lives and the diversity of grandparents' circumstances, roles, and obligations. Overall, it was clear from the accounts of most of the grandparents that they were offering a range of support for their families, most of it willingly but sometimes because there was no alternative.

## REFERENCES

Bloom, D. E., & Steen, T. P. (1996). Minding the baby in the United States. In K. England (Ed.), *Who will mind the baby? Geographies of child care and working mothers*. New York: Routledge.

Bowling, A. (1995). The most important things in life: Comparisons between older and younger population age groups by gender. Results from a national survey of the public's judgments. *International Journal of Health Science, 6,* 169–175.

Bradshaw, J., & Millar, J. (1991). *The employment of lone parents: A comparison of policy in 20 countries.* London: Family Policy Studies Centre.

Burton, L. (1992). Black grandparents rearing children of drug-addicted parents: Stressors, outcomes and social services needs. *Gerontologist, 32*(6), 744–751.

Casper, L. M., & Bryson, K. R. (1998). *Co-resident grandparents and their grandchildren: Grandparent maintained families* (Population Division Working Paper No. 26). Washington, DC: U.S. Census Bureau.

Chalfie, D. (1994). *Going it alone: A closer look at grandparents parenting grandchildren.* Washington, DC: American Association of Retired Persons.

Clarke, L., & Cairns, H. (2001). Grandparents and the care of children: The research evidence. In B. Broad (Ed.), *Kinship care: The placement choice for children and young people.* Lyme Regis, UK: Russell House.

Clarke, L., & Roberts, C. (2003). *Grandparenthood: Its meaning and its contribution to older people's lives.* Economic and Social Research Council, Growing Older Programme Findings Number 22. Retrieved from http://www.growingolder.group.shef.ac.uk/GOFindings22.pdf

Cotterill, P. (1992). But for freedom, you see, not to be a babyminder: Women's attitudes towards grandmother care. *Sociology, 26*(4), 603–618.

Cunningham-Burley, S. (1985). Constructing grandparenthood: Anticipating appropriate action. *Sociology, 19*(3), 421–436.

Dench, G., Ogg, J., & Thomson, K. (1999). The role of grandparents. In R. Jowell, J. Curtice, A. Park, & K. Thomson (Eds.), *British social attitudes: The 16th report.* Aldershot, UK: Ashgate.

Dex, S. (Ed.). (1999). *Families and the labour market: Trends, pressures and policies.* London: Joseph Rowntree Foundation, Family Policy Studies Centre.

Emick, M. A., & Hayslip, B. (1999). Custodial grandparenting: Stresses, coping skills and relationships with grandchildren. *International Journal of Aging and Human Development, 48*(1), 35–61.

Finch, J., & Mason, J. (1993). *Negotiating family responsibilities.* London: Routledge.

Fischer, L. R. (1983). Transition to grandmotherhood. *International Journal of Aging and Human Development, 16,* 67–78.

Fisher, C. (1996). Grandparents give of themselves. *American Demographics, 18*(6), 13–15.

Fuller-Thomson, E., Minkler, M., & Driver, D. (1997). A profile of grandparents raising grandchildren in the United States. *Gerontologist, 37*(3), 406–411.

Hagestad, G. O. (1985). Continuity and connectedness. In V. L. Bengston & J. F. Robertson (Eds.), *Grandparenthood.* London: Sage.

Harden, A. W., Clark, R. L., & Maguire, K. (1997). *Informal and formal kinship care.* Washington, DC: U.S. Department of Health and Human Services.

Home Office. (1998). *Supporting families: A consultation document.* London: Stationery Office.

Jendrek, M. P. (1993). Grandparents who parent their grandchildren: Effects on lifestyle. *Journal of Marriage and the Family, 55,* 609–621.

Laws, S., & Broad, B. (2000). *Looking after children within the extended family: Carers' views.* Leicester, UK: De Montfort University.

Mason, J., May, V., & Clarke, L. (in press). Ambivalence and the paradoxes of grandparenting. *Sociological Review.*

Marx, J., & Solomon, J. C. (2000). Physical health of custodial grandparents. In C. B. Cox (Ed.), *To grandmother's house we go and stay: Perspectives on custodial grandparents.* New York: Springer.

Minkler, M., & Roe, K. (1993). *Grandmothers as caregivers*. Newbury Park, CA: Sage.

Minkler, M., Roe, K., & Price, M. (1992). The physical and emotional health of grandmothers raising grandchildren in the crack cocaine epidemic. *Gerontologist, 32,* 752–761.

Pearlin, L. I., & Schooler, C. (1978). The structure of coping. *Journal of Health and Social Behaviour, 19,* 2–21.

Pitcher, D. (1999). *Grandparents who care for their grandchildren: Issues for children, families, and those working with them*. Plymouth, UK: Social Services, Plymouth City Council.

Rasmussen, B. (1983). *Aldre undervurderver deres rolle i familien* (p. 115). Copenhagen: Berlingske Tidende.

Robertson, J. F. (1977). Grandmotherhood: A study of role conceptions. *Journal of Marriage and the Family, 39,* 165–174.

Rutrough, T. S., & Ofstedal, M. B. (1997). Grandparents living with grandchildren: A metropolitan-nonmetropolitan comparison. In L. M. Casper & K. R. Bryson (Eds.), *Co-resident grandparents and their grandchildren: Grandparent maintained families* (Population Division Working Paper No. 26). Washington, DC: U.S. Census Bureau.

Saltzman, G. A. (1992). Grandparents raising grandchildren. *Creative Grandparenting, 2*(4), 2–3.

Troll, L. (1983). Grandparents: The family watchdogs. In T. Brubaker (Ed.) *Family relationships in later life*. Beverly Hills, CA: Sage.

Tunaley, J. (1998, December 15). *Grandparents and the family: Support versus interference*. Paper presented at the BPS Conference, London.

Wilson, G. (1987). Women's work: The role of grandparents in intergenerational transfers. *Sociological Review, 35*(4), 703–720.

# CHAPTER 22

# Poor Fathers' Involvement in the Lives of Their Children

## MELVIN N. WILSON

An increasingly important area of study in the development of children born to single women is the area of father-child interactions. Historically, children in single-parent families were studied using a deficit model, examining the negative consequences of father absence on child development (Garcia Coll, Meyer, & Brillon, 1995; McLoyd & Randolph, 1985). Researchers are now examining relationships children have with their fathers and finding that low-income, nonresident fathers do, in fact, maintain contact with children (King & Sobolewski, 2006; Mincy, 2002). The father-child interaction is an important predictor in many areas of a child's life as well as father's well-being (Marsiglio, Day, & Lamb, 2000) and functioning (Kalil, Ziol-Guest, & Coley, 2005). Unfortunately, there is a dearth of knowledge regarding the contribution of young, low income, and unwed fathers' role in the care and socialization of their children.

Although child care and socialization are vital parental responsibilities, for the most part providing physical care and socialization has been the responsibility of mothers rather than fathers. Much research has approached the study of families by interviewing mothers as the major source of family information. Inasmuch as fathers are an important part of the familial context, fathers' perspective in family life has gone largely unrecorded. Paternal behaviors and interactions with children may be especially important for children who live in divorce or never-married family situations. Moreover, it is conceivable that other paternal influences on children are not directly a result of fathers' presence in the home but, rather, that these paternal influences affect parenting and parent-child relationships.

Our understanding of low-income father involvement has been based on the traditional societal role of "provider" whereby father involvement has been characterized as the provision of economic resources to the family (Amato, 1998; Eggebeen, 2002; Marsiglio, 1993; McAdoo, 1986). Recent research on father involvement has begun to expand beyond the provider role to examine a diverse array of father involvement activities (e.g., playing, direct care, helping with homework, and scheduling doctor's appointments). Research on low-income fathers' involvement with their families and children has been plagued by two research caveats. First, the traditional role of fathers in families has been limited to the provision of economic and material supplies (Coley, 2001). Second, the nature of fathers' involvement in families has not generally considered fathers' emotional and behavioral involvement in families (Amato & Gilbreth, 1999; Hawkins & Eggebeen, 1991). Similarly, fathers who do not live with the child are not considered to be a part of the child's life. Thus, it can be the case that the amount of time that fathers spend with their children varies across fathers and fathering situations.

Research has traditionally focused on mothers and their interactions with their children but neglected the father's role in child rearing (Eggebeen, 2002; Mott, 1990). Mothers have long been assumed to be primarily responsible for raising children and this perception has led to a tendency to focus on mothering and its relationship to child outcomes (Cohen, 1993; Marsiglio, 1993; McAdoo, 1986, 1993; McBride & Rane, 1997).

Marsiglio (1993) points out that society is partially responsible for relegating fathers to the role of breadwinner. Historically, men's most important role in the family has been that of economic provider whereas women have been seen as the socio-emotional leaders of the family who are solely responsible for fulfilling the emotional needs of the family (Marsiglio, 1993). As a result, the traditional man's role in the family has been linked to the public sphere whereas the traditional woman's role has traditionally been linked to the private, household sphere.

Researchers have begun to consider fathers' involvement in the domestic life of their families. For instance, Hossain, Field, Pickens, Malphurs, and Del Valle (1997) examined father involvement in terms of fathers' primary caregiving activities with 5-month-old infants. Hossain and colleagues (1997) found that mothers demonstrated higher engagement in each basic caregiving activity (bedtime routine, physical care, feeding, soothing), but mothers and fathers did not differ in the amount of time they spent singing to and playing with their infants. Other researchers have obtained similar results (Deutsch, Lussier, & Servis, 1993; Feldman, Nash, & Aschenbrenner, 1983; Hossain & Roopnarine, 1994; Jain, Belsky, & Crnic, 1996). That is, although mothers spent more time engaged in the feeding and physical care of the infant, mothers and fathers did not differ in the amount of time they spent playing with the infant.

Recent research has demonstrated that the provider role shares importance with, and is sometimes even superseded by, the importance of nurturance, emotional, and social fathering behaviors (McLanahan, 2006). Cohen (1993) and Hamer (1997) obtained similar results regarding father's conceptualization of the paternal role. Fathers placed primary importance on social and emotional components of fatherhood (e.g., engaging in recreational activities, teaching, showing affection). Although fathers acknowledged economic contributions as part of the paternal role, they considered the provider's role to be a relatively unimportant component of fatherhood. In contrast, mothers tended to emphasize the provision of financial support as one of the most important components of fatherhood. Fathers in the Cohen and Hamer studies reported that socio-emotional and nurturing behaviors are critical aspects of fathering. The discrepancy between mothers' and fathers' perceptions of the father role often leads to detrimental effects on fathers' degree of engagement in their children's lives (Cohen, 1993; Hamer, 1997). Moreover, fathers who would like to be involved in the care and development of their children but who are unable to provide economic support may be restricted from interacting with their children. That is, a mother will limit a father's contact with his child if he does not provide sufficient economic support (Fox, 1985).

## FACTORS INFLUENCING PERFORMANCE OF THE FATHER ROLE

Research has examined several factors associated with differences in fathers' patterns of involvement in child-care activities. Such factors include family demographics; father's relationship with the mother of his child; child characteristics and temperament; father's mental health, motivation, self-confidence, and competence in the fathering role; father's social support; and parents' sex-role attitudes (Deinhart, 1998; Jain et al., 1996; Mincy, 2002; Roopnarine & Ahmeduzzaman, 1993).

## DEPRESSION FACTORS AND FATHER INVOLVEMENT

Although a wealth of literature examines the effect of the father's depression on the child's well-being (Cohen, 1993; Hamer, 1998), few studies have examined the nature of depressed fathers' interactions with their children. Past research has demonstrated that depressed mothers engage in more negative interactions with their children and are less involved in their children's lives (Field, Hossain, & Malphurs, 1999; Hammen & Goodman-Brown, 1990). Hence, the presence of depression in a parent negatively affects that parent's ability to be positively engaged in his or her child's life.

Roggman, Benson, and Boyce (1999) examined depression and father's involvement with their 10- to 14-month-old infants. The findings indicated that father's depression was negatively correlated with father involvement. On the other hand, Field et al.

(1999) examined parent-child interactions in families of depressed or nondepressed mothers and fathers of infants. Field and colleagues (1999) found that depressed mothers demonstrated lower levels of engagement with their infants than did nondepressed mothers. Interestingly, depressed fathers demonstrated higher levels of engagement with their infants than did the depressed mothers of these same infants. Depression did not seem to be a factor that greatly influenced their interactions with their infants. Field and her colleagues suggested that depressed fathers may tend to compensate for their depressed behavior in interactions with their child in a way that depressed mothers do not.

## NONRESIDENT FATHERS AND FATHER INVOLVEMENT

Many studies of fathering are based on samples of married couples. Relatively little attention has been given to fathers who are not involved in a marital relationship with their child's mother or who do not share a residence with the family. Hamer (1997) pointed out that, similar to general descriptions of the father's role, the role of the nonresident father is poorly defined. The nonresident father's role is almost always viewed in terms of the provision of economic resources. Because nonresident fathers are limited in the amount of daily interactions with their children, there are few opportunities to measure social and affective aspects of these interactions. Hence, there is a tendency to focus on easily observable fathering behaviors, which include primarily the provision of financial resources.

The few studies that do examine parenting behavior in nonresident fathers indicate that nonresident fathers demonstrate only minimal engagement in various interactions with their children (Hamer, 1997; Minton & Pasley, 1996). For example, Seltzer (1991) found that

30% of nonresident fathers reported no contact with their children in the last 12 months. Another third of fathers indicated that they saw their children several times or less during the last 12 months. Only about 25% of fathers indicated that they saw their children at least once a week. Seltzer (1991) also found that less than half of the fathers in the study paid any child support in the last year.

## SOCIOECONOMIC FACTORS AND FATHER INVOLVEMENT

Erickson and Gecas (1991) examined research on the relationship between social class and fathers' attitudes toward father involvement. They found that studies conducted before the 1980's consistently demonstrated differences in father role attitudes between working-class and middle-class fathers. Middle-class fathers equated fatherhood with providing support and encouragement to their child, whereas working-class fathers valued discipline and control in childrearing practices (Kohn, 1977). Past research also indicated that middle-class fathers were more likely to desire active, interactional involvement in their children's lives than were working-class fathers (Kohn & Carroll, 1960; Lerman & Sorenson, 2000; Lewis & Weinraub, 1976).

Although past research consistently demonstrated differences in father role attitudes for low- and middle-income fathers, more recent research suggests that attitude differences may not extend to differences in fathering behavior. Hossain and his colleagues (1997) found that neither income nor education were significant predictors of father involvement. They also pointed out that low-income fathers reported spending approximately 49% as much time as their wives in caregiving activities. In contrast, past research indicates that middle-income fathers reported spending about 25 to 33% as much time as their wives in caregiving

activities. Thus, low-income fathers reported levels of involvement equal to or greater than those reported by middle-income fathers.

Hossain and Roopnarine (1994) noted that their failure to find socioeconomic differences in fathering may be the result of their sample, in which the fathers were fairly well-educated and economically stable. In contrast, Jain and his colleagues (1996) found contrasting results in their study of 69 middle-class white fathers with 15-month-old infants. The researchers clustered fathers into the four groups based on their engagement in child-care activities: caretakers, playmates/teachers, disciplinarians, and disengaged fathers. Results indicated that fathers classified in the caretaker or playmate/teacher clusters had more education and a higher job status than did those fathers in the disciplinarian or disengaged clusters. These findings suggested that socioeconomic status may be associated with differences in involvement for specific types of fathering.

## FATHER INVOLVEMENT AND AGE

Few studies exist that discuss the impact of fathers' age or the age he became a father on his involvement with his children. Studies that do examine age as a factor influencing men's engagement in their children's lives usually focus on young fathers' ability to care for their children. Such research is sparse, however, because of the difficulty of recruiting young fathers to participate in studies (Danziger & Radin, 1990). Adams, Pittman, and O'Brien (1993) pointed out that it is very difficult to obtain information on young fathers for several reasons. First, young fathers are often partners of young or adolescent girls, and historically, researchers have focused more on adolescent and young mothers rather than adolescent or young fathers. In addition, young fathers are less likely to have legally established paternity

(Danziger & Radin, 1990) and often, contact with young fathers depends on mothers' desire to identify the father. Thus, young fathers are less likely to participate in studies examining adolescent parenting.

Several studies suggest that approximately 60% of teen mothers married the father of their child within 1 year of the child's birth (Adams et al., 1993). For those young mothers who remain unmarried, approximately half report that the fathers of their children remain in contact with the child. However, this finding is limited because it does not provide information about the nature of the father-child contacts. In addition, contact with the child often depends on the quality of the mother-father relationship. Therefore, if the relationship between the parents is poor or nonexistent, there is often little father-child contact.

Danziger and Radin (1990) examined father involvement in a sample of teen mothers who lived separately from their child's father. Danziger and Radin examined the impact of the quality of the father-child relationship, diversity of child-care chores the father engaged in, and the extent to which the mother discussed the child with the father on father involvement. Results indicated that, for minorities, the younger the father, the more likely he was to be involved in parenting. The researchers suggest that this difference may be because the minority father's absence might not be as strongly related to an absence from the child's life compared with that of white fathers.

Marsiglio (1993) found that teen fathers and young fathers in their 20s were more likely to experience higher levels of unemployment and lower levels of educational attainment than were young men who were not fathers. Sullivan (1985) asserted that young men with unstable or nonexistent means of supporting the child may be reluctant to establish paternity or to demonstrate involvement in their children's lives. Many young men may withdraw from the father role altogether when they are unable to provide the child with economic resources. In addition, young men who have a difficult time providing financial support may face the mother's objection to his seeing the child.

## AN ACTUARIAL PERSPECTIVE

For this analysis, variables of interest include socio-demographic factors, measures of psychological well-being, and whether or not the father was ever incarcerated. Sociodemographic characteristics include race, age, household income, immigration status (i.e., born in the United States), and the number of children. Psychological well-being was measured by fathers' perceived health status, satisfaction with life, sense of personal efficacy, depressive symptoms, substance use, feelings of cultural attachment, and church attendance. This analysis examines factors that distinguish a group of similar fathers who are involved frequently with their children from those who are not frequently involved with their children. That is, it assumes that within a group of obviously similar men, some characteristics will vary across the group. Given that this sample is screened for a demographic group of young, low-income women who are having either their first or second child, the fathers will also likely be young, low-income, and less educated. The analysis represents both a cross-sectional and longitudinal evaluation that examines the relationship between social and psychological characteristics and paternal behaviors.

Classification and regression tree technology (CART; Breiman, Freidman, Olshen, & Stone, 1984; Steinberg & Colla, 1995) was employed to classify a sample of similar men as accurately and reliably as possible. CART is a data analysis procedure that permits a stepwise examination of the relationship between an outcome variable and multiple predictor variables. CART analysis typically results in the categories of characteristics that are associated with the presence or absence of the primary outcome. CART methodology employs a binary decision tree as a classifier; this form of binary recursive partitioning separates the sample into subsamples. CART represents an advanced actuarial approach to understanding variables and factors influencing father involvement (Lewis, 2000; Steinberg & Colla, 1995;Yohannes & Hoddinott, 1999). For the current study, the decision tree is constructed by refining the single characteristic that provides the best split between the proportions of the men who were and were not frequently involved with their children.

## METHOD

### Procedures and Sample Recruitment

This study is a classification examination of fathers' social and psychological well-being characteristics that are associated with involvement with children. The data is drawn from a larger study, which is referred to as the Fragile Families and Child Well-Being (FFCWB) Project (McLanahan, Garfinkel, Brooks-Gunn, & Tienda, 2000), and is investigating the family formation of single parents. The FFCWB is a national study that is designed to examine the consequences of nonmarital childbearing in low-income families, and to examine the consequences of welfare reform and the role of fathers in unwed families.

A common data collection procedure was employed to recruit low-income, nonresident mothers and fathers in 20 U.S. cities. Within each city, participants were recruited from as many as five hospitals to obtain a sample of 250 nonmarital births and 75 marital births. All participants were parents who were having their first or second child and were either receiving or eligible to receive public welfare assistance. Mothers and most fathers were interviewed in the hospital within 24 hours after giving birth. Those fathers not interviewed in the hospital were interviewed shortly after the mother left the hospital. Data collection began in 1999, 3 years after the implementation of the Personal Responsibility and Reconciliation Act.

### Measures of Interest

The measures consisted of items that addressed social demographic characteristics including race, age, income earned in the last year, residential status, number of children and immigration status. Health and psychological well-being measures represented levels of life satisfaction, personal efficacy, alcohol and substance use, depressive symptom characteristics, and health status. Social characteristic variables included respondents' race/ethnicity, residence with the child, income category, and age.

The measures were similar to scales that have been used in other studies of paternal psychological well-being and father involvement (e.g., Collins, 1986; Gove, 1973; Umberson & Williams, 1993). Fathers' health status was created from questions that asked respondents to indicate general level of health, and use of alcohol, drug, and tobacco products. Whereas the health questions asked the respondents to indicate their general level of physical health, the substance abuse items ask respondents to report how many days they had used alcohol, tobacco, and drugs during the past 3 months.

Fathers' psychological well-being was measured by questions assessing his level of depressive symptoms, whether he had mental health problems, his sense of life satisfaction, his sense of personal efficacy, and his incarceration history. The measures of depressive symptoms are adapted from the Center for Epidemiologic Studies Depression Scale

(CES-D; Radloff, 1977, 1991). These questions asked the respondents to report on the number of days that they experienced depressive symptoms during the past week. Life satisfaction addressed the respondents' feelings about their lives as a whole. The respondents' level of perceived empowerment represented their sense of personal efficacy.

The dependent variable was a measure of paternal involvement in child-care activities administered during the 12-month follow-up questions that asked about fathers' participation in child-care behaviors that are directed at caring for and playing with the child.

## DESCRIPTIVE FINDINGS

Table 22.1 presents the social characteristics of the fathers. The sample consists *primarily* of African American and Hispanic American men who are 25 years old or younger, born in the United States, who have one child, and who are either cohabiting with or married to their child's mother. The mean of the men's income is between $10,000 and $34,999, with Caucasian fathers earning more than did African American or Latino fathers. The mean education level was high school graduate. The men were in very good or excellent health, expressing a sense of life satisfaction and personal efficacy. They also reported few symptoms of depression. The men reported using tobacco products (39% of sample smoked) and alcohol (several times a month and less than monthly). About 30% of sample reported having ever been incarcerated.

The CART analysis produced two types of nodes, or branches; parent nodes represent the primary points of partitioning the sample, and terminal nodes represent endpoint of the partitioning process. This CART analysis represents an 18–terminal node or branch tree with primary splits occurring on incarceration, immigrant status, substance problem, race/ethnicity, number of children, earning group, alcohol use, and father's age. Figure 22.1 depicts the output of the CART analysis. Although the predictions were modest, the prediction of fathers' frequent involvement in child-care activities was interesting. The questions ever incarcerated, immigration status, and alcohol use variables were consistent predictors. Table 22.2 presents the 17 parent nodes and 18 terminal nodes that branch from the parent nodes. Table 22.3 presents the relative importance for each of the independent variables.

Figure 22.1 outlines the various clusters of men. The deciding variables of incarceration, immigrant status, income group, residence with child, and alcohol use served as the primary branch nodes in the developing classification tree. Frequently involved fathers were separated from infrequently involved fathers most decidedly by whether or not the fathers had ever been incarcerated, ever had a substance problem, or whether the father was an immigrant. Frequently involved fathers, additionally, were described as being of Hispanic origin. Infrequently involved fathers were described as heavy alcohol users. Optimally, there were 18 different clusters of fathers, which were divided between frequently and infrequently involved fathers. The clusters were formed by first culling the sample for incarcerated, substance problem, and immigration status because those variables represent the base branches of the tree. Interestingly, ever incarcerated and immigration status were associated with being African American and Latino, respectively.

The classification accuracy on this sample was 65% for predicting infrequently involved and 81% for predicting frequently involved fathers. Cross validation tells us how accurately the tree would predict if it were applied to a new data asset. Table 22.2 presents the parent and terminal nodes' classification characteristics. Splitters and characteristics indicate the specific variable and interacting variables on which the data separated. Classification indicates the proportion of the split sample that had

**Table 22.1**  Fathers' Capacities and Well-Being in 20 Cities: Definition of Variables in Analyses

| Characteristic | N | % | Characteristic | N | % |
|---|---|---|---|---|---|
| Race | | | Personal Efficacy | | |
| White | 785 | 21 | Yes | 3247 | 85 |
| Black | 1789 | 47 | No | 564 | 15 |
| Hispanic | 1048 | 28 | | | |
| Other | 165 | 4 | Ethnic Attachment | | |
| | | | Yes | 2969 | 80 |
| Residence | | | No | 761 | 20 |
| With Child | | | | | |
| No | 1069 | 28 | Church Attendance | | |
| Yes | 2734 | 72 | Infrequent | 1757 | 46 |
| | | | Frequent | 2063 | 54 |
| Father's Age (years) | | | Depressive Symptoms | | |
| < 20 | 318 | 8 | No symptoms | 616 | 16 |
| 20–24 | 1158 | 31 | Low endorsement | 1594 | 42 |
| 25–29 | 934 | 25 | Moderate | | |
| 30–35 | 803 | 21 | endorsement | 938 | 25 |
| 36+ | 584 | 15 | High endorsement | 635 | 17 |
| Father's Income ($) | | | Mental Health | | |
| < 5,000 | 360 | 9 | Problems | | |
| 5,000–9,999 | 322 | 9 | Yes | 258 | 7 |
| 10,000–19,999 | 742 | 19 | No | 3395 | 93 |
| 20,000–34,999 | 933 | 24 | | | |
| 35,000–49,999 | 570 | 15 | Tobacco Use | | |
| 50,000–74,999 | 517 | 14 | Yes | 1493 | 39 |
| 75,000+ | 386 | 10 | No | 2327 | 61 |
| Born in the U.S. | | | Frequency of | | |
| Yes | 3076 | 81 | Alcohol Use | | |
| No | 746 | 19 | Each day | 143 | 5 |
| | | | Several times a week | 464 | 18 |
| Number of | | | Several times | | |
| Children | | | a month | 1020 | 38 |
| 1 Child | 1112 | 51 | Less than monthly | 1031 | 39 |
| 2 Children | 608 | 28 | | | |
| 3 Children+ | 474 | 21 | Substance Abuse | | |
| | | | Problems | | |
| Health Quality | | | Yes | 252 | 7 |
| Poor | 24 | 1 | No | 3390 | 93 |
| Fair | 267 | 7 | | | |
| Good | 785 | 21 | Incarcerated | | |
| Very good | 1433 | 36 | Yes | 1186 | 29 |
| Excellent | 1314 | 34 | No | 2905 | 71 |
| Life Satisfaction | | | Child-Care Duties | | |
| Yes | 2850 | 25 | Never/seldom | 1897 | 53 |
| No | 963 | 75 | Often/each day | 1664 | 45 |

the characteristics, and probability represents their proportion in the whole sample.

The infrequently involved men represent the easily describable clusters. The main cluster for the infrequently involved included men who are labelled as incarcerated, native born and substance users. As seen in Table 22.2 and Figure 22.1, terminal nodes 13, 14, 16, 17, and 18 accounted for 35% of the sample. Conversely, the frequently involved men

**Table 22.2**   Parent and Terminal Nodes Characteristics and Classification

| Parent Node | Node Classification | Splitters | Characteristics | Classification | Probability |
|---|---|---|---|---|---|
| 1 (N = 3,577) | Frequent | Incarceration | Not incarcerated | 67.2 | .74 |
| 2 (N = 2,749) | Frequent | Immigration | Foreign born | 71.3 | .64 |
| 3 (N = 2,320) | Frequent | Substance problem | No substance problem | 73.0 | .63 |
| 4 (N = 2,280) | Frequent | Race | African American, Other | 74.6 | .44 |
| 5 (N = 1,577) | Frequent | Children | 2 or 3 children | 72.9 | .36 |
| 6 (N = 1,295) | Frequent | Income group | Low-middle income | 73.2 | .34 |
| 7 (N = 1,224) | Frequent | Fathers' age | Young (less than 24) | 73.2 | .26 |
| 8 (N = 933) | Frequent | Alcohol use | ≤ Monthly | 72.8 | .26 |
| 9 (N = 920) | Frequent | Residence w/child | No | 71.3 | .21 |
| 10 (N = 783) | Frequent | Alcohol use | < Daily | 71.5 | .19 |
| 11 (N = 691) | Frequent | Children | 2 children | 70.6 | .18 |
| 12 (N = 648) | Frequent | Income group | <5,000 | 70.9 | .18 |
| 13 (N = 638) | Frequent | Church | No | 70.9 | .17 |
| 14 (N = 618) | Frequent | Life satisfaction | Yes | 70.0 | .17 |
| 15 (N = 612) | Frequent | Alcohol use | < Daily | 70.9 | .17 |
| 16 (N = 71) | Frequent | Children | 3 children | 67.6 | .02 |
| 17 (N = 58) | Frequent | Fathers' age | –24 years | 72.4 | .02 |

| Terminal Node | Node Classification | Splitters | Characteristics | Classification | Probability |
|---|---|---|---|---|---|
| 18 (N = 828) | Infrequent | Incarceration | Incarcerated | 46.4 | .23 |
| 17 (N = 429) | Infrequent | Immigration | Native born | 38.0 | .11 |
| 16 (N = 40) | Infrequent | Substance problem | Yes | 42.5 | .01 |
| 15 (N = 703) | Frequent | Race | White and Hispanic | 70.3 | .19 |
| 14 (N = 13) | Infrequent | Children | 2 children | 53.8 | .003 |
| 13 (N = 25) | Infrequent | Fathers' age | <20 | 48.0 | .007 |
| 12 (N = 33) | Frequent | Fathers' age | –24 | 87.9 | .009 |
| 11 (N = 291) | Frequent | Fathers' age | –24 | 87.9 | .08 |
| 10 (N = 92) | Frequent | Alcohol use | Daily | 68.5 | .026 |
| 9 (N = 43) | Frequent | Children | 3 children | 74.4 | .012 |
| 8 (N = 6) | Infrequent | Satisfaction w/life | Not satisfied | 70.6 | .001 |
| 7 (N = 110) | Frequent | Alcohol use | Several times a week | 76.4 | .03 |
| 6 (N = 502) | Frequent | Alcohol use | Several times a month | 81.3 | .14 |
| 5 (N = 20) | Frequent | Church | Frequent | 85.0 | .005 |
| 4 (N = 10) | Frequent | Income group | 5,000–9,999 | 100.0 | .002 |
| 3 (N = 137) | Frequent | Residence w/child | Yes | 81.8 | .04 |
| 2 (N = 13) | Frequent | Alcohol use | No alcohol | 92.3 | .003 |
| 1 (N = 282) | Frequent | Children | 1 child | 82.3 | .08 |

**Table 22.3** Variable Importance

| Variable | Relative Importance |
|---|---|
| Alcohol Use | 100.000 |
| Incarceration | 94.765 |
| Life Satisfaction | 92.452 |
| Income Group | 90.272 |
| Children | 80.069 |
| Church | 59.867 |
| Tobacco | 56.530 |
| Health Status | 43.807 |
| Immigrant | 29.399 |
| Race/Ethnicity | 23.203 |
| Father's Age | 20.964 |
| Sense of Efficacy | 20.428 |
| Residence With Child | 18.695 |
| Ethnic Attachment | 16.243 |
| Substance Problem | 15.975 |
| Mental Health Problem | 13.957 |
| Depressive Symptoms | 11.013 |

men with a wide variety of characteristics not readily describable without considering all the associated relevant interactions represented by the various parent nodes.

In addition to identifying the main predictor variables, CART identifies the relative importance for each of the independent variables. Variables are scored based on the improvement each variable makes to overall prediction of the outcome. This allows for identification of variables that are important but whose significance is masked or hidden by other variables during the tree building process.

## DISCUSSION AND CONCLUSIONS

Overall, the findings that father involvement variables are associated with social characteristics is in accordance with previous studies.

That is, fathers who had never been incarcerated, who were immigrants, who were not substance users, and who lived with the child were more likely to be classified as frequently involved compared with the other fathers. In addition, fathers who infrequently attended church, who perceived their lives as satisfying, and who were modest alcohol consumers were likely to be frequently involved with their child. Past literature has castigated men who are poor as absent in the lives of their children (Amato, 1998; McAdoo, 1986, 1993). However, the finding of this study paints a different picture. Surprisingly, low-income fathers were as likely to be classified as frequently involved with their children as were middle-class and upper-middle-class fathers. Men's economic contributions to family life and residence with their children are important characteristics of paternal involvement. However, other characteristics interacted in important ways to produce paternal involvement. For instance, modest alcohol use, low income, infrequent church attendance, and a perception of satisfaction with life were also characteristics of frequently involved fathers. Frequently involved fathers also included fathers who earned more than $50,000, live with their children, consume a moderate level of alcohol, and attended church. The infrequently involved fathers were likely to be men who reported being ever-incarcerated, native born, having a substance problem. The interesting point is that the variations of frequently involved fathers are broad and include characteristics that are typically used to describe fathers who have no contact with their children (Adams et al., 1993; Amato, 1998; Bowman, 1993; Hyde & Texidor, 1988; Mincy, 2002).

Future research should continue to investigate the role that young, low-income, and nonresident fathers play in the lives of children. The growing number of single-parent families warrants further examination of paternal involvement in families, and especially paternal involvement in the lives of

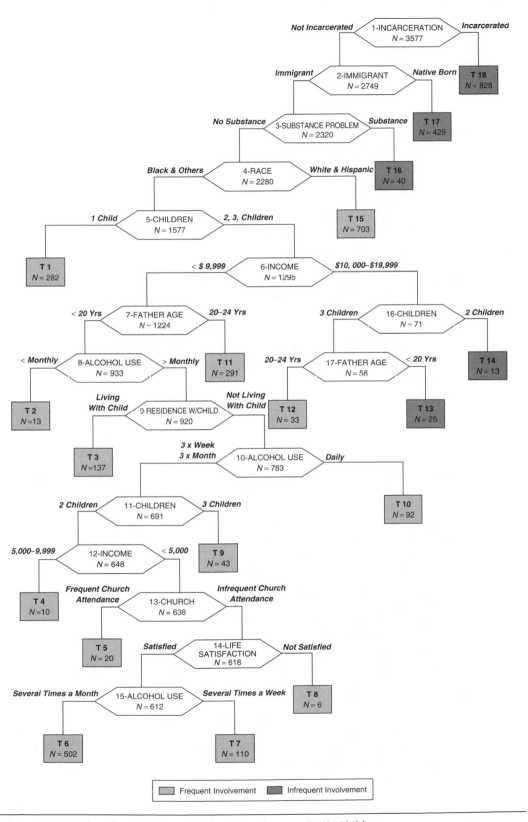

**Figure 21.1** Classification Tree of Fathers' Involvement With Children

children. Society can no longer afford to hold the belief that low-income, nonresident fathers are not important contributors to the well-being of their children. On the contrary, research must explore the multiple ways that fathers interact with their children (Cabrera & Peters, 2000; Cabrera, Tamis-LeMonda, Bradely, Hofferth, & Lamb, 2000).

## REFERENCES

Adams, G., Pittman, K., & O'Brien, R. (1993). Adolescent and young adult fathers: Problems and solutions. In A. Lawson & D. L. Rhode (Eds.), *The politics of pregnancy: Adolescent sexuality and public policy* (pp. 261–237). New Haven, CT: Yale University Press.

Amato, P. R. (1998). More than money? Men's contributions to their children's lives. In A. Booth & A. C. Crouter (Eds.), *Men in families* (pp. 241–278). Mahwah, NJ: Erlbaum.

Amato, P. R., & Gilbreth, J. G. (1999). Nonresident fathers and children's well-being: A meta-analysis. *Journal of Marriage and the Family, 61,* 557–573.

Bowman, P. J. (1993). The impact of economic marginality among African American husbands and fathers. In H. P. McAdoo (Ed.), *Family ethnicity* (pp. 120–137). Newbury Park, CA: Sage.

Breiman, L., Freidman, J., Olshen, R., & Stone, C. (1984). *Classification and regression trees.* Belmont, CA: Wadsworth.

Cabrera, N., & Peters, H. E. (2000). Public policies and father involvement. *Marriage and Family Review, 29*(4), 295–314.

Cabrera, N. J., Tamis-LeMonda, C. S., Bradely, R. H., Hofferth, S., & Lamb, M. E. (2000). Fatherhood in the twenty-first century. *Child Development, 71*(1), 127–136.

Cohen, T. F. (1993). What do fathers provide? In J. C. Hood (Ed.), *Men, work, and family* (pp. 1–22). Newbury Park, CA: Sage.

Coley, R. L. (2001). (In)visible men: Emerging research on low-income unmarried, and minority fathers. *American Psychologist 56*(9), 743–753.

Collins, P. H. (1986). The Afro-American work/nexus: An exploratory analysis. *Western Journal of Black Studies, 10*(3), 148–156.

Danziger, S. K., & Radin, N. (1990). Absent does not equal uninvolved: Predictors of fathering in teen mother families. *Journal of Marriage and the Family, 52,* 636–642.

Deinhart, A. (1998). *Reshaping fatherhood: The social construction of shared fathering.* Thousand Oaks, CA: Sage.

Deutsch, F. M., Lussier, J. B., & Servis, L. J. (1993). Husbands at home: Predictors of paternal participation in childcare and housework. *Journal of Personality and Social Psychology, 65*(6), 1154–1166.

Eggebeen, D. (2002) The changing course of fatherhood: Men's experience with children in demographic perspective. *Journal of Family Issues, 23,* 486–506.

Erickson, R. J., & Gecas, V. (1991). Social class and fatherhood. In F. W. Bozett & S. M. H. Hanson (Eds.), *Fatherhood and families in cultural context* (pp. 114–137). New York: Springer.

Feldman, S. S., Nash, S. C., & Aschenbrenner, B. G. (1983). Antecedents of fathering. *Child Development, 54,* 1628–1636.

Field, T. M., Hossain, Z., & Malphurs, J. (1999). Depressed fathers' interactions with their infants. *Infants Mental health Journal, 20*(3), 322–332.

Fox, G. L. (1985). Noncustodial fathers. In S. M. H. Hanson & F. W. Bozett (Eds.), *Dimensions of fatherhood* (pp. 393–415). Beverly Hills, CA: Sage.

Garcia Coll, C. T., Meyer, E. E., & Brillon, L. (1995). Ethnic and minority parenting. In M. H. Bronstein (Ed.), *Handbook of parenting: Vol. 2. Biology and ecology of parenting* (pp. 189–209). Mahwah, NJ: Erlbaum.

Gove, W. R. (1973). Sex, marital status, and morality. *American Journal of Sociology, 79,* 45–67.

Hamer, J. F. (1997). The fathers of "fatherless" black children. *Families in Society: The Journal of Contemporary Human Services, 78*(6), 564–578.

Hamer, J. F. (1998). The definition of fatherhood: In the words of never-married African American custodial mothers and the noncustodial fathers of their children. *Journal of Sociology & Social Welfare, 25,* 81–104.

Hammen, C., & Goodman-Brown, T. (1990). Self-schemas and vulnerability to specific life stress in children at risk for depression. *Cognitive Therapy and Research, 14, 215–227.*

Hawkins, A. J., & Eggebeen, D. J. (1991). Are fathers fungible?: Patterns of co-resident adult men in maritally disrupted families and young children's wellbeing. *Journal of Marriage and the Family, 53, 958–972.*

Hossain, Z., Field, T., Pickens, J., Malphurs, J., & Del Valle, C. (1997). Fathers' caregiving in low-income African American and Hispanic American families. *Early Development and Parenting, 6*(2), 73–82.

Hossain, Z., & Roopnarine, J. L. (1994). African American fathers' involvement with infants: Relationship to their functioning style, support, education, and income. *Infant Behavior and Development, 17,* 175–184.

Hyde, B. L., & Texidor, M. S. (1988). A description of the fathering experience among black fathers. *Journal of Black Nurses Association, 2,* 67–78.

Jain, A., Belsky, J., & Crnic, K. (1996). Beyond fathering behaviors: Types of dads. *Journal of Family Psychology, 10*(4), 431–442.

Kalil, A., Ziol-Guest, K., & Coley, R. L. (2005) Perception of father involvement patterns in teenage mother families: Predictors and links to mother's psychological adjustment. *Family Relations, 54,* 197–211.

King, V., & Sobolewski, J. M. (2006). Nonresident fathers' contribution to adolescent well-being. *Journal of Marriage and the Family, 68,* 537–557.

Kohn, M. (1977). *Class and conformity: A study in values.* Homewood, IL: Dorsey Press.

Kohn, M., & Carroll, E. E. (1960). Social class and the allocation of parental responsibilities. *Sociometry, 23,* 372–392.

Lerman, R., & Sorenson, E. (2000). Father involvement with their nonmarital children: patterns, determinants, and effects on their earnings. *Marriage and Family Review, 29,* 137–158.

Lewis, M., & Weinraub, M. (1976). The father's role in the child's social network. In M. E. Lamb (Ed.), *The role of the father in child development* (pp. 157–184). New York: Wiley.

Lewis, R. J. (2000). *An introduction to classification and regression (CART) analysis.* Paper presented at the meeting of the Society for Academic Emergency Medicine, San Francisco, CA. Retrieved August 9, 2002, from http://www.saem.org/download/lewis1.pdf

Marsiglio, W. (1993). Contemporary scholarship on fatherhood: Culture, identity, and conduct. *Journal of Family Issues, 14*(4), 484–509.

Marsiglio, W. Day, R., & Lamb, M. (2000). Exploring fatherhood diversity: Implications for conceptualizing father involvement. *Marriage and Family Review, 29,* 269–293.

McAdoo, J. L. (1986). A black perspective on the father's role in child development. *Marriage & Family Review, 9*(3–4), 117–133.

McAdoo, J. L. (1993). The roles of African American fathers: An ecological perspective. *Families in Society: The Journal of Contemporary Human Services, 74,* 28–35.

McBride, B. A., & Rane, T. R. (1997). Role identity, role investments, and paternal involvement: Implications for parenting programs for men. *Early Childhood Research Quarterly, 12,* 173–197.

McLanahan, S. (2006). Fragile families and the marriage agenda. In L. Kowalski-Jones & N. Wolfinger (Eds.), *Fragile families and the marriage agenda* (pp. 1–21). New York: Springer.

McLanahan, S., Garfinkel, I., Brooks-Gunn, J., & Tienda, M. (2000). *The fragile families and child well-being study.* Retrieved from http://www.columbia.edu/cu/ssw/grants/indivproj/garf2.html

McLoyd, V. C., & Randolph, S. (1985). Secular trends in the study of Afro-American children: A review of *Child Development,* 1936–1980. In A. B. Smuts & J. W. Hagen (Eds.), History and research in child development. *Monographs of the Society for Research in Child Development, 50*(4–5, Serial No. 211), 78–92.

Mincy, R. (2002). *Who should marry whom? Multiple fertility among new parents* (Working Paper #2002-03-FF). Princeton, NJ: Center for Research on Child Well-being.

Minton, C., & Pasley, K. (1996). Fathers' parenting role identity and father involvement: A comparison of nondivorced and divorced, nonresident fathers. *Journal of Family Issues, 17*(1), 26–45.

Mott, F. (1990). When is father really gone? Paternal-child contact in father absent families. *Demography, 27,* 499–518.

Radloff, L. S. (1977). The CES-D scale: A self-report depression scale for research in the general population. *Applied Psychological Measurement, 1*(3), 385–401.

Radloff, L. S. (1991). The use of the Center for Epidemiologic Studies Depression Scale in adolescent and young adults. *Journal of Youth and Adolescence, 20*(2), 149–166.

Roggman, L. A., Benson, B., & Boyce, L. (1999). Fathers with infants: Knowledge and involvement in relation to psychosocial functioning and religion. *Infant Mental Health Journal, 20*(3), 257–277.

Roopnarine, J. L., & Ahmeduzzaman, M. (1993). Puerto Rican fathers' involvement with their preschool-age children. *Hispanic Journal of Behavioral Sciences, 15*(1), 96–107.

Seltzer, J. (1991). Relationships between fathers and children who live apart: The father's role after separation. *Journal of Marriage and the Family, 53*(1), 79–101.

Steinberg, D., & Colla, P. (1995). *CART: Tree structured non-parametric data analysis.* San Diego, CA: Salford Systems.

Sullivan, M. L. (1985). *Teen fathers in the inner city.* New York: Vera Institute of Justice.

Umberson, D., & Williams, C. L. (1993). Divorced fathers: Parental role strain and psychological distress. *Journal of Family Issues, 14,* 378–400.

Yohannes, Y., & Hoddinott, J. (1999). *Classification and regression trees: An introduction.* Washington, DC: International Food Policy Research Institute. Retrieved August 2002 from http://www.ifpri.org

# CHAPTER 23

# The Health-Care Safety Net for Mexican-Origin Families

RONALD J. ANGEL, JACQUELINE L. ANGEL, AND LAURA LEIN

In the United States, employer-sponsored health insurance represents the largest source of health-care coverage for the working age population. In 2001, approximately 71% of the insured population had private coverage, and of those, approximately 63% were covered by employer-sponsored plans (Mills, 2002). For those without private coverage, the federal government is the insurer of last resort. In 2001, slightly more than 13% of insured Americans were covered by Medicare, and an additional 11% received Medicaid. The military and other sources cover a relatively small fraction of the population, leaving more than 40 million Americans, or more than 14% of the population, without health insurance (Mills, 2002). This is a startling figure in and of itself, but it masks an even more serious problem that arises from the fact that although the proportion of uninsured Americans is high across the board, the proportion of uninsured is even higher among minority Americans (Angel & Angel, 1996; Mills, 2002; Weinick, Zuvekas, & Cohen, 2000), among whom Mexican Americans face unique problems of

seriously inadequate coverage (Berk, Albers, & Schur, 1996; De la Torre, Friis, Hunter, & Garcia, 1996; Doty & Ives, 2002; Giachello, 1992; Halfon, Wood, Valdez, Pereyra, & Duan, 1997; Iannotta, 2002; Santos & Seitz, 2002; Valdez, Giachello, Rodriguez-Trias, Gomez, & De la Rocha, 1993).

In this discussion, we examine the health-care coverage of the Mexican-origin population of the United States and compare it with the situation of blacks and non-Hispanic whites, as well as with that of other Hispanic groups. Rather than focusing solely on any one age group or one source of health-care coverage, we examine coverage through the life course and summarize rates of public and private coverage for children, pre-retirement age adults, and the elderly. One serious consequence of our current system of health-care financing for families that do not have full family coverage from an employer's group plan, either because it is not offered or because they cannot afford it, is that often some members of the family are covered but others are not. Medicaid and the new State Children's Health Insurance

Program (SCHIP) provide coverage for pregnant women, infants, and children up to the age of 19 in families with incomes even somewhat above the federal poverty line (Starfield, 2000). No such programs exist for nondisabled adults, and in the absence of employer-based or private coverage they must do without care, rely on charity, or incur often crushing medical debt. In the United States today, medical debt is the leading cause of bankruptcy (Himmelstein, Warren, Thorne, & Woolhandler, 2005; Sullivan, Warren & Westbrook, 2000).

Although after the age of 65, all citizens qualify for Medicare, difficulties in paying for health care do not end. Individuals who do not own supplemental Medigap plans to pay for what Medicare does not cover face the risk of large medical debt or having to do without needed care. Mexican Americans are at elevated risk of inadequate coverage at all ages. The data clearly reveal that health coverage disadvantages among minority elders represent the continuation of lifelong disadvantages that begin in the earliest years of life. An important motivation for a comparison of the health-care needs of different age groups also arises from the fact that given a finite economic pie, different age groups necessarily compete for resources (Hayes-Bautista, Chapa, & Schink, 1988). Ethnic differences in access to health care, then, are confounded with age-based differences in coverage. Although nearly three-quarters of Medicaid participants are children in poor families, more than three-quarters of Medicaid revenues go to pay for the long-term care of the elderly and disabled (Liska, 2003). That minority Americans, including Mexican Americans, are at elevated risk of inadequate health-care coverage at all ages adds an ethnic dimension to age differences in health-care financing.

In this chapter, we draw on three data sets: the first a recently completed study of the lives of families in poverty and their response to welfare reform, the second an ongoing longitudinal study of the older Mexican American population of the Southwest that is now in its 10th year, and the third the Health and Retirement Study (HRS), which includes an oversample of Hispanics. We employ each to identify major correlates of economic vulnerability and of inadequate health-care coverage among these three age groups. We begin our examination, though, with data from the 2001 Current Population Survey (CPS) to identify the major sources of health-care coverage for children and adults from the three major Hispanic groups—Mexican Americans, Cuban Americans, and Puerto Ricans—and to compare their coverage with that of non-Hispanic blacks and whites.

In Table 23.1, we examine patterns of health insurance coverage among Hispanics of three age groups: children and adolescents younger than 18, working-age adults, and elderly persons 65 and older. The data reveal that although 75% of non-Hispanic white children are covered by a parent's employer-sponsored plan, only about half of non-Hispanic black and Cuban American children are covered by such private insurance. Forty-five percent of Puerto Rican and only 39% of Mexican American children are covered by their parents' plans. In the absence of employer-based coverage, Medicaid represents the most obvious alternative, and thus, the four minority groups display high rates of use of this program. Despite the relatively high rate of Medicaid coverage, though, the results show that substantial percentages of minority children do not participate. This also demonstrates the seriousness of the problem among Mexican American children and adolescents, more than a quarter of whom have no insurance of any sort.

The middle panel of Table 23.1 presents data on health insurance coverage among adults 18 to 64. Although a clear majority of non-Hispanic white adults report employer-sponsored health insurance, fewer than half of Mexican American or Puerto Rican adults report such coverage. The data clearly show

**Table 23.1**   Selected Type of Health Insurance Coverage for Persons Under 18 Years:
2001 by Race and Hispanic Ethnicity

| Type of Coverage | Under 18 Years | | | | |
|---|---|---|---|---|---|
| | Non-Hispanic White | Non-Hispanic Black | Mexican Origin | Cuban American | Puerto Rican |
| Employer | 75% | 51% | 39% | 52% | 45% |
| Medicaid | 15% | 38% | 35% | 27% | 42% |
| None | 7% | 14% | 26% | 18% | 11% |
| Total (in thousands) | 44,378 | 11,227 | 9,314 | 270 | 987 |
| | *Aged 18–64 Years* | | | | |
| Employer | 65% | 58% | 43% | 57% | 49% |
| Medicare | – | – | 2% | 4% | 5% |
| Medicaid | 5% | 14% | 8% | 8% | 22% |
| None | 13% | 24% | 45% | 25% | 23% |
| Total (in thousands) | 122,470 | 20,648 | 14,768 | 795 | 2,021 |
| | *65 Years and Older* | | | | |
| Employer | 36% | 29% | 17% | 15% | 17% |
| Medicare | 97% | 93% | 91% | 92% | 97% |
| Medicaid | 7% | 20% | 22% | 31% | 37% |
| None | .03% | 2% | 5% | 3% | .04% |
| Total (in thousands) | 27,973 | 2,801 | 992 | 311 | 213 |

SOURCE: U.S. Census Bureau, *Annual Demographic Supplement*, 2002, and unpublished tabulations for Hispanic subgroups.

NOTE: Respondents 15 and older were asked to indicate all forms of coverage a child living in the household had. We present only the most frequently reported. Categories may overlap.

that for adults publicly funded health-care coverage does not make up for the lack of private coverage. Although a substantial fraction of non-Hispanic blacks (14%) and Puerto Ricans (22%) report receiving Medicaid, among all groups rather large percentages report no coverage, a situation that is particularly serious for the four minority groups. Approximately one-quarter of black, Cuban American, and Puerto Rican adults report that they have no health insurance. The situation is even worse for Mexican Americans, though, 45% of whom report that they have no health insurance. This striking difference among Hispanics shows that Mexican Americans face rather unique and serious risks for inadequate coverage (Angel & Angel, 1996; National Council of La Raza, 1992; Valdez, Morganstern, et al., 1993).

These statistics underscore the complexity of the health-care coverage system in the United States and the differential vulnerability of various groups. The situation of Mexican Americans reveals that even among minority populations, other risk factors that are still poorly understood place certain groups at seriously elevated risk of inadequate health coverage. Such factors may relate to regional concentration and labor market differences, immigration status, language difficulties, and other barriers that increase the risk of inadequate coverage (Berk et al., 1996; Berk & Schur, 2001; Berk, Schur, Frankel, & Chavez, 2000). Mexican Americans are far less likely than any other group to be employed in managerial or professional occupations (National Council of La Raza, 1992). Mexican origin adults, and especially immigrants, are overrepresented in the service sector in which they are usually not offered employer-sponsored health insurance, or in which the premiums required for individual or family coverage place such coverage out of reach (Schur & Feldman, 2001).

The bottom panel of Table 23.1 provides coverage data for adults 65 and older, which clearly shows the equalizing effects of universal health insurance, in this case Medicare, which covers over 90% of each group. Yet important group differences remain. Although approximately 36% of non-Hispanic whites and 29% of non-Hispanic blacks report employer-based insurance, only about 15% of any of the three Hispanic groups report employer-based coverage. Such coverage can reflect continuing employment past age 65, but more importantly, it usually reflects the ownership of supplemental Medigap or long-term care insurance that covers health-care costs such as those for long-term care or prescription drugs and appliances that Medicare does not pay. Individuals without supplemental private coverage can face serious medical expenditures. Increasingly, private long-term care insurance is necessary to ensure that even a substantial middle-class estate is not consumed by nursing home costs. For middle-class retirees, such supplemental coverage is often part of a generous retirement package. Even when it is not part of a retirement package, middle-class incomes make the purchase of supplemental Medigap plans possible.

For the destitute elderly, Medicaid pays the premiums and other expenditures not covered by Medicare. Such dual eligibility reflects economic marginality and the table shows that older blacks and Hispanics are at elevated risk of falling into this category. As among other age groups, the working poor—or in the case of the elderly those with low retirement incomes that are too high to allow them to qualify for Medicaid—face particularly serious health-care financing problems. Both working age and retirement age minority group members often find themselves in this situation. In the CPS, more than 5% of older Mexican Americans report that they have no health insurance coverage. Whether this figure represents a misunderstanding of the survey question, a failure to qualify for Medicare, or simple nonparticipation is not clear. Nonetheless, that even a small fraction of older individuals do not participate in a universal program emphasizes the unique vulnerability of the entire group (Therrien & Ramirez, 2000; U.S. Census Bureau, 2003).

## WELFARE, CHILDREN, AND FAMILIES: A THREE-CITY STUDY

Given this clear Mexican American health-care financing disadvantage that persists over the life course, it would be useful to examine the correlates of inadequate coverage. As before, let us begin with children. A recently completed study of the response to welfare reform of poor Hispanic, African American, and non-Hispanic white families in Boston, Massachusetts, Chicago, Illinois, and San Antonio, Texas, provides new information about the health-care coverage of minority children. These three cities have diverse populations and very different welfare policies (Winston et al., 1999). The study was begun in 1999 and includes an intensive survey of approximately 2,400 poor families with children, approximately 40% of which were receiving cash welfare payments when they were interviewed. Seventy-seven percent of the families had incomes below the poverty line, and 73% were headed by single mothers (Winston et al., 1999). Extensive baseline information was obtained on one child per household and his or her caregiver, usually the mother. For present purposes, we focus upon the extent of health-care coverage among poor families. Detailed ethnographic interviews were completed with at least 50 families in each of the three cities, and family accounts of health insurance problems emerged frequently. The ethnography provides useful insights into the system and community-level barriers that poor families face in acquiring health care (Angel, Lein, & Henrici, 2006).

## Health-Care Coverage for Poor Children

One of the major reasons for the large number of uninsured children in the United States is that many children in poor families are not enrolled (Selden, Bantin, & Cohen, 1998). Differences in state eligibility criteria, as well as local administration of the program, are of major importance in determining who enrolls. Table 23.2 shows the rather dramatic differences among cities in Medicaid coverage among families with children. In Boston, 82% of families with incomes below 100% of poverty include a child who receives Medicaid, a figure similar to that for Chicago. In San Antonio, on the other hand, only 64% of families with household incomes below

100% of poverty receive Medicaid. The figure for the United States as a whole from the March 2000 Current Population Survey is 60%. As family income increases, Medicaid participation decreases, although it remains much higher in Boston than in Chicago or San Antonio. In San Antonio, only 5% of children in families with incomes between 150% and 200% of poverty receive Medicaid (Angel et al., 2006).

Hispanics in San Antonio are primarily of Mexican origin, so one might ask if the lower rates of coverage among Mexican American children generally reflect the fact that this group is heavily concentrated in Texas. Table 23.3 presents the results of two logistic regressions of (1) any health insurance and (2) Medicaid participation on several factors that potentially influence coverage among the poor, including race and Hispanic ethnicity, citizenship status of both mother and child, mother's marital status, the child's age, and city. In each Three-City Study household, extensive information was collected on one randomly selected "focal" child. These analyses refer to that child. The results are rather dramatic and reveal that even when these other factors are controlled, Mexican-origin children are only 29% as likely to be covered by any form of health insurance and 43% as likely to be covered by Medicaid as non-Mexican Hispanics, the reference group.

Table 23.3 reveals some interesting associations that reflect national and state policy

**Table 23.2**    Children Covered by Medicaid

| Family Income Relative to Federal Poverty | All 3 Cities | Boston | Chicago | San Antonio | March 2000 CPS |
|---|---|---|---|---|---|
| < 100% | 77% | 82% | 82% | 64% | 60% |
| 100–124% | 58% | 86% | 59% | 30% | 42% |
| 125–149% | 53% | 63% | 61% | 35% | 33% |
| 150–199% | 34% | 64% | 35% | 5% | 23% |

SOURCE: Adapted from Angel, Lein, and Henrici, 2006.

**Table 23.3** Determinants of Health Insurance Coverage for Children 18 and Younger Below 200% Poverty

| Independent Variable | Any Health Insurance | | Any Medicaid | |
|---|---|---|---|---|
| | Odds Ratio | Confidence Interval | Odds Ratio | Confidence Interval |
| Race/Hispanic Ethnicity | | | | |
| Mexican Origin | .29 | (.15–.56) | .43 | (.28–.67) |
| Black | .97 | (.54–1.75) | .89 | (.63–1.28) |
| Non-Hispanic Whites (Non-Mexican Hispanic) | 1.16 | (.48–2.78) | .54 | (.34–.86) |
| Citizenship Status | | | | |
| Child U.S. Citizenship | 4.29 | (2.41–7.63) | 2.21 | (1.34–3.66) |
| Mother U.S. Citizenship | .76 | (.51–1.15) | .59 | (.42–.82) |
| City | | | | |
| San Antonio | .49 | (.27–.90) | .60 | (.40–.89) |
| Chicago (Boston) | .85 | (.51–1.42) | .97 | (.71–1.31) |
| Mother's Marital Status | | | | |
| Cohabitating | .72 | (.40–1.28) | .63 | (.41–.97) |
| Spouse Present | .75 | (.55–1.03) | .45 | (.35–.57) |
| Spouse Absent (mother, never married) | .81 | (.50–1.31) | .57 | (.41–79) |
| Child's Age (in years) | .98 | (.95–1.00) | .92 | (.91–.94) |
| Sample size = 2,140 | | | | |

SOURCE: Three-City Study, New Analysis.

related to health-care coverage. Although mother's citizenship status is not significant at conventional levels in predicting insurance of any sort, the children of mothers who are U.S. citizens are only 59% as likely as those whose mothers are not citizens to receive Medicaid. This probably reflects an immigrant parent's greater reliance on public health coverage. On the other hand, the child's citizenship status greatly influences the probability that he or she will be covered by some form of health insurance. Citizen children are far more likely to have health insurance, including Medicaid, than are noncitizens. Most public programs base eligibility on U.S. citizenship, so this finding is to be expected (Zambrana & Logie, 2000). The table also reveals that children in San Antonio are less than half as likely as children in Boston, the reference category, to

be covered by any form of health insurance and only 60% as likely to be covered by Medicaid. Although the coefficient is slightly short of statistical significance, having a spouse present reduces the likelihood of having any form of health insurance. For Medicaid, on the other hand, the presence of a partner, whether he is living in the household or not, greatly reduces the probability of coverage. If a spouse is present in the household, the child is only 45% as likely as a child whose mother has never been married to be covered, revealing the serious marriage penalty that is part of the Medicaid program.

### Pre-Retirement Age Hispanics: Asset Poor

The health insurance disadvantage among Mexican-origin children continues into adulthood and old age. Ethnographic, as well as survey data from the Three-City Study, reveal a serious lack of coverage for the parents of the children in households with incomes below 200% of poverty. Except during pregnancy or as a result of serious chronic illness or disability, the United States provides no health-care safety net for adults. In the Three-City Study, mothers went without care or had incomplete care for serious illnesses that interfered with their ability to work. If occupational disadvantage and the lack of health insurance were confined to early adulthood, the situation of the group might not have serious long-term consequences. If, on the other hand, that disadvantage persists into mature adulthood, the situation has much more serious implications for health. For most families, the decade preceding retirement represents the pinnacle of economic achievement and security. This period of the life course also represents the launching pad for the retirement years. Economic uncertainty and inadequate health-care coverage in the 50s and early 60s bode ill for the retirement years.

To determine the extent and type of health insurance coverage among pre-retirement age Hispanics, we employ the first wave of the HRS, a nationwide survey of employment, assets, health, health insurance, and retirement plans among a nationally representative sample of 12,654 individuals aged 51 to 61 including oversamples of 2,064 blacks and 1,174 Hispanics. In this survey, health insurance included employer-based plans, privately purchased plans, Medicare, Medicaid, and veterans insurance.

Figure 23.1 presents data on the type of health insurance coverage among one cohort of pre-retirement age adults by race and Hispanic ethnicity. In this table, private includes both privately purchased plans, which constitute a small fraction of all insurance

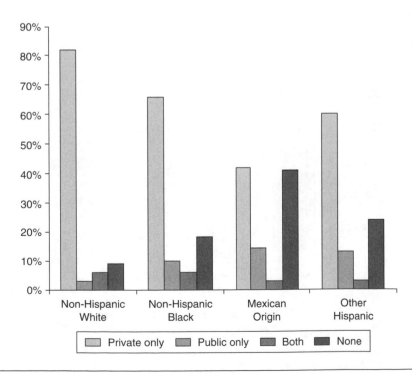

**Figure 23.1**   Health Insurance Coverage Among Persons 51–61 Years Old in 1992

SOURCE: Health and Retirement Study (HRS).

coverage, and employer-sponsored group plans. The figure reveals a high rate of private coverage among non-Hispanic white adults, but much lower levels of coverage among non-Hispanic blacks and other Hispanics. Among Mexican-origin individuals private (employer based) coverage is basically half of that of non-Hispanic whites. Forty percent report no health insurance of any form. The lack of health insurance at this age range places many of these individuals at serious risk of ill health and its longer-term consequences (Schur, Albers, & Berk, 1995). This is the point in the life course during which the consequences of chronic diseases, such as diabetes and hypertension, begin to take their toll.

The lack of health insurance is part of a package that includes low income and asset accumulation. By the time an individual or a couple reach the ages of 51 to 61, they have accumulated most of the wealth that they will ever have. Homes are close to being paid off and one's income is as high as it will probably get. Differences in wealth between groups during the pre-retirement years mean large differences in economic well-being and health during retirement. These differences have particularly profound implications for options in long-term care. Low income and a lack of retirement health benefits place minority Americans at serious risk of dependency on family or of incomplete and inadequate health care in old age.

Figure 23.2 presents data on the total value of the assets owned by families in different household types defined by race and Hispanic ethnicity, as well as by the marital status of the head. Female headship represents a major dimension of economic disadvantage given the traditionally lower lifetime earnings of women and the fact that many have not been continuously employed. This figure reveals stark differences in the total asset value of minority and nonminority households as well as between

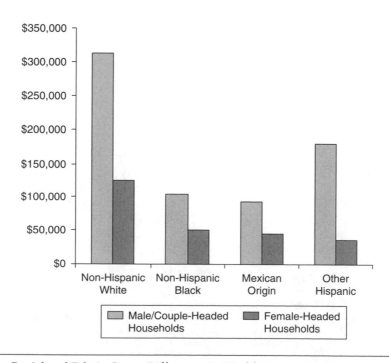

Figure 23.2    Racial and Ethnic Group Differences in Wealth Among Pre-Retirement Age Individuals in 1992

SOURCE: Health and Retirement Study (HRS)–Wave 1.

those headed by a couple or a male and those headed by a female. Even though the average pre-retirement age non-Hispanic white couple in the mid 1990s had more than $300,000 in total assets, the average Mexican American couple had less than $100,000 in wealth. Female-headed households in all groups are seriously asset poor. Analyses of employment patterns among the elderly by Flippen and Tienda (1996) suggest that retirement for older Hispanics is not the voluntary termination of a career but, rather, the end stage of a long period of unstable employment and joblessness. Such a career trajectory is one that results in inadequate asset accumulation and a high risk of late-life poverty (Flippen & Tienda, 1996).

## Elderly Hispanics: A Lack of Medigap Coverage

To assess health-care coverage among older Mexican American individuals, we employ data from a 10-year longitudinal study carried out in the southwestern United States (Angel, Angel, & Markides, 2002). The study, titled the Hispanic Established Population for Epidemiologic Studies of the Elderly (Hispanic-EPESE), has followed a cohort of 3,050 Mexican-origin individuals who were 65 or older and who lived in Arizona, California, Colorado, New Mexico, and Texas at the time of the first interview in 1993 and 1994. Detailed information on household demographics, economics, health status and health-care use was collected. The sample was re-contacted and much of the same information collected again in 1995–1996, 1998–1999, and 2000–2001. At each wave, information on individuals who were too incapacitated to respond for themselves was collected from a knowledgeable proxy. Nearly half of the sample was foreign-born, and more than half had household incomes below the poverty level.

Figure 23.3 presents information on health insurance coverage in this relatively poor sample of older Mexican Americans. It shows that Mexican-origin elderly are particularly dependent on Medicaid and that only 19% have private Medigap plans. Forty-one percent depend on Medicare alone. The lack of supplemental coverage places these individuals at serious risk of not receiving the care they need (Angel & Angel, 1997). Medicare physician coverage requires the payment of a monthly premium and a substantial fair-share cost is associated with hospital stays. In addition, Medicare does not cover the cost of eyeglasses, hearing aids, or other specialized medical devices and appliances. The costs of a medical encounter for an older person without supplemental coverage can be quite high. As at other ages, the lack of a supplemental Medigap plan is part of a package that includes a lifetime of employment in jobs that do not provide retirement health plans and a retirement income that can make the purchase of private coverage prohibitively expensive.

Medicaid represents the health-care safety net for the poor elderly. For those with incomes below or slightly above poverty Medicaid covers the costs of premiums and other costs associated with Medicare. Such individuals have come to be referred to as "dual eligible" because they qualify for both Medicare and Medicaid. Dual eligibility, therefore, is itself an indicator of vulnerability. Unfortunately, for those individuals with incomes above 200% of poverty, Medicaid is not available and if they do not have a private Medigap plan, these older individuals must rely on their own resources to pay for what Medicare will not. For that reason, the accumulated assets are particularly important.

What is particularly striking about Figure 23.3 is that 7% of these elderly Mexican American respondents report no health insurance of any kind, a figure higher than that for the nation as a whole (cf. Table 23.1) that reflects the unique disadvantage of those older individuals living along the U.S.–Mexico border. To make

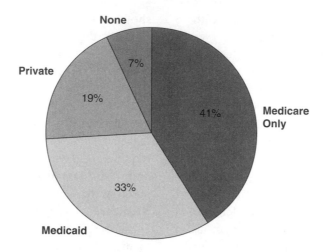

**Figure 23.3**     Health Insurance Coverage for Older Mexican Americans in the Southwestern United States

SOURCE: Hispanic EPESE–Version 2.

some sense of these findings, we present type of health insurance by nativity in Figure 23.4. Among the foreign-born, 12% report no insurance and only 10% report that they have any private Medigap insurance. Thirty-six percent are dual eligible. The data show, then, that nativity interacts with region and other factors to place Mexican-origin individuals in poorly paid service sector jobs in which they do not receive benefits. The disadvantage this group faces, therefore, arises from multiple sources and for a large fraction is life-long. This hardened disadvantage presents policymakers with a serious challenge in pro-viding adequate health-care coverage to the Mexican-origin population.

## DISCUSSION: EXPANDING HEALTH INSURANCE COVERAGE TO THE UNINSURED MEXICAN-ORIGIN POPULATION

We are left with the question of how the specific health-care financing needs of Mexican Americans of all ages can be addressed. A com-prehensive national health insurance system that would provide coverage to all residents on an equal basis would be the most direct solu-tion, albeit one that has proved to be politically unattainable. Short of that, we might suggest modifications to existing programs to help address the serious gaps in the health-care safety net that poor Americans, including those of Mexican origin, face. Among these sugges-tions are the following:

*Increase Outreach Efforts to Publicize State Children's Health Insurance Program.* The state funded health insurance program for low-income children (SCHIP) is one obvi-ous way to help address the health-care needs of children who do not qualify for Medicaid. Unfortunately, not all eligible children are covered. In Texas, for example, although more than 3.3 million children were covered by the state's program in 2000, more than 2 million low-income children who were eligible were not enrolled (Perry, Kannel, Valdez, & Chang, 2000). As part of a general solution, the fed-eral Medicare, Medicaid, and SCHIP Benefits Improvement and Protection Act of 2000 (BIPA) was enacted in December 2000 to improve outreach efforts. States were given permission to retain as much as 10%

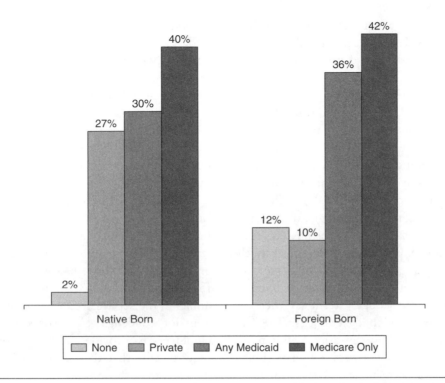

**Figure 23.4**    Health Insurance Coverage of Mexican-Origin Elderly Individuals by Nativity

SOURCE: Hispanic EPESE–Version 2.

of their 1998 SCHIP allotment for outreach activities. This gave states greater flexibility in identifying and enrolling children eligible for SCHIP (Centers for Medicare and Medicaid Services, 2002). It remains to be seen whether all states will take full advantage of this opportunity.

Despite ambitious state mass-media campaigns to encourage SCHIP enrollment, studies have shown that the lack of information, confusion about eligibility requirements, and administrative obstacles continue to pose significant barriers to participation (Carpenter & Kavanagh, 1998; Ross & Cox, 2000). Although health-care organizations, including hospitals and health departments, traditionally have played important roles in identifying children who are eligible for public insurance, other organizations including schools, employers, and community and religious groups are increasingly helping

children gain coverage (Felland & Benoit, 2001). In addition, most states have simplified complicated enrollment procedures for SCHIP and require re-certification only every 12 months (Ross, 2001). Unfortunately, as with Medicaid coverage, states differ in the extent to which they have succeeded in enrolling eligible children (Wiener & Brennan, 2002). Less complicated procedures for moving among insurance plans would also make access easier. In particular, families report confusion over the process by which they change from Medicaid to SCHIP to other insurance plans as the eligibility and access of different family members to different insurance plans change. Both survey and interview data from the Three-City Study indicate that households with medical insurance vary in both the source and amount of medical insurance coverage available to different family members.

Programs to reach rural children, including efforts in Texas, are potentially useful. In Texas, an experimental program along the U.S.–Mexico border named the Border Vision Fronteriza (BVF) program that was carried out in 1999 employed trained volunteers or promotores, the Spanish word for "promoter," which in this case refers to "health promoter," to educate Hispanic families about Medicaid and SCHIP. The project enrolled more than 10,325 children, greatly exceeding its initial goal of 4,500 children (Ross, 2002). Unfortunately, such efforts are expensive and administratively complex, and growing federal and state budget deficits will make them difficult to carry out over the longer term (Office of Management and Budget, 2002). The fact that many rural Mexican-origin children live in medically underserved counties limits the actual health impact of such outreach programs.

*Targeted Public Subsidies for Low-Income Adults.* As we noted earlier, Mexican-origin workers, like minority Americans generally, have lower access to employer-based healthcare coverage than more affluent groups. Under our present system, adults have limited access to public financing. Only pregnant women are routinely covered. In October 2002, Health and Human Services Secretary Tommy G. Thompson issued a new regulation that allows states to use the SCHIP to provide health coverage for prenatal care and delivery to women who do not qualify for Medicaid. The new rules allow states to provide coverage regardless of the mother's immigration status. New Jersey, Rhode Island, and Colorado had already obtained waivers to cover pregnant women using SCHIP funds. Because Hispanics have a high fertility rate and more than one-third of pregnant women in working families lack health insurance, they could benefit greatly (Guyer, Broaddus, & Dude, 2001). Once again, though, providing

adult coverage under SCHIP creates serious budgetary problems for states that not all will accept (National Governor's Association, 2002). Furthermore, family interviews in the Three-City Study indicate that medical coverage that ceases soon after delivery leaves women who experience chronic conditions exacerbated by pregnancy and delivery without medical coverage, often while they are still in treatment (Angel et al., 2006).

Except in the case of pregnancy, publicly financed health coverage for adults is almost nonexistent. For adults, employment remains the primary source of insurance, and this is likely to remain the case for the foreseeable future. Extending coverage to adults in the service sector has proved to be a major challenge. Short of subsidies for employers to provide coverage, along with requirements that they do so, it is hard to imagine that those who are not currently covered will soon be. Medical savings accounts, tax incentives for employers, and the other proposals that have been offered will probably not allow a working family to save enough for extensive care nor motivate service sector employers to shoulder large increases in employee compensation. Furthermore, such incentives for employee coverage have minimal effect on the large number of Mexican-origin workers who are self-employed or working for very small and family-operated businesses. Interviews with families in the Three-City Study indicate that workers who juggle several part-time or seasonal jobs remain either uncovered or have gaps in their medical insurance coverage. In our current political and economic environment, then, coverage for Mexican-origin working age adults remains elusive.

*Information and Outreach for Older Adults.* Lower rates of ownership of supplemental Medigap coverage among Mexican-origin seniors means that many lack access to the full range of services they need. What seems like a moderate individual contribution for a middle-class couple or individual may simply be more than a Mexican-origin Medicare beneficiary can afford. For this reason, it is important that all low-income families have the information they need about state assistance programs. Currently, several programs help pay Medicare premiums, deductibles, and coinsurance for eligible low-income Medicare beneficiaries. The most generous is the Qualified Medicare Beneficiaries (QMB) program, which pays Medicare Part A and B premiums, deductibles, and co-insurance. As is the case for all programs with state contributions, states vary in eligibility criteria and amount paid. To qualify for this program in Texas, an individual must have a modest income, less than $736 per month. As with programs for children, outreach efforts can increase participation among those who are eligible. Efforts by the Texas Department on Aging (now called the Department of Disability and Aging Services) to increase access to Medicaid services for "dual eligible" Hispanic retirees along the U.S.–Mexico border suggest that state and local partnerships that include community and faith-based organizations and other nongovernmental agencies, and that employ bilingual outreach specialists, can increase enrollment (Stockton, Bryant & Santoyo, 2001). As has been demonstrated with programs for children, administrative streamlining also helps. Making the application process easier for applicants, including a Spanish language version of a single application that combines eligibility requirements for both federal and state programs would make it easier for elderly Mexican Americans to apply (Carliner, 2002). Three City Study family interviews indicate that the lack of medical coverage among older adults has potentially serious implications for poor families that include an older grandparent or that assume other responsibilities for aging adults. In these families working mothers of young children are often burdened with the additional responsibility of providing care to older relatives who often do not receive the medical treatment they need or do not receive financing for goods and services that would simplify the care giving task for the care provider.

## CONCLUSION

The United States is unique among developed nations in having no universal health-care financing program for all citizens and in linking health insurance coverage almost exclusively to employment. The definition of a good job in the United States has evolved to include generous retirement and health benefits. In the best of circumstances, those health benefits continue into old age as part of a generous retirement package. A large body of research reveals the shortcomings of this system, especially for the unemployed and those employed in the service sector. If health insurance is a job benefit toward which both the employer and employee must contribute, it is unlikely to be part of the package offered to low-income workers or to be something that they could afford if it were offered.

The findings of the Three-City Study, the HRS, and the Hispanic-EPESE, and other data all show that from birth to death group-specific factors influence a family's ability to pay for health care (Angel et al., 2006). Mexican American children face barriers to enrollment in Medicaid and other health insurance programs that we do not yet fully understand. For adults, factors related to nativity, citizenship status, and literacy play a role. Among the elderly, similar factors reduce access to Medigap coverage. What is clear from the Three-City Study is that the lives of the poor are highly unstable and that relatively minor adversities can disrupt routines and place a family at risk of inadequate coverage (Angel et al., 2006). When illness strikes a middle-class family, employer-sponsored health insurance covers the cost, and the family itself usually has other resources with which to adapt. Among the poor, health crises are often disastrous, and given their low incomes and few assets, such families have few material resources with which to cope. Many observers have noted what has been called "churning" in health-care coverage among the poor as families move from private sources of coverage to public sources to no coverage at all. The only comprehensive solution for our nation's health-care coverage crisis would be governmentally sponsored financing as in Canada. Barring such a comprehensive approach, the only solutions are partial and entail efforts to facilitate the enrollment of eligible individuals in existing programs. Unfortunately, for working age adults, the options remain limited.

## REFERENCES

Angel, R. J., & Angel, J. L. (1996). The extent of private and public health insurance coverage among adult Hispanics. *Gerontologist, 36*(3), 332–340.

Angel, R. J., & Angel, J. L. (1997). *Who will care for us? Aging and long-term care in multicultural America.* New York: New York University Press.

Angel, R. J., Angel, J. L., & Markides, K. S. (2002). Stability and change in health insurance among older Mexican Americans: Longitudinal evidence from the Hispanic EPESE. *American Journal of Public Health, 92*(8), 1264–1271.

Angel, R. J., Lein, L., & Henrici, J. (2006). *Poor families in America's health care crisis.* New York: Cambridge University Press.

Berk, M. L., Albers, L. A., & Schur, C. L. (1996). The growth in the U.S. uninsured population: Trends in Hispanic subgroups, 1977 to 1992. *American Journal of Public Health, 86*(4), 572–576.

Berk, M. L., & Schur, C. (2001). The effect of fear on access to care among undocumented Latino immigrants. *Journal of Immigrant Health, 3*(3), 151–156.

Berk, M. L., Schur, C., Frankel, M., & Chavez, L. (2000). Health care use and undocumented Latino immigrants. *Health Affairs, 19*(4), 51–64.

Carliner, D. (2002). Getting the elderly their due. *Health Affairs, 21*(6), 198–201.

Carpenter, M. B., & Kavanagh, L. (1998). *Outreach to children: Moving from enrollment to ensuring access.* National Education Center in Maternal and Child Health. Washington, DC: Georgetown University.

Centers for Medicare and Medicaid Services. SMDL #01-021. Retrieved November 11, 2002, from http://cms.hhs.gov/schip/sho7051a.asp

De la Torre, A., Friis, R., Hunter, H. R., & Garcia, L. (1996). The health insurance status of U.S. Latino women: A profile from the 1982–84 HHANES. *American Journal of Public Health, 86*(4), 533–537.

Doty, M. M., & Ives, B. L. (2002). *Quality of health care for Hispanic populations: Findings from the Commonwealth Fund 2001 Health Care Quality Survey.* Publication #526. New York: Commonwealth Fund.

Felland, L. E., & Benoit, A. (2001). *Communities play key role in extending public health insurance to children:* Issue Brief No. 44. Washington, DC: Center for Studying Health System Change.

Flippen, C., & Tienda, M. (1996). Labor force behavior of Hispanic elderly: Insights from the HRS. *HRS/AHEAD Working Paper Series 96–032.* Ann Arbor: University of Michigan.

Giachello, A. L. (1992). Hispanics and health care. In P. S. Cafferty & W. C. McCready (Eds.), *Hispanics in the United States* (pp. 159–194). New Brunswick, NJ: Transaction.

Guyer, J., Broaddus, M., & Dude, A. (2001). *Millions of mothers lack health insurance coverage.* Washington, DC: Center on Budget and Policy Priorities.

Halfon, N. D., Wood, L., Valdez, R. B., Pereyra, M., & Duan, N. (1997). Medicaid enrollment and utilization of appropriate health services by Latino children in inner-city Los Angeles. *Journal of the American Medical Association, 277*(8), 636–641.

Hayes-Bautista, D. E., Chapa, J., & Schink, W. O. (1988). *The burden of support: Young Latinos in an aging society.* Stanford, CA: Stanford University Press.

Himmelstein, D. U., Warren, E., Thorne, D., & Woolhandler, S. (2005). MarketWatch: Illness and injury as contributors to bankruptcy. *Health Affairs Web Exclusive.*

Iannotta, J. G. (Ed.). (2002). *Emerging issues in Hispanic health: Summary of a workshop.* Washington, DC: National Academies Press.

Lillie-Blanton, M. D., Leigh, W. A., & Alfaro-Corre, I. A. (1996). *Achieving equitable access: Studies of health care issues affecting Hispanics and African Americans.* Washington, DC: Joint Center for Political and Economic Studies.

Liska, D. (2003). Number A-8 in Series, *Assessing new federalism: Issues and options for states.* Washington, DC: Urban Institute. Retrieved January 11, 2003, from http://newfederalism.urban.org/html/anf_a8.htm

Mills, R. J. (2002, September). U.S. Census Bureau, health insurance coverage: 2001. *Current Population Reports,* P60-220. Retrieved June 4, 2007, from http://www2.census.gov/prod2/popscan/p60-220.pdf

National Council of La Raza. (1992). *Hispanics and health insurance.* Washington, DC: Labor Council for Latin American Advancement.

National Governor's Association. (2002). HR-15. *The state children's health insurance program (S-CHIP) policy.* Retrieved June 4, 2007, from http://www.nga.org/portal/site/nga/menuitem.8358ec82f5b198d18a27811050 1010a0/?vgnextoid=20da9e2f1b091010VgnVCM1000001a01010aRCRD

Office of Management and Budget. (2002). *Analytic perspectives: Budget of the U.S. government, fiscal year 2003* (p. 297). Washington, DC: Author.

Perry, M., Kannel, S., Valdez, R. B., & Chang, C. (2000, January). *Medicaid and children: Overcoming barriers to enrollment.* Kaiser Commission on Medicaid and the Uninsured.

Ross, D. C. (2001). Reducing the number of uninsured children: Outreach and enrollment efforts. Testimony from Center on Budget and Policy Priorities before the Senate Finance Committee, March 15. Retrieved November 11, 2002, from http://www.cbpp.org/3-15-01dcrtest.htm#N_2_

Ross, D. C., & Cox, L. (2000, October). *Making it simple: Medicaid for children and CHIP income eligibility guidelines and enrollment procedures.* Washington, DC: Center on Budget and Policy Priorities. The Kaiser Commission on Medicaid and the Uninsured.

Ross, H. (2002). Border Vision Fronteriza: Tapping into community workers and volunteers. *Closing the Gap Newsletter,* 9. Washington, DC: U.S. Department of Health and Human Services.

Santos, R., & Seitz, P. (2002). Benefit coverage for Latino and Latina workers. In S. M. Perez (Ed.), *Moving up the economic ladder: Latino workers and the nation's future prosperity.* Washington, DC: National Academies Press.

Schur, C., & Feldman, J. (2001). *Running in place: How job characteristics, immigrant status, and family structure keep Hispanics uninsured*. New York: Commonwealth Fund.

Schur, C. L., Albers, L. A., & Berk, M. L. (1995). Health care use by Hispanic adults: financial vs. non-financial determinants. *Health Care Financing Review, 17*(2), 71–88.

Selden, T. M., Bantin, J. S., & Cohen, J. W. (1998). Medicaid's problem children: Eligible but not enrolled. *Health Affairs, 17*(3), 192–200.

Starfield, B. 2000. Evaluating the state children's health insurance program: Critical considerations. *Annual Review of Public Health, 21,* 569–585.

Stockton, J., Bryant, R., & Santoyo, L. (2001, December). *Enrollment of Hispanic dual-eligibles on the U.S./Mexico border*. Austin: Texas Department on Aging.

Sullivan, T. A., Warren, E., & Westbrook, J. L. (2000*). Fragile middle class: Americans in debt*. New Haven, CT: Yale University Press.

Therrien, M., & Ramirez, R. (2000). The Hispanic population in the United States. March 2000: *Current Population Reports*. P-20-535. Retrieved November 20, 2002, from http://www.census.gov/population/socdemo/hispanic/p20-535/p20-535.pdf

U.S. Census Bureau. (2003, January 2). Unpublished tabulations, Robert J. Mills. Washington, DC.

Valdez, R. B., Giachello, A., Rodriguez-Trias, H., Gomez, P., & De la Rocha, C. (1993). Improving access to health care in Latino communities. *Public Health Reports, 108,* 534–539.

Valdez, R. B., Morganstern, H., Brown, R., Wyn, R., Wang, C., & Cumberland, W. (1993). Insuring Hispanics against the costs of illness. *Journal of the American Medical Association, 269*(7), 889–894.

Weinick, R. M., Zuvekas, S. H., & Cohen, J. W. (2000). Racial and ethnic differences in access to and use of health care services, 1977 to 1996. *Medical Care Research and Review, 57*(1), 36–54.

Wiener, J. M., & Brennan, N. (2002). *Assessing the new federalism: Recent changes in health policy for low-income people in Texas, 23,* 12.

Winston, P., Angel, R. J., Burton, L. M., Chase-Lansdale, P. L., Cherlin, A. J., Moffit, R. A., et al. (1999). *Welfare, children and families: A three-city study—overview and design*. Baltimore: Johns Hopkins University. Retrieved January 11, 2003, from http://www.jhu.edu/~welfare?overviewanddesign.pdf

Zambrana, R. E., & Logie, L. A. (2000). Latino child health: Need for inclusion in the U.S. national discourse. *American Journal of Public Health, 90*(12), 1827–1833.

# CHAPTER 24

# Federal Policy Efforts to Improve Outcomes Among Disadvantaged Families by Supporting Marriage and Family Stability

M. Robin Dion and Alan J. Hawkins

There is broad consensus that family structure is inextricably linked with poverty and the well-being of children. These factors go hand-in-hand so often that it becomes difficult to disentangle how they relate to one another. For example, does the relationship between single parenting and low income mean that rearing children without a partner is likely to lead to poverty, or is poverty itself likely to lead to single-parent family structures? Does the influence flow in both directions? Regardless of the direction of the association between income and family structure, studies show that children who grow up poor or without one of their biological parents are more likely than others to be at risk for adverse developmental outcomes. This paper reviews the connections between poverty, family structure, and child well-being, explains the rationale for a new policy strategy that is focused on intervening more directly at the level of family structure, and describes several major federal initiatives underway to develop and test the new strategies.

## FAMILY STRUCTURE, POVERTY, AND CHILD WELL-BEING

### Family Structure and Poverty

Numerous studies show that single-parent families are generally at greater risk for being poor than are families that are headed by married parents (McLanahan, 1997; McLanahan & Sandefur, 1994; Waite & Gallagher, 2000). According to a congressional report, the poverty rate for single mothers with children in 1998 was 39.2%, compared with 7.8% for families in which an adult male was present (U.S. House of Representatives, 2001). Both marital dissolution and failure to form marital unions are substantial contributors to children's developmental problems and poverty. Moreover, nonmarital childbearing is strongly associated with welfare dependence. Data collected on the nation's welfare program in 1999 showed that most recipients were single mothers and nearly three-quarters had never been married (U.S. Census Bureau, 2000). Thus, only about 24% of single mothers receiving welfare were divorced, separated, or widowed—whereas in the general population over 50% of single mothers had been married at some point (Jacobson, 2002). Fully one-third of all births in the United States today are to individuals who are not married. Although many of these parents may be cohabiting with a partner at the time of the conception, cohabitation is known to be a less stable form of family structure (Graefe & Lichter, 1999; Seltzer, 2000; Smock, 2000), meaning that many children are ultimately at risk of being raised without one of their parents and in poverty.

The association between family structure and poverty is thought to be bidirectional. Raising children without the benefit of a second adult's income is likely to lead to lower overall income. Although payment of child support has increased considerably, families at the lower rungs of the economic ladder are less likely to receive child support. Looking at the correlation in the reverse direction, poverty may lead to nonmarital childbearing and divorce. Poor women may feel that they have few choices when it comes to finding a "marriageable" partner, and yet be reluctant to give up on childbearing (Edin, 2000; Edin & Kefalas, 2005). The stresses of living in poverty may also make it more difficult to maintain positive relationships of the type that could lead to (or maintain) stable and satisfying marriages. Individuals raised by lone parents in poverty may have little exposure to models of healthy marriage and perhaps may lack understanding of how to work as a team in a relationship without sacrificing one's own needs.

## Family Structure and Child Well-Being

Multiple analyses of data from large, nationally representative samples confirm that family structure matters for children's development. Regardless of whether single parenthood arises because of divorce or a lack of marriage, data indicate that children growing up with an unmarried parent are at greater risk for less favorable developmental outcomes. McLanahan and Sandefur (1994) found that children who lived with their own married parents at least through age 16 were more likely to graduate from high school or college, more likely to become economically self-sufficient as adults, and less likely to become teen parents or to be involved in drug and alcohol abuse or juvenile delinquency than children who grew up without one of their biological parents in the home. With the exception of widowhood, the effects of this study, even controlling for a range of background characteristics, were consistent regardless of whether the single mother was divorced or separated or had never married at all.

Other research confirms that the outcomes for children of divorce are unfortunately similar to those of children whose parents never marry. For example, a meta-analysis of 92 studies comparing children of divorced parents with children whose parents were continuously married showed that the former had significantly less favorable academic achievement, psychological adjustment, behavior, self-concept, and social relationships, including the quality of relationships with parents (Amato, 2001; Amato & Booth, 1997; Amato & Keith, 1991).

## Poverty and Child Well-Being

Researchers have asked which is more important—family structure or poverty—in predicting children's developmental outcomes. An analysis conducted by 12 research teams relying on 9 separate data sources supported previous findings that a non-intact family structure has negative consequences for children across a broad range of outcomes (Duncan & Brooks-Gunn, 1997). Across these analyses, children of divorced or never-married mothers nearly always had lower educational attainment and more behavioral and psychological problems. When income and other key background factors of families were considered in the analyses, these effects were attenuated somewhat, but single parenting was still associated with less favorable child development outcomes.

## THE HOPE OF INTERVENTION

Figure 24.1 shows the linkages among family structure, poverty, and child outcomes. To address the problem of poverty, policymakers have focused primarily on intervening at the economic level—the right side of the diagram. A key goal of the 1996 welfare reform legislation and its reauthorization a decade later was to encourage employment and economic self-sufficiency among poor families. Theoretically, improving the family economic situation can also lead to improved child well-being and more stable family structure. Several experimental studies have been conducted to examine the effects of welfare reform on both family formation decisions and child well-being (for reviews, see Bos, Crosby, Duncan, Huston, & Morris, 2001; Grogger, Karolyn, & Klerman, 2002).

In general, the results of experimental studies from a broad range of states show little evidence that requiring welfare recipients to work has resulted in either extensive harm or widespread benefit to children. Effects tended to depend on child age and generosity of welfare benefits. Only one of a range of experimental studies of the effects of welfare reform showed positive impacts on family structure. In that study, married or cohabiting couples in the intervention group received greater economic incentives for employment compared with those in the control group and were less likely to be divorced 7 years later (Genettian, 2003). On a national level, helping single parents go to work has clearly reduced their dependence on government benefits, but it remains unclear how many of these families have been lifted out of poverty, and most welfare recipients remain single parents.

Intervening on the left side of the diagram is the new policy approach that is being implemented as an addition to the antipoverty strategy of increasing attachment to the labor force. This emerging policy focuses directly on preventing the causes of family instability by intervening at the level of the couple's relationship. Policymakers do not appear to be conceiving of this strategy as a substitute for interventions that provide supports for work (Haskins & Sawhill, 2003). Rather, using policy to help families gain the skills and information needed to maintain (or enter and maintain) stable and healthy marriages is being considered because there are strong reasons

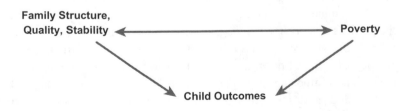

**Figure 24.1**   Linkages Among Family Structure, Poverty, and Child Outcomes

to think such an approach would have additional beneficial effects on both child well-being and poverty. These policies at the federal level are circumscribed under the rubric of the government's "Healthy Marriage Initiative."

## RATIONALE FOR SOCIAL POLICY EXPERIMENTATION TO STRENGTHEN MARRIAGE

As part of the Healthy Marriage Initiative, policymakers have been exploring how interventions could be developed to help couples form and sustain healthy marriages to provide children with greater emotional and economic stability and potentially reduce poverty. Specifically, policymakers are considering such things as promoting marriage education services for disadvantaged couples, supporting communitywide campaigns to strengthen marriages and reduce divorce, and changing tax policies and social service program participation rules that penalize the choice to marry. Understandably, scholars' reactions to this new line of policy experimentation run the gamut from hostility (Coltrane & Adams, 2003; Duggan, 2004) to skepticism (Coontz & Folbre, 2002) to constructive criticism and cautious optimism (Ooms, 2002; Parke, 2003) to enthusiasm (Gallagher, 2004). Moreover, dozens of journalists have weighed in on this policy experimentation as well (Whitehead & Blankenhorn, 2004), with most arguing that the initiative was foolhardy, an untested "brave new world," or fiscally irresponsible. A few journalists argued that the initiative was a logical next step in addressing poverty and helping children and families (Winkler, 2004).

Much of the public's reactions to marriage promotion policy, however, come from misperceptions of the policies and the rationale behind them. Thus, it is important to understand the background and context from which the current policies and initiatives have sprung.

First, researchers have increasingly recognized that a stable, healthy marriage is the optimal environment for children's positive development. Although many children do well outside the protective boundaries of marriage, non-intact family structures are still associated with increased risks for children's social, intellectual, and moral development (Amato & Booth, 1997; Hetherington & Kelly, 2002; McLanahan & Sandefur, 1994). Moreover, marriage is associated with men's and women's well-being. Of course, the more positive outcomes among married families exist at least in part because those who are better off are more likely to select into marriage and maintain that marriage anyway. But good research that controls for this possibility still shows positive outcomes for marriage beyond selection effects (Nock, 1997; Waite & Gallagher, 2000).

One way to look at the new policies and programs for supporting marriage is that they may simply enhance and increase the naturally occurring selection process. That is, if programs prepare couples to have healthier relationships and equip them with the skills and supports known to be associated with healthy marriage, the result could be that more "select into" marriage (or employ the skills and supports to maintain a healthy marriage). The Healthy Marriage Initiative in some ways is intended to do just that: not to push people into marriage but, rather, to provide support for those who want to build or keep a solid and stable marriage.

Second, this growing recognition that stable, healthy marriages are a critical element of the social infrastructure was recognized in the 1996 Temporary Assistance for Needy Families (TANF) welfare reform legislation. One of the important goals of the legislation was to promote married, two-parent families. Thus, the passage of this legislation motivated policymakers to think more directly about family structure as a point of policy intervention. In addition, legislation reauthorizing TANF, which passed and was signed into law in 2006, addresses this issue more concretely by allocating $500 million over 5 years to fund a set of efforts to support the formation and maintenance of healthy marriages and reduce divorces. Much of the marriage support funds will be spent on programs to make marriage education services available to a wider audience, especially to more disadvantaged individuals and couples. Legislation specifies that these funds are to be used to support eight allowable activities: (1) media campaigns to raise awareness of the importance of marriage and the skills needed to increase marital stability and health; (2) education in high schools on the value of marriage, relationship skills, and budgeting; (3) marriage education, marriage skills, and relationship skills programs (that may include parenting skills, financial management, conflict resolution, and job and career advancement) for nonmarried pregnant women and nonmarried expectant fathers; (4) pre-marital education and marriage skills training for engaged couples and for couples or individuals interested in marriage; (5) marriage enhancement and marriage skills training for married couples; (6) divorce reduction programs that teach relationship skills; (7) marriage mentoring programs that use married couples as role models and mentors in at-risk communities; and (8) programs to reduce the disincentives to marriage in means-tested aid programs, if offered in conjunction with any activity described previously.

Federal policymakers point out that the Healthy Marriage Initiative funding is not subtracting from other funding for single parents, like cash assistance or child-care support. Rather, the funds are being reallocated from other sources, such as the so-called Out-of-Wedlock-Childbirth Bonus. In addition, as much as $50 million a year for 5 years will be allocated for fatherhood programs to support efforts to strengthen father-child relationships, especially in at-risk communities. Many of these programs also may include efforts to strengthen the relationship between fathers and mothers.

A growing marriage education movement in the United States is a third part of the rationale for experimenting with social policy to strengthen marriages (Institute for American Values, 2004). Unlike marital therapy, marriage education is primarily preventative intervention and is often done in group settings rather than one-on-one therapeutic settings. Although programs differ in several respects, they generally seek to teach couples the skills shown in empirical research to be associated with successful relationships, such as constructive communication and conflict management, and strategies for building empathy, affection, and commitment (see Dion, 2005, and Dion et al., 2003, Chapter III, for reviews). Marriage educators intervene at various times in the life course and use a range of settings with different target populations with the purpose of enhancing marital relationships and preventing marital breakdown (Hawkins, Carroll, & Doherty, 2004).

Increasing evidence indicates that research-based principles of healthy relationships and marriage can be taught and learned to improve relationships and prevent some divorce. Previous meta-analytic studies have concluded that relationship and marriage education efforts are generally effective (Carroll & Doherty, 2003; Giblin, Sprenkle, & Sheehan, 1985; Reardon-Anderson, Stagner, Macomber, & Murray, 2005; Wampler & Butler, 1999). These meta-analytic studies have some limitations because they reviewed a narrow portion of the marriage education spectrum (e.g., premarital education only, Carroll & Doherty, 2003); they focused only on one particular program (e.g., Couples Communication; Wampler & Butler, 1999); they failed to differentiate marital therapy from marital education programs (Reardon-Anderson et al., 2005), or they were conducted more than 20 years ago and thus do not include more recent programs (Giblin et al., 1985). Nevertheless, the most recent and comprehensive meta-analytic study of the effectiveness of marriage education addresses these limitations and confirms that relationship and marriage education programs are generally effective (Fawcett, Hawkins, & Blanchard, 2006).

Although marriage education programs generally appear to be effective, important questions have yet to be adequately addressed. Perhaps most important among those unanswered questions is how effective these efforts will be to help disadvantaged and culturally diverse individuals and couples to form and sustain healthy relationships and marriages. A substantial number of high-quality studies are underway now to address this important gap in the research literature. (We discuss some of these efforts later in this chapter.)

Similarly, a fourth part of the rationale for experimenting with social policy to strengthen marriages comes from high-quality research on the aspirations of lower-income, unmarried couples with children, or fragile families. More than one-third of all births in the United States today are to unmarried parents, with proportions far higher in particular subgroups. However, findings from the national Fragile Families and Child Wellbeing Study show that a large proportion—more than 80%—of unwed parents in urban settings are living together or romantically involved at the birth of their child, and most of these—about half—expect to marry (Bendheim-Thoman Center for Research on Child Wellbeing, 2002; 2003). Longitudinal data with these families show that without intervention, they fail to achieve their aspirations for marriage. This work has encouraged policymakers to think about ways they could assist these fragile families to achieve their dreams of a stable, healthy marriage rather than maintain a laissez-faire attitude about family structure.

A fifth part of the rationale for social policy experimentation comes from research showing that disadvantaged married couples face greater challenges to maintaining their marriages. Many disadvantaged men and women marry (Fein, Burnstein, Fein, & Lindberg, 2003), but face higher risks of marital dissolution (Bramlett & Mosher, 2002, Table 21; Heaton, 2002; Lichter, Graefe, & Brown, 2003; Raley & Bumpass, 2003). And disadvantaged women who marry but later divorce appear to experience deeper poverty than their never-married counterparts do (Lichter et al., 2003). Lichter and his colleagues conclude from their research: "Without also strengthening fragile *marriages,* marriage promotion initiatives are unlikely to provide a long-term solution to poverty; indeed, they could make matters worse for disadvantaged women if they separate or divorce" (2003, p. 80, italics added). Recognizing this challenge, policymakers have planned to support programs and policies that will strengthen and nurture relationships among disadvantaged married couples.

To summarize, the rationale for the federal Healthy Marriage Initiative includes at least five points: (1) stable, healthy marriages are optimal developmental contexts for children (and adults); (2) TANF legislation calls for promoting two-parent, married families; (3) a marriage education movement is showing some success at providing couples with the skills and knowledge needed to form and sustain healthy marriages; (4) most fragile family couples have aspirations for marriage; and (5) disadvantaged, married couples face greater challenges in maintaining a healthy marriage. The following section outlines some of the federal policy experimentation to strengthen marriages.

## CURRENT POLICY EXPERIMENTATION TO STRENGTHEN MARRIAGE

Although many privately sponsored marriage education programs exist across the country, they are often small and only recently have a few begun to cater to disadvantaged populations. The Administration for Children and Families (ACF) of the U.S. Department of Health and Human Services has been encouraging and overseeing the development of healthy marriage initiatives in a variety of ways, including making grants to state and local government agencies as well as community and faith-based organizations to add marriage and relationship strengthening services to existing public sector service systems, including child welfare, child support, refugee resettlement, and financial literacy and asset development programs. With the substantial new funding reserved especially for marriage-support activities, the agency is poised to award a large number of grants, on a competitive basis, to states and local organizations to develop and implement programs in accordance with the eight allowable activities specified in the Deficit Reduction Act of 2006.

To learn what works, ACF is also encouraging the careful and systematic development of specific policies and programs that will be subjected to rigorous evaluation to determine effectiveness. The agency's Office of Planning, Research, and Evaluation has already funded a handful of large-scale projects that will involve the demonstration and evaluation of multiple programs across the country, in partnership with state agencies or private organizations. Within each large project, multiple local programs will use similar strategies and approaches to ensure a fair and adequate test of the intervention model. In addition, ACF also is funding the National Healthy Marriage Resource Center. Each of these initiatives is described later.

## Building Strong Families Project

Building Strong Families (BSF) was the first of the three major demonstration/ evaluation projects to be funded. It was awarded in October 2002 to prime contractor Mathematica Policy Research. The research team includes a wide range of expert consultants and subcontractors: Manpower Demonstration Research Corporation (MDRC), the Urban Institute, Decision Information Resources, and Public Strategies. The foundation for the project was developed from two earlier Mathematica studies begun in early 2000 that developed a conceptual framework for designing, implementing, and evaluating a large-scale program for unmarried couples who are expecting or have just had a child together (Dion et al., 2003). The motivation for these projects flowed directly from the recognition that (1) a substantial proportion of all births are to unmarried parents, (2) the children in these families are at high risk for family instability, poverty, and poor developmental outcomes, and (3) intriguing new findings suggest that most unwed couples are in fact romantically involved and interested in marriage around the time their child is born (Carlson, McLanahan, & England, 2004).

BSF is a 9-year project that involves two major phases: (1) program design, development, and implementation, and (2) process study and rigorous random-assignment evaluation of outcomes. The program development phase of the project has been an intensive and substantial effort because marriage education programs to help unmarried expectant couples improve their relationships and explore marriage did not widely exist before BSF. Traditional social services programs lacked a focus on couples, instead serving either single mothers or single fathers. Standard marriage education programs did focus on couples, but were rare or nonexistent in culturally diverse, low-income communities.

Unmarried couples with children are often racially and ethnically diverse (almost 70% of all births to African Americans are nonmarital), have lower levels of educational attainment and earnings, and many have children by former partners (Carlson et al., 2004). Because most marriage education programs have been used with white, middle-class engaged or married couples, BSF sponsored the development and adaptation of research-based curricula for unmarried parents by bringing together two kinds of expert researchers and practitioners: those who focus on low-income unwed parent families, and those who focus on marriage and relationships. These experts adapted and tailored the curriculum materials to be specific to the unique needs of low-income, culturally diverse, romantically involved unmarried couples expecting a child.

Although focusing directly on couples' relationship skills and interaction is the core and central component of BSF, research shows that fragile families experience a range of challenges that can impinge upon the successful development of relationships and marriage. For example, lack of employment among men may serve as a deterrent to marriage (Testa & Krogh, 1995; Wilson, 1987). In recognition of these challenges, the BSF program model includes support for other needed family services. The model includes three major components:

• *Skills, Information and Knowledge to Support Healthy Couple Relationships and Marriage.* Research-based curricula adapted and supplemented specifically for the target population is used to teach relationship skills and support marriage in this core program component. Material covers standard topics such as communication and conflict management skills, as well as strategies for building fondness, affection, and mutual trust. Issues shown in research and practice to be of particular relevance for low-income unwed parents are also included, such as how to build commitment, how to manage emotions to prevent the escalation of conflicts, and the use of strategies for dealing constructively with the parents of children from previous relationships.

• *Family Support Services to Enhance Marriageability.* Depending on each family's needs, services are provided for employment issues, parenting education, mental health conditions, substance abuse, or other personal or family challenges that can impede the formation and maintenance of strong relationships and marriage.

• *Family Coordinators to Assess Needs and Provide Ongoing Support.* Specially trained coordinators assess each family's needs and match them to the most appropriate services, encourage ongoing program participation and completion, provide sustained emotional support, and reinforce the skills couples learn in the core educational sessions.

After a period of identifying numerous potential program sponsors at the local level and guiding development of their programs, sites in seven states were selected to participate in the BSF pilot. Most of these organizations already served low-income families in various other ways and were interested in building a focus on relationships and marriage into their services. A study of the pilot sites' experiences implementing the program has provided information on lessons learned during this early stage (Dion, Avellar, Zaveri, & Hershey, 2006). After this period of program development, implementation, and pilot testing, the project team selected all seven sites to participate in the full experimental evaluation (Baton Rouge; Baltimore; Orange and Broward Counties in Florida; Marion, Lake, Allen, and Miami Counties in Indiana; Oklahoma City; Atlanta; and Houston and San Angelo, Texas). As many as 6,000 couples who volunteer for the program are being randomly assigned to either the BSF intervention or to a control group. Their outcomes are being followed over a period of 3 to 5 years, including longitudinal assessments of family structure, quality of couple relationships, marital stability, economic well-being, parenting behavior, and engagement of fathers. The couples' children will also be assessed for their development along several dimensions, including cognitive, social, and emotional outcomes.

## Supporting Healthy Marriages Project

Helping unmarried parents prepare for a healthy marriage cannot be the only strategy to address issues of family formation in the low-income population. Many low-income individuals do marry, and research suggests that they are at higher risk for dissolution than other couples. More than 8 million married couples live below 200% of the federal poverty level. Therefore, a second ACF project specifically targets low-income married couples: Supporting Healthy Marriages (SHM). In late 2003, ACF contracted with MDRC and subcontractors Abt Associates and Child Trends to conduct a major, long-term research project of the potential of marriage education services to positively affect low-income married couples and couples planning to marry. The project brings together an experienced group of social policy researchers and an impressive consulting group of national scholars.

Like the BSF project, the project has two major phases: (1) program design, development, and implementation and (2) rigorous evaluation, including both process and impact evaluation. Careful, up-front work with a nationally recognized team of expert consultants has developed a program model that includes a mandatory marriage education component, an optional component with links to supplemental services, and an optional set of policy changes to reduce policy disincentives for marriage. The target population for SHM programs is low-income couples with children or of childbearing age, who are married or planning to marry. Curriculum appropriate to this target population is being developed or modified from existing programs. Again like BSF, considerable program development work will be required because of the small number of organizations providing marriage education to disadvantaged populations. After a period of pilot testing, the research team will identify as many as eight sites for developing, implementing, and evaluating the SHM program. Thousands of volunteer couples will be randomly assigned to treatment groups with marriage education programs and support services, or to a control group. These couples will be followed for 5 years to gather a rich array of data on a range of relationship measures and child outcomes (when children are a part of the unions). The study eventually will be able to address the potential of marriage education programs to help disadvantaged married couples strengthen their relationships, increase communication skills, overcome barriers, prevent divorce, and ultimately improve child well-being.

## Community Healthy Marriage Initiative (CHMI) Project

The policy interest in strengthening marriages goes beyond programmatic intervention aimed at disadvantaged married and unmarried couples. In addition, federal policymakers will evaluate the potential of broad, communitywide approaches intended to reinforce societal support for marriage. This approach, which emerged from within the growing marriage movement, focuses on creating cultural-level change as well as increasing the supply of various types of marriage education services within specific communities. The strategy seeks to shift the culture from one that sees marriage as only a private concern to one that sees marriage as an important part of a healthy civic infrastructure. In this approach, interventions are directed by community-based coalitions of government agencies, nonprofits, and faith-based organizations and focus on efforts to saturate the community with messages about the importance of healthy marriages and what can be done to foster them. Coalitions work with local media, businesses, religious and civic institutions, and other organizations to produce a sustained, communitywide effort to promote healthy marriage. Experimentation with this kind of intervention rests on an emerging body of scholarship in public health and health communications demonstrating that community health promotion campaigns can, indeed, positively affect social behavior (Hornik, 2002). Very little work has explored marriage-related behaviors, but one recent study comparing communities with marriage initiatives to matched communities without such initiatives suggests that these kinds of community interventions may contribute to decreasing divorce rates (Birch, Weed, & Olsen, 2004).

Recognizing the potential of this growing, community-saturation approach to strengthening marriage, ACF has contracted with RTI International and the Urban Institute to conduct a study of the implementation and effectiveness of selected community healthy marriage initiatives, beginning October 2003. They will evaluate as many as 12 sites, including sites that implement child support waiver demonstrations. Outcomes to be measured include marriage and divorce rates, economic circumstances of families, child and family well-being, and marital quality and stability. In child support waiver sites, outcomes related to the child support program will be included, such as the rate of paternity establishment and payment of child support.

Everyone within each CHMI community has the potential for being exposed to the media messages about the value of healthy marriage, so non-experimental methods must be used to evaluate the impact of the strongest sites. The project team will seek to answer an array of questions about changes in the community based on

appropriate comparison communities without formal initiatives, and track key social indicators. The evaluation will examine effects of both individual and community-level strategies intended to promote healthy marriages.

## National Healthy Marriage Resource Center

The National Healthy Marriage Resource Center (NHMRC) is a national resource and Web-based clearinghouse for information and research relating to forming and sustaining healthy marriages. The NHMRC is a central point of support for the federal Healthy Marriage Initiative. The NHMRC's Web site was launched in early 2006 (www.healthymarriageinfo.org). Target populations for the NHMRC include educators, practitioners, individuals and couples, and other interested entities. Working with the NHMRC is a team of prominent marriage education scholars and practitioners from various universities, research and policy groups, and other organizations.

The work of the NHMRC is guided by five primary goals: (1) to provide current information and resources for the public about what it takes to have a healthy marriage; (2) to provide resources for practitioners and organizations wanting to implement healthy marriage programs and activities; (3) to provide resources for organizational leaders interested in building community healthy marriage initiatives; (4) to provide resources for individuals working to strengthen marriages through public policy; and (5) to provide research reviews and findings for individuals, couples, practitioners, organizational leaders, and researchers.

Among other tasks, the NHMRC (1) collects, analyzes, organizes, and disseminates the best information on marriage research and educational practice; (2) provides individuals and couples with a road map for finding information about local marriage education programs and healthy marriage initiatives and activities; (3) creates resources and tools to aid marriage educators, practitioners, community leaders, and other interested individuals and groups; (4) collects, fosters, and articulates best practices for practitioners; (5) offers academicians and researchers, as well as leaders of local community and faith-based marriage initiatives, a centralized information hub to support the exchange of ideas; and (6) fosters discussion about the culture and status of healthy marriage across academic disciplines and among diverse social groups in the country. A new task being added to the NHMRC in 2007 is to provide technical assistance to ACF's Healthy Marriage Initiative grantees and other interested organizations to increase their expertise and competence in their efforts to strengthen marriages in their communities.

## POTENTIAL CONCERNS ABOUT HEALTHY MARRIAGE INITIATIVES

Individuals have raised various concerns about the potential for healthy marriage initiatives to achieve their stated goals without causing harm. Many of these concerns are understandable and, in some cases, have led to deeper thinking about how programs will be designed or implemented. In other cases, the concerns reflect an inadequate understanding of what is being considered. For example, one of the earliest misunderstandings was that the programs would somehow be coercive and require couples to marry who otherwise would not do so. Some feared that receipt of government benefits would be conditioned on participation in marriage education programs, or worse, on marriage itself. Others worried that those who are persuaded to marry will simply divorce later, creating even more family instability. In reality, the programs described in this paper will

be offered as a service—not previously available on a widespread basis—for low-income couples who are interested and voluntarily choose to participate. The primary objective of healthy marriage programs is to provide couples with the skills they need should they desire to enter into or strengthen their marriage. Actually, the term *promoting marriage* refers to supporting the institution of marriage as a valuable context within which to raise children. The term is not intended to reflect the promotion of specific marriages, which are individual decisions.

Another serious concern is that the programs may inadvertently encourage marriages in which domestic violence may be a factor. Yet the goal of the programs supported by the Healthy Marriage Initiative is not to support any kind of marriage, but rather healthy marriage—those characterized by love and strong commitment and effective management of conflicts. The research is clear that marital conflict is destructive for the couple and for the children (Cummings, 1998). Thus, if child well-being is the ultimate goal of healthy marriage initiatives, it would make little sense to encourage marriage at all costs. The major initiatives (BSF, SHM, and CHMI) require programs to have in place clear protocols for systematic assessment and referral in cases of domestic violence. Other programs funded under the Healthy Marriage Initiative are also required to show evidence that they are prepared to directly address the problem of domestic violence. As a result of such programs, relationship and marriage programs might uncover individuals who otherwise would not have come to the attention of organizations that can help them with abusive situations, thus potentially reducing, rather than encouraging, the incidence of domestic violence.

Other issues relate to the "barriers" to marriage for low-income families. These include issues that have been identified in ethnographic research with fragile families, such as the "high economic bar" for marriage, fear of divorce, a lack of maturity or readiness for marriage among some men and women, and issues related to distrust and infidelity. The identification of such challenges is useful because it can lead to well-designed interventions and curricula that are tailored to address these specific issues.

## CONCLUDING THOUGHTS

The research suggests that poverty and its relation to child well-being is too significant a public policy issue to accept the status quo. Although the causes of poverty are multidimensional, it does not seem to make sense to exclude an important factor, such as family structure, from the intervention equation. In the words of one of the BSF site partners, "Although we do not yet know exactly what will work to strengthen and support healthy marriage in low-income families, the evidence about poverty and family structure is compelling enough to make a good try, and test whether it works."

Yet planning programs and implementing them are two different things. Will couples voluntarily agree to participate in the demonstration/evaluations? Our best guidance about whether relationship and marriage programs are needed by low-income families is likely to come from asking couples themselves. Several states have now fielded surveys of their broad populations to determine the level of interest in participating in such programs (Heath, Bradford, Whiting, Brock, & Foster, 2004; Johnson et al., 2002; Karney, Garvan, & Thomas, 2003; Schramm, Marshall, Harris, & George, 2003). The emerging data suggest widespread interest, which is sometimes greatest among the low-income population (Dion, Hesketh, & Harrison, 2004; Johnson et al., 2002; Schramm et al., 2003). Moreover, the level of interest and effort that many organizations

serving low-income families are now putting into preparing to build or integrate healthy marriage programs suggests that organizations see this as a gap or a need that is presently not being met. This is confirmed in a recent early report on the implementation of the BSF programs (Dion et al., 2006). The report also describes the strong interest and engagement of participating couples, most of whom responded positively and enthusiastically to the BSF program, even during the pilot period. If we are patient, the federal projects reviewed in this paper will tell us a great deal about whether disadvantaged couples can benefit from marriage education efforts, and whether public policy directly addressing family structure can play an important, contributing role in the fight against poverty and efforts to promote children's optimal development.

It is also encouraging that the federal Healthy Marriage Initiative, overall, is producing a working coalition of the ideological left and right rather than contributing further to a cultural war. On the left, many liberals appreciate a progressive position toward helping disadvantaged families, and that the federal Healthy Marriage Initiative has been sensitive to potential pitfalls of efforts to strengthen marriage. On the right, many conservatives appreciate the acknowledgment of marriage as central to the problem of poverty and child well-being. Both sides can appreciate a modest beginning to public policy efforts with substantial commitment to careful evaluation of what works and what doesn't by some of the country's foremost social experiment researchers and expert advisors. Perhaps it is too idealistic to hope that new policies to strengthen marriage, especially among disadvantaged groups, will plow fertile ground for a new era of antipoverty public policy that brings together the left and right. If it does accomplish this feat, however, children and families will be the clear winners.

# REFERENCES

Amato, P. R. (2001). Children of divorce in the 1990s: An update of the Amato and Keith (1991) meta-analysis. *Journal of Family Psychology, 15*(3), 355–370.

Amato, P. R., & Booth, A. (1997). *A generation at risk: Growing up in an era of family upheaval.* Cambridge, MA: Harvard University.

Amato, P. R., & Keith, B. (1991). Parental divorce and the well-being of children: A meta-analysis. *Psychological Bulletin, 110,* 26–46.

Bendheim-Thoman Center for Child Wellbeing. (2002, July). Is marriage a viable option for fragile families? *Fragile Families Research Brief, No. 9.* Princeton, NJ: Princeton University Press.

Bendheim-Thoman Center for Child Wellbeing. (2003, January). Union formation and dissolution and in fragile families. *Fragile Families Research Brief, No. 14.* Princeton, NJ: Princeton University Press.

Birch, P. J., Weed, S. E., & Olsen, J. (2004). *Assessing the impact of community marriage policies on the U.S. county divorce rates.* Working paper, Institute for Research and Evaluation, Salt Lake City, UT.

Bos, J., Crosby, D., Duncan, G., Huston, A., & Morris, P. (2001). *How welfare and work policies affect children: A synthesis of research.* New York: Manpower Demonstration Research Corporation.

Bramlett, M. D., & Mosher, W. D. (2002). Cohabitation, marriage, divorce, and remarriage in the United States. *Vital and Health Statistics, 23*(22). Hyattsville, MD: National Center for Health Statistics.

Carlson, M., McLanahan, S., & England, P. (2004). Union formation and dissolution in fragile families. *Demography 41*(2), 237–262.

Carroll, J. S., & Doherty, W. J. (2003). Evaluating the effectiveness of premarital prevention programs: A meta-analytic review of outcome research. *Family Relations, 52,* 105–118.

Coltrane, S., & Adams, M. (2003). The social construction of the divorce "problem": Morality, child victims, and the politics of gender. *Family Relations, 52,* 363–372.

Coontz, S., & Folbre, N. (2002). *Marriage, poverty, and public policy.* A discussion paper from the Council on Contemporary Families, prepared for the Fifth Annual CCF Conference, April 26–28, 2002.

Cummings, E. M. (1998). Children exposed to marital conflict and violence: Conceptual and theoretical directions. In G. Holden, R. Geffner, & E. Jouriles (Eds.), *Children and family violence.* Washington, DC: American Psychological Association.

Dion, M. R. (2005). Healthy marriage programs: Learning what works. *Future of Children, 15,* 2.

Dion, M. R., Avellar, S. A., Zaveri, H. H., & Hershey, A. M. (2006). *Implementing marriage programs for unmarried couples with children: Early lessons from the Building Strong Families project.* Washington, DC: Mathematica Policy Research.

Dion, M. R., Devaney, B., McConnell, S., Ford, M., Hill, H., & Winston, P. (2003). *Helping unwed parents build strong and healthy marriages: A conceptual framework for interventions.* Washington, DC: Mathematica Policy Research.

Dion, M. R., Hesketh, H., & Harrison, C. (2004). *Marriage and family formation in four state surveys.* Presentation for the National Governor's Association, Center for Best Practices, Washington, DC.

Duggan, L. (2004). Holy matrimony. *The Nation.* Retrieved February 26, 2004, from http://www.thenation.com/doc/20040315/duggan

Duncan, G. J., & Brooks-Gunn, J. (1997). *Consequences of growing up poor.* New York: Russell Sage.

Edin, K. (2000). Few good men: Why low-income single mothers don't get married. *American Prospect, 11,* 26–31.

Edin, K., & Kefalas, M. (2005). *Promises I can keep: Why poor women put motherhood before marriage.* Berkeley: University of California Press.

Fawcett, E. B., Hawkins, A. J., & Blanchard, V. S. (2006). *Are marriage education programs effective? A conceptual and meta-analytic review of marriage education programs.* Washington, DC: National Healthy Marriage Resource Center.

Fein, D. J., Burnstein, N. R., Fein, G. G., & Lindberg, L. D. (2003). *The determinants of marriage and cohabitation among disadvantaged Americans: Research findings and needs.* Bethesda, MD: Abt Associates.

Gallagher, M. (2004). *Can government strengthen marriage? Evidence from the social sciences.* New York: Institute for American Values.

Genettian, L. (2003). *The long-term effects of the Minnesota Family Investment Program on Marriage and Divorce Among Two-Parent Families.* New York: MDRC.

Giblin, P., Sprenkle, D. H., & Sheehan, R. (1985). Enrichment outcome research: A meta-analysis of premarital, marital and family interventions. *Journal of Marital and Family Therapy, 11*(3), 257–271.

Graefe, D., & Lichter, D. (1999). Life course transitions of American children: Parental cohabitation, marriage, and single motherhood. *Demography, 36*(2), 205–17.

Grogger, J., Karoly, L., & Klerman, J. (2002). *Consequences of welfare reform: A research synthesis.* Los Angeles: RAND.

Haskins, R., & Sawhill, I. (2003, September). Work and marriage: The way to end poverty. *Brookings Institution Policy Brief: Welfare reform and beyond #28* (pp. 1–8). Washington DC: Brookings Institution.

Hawkins, A. J., Carroll, J. S., & Doherty, W. H. (2004*). A comprehensive framework for marriage education.* Washington DC: Administration for Children and Families.

Heath, C. J., Bradford, K., Whiting, J., Brock, G., & Foster, S. (2004). *The Kentucky Marriage Attitudes Study: 2004 baseline survey.* Lexington: Research Center for Families and Children, University of Kentucky.

Heaton, T. B. (2002). Factors contributing to increasing marital stability in the United States. *Journal of Family Issues, 23,* 392–409.

Hetherington, E. M., & Kelly, J. (2002). *For better or worse: Divorce reconsidered.* New York: W.W. Norton.

Hornik, R. C. (2002). *Public health communication: Evidence for behavior change.* Mahwah, NJ: Erlbaum.

Institute for American Values. (2004). *What next for the marriage movement?* New York: Institute for American Values. Retrieved May 6, 2006, from http://center.americanvalues.org/?p=11

Jacobson, J. (2002). Unpublished tabulations using FY 1999 ACF TANF Emergency Datafile. Washington DC: Mathematica Policy Research.

Johnson, C. A., Stanley, S. M., Glenn, N. D., Amato, P. R., Nock, S. L., Markman, H. J., et al. (2002). *Marriage in Oklahoma: 2001 baseline statewide survey on marriage and divorce.* Stillwater: Oklahoma State University Bureau for Social Research.

Karney, B. R., Garvan, C. W., & Thomas, M. S. (2003). *Family formation in Florida: 2003 baseline survey of attitudes, beliefs, and demographics relating to marriage and family formation.* Gainesville: University of Florida.

Lichter, D. T., Graefe, D. R., & Brown, J. B. (2003). Is marriage a panacea? Union formation among economically disadvantaged unwed mothers. *Social Problems, 50,* 60–86.

McLanahan, S. (1997). Parent absence or poverty: Which matters more? In G. J. Duncan & J. Brooks-Gunn (Eds.), *Consequences of growing up poor.* New York: Russell Sage.

McLanahan, S., & Sandefur, G. D. (1994). *Growing up with a single parent: What hurts, what helps.* Cambridge, MA: Harvard University Press.

Nock, S. L. (1997). *Marriage in men's lives.* New York: Oxford University Press.

Ooms, T. (2002, April 8). Marriage plus. *American Prospect, 13*(7).

Parke, M. (2003, May). Are married parents really better for children? What research says about the effects of family structure on child well-being. *CLASP Policy Brief,* Couples and Marriage Series, Brief No. 3, 1–7.

Raley, K., & Bumpass, L. (2003). The topography of the divorce plateau: Levels and trends in union stability in the United States after 1980. *Demographic Research, 8,* 245–259.

Reardon-Anderson, J., Stagner, M., Macomber, J. E., & Murray, J. (2005). *Systematic review of the impact of marriage and relationship programs.* Washington, DC: Urban Institute. Retrieved February 5, 2006, from http://www.urban.org/url.cfm?ID=411142

Schramm, D. G., Marshall, J. P., Harris, V. W., & George, A. (2003). *Marriage in Utah: 2003 baseline statewide survey on marriage and divorce.* Salt Lake City: Utah Department of Workforce Services.

Seltzer, J. A. (2000). Families formed outside of marriage. *Journal of Marriage and the Family, 62*(4), 1247–1268.

Smock, P. J. (2000). Cohabitation in the United States: An appraisal of research themes, findings, and implications. *Annual Review of Sociology, 26,* 1–20.

Testa, M., & Krogh, M. (1995). The effect of employment on marriage among black males in inner-city Chicago. In M. B. Tucker & C. Mitchell-Kernan (Eds.), *The decline in marriage among African Americans.* New York: Russell Sage.

U.S. Census Bureau. (2000, March). *One-parent family groups with their own children under 18, by marital status, and race and Hispanic origin of the reference person,* Table FG6. Washington, DC: Author.

U.S. House of Representatives, Committee on Ways and Means. (2001). *2001 green book: Background material and data on programs within the jurisdiction of the Committee on Ways and Means,* Table H-6, p. 1289. Washington, DC: U.S. Government Printing Office.

Waite, L. J., & Gallagher, M. (2000). *The case for marriage.* New York: Doubleday.

Wampler, K. S., & Butler, M. H. (1999). A meta-analytic update of research on the couple communication program. *American Journal of Family Therapy, 27*(3), 223–237.

Whitehead, B. D., & Blankenhorn, D. (2004). *Media coverage of the administration's healthy marriage initiative: January 14, 2004–February 9, 2004.* Retrieved February 19, 2004, from http://www.americanvalues.org

Wilson, W. J. (1987). *The truly disadvantaged: The inner city, the underclass, and public policy.* Chicago: University of Chicago Press.

Winkler, C. (2004). Marriage of convenience: How the *New York Times* got the president's marriage initiative wrong. *Weekly Standard.* Retrieved from http://www.weeklystandard.com/Utilities/printer_preview.asp?idArticle=3750&R=9D1A191B0

# CHAPTER 25

# Microenterprise

## Building Well-Being Among Poor U.S. Families

### Warner P. Woodworth

aria Luisa is a 43-year-old Hispanic immigrant who struggled for several years after arriving in the United States from Central America. Together with her husband and three children, she moved to Provo, Utah, hoping to find the American dream—secure careers, school for the children, a decent home, food security, and a better quality of life than before. But life was hard. Neither Maria Luisa nor her spouse was able to obtain middle-class wage jobs. Poverty led to numerous stresses and strains. Eventually, her husband abandoned his family and moved on, leaving no forwarding address.

The uncertainties of a bleak future, unanswered questions, and practical matters like how to pay the rent all heightened Maria Luisa's worries. Unable to speak English combined with no income led to having to move to another dilapidated rental unit. This meant a loss of the children's few friends, as well as having to begin anew in the middle of the academic year at a new school.

After further difficulties, Maria Luisa heard about a local community nonprofit organization, Mentores para la Microempresa (Micro Business Mentors). That group was launching a program to train Spanish-speaking immigrants who sought to start income-generating projects. Beginning to feel she might not be successful in obtaining employment in the formal economy of Utah, becoming self-employed might be a viable alternative, she thought.

A year later, after small business training and a microloan of $500, Maria Luisa is able to stand on her own two feet. She used the loan to purchase haircutting equipment: Clippers, combs, electric hair-styling brushes, trimmers, a curling iron, razors, hair tonics, talc, gels, and a shoulder bag. She makes a living going door to door carrying the tools of her new trade. She solicits customers who would enjoy a low-cost, nicely done haircut within the comfort of their own homes.

Maria Luisa was able to pay off her loan 100%, on time. She started out her microenterprise by bringing in about $300 the first month. With Micro Business' ongoing consulting assistance, her business has grown so that she now grosses some $1,500 per month. Her family has been able to remain in the same apartment so the children can continue to stay in the same school, keep their friends, and worship at the same church. All this gives the family stability and a degree of security that they never had before.

Each month Maria Luisa saves a percentage of her income to maintain the business and prepare for a better future. Eventually, she hopes to go to beauty school and then open her own shop.

The case of Maria Luisa is real. It grew out of a project that my Brigham Young University students and I developed during the past several years to address the challenges of family poverty in our own community. This chapter elucidates the growing phenomenon of U.S. microenterprise—what it is, how it strengthens poor families, where it works, how it is structured, and the extent of its impacts.

Many Americans talk about "moral values" such as overthrowing Saddam Hussein in the Iraq War, blocking stem cell research, and dealing with terrorism. But for me, alleviating family poverty is a moral value of top priority. So let us turn to a new tool for aiding poor families, the strategy of microenterprise.

## LIFTING POOR FAMILIES THROUGH MICROENTERPRISE

Although many American families experience the stress and strain of poverty, new solutions are being implemented to help overcome the debilitating effects of joblessness. One of the most innovative is microenterprise and its related tactics to empower the poor and enable those who struggle to enjoy greater incomes, experience a sense of dignity, solidify family relationships, and improve their quality of life.

This approach differs from large-scale, expensive programs that broadly assert that their objective is to eliminate poverty, in general. Instead, this is a sort of boutique strategy that has narrower goals. It uses a business model, not charity, to lift the poor, and it accomplishes this one family at a time. In doing so, the poor experience a better life, feel more dignity, and are not dependent on huge government programs. The phrase I often use in my consulting and working with microenterprise organizations is that it gives the poor "a hand-up, not a handout."

To begin with, let us clarify several terms. First, microenterprise is usually created through *nongovernmental organizations* (NGOs), an increasingly used expression for what Americans typically have referred to as nonprofit foundations. The most commonly used word is *microenterprise*. I use it to signify one's very small business, usually operated by just one or two family members. Next is the word, *microcredit,* by which I mean "microlending" only—tiny amounts of capital loaned for income-generating projects. *Microentrepreneur* is the term for the recipient of microcredit, that is, an individual who seeks a small loan with which to start or expand one's business. *Microfinance* is a more encompassing word that may include microcredit for the microenterprise operated by the microentrepreneur. It may also include other economic services for the poor such as a microentrepreneur's savings account, microloans for housing or education, micro-insurance, small-scale agriculture loans for seed or tools. NGOs that provide this broader array of financial services are often described as *microfinance institutions* (MFIs). One may wonder where these new financial strategies came from.

## GLOBAL ORIGINS OF MICROENTERPRISE

Three financial experiments gave rise to this movement. One MFI that claims it was the first is ACCION International, an NGO that was doing traditional development work in Latin America during the 1970s. ACCION began to provide simple, tiny loans for start-up economic activity in 1972 in Brazil. As a result of a small amount of credit helping a poor family improve, the practice began to spread. Though ACCION's early efforts were limited to Latin America, it eventually began to expand—launching start-up offices in the United States, Africa, and, most recently, India.

Another pioneer was the Grameen Bank of Bangladesh, based in the capital city, Dhaka. This was the first microenterprise support organization to achieve major growth and substantial scale. Founded in 1976 by Professor Muhammad Yunus, a U.S.–trained economist, Grameen created a peer-lending structure where five to six women each received individual loans and jointly guaranteed all the loans in their group. Weekly payments were small and easy to understand, and all loans were 1 year in length. The groups met weekly in a designated center, meeting with five to seven other groups, to make loan and interest payments and to support each other's business success. This group structure fostered self-esteem and a culture of mutual accountability that supported high loan repayment rates, high savings rates, and low levels of business failure.

Today, Grameen has more than 5 million clients, 96% of them women. One of the most important features of Grameen is its openness and commitment to helping other NGOs start microcredit programs. Today, hundreds of replication efforts in many nations were built off the Grameen model.

The third MFI, Foundation for International Community Assistance (FINCA International), did not become a major organization in the emerging microcredit field until 1990. But the founder, Dr. John Hatch, was a key player in the efforts to generate interest and public attention for the MFI field, beginning in 1983. Indeed, without any knowledge

of the Grameen Bank in far-off Bangladesh, or of the microcredit experiments by ACCION in Latin America, Hatch invented another type of solidarity group that he called *village banking*. In his model, the loan officer would go to a village, explain the concept, and ask the village elders to choose 30 to 40 impoverished women who each needed a $50 loan to start or expand a business. Later the loan officers returned for the repayment.

FINCA's model was implemented in those early years in several Latin American locales, but more recently has expanded to Africa and the former Soviet Union. Today, it has more than 300,000 clients who constitute some 24,000 village bank groups of mostly poor women living in 23 nations. Further details about the rise of microenterprise through ACCION, Grameen, and other cases may be obtained in Woodworth (2000).

This strategy for empowering poor families has become perhaps the most innovative development tool to globally empower millions of poor families in the last decade. This is impressive for several reasons: It defies the traditional assumption that solutions are best invented in industrialized nations and that top-down development is required because national political leaders' support is essential for success. Instead, microfinance essentially turns traditional borrowing and finance for families upside down.

## MFI GROWTH AND ACCELERATION

From its humble, experimental beginnings, microcredit has grown into a development strategy involving millions of poor women and men who access the services of thousands of microfinance institutions. These MFIs come in various forms. Most are NGOs directly operating as microcredit practitioners. That is, they acquire funds and provide microcredit services. Some are commercial banks such as

Mibanco in Peru and Banco Sol in Bolivia. These are specialized, for-profit banks set up to provide financial services to impoverished families. Many credit unions are also starting to participate in the microcredit movement.

As microcredit has been increasingly recognized for its contribution to poverty alleviation, many government and multilateral organizations (such as the U.S. Agency for International Development, the World Bank, the United Nations) have become involved. Likewise, important microenterprise industry research and policy organizations are helping further the impact of microcredit for the poor: They include the UN's "International Year of Microcredit" (United Nations, 2005), the Consultative Group to Help the Poorest (CGAP), the Small Enterprise Education and Promotion Network (SEEP), and the Microcredit Summit established in 1997 that since has accelerated microloans to more than 92 million families (Harris, 2005).

## U.S. MICROCREDIT

Microcredit strategies emerged in America during the mid-1980s in response to the desires of low-income people, women, minorities, and persons with disabilities who wanted to achieve the American dream of self-employment. In a curious historical twist of the usual pattern in which U.S. aid organizations go abroad to advise Third World countries about how to improve their economies through "modern" innovations, it was just the opposite in the case of microfinance. NGOs from poor nations came to North America to share their expertise on how the peer lending approach to microentrepreneurship could be applied in the states, as well as Canada (Nelson, 1994). Grameen and two other successful Bangladeshi MFIs led the discussions.

As the western organizations learned from Asian practitioners, innovations followed, despite the general opinion that so-called industrialized societies would never embrace group borrowing techniques. Over time, some applications of Third World approaches have succeeded in the United States. Microfinance has helped people transform their family lives and improved the economic well-being of their communities. The field has grown rapidly and now exceeds hundreds of programs operating in virtually all states and Washington, D.C.

In the process, microcredit has gained the attention of local, state, and national legislators of both political parties. It has captured the interests of economic development, human services, and other professionals. The enactment of welfare reform laws in 1996, with their time limits and work requirements, has increased the urgency of creating economic opportunities for low-income people. Microenterprise represents an important new option for many of these individuals.

Currently, a microenterprise in the U.S. economy is usually defined as a business with five or fewer employees that is small enough to require initial capital of $35,000, or less. Most microenterprises are sole proprietorships, which create employment for the owner, and often, other family members. However, some microenterprises grow into larger businesses and eventually employ other members of the community.

There seem to be several reasons why I and others view the rise of microfinance within the U.S. context as both viable and desirable:

1. Self-employment allows people in low wage regular jobs to supplement their income.

2. Microcredit enables the entrepreneurial spirit to flourish among society's poorest families and promote their development (Nelson, 1994).

3. Structural unemployment, such as plant closings and corporate downsizing, has dislocated many workers, leading many to create their own jobs.

4. Banks in the United States find it difficult to make profitable microenterprise loans under $35,000, most of which are not 100% collateralized. Reasons for this include the cost of conducting due diligence on loan applications, high transaction costs on loans, and compliance with "safety and soundness" issues of federal and state regulators.

5. For a low-income person, self-employment offers opportunities to use one's talents and find personal fulfillment. These opportunities may be difficult to find through low-wage employment (Nelson, 2000).

6. Self-employment offers women the flexibility to balance work and family responsibilities.

7. Immigrants and refugees frequently lack the certifications, licenses, or English proficiency needed to obtain professional jobs for which they may qualify. Creating a self-employment business related to their professional training is often preferable to a low-wage job in another field.

Thus, MFIs provide business development services to people who are currently operating or are interested in starting a microenterprise. The programs are operated by a wide variety of nonprofit organizations. They range from those for which microcredit is their primary activity, to those whose programs include various other employment, economic development, and antipoverty strategies. MFI programming fits well into the service mix of these organizations because most microcredit programs focus on community development, business development, or poverty alleviation. Such organizations include community development corporations, loan funds, community action agencies, women's business centers, community development financial institutions, small business development centers, and many others.

## MFI Services

A number of useful supports for microenterprise are provided by MFIs.

*Business Training and Technical Assistance.* These programs help participants build the skills needed to plan, market, and manage their microbusinesses. The business training and technical assistance usually results in the participants developing their ideas into feasible enterprises and writing formal business plans. In addition to helping individuals learn to research the market, conduct financial analyses, and plan marketing strategies, the training and technical assistance addresses personal development issues such as family budgeting, control of personal finances, and appropriate managerial behavior.

*Access to Credit.* Microfinance helps participants obtain access to funding for their businesses. Many MFIs operate in-house lending programs. Others link participants with loans from collaborating banks, public loan funds, or other financing sources with which they have formal relationships. Most loans are made to individual business owners, but some programs use a peer-lending model. This assistance to accessing credit is crucial because federal and state banking regulations and underwriting criteria often prevent commercial banks from making loans to poor families.

*Ongoing Business Assistance.* Continuing consulting is provided to microentrepreneurs after they start or expand their family firms to address issues that the businesses face as they move through each stage of development, as well as specific difficulties that they encounter.

*Access to Markets.* Microcredit technical assistance helps participants find markets that will increase sales and profitability. This assistance often provides training on marketing and sales concepts, but may also encourage clients to participate in trade shows, develop catalogs of their products, and advertise their businesses on the Internet. Some programs have started incubators for certain types of firms, such as technology or food businesses. Incubators provide business owners with a place to operate their firms, as well as with support services, such as administrative services and technical assistance.

*Asset Development and Economic Literacy.* MFIs help clients increase their understanding of banking and savings principles. Some offer participants the option to open Individual Development Accounts (IDAs)— savings accounts that can be used by low-income households for certain purposes, such as to purchase a home or start a business. These accounts are matched—usually $1 to $3 for every dollar saved—with funds from either private or government sources.

Microentrepreneurs may choose to start a wide range of businesses—those that fit their interests and abilities. Common types of businesses are repair services, cleaning services, specialty foods, jewelry, arts and crafts, gifts, clothing and textiles, computer technology, child care, and environmental products and services. Let us examine several examples of MFIs that support such small U.S. firms, the first being a case of Native American family microcredit.

## Lakota Fund, South Dakota

The typical U.S. approach to native economic development consists of top-down, government-operated, large grants of money that go to tribal officials, as well as often to their expensive Anglo consultants. These generally only last for the short term and many suffer from governmental bureaucracies and inefficiencies, as well as corruption. In contrast, independent Native American microcredit could become a viable alternative. Indeed, small, grassroots-operated microenterprise development may become a catalyst for achieving greater tribal self-sufficiency. The Lakota Fund, albeit small, is a case in point (Lakota Fund, 1998; Woodworth, 2004).

The Lakota Fund became the first microcredit financing for Native Americans in 1986. This effort on the Pine Ridge Indian

Reservation was established because the region in South Dakota was among the poorest within the United States. Unemployment tended to range between 70% and 85%.

In the past, the 22,000 Native Americans at Pine Ridge have largely survived on federal funds to schools, health care, and tribal government. Otherwise, agriculture has been the only source of income except for a few small private firms. The Lakota Fund was established in Kyle, a central village in the reservation. During the past two decades, hundreds of tiny loans have been accessed by tribal members starting new microenterprises.

It began as a 1986 project of the First Nations Development Institute based in Fredericksburg, Virginia. Channeling loan capital to the Lakota Fund has been one of its greatest successes. More than 1,600 loans totaling some three million dollars have been given to would-be microentrepreneurs at Pine Ridge through several mechanisms.

*Lakota Circle Banking.* One strategy is that of "Circle Banking," based on the group lending model of the Grameen Bank. Small peer groups of 4 to 10 individuals form a group and participate in five microentrepreneurial training sessions. Most participants would not be considered "credit worthy" according to traditional U.S. banking criteria.

Upon completion of the Circle business education, the group is "certified" and its members then determine who will receive what amount of loans, usually ranging from $400 to $1,000, with which to start. Lakota uses the social collateral of others in the Circle to guarantee that each loan is repaid. As co-debtors, this practice ensures a loan repayment rate of about 90%. As loans are repaid, another larger amount may be borrowed to expand one's microenterprise.

An example illustrates the type of borrowers and businesses financed through microlending. Roselyn Spotted Eagle is an older woman who lives on the Pine Ridge Reservation in a two-room house without running water or decent heating. She supports a grandson who is afflicted with fetal alcohol syndrome. Ms. Spotted Eagle makes beautiful beaded crafts for the tourist market, and through microcredit, she has been able to purchase new tools and a greater inventory of beads and other materials to expand her microenterprise.

What features help to explain Lakota Circle Banking success? First, it is not just about money, but also about training and education. The course modules include basic business skills such as budgeting, marketing and sales, quality, tax and licensing, and so forth. Borrowers also may participate in life-skills education that covers topics such as problem-solving, goal setting, drug abuse, and alcoholism issues. Elsie Meeks, executive director, reports, "If I were to identify the one most valuable aspect of Circle Banking, I would have to say that learning to deal with and solve problems is more important than even the loans" (Sustainable Communities Network [SCN], 1997, p. 91).

Another facet of Lakota Fund's achievements is its native control. Rather than be operated by Anglos or other outside "experts," the fund has a staff of four members from the tribe. They are overseen by a nine-person board of directors, most of whom also live on the reservation as tribal members. Thus, indigenous values and culturally appropriate policies are embedded and maintained over the years (Meeks, 2000).

A third element that ensures the Lakota Fund's achievements is strict adherence to the Grameen model, rather than a U.S. variation. The Lakota Fund also insists that borrowers deposit at least $5 every 2 weeks as a nest egg of personal savings, also a replication of the Grameen system.

*Small Business Loans.* The second mechanism for entrepreneurial start-up is the Lakota Fund's Small Business Loan (SBL) program. In contrast to microcredit for Circle Banking

enterprises, SBL started by giving initial loans for as much as $25,000, much more money than that of the microenterprise level. However, candidates have to first participate in a 7-week training program where they obtain the basics of small business success and develop a feasibility plan. Examples of small businesses needing more capital than Circle Banking include construction, electronic repairs, and restaurants (Garr, 1996). From the reservation, we shift to microenterprise in the southern United States.

## Micro-Business USA, Florida

Another American MFI that provides microfinance services is based in the Miami area of south Florida. It was first established by my colleague, Kathleen Gordon, as a branch of Working Capital more than a decade ago. Micro-Business USA (MB-USA) has grown gradually ever since and today serves multiple families in three languages: Creole, Spanish, and English. Its clients include low-income whites, Hispanic immigrants, especially large populations from the Dominican Republic and Cuba, as well as Haitian and other Caribbean refugees.

From Gordon's presentations at Brigham Young University's annual microcredit conferences, speeches to students in my courses, and personal conversations, the following picture about MB-USA emerges (Gordon, 1997). The organization only provides microloans to U.S. citizens or permanent residents with low incomes. Most are self-employed, but a few also have other jobs in the formal economy, so their microenterprise becomes a second income. The MFI's mission is to support financial self-sufficiency for low-income families. It is established as a not-for-profit corporation with the state of Florida, and is qualified as an IRS Section 501(c)(3) tax-exempt firm. This enables donors to claim a charitable tax deduction on their federal filings for monies given to support microcredit in Florida.

*Basics of MB-USA.* In addition to headquarters in Miami, MB-USA has additional offices in North Miami, Broward County, Fort Lauderdale, and St. Petersburg. It has provided training in peer-group lending processes to some 6,000 individuals, given out more than 2,500 loans, and enjoys a rate of repayment in excess of 95%. Poor individuals begin the MB-USA program with 12 hours of training and a $500 microloan. Little by little, they build a credit history in the ensuing weeks and months as the loan payments are made on time, until it is fully repaid. Clients also continue to participate in the MFIs microenterprise training to learn marketing and sales, leadership, accounting, and other critical dimensions of entrepreneurship (MB-USA, 2006).

At this stage, firms are often part-time income-generating projects. Recipients develop their talents and skills, apply ideas, and enjoy the experience of nurturing their own microenterprises. They overcome self-doubt and economic hardships, and begin to feel greater self-worth, according to Gordon.

*Client Success.* One illustration of a positive case that typifies MB-USA's (2006) impact is Gammons Seasonings started by Larry Gammons in 2001. With a $500 loan and a small business license, the founder began in his kitchen. A second loan for $1,000 enabled him to purchase more supplies, develop a bar code for tracking products, and build a Web site. He even began running a low-cost television commercial through a local cable station. As business continued to grow, he qualified for another MB-USA credit line for $2,500 so he could purchase liability insurance and began placing his seasonings in grocery stores. Finally, Gammons' spices began to be bottled and sent out through an area distribution firm, ensuring a growing income and a more secure future for the Gammons family. He now is known as an African American success in Florida and specializes in barbecue herbs and seasonings, and each of his family members is a beneficiary (Black Miami, 2006).

Building assets in a microenterprise gives poor Florida residents security. In the case of a small firm, it may also generate thousands of dollars in extra annual income. Studies suggest that for poor families this may translate into better health care, an improved living environment, perhaps a car that actually operates, and other family outcomes such as nutrition and children's education.

### Microbusiness Mentors, Utah

One offshoot of MB-USA is that it has inspired other groups to design and implement community-based microcredit programs like the one my students and I established for poor families in Provo, Utah. With advice from Gordon, who shared materials and her experience, we began to design an MFI as a university laboratory for service learning in 2003, as noted in this chapter's beginning, the vignette about Maria Luisa.

*Initial Research.* For my social entrepreneurship course, a team of graduate students worked with others across campus to conduct a needs assessment of the growing inner-city Latino community. What we found were a number of problems facing residents in that area, in contrast to other neighborhoods: median family incomes under $20,000, higher violent crime rates, lower high school GPAs, more public-assisted housing subsidies, official poverty rates of 52% to 84%, family English as a Second Language (ESL) of 28% to 51% in that area's elementary schools, and student mobility that ranged between 50% and 64% (Brigham Young University, 2002).

In our surveys of Provo inner-city Latino families, we learned that 48% reported having no savings, and 71% had annual incomes of under $30,000. When we inquired about their potential interest in becoming self-employed, 81% answered in the affirmative. Likewise, 78% reported they would be interested in receiving business training. Yet, surprisingly to us, only 55% expressed interest in obtaining a loan (Woodworth et al., 2003). Thus, we began to feel that the delivery of business skills might best be our first priority. Based on these data, Microbusiness Mentors was created. Its nickname, "M & Ms," began to be used for marketing our services.

*M & Ms Process.* We designed a four-pillar system for operating its program: training, group support, mentors, and loans. Briefly put, training seemed to be of interest to 78% of Latino adults in our survey. So we designed eight modules, one to be taught each week for 8 weeks. During these weeks, the participants learn about each other, work on training cases as a team, share ideas and experiences, all culminating in the creation of one's microenterprise plan. This system of mutual support builds solidarity and trust. If group members go on to complete the eight sessions of training and qualify for $500 loans, a graduation ceremony is held, certificates of completion are given, as well as the loans. Each member of the group signs a commitment to repay each others' loans, in addition to one's own, the group thereby acting as social collateral. This technique is sometimes referred to as "peer-lending" or "solidarity group loans." Group commitment and peer pressure minimize borrower default rates. Also, they teach responsibility and the importance of repayment on time and in full for the amount due. After graduating and obtaining their first loans, M & Ms microentrepreneurs next turn to launching their tiny businesses, and each is assigned a volunteer mentor who agrees to coach them at least monthly during the next year.

As of now, M & Ms seems to be quite promising. Hundreds of Utah Latinos have received orientation or training. Those who completed the training have received loans, started microenterprises, and, at least so far, 100% of them have paid back their microcredit debts. Currently, M & Ms is seeking to become a legal 501(c)(3) MFI in Utah so it may expand its services and loan capital to greater numbers of poor families. But does this approach to alleviating family poverty work beyond the cases cited previously? We turn next to several more systematic studies that indicate answers.

## RESEARCH ON U.S. MICROCREDIT

Although there are numerous articles regarding Third World microfinance, U.S. research is limited. However, the following paragraphs synthesize a number of benefits and effects from MFI efforts:

1. Microcredit supplements family income. Research shows that clients of one organization in the northeast, Working Capital, a Massachusetts MFI, enjoyed more than $5,000 in additional income annually, a considerable figure for many poor families (Ashe, 2000).

2. Microcredit increases family assets. An Aspen Institute study (Clark & Kays, 1999) found that average household assets over 5 years grew by $13,623 among all study respondents. A low-income subgroup experienced a significantly higher increase in assets, averaging $15,909 during the same period.

3. Microcredit pares down one's reliance on government welfare. Two studies, one by the Self-Employment Investment Demonstration (SEID) project (Raheim & Alter, 1995), and the other by the Aspen Institute (Clark & Kays, 1999), found that many welfare recipients who participated in microenterprise development programs left Aid to Families with Dependent Children (AFDC) as well as food stamps programs. In the Aspen Institute's study, 61% of the low-income

group stopped receiving AFDC. In the SEID study, 43% were not receiving food stamps, and 52% of the study participants no longer received AFDC benefits.

4. Microcredit through group lending ensures greater enterprise survival rates, including sales and profits, than typical individual-based small businesses (Barsky, 2000).

5. Microcredit builds family income and moves the poor out of poverty. A 5-year tracking study by the Aspen Institute (Clark & Kays, 1999) of longitudinal data from seven MFIs between 1991 and 1997 was conducted. Average household incomes of low-income program participants increased by $8,484 over 5 years. This resulted in 53% of participants moving out of poverty.

6. Miscellaneous other outcomes. Microcredit services improve microentrepreneurs' self-esteem, their quality of life, and their participation in the community. Barsky's (2000) research demonstrated that involvement in a borrower solidarity group results in increased self-confidence, better family relationships, and improved leadership and communication skills. Through their business activities, microentrepreneurs are more able to provide for their families. They serve as positive role models for their children and for the community. Many successful microentrepreneurs become mentors and advisors to others who seek to become self-employed.

7. The studies by Ashe concluded that peer lending creates jobs for not only the poor microentrepreneur, but also one's friends and neighbors. It opens new access to sources of credit, and builds better management capabilities, as well (Ashe, 2000).

8. Families and individuals in ACCION programs report more self-respect, dignity, and independence through group lending processes (Himes & Servon, 1998).

9. Microcredit adds to the net worth of poor families. The Clark and Kays research (1999) showed higher amounts of family net worth, growing at an average level of $1,519 by the end of a 5-year period.

## MICROCREDIT AS A MODEL FOR POOR FAMILIES

U.S. microenterprise programs use a business model for fighting poverty. These programs are not a tool for welfare, handouts, or other approaches to charity. Rather, they seek to operate using free market principles; the underlying assumption being that by empowering poor families with economic knowledge, small business skills, and capital, poor families will be able to raise themselves above the suffering and lack of dignity many feel throughout the years of their economic struggles.

American MFIs focus on underserved families who have had difficulty accessing business development services of credit through traditional institutions. They often channel their services toward a specific target population, such as women, members of minority communities, people with low incomes, immigrants and refugees, or welfare recipients.

A core assumption is that by supporting parents in starting or expanding an income-generating enterprise, their examples may motivate their children later. MFIs can help parents to increase their income, assets, and net worth. As a result, their reliance on welfare may be reduced, enabling them to move out of poverty. Self-employment activities can also result in individuals' increased self-esteem, improved quality of life, and greater involvement in their own communities. Such programs also benefit one's home town. They help to revitalize downtown areas, enhance regional economies in rural areas, and may lead to additional results for good.

A question often raised is how U.S. MFIs are capitalized. Early in the movement during the 1980s, funding for microcredit programs mostly came from foundations. Over time, however, existing agencies whose work focused on poverty alleviation and historically relied on public funding, found that some of the public dollars available to them could support these efforts. By the early 1990s, microfinance was recognized as a distinct field, and supporting legislation and appropriations began to be passed by Congress. Today, the federal government channels money through such avenues as the Small Business Administration (SBA) Microloan Fund, and other agencies such as agriculture and housing also offer funding. In the latest fiscal year of federal funding for 2006, Congress authorized $12.7 million for SBA loans, along with $13 million in technical assistance for supporting microenterprise development. Also, corporations such as American Express and Levi Strauss provide philanthropic grants to MFIs, as do nonprofits such as the United Way. In addition, churches and individuals are becoming more interested in funding such efforts to empower the family.

Regarding the scope of today's MFI programs, the size varies considerably, as do the types of agencies that host them, and in the extent to which they identify with the field. This makes hard data nearly impossible to ascertain. Various observers estimate there are between 500 and 700 formal microcredit programs in America. With respect to numbers of microenterprises, the Association for Enterprise Opportunity (AEO) generously estimates on its state fact sheets that more than 21 million such firms exist (AEO, 2006).

AEO also claims that the total number of microentrepreneurs makes up 17.2% of all private sector jobs in the nation. In contrast, Edgecomb and Klein (2005) in their latest study suggest the number to be about half that, approximately 10 million microentrepreneurs. Others argue for different totals—their disputes, of course, arising from alternative definitions of how many employees, or how much capital is involved.

Microfinance is becoming institutionalized in America and is increasingly supported by the business community. Members of both political parties have sponsored legislation and appropriations with the objective of strengthening the family through countering poverty. Back when he was governor, former President Bill Clinton and wife, Hillary, helped to establish one of the first microcredit nonprofits in America, the Good Faith Fund, in Arkansas (Taub, 2004). Later serving in the White House, Clinton affirmed the importance of microenterprise development in giving families an opportunity to participate in America's economic prosperity by initiating Presidential Awards for Excellence in Microenterprise Development, presenting the awards to outstanding programs in 1997 and 1999.

## CRITICISMS OF MICROCREDIT

Although the growth of microfinance has been dramatic, it has also had some problems. Some of the early organizational players have shut their doors. Symptoms of problems vary—leveling off of growth, board and staff infighting, inability to raise more grant money, and aggressive marketing by new MFIs entering the movement, among other factors. In certain instances, MFI managers belatedly realized that domestic applications of microcredit were more complex, necessitated greater sophistication, and so forth. For instance, FINCA spent 3 years and considerable money seeking to build a U.S. strategy, but finally abandoned the idea and refocused on its more successful global outreach. One notable case of MFI dissolution was the Coalition for Women's Economic Development (CWED) in Los Angeles, one of the seven core programs in the Self-Employment Learning Project (Huemann & Wiley, 1999). After some years, it completely disintegrated. (Factors leading to its demise included staff conflicts, poor managerial decisions, and public sector bureaucracy, which hampered the organization's capacity to change with new economic conditions.)

Finally, when trends such as dropping U.S. unemployment rates and rising availability of decent wage/salary jobs occur, there will be a decrease in the number of people who seek to create microcredit-based self-employment options.

A number of conservative U.S. think tanks have heavily criticized the rise of microcredit. One of them, the Mises Institute, was established to eulogize the legendary thinking of Ludwig von Mises, and takes a decidedly libertarian stance on economic and political issues. The writer complains that microcredit is a type of "cult," and complains, "Despite a massive governmental push . . . very few borrowers receive any benefit at all." He concludes hyping traditional finance by raising a rhetorical question: "Is this the kind of program that will uplift the poor in the United States? We are better off sticking with old-fashioned banks that turn a profit, don't need subsidies, treat their borrowers like human beings rather than minions in a vast political organizing effort" (Tucker, 1999, p. 2).

But even mainstream business sources have their doubts about microcredit. For instance, in 2001 the *Wall Street Journal* published one of the most widespread attacks on the movement. Its authors alleged that Grameen Bank suffered from loan repayment problems and lateness or nonpayment, and that its accounting processes hid financial irregularities (Pearl & Phillips, 2001). The world's largest MFI defended itself in the press by pointing out that it adheres 100% to Bangladeshi corporate accounting practices, and pointed out that the nation's Central Bank officials constantly audit its books, resulting in two decades without a single irregularity. In fact, the MFI has continually published its financial information every month to anyone interested, making it one of the most transparent banks in the world (Yunus, 2001).

With respect to late payments and nonpayment of some loans, Grameen reported that indeed, it did suffer a onetime hit, but it was because of the devastating 1998 floods that inundated half of the country, killing thousands, destroying microenterprises, and leaving millions of homes under water for nearly three months. As a socially conscious MFI, Grameen forgave thousands of microloans and wrote them off as an expense. Repayment rates had indeed dropped to approximately 90%, but rebounded within a year and were again operating at 99% (Yunus, 2001).

Although the *Journal* debated has subsided, other skeptics and their criticisms remain. Summarizing some of the issues includes the following oft-repeated assertions: (a) Providing loans to women only may disrupt the traditional family structure, (b) tiny amounts of microcredit are too small to generate significant new jobs and lift the poor out of poverty, and (c) many more youth and young adults are unemployed globally, and microfinance is not sufficient to solve this crisis, and so forth.

My frequent response to such critiques is the observation that microcredit is not a silver bullet with which to solve all problems. It is but one tool, albeit a radically different idea, for reducing family poverty in many sectors of society. With respect to the previous three issues, my rebuttals are synthesized as follows:

1. Although skeptics may worry about female-focused microcredit disrupting families, some data suggest that microcredit makes women more equal and gives them a sense of dignity. Studies imply that marriages are stronger when there is a more level playing field between the partners. The female entrepreneurs begin to accumulate assets, and these assets can be used to provide better education and health care for their children. Furthermore, a number of MFIs have begun to change their client mix by moving toward a more 50-50 ratio of male and female borrowers. Actually, one in India, BASIX, now gives preferential treatment in giving loans to male microentrepreneurs first (BASIX,

2005). A number of other MFIs are beginning to do the same.

2. The second complaint is from critics who argue that small microloans are insignificant in generating new jobs. To this, I would agree to an extent, depending on what is meant by "insignificant." At one level, I would argue that helping even just a few families is a good thing. Maybe even one. But the impact problem of numbers is the result of the lack of capital, not the methodology. In the future, as the formal financial markets further embrace this movement, we will see much more significant effects from it on a nation's economy. In Bangladesh, where millions have received microloans, approximately a third of recipients have moved above the official poverty line (Yunus, 2000). I am told that similar effects have occurred in Bolivia and Peru. As MFI access to larger amounts of capital becomes easier, more families will rise above poverty, including the U.S. poor.

3. With respect to the third criticism that new employment creation is not keeping up with the demand, especially regarding youth, I concur. But the size of the problem is immense. Should we abandon traditional capitalist companies because they do not provide all the jobs society needs? The International Labour Organization (ILO) estimates that there are some 200 million unemployed people globally, and nearly half are the ages of late teens and early adults. Even worse, the proportion has greatly accelerated in just the past decade, making the future even more bleak (ILO, 2004). So I would suggest that MFIs are more needed now than ever. Microenterprises, more so than huge multinational corporations, are going to help answer this challenge. Large companies have been downsizing for a decade in much of the world, and those jobs will not return. This is likely to be a growing crisis facing the U.S. economy as well. One of the most viable solutions is clearly going to

be microcredit. To meet the demand, however, MFIs must turn their attention to this growing new, younger target population, a group that it typically has overlooked. Doing this will require new strategies, youth-centered training programs, and other innovations to strengthen the next generation of microentrepreneurs.

## NEXT STEPS

Of course, other issues regarding microenterprise could be addressed were it not for the constraints of space and deadlines for this chapter. Among them are my personal concerns about *mission drift,* that is, the tendency of U.S. microcredit to flow to the upper-level segments of the poor rather than to those truly at the bottom. This phenomenon tends to occur because very poor families are perceived as higher risks, less educated, and may, therefore, not repay their loans on time, in full.

But I argue that considerable effort should be made to focus on America's most vulnerable families and that by designing effective strategies they can and will be responsible clients. To what extent this is possible within the current U.S. economic context is clearly a matter of debate, owing at least, in part, to the cold reality that serving the poorest microentrepreneurs with tiny loans is not just risky, but also more expensive.

Future research needs to be done, but I think the data will bear out my assertion that the poor can become bankable. Better studies are badly needed on viable MFI tools for alleviating U.S. family poverty. Which methods are indeed best? How may greater amounts of capital ramp up this movement within our own country? What does not work, and why? How might it be changed? In addition, I would suggest that U.S. microfinance needs to move beyond government support and private donations. What will be required increasingly in the future is to build MFI strategies that not only reach out to poor families, but that can become sustainable for the long run. To continue depending on government subsidies, fund-raising campaigns and annual donor requests will not fully do the job. Nor will simply reaching a break-even point be sufficient. Over time, U.S. MFIs may need to be transformed into institutions of the capital markets, in which they are no longer operate as mere nonprofit foundations, but become morphed into for-profit companies working parallel with the traditional banking sector.

In conclusion, my sense is that microenterprise tools have made inroads for alleviating family poverty in America. They are elements of an economic self-reliance strategy that is here to stay. Microenterprise is based on the premise of a business model, not welfare. If we envision economic development as a ladder, what we have had historically is rungs toward the top that served the upper middle classes and elites—those who had decent jobs, or great jobs, sufficient or huge wealth, who worked in corporations, government, or the financial zenith of Wall Street. These families have enjoyed great access to banks and other upper echelon financial services, reiterating the old adage that it takes money to borrow money.

In contrast, at the very bottom of the economic ladder are the poorest families—the disabled, the unemployed, the immigrants. They have subsisted on the lower rungs because of government antipoverty tools such as job services, food stamps, AFDC, and other programs. But these have not been enough to help many of the poor climb up. Instead, they have stayed at the bottom—stagnant, dependent, and unable to progress.

U.S. microenterprise adds a couple of new rungs to the ladder, above those of welfare, but below the rungs of the upper and middle classes. It can be a facilitator for improving a family's quality of life. What is different, however, is that microcredit empowers the poor family's capital investment, even in a microenterprise. As we have seen in south Florida, Hispanic Utah, and the Lakota reservation in the Midwest, it generates a sense of ownership and hope. Bit by bit, along with entrepreneurial training and consulting, in addition to a microloan, the impoverished family of today may rise beyond mere survival toward a sense of dignity tomorrow, and eventually enjoy the blessing of having control over one's own economic future. This is the promise of microenterprise for poor U.S. families.

## REFERENCES

Ashe, J. (2000). Microfinance in the United States: The Working Capital experience—Ten years of leading and learning. *Journal of Microfinance, 2,* 22–60.

Association for Economic Opportunity. (2006). *State fact sheets.* Washington, DC: Author.

Barsky, J. S. (2000). *Getting it together: Working Capital's group model and its effects on microentrepreneurs, their businesses, and their communities.* Cambridge, MA: Working Capital.

BASIX. (2005). *Annual report.* Retrieved July 1, 2006, from http://www.basixindia .com/basix2004–05.pdf

Black Miami. (2006). *Gammons seasonings.* Retrieved April 2, 2006, from http://www.blackmiami.tripod.com/wholesale.html

Brigham Young University. (2002). *Hispanic inner city report.* Unpublished Report, College of Education, Brigham Young University.

Clark, P., & Kays, A. (1999). *Microenterprise and the poor*. Washington, DC: Aspen Institute.

Daley-Harris, S. (Ed.). (2005). *State of the Microcredit Summit Campaign report 2005*. Washington, DC: Microcredit Summit Campaign.

Edgecomb, E., & Klein, J. (2005). *Opening opportunities, building ownership: Fulfilling the promise of microenterprise in the United States*. Washington, DC: Aspen Institute.

Garr, R. (1996). *Groups that change communities: The Lakota Fund*. Retrieved May 1, 2004, from http://www.grass-roots.org/usa/lakotafund.shtml

Gordon, K. (1997–2005). Presentations, speeches, and conversations with W. Woodworth, Brigham Young University, Provo, UT.

Himes, C., & Servon, L. J. (1998). *Measuring client success: An evaluation of ACCION's impact on microenterprises in the United States* (The U.S. Issues Series, Document #2). Washington, DC: ACCION International.

Huemann, E., & Wiley, J. (1999). *The challenge of microenterprise: The CWED story*. Oakland, CA: National Economic Development & Law Center.

International Labour Organization (ILO). (2004, August 12). *Global unemployment trends for youth*. Geneva: Author.

Lakota Fund. (1998). *About the fund*. Retrieved May 3, 2004, and June 17, 2006, from http://www.lakotafund.org/about/htm

Meeks, E. (2000). A conversation. *Community Dividend*. Federal Reserve Bank of Minneapolis, Issue No. 2.

Micro-Business USA. (2006a). *Micro-Business success*. Retrieved May 30, 2006, from http://www.microbusinessusa.org/success.htm

Micro-Business USA. (2006b). *Micro-Business USA*. Retrieved May 28, 2006, from http://www.microbusinessusa.org/programs.htm

Nelson, C. (1994). *Going forward: The peer group lending exchange*. Toronto: Calmeadow.

Nelson, C. (Ed.). (2000). Microenterprise fact sheet series, Issue 1. *Microenterprise self-employment*. Fund for Innovation, Effectiveness, Learning and Dissemination (FIELD) at the Aspen Institute, and the Association for Enterprise Opportunity (AEO). Washington, DC: Aspen Institute.

Pearl, D., & Phillips, M. M. (2001, November 27). Grameen Bank, which pioneered loans for the poor, has hit a repayment snag. *The Wall Street Journal*.

Raheim, S. & Alter, C. F. (1995, April). *Self-employment investment demonstration final evaluation report Part I: Participant survey*. Iowa City: University of Iowa School of Social Work.

Sustainable Communities Network (SCN). (1997). *The Lakota Fund, 91–92*. Retrieved May 1, 2004, from http://www.sustainable.org/casestudies/SIA_PDFs/SIA_South_Dakota.pdf

Taub, R. P. (2004). *Doing development in Arkansas: Using credit to create opportunity for entrepreneurs outside the mainstream*. Fayetteville: University of Arkansas Press.

Tucker, J. (1999). Microcredit meltdown. *The free market, 2*. Retrieved July 8, 2006, from http://www.mises.org/story/337

United Nations. (2005). International Year of Microcredit 2005. Retrieved July 19, 2006, from http://www.yearofmicrocredit.org

Woodworth, W. (Ed.). (2000). *Small really is beautiful: Micro approaches to third world development—Microentrepreneurship, microenterprise, and microfinance*. Ann Arbor, MI: Third World Thinktank.

Woodworth, W. (2004, October). *Tribal entrepreneurship: Microfinance for Indian self-reliance.* Paper presented at the International Academy for Management and Business Conference (IAMB), Las Vegas, NV.

Woodworth, W., Brown J., Heaton, T., Morris, L., Munyon, J., Okerlund, M., et al. (2003). *Latino community service learning data.* Mayor's unpublished presentation at the Marriott School, Brigham Young University.

Yunus, M. (2000). The Grameen Bank model for lifting the poor. In W. Woodworth (Ed.), *Small really is beautiful: Micro approaches to third world development—Microentrepreneurship, microenterprise, and microfinance* (pp. 32–43). Ann Arbor, MI: Third World Thinktank.

Yunus, M. (2001, December 12). The Grameen Bank, micro-credit, and the *Wall Street Journal. The Wall Street Journal.*

# CHAPTER 26

# Working With Families in Poverty

## Toward a Multilevel, Population-Based Approach

MATTHEW R. SANDERS AND WILLIAM BOR

The quality of parent-child relationships is recognized as an important influence on future child and adolescent development (Collins, Maccoby, Steinberg, Hetherington, Bornstein, 2000; Hill, 2002; Maccoby, 2000). Many initiatives targeting the prevention of antisocial behavior, mental health problems including depression and suicide, and drug abuse point to the importance of implementing evidence-based programs to improve parenting skills and thereby reduce the exposure of children to adverse environmental factors. Parenting interventions based on social learning models have repeatedly been demonstrated to be effective in helping many parents to become more positive in their interactions with their children and to reduce dysfunctional parenting practices (Sanders, 1999). This approach involves use of active skills training methods such as modeling, practice, and feedback to teach parents to increase positive interactions and be more consistent and contingent in disciplining children. However, when parents raise their children in an environment of

financial hardship and the consequent adversities that stem from being poor, the parenting task is complicated and becomes more stressful.

This chapter explores the relationship between poverty, parenting, and child outcomes, especially behavior problems. It also discusses the implications of this research for the development and implementation of parenting programs. Particular challenges in working with poor families are identified and possible solutions to these challenges are discussed. In particular, we argue that a population approach is a strategy better suited to the needs of poor families. Research relating to the use of the Australian-developed Triple P-Positive Parenting Program with poor families is used to illustrate principles and issues involved in addressing the parenting concerns of families.

## The Impact of Poverty on Child and Adolescent Development

The term *poverty* is used in this paper in a generic sense signifying a family's lack of resources, low income, low occupational status of parents, or a more composite measure of disadvantage. Much of the empirical evidence relevant to English-speaking developed economies on the negative impact of poverty on children has emerged from research in the United States, Canada, and the United Kingdom (Bradshaw, 2002; Duncan & Brooks-Gunn, 1997).

North American studies indicate that a strong relationship exists between low family income and poor academic attainment (Duncan & Magnuson, 2003). Other outcome measures (behavior, health) are weakly predicted by income. The experience of poverty in early and middle childhood rather than later poverty is more important in influencing later cognitive and achievement outcomes as well as completed schooling. The effect of poverty is not linear, with most of the burden falling on disadvantaged families, especially in relation to low achievements. Comparisons between poor and nonpoor children reveal that poor children have twice the risk of failing to complete or dropping out of high school, 1.4 times risk for learning disability, and 6.8 times risk for reported child abuse and neglect (Duncan & Magnuson, 2003).

The picture in the United Kingdom is somewhat different than the North American experience (Bradshaw, 2002). Using various estimates, the United Kingdom has higher rates of child poverty compared with its European neighbors. The social characteristics of poor children in the United Kingdom are dominated by families with no employment and single-parent status, large families with three or more children, and families belonging to minority ethnic groups. Child poverty is concentrated in various geographical areas (e.g., northern United Kingdom). Review of the outcomes for children during the last two decades reveals probable increases in child mortality, child accidental deaths, increases in youth suicide and poorer educational outcomes.

## Mechanisms

Although the association between poverty (variously measured) and poor child outcomes are relatively uncontroversial, what remains uncertain are the mechanisms by which poverty produces its negative effects on child development. Different components of socioeconomic status (SES) can have different effects (Duncan & Magnuson, 2003). For example, as noted previously, low family income is more strongly associated with poor academic outcomes than with mental health or physical health outcomes. It appears that low family income early in childhood has greater negative effects than it does during adolescence. Persistent poverty has the greatest impact on child outcomes in contrast to changing parental income status (Blau, 1999). Parent education status, though considered predominantly functioning through parent-child interaction and subsequent cognitive skills development, can also influence child development through parental organizational skills (Duncan & Magnuson, 2003).

Mechanisms can include poor nutrition, poorly stimulating home environment, parental mental health problems, adverse neighborhood influences, and parent-child interaction difficulties (Bradley & Corwyn, 2002). Parenting behaviors in low socioeconomic households can include deficits in stimulation of child cognitive skills, poor supervision, poor parental regulation of affect, punitive or irritable interaction, and low parental self-efficacy, helplessness and frank neglect.

## Parenting, Poverty, and Child Outcomes

Any examination of the link between poverty, parenting, and child outcomes assumes the importance of the role of parents in child socialization and well-being. Early research into the impact of parenting on children and adolescents emphasized the impact on well-being through a combination of warmth, supervision, and consistent non-violent discipline (Baumrind, 1966; Maccoby & Martin, 1983). Although this early research was criticized for neglecting other explanatory factors such as heredity, peer group influences, and broader social factors, research using sophisticated designs has confirmed the importance of parenting (Collins et al., 2000; Maccoby, 2000; Rutter, 2004).

One well-researched aspect of the relationship between poverty, parenting, and child outcomes is the investigation of the impact of economic loss on child and adolescent behavior. One stream of research within this area comprised a series of American longitudinal studies that examined the impact of economic loss on families with children and adolescents of different ages, across different historical periods (Conger & Elder, 1994; Elder, 1999). From these empirical investigations emerged the "Family Stress Model" (FSM) (Conger, Ge, Elder, Lorenz, & Simons, 1994), a dynamic understanding of the role of economic loss, the experience of economic pressure, changes in parents' mood, marital relationship and parenting behavior, which resulted in child and adolescent socio-emotional difficulties. Detailed assessment of the FSM has established a clear link between economic pressure and harsh parenting (Simons, Whitbeck, Melby, & Wu, 1994). The FSM has been replicated in countries with different social security structures from the United States, such as during the Finland recession of the 1990s (Solantaus, Leinonen, & Punamaki, 2004).

A second stream of research includes a group of American studies, both cross-sectional and longitudinal in design, that examined the impact of poverty on minority ethnic groups and on the geneses of conduct and delinquency problems. McLoyd and Wilson (1991) carried out a cross-sectional study on 92 children and African American mothers on welfare. The study collected information

about a number of aspects of mother-child functioning, including child behavior, maternal mental state, and parenting. The multivariate modeling confirmed that low nurturance made a significant contribution beyond other confounders to poor child outcomes in this population. In a later, larger cross-sectional study focusing on single poor African American mothers and children, Ceballo and McLoyd (2002) sought to clarify the impact of neighborhood functioning, social support, and parenting in poor families. The study found that poorer neighborhoods reduced the positive impact of social support on parenting. The FSM was assessed in urban poor single parents with preadolescent children from a diverse racial background (Mistry, Vandewater, Huston, & McLoyd, 2002). The findings were in the expected direction with economically pressured parents experiencing distress and dysfunctional parenting.

Other research has confirmed the importance of parenting as a mediator of poor child outcomes. Dodge, Pettit and Bates (1994) found that increases in disadvantage were associated with increasingly poor socialization of children across multiple domains such as discipline, warmth, and cognitive stimulation. Harsh discipline stood out as having one of the strongest effects on later behavior. Sampson and Laub (1994) reexamined data from the Glueck cohort study, which compared the outcomes of 500 matched delinquent youth, confirming that family process factors (parent-child attachment, supervision, and harsh discipline) mediated two-thirds of the influence of poverty on later delinquency.

In summary, research, especially from the United States, has demonstrated an important and enduring link between poverty, economic pressure, parenting, and child and adolescent mental health outcomes. Although not all family poverty studies have confirmed the link (Hanson, McLanahan & Thomson,

1997), the main findings have been replicated in different ethnic groups and in different countries. The implications of the link between poverty, parenting and adverse child mental health outcomes for the development of effective family-based interventions, especially for poor families, is discussed later.

## Parenting Programs for Poor Families

The need of poor families for evidence-based parenting and family support interventions has to be seen in the larger scientific context of research into the effects of parenting programs. Several recent comprehensive reviews have documented the efficacy of family-based interventions or Behavioral Family Intervention (BFI) based on social learning, functional analysis, and cognitive-behavioral principles as an approach to treating children and their families (Lochman, 1990; McMahon, 1999; Sanders, 1996, 1998; Taylor & Biglan, 1998). This literature will not be revisited here in detail. Evidence indicates that BFI can benefit children with disruptive behavior disorders, particularly children with oppositional defiant disorders (ODD), and their parents (Forehand & Long, 1988; McMahon & Wells, 1998; Webster-Stratton, 1994). The empirical basis of BFI is strengthened by evidence that the approach can be successfully applied to many other clinical problems and disorders, including attention deficit hyperactivity disorder (Barkley, Guevremont, Anastopoulos, & Fletcher, 1992), persistent feeding difficulties (Turner, Sanders, & Wall, 1994), pain syndromes (Sanders, Shepherd, Cleghorn, & Woolford, 1994), anxiety disorders (Barrett, Dadds, & Rapee, 1996), autism and developmental disabilities (Schreibman, Kaneko, & Koegel, 1991), achievement problems, and habit disorders, as well as everyday problems of normal children (see Sanders, 1996; Taylor & Biglan, 1998, for reviews of this literature).

Parenting and family-oriented interventions have also been increasingly used with parents of adolescents at risk of drug abuse, conduct problems and delinquency, attention deficit disorder, eating disorders, depression, and chronic illness (Dishion & Andrews, 1995; Irvine, Biglan, Smolkowski, Metzler, & Ary, 1999; Spoth, Redmond, & Shin, 2001).

Meta-analyses of treatment outcome studies of family focused interventions often report large effect sizes (Serketich & Dumas, 1996), with good maintenance of treatment gains (Forehand & Long, 1988). Treatment effects have been shown to generalize to school settings (McNeil, Eyberg, Eisenstadt, Newcomb, & Funderburk, 1991) and to various community settings outside the home (Sanders & Glynn, 1981). Parents participating in these programs are generally satisfied consumers (Webster-Stratton, 1989).

It is also becoming increasingly evident that the benefits of parenting programs are not restricted to children, with several studies now reporting effects in other areas of family functioning, including reduced maternal depression and stress, increases in parental satisfaction and efficacy, and reduced marital conflict over parenting issues (e.g., Nicholson & Sanders, 1999; Sanders, Markie-Dadds, Tully & Bor, 2000; Sanders & McFarland, 2000; Webster- Stratton, 1998).

## A POPULATION PERSPECTIVE ON PREVENTION AND FAMILY INTERVENTION

Parenting interventions that target poor families are particularly likely to benefit from a population-based strategy that makes parenting support available to all families in a community, neighborhood, or geographical catchment area. This strategy needs to be designed to enhance parental competence, prevent dysfunctional parenting practices, promote better teamwork between partners, and thereby reduce an important set of family risk factors associated with behavioral and emotional problems in children and adolescents. Before such a population approach can be effective, several scientific and clinical criteria need to be met (Taylor, 1999).

## Knowledge of the Prevalence and Incidence of Family Risk Factors

Some studies that have established the incidence and prevalence of child behavior problems have also examined parenting practices, disciplinary styles, psychological adjustment, and marital conflict. For example, Sanders et al. (1999) found that 70% of parents with children younger than age 12 years reported they spank their children at least occasionally, 3% reported hitting their child with an object other than their hand, and 25% of parents reported significant disagreements with partners over parenting issues. Ralph et al. (2003) found that between 14% and 21% of parents of young adolescents aged between 12 and 14 reported feeling nervous, down in the dumps, or downhearted and blue much of the time, with between 30% and 40% reporting high levels of emotional dependence on their adolescents' well-being.

## Knowledge That Changing Specific Family Risk and Protective Factors Leads to a Reduction in Prevalence and Incidence of Targeted Child Problems

An effective population level parenting strategy must make explicit the kinds of parenting practices that are considered harmful or beneficial to children. The core constructs believed to underpin competent parenting need to be articulated so that targets for intervention can be specified. The validity of an intervention model would be greatly strengthened if improvements in child functioning were shown to be directly related to specific decreases in dysfunctional parenting and increases in competent parenting variables specified by the model. For example, considerable evidence now supports the proposition that teaching parents positive parenting and consistent disciplinary skills results in significant improvements in behavior for most oppositional and disruptive children, particularly young children, attesting to the importance of reducing patterns of coercive parent-child interaction (Patterson, 1982).

## Family Interventions Must Be Culturally Appropriate

An effective population-level strategy should be tailored in such a way that it is accessible, relevant, and respectful of the cultural values, beliefs, aspirations, traditions, and identified needs of different ethnic groups. Factors such as family structure, roles and responsibilities, predominant cultural beliefs and values, child raising practices and developmental issues, sexuality, and gender roles may be culturally specific and need to be addressed. Although there is much to learn about how to achieve this objective in a multicultural context, it is likely that sensitively tailored parenting programs can be effective with a variety of cultural groups. It is important that the multicultural context within which assessment, intervention, and research programs operate is made clear in evaluations. There is an ethical imperative to ensure that interventions designed to provide skills to parents and children in the dominant culture are not at the expense of language and other competencies or values in the child's own culture.

## Interventions Need to Be Widely Available

A key assumption of a population-based approach is that parenting and other family intervention strategies should be widely accessible in the community. Barriers to accessing parenting and other family intervention programs for poor families must be reduced. Families most in need of help with emotional and behavioral problems often do not seek or gain access to support services. Families who are socially and economically disadvantaged are less likely to refer themselves for help. In addition, parenting services may be viewed as coercive and intrusive, rather than helpful. Use of media, the Internet, and CD-ROM–based applications all have the potential to increase the reach of interventions to hard-to-access groups, although such approaches require systematic evaluation.

## A POPULATION APPROACH TO PREVENTION: THE TRIPLE P-POSITIVE PARENTING PROGRAM

Approaches to prevention are now typically conceptualized as falling into one of three categories: universal, selective, or indicated (Mrazek & Haggerty, 1994). A *universal* prevention strategy targets an entire population (e.g., national, local community, neighborhood, or school), *selective* prevention programs refer to strategies that target specific subgroups of the general population that are believed to be at greater risk than others for developing a problem (e.g., poor families, young single mothers), and *indicated* preventive interventions target high-risk individuals who are identified as having detectable problems, but who do not yet meet diagnostic criteria for a behavioral disorder (e.g., disruptive and aggressive children). The Triple P-Positive Parenting Program is a multilevel parenting and family support strategy developed by the first author and his colleagues at The University of Queensland in Brisbane, Australia. The program aims to prevent severe behavioral, emotional, and developmental problems in children by enhancing the knowledge, skills,

and confidence of parents. It incorporates universal, selective, and indicated interventions organized across five levels on a tiered continuum of increasing strength (see Table 26.1) for parents of children from birth to age 12. Recently the program has been extended in collaboration with the second author to provide the same levels of support for parents of teenagers aged 12 to 16.

Level 1, a universal parent information strategy, provides all interested parents with access to useful information about parenting through a coordinated media and promotional campaign using print and electronic media, as well as user-friendly parenting tip sheets and videotapes that demonstrate specific parenting strategies. This level of intervention aims to increase community awareness of parenting resources, receptivity of parents to participating in programs, and to create a sense of optimism by depicting solutions to common behavioral and developmental concerns. Level 2 is a brief primary health-care selective intervention providing anticipatory developmental guidance to parents of children with mild behavior difficulties. This level of intervention can be delivered individually (one to two sessions), or to large groups of parents as three 90-minute seminars. Level 3, a four-session more intensive selective intervention, targets children with mild to moderate behavior difficulties and includes active skills training for parents. Level 4 is an indicated intensive 8- to 10-session individual or group training program for parents of children with more severe behavioral difficulties, and Level 5 is an enhanced behavioral family intervention program for families where parenting difficulties are complicated by other sources of family distress (e.g., marital conflict, parental depression, high levels of stress, or teenage relationship problems).

In summary, this multilevel strategy recognizes differing levels of dysfunction and behavioral disturbance in children and

**Table 26.1** The Triple P Model of Parenting and Family Support

| Level of Intervention | Target Population | Intervention Methods | Practitioners |
|---|---|---|---|
| Level 1 Media-based parent information campaign Universal Triple P | All parents interested in information about parenting and promoting their child's development. | Coordinated media and health promotion campaign raising awareness of parent issues and encouraging participation in parenting programs. May involve electronic and print media (e.g., community service announcements, talk-back radio, newspaper and magazine editorials). | Typically coordinated by area media liaison officers or mental health or welfare staff. |
| Level 2 Health promotion strategy/brief selective intervention Selected Triple P Selected Teen Triple P | Parents interested in parenting education or with specific concerns about their child's development or behavior. | Health promotion information or specific advice for a discrete developmental issue or minor child behavior problem. May involve a group seminar process or brief (up to 20 minutes) telephone or face-to-face clinician contact. | Parent support during routine well-child health care (e.g., child and community health, education, allied health, and childcare staff). |
| Level 3 Narrow focus parent training Primary Care Triple P Primary Care Teen Triple P | Parents with specific concerns as above who require consultations or active skills training. | Brief program (about 80 minutes over four sessions) combining advice, rehearsal, and self-evaluation to teach parents to manage a discrete child problem behavior. May involve telephone or face-to-face clinician contact or group sessions. | Same as for Level 2. |
| Level 4 Broad focus parent training Standard Triple P Group Triple P; Group Teen Triple P; Self-Directed Triple P; Self-Directed Teen Triple P | Parents wanting intensive training in positive parenting skills. Typically parents of children with behavior problems such as aggressive or oppositional behavior. | Broad focus program (about 10 hours over 8–10 sessions) focusing on parent-child interaction and the application of parenting skills to a broad range of target behaviors. Includes generalization enhancement strategies. May be self-directed or involve telephone or face-to-face clinician contact or group sessions. | Intensive parenting interventions (e.g., mental health and welfare staff, and other allied health and education professionals who regularly consult with parents about child behavior). |
| Stepping Stones Triple P | Families of preschool children with disabilities who have or are at risk of developing behavioral or emotional disorders. | A parallel 10-session individually tailored program with a focus on disabilities. Sessions typically last 60–90 minutes (with the exception of three practice sessions, which last 40 minutes). | Same as above. |
| Level 5 Intensive family intervention modules Enhanced Triple P | Parents of children with behavior problems and concurrent family dysfunction such as parental depression or stress, or conflict between partners. | Intensive individually tailored program with modules (60- to 90-minute sessions) including practice sessions to enhance parenting skills, mood management and stress coping skills, and partner support skills. | Intensive family intervention work (e.g., mental health and welfare staff). |
| Pathways Triple P | Parents at risk of maltreating their children. Targets anger management problems and other factors associated with abuse. | Modules include attribution retraining and anger management. | Same as above. |

adolescents, and that parents have differing needs and desires regarding the type, intensity, and mode of assistance they may require. The multilevel strategy is designed to maximize efficiency, contain costs, avoid waste and over servicing, and ensure the program has wide reach in the community. The program targets five different developmental periods from infancy to adolescence, and within each developmental period, the reach of the intervention can vary from being very broad (targeting an entire population) or quite narrow (targeting only high-risk children). Also, the multidisciplinary nature of the program involves the better use of the existing professional workforce in the task of promoting competent parenting.

## RELATIONSHIP BETWEEN DISADVANTAGE AND RESPONSE TO PARENTING INTERVENTIONS

When parents do participate in a parenting program, the impact of the intervention is compromised by lower than desirable completion rates (Fontana, Fleischman, McCarton, Meltzer, & Ruff, 1988; Weinberger, Tublin, Ford, & Feldman, 1990). Research examining how to improve engagement and decrease noncompletion is needed to strengthen the population level value of parenting programs as preventive interventions BFI (Biglan & Meltzer, 1998; Prinz & Miller, 1996; Spoth, Goldberg, & Redmond, 1999).

*Engagement* can be defined at a number of levels, beginning with the initial reach of a program or intervention, to subsequent completion of the particular intervention. *Intervention reach* is defined as the percentage of parents in a given population who are attracted to the intervention. *Completion* refers to adherence to the content and process of the intervention.

Low completion rates pose challenges for preventive interventions. The success of an intervention rests in its ability to lead to individual change, as well as the capability to deliver population level shifts away from clinical levels of difficulty. Engagement of low-income parents is critical for reducing the prevalence rates of adverse outcomes including childhood mental health problems. To achieve these objectives, the intervention needs to reach parents whose children are at risk of developing problems and ensure that parents complete a sufficient intervention dose. To decrease the prevalence rates of conduct problems in preschool-aged children, sufficient numbers of families need to be exposed to the intervention, and of those exposed, high completion rates are needed to optimize the yield from the investment in the intervention.

Low completion rates (e.g., 50% or worse) reduce the clinical outcomes of services, waste scarce clinical resources, and adversely affect the professionals involved in delivering the intervention. Practitioners experiencing high noncompletion rates can become disillusioned and frustrated and develop negative appraisals of clients and may disown responsibility for the intervention outcomes they achieve. Finally, low engagement and high noncompletion in research trials can lead to inadequate sample sizes that limit conclusions and generalizability (Hinshaw et al., 2004). Relatively few studies address the issue of engagement (Spoth & Redmond, 2000). Although some research has examined the relationships between recruitment, engagement, and appointment keeping and factors of socioeconomic status, few causal links have been established (e.g., Dubinsky, 1986).

Some research has shown that the completion rates of parents undertaking a group version of Triple P is related to parent characteristics. For example, Zubrick et al. (2005) found that even though the program was effective in reducing the prevalence of conduct problems when offered universally to all parents in a disadvantaged catchment area, parents were less likely to complete the program if they were sole parents, had less than 10 years of education, earned less than $20,000 per year in family income and if the family was a step or blended family. Parents who did not complete the program also reported higher levels of depression, anxiety, and stress. Similarly, Heinrichs, Bertram, Kuschel, and Hahlweg (2005) found a number of socio-demographic factors such as single parenthood and low social status related to program participation. These findings have also been demonstrated cross-culturally (Leung, Sanders, Ip, & Lau, 2006).

These findings are important because these same characteristics are related to increased risk of children developing problems in the first place. However, these studies examined only a limited range of socio-demographic predictors and did not examine reasons for the relationship between factors such as single parenting and program completion. This evidence collectively suggests that special efforts are needed to engage poor families and to tailor universally offered parenting programs to their needs.

## Implications

Part of the challenge in working with poor families is the recognition that many parents may be at risk of not completing the intervention and may benefit from additional strategies to promote engagement. Table 26.1 outlines a consultation framework for working collaboratively with parents. Table 26.2 outlines possible strategies that have been found helpful in working with poor families at risk of child maltreatment.

To improve the efficacy of parenting programs with poor parents, a range of strategies can be employed to improve retention:

1. *Increase parental self-efficacy:* Use of individualized selection of graded homework tasks to ensure early success; using a self-regulatory model in goal selection;

individual clarification of goals; reinforcement of attendance (verbal and social).

2. *Enhance motivation:* Individual clarification of obstacles to change; use of testimonials from other low-income parents to assist in anticipating obstacles and increasing perceived benefits; use of motivational interviewing techniques before commencing the intervention.

3. *Create favorable outcome expectancies:* Individual clarification of expectations and obstacles; clarification of purpose and process of intervention; clarification of the nature of expected outcomes for parent, child, and family.

Strategies used in enhancing engagement can be based on the specific risk factors identified for each individual family, and may thus differ between individuals in a parenting group. For example, where parents' expectations about the program form an obstacle to engagement, practitioners can contact the parent and clarify expectations, obstacles, and commitment to the process before the commencement of the group. Similarly, if motivation to change is low, practitioners can contact parents before the group, establish rapport and trust, clarify expectations, and enhance parents' motivation to attend. Ensuring early sense of achievement and working from a competency-based model (Sanders & Cann, 2002) may engage those parents with low self-efficacy. Practitioners can use additional social reinforcement (e.g., acknowledging attendance and effort, praising for homework completion) and encouragement during the group sessions to enhance perceptions of self-efficacy. Approaches can be tailored to the family characteristics; for example, some low-income parents with low intervention expectancies may benefit from additional attention to the credibility of treatment. In contrast those with low expectancies and high levels of child problem behaviors may benefit most from a description of the likely impact of the

**Table 26.2**    Process Issues and Engaging Poor Parents

| *Domain* | *Description* | *Possible Strategies* |
|---|---|---|
| Building rapport | Participants may be reluctant, resentful, suspicious, and hostile. | Normalize the process of attending a parenting program and point out benefits to participants. |
| | | Allow sufficient time for first home visits to build a relationship with participant in a relaxed atmosphere. |
| Strengthening motivation | There is a high incidence of disruption in participants' lives, and attending group sessions is a significant demand on their time. | Build rapport with participants. Add small material incentives (e.g., lucky dip or door prize for attendance). |
| | | Phone participants each week to encourage attendance at next session. |
| | | Provide certificates to those who complete the program (including home visits and assessment). |
| Reducing barriers to attending group sessions | Poor planning and organizational skills.Transport problems. | Remind participants frequently about group sessions and home visit appointments. |
| | | Provide transport assistance (e.g., taxis, bus). |
| Managing disruptions to involvement in program | Participants' lives can be chaotic and unpredictable, creating obstacles to attending groups and keeping appointments for home visits. | Allow flexibility in the program. Allow participants to switch groups if required. |
| | | Be prepared to reschedule home visits a number of times while maintaining rapport with participant. |
| Literacy Issues | Participants may have very poor literacy, particularly from non-English speaking backgrounds. They find it difficult to complete questionnaires and written exercises during sessions. | Give more one-on-one attention (e.g., read out questionnaires question by question) in group sessions. |
| | | Co-facilitators assist with any exercises involving writing. |

intervention on their child's behavior (Nock & Kazdin, 2001).

An active pursuit of avoiders and noncompleters can also be used to reduce barriers and obstacles to participation. This could involve individualized contact with each parent following non-attendance at a group session and clarification of concerns and obstacles. This needs to be done in a nonblaming and supportive manner, such that an attitude of acceptance will be communicated. Similarly, practitioners will be taught strategies to avoid power struggles over task and homework completion, using an acceptance approach.

## CONCLUSION

Family conflict and poor parenting are generic risk factors associated with a wide variety of adverse developmental outcomes in children including increasing risk for conduct problems, drug abuse, delinquency, and academic underachievement. Considerable evidence shows that although financial hardship contributes to adverse outcomes in children, the quality of parenting mediates the effects of poverty on children. This chapter makes the case for assisting disadvantaged families through a population level perspective specifically designed to address parenting and family risk factors related to the development of child psychopathology. A comprehensive, evidence-based, multilevel model of parenting and family support is presented. The evidence reviewed shows significant effects on both child and parent mental health outcomes. Challenges in disseminating empirically supported parenting interventions and future directions for family intervention research, policy, and practice are highlighted.

When poor parents experience difficulties with their children, it is tempting to assume that because there may be many additional problems present (e.g., mental health problems, drug or alcohol abuse, relationship violence, unemployment, unsafe neighborhoods) that all of these risk factors need to be attended to so parents can derive any benefit from participation. However, when families present for assistance, it is often difficult to determine which of a range of problems are of primary etiological significant and which

are secondary. For example, a poor parent of a preschooler with severe behavior problems may present as being depressed, anxious, in conflict with a partner, and worried about her finances. However, the depression and partner conflict and a substantial level of stress could be sequelae of living with a child who is aggressive and out of control. Other difficulties commonly seem much more manageable when the parent gets a good night's sleep without their sleep pattern being disrupted by the child and partner conflict often decreases once the parents agree on a strategy to use with the child. Furthermore, the principle of sufficiency argues for the need to identify the minimally sufficient level of intervention support required by the parent. Complex multicomponent treatments can be time consuming, costly to deliver, and burdensome on parents' time, and not necessarily more effective than targeting a more limited subset of problems that the parent experiences success with. Our experience in working with poor parents is that a better relationship with their children is extremely important to them. Achieving success in the parenting domain can increase a more global sense of personal efficacy and agency that can potentially generalize to other areas of their lives.

## REFERENCES

Barkley, R. A., Guevremont, D. C., Anastopoulos, A. D., & Fletcher, K. E. (1992). A comparison of three family therapy programs for treating family conflicts in adolescents with attention-deficit hyperactivity disorder. *Journal of Consulting and Clinical Psychology, 60*(3), 450–462.

Barrett, P. M., Dadds, M. R., & Rapee, R. M. (1996). Family treatment of childhood anxiety: A controlled trial. *Journal of Consulting and Clinical Psychology, 65*, 627–635.

Baumrind, D. (1966). Effects of authoritative parent control on child behavior. *Child Development, 37*(4), 887–907.

Biglan, A., & Metzler, C. W. (1998). A public health perspective for research on family-focused interventions. In R. S. Ashery, E. B. Robertson, & K. L. Kumpfer (Eds.), *Drug abuse prevention through family interventions. NIDA Research Monograph 177* (pp. 430–458) (NIH Publication No. 99-4135). Washington, DC: National Institute on Drug Abuse.

Blau, D. M. (1999). The effect of income on child development. *Review of Economics and Statistics, 81*(2), 261–276.

Bradley, R. H., & Corwyn, R. F. (2002). Socioeconomic status and child development. *Annual Review of Psychology, 53,* 371–399.

Bradshaw, J. (2002). Child poverty and child outcomes. *Children and Society, 16,* 131–140.

Ceballo, R., & McLoyd, V. C. (2002). Social support and parenting in poor, dangerous neighborhoods. *Child Development, 73*(4), 1310–1321.

Collins, W. A., Maccoby, E. E., Steinberg, L., Hetherington, E. M., & Bornstein, M. H. (2000, February). The case for nature and nurture. Contemporary research on parenting. *American Psychologist,* pp. 218–232.

Conger, R. D., & Elder, G. H., Jr. (1994). Families in troubled times: The Iowa Youth and Families Project. In R. D. Conger & G. H. Elder, Jr. (Eds.), *Families in troubled times. Adapting to change in rural America* (pp. 3–19). New York: Aldine de Gruyter.

Conger, R. D., Ge, X., Elder, G. H., Lorenz, F. O., & Simons, R. L. (1994). Economic stress, coercive family process and developmental problems of adolescents. *Child Development, 65,* 541–561.

Dishion, T. J., & Andrews, D. W. (1995). Preventing escalation in problem behaviours with high-risk young adolescents: Immediate and 1-year outcomes. *Journal of Consulting and Clinical Psychology, 63,* 538–548.

Dodge, K. A., Pettit, G. S., & Bates, J. E. (1994). Socialization mediators of the relation between socioeconomic status and child conduct problems. *Child Development, 65,* 649–665.

Dubinsky, M. (1986). Predictors of appointment non-compliance in community mental health patients. *Community Mental Health Journal, 22*(2), 142–146.

Duncan, G. J., & Brooks-Gunn, J. (Eds.). (1997). *Consequences of growing up poor.* New York: Russell Sage.

Duncan, G. J., & Magnuson, K. A. (2003). Off with Hollingshead: Socioeconomic resources. Parenting and child development. In M. H. Bornstein & R. H. Bradley (Eds.), *Socioeconomic status, parenting and child development* (pp. 83–106). Mahwah, NJ: Erlbaum.

Elder, G. H. (1999). *Children of the Great Depression: Social change in life experience. 25th anniversary edition.* Boulder, CO: Westview Press.

Fontana, C. A., Fleischman, A. R., McCarton, C., Meltzer, A., & Ruff, H. (1988). A neonatal preventative intervention study: Issues of recruitment and retention. *Journal of Primary Prevention, 9,* 164–176.

Forehand, R. L., & Long, N. (1988). Outpatient treatment of the acting out child: Procedures, long-term follow-up data, and clinical problems. *Advances in Behaviour Research and Therapy, 10,* 129–177.

Hanson, T. L., McLanahan, S., & Thomson, E. (1997). Economic resources, parental practices, and children's well-being. In G. J. Duncan & J. Brooks-Gunn (Eds.), *Consequences of growing up poor* (pp. 190–238). New York: Russell Sage.

Heinrichs, N., Bertram, H., Kuschel, A., & Hahlweg, K. (2005). Parent recruitment and retention in a universal prevention program for child behavior and emotional problems: Barriers to research and program participation. *Prevention Science, 6,* 275–286.

Hill, J. (2002). Biological, psychological and social processes in the conduct disorders. *Journal of Child Psychology and Psychiatry, 43*(1), 133.

Hinshaw, S. P., Hoagwood, K., Jensen, P. S., Kratochvil, C., Bickman, L., Clarke, G., et al. (2004). AACAP 2001 Research Forum: Challenges and recommendations regarding recruitment and retention of participants in research investigations. *Journal of the American Academy of Child & Adolescent Psychiatry, 43*(8), 1037–1045.

Irvine, A. B., Biglan, A., Smolkowski, K., Metzler, C. W., & Ary, D. V. (1999). The effectiveness of a parenting skills program for parents of middle-school students in small communities. *Journal of Consulting and Clinical Psychology, 67*, 811–825.

Leung, C., Sanders, M. R., Ip, F., & Lau, J. (2006). Implementation of Triple P-Positive Parenting Program in Hong Kong: Predictors of program outcome. *Journal of Children's Services, 1(2)*, 4–17.

Lochman, J. E. (1990). Modification of childhood aggression. In M. Hersen, R. M. Eisler, & P. M. Miller (Eds.), *Progress in behavior modification* (Vol. 25, pp. 47–85). New York: Academic Press.

Maccoby, E. E. (2000). Parenting and its effects on children: On reading and mis-reading behavior genetics. *Annual Review of Psychology, 51*, 1–27.

Maccoby, E. E., & Martin, J. A. (1983). Socialization in the context of the family: Parent-child interaction. In E. M. Hetherington (Ed.), *The handbook of child psychology*. New York: Wiley.

McLoyd, V. C., & Wilson, L. (1991). The strain of living poor: Parenting, social support and child mental health. In A. C. Huston (Ed.), *Children in poverty: Child development and public policy* (pp. 105–135). New York: Cambridge University Press.

McMahon, R. J. (1999). Parent Training. In S. W. Russ & T. Ollendick (Eds.), *Handbook of psychotherapies with children and families*. New York: Plenum Press.

McMahon, R. J., & Wells, K. C. (1998). Conduct problems. In E. J. Mash and R. A. Barkley (Eds.), *Treatment of childhood disorders* (2nd ed.). (pp. 111–207). New York: Guilford Press.

McNeil, C. B., Eyberg, S., Eisenstadt, T. H., Newcomb, K., & Funderburk, B. W. (1991). Parent-child interaction therapy with behavior problem children: Generalization of treatment effects to the school setting. *Journal of Clinical Child Psychology, 20(2)*, 140–151.

Mistry, R. S., Vandewater, E. A., Huston, A. C., & McLoyd, V. C. (2002). Economic well-being and children's social adjustment: The role of family process in an ethically diverse low-income sample. *Child Development, 73*, 935–951.

Mrazek, P., & Haggerty, R. J. (1994). *Reducing the risks for mental disorders*. Washington, DC: National Academy Press.

Nicholson, J. M., & Sanders, M. R. (1999). Randomized controlled trial of behavioral family intervention for the treatment of child behavior problems in step-families. *Journal of Divorce and Remarriage, 30(3–4)*, 1–23.

Nock, M. K., & Kazdin, A. E. (2001). Parent expectancies for child therapy: Assessment and relation to participation in treatment. *Journal of Child & Family Studies, 10(2)*, 155–180.

Patterson, G. R. (1982). *Coercive family process*. Eugene, OR: Castalia Press.

Prinz, R. J., & Miller, G. E. (1996). Parental engagement in interventions for children at risk for conduct disorder. In R. D. Peters & R. J. McMahon (Eds.), *Preventing childhood disorders, substance abuse, and delinquency* (pp. 161–183). Thousand Oaks, CA: Sage.

Ralph, A., Toumbourou, J. W., Grigg, M., Mulcahy, R., Carr-Gregg, M., & Sanders, M. R. (2003). Early intervention to help parents manage behavioural and emotional problems in early adolescents: What parents want. *Australian e-Journal for the Advancement of Mental Health, 2(3)*. Retrieved from http://www.auseinet.com/journal/vol2iss3/ralph.pdf

Rutter, M. (2004). Environmentally medicated risks for psychopathology: Research strategies and findings. *Journal of the American Academy of Child and Adolescent Psychiatry, 41*(1), 3–18.

Sampson, R. J., & Laub, J. H. (1994). Urban poverty and the family context of delinquency: A new look at structure and process in a classic study. *Child Development, 65*, 523–540.

Sanders, M. R. (1996). New directions in behavioural family intervention with children. In T. H. Ollendick & R. J. Prinz (Eds.), *Advances in clinical child psychology* (Vol. 18, pp. 283–330). New York: Plenum Press.

Sanders, M. R. (1998). The empirical status of psychological interventions with families of children and adolescents. In L. L'Abate (Ed.), *Family psychopathology: The relational roots of dysfunctional behavior.* New York: Guilford Press.

Sanders, M. R. (1999). The Triple P-Positive parenting program: Towards an empirically validated multilevel parenting and family support strategy for the prevention of behavior and emotional problems in children. *Clinical Child and Family Psychology Review, 2*(2), 71–90.

Sanders, M. R., & Cann, W. C. (2002). Promoting positive parenting as an abuse prevention strategy. In K. Browne, H. Hanks, P. Stratton, & C. Hamilton (Eds.), *Early prediction and prevention of child abuse: A handbook* (pp. 145–163). Chichester, UK: Wiley.

Sanders, M. R., & Glynn, E. L. (1981). Training parents in behavioural self-management: An analysis of generalization and maintenance effects. *Journal of Applied Behavior Analysis, 14*, 223–237.

Sanders, M. R., Markie-Dadds, C., Tully, L., & Bor, B. (2000). The Triple P-Positive Parenting program: A comparison of enhanced, standard and self-directed behavioural family intervention for parents of children with early onset conduct problems. *Journal of Consulting and Clinical Psychology, 68*, 624–640.

Sanders, M. R., & McFarland, M. L. (2000). The treatment of depressed mothers with disruptive children: A controlled evaluation of cognitive behavioural family intervention. *Behavior Therapy, 31*, 89–112.

Sanders, M. R., Shepherd, R. W., Cleghorn, G., & Woolford, H. (1994). The treatment of recurrent abdominal pain in children. A controlled comparison of cognitive-behavioural family intervention and standard pediatric care. *Journal of Consulting and Clinical Psychology, 62*, 306–314.

Sanders, M. R., Tully, L. A., Baade, P., Lynch, M. E., Heywood, A., Pollard, G., & Youlden, D. (1999). A survey of parenting practices in Queensland: Implications for Mental Health Promotion. *Health Promotion Journal of Australia, 9*, 105–114.

Schreibman, L., Kaneko, W. M., & Koegel, R. L. (1991). Positive affect of parents of autistic children: A comparison across two teaching techniques. *Behavior Therapy, 22*(4), 479–490.

Serketich, W. J., & Dumas, J. E. (1996). The effectiveness of behavioural parent training to modify antisocial behaviour in children: A meta-analysis. *Behavior Therapy, 27*, 171–186.

Simons, R. L., Whitbeck, L. B., Melby, J. N., & Wu, C. (1994). Economic Pressure and Harsh Parenting. In R. D. Conger & G. H. Elder, Jr. (Eds.), *Families in troubled times. Adapting to change in rural America* (pp. 207–222). New York: Aldine de Gruyter.

Solantaus, T., Leinonen, J., & Punamaki, R. L. (2004). Children's mental health in times of economic recession: Replication and extension of the Family Economic Stress Model in Finland. *Developmental Psychology, 40*(3), 412–429.

Spoth, R., Goldberg, C., & Redmond, C. (1999). Engaging families in longitudinal preventive intervention research: Discrete-time survival analysis of socioeconomic and social-emotional risk factors. *Journal of Consulting and Clinical Psychology, 67*(1), 157–163.

Spoth, R. L., & Redmond, C. (2000). Research on family engagement in preventive interventions: Toward improved use of scientific findings in primary prevention practice. *Journal of Primary Prevention, 21*(2), 267–284.

Spoth, R. L., Redmond, C., & Shin, C. (2001). Randomised trial of brief family interventions for general populations: Adolescent substance use outcomes 4 years following baseline. *Journal of Consulting and Clinical Psychology, 67,* 619–630.

Taylor, C. B. (1999, September). *Population-based psychotherapy: Issues related to combining risk factor reduction and clinical treatment in defined populations.* Paper presented at the 29th Annual Congress of the European Association of Behavioural and Cognitive Therapies, Dresden, Germany.

Taylor, T. K., & Biglan, A. (1998). Behavioural family interventions for improving child-rearing: A review of the literature for clinicians and policy makers. *Clinical Child and Family Psychology, 1*(1), 41–60.

Turner, K. M. T., Sanders, M. R., & Wall, C. R. (1994). Behavioural parent training versus dietary education in the treatment of children with persistent feeding difficulties. *Behaviour Change, 11*(4), 242–258.

Webster-Stratton, C. (1989). Systematic comparison of consumer satisfaction of three cost effective parent training programs for conduct problem children. *Behavior Therapy, 20,* 103–115.

Webster-Stratton, C. (1994). Advancing videotape parent training: A comparison study. *Journal of Consulting and Clinical Psychology, 62*(3), 583–593.

Webster-Stratton, C. (1998). Preventing conduct problems in Head Start children: Strengthening parenting competencies. *Journal of Consulting and Clinical Psychology, 66*(5), 715–730.

Weinberger, D. A., Tublin, S. K., Ford, M. E., & Feldman, S. S. (1990). Preadolescents' social-emotional adjustment and selective attrition in family research. *Child Development, 61,* 1374–1386.

Zubrick, S. R., Ward, K. A., Silburn, S. R., Lawrence, D., Williams, A. A., Blair, E., et al. (2005). Prevention of child behavior problems through universal implementation of a group behavioral family intervention. *Prevention Science, 6*(4), 287–304.

# CHAPTER 27

# Increasing Marriage Would Dramatically Reduce Child Poverty

ROBERT E. RECTOR, KIRK A. JOHNSON, AND PATRICK F. FAGAN

I n 2001, 1.35 million children were born outside marriage in the United States. This represents 33.5% of all children born in the United States in that year. Children raised by never-married mothers are seven times more likely to be poor when compared with children raised in intact married families. The obvious nexus between single-parent families and child poverty has led President George W. Bush to propose a new trial program aimed at increasing child well-being and reducing child poverty by promoting healthy marriage.

Critics have rejected President Bush's proposal as illogical. They argue that increasing marriage would not significantly reduce child poverty for two reasons: first, there is a substantial shortage of suitable males for single mothers to marry, and second, even if single mothers married the father of their children, the earnings of the fathers are so low that they would not lift the family out of poverty.

However, new light has been shed on the status of nonmarried parents through the recent Fragile Families and Child Wellbeing Study.[1]

The Fragile Families survey is a nationwide effort to collect data on both married and non-married parents at the time of a child's birth. The survey reveals that most of the claims about marriage and nonmarried fathers made by the opponents of the Bush "healthy marriage" proposal are wildly inaccurate.

The Fragile Families Study shows the following:

- The median age of nonmarried mothers is 22 at the time of birth of the child. Nearly three-quarters of nonmarried mothers are in a relatively stable romantic relationship with the expectant father at about the time of birth of their child.
- The expectant nonmarried fathers who have a romantic involvement with the mother-to-be are quite "marriageable." Very few have drug, alcohol, or physical abuse problems.
- On average, the earnings of nonmarried expectant fathers are higher than the earnings of expectant mothers in the year before the child's birth.
- The median annual earnings of nonmarried fathers are approximately $17,500 per year.

In this study, the Fragile Families data are used to calculate how much marriage could reduce poverty among couples who are not married at the time of the child's birth. This analysis finds that marriage would dramatically reduce poverty among the nonmarried mothers who are romantically involved with the fathers at the time of the child's birth.

Specifically, if these mothers do not marry but remain single, about 55% will be poor. By contrast, if all the mothers married the child's father, the poverty rate would fall to less than 17%. Thus, on average, marriage would reduce the odds that a mother and a child will live in poverty by more than 70%.

The contention, made by critics of the president's marriage-strengthening policy, that increased marriage will not reduce child poverty because fathers do not earn enough to lift a family out of poverty is inaccurate. Even though marriage of mothers and fathers would not eliminate child poverty in every case, in most cases, marriage would lift families out of poverty. Overall, the insights culled from the Fragile Families dataset and described in this study strongly indicate that a policy aimed at promoting healthy marriage among young parents has enormous potential to reduce child poverty.

## ANALYSIS

The data used in this analysis are taken from the Fragile Families and Child Wellbeing Study, developed jointly by Princeton University's Center for Research on Child Wellbeing and Columbia University's Social Indicators Survey Center.[2] The Fragile Families Study provides the best data available on the characteristics of nonmarried parents about the time of a child's birth.

These couples are of particular public policy interest because they are likely to be a high-priority target group for President Bush's proposed program to promote healthy marriage. Thus, the nonmarried parents in the Fragile Families survey are an excellent population for assessing the potential economic consequences of increasing marriage.

## CHARACTERISTICS OF NONMARRIED PARENTS

Some 38% of the mothers in the Fragile Families Study were not married at the time of their child's birth. Popular opinion sees out-of-wedlock childbearing as occurring mainly to young girls of high-school age who lack stable relationships with their child's father. This perception is erroneous. The median age for mothers who give birth outside marriage is 22.

Nor are nonmarried mothers alone and isolated at the time of birth. As Table 27.1 shows, nearly 50% of these mothers are cohabiting with the expectant father at around the time of the child's birth. Another 23% describe themselves as "romantically involved" with the father, although the couple is not cohabiting.

The characteristics of nonmarried fathers who are cohabiting or romantically involved with the mother are generally more favorable than the popular stereotype (see Table 27.2). Around 67% of the fathers have at least a high-school degree. Some 97% were employed during the prior year, and 82% were employed at the time of the child's birth. The median annual income of these romantically involved/cohabiting fathers was $17,500.

Among romantically involved or cohabiting couples, physical abuse is rare: A full 98% of the women in this group report that the father has never slapped them when angry. Although some fathers do have drug and alcohol problems, the level is less than might be expected: Around 12% of the mothers report arguing with their boyfriends about a drug or alcohol problem in the last month; 2.5% report that drugs or alcohol impede the boyfriend's ability to hold a job.

On average, the nonmarried expectant fathers have higher earnings than the expectant

**Table 27.1** Relationship Between Unmarried Mother and Father

|  | *Black* | *All* |
|---|---|---|
| Cohabitating and romantically involved | 35.4% | 49.7% |
| Not cohabitating but romantically involved | 32.2% | 23.0% |
| "On-again, off-again" relationship | 13.9% | 10.6% |
| Just friends | 10.7% | 8.1% |
| Hardly ever or never talk to each other | 7.8% | 8.6% |
| Total | 100.0% | 100.0% |

SOURCE: Fragile Families and Child Wellbeing Study.

**Table 27.2** Characteristics of Unmarried Fathers Who Are Romantically Involved With Mothers

| *Indicator* | *Black* | *All* |
|---|---|---|
| Father's median age at baby's birth | 25 | 25 |
| Father's median annual income | $17,500 | $17,500 |
| Father's median weeks worked last year | 48 | 50 |
| Percent employed during year | 96.1% | 97% |
| Percent employed at baby's birth | 73.0% | 82% |
| Percent high school graduate or higher education | 66.2% | 66.7% |
| Percent "hit or slap" mother "sometimes" or "often" | 1.3% | 1.8% |
| Percent argued "often" or "sometimes" about drug/alcohol problem in past month | 14.1% | 12.2% |

SOURCE: Fragile Families and Child Wellbeing Study.

mothers in the year before the child's birth. The median wage rate of fathers is $8.55 per hour, compared with $7.00 per hour for the mothers.[3]

Nearly all couples that are romantically involved or cohabiting are interested in developing a long-term, stable relationship. Some 95% believe that there is at least a 50-50 chance they will marry in the future.

## MARRIAGE SIMULATION

The purpose of this study is to calculate the reduction in poverty that would occur if non-married women married the fathers of their new children around the time of the child's birth. As shown in Table 27.1, some non-married pregnant women do not have positive and stable relationships with their child's father. In these cases, marriage is not, for the most part, a reasonable option. Therefore, we have restricted our initial marriage simulation to the 73% of nonmarried couples who were cohabiting or romantically involved but living apart at the time of their child's birth. We shall henceforth refer to these couples as the "marriageable group."

To determine the impact of marriage on the poverty of children and mothers, we first estimate what the poverty rate of the mothers would be if they remained single. We then calculate what the poverty rate would be if the mother and father marry. The difference between the poverty rate of the mothers when single and the rate for mothers when married demonstrates the potential for marriage to reduce child poverty and maternal poverty.

## EMPLOYMENT AND EARNINGS

The Fragile Families survey contains data on the annual earnings of new fathers during the year in which the child was born. We employ these annual earnings figures in our analysis. The study also provides annual earnings for mothers in the year before birth. However, women's participation in the labor force may be altered significantly by the birth of a child. Because of this, the paper estimates mothers' post-birth earnings based on a range of assumptions concerning the hours of employment.

Specifically, we have calculated the effect of marriage on poverty according to three separate scenarios relating to the mothers' employment after the child's birth.

- Scenario #1: The mother has zero annual employment after the birth.
- Scenario #2: The mother is employed part-time for a total of 1,000 hours per year after the birth.
- Scenario #3: The mother is employed full-time throughout the year after the birth for a total of 2,000 hours.

In each scenario, the annual earnings of the fathers are assumed to be the same as the earnings in the year before the child's birth. The annual earnings of the mother are derived by multiplying the mother's hourly wage rate by the specified hours worked. In each scenario, the employment and earnings of a mother are assumed to be unchanged by marriage; that is, the mother is assumed to earn the same amount when married as when single.[4]

## WELFARE BENEFITS

The simulation assumes that single mothers will be eligible for Temporary Assistance for Needy Families (TANF), Earned Income Tax Credit (EITC), and food stamps. The level of benefits that a single mother would receive from each program is determined by the number of children in the family and the mother's annual earnings. Simulations for married couples assume that they are eligible only for food stamps and the EITC. The couple's earnings and family size determine the value of benefits. It is assumed that no married couples will receive TANF benefits.

## RESULTS OF THE MARRIAGE SIMULATION

Under each scenario, we calculate the percentage of mothers who would be poor if they lived as single parents and the percentage who would be poor if they were married to the child's father.[5]

*Scenario #1: The Mother Is Unemployed.* Table 27.3 shows the impact of marriage on maternal and child poverty under Scenario #1. In this scenario, the mothers are not employed after the birth of the child. When single, the mothers are solely dependent on welfare (TANF and food stamps). When married, the mothers are solely dependent on the father's earnings plus EITC and food stamps.

As Table 27.3 shows, if mothers remain single and unemployed, they will be poor 100% of the time. This is because welfare benefits alone rarely, if ever, provide enough income to raise a family above the poverty level. By contrast, if the mother marries the child's father, the poverty rate drops dramatically to 35%. In other words, nearly two-thirds of the nonmarried fathers within the marriageable group earn enough by

**Table 27.3**     Results of Marriage Simulation Among Marriageable Couples

| | Family Income Below 100% of Poverty | Family Income Between 100% and 150% of Poverty | Family Income Over 150% of Poverty | Total |
|---|---|---|---|---|
| Scenario 1: Mother is not employed | | | | |
| If mother remains single | 100.0% | 0.0% | 0.0% | 100.0% |
| If mother and father marry | 35.0% | 35.4% | 29.6% | 100.0% |

SOURCE: Fragile Families and Child Wellbeing Study.

themselves to support a family above poverty without any employment on the part of the mother.

Under the conditions of Scenario #1, marriage more than doubles the family income of mothers and children. If unmarried, the mothers would have a median income of around $8,800. Marriage would raise the mothers' median family income by more than $11,000 to $20,226 (see Table 27.6).

*Scenario #2: The Mother Is Employed Part-Time.* Table 27.4 shows the impact of marriage on child poverty under Scenario #2. In this scenario, mothers are assumed to be employed part-time for a total of 1,000 hours per year after the birth of their child. This scenario closely matches the employment rates of single mothers with young children as reported by the U.S. Census Bureau.[6] Thus, this is the most realistic of the three scenarios.

Single mothers are assumed to receive income from earnings, EITC, food stamps, and, in some cases, TANF.[7] Married couples are assumed to receive income from earnings, EITC, and food stamps. In this scenario, mothers are assumed to work 1,000 hours per year, whether single or married.

As Table 27.4 shows, 55% of the mothers in the Fragile Families study will live in poverty if they remain single and are employed part-time. By contrast, if the mothers marry, their poverty rate plummets to 17%. In other words, the father's normal earnings, combined with the part-time earnings of the mother, are sufficient to raise 83% of the families above the poverty line.

Under conditions of part-time maternal employment in Scenario #2, marriage increases family income by 75%. If unmarried, mothers would have a median income of around $13,500. Marriage would raise

**Table 27.4**     Results of Marriage Simulation Among Marriageable Couples

| | Family Income Below 100% of Poverty | Family Income Between 100% and 150% of Poverty | Family Income Over 150% of Poverty | Total |
|---|---|---|---|---|
| Scenario 2: Mother is employed part-time | | | | |
| If mother remains single | 55.1% | 41.3% | 3.6% | 100.0% |
| If mother and father marry | 16.9% | 37.2% | 45.9% | 100.0% |

SOURCE: Fragile Families and Child Wellbeing Study.

the mothers' median family income by around $10,000 to a level of $23,700.[8]

Marriage combined with part-time maternal employment not only raises nearly all families above poverty, but in many cases also raises family income well above the poverty level. For example, under Scenario #2, less than 4% of single mothers would have family incomes above 150% of the poverty level. By contrast, about 46% of married couples would have an income above 150% of the poverty level.[9]

*Scenario #3: The Mother Is Employed Full-Time.* Full-time, full-year employment is effective in reducing poverty among single mothers. Some 90% of single mothers could maintain their families above poverty if they worked full-time throughout the year. (Full-time, full-year employment is equivalent 2,000 annual hours of employment or 40 hours per week for 50 weeks.) Census Bureau data (again from the Current Population Survey) reveal that approximately 30% of single mothers with children younger than 4 are employed 2,000 hours or more per year.

Very few single mothers who were employed full-time, full-year would remain poor, so marriage has little effect in reducing poverty in this scenario. (Nearly 96% of married couples would have incomes above the poverty level, compared with 90% of single mothers.) However, marriage would raise the family incomes of many full-time working mothers well above poverty and into middle-class levels.

Full-time working mothers would have a median income of around $17,500 per year. If these mothers married their child's father, median family income would rise to $29,000 per year. As Table 27.5 shows, nearly two-thirds of these married couples would have incomes above 150% of the poverty level. By contrast, only 20% of full-time working single mothers would have incomes above that level.

## SUMMARY OF RESULTS[10]

Tables 27.6 and 27.7 summarize the results of the three scenarios for marriageable couples. As Table 27.6 shows, marriage would increase median family income of mothers in the study by between $10,200 and $11,400 per year. (The increase in median family income is less than the median annual earnings of the fathers—$17,500—because marriage entails an offsetting loss of welfare benefits for the mother.)

Table 27.7 summarizes the impact of marriage on poverty. In each scenario, marriage reduces the probability that mothers will live in poverty by at least two-thirds. Marriage would lift the incomes of many mothers above 150% of the poverty level. In Scenario #1, some 30% of married families would have incomes above 150% of the poverty level. In

**Table 27.5**    Results of Marriage Simulation Among Marriageable Couples

|  | Family Income Below 100% of Poverty | Family Income Between 100% and 150% of Poverty | Family Income Over 150% of Poverty | Total |
|---|---|---|---|---|
| Scenario 3:  Mother is employed full-time |  |  |  |  |
| If mother remains single | 9.8% | 69.9% | 20.3% | 100.0% |
| If mother and father marry | 4.4% | 31.6% | 64.0% | 100.0% |

SOURCE: Fragile Families and Child Wellbeing Study.

**Table 27.6**    Median Family Income Before and After Simulation*

|  | *Before Simulation* | *After Simulation* | *Net Increase in Family Income Due to Marriage* |
|---|---|---|---|
| Scenario 1 | $8,844 | $20,266 | $11,422 |
| Scenario 2 | $13,578 | $23,777 | $10,199 |
| Scenario 3 | $17,491 | $29,090 | $11,599 |

* Result of simulation among marriageable couples.

SOURCE: Fragile Families and Child Wellbeing Study.

**Table 27.7**    Results of Marriage Simulation Among Marriageable Couples

|  | *Family Income Below 100% of Poverty* | *Family Income Between 100% and 150% of Poverty* | *Family Income Over 150% of Poverty* | *Total* |
|---|---|---|---|---|
| Scenario 1: Mother is not employed |  |  |  |  |
| If mother remains single | 100.0% | 0.0% | 0.0% | 100.0% |
| If mother and father marry | 35.0% | 35.4% | 29.6% | 100.0% |
| Scenario 2: Mother is employed part-time |  |  |  |  |
| If mother remains single | 55.1% | 41.3% | 3.6% | 100.0% |
| If mother and father marry | 16.9% | 37.2% | 45.9% | 100.0% |
| Scenario 3: Mother is employed full-time |  |  |  |  |
| If mother remains single | 9.8% | 69.9% | 20.3% | 100.0% |
| If mother and father marry | 4.4% | 31.6% | 64.0% | 100.0% |

SOURCE: Fragile Families and Child Wellbeing Study.

Scenario #3, nearly two-thirds of married families would have incomes above that level.

## ALTERNATIVE MARRIAGE SIMULATION FOR ALL NONMARRIED COUPLES

As noted, the marriage simulation data presented in Tables 27.3 through 27.7 pertain to the "marriageable" couples within the Fragile Families survey—that is, those who, at the time of the child's birth, are cohabiting or living separately but are still romantically involved. These couples represent 73% of all nonmarried couples at the time of a child's birth.

Expectant mothers and fathers in the marriageable group have somewhat higher earnings than do other nonmarried couples in the year before their child's birth. Therefore, marriage may have a substantially greater effect in reducing poverty among the marriageable group than among nonmarried couples in general.

To investigate that possibility, the marriage simulation was rerun for all nonmarried couples in the Fragile Families survey; thus, the new simulation included both the "marriageable" and " nonmarriageable" couples. The results of this expanded simulation were extremely similar to those for the marriageable subset. For example, under

Scenario #2, 56.5% of mothers will be poor, if unmarried, compared with 18.4% of mothers, if married. (For the marriageable subgroup, the figures were 55.1% and 16.9%, respectively.) The complete results of the expanded simulation for all nonmarried couples are shown in Table 27.8.

## DISCUSSION

Each year, more than 1.3 million children in the United States are born outside marriage. This represents 33.5% of all births. The Fragile Family survey shows that in 73% of out-of-wedlock births, the mother and father are romantically involved and have a relatively stable relationship.

Nearly half of nonmarried expectant mothers are cohabiting with the father at about the time of their child's birth. Overall, some 95% of nonmarried mothers express positive attitudes about marrying their new baby's father in the future. Yet only 9% of couples will actually marry within a year after their child's birth. Within a few years,

the relationships of most of the nonmarried parents will deteriorate and the mother and father will split up.

As a new strategy for reducing child poverty and improving child well-being, President Bush has proposed a new pilot program to promote healthy marriage. A principal target population of the president's proposed program would be romantically involved nonmarried couples at or around the "magic moment" of a child's birth. This target group is the precise population analyzed in this study.

Participation in the president's marriage program would be voluntary. The program would seek to increase healthy marriage by providing target couples with the following:

- Accurate information on the value of marriage in the lives of men, women, and children
- Marriage-skills education that will enable couples to reduce conflict and increase the happiness and longevity of their relationship
- Experimental reductions in the current financial penalties against marriage that are contained in all federal welfare programs

**Table 27.8** Results of Marriage Simulation Among All Single Couples*

| | Family Income Below 100% of Poverty | Family Income Between 100% and 150% of Poverty | Family Income Over 150% of Poverty | Total |
|---|---|---|---|---|
| Scenario 1: Mother is not employed | | | | |
| If mother remains single | 100.0% | 0.0% | 0.0% | 100.0% |
| If mother and father marry | 36.6% | 34.8% | 28.6% | 100.0% |
| Scenario 2: Mother is employed part-time | | | | |
| If mother remains single | 56.5% | 40.1% | 3.4% | 100.0% |
| If mother and father marry | 18.4% | 37.3% | 44.3% | 100.0% |
| Scenario 3: Mother is employed full-time | | | | |
| If mother remains single | 10.5% | 69.9% | 19.6% | 100.0% |
| If mother and father marry | 5.1% | 33.2% | 61.7% | 100.0% |

* Cases with missing data excluded from analysis.

SOURCE: Fragile Families and Child Wellbeing Study.

The programs would use existing marriage-skills education programs that have proven effective in decreasing conflict and increasing happiness and stability among couples. The pro-marriage initiative would not seek merely to increase marriage rates among target couples, but would provide ongoing support to help at-risk couples maintain healthy marriages over the long term.

The president proposes spending $300 million per year on his pilot program to promote healthy marriage. This modest sum represents spending only 1 cent to promote healthy marriage for every 5 dollars the government currently spends subsidizing single-parent families.

The analysis presented in this paper shows that marriage has an enormous potential to reduce poverty among couples who are unmarried at the time of their child's birth. In general, a 10% increase in the marriage rate of poor single mothers would reduce poverty among that group by 7 percentage points.

Increasing the number of healthy marriages would also have substantial non-economic benefits for children. Children who are raised in marriage by their biological mother and father are dramatically less likely to have emotional and behavioral problems, to be physically abused, to become involved in crime, to fail in school, to abuse drugs, and to end up on welfare as adults.[11]

## CRITICISM OF MARRIAGE PROGRAMS TO ALLEVIATE POVERTY

Critics of President Bush's proposal have charged that increasing the number of healthy marriages would not reduce child and maternal poverty. These claims are false and misleading.

For example, in a widely publicized paper titled "Let Them Eat Wedding Rings: The Role of Marriage Promotion in Welfare Reform," an organization called Alternatives to Marriage asserted, "Marriage is not an effective solution to poverty" (Solot & Miller, 2002, p. 1). However, the actual study cited in the paper shows the opposite: Marriage would eliminate poverty for most poor single mothers surveyed. Nevertheless, Alternatives to Marriage argues that marriage is not "an effective solution to poverty" because marriage would not eliminate poverty in every instance. The error of such an argument needs no further elaboration.

Additionally, some critics argue that societal structures preclude single women from rising up the economic ladder. By way of this argument, poverty would be the lack of economic resources, not single parenthood per se. Richters (1994) is a strong proponent of this argument, noting that female households lack sufficient education and skills capital to command the type of wages sufficient to raise them out of poverty.

This argument tends to ignore the synergistic effects of marriage on family finances. A married family can more easily manage the demands of home and work life when two parents share responsibilities of work and family. Also, it is easier to rise above the poverty line with two potential earners in a married family, rather than only a single parent. It is not at all surprising, then, to see poverty rates among individuals in married families to be far lower than poverty rates among single female-headed (single) families. According to 2004 Census Bureau estimates, poverty among those in female-headed families was more than 30%, whereas poverty in married families was only 6.4%. Additionally, child poverty is much lower in married families; although 9% of children in married families were poor, nearly 42% of children in female-headed families were poor in 2004 (U.S. Census Bureau, n.d.).

## FUTURE RESEARCH

The next step to this research is to evaluate the efficacy of programs that would likely be included in the president's Healthy Marriage Initiative. An assortment of smaller studies does exist and has been documented recently (Fagan, 2001); the impetus for some of these studies has been state and local initiatives whose aim is to reduce illegitimacy, reduce divorce, or both. Although these studies show that these programs are effective in decreasing divorce or illegitimacy, they do not establish that these programs would work on a widespread level.

Ideally, two types of programs should be evaluated. The first is pre-marital counseling programs aimed at low-income couples. The second program should be marital skills and education programs generally. Do these programs help form or maintain healthy marriages? Do they help stem illegitimacy?

It should go without saying that any federal program should have a strong evaluation component. More importantly, though: Evaluation of the program should be undertaken by qualified research organizations or academics that can spend the time necessary to collect the right kinds of data and generate appropriate statistical tests. Generally speaking, program administrators should not be evaluating their own programs. Not only may they lack the time or statistical acumen for such an endeavor, but also the study itself risks being biased. It is arguable that having a federal social program such as the president's Healthy Marriage Initiative without a strong evaluation component is not worth having at all.

## CONCLUSION

The erosion of marriage and the increase in single-parent families are major causes of child poverty and welfare dependence in the United States. Nearly three-quarters of government means-tested welfare aid to children goes to single-parent families (Fagan, Rector, Johnson, & Peterson, 2002). More than 80% of long-term child poverty occurs in broken or never-married families.

There is a widespread misconception that single mothers have little contact with the fathers of their children. In reality, surveys show that most nonmarried expectant mothers are romantically involved with their child's father at around the time of the child's birth. Most of these couples express positive attitudes about marriage and hope to become married in the future. Yet relatively few will, in fact, marry. Most will split apart a few years after the child's birth.

President Bush has proposed a pilot program aimed at promoting healthy marriage, especially in low-income communities. A key target group for this policy would be nonmarried mothers and fathers around the time of the "magic moment" of a child's birth. This study demonstrates that policies to increase marriage among these parents could have a large impact in reducing child poverty. In general, a 10% increase in marriage among poor single mothers would reduce child poverty within that group by 7 percentage points.

Healthy marriage is critical to the well-being of children, women, and men. President Bush's marriage-strengthening initiative should therefore be an essential part of any future welfare policy.

## TECHNICAL APPENDIX

As noted in the text, this study is based on data from the Fragile Families database (sometimes called the Survey of New Parents) conducted by the Center for Research on Child Wellbeing at Princeton University and the Social Indicators Survey Center at Columbia University. The survey poses questions to roughly 3,500 families to gauge a nationally representative sample of parents, especially regarding the nature of the relationship between unwed mothers and fathers.

In that respect, this is an especially useful database with which to simulate the effects of marriage on child poverty, especially given that the time near a child's birth is seen as a "magic moment" where unwed parents may decide to get married.

The data employ a national population weight that is designed to estimate properly the number of births in major U.S. cities (those with populations of at least 200,000). On a weighted basis, these data represent some 1.2 million babies; however, because most births in America are to married couples, only about 38% of the births in the Fragile Families survey are to unwed mothers.

Of the out-of-wedlock births, nearly 73% of children are born to parents who are romantically involved with each other. (See Table 27.1.) Marriage is likely to fail if no romantic involvement exists between the mother and the father. For that reason, only mothers who self-report a current romantic involvement with the father of the child are included in the analysis.

To conduct the analysis properly, data are needed both on the number of the mother's children who live with her (if this is not her first birth) and on earnings for the mother (for her last paying job before any maternity leave) and the father. In some cases, surveys were completed for the mother but not the father, rendering those observations unusable. Further, some surveys were completed, but questions relating to earnings or income were not reported either by the mother or by the father. Because of these data limitations, this analysis includes only cases for just over 225,000 children, on a weighted basis. On an unweighted basis, the simulation includes nearly 1,250 observations, or about two-thirds of the "romantically involved but not married" subset of the survey.

The analysis simulates the child poverty rates these mothers are likely to experience if they remain single versus their poverty rates if they married the child's father. Income for the father is assumed to remain unchanged from the last year reported in the survey. Income for the mother is based on three core scenarios:

- Scenario #1: The mother does not work.
- Scenario #2: The mother works 1,000 hours per year (or an average of 20 hours per week during 50 weeks per year).
- Scenario #3: The mother works 2,000 hours per year (or an average of 40 hours per week during 50 weeks per year).

The Fragile Families data allow an hourly earnings figure to be computed for the mother to facilitate this analysis. In a few rare cases, the computed hourly income figure is less than the statutory federal minimum wage of $5.15 per hour. In those cases, the hourly rate is set at $5.15 per hour and the analysis is continued. The poverty rates are then calculated based on two family outcomes:

- Outcome A: The mother does not marry the father of her new baby (and does not marry anyone else).
- Outcome B: The mother does marry the father of her new baby.

One of the valid criticisms of the simple use of income as the basis for poverty determination is that it ignores program benefits and tax effects. When low-income families receive food stamps, for instance, their ability to consume increases and their economic situation is thereby improved.[12] Because of this, income is adjusted to consider the following four factors:

*TANF.* Cash welfare benefits are added to any income of single women (in this simulation, no married couples may receive TANF and, operationally, few married couples qualify for cash TANF benefits). Actual TANF benefits do vary from state to state, so the reasonable median-benefit state of Kansas is used in the simulation. In Kansas, a single mother with two children who has no income would have received $429 per month (or $5,148 per year) in benefits in 1999. TANF benefits are assumed to fall by 50 cents for every dollar earned. (Put another way, the TANF "disregard rate" is set at 50%.) If a single mother earns more than $10,296, she will not receive any TANF benefits.

*Food Stamps.* Food stamps are calculated on the basis of the 1999 formula benefit levels. In 1999, a family of three could receive a maximum of $329 in food stamps per month. The Food Stamp Program counts TANF as income for purposes of benefit calculation, so any TANF is counted against food stamp eligibility. This simulation assumes that if families qualify for food stamps and/or TANF, they will apply for and receive benefits under current law formulas.

*Earned Income Tax Credit.* If a family (whether married or not) has earnings, the EITC is calculated and included as income for purposes of poverty determination. The EITC has no interaction with either TANF or food stamps.

*Payroll (FICA) Taxes.* Payroll taxes on earnings (employee side only) are subtracted from income as a last step before determining poverty rates.

Initial interviews for the Fragile Families survey took place during 3 years in the late 1990s and 2000, so the data from the midpoint year of 1999 were chosen for income, program participation, and poverty calculation. The poverty thresholds are those published for that calendar year by the Census Bureau.[13]

In all cases, poverty rates drop substantially with an increase in marriage. Tables 27.6 and 27.7 show how marriage would lift many of these families out of poverty—in some cases to more than 150% of the poverty level. (For a family of four, 150% of the poverty level is $25,543 per year.)

## NOTES

1. For a detailed description of the Fragile Families and Child Wellbeing Study, see http://www.fragilefamilies.princeton.edu/about.asp. The Fragile Families Study is a survey of roughly 4,700 new and, in many cases, unwed parents. Information about them and their new children will be tracked for 5 years. The analysis here deals only with the first year or "baseline" survey.

2. The survey of new births was collected to garner information on the changing relationships of unwed parents. As noted previously, these births will be tracked for 5 years to analyze changing dynamics. This analysis deals only with the first-year "baseline" data of the mothers and fathers.

3. The wage rates for the mothers are inferred, based on the last job they held, given that most of these women would be on maternity leave or another work break at the time of the survey.

4. In reality, some mothers might choose to work less when married. For these mothers, marriage would produce an increase in both income and "leisure." For simplicity of presentation, this option of working less after marriage has not been included in the simulation.

5. According the U.S. Census Bureau, a family is deemed poor if its annual income falls below specified poverty income thresholds. These thresholds vary according to family size. In 1999, the government's poverty income thresholds

were $13,423 for a three-person family, $16,954 for a four-person family, and $19,882 for a five-person family. If a father and mother marry, the father is added to the count of family members and the poverty income threshold is increased accordingly; the average increase in the poverty threshold is roughly $3,000 per additional family member. Thus, if a father adds more than $3,000 in net income to a family, marriage will reduce the probability that the mother and children will be poor. See U.S. Census Bureau (2000), p. A4.

6. According to data from the Census Bureau's Current Population Survey (2000), the median annual number of hours of employment for single mothers with children younger than 4 years is about 1,040.

7. The benefits a mother would receive from EITC, food stamps, and TANF are contingent on her annual earnings, which are calculated by multiplying her hourly wage rate (as reported in the Fragile Families survey) by 1,000 hours.

8. The increase in family income as a result of marriage is less than the median earnings level of the father because the couple would suffer a substantial reduction in welfare benefits if they marry.

9. In 1999, a family of four would have an income above 150% of the poverty level if it had an income above $25,342. A family of three would have an income above 150% of the poverty level if it had an income of $20,135.

10. As noted, nearly 50% of the nonmarried couples in the "marriageable group" are cohabiting at the time of the child's birth. According to Census Bureau methodology, cohabiting fathers are not considered as part of the mother's family unit. Thus, neither the father nor his earnings would be counted when determining whether the mother is poor. If a couple marries, the father and his income are included as part of the family unit. In practice, nonmarried cohabiting fathers are likely to contribute some income to the mother and child. This means that the government is likely to overestimate the de facto poverty rate of single mothers who are cohabiting. Consequently, the short-term impact of marriage in reducing poverty of single mothers may be somewhat overstated. On the other hand, the relationships of cohabiting parents are unstable. Such couples are likely to separate within a short period, and the mother and child will fall into true poverty. Healthy marriage–promotion policies are intended to increase not merely marriage, but also a couple's commitment and stability. By increasing the stability and longevity of the parents' relationships, marriage-promotion programs would have a substantial effect in reducing long-term poverty among mothers and children.

11. Sigle-Rushton (2001) also employs data from the Fragile Families survey and obtains results similar to those presented in this study. For example, the study estimates that 95% of single mothers would escape poverty if they were married and worked part-time.

12. For an elongated critique of these income issues, see Rector and Hederman (1999).

13. For the official 1999 poverty thresholds, see http://www.census.gov/hhes/www/poverty/threshld/thresh99.html (as of May 20, 2003). This analysis used the "weighted average" thresholds.

---

# REFERENCES

Fagan, P. F. (2001). *Encouraging marriage and discouraging divorce.* (Backgrounder #1421). Washington, DC: Heritage Foundation.

Fagan, P. F., Rector, R. E., Johnson, K. A., & Peterson, A. (2002). *The positive effects of marriage: A book of charts*. Washington, DC: Heritage Foundation.

Rector, R. E., & Hederman, R. S., Jr. (1999). *Income inequality: How census data misrepresent income distribution* (Center for Data Analysis Report No. 99-07). Washington, DC: Heritage Foundation.

Richters, A. (1994). Building a new paradigm: Gender, health and development. *Women's Health Journal (ISIS International), 2–3,* 40–46.

Sigle-Rushton, W. (2001). *For richer or poorer* (Center for Research on Child Well-Being Working Paper 301–17 FF). Princeton, NJ: Princeton University.

Solot, D., & Miller, M. (2002). *Let them eat wedding rings: The role of marriage promotion in welfare reform*. Boston: Alternatives to Marriage Project.

U.S. Census Bureau. (2000). *Poverty in the United States 1999* (Current Population Reports Series P60-210). Washington, DC: U.S. Government Printing Office.

U.S. Census Bureau. (n.d.). *Detailed poverty tables 2004* (Table POV02). Retrieved from http://pubdb3.census.gov/macro/032005/pov/new02_100_01.htm

# Index

# About the Editors

D. Russell Crane is Professor of Marriage and Family Therapy in the School of Family Life at Brigham Young University. He has written one sole-author text, *Fundamentals of Marital Therapy* (1996), co-edited another, *Handbook of Families and Health: Interdisciplinary Perspectives* (2006), and more than 50 refereed journal articles and book chapters. His work has appeared in leading scholarly journals including the *Journal of Marital and Family Therapy; Journal of Marriage and Family; Journal of Family Issues; Family Relations; American Journal of Family Therapy; Family Process; Clinical Child Psychology and Psychiatry; Families, Systems and Health; Contemporary Family Therapy;* and *Family Therapy.* He has recently completed a 6-year term (2000–2006) as the Director of the Families Studies Center and Associate Director for Research in the School of Family life at Brigham Young University. In addition, he has completed a 6-year term (2000–2006; 2006 as chair) as a member of the Commission on Accreditation for Marriage and Family Therapy Education of the American Association for Marriage and Family Therapy.

Tim B. Heaton is Professor in the Department of Sociology and Associate Director of the Family Studies Center at Brigham Young University. His major research focuses on the relationship between family characteristics on children's health in Latin America. In addition to analysis of the extensive data provided by the demographic and health surveys, he has helped collect data on mothers with children younger than age 5 in Bolivia and Colombia. He also continues to be interested in family demographics. Current work focuses on the divorce generation—the cohort married in the late 1960s and the early 1970s that experienced unprecedented divorce rates. Now half of this cohort has experienced marital disruption. He has authored more than 100 articles and chapters, and authored or edited 11 books.

# About the Contributors

**Angela Abela** is a senior lecturer at the University of Malta where she is Course Director of the professional Masters Programme in Clinical, Counseling and Educational psychology. She has published on marital conflict, children, and families. She is also a practicing clinical psychologist and a family therapist and supervisor. Between 2002 and 2006, she chaired the National Family Commission. In 2005, she was appointed by the Council of Europe to be part of a European Working Party on Parenting Children at Risk of Social Exclusion. She holds a PhD from the Tavistock Clinic and the University of London, and a Masters degree in Clinical Psychology from the Université de la Sorbonne Paris V.

**Jacqueline L. Angel** earned her PhD from Rutgers University and is Associate Professor at the LBJ School of Public Affairs and Sociology, the University of Texas at Austin. Her research focuses on health and social welfare policy issues with a special emphasis on populations of Hispanic origin. Currently, she is collaborating with investigators from the UT medical schools in Galveston and San Antonio on a benchmark study of elderly Mexican Americans' health in the southwestern United States. She has also recently completed a National Institute on Aging funded study on the health and economic well-being of older immigrants in the United States. Some recent publications from this work appear in the *American Journal of Public Health, International Migration Review, Journal of Gerontology: Social Science,* and *Public Administration Review* and also in a forthcoming edited collection titled *The Health of Aging Hispanics: The Mexican-Origin Population.*

**Ronald J. Angel** received his PhD from the University of Wisconsin in 1981. Currently, he is Professor of Sociology at the University of Texas at Austin. His research focuses on the role of culture and social class on health and health-care use, and he has published extensively on these and other topics. He is a former editor of the *Journal of Health and Social Behavior.* Currently, in collaboration with colleagues at the medical schools at Galveston and San Antonio, he is Principal Investigator of the Austin site on a benchmark study of the health of elderly Mexican Americans in the southwestern United States. He is also a Principal Investigator on a major study of the impact of welfare reform on children and families funded by the National Institute for Child Health and Human Development and several private foundations. His most recent book is *Poor Families in America's Health Care Crisis* (2006).

**Stephen J. Bahr** is Professor of Sociology at Brigham Young University. He received his PhD from Washington State University and previously taught at the University of Texas

484

at Austin. In recent years, his research has focused on three major areas. First, he has studied the process of prisoner reentry into society and characteristics associated with successful reentry. Second, he has done research on risk factors that are associated with adolescent drug use. Finally, he is currently analyzing changes in divorce rates and the process of marital and relationship dissolution.

**R. Gabriela Barajas** is a doctoral student in Developmental Psychology at Teachers College, Columbia University and a graduate research fellow at the National Center for Children and Families. Her research interests include the effects of poverty and maternal depression on child development. She is particularly interested in the health and scholastic achievement of children in "at risk" environments. Ms. Barajas earned her B.A. in Human Biology from Stanford University (2001) and her MA in Developmental Psychology at Teachers College (2005). At the Center, Ms. Barajas works on the Yonkers Family and Community Project and the Fragile Families study.

**Douglas J. Besharov**, JD, LLM, is Professor at the University of Maryland School of Public Policy and the Joseph J. and Violet Jacobs Scholar at the American Enterprise Institute. Professor Besharov was the first director of the U.S. National Center on Child Abuse and Neglect. His most recent book is *Recognizing Child Abuse: A Guide for the Concerned* (1990), a book designed to help professionals and laypersons identify and report suspected child abuse. He has written or edited 14 other books, and has contributed to the *New York Times, Washington Post, Wall Street Journal,* and *Los Angeles Times.*

**Ana Birkhead**, WHNP, is an instructor in the Brigham Young University College of Nursing and earned her PhD from the University of California at San Francisco. Her research focus is the health and well-being of Hispanic immigrant women.

**Kevin D. Blair** received his MSW from the University of Chicago and his PhD from the University at Buffalo. Dr. Blair is also a graduate of the Chicago Institute for Psychoanalysis. Dr. Blair's practice experience includes work as a school social worker, and in crisis intervention, divorce mediation, family therapy, and community organizing. His research interests include the practice of social work in schools and linkages between anthropology and social work. Dr. Blair has published several articles that examine the practice of social work in schools. Recently Dr. Blair has focused his attention on the Child Only component of the Temporary Assistance to Needy Families (TANF) program. He is currently engaged in a study of the strengths and stressors associated with being a kinship caregiver who is involved in the TANF program.

**William Bor**, DPM, is the Director of KidsinMind Research (www.kidsinmind .org.au) at the Mater Hospital, Brisbane, Australia. He is a certified Child and Adolescent Psychiatrist and Senior Lecturer with the Department of Psychiatry, University of Queensland. Dr. Bor's research interests include the developmental origins, trajectory, and treatment of severe aggression and antisocial behavior. Dr. Bor is involved in two longitudinal studies, a prevention program with disruptive preschoolers and a large-scale birth cohort study beginning in 1981. Dr. Bor is part of team implementing a trial of Multisystemic Therapy for abused and neglected children. Dr. Bor has coauthored 50 papers in peer-reviewed journals.

**Jeanne Brooks-Gunn**, PhD, is the Virginia and Leonard Marx Professor of Child Development and Education at Teachers

College and the College of Physicians and Surgeons at Columbia University. She is also co-director of the National Center for Children and Families at Columbia (policyforchildren .org). Dr. Brooks-Gunn Received an EdM from Harvard University and her PhD from the University of Pennsylvania. As a developmental psychologist, she conducts policy-relevant research on children, youth, and families and is the author of more than 400 articles, 4 books, and numerous edited volumes.

**Gary Bryner** is Professor in the Political Science Department and Public Policy Program at Brigham Young University (BYU), where he teaches courses in public policy, American politics, constitutional law, and environmental and natural resources policy. He has been a research fellow at the Natural Resources Defense Council, the National Academy of Public Administration, and the Brookings Institution, and has worked with the Rockefeller Institute of Government on studies of state welfare and Medicaid policy. He has BS and MA degrees in Economics from the University of Utah, a PhD in Government from Cornell University, and a JD from BYU.

**Kevin Ray Bush** is Associate Professor of Family Studies at Miami University in Oxford, Ohio. His research interests focus on child and adolescent development in the contexts of family and culture including self-concept, self-efficacy, academic achievement, internalizing and externalizing issues. He has conducted studies with U.S. (Appalachian, African American, Asian American, and Latinos) and international (e.g., Chinese, Mexican, South Korean, and Russian) samples of children, adolescents, and parents.

**Lynn Clark Callister**, RN, PhD, FAAN, is Professor in the Brigham Young University College of Nursing and a Fellow in the American Academy of Nursing. She has conducted cross-cultural research with childbearing women for the past 20 years in North and Central America, Scandinavia, the Middle East, the People's Republic of China, and the Russian Federation. She was a 2004 Fulbright Scholar to the Russian Federation. Dr. Callister has a master's degree from Wichita State University and a doctorate from the University of Utah.

**Michael Chavez**, MA, is a graduate student in the Department of Sociology at the University of California, Riverside. His current work focuses on the stress that disease can cause within intimate relationships. More specifically, he is concerned with certain types of relapsing or remitting diseases because these types of illnesses may prove to have fundamentally different implications on otherwise healthy relationships. He also does research on discrimination toward language minority students in the local educational system.

**Lynda Clarke** is a Senior Lecturer in Demography and Head of the Centre of Population Studies, London School of Hygiene and Tropical Medicine, the renowned postgraduate public health institution of the University of London. Dr. Clarke specializes in family demography in developed countries, being particularly interested in the changing family circumstances of children and the policy implications of family change. Previous work includes research into mothers, work and child care, childbearing decisions and teenage pregnancy. Currently, Dr. Clarke is the UK expert for the *EU Monitor* on the "Social Situation of the EU," directing a study of fatherhood in South Asian families and collaborating in international studies of men in prison and a study of fatherhood in South Africa.

**Scott Coltrane**, PhD, is Professor of Sociology and Associate Director of the

Center for Family Studies at the University of California, Riverside. His research focuses on families, gender, and social inequality. He is past president of the Pacific Sociological Association and is author of *Family Man, Gender and Families* (1996) and *Sociology of Marriage and the Family* (2001) and editor of *Families and Society* (2004). His most recent NIH-funded research projects investigate the impact of economic stress and the meaning of fatherhood in Mexican American and European American families.

**Katherine Jewsbury Conger**, PhD, is Assistant Professor of Human Development and Family Studies at the University of California, Davis (UCD). Dr. Conger's program of research focuses on the antecedents, correlates, and consequences of economic stress on family functioning and individual well-being. In particular, she examines the interpersonal processes in sibling and parent-child relationships that influence the onset and change in problem behaviors and important competencies during adolescence and early adulthood. During the past 15 years, her research has been supported by grants from the National Institute of Mental Health, National Institute on Drug Abuse, and National Institute of Child Health and Human Development as well as UCD and has been published in numerous book chapters and journal articles.

**Rand D. Conger** is Distinguished Professor of Human Development and Family Studies at the University of California, Davis. Dr. Conger's research focuses on social, cultural and individual characteristics that influence risk for problem behavior, substance abuse, and psychiatric disorders over time. He has published his research in more than 200 books, book chapters, and journal articles. During the past 30 years, his research has been supported by a series of federal grants from the National

Institutes of Health. In addition, the significance of his scholarly activities has been recognized through several awards from professional organizations including the National Association for Rural Mental Health, the National Council on Family Relations, the Family Sociology Section of the American Sociological Association, the International Association for Relationship Research, the Rural Sociological Society, and by election to the status of Fellow in the American Psychological Association and the National Council on Family Relations.

**Martha L. Crowley**, PhD, is Assistant Professor at Department of Sociology and Anthropology at North Carolina State University. Her research focuses on how class, race, and gender stratification play out in social institutions, including work, education, and the family. She is currently investigating worker control techniques, their impact on the experience of work, and variation along lines of class, race, and gender. Other recent research addresses the organizational foundations of sexual harassment, Mexican migration into new settlement destinations, and variation in educational resources, investment and outcomes across rural, urban, and suburban locales. She currently serves on the editorial board of *Family Relations*.

**M. Robin Dion** is a Senior Researcher at Mathematica Policy Research in Washington, D.C. Since earning an MA degree in Social Psychology in 1994, she has studied family formation in the low-income population. She was at the vanguard of early federal and state interest in supporting healthy marriage among disadvantaged groups, creating research-based conceptual frameworks and guiding and analyzing the development of various efforts. Ms. Dion is Principal Investigator for Building Strong Families, a large-scale federally sponsored demonstration and rigorous

9-year evaluation of multiple programs to support healthy couple relationships and marriage among unwed parents. She also directs the process evaluation of the Oklahoma Marriage Initiative, the largest and most long-standing statewide initiative. A frequent speaker and author, she serves on the advisory groups of several state marriage initiatives.

**Patrick F. Fagan** is the William H. G. FitzGerald Research Fellow in Family and Cultural Issues at the Heritage Foundation. A former Deputy Assistant Secretary of Health and Human Services during the Bush administration, Mr. Fagan examines the relationship between family, community, and social problems. He also studies urban policy, the breakdown of the family in America, crime, and cultural issues. He has served as a legislative analyst for Senator Dan Coats of Indiana and, before becoming involved in public policy, was a family therapist and clinical psychologist in the inner city and elsewhere. Fagan, a native of Ireland, earned his master's degree in psychology at University College Dublin and has pursued doctoral studies at American University. He is presently doing doctoral work at University College Dublin.

**Rebecca Glauber** is a PhD candidate in Sociology at New York University. Her research interests include stratification, families, gender, and labor markets. Her dissertation, which she is currently completing, examines the effect of becoming a father on men's employment outcomes and on gender labor market inequality over the life course.

**Anjali E. Gupta** is a doctoral student of Human Development and Family Sciences at the University of Texas at Austin. Her research interests are child and family policy, specifically, the mental health and work of low-income women. She has a master's degree in Public Administration from Indiana University at Bloomington. Before starting her doctoral work, she was a research analyst at the Chapin Hall Center for Children at the University of Chicago where she analyzed data from minority and poor populations. In addition, she was a Fulbright Scholar based in Kingston, Jamaica, and a VISTA volunteer in Denver, Colorado.

**Alan J. Hawkins** is Professor of Family Life at Brigham University. He received his PhD in Human Development and Family Studies at The Pennsylvania State University in 1990. He has published extensively on issues related to fathering and marriage. His recent scholarship has focused on exploring ways to strengthen marriage through education and policy. In 2003–2004, he was a visiting scholar with the Administration for Children and Families, U.S. Department of Health and Human Services, working on the federal Healthy Marriage Initiative. He also helped build the National Healthy Marriage Resource Center, a federally funded, Web-based clearinghouse of information to support efforts to help couples form and sustain healthy marriages. He is also a member of the Utah Commission on Marriage.

**Charles B. Hennon** received his PhD in Sociology from Case Western Reserve University). He is Professor of Family Studies, Miami University, Oxford, Ohio. Previously, he was professor of Child and Family Studies, University of Wisconsin–Madison. The author or editor of 6 books and more than 60 articles/book chapters, he is founding editor of the *Journal of Family and Economic Issues*. Dr. Hennon was a recipient of the 2006 Richard T. Delp Outstanding Faculty Award (Miami University) in recognition of significant contributions in influencing the lives of students, in scholarship, and in service.

**Caeli A. Higney** was a research assistant at the American Enterprise Institute (AEI) from 2004 to 2006. Now attending Stanford Law School, she is the coauthor of "Federal and State Child Care Expenditures (1997–2004): Rapid Growth Followed by Steady Spending" (with Douglas J. Besharov), and "Summaries of Twenty Early Childhood Evaluations" (with Douglas J. Besharov and Peter Germanis).

**Harvey Hillin** is a policy analyst for Kansas Health Policy Authority (Medicaid). He graduated from the University of the South, Sewanee, Tennessee, has an MSW from the University of Kansas, and a PhD in Education from Kansas State University. He has worked in child welfare, mental health, and substance abuse treatment settings. He is author of *Better Living Through Chemistry? What You Should Know About Addiction* (2002), and coauthor (with Mary Hillin, PhD) of three other books. He also practices as a licensed clinical social worker and substance abuse counselor serving parolees for the U.S. Department of Justice.

**Aletha C. Huston,** PhD, is the Priscilla Pond Flawn Regents Professor of Child Development at the University of Texas at Austin and president of the Society for Research in Child Development. She specializes in understanding the effects of poverty on children and the impact of child care and income support policies on children's development. Her books include *Children in Poverty: Child Development* (1991); *Public Policy, Big World, Small Screen: The Role of Television in American Society* (1992); and *Developmental Contexts in Middle Childhood: Bridges to Adolescence and Adulthood* (2006) (http://www.utexas.edu/research/critc).

**Anna D. Johnson** is pursuing a doctoral student at Columbia University Teachers College, pursuing a PhD in Developmental Psychology under the advisement of Dr. Jeanne Brooks-Gunn. As a graduate research fellow at the National Center for Children and Families, a research center co-directed by Dr. Brooks-Gunn, Ms. Johnson works on a variety of large, longitudinal, and multisite studies that aim to inform policy decisions that impact children and families. Before beginning her doctoral work, she was a trial preparation assistant in the Child Abuse and Family Violence Bureau at the Manhattan District Attorney's Office.

**Eric D. Johnson** is currently Assistant Professor in the Programs in Couple and Family Therapy, Drexel University, where he is the Interim Director of the PhD Program. He holds a PhD in Social Work from Rutgers University (1996), a MSW from Syracuse University (1975), and a MDiv from Princeton Theological Seminary (1971). During the past 25 years, he has been a consultant to numerous organizations in the areas of community mental health, child services, juvenile justice, and corrections. His primary clinical and research interests focus on services to underserved populations, including minority, low-income, mentally ill, and jail populations. He has published several journal articles and book chapters on families of the seriously mentally ill.

**Kirk A. Johnson,** PhD, was Senior Policy Analyst for the Heritage Foundation's Center for Data Analysis in Washington, D.C. While he was there, he conducted statistical research on a broad range of topics, including marriage and family, welfare, academic achievement, labor, and consumer finance issues. He has also held positions at George Mason University, the Mackinac Center for Public Policy, the U.S. Census Bureau, and the University of North Texas.

**Laura Lein** received her PhD in Social Anthropology from Harvard University in

1973. She is Professor in the School of Social Work and the Department of Anthropology at the University of Texas at Austin. Her research focuses on the interface between families in poverty and the institutions that serve them. She recently coauthored with Ronald Angel and Jane Henrici *Poor Families in America's Health Care Crisis* (2006). Recent publications on families in poverty have appeared in the *Washington University Journal of Law & Policy* (2006), *Human Behavior in the Social Environment* (2006), and *Community, Work and Family* (2005). She is also continuing work on the experience of welfare reform among groups in Texas and on the experience of poverty among families living in the Monterrey–San Antonio corridor.

**Daniel T. Lichter** is the Ferris Family Professor in the Department of Policy Analysis and Management at Cornell University. He also directs the University's Bronfenbrenner Life Course Center. His research focuses on welfare reform and child poverty, marriage promotion policies, and the family formation behaviors of low-income unwed mothers. He is coauthor with Zhenchao Qian of *Marriage and Family in a Multiracial Society* (2004), published by the Population Reference Bureau and Russell Sage Foundation, and he is currently studying racial diversity and immigration in America's new rural destinations. He is past editor of *Demography*.

**Shoon Lio** is a PhD candidate in Sociology at the University of California, Riverside. His research interest is in how the boundaries of American citizenship are constituted by racial projects such as the formation of collective memory and the construction of moral panics over racialized "others." He is also conducting research on neighborhoods as the context for child development, collective identity and youth violence, and Asian American social movements. He is interested in the sociology of citizenship, race and ethnic relations, social theory, urban sociology and social psychology.

**David F. Marks** is Professor of Psychology at City University, London. Before that, he held appointments at the University of Sheffield, United Kingdom, the University of Otago, New Zealand, and Middlesex University, United Kingdom. His books include *The Health Psychology Reader* (2002), *Research Methods for Clinical and Health Psychology* (2004, with L. Yardley), *Health Psychology: Theory, Research, Practice* (2005, with M. Murray, B. Evans, C. Willig, C. Woodall, and C. Sykes), and *Overcoming Your Smoking Habit* (2005). He is editor of the *Journal of Health Psychology*.

**Ryan Martin** is a specialist focusing on the Temporary Assistance for Needy Families program in the Administration for Children and Families, U.S. Department of Health and Human Services. He is a graduate of the Presidential Management Fellowship program, the premier program for leadership development in the federal civil service. His has researched state policy choices regarding work incentives for low-income individuals, as well as methods of increasing the involvement of noncustodial parents in the lives of their children. He received a MPP and a BS in Economics from Brigham Young University.

**Lawrence M. Mead** received his PhD in Political Science from Harvard University and is Professor of Politics at New York University, where he teaches public policy and American government. He has been a visiting professor at Harvard, Princeton, and the University of Wisconsin. An expert on the problems of poverty and welfare in the United States, he was the principal academic exponent of work requirements in welfare, the approach that now dominates national policy. He is also a leading scholar of the politics and implementation of welfare reform. His works have helped shape welfare reform in the United States and abroad.

**Michael Murray** is Chair of Applied Social and Health Psychology at Keele University, United Kingdom. Previously, he held appointments at St. Thomas' Hospital Medical School, London, the University of Ulster, Northern Ireland, and Memorial University of Newfoundland, Canada. He has published extensively on social psychological aspects of health and illness including *Health Psychology: Theory, Research, Practice* (2005, with D. F. Marks, B. Evans, C. Willig, C. Woodall, and C. Sykes), *Qualitative Health Psychology: Theories and Methods* (1999, with K. Chamberlain), and *Critical Health Psychology* (2004).

**W. Sean Newsome**, MSW, PhD, is Assistant Professor and BSW Program Director at Miami (Ohio) University. Currently, Dr. Newsome teaches social work practice, human behavior in the social environment (HBSE) and social welfare and its impact on diverse groups. His applied research interests include the use of solution focused brief therapy (SFBT) with at-risk K–12 populations, school-family-community partnerships, risk and protective factors associated with school truancy, bullying behavior and school violence, and the impact of grandparents raising grandchildren in K–12 settings. Before pursuing his doctorate work in social work, he practiced as a treatment coordinator for Boysville of Michigan and as a school social worker in Birmingham, Michigan. He received his doctorate in social work from The Ohio State University.

**Martha N. Ozawa**, PhD, is Bettie Bofigner Brown Distinguished Professor of Social Policy and Director of the Martha N. Ozawa Center for Social Policy Studies at George Warren Brown School of Social Work, Washington University in St. Louis. She obtained her MSSW in 1966 and PhD in Social Welfare in 1969 from University of Wisconsin–Madison. Her recent research focuses on the economic well-being of elderly persons and children, the effect of disability on income status in old age and on labor force participation among adults, distribution of income and wealth, and volatility in income status in the United States.

**Ross D. Parke** is Distinguished Professor of Psychology and Director of the Center for Family Studies at the University of California, Riverside. He received his MA from the University of Toronto and PhD from the University of Waterloo. He is past president of the Society of Research in Child Development and former editor of the *Journal of Family Psychology*. In addition to his long-standing interest in fathers, his current work focuses on the links between family and peer social systems and on families and children of diverse ethnic backgrounds. He is author of *Fatherhood* (1996) and coauthor of *Throwaway Dads* (1999) and *Child Psychology* (6th ed., 2005).

**Gary "Pete" Peterson**, PhD, is Professor and Chair of Family Studies and Social Work at Miami University–Ohio. His areas of teaching and scholarly interest are parent-child/adolescent relations, adolescent development, and family theory. Specific topics have included family (parental) contributors to adolescent social competence, family influences on adolescent autonomy development from parents, family influences on adolescent conformity to parents, and family influences on the status attainment of adolescents and young adults from rural Appalachia. His scholarly articles have appeared in the *Journal of Marriage and the*

*Family*; *Family Relations*; *Journal of Adolescent Research*; *Youth and Society*; *Family Science Review*; *Family Process*; *Sociological Inquiry*; and *Family Issues*. Currently, he is examining parent-adolescent relations within samples of adolescents from the People's Republic of China, Russia, India, Kenya, Mexico, Chile, and the United States as part of the *Cross-National Adolescent Project*. He is a co-editor of the books *Handbook of Marriage and the Family* (2nd ed., 1999) and *Adolescents in Families* (1986), and editor of the journal *Marriage and Family Review* and the general editor of the handbook series for Haworth Press titled *The Haworth Series on Marriage and Family Studies*.

**Nina Philipsen** is a doctoral student in Developmental Psychology and a graduate research fellow at the National Center for Children and Families (NCCF). Ms. Philipsen graduated from the University of Texas with a BA in Psychology in 2003 and earned a masters degree from Purdue University in Child Development and Family Studies. At NCCF, Nina works on the Fragile Families project. Her primary research interests include early child health, education, and care policy.

**Zhenchao Qian**, PhD, is Professor of Sociology and Research Associate of Initiative in Population Research at The Ohio State University. His research focuses on changing patterns of union formation and assortative mating. He has published work on changes in cohabitation and marriage, racial differences in intermarriage, and racial identification of biracial children. He is coauthor with Daniel T. Lichter of "Social Boundaries and Marital Assimilation: Interpreting Trends in Racial and Ethnic Intermarriage" in *American Sociological Review* (2007).

**Robert E. Rector**, Senior Policy Analyst, Welfare and Family Issues, the Heritage Foundation examines such issues as welfare reform, marriage and illegitimacy, tax reform to assist families, and poverty in America. A graduate of the College of William and Mary, Mr. Rector earned his master's degree in political science from Johns Hopkins University. He recently authored *America's Failed $5.4 Trillion War on Poverty* (1995), which examines the U.S. welfare system. He has published articles the *Wall Street Journal,* the *Los Angeles Times,* and hundreds of other newspapers. Mr. Rector's writings have also appeared in *National Review, Policy Review, The World and I, The American Enterprise, Insight, Human Events,* the *Harvard Journal on Legislation,* and other magazines. He previously worked as a management analyst at the U.S. Office of Personnel Management.

**Matthew R. Sanders**, PhD, is Professor of Clinical Psychology and Director of the Parenting and Family Support Centre at the University of Queensland. He is founder of the Triple P-Positive Parenting Program. This internationally recognized program has twice won the National Violence Prevention Award from the Commonwealth Heads of Governments in Australia. He conducts research in the area of parenting, family psychology, and the treatment and prevention of childhood psychopathology. The Parenting and Family Support Centre is involved in conducting a number of randomized controlled trials evaluating the effects of family-based interventions for children and adolescents. Current research projects focus on evaluating family interventions for children at risk for the development of severe conduct problems, children with challenging behavior and developmental disabilities, parental maltreatment, parental depression, and marital conflict. He is author of the popular book *Every Parent: A Positive Approach* to *Children's Behaviour* (2004), and has published extensively on the nature, causes, prevention, and treatment of behavioral disturbance in children. In 1996, he was awarded a Distinguished Career Award from the Australian Association for Cognitive Behaviour Therapy. He has served as a consultant for several government departments and agencies both within Australia and internationally interested in the adoption of population-level, evidence-based parenting and family support strategies. He is also a member of the National Suicide Prevention Council.

**Thomas J. Schofield**, MA, is a graduate student in the Department of Psychology at the University of California, Riverside, working toward completion of a dissertation examining the predictors and possible effects of changes in parenting across time among Mexican Americans and European Americans. His interests include the family unit, as studied across levels of analysis including dyadic, triadic, and family-level, as well as the interaction between the nature of family functioning and contexts, both perceived (culture, religion) and physical (neighborhoods).

**Carmel Tabone**, OP, is Senior Lecturer in the Department of Social Policy and Social Work and the Department of Public Policy at the University of Malta. He holds an S.Th.L. from St. Thomas Aquinas College, Malta, and S.Th.Lic. (Moral Theology) and Sc.Soc.D. from the Pontifical University of St. Thomas Aquinas (Angelicum) in Rome. He was a visiting scholar at Templeton College, University of Oxford, and at the Pontifical University of St. Thomas Aquinas in Rome. He served as chairman of the Family Study and Research Commission of the Ministry for Social Development in Malta. Dr. Tabone is Vice Chairperson of the National Family Commission and is a member of the National Commission for

the Advancement of Women. He also served as co-coordinator of the Mediterranean Social Sciences Network and editor of the Mediterranean Social Sciences Journal. He is author of *The Secularization of the Family in Changing Malta* (1987) and *Maltese Families in Transition* (1995), and a series of articles dealing with the family and development.

**Kate Tarrant**, MPA, is a doctoral student in Curriculum and Teaching, concentrating on early childhood policy, and a graduate research fellow at the National Center for Children and Families at Teachers College, Columbia University. Ms. Tarrant earned her Masters degree in Public Administration at Columbia University. Her research interests include the impact of early childhood policy for teachers, families, and children in different early learning settings, particularly home-based settings.

**David B. Taylor** earned a PhD in Social Ecology from the University of California, Irvine in 1999. He is Associate Professor of Criminology and Criminal Justice at Niagara University. His primary research emphasis is on kinship caregiving, and he is currently conducting research on the implementation of strengths-based approaches in case management. Dr. Taylor is the recipient of several nationally recognized funding awards, has served as a consultant on several other national grants, and has reviewed and edited proposals in a broad range of areas. He is a member of the American Society of Criminology and a lifetime member of the Academy of Criminal Justice Sciences.

**Shigueru J. Tsuha**, MA, is a graduate student in the Department of Sociology at the University of California, Riverside. His interests include the study of race and class in the United States and at a global level, work, organizations, exploitation, labor, and social movements. Shigueru is conducting dissertation research on racial identities and racism as they are experienced by Japanese descendants born in Peru now living in the United States, Peru, and Japan.

**Jessica Thornton Walker** is a doctoral student of Human Development and Family Sciences at the University of Texas at Austin, where she is the 2005 recipient of the University's Preemptive Fellowship, the Zeifman Graduate Fellowship, and the Dean's Excellence Award. Her research focuses on the intersection of poverty, policy, and child development with particular attention to children's academic performance. Before her doctoral studies, she worked as a research assistant at Georgetown University, examining parenting among low-income and adolescent mothers, and at Children's National Medical Center in Washington, D.C., examining the academic and behavioral consequences of traumatic brain injury.

**Carol Ward** received her PhD from the University of Chicago in 1992. She was a research specialist for the Administration for Native Americans in Washington, D.C. for 5 years and also completed a dropout study on the Northern Cheyenne Indian reservation that was published as a monograph, *Native Americans in the School System* (2005). She joined the Sociology faculty at Brigham Young University in 1990 but still works with the Northern Cheyenne on issues related to education, substance abuse recovery, welfare reform, and food assistance programs. She teaches classes in racial and ethnic relations, sociology of education, community, qualitative and survey methods.

**Erin Feinauer Whiting** received her MS in Sociology from Brigham Young University (1999) and her PhD in Rural Sociology at the University of Missouri–Columbia (2006). She has worked on a variety of research endeavors on the Northern Cheyenne Reservation since she first visited in autumn of 1998. She is interested in all aspects of poverty and especially hunger. Additionally, she is interested in the importance of places in social life and the organization of social spaces, as well as community organization and development.

**Melvin N. Wilson**, PhD, is Professor in the Department of Psychology at the University of Virginia. Dr. Wilson has an extensive background in academic, research and training activities generally focused on understanding contextual processes and outcomes in African American families and children. He has conducted analyses on young, low-income, unwed, and nonresident fathers and their involvement with their children. In addition, he has developed intervention protocols aimed at helping young men meet family responsibilities and involvements and services to men who are court-ordered for treatment of wife-battering. Currently, Dr. Wilson is conducting a preventive intervention involving families with toddlers at risk for conduct disorder.

**Stephan M. Wilson**, earned his PhD in Family Relations and Human Development from the University of Tennessee, Knoxville, and is Professor of Human Development and Family Studies and Senior Associate Dean in the College of Health and Human Sciences at the University of Nevada, Reno. He has been on the faculty at the University of Kentucky, Virginia Tech, Montana State, and Kenyatta (in Kenya) universities. He is author of more than 60 articles and book chapters, editor of 2 edited books and 30 other publications, and serves on the editorial board of *Family Relations* and *Marriage and Family Review* as well as serving as an occasional reviewer for several other journals. In 2005, Dr. Wilson was awarded Fellow status in the National Council on Family Relations.

**Warner P. Woodworth** earned his PhD in Psychology from the University of Michigan and is a social entrepreneur and Professor of

Organizational Leadership and Strategy at the Marriott School, Brigham Young University. He is a consultant to corporations, governments, trade unions, and social enterprises worldwide. Teaching MBAs and doing action research, he has published 10 books and more than 160 articles, many on microenterprises and NGOs. During the last decade, he has been founder or director of 15 NGOs that raised in excess of $24 million and gave out some 920,000 microloans to empower the poor and build self-reliance in 21 countries.

**W. Jean Yeung**, PhD, is Research Professor and Senior Research Scientist at the Center for Advanced Social Science Research, Department of Sociology in New York University. She is a co-principal investigator of the Panel Study of Income Dynamics and an affiliated scholar at the National Poverty Center of the Gerald Ford School of Public Policy in the University of Michigan and the RAND Policy Research Corporation. Her research focuses on intergenerational studies, family and children's well-being and policies, Demography, and research methods. Her recent publications include the effects of child poverty, family wealth, fathers' involvement on children's behavior and achievement.

**Hong-Sik Yoon** is Assistant Professor in the Department of Social Welfare, College of Social Science at Chonbuk National University in Deuckjin-Gu, Jeonju, Korea.